CULTURE

Popular Culture: 1900–1919

Jilly Hunt

www.raintreepublishers.co.uk
Visit our website to find out more information about Raintree books.

To order:
Phone 0845 6044371
Fax +44 (0) 1865 312263
Email myorders@raintreepublishers.co.uk

Customers from outside the UK please telephone +44 1865 312262

Raintree is an imprint of Capstone Global Library Limited, a company incorporated in England and Wales having its registered office at 7 Pilgrim Street, London, EC4V 6LB – Registered company number: 6695582

First published in hardback in 2013

Edited by Adam Miller, Andrew Farrow, and Adrian Vigliano
Designed by Richard Parker
Original illustrations © Capstone Global Ltd 2013
Illustrations by Richard Parker
Picture research by Mica Brancic
Originated by Capstone Global Library Ltd
Printed and bound in China

ISBN 978 1 406 24020 7
16 15 14 13
10 9 8 7 6 5 4 3 2

British Library Cataloguing in Publication Data
TO COME
A full catalogue record for this book is available from the British Library.

Acknowledgements
We would like to thank the following for permission to reproduce photographs: Alamy p. 25 (© Lebrecht Music and Arts Photo Library); Art Archive p. 34 (The Owen Trust); Corbis pp. 18 (© Bettmann), 37 (© Robert Landau); Getty Images pp. 15 (Archive Photos/Buyenlarge), 31, 33, 42 (Archive Photos/Buyenlarge), 29 (Buyenlarge), 38 (Frank Lloyd Wright Preservation Trust), 17 (Gamma-Keystone), 21, 30 (Gamma-Keystone/Keystone-France), 26, 45 (Hulton Archive), 7, 13 (Hulton Archive/Apic), 27 (Hulton Archive/Central Press), 6, 49, 51 (Hulton Archive/Topical Press Agency), 5 (Hulton Archive/Topical Press Agency/A. R. Coster), 52 (Popperfoto/Bob Thomas), 35 (Popperfoto/Paul Popper), 11 (Science & Society Picture Library), 53 (Sean Gallup), 9 (Sean Sexton), 23 (Redferns/GAB Archive); Library of Congress pp. 41 [Lewis Hine/Photographs from the records of the National Child Labor Committee (U.S)], 46 (Prints and Photographs Division); Mary Evans Picture Library p. 43 (Onslow Auctions Limited); Photoshot p. 39 (© UPPA); The Kobal Collection p. 16 (EDISON). Background images and design features reproduced with permission of Shutterstock.

Cover photograph of four women laughing while running on a beach reproduced with the permission of Getty Images (Harold M. Lambert).

Every effort has been made to contact copyright holders of any material reproduced in this book. Any omissions will be rectified in subsequent printings if notice is given to the publisher.

Contents

POPULAR CULTURE

Some words are printed in bold, **like this**. You can find out what they mean by looking in the glossary.

What is popular culture?

What do you enjoy doing in your free time? Do you enjoy watching a film or some television? Or perhaps you like reading a good book or flicking through the pages of a magazine to find out about the latest fashions? Chances are that a lot of other people like the same films, television programmes, books, or magazines as you. This makes these pastimes part of a popular culture.

The word *culture* can be used in many ways, but in this book we mean culture to be the arts, such as films, music, books, and design. Culture can also include elements that are part of everyday life such as travel and the clothes people wear.

Popular culture really came into being with the introduction of mass communication such as television and radio. In the years between 1900 and 1919, mass communication was just beginning. This was an exciting time of inventions and technological advances. Can you imagine a world without television? Well, that was our world during this time. Television wasn't widely introduced until the 1920s. Going to a cinema was a new experience in the early 1900s, since films were only available to the general public from about 1896.[1] Can you imagine what it would have been like to see your first "moving picture", as they were called then, projected on to a big screen?

Where does popular culture start?

Popular culture might vary in different countries or there might be trends that appeal to lots of people around the world.

Sometimes an advance in technology means that an item, such as the car, will become more affordable. This will have an impact on how people live their lives. A new car means that travelling to see friends or relatives may become a lot easier. Many new cars on the road may also mean traffic jams and an increase in pollution.

Sometimes trends, such as designer fashion, start with the elite. A new look is then adapted to make it accessible and affordable to the mainstream public. The reverse of this might also happen. A trend might start with a particular subgroup of people and spread to become widely popular. For example, ragtime and jazz music developed within the African American community. During the early 1900s, racism among the wealthy social elite (and throughout society) caused people to view blacks and their culture as

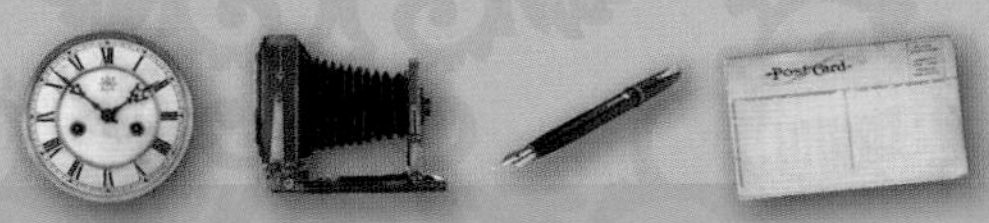

taboo. However, ragtime and jazz soared to popularity among the elite and other groups.

The appeal of cinemas spread around the world, and they became a key part of popular culture. This crowd is waiting to enter a "kinema" (an old spelling of "cinema") in London in 1918.

What was the world like in the 1900s and 1910s?

The twentieth century started out with Britain being the most powerful nation in the world. But by 1919 the world had become a very different place. **World War I** (1914–1918) was on a scale not seen before.

Age of imperialism

At the turn of the century, the British **Empire** was at its height. This was the age of **imperialism**. Great Britain, under the rule of Queen Victoria, had many **colonies** around the world, including India, Canada, New Zealand, Australia, and South Africa. This meant Great Britain had a strong global influence. What was popular in the United Kingdom would be spread around the world to its colonies.

These British soliders are returning home from fighting in World War I in 1915.

Around this time, the global influence of the United States began to strengthen. It was the beginning of the "American Century", in which American manufacturing power would overtake the European industrial powers and empires of the United Kingdom, Germany, and France.

World War I

The big event that affected people all over the world was World War I (1914–1918). About 8.5 million people were killed and more than 21 million wounded.[2] It was the first industrial war, though people had thought that new technologies would stop wars. Instead, technological advances and mass production made World War I one of the most brutal and horrific wars the world had ever seen. The war changed the way people thought. The social restrictions in place before the war now seemed less important. When people were dying, what did it matter what style of jacket one wore to a formal dinner? The general public wanted to be freer from these restrictions, and this was displayed in various ways: from the way people dressed to the type of music they enjoyed.

Fight for the right to vote

Women around the world had been fighting for their right to vote since the nineteenth century, particularly in the United Kingdom and United States. However, other countries gave women the right to vote earlier than the United Kingdom and United States did. For example, New Zealand granted the right in 1893, Australia in 1902, Finland in 1906, and Norway in 1913.[3]

Bicycles became a symbol of new freedom and rights for women (see page 47).

Campaigners for women's rights would often hold demonstrations and perform militant actions in order to draw attention to their plight. In the United Kingdom, campaigners chained themselves to railings, refused to pay taxes, and went on hunger strike if they were imprisoned. One **suffragette**, Emily Davidson, died after she threw herself under the king's horse.[4]

World War I sped up the **franchise** of women, because while men were away fighting, women did many of the jobs that the men had left.

Time to travel

This was an exciting time for technical advances in transport. Previously travel had only been for the very rich, but transport was becoming more affordable. In the late nineteenth century the main way to travel was by horse and cart or horse-drawn carriages.[5] As the twentieth century progressed, the options for travel increased. Public transport also grew with the opening of underground railway systems in cities around the world. Train travel became more accessible as the rail networks in the United States and Europe neared completion. Ocean travel became faster and people were taking to the air in the first planes.

These developments in travel also influenced popular culture, especially for the middle classes. An increase in prosperity meant that people had more time available for leisure activities, including going on holiday. The railways made it possible for people to travel larger distances in a shorter time. Seaside holidays, if only for a day, became very popular, especially in the United Kingdom.

Sinking of the unsinkable

The *Titanic* was hailed by its owner, White Star Line, as being unsinkable. However, on its first voyage across the Atlantic Ocean in April 1912, the *Titanic* hit an iceberg and sank, killing around 1,490 people. This tragic loss of life led to new regulations about the number of lifeboats ships would carry. The events of the *Titanic* have inspired numerous stories, films, songs, and works of art, and the story continues to fascinate people today.

Travelling trends

The accessibility of travel meant that popular trends spread further and more quickly. For example, the expanding train system and the riverboats of the Mississippi River helped the popularity of ragtime and early jazz spread up from New Orleans, Louisiana, in the south to the northern cities of the United States.[6]

Travelling for work

Underground railways developed at the turn of the century. They linked urban and suburban areas, providing faster travel and allowing people to commute into city centres for work or leisure. London had the first underground train line, which opened in 1863 using steam locomotives.[7] London's first electric underground train was in service in 1890, and more lines were electrified through the early 1900s.[8] Cities around the world started developing underground railways: Budapest's subway opened in 1896, Paris's Metro in 1900, Boston's subway in 1897, and New York City's subway in 1904.[9]

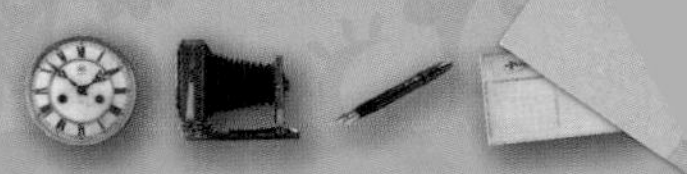

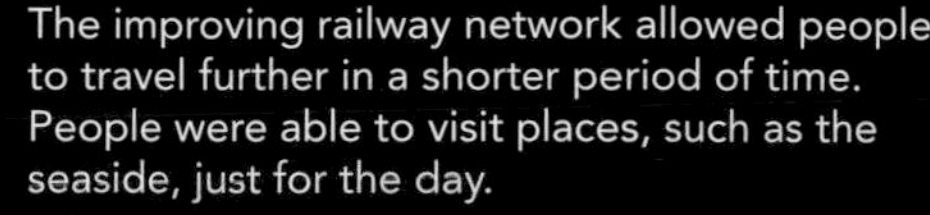

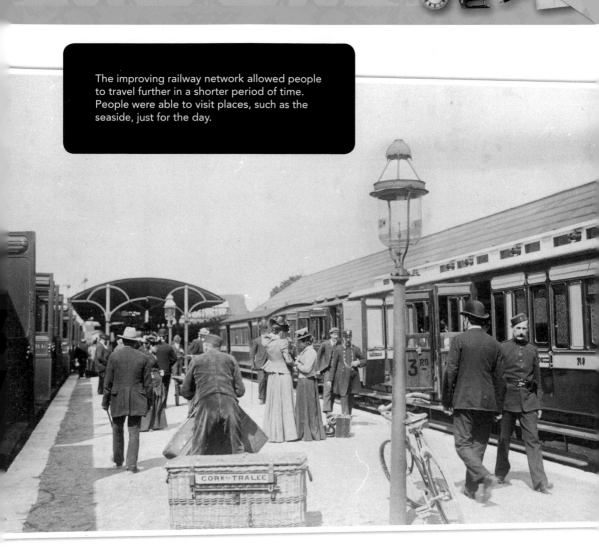

The improving railway network allowed people to travel further in a shorter period of time. People were able to visit places, such as the seaside, just for the day.

Air travel takes off

The desire to fly has been around for centuries, but in 1903 Orville and Wilbur Wright made the first successful engine-powered, heavier-than-air flight carrying a person.[10] From 14 to 15 June, 1919, John Alcock and Arthur Whitten Brown made the first non-stop Atlantic flight. It took 16 hours and 27 minutes from Newfoundland, Canada, to Clifden, Ireland.[11] Aircraft were used in World War I, but it wasn't until the second half of the twentieth century that **commercial flights** were inexpensive enough to be a travel option.

Impact of the car

The rich were traditionally the only people who could afford private transport up until the late nineteenth century. In the first few decades of the twentieth century this was beginning to change. In 1903, the Ford Motor Company sold its first cars.[12] In 1908, Ford released the Model T, and it proved so popular that Henry Ford had to think about ways he could produce the car in large quantities but at low cost. In 1913, Ford opened the first moving **assembly line** in Michigan.[13] This revolutionized manufacturing techniques for all kinds of goods, not just cars. Goods could now be made more cheaply, and therefore would be more affordable to the masses.

Initially cars weren't very popular to the everyday person. They were seen as noisy and dangerous. In Britain, the 1903 Motor Car Act set a top speed of 32 kilometres per hour (20 miles per hour), which seems very slow compared to today's speeds.

However, the car changed society. It made people more mobile and gave them the freedom to go where they wanted. It created the need for roads and changed the appearance of towns and cities. It allowed people to live further away from their jobs and drive to them. Ford's idea of turning the car from a luxury into an everyday essential by making it cheap enough for many people to afford was realized.[14]

Travel as immigrants

Popular culture was also spread by the increase in immigration around the world. In 1901, the Australian government encouraged British **emigrants** to Australia by offering land.[15] In the early twentieth century,[16] large numbers of European emigrants went to the United States. Over 2 million Italians, 1.5 million Jews, and 0.5 million Slavs[17] emigrated to the United States, looking to escape economic and religious persecution. Many of the poorer **immigrants** were not educated and could not speak the language of their new country. They often had to take the low-paying jobs offered by expanding industries. Even so, they contributed to the culture of the United States and added to it with their own forms of popular culture. For example, there was a strong Jewish theatre and **vaudeville** scene (see pages 20-21).

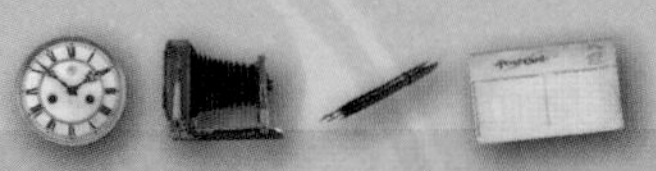

Ford's Model T became hugely popular. Only one paint, Japan black enamel, would dry fast enough to cope with the speed of the production line, so customers could have "any colour they want so long as it's black".

Assembly lines

Assembly lines are set up so that a worker performs a specific task. An assembly line building a car starts with a bare chassis. Then the different components are added by the workers along the line in a specific order. This method speeds up production because each worker does only one specific task, has the equipment needed for that task, and becomes skilled at doing it.

Children's entertainment

The world of children's entertainment in the 1900s and 1910s might seem very different to you because there were no computer games or television. Instantly recognizable characters such as Buzz Lightyear and Spider-Man didn't exist. However, you are probably also very familiar with some of the popular toys from these decades.

Jigsaw puzzles have been around since the eighteenth century, but it wasn't until the 1860s and 1870s that popular pictures were used as jigsaws in the United Kingdom and United States. These puzzles became extremely popular in the early 1900s.[1]

Did you know?

The teddy bear was named after US president Theodore Roosevelt. While on a hunting trip in 1902, Roosevelt refused to shoot a bear cub. This inspired a toy maker to name a stuffed bear after him – his nickname was Teddy. The craze for teddy bears began![2]

Have you ever created a picture using wax crayons? In 1903, Crayola crayons were made by Edwin Binney and C. Harold Smith.[3]

The Meccano set, or Erector set, was invented by Frank Hornby in Liverpool, England, in 1901.[4] This was a construction set consisting of a variety of reusable parts such as metal strips, plates, wheels, **axles**, and gears, along with nuts and bolts to connect it all together. The users could build working models and mechanical devices and be like real engineers. These sets are still available to buy today.

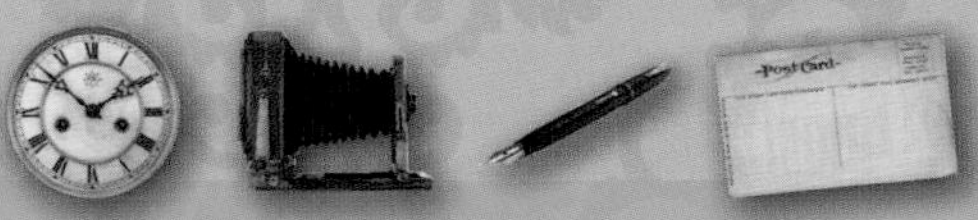

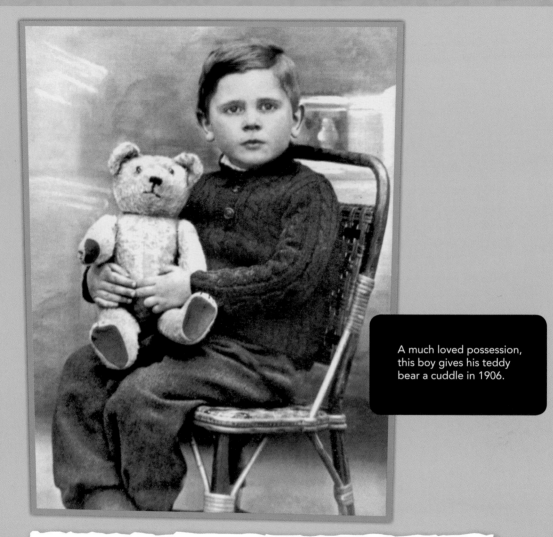

A much loved possession, this boy gives his teddy bear a cuddle in 1906.

CULTURE IN CONTEXT

At the beginning of the twentieth century it was still common for children from working-class families to have to go to work, often in factories, shipbuilding yards, or in mines. The 1900 US census showed that about two million children were employed.[5] **Child labour** was also common in the United Kingdom at this time, but the introduction of compulsory education helped reduce the number of child labourers. It wasn't until 1918 that compulsory education became law in every state in the United States.[6] There would be little time for play for some working-class children.

Film and light entertainment

Going to the cinema became a hugely popular form of entertainment in the first few decades of the twentieth century. Motion pictures had a big impact on popular culture, with people following the careers of their favourite stars and wanting to look like them. Going to the cinema wasn't expensive, so it was accessible to a large part of the population.

Early beginnings

Motion pictures became available to the general public around 1896. At first, the short films were shown as part of music hall shows, also called vaudeville (see pages 18-19), or circus shows. In 1902 in Los Angeles, California, a shop opened that showed only moving pictures and was a great success. This led to the opening of movie houses throughout the United States. In Pittsburgh, Pennsylvania, in 1905 the first cinema was opened. It cost a nickel to get in so it became known as the nickelodeon.[1] The first nickelodeons appealed to the working class but gradually became popular with the middle class as well.

Did you know?

During World War I, film production in the United Kingdom was much higher than it is today.

The early film industry

Up until 1914, the film industry was international and led by the United States, France, Britain, and Italy. European films were dominated by Charles Pathé and his brother.[2] Their company commissioned its own studio camera, which was better than other cameras. They also built a production facility in France where films could be made using an assembly line approach.[3]

World War I changed things. There was an increased demand for films, because people wanted to escape the reality of everyday life. With the Europeans at war, they couldn't meet this demand. The United States took the lead and became the foremost filmmaking country in the world. Perhaps when you think of US filmmaking you think of Hollywood, California. However, the first US studios were in New York City and Chicago, Illinois, because of the pool of theatre actors available in those cities.

An advertisement for a motion picture from the 1900s based on Edgar Allen Poe's *The Raven*.

A move to warmer climates

It was the high demand for films that led to the film industry's move to Hollywood. Film companies needed to be able to film year-round. Since most movies were shot outdoors in available light, the winter conditions in New York and Chicago weren't ideal. The film industry needed to move to a warmer climate with clearer skies. They needed a new centre, and a suburb of Los Angeles called Hollywood proved to be just the place.

Silent movies

Early films were very different from the films we are used to today. They were short, silent comedies, dramas, or documentaries. Music would be played, usually by a live pianist in front of the screen. The actors would not speak. In between scenes, **title cards** appeared on-screen explaining what was happening or providing **dialogue**.

Initially films were only a few minutes long – more like today's advertisements. In 1903, Edwin S. Porter revolutionized filmmaking by editing films to tell a story in different locations. His 1903 film *Life of an American Fireman*[4] was the first US documentary movie and contained film of actual fire scenes combined with actors playing the role of fire chief–hero and a trapped mother and child. He created the feeling of suspense by cutting back and forth between the frightened mother and the brave firefighters.

The first blockbuster

D. W. Griffith's 1915 silent movie *The Birth of a Nation*[5] is considered the first Hollywood blockbuster. It was the most profitable movie of its time. The film is about the American Civil War (1861–1865) and was admired for its technical and dramatic innovations, but was condemned for the racism contained within its story. The movie cost $100,000[6] to make, which was a lot of money at the time, but it was so successful that it made millions of dollars in profit.[7] *The Birth of a Nation* showed the power and popularity of movies and that going to the cinema was now a middle-class pastime. It was clear that there was money to be made in the film industry.

Porter's *The Great Train Robbery* (1903)[8] was a highly influential movie. It used the first close-up – a shot of a gunman shooting straight at the camera, or audience. Early audiences were terrified that they were being shot at!

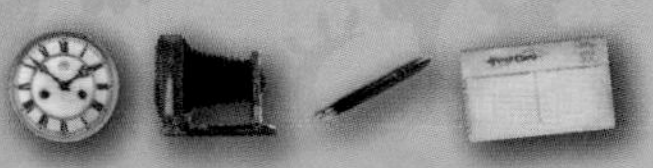

Fluctuation in cinema audience numbers in the United Kingdom[9]

Year	Number of viewers
1916	20 million
1946	1.6 billion
1956	1.1 billion
1960	501 million

Charlie Chaplin was one of the stars of the silent movies.

The star system

Today we are all very familiar with the names of big movie stars. However, it wasn't always this way. In 1909,[10] film producer Carl Laemmle introduced the star system to the United States by promoting actress Florence Lawrence. Before this, actors were not known by name. For example, the actress Mary Pickford, who became one of the richest and most famous women in the United States, was initially known only as the "Biograph Girl with the Curls".[11] Other film studios saw that promoting actors and actresses could improve business, so they started distributing **publicity stills**. The star system was born and has developed into the multimillion dollar global business that it is today.

Animation

In 1906, the first animated cartoon was produced by J. Stuart Blackton. It was called *Humorous Phases of Funny Faces*. Other animators followed, such as Winsor McCay with *Gertie the Dinosaur*. The first star of **animation** was probably Felix the Cat, created by Otto Messmer in 1919.[12]

Music hall and vaudeville

The movies started as part of the entertainment in shows called vaudeville, as they were known in the United States, or music hall in the United Kingdom. These were a kind of **variety show**. Both shows were a similar form of light entertainment. They included a series of individual acts featuring singers, dancers, jugglers, magicians, acrobats, comedians, and trained animals.

A music hall performance in progress.

Origins

Music hall in the United Kingdom came from the working-class concerts given in pubs during the eighteenth and nineteenth centuries. Eventually this style of entertainment moved to music clubs, theatres, and concert halls. In the United States, vaudeville started in the 1850s and 1860s in beer halls and was aimed mainly at men. By the late nineteenth century it had become more respectable, was held in theatres, and was considered family entertainment. Music hall was the height of fashion in entertainment from about the mid-1890s to the early 1930s.

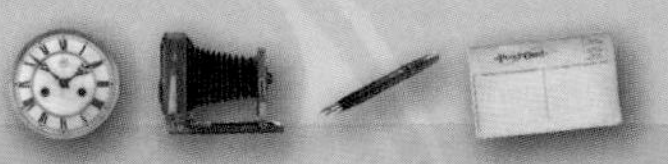

Future stars

Music hall and vaudeville made stars of many performers. W. C. Fields was an American juggler and comedian. He appeared in vaudeville and in *Ziegfeld Follies* **revues** between 1915 and 1921, before he became established in films as an internationally famous comic.[13]

Harry Houdini, the great escape artist, took part in vaudeville shows as a trapeze artist, but he wasn't very successful. It was his daring escape attempts while shackled with ropes, chains, and handcuffs and submerged underwater or suspended upside down high above the ground that gained him an international reputation.

Buster Keaton, who became a silent film star, began performing in vaudeville acts when he was just three years old. His parents were also vaudeville performers who specialized in a type of acrobatics called knockabout. His father used Buster as a "human mop".[14]

The end of music hall

The huge popularity of cinema gradually edged out music hall. Films started to dominate the shows, and by about 1927 the shows consisted mostly of full-length motion pictures with added music hall acts.[15]

Ziegfeld's revues

Florenz Ziegfeld was an American theatrical producer who made a big impact with his revues, starting in 1907.[16] His slogan was "Glorifying the American Girl". These shows featured semi-nudity, **pageantry**, and comedy. The *Ziegfeld Follies* were based on the Folies Bergère of Paris but were less **risqué**. (The Folies Bergère was a Parisian music hall famed for its displays of female nudity.) Ziegfeld developed stars such as singer and comedienne Fanny Brice, and comedians Eddie Cantor, Will Rogers, and Bert Williams.

Jewish influence

At the turn of the century, the United States was the destination of many of Europe's emigrants. There were large numbers of Italians, Slavs, and Jews leaving Europe in the hope of escaping poverty and persecution and living the American dream of freedom and opportunity. The different nationalities brought with them their own cultures, which influenced the popular culture of the areas they settled in. Many Jewish immigrants settled in America's north-east, in cities such as New York and Boston. In the big cities the popular forms of entertainment such as vaudeville and theatre were well established but the film industry was still growing. Jewish immigrants got involved in all areas of the entertainment industry and heavily influenced popular culture.

Many Jewish performers became part of American vaudeville, including such big-name stars as Fanny Brice, Eddie Cantor, and Al Jolson. A separate circuit of vaudeville, called Yiddish vaudeville, was named after the Yiddish language spoken by many of the eastern European Jews.

Anti-semitism

During this time there were a lot of negative feelings towards Jews and they were often persecuted. This is called **anti-semitism**. Many of the Jewish performers of vaudeville made their religion the main part of their act in a humorous way. This helped bring a greater understanding of the Jewish culture to the audience and helped to soften anti-semitic attitudes.

The move to Hollywood

It was a natural move for many of these performers to go to Hollywood when the film industry relocated there. For example, theatre and screen star Paul Muni achieved great success in Hollywood. His reputation as a stage actor meant that Hollywood couldn't stereotype him into certain roles, so he had the rare luxury of approving the scripts of the films he worked on.[17]

Many Jewish immigrants, such as filmmaker and producer Samuel Goldwyn and motion picture executive Louis B. Mayer, were involved behind the scenes in the Hollywood film industry. Together with Marcus Loew, who owned Metro Pictures, they formed the company Metro-Goldwyn-Mayer, or MGM, which is still a big name in the film industry today.[18]

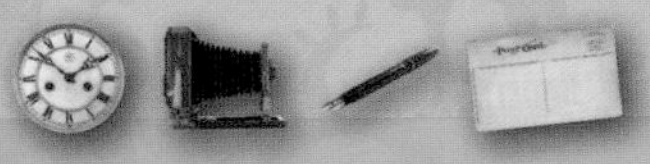

Al Jolson (1886-1950)

Al Jolson was born in Russia in 1886 but lived in the United States from the age of seven. He made his first stage appearance in 1899 in a vaudeville act with his brother. Jolson became a popular New York entertainer and singer. In 1927, he starred in *The Jazz Singer*, which was the first feature film to have **synchronized** speech. The film is about a boy struggling to balance Jewish life with his love of performing.

Music

The early 1900s was an exciting time for music. Famous writers and performers, such as composers Claude Debussy, Gustav Mahler, Richard Strauss, Igor Stravinsky, and opera singers Caruso and Nelly Melba, were busy creating and entertaining. However, there were talented musicians who couldn't make it in this musical world because of the colour of their skin. African Americans were treated as second-class citizens and weren't permitted to take part in or contribute to the white music of high society. African American musicians formed their own musical styles with ragtime, blues, and jazz. These styles would soon have a big influence around the world.

Ragtime music

Ragtime was an incredibly popular form of music in the United States from 1899 to 1917.[1] It was the forerunner of jazz. Ragtime emerged from various forms of African American music and was influenced by folk and brass band music, as well as black and white minstrel shows (see box on page 24).

The main instrument in ragtime music is the piano. Ragtime is a style of playing based on **honky-tonk** piano playing. In ragtime, the right-hand beat is syncopated, which means the strong beat gets weaker and the weak beat gets stronger. The fresh rhythms and smooth sounds of ragtime appealed to millions of Americans.

Ragtime on paper

By the turn of the century, ragtime music began to be published. The first "rag" published was called "Harlem Rag" and was by Tom Turpin.[2] Easy-to-read versions of ragtime music were published for people to play on their pianos at home. As the leisure time of middle-class Americans increased, so did the demand for sheet music. The piano was a popular addition in the parlour of many American homes. It served as a form of entertainment and also a status symbol.[3] Ragtime was an African American music form that transferred easily to the white mainstream because it was instrumental. Scott Joplin was a popular ragtime composer whose music sold in the thousands.

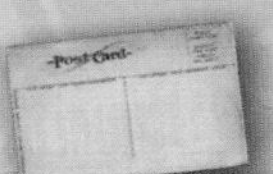

Did you know?

Scott Joplin's "Maple Leaf Rag" was published in 1899 and sold 75,000 copies in the first year.[4]

Scott Joplin became one of the first African Americans to enjoy widespread fame.

Scott Joplin (1868-1917)

Scott Joplin was a talented American pianist and composer. He taught himself to play the piano before getting formal lessons at the age of eleven.[5] Joplin was a leading figure in ragtime and was known as the King of Ragtime. He was one of the first ragtime musicians to write down the music. His hits included "Maple Leaf Rag", "Swipesy Cakewalk", and "The Entertainer". He died in 1917. Joplin's popularity and that of ragtime were revived in the 1970s when "The Entertainer" was used in a very popular film, *The Sting*.

Early jazz

Ragtime developed before jazz and continued to be popular along with early jazz. Some ragtime musicians were involved in the creation of early jazz. But jazz took off in a big way and has been a major influence on popular culture around the world ever since.

Jazz developed in the southern United States in the early twentieth century. Like ragtime, it started with African American musicians and its appeal quickly spread to a large section of society. It was the popular music to listen to and dance to in bars and saloons, and it remains popular today.

What is jazz?

Jazz is an informal sound that often utilizes up-tempo rhythms. It is a combination of West African rhythms with elements from ragtime, brass bands, blues, and **work songs**. The work songs that influenced jazz are the songs sung by African American slaves and workers to relieve the boredom of a repetitive task. They were often spiritual in nature.

Brass band music, particularly that of New Orleans marching bands, is an important part of jazz. Brass bands would play for a variety of functions, but usually for funerals. On the way to the burial, the band would play mournful music known as a dirge. On the way back, they would play happy, faster music. These bands would play **improvised** tunes, which are a key element in jazz. The musicians did not play from written sheet music. Instead, each musician played the tune in a different way. Some of jazz's legendary figures, such as Buddy Bolden and King Oliver, were involved in these marching bands.

CULTURE IN CONTEXT: Black and white minstrel show

Minstrel shows were travelling bands of entertainers who performed songs and music of African American origin. These bands are now controversial because the performers were white people with their faces blackened by make-up in order to appear African American. The humour, based on racial stereotypes, is now considered offensive.

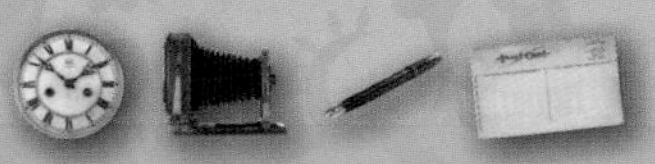

King Oliver (with trumpet, back row) was a leading figure in early jazz. He was also the person who saw the talent and potential in the young musician Louis Armstrong (kneeling, centre). Armstrong became one of the most famous jazz trumpeters ever.

Birth of the blues

The blues emerged at the same time as jazz, and the two music forms influenced each other. Like jazz, early blues was played in the southern United States by African American musicians at the turn of the century. Blues musicians mixed work songs with African and white folk music. The first blues **record** was published in 1912. It was called "Memphis Blues" and was by W. C. Handy.[6]

Dance

In the early twentieth century, some Americans were looking for new dances. As ragtime music became more acceptable, high society ballrooms started to do the cakewalk. This dance involved couples forming a square, with men on the inside. The couples then strutted around the square to the music. Judges evaluated the dancers based on their elegance, grace, and inventiveness, gradually eliminating the couples who were not the best dancers. The winning couple was presented with a cake.[7] Scott Joplin's "Swipesy Cakewalk" was a popular tune for this dance.

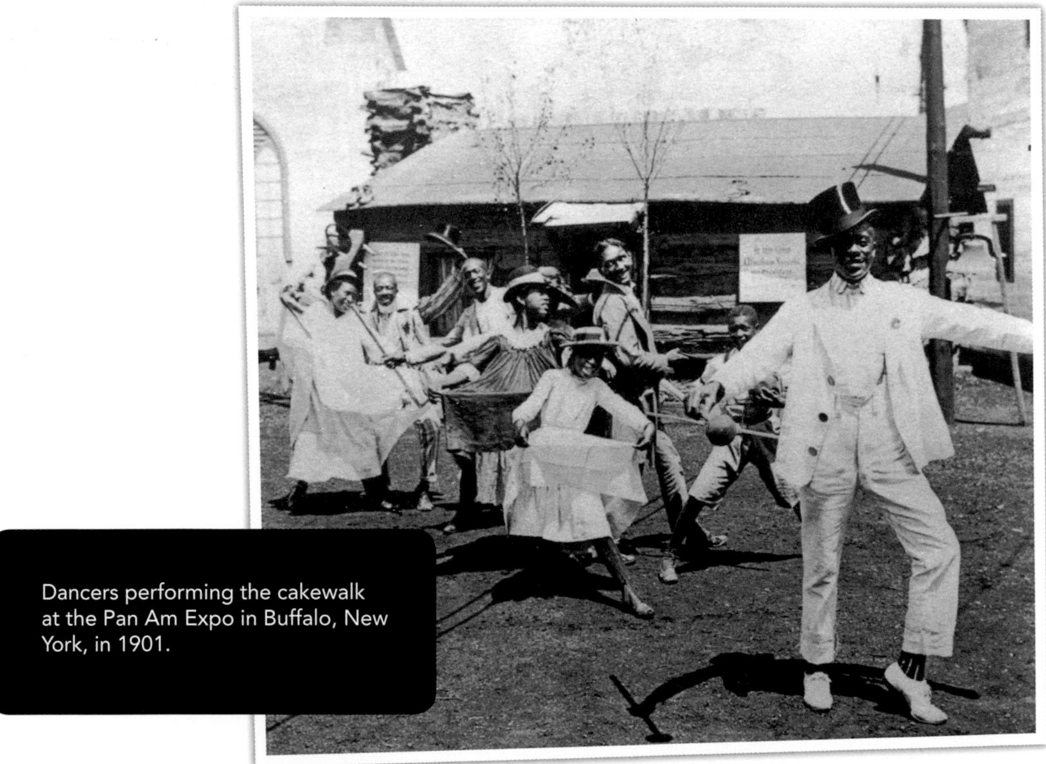

Dancers performing the cakewalk at the Pan Am Expo in Buffalo, New York, in 1901.

The dances performed to ragtime were mainly the one-step. This is where a couple walked one step to each beat of the music. Its simplicity was part of its popularity because everyone could do it. Those who were more skilled in dance could also choose from the Argentine tango, the hesitation waltz, the Brazilian maxixe, or the foxtrot.

In Europe, the younger generation embraced the more lively, exciting dances coming from the United States. They took up the one-step, two-step, the turkey trot, the foxtrot, and the quickstep.[8]

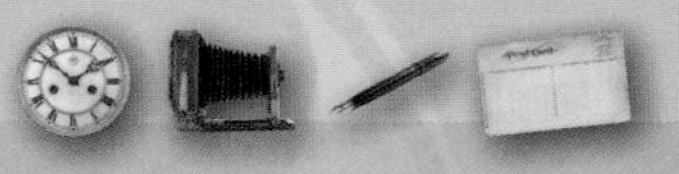

A gramophone is being used to attract attention to a recruitment drive in London for World War I soldiers.

The music business

In the early twentieth century, the music industry was very different to how it is now. The most common way for people to buy music was as sheet music so that they could play the tune themselves. A popular social activity was gathering at someone's home and singing songs around a piano.

People had been experimenting with different ways of recording and playing back sounds and music since the mid-1850s.[9] But it wasn't until 1887 that the record was invented. These records were flat disks that held sound grooves in a spiral. They could be played back on a gramophone. By 1915, the 78 **rpm (revolutions per minute)** record had been introduced and it allowed a playing time of about four and a half minutes per side, which was enough for one or two songs per side.

Improvements in recording and playback technology allowed people to reproduce music on a larger scale for the general public. Recorded music and sheet music sales increased as people had more and more free time. The pleasure and escapism provided by popular music was especially in demand after World War I.

CULTURE IN CONTEXT: Development in radio

Experiments with radio technology led to big advances in the early twentieth century, but it wasn't until about 1912 that the concept of **broadcasting** was realized. In 1916, the possibility of a radio broadcast receiver in every home was proposed.[10] Radio was increasingly used in World War I, but commercial broadcasting did not start until around 1920.[11]

The printed word

By 1900, new techniques for printing, binding, typesetting, and producing paper made the mass production of books, newspapers, and magazines possible. Mass production made the printed word more affordable and reading was an increasingly popular pastime, boosted by an increase in literacy rates.

Pulp magazines

There was a type of magazine called a pulp magazine that was named after the cheaper pulp paper on which it was printed. This pulp paper allowed the price of magazines to drop, making them more affordable. The first pulp magazine, called *The Golden Argosy*, was published in 1882 and was aimed at children. This magazine evolved into a new fiction magazine for adults, called *The Argosy*. It was nearly 200 pages long and packed with fiction and poetry. It became a great success. Pulp magazine publishers expanded and began to specialize in crime stories, westerns, romances, adventures, and fantasies with magazines such as *Detective Story Magazine* and *New Buffalo Bill Weekly*.

Miscellany periodicals

One of the most popular forms of magazine was the **miscellany** periodical. These magazines were a combination of short stories and articles on travel, political events, and technological oddities. They provided people who could not afford to travel the opportunity to read and learn about places near and far. They also supplied those with even the smallest sum of disposable income with ideas for entertainment. These periodicals popularized short stories such as Arthur Conan Doyle's Sherlock Holmes mysteries (see pages 32–33). Unlike serial stories, these short stories didn't require any previous knowledge on the part of the reader. They were also just the right length for the commute that people were making on the new underground trains.

The dime novel

In the United States dime novels were popular until about 1915. These were usually inexpensive paperbacks containing adventure fiction, usually with a western theme or a science fiction element.[1]

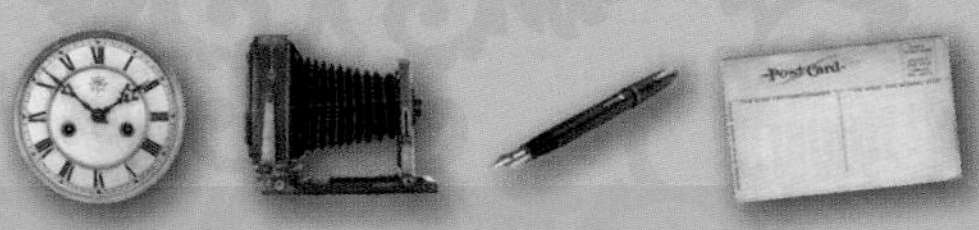

COMPLETE NEW SHERLOCK HOLMES STORY
The Adventure of the Sussex Vampire

THE STRAND MAGAZINE

A TIP FOR THE TONGUE
SEE PAGE 6

ALSO
CONAN DOYLE
ON
SHERLOCK HOLMES
IN HIS REMINISCENCES

Short stories featuring the detective Sherlock Holmes were popular in miscellany periodicals.

Women's magazines

Looking at a newsagent's magazine shelf today you might be surprised to learn that many of today's women's magazines were being published in the early twentieth century. For example, *Good Housekeeping* was founded in 1885, *Vogue* was founded in 1892, *Harper's Bazaar* in 1867, and *Vanity Fair* first appeared in 1859 and was reintroduced in 1914.[2] The 1914 version of *Vanity Fair* was a cultural force during the Jazz Age, because it published the work of modern artists, illustrators, and writers.[3]

Vogue was originally intended to be a weekly high-society journal for New York City's social elite. However, when Condé Nast bought *Vogue* in 1909 he transformed it into an influential women's fashion magazine focused on beauty, conduct, and etiquette.

Condé Nast became the first person to publish international editions of magazines when he published a British *Vogue* in 1916.[4]

Condé Nast (1873-1942)

Condé Nast and his company had a worldwide influence on popular culture. Nast built on the success of *Vogue* by buying other magazines, such as *Vanity Fair* and *House & Garden*. His innovative publishing theory was the concept of specialized publishing. This is when a publication is aimed at a particular group of people who share common interests. By aiming these magazines at certain specialized groups, Nast created magazines that were sophisticated and glamorous and influential on fashionable trends.

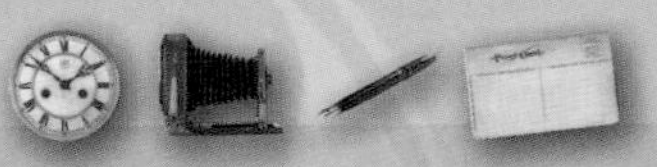

Comics

What we think of as the comic strip developed in the United States. However, before this, European newspapers, magazines, and books published stories in cartoon form. Swiss artist Rodolphe Töpffer divided his picture stories into frames and added narrative to each frame. Picture stories with the title characters of such comic strips as *Max und Moritz* and *Ally Sloper* became popular in Germany and the United Kingdom.[5]

In the United States comics grew in popularity between 1895 and 1905,[6] when the comic strip was used in newspaper **circulation wars**. Improvements in colour printing led to the introduction of **colour supplements** in US Sunday papers. These Sunday supplements featured comic strips. There was such a big demand for these comics that by 1910 newspapers were publishing small books that contained previously published comic strips.[7]

Rudolph Dirks was the first person to create what we now recognize as a comic strip with speech balloons and cartoon panels. His strip *The Katzenjammer Kids* appeared in the *Journal American* on December 12, 1897.[8] Many other artists turned their attention to the comic strip. A cartoon mouse called Teddy Tail was the main character in the first British daily comic strip. The cartoon was first printed in the Daily Mail in 1915.

The first successful daily newspaper comic strip was created in 1907 by Bud Fisher. *Mutt and Jeff* went on to be a favourite with US audiences for decades. There has even been sheet music created based on the *Mutt and Jeff* characters!

Literature

People interested in literature were reading work by authors such as Virginia Woolf, E. M. Forster, James Joyce, Somerset Maugham, D. H. Lawrence, Henry James, and Mark Twain.

New types of fiction were becoming popular in these decades. The mainstream fiction of the **Victorian era** was typically a three-volume novel about domestic life. The popularity of these was replaced with the more accessible single-volume, faster-paced literature, such as adventure and detective stories and the science fiction novel.[9]

Science fiction

Science fiction was a popular **genre** of novels during these decades. The novels of author H. G. Wells shaped the way many people thought and behaved. Wells's science fiction novels contained predictions of air combat, contact between planets, and eugenics – the practice of altering a population by controlled breeding. Examples of his science fiction work include *The War of the Worlds* (1898), *The War in the Air* (1908), and *The First Men in the Moon* (1901).[10] Wells also wrote popular comic novels, including *Kipps* (1905) and *The History of Mr. Polly* (1910),[11] about how the lower middle class lived.

Adventure stories

Adventure stories, such as Rudyard Kipling's *The Jungle Book* (1894) and *Just So Stories* (1902), added a bit of excitement to life and kept the reader gripped. In 1907, Kipling was awarded the Nobel Prize for Literature, becoming the first writer in English to receive it.[12] Kipling wrote about India at the height of the British Empire. His stories were often romantic and sentimental. Another English writer known for his adventure novels was Henry Rider Haggard. Many of his stories were set in Africa. He is best known for his books *King Solomon's Mines* (1885) and *She* (1889).[13]

Detective novels

The detective novel was a new form of fiction. Detective stories became popular in magazines in the late nineteenth century but didn't become popular as novels until the twentieth century. Then they took off in a big way.[14] Arthur Conan Doyle's famous detective, Sherlock Holmes, first appeared in 1887 but remained popular for decades to come. There was such an outcry from the public when Conan Doyle killed off Holmes that he had to resurrect this popular character in *The Hound of the Baskervilles*, published in 1902.[15]

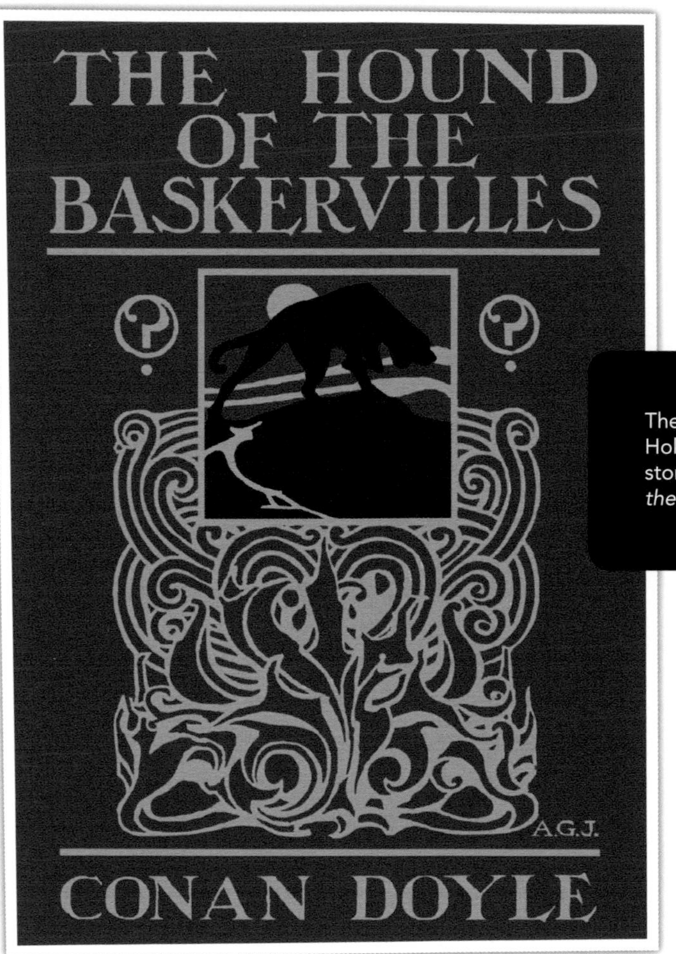

The fictional detective Sherlock Holmes appeared in over 50 stories, including *The Hound of the Baskervilles*.

Fan magazines

Fan magazines first appeared in 1911. *Motion Picture Story Magazine* was launched in the United States with the intention of advertising films. It provided short pieces of fiction to promote the important movies of one of the major film companies, Vitagraph. In the United Kingdom, *The Pictures* used a similar approach. People liked these magazines because they felt that they were getting privileged information. The short stories also helped cinema-goers understand what was happening in the films since there was no spoken dialogue in the early motion pictures.

Wartime literature

World War I affected all areas of people's lives. The tragic, brutal events that occurred made some people want to write about their experiences. Sometimes people weren't able to do this, though, until some time had elapsed since the war. Other people whose lives had also been dominated by the war wanted to read these works.

Poetry

Poetry is a popular way of expressing feelings. Siegfried Sassoon was an English poet and writer who wrote poetry about the stark reality of war while he was serving in the British Army. He wrote about his compassion for his fellow soldiers as well as his contempt for the war leaders and what he thought was their insincere patriotic talk. While Sassoon was hospitalized in 1917[16] he met the poet Wilfred Owen. Sassoon gave Owen encouragement to write about the war. Owen's poems are about the horrors of war and his pity for the victims. Sadly, Owen became one of these victims when he was killed in 1918 during the final days of battle. Only five of Owen's poems were published during his lifetime, but his reputation grew when Sassoon published Owen's work in 1920. Owen's most famous work includes "Strange Meeting" and "Anthem for Doomed Youth".[17]

The Canadian John McCrae wrote the famous poem "In Flanders Fields". It is from this poem that poppies have become associated with World War I. In it, McCrae writes of poppies blowing between the crosses that act as gravestones. Paper poppies are now sold in many countries to raise money for war veterans and people wear them to show their remembrance of those who died in World War I and World War II.

This portrait of Wilfred Owen was taken around 1916.

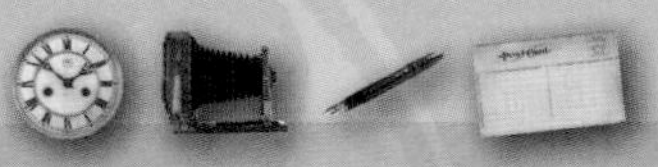

Prose

Some people wrote about their wartime experiences in the forms of memoirs and diaries. *Le Feu* (*Under Fire*) (1917)[18] by Henri Barbusse is a firsthand account of the life of French soldiers. Robert Graves wrote a memoir titled *Good-bye to All That* (1929).[19] Others used World War I as the setting for their novels, including Erich Maria Remarque with *All Quiet on the Western Front* (1929).[20] A film version of this successful novel is often shown on television today. Rebecca West's *The Return of the Soldier* (1918)[21] is about life on the **home front**, and John Dos Passos's *Three Soldiers* (1921) is based on his experience as an ambulance driver during the war.

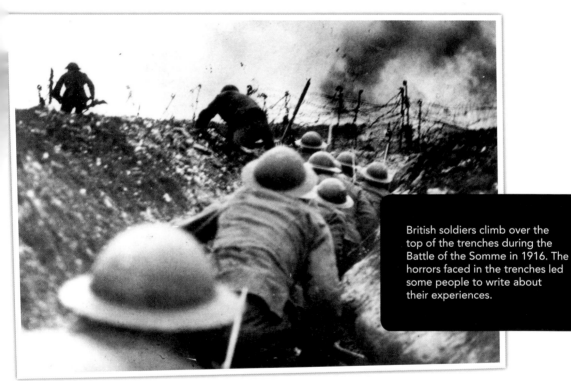

British soldiers climb over the top of the trenches during the Battle of the Somme in 1916. The horrors faced in the trenches led some people to write about their experiences.

World War I songs

World War I inspired many songs. Some of them were about the war, others were written to keep up morale. Popular songs of the time included:

- "It's a long way to Tipperary"
- "Oh! It's a lovely war"
- "Over there"
- "Pack up your troubles in your old kit bag"

Art and design

If you were to look up which artists were working between 1900 and 1919, you would find some famous names. Pablo Picasso and Georges Braque were inventing **cubism**. Wassily Kandinsky was painting early abstract art. Henri Matisse was experimenting with colour. Marcel Duchamp was shocking the art world with his ready-made piece called *Fountain*, which was just a urinal signed "R. Mutt". The **surrealists**, such as Salvador Dalí and René Magritte, were forming and experimenting with the link between reality and dreams. However, the ordinary person in the years from 1900 to 1919 would probably not have even heard of these artists. Until the 1960s with the rise of pop art, art was not accessible to the general public. Only a few wealthy individuals were able to afford to buy art. However, what the artists were doing played a significant role in the look and style of the era.

Art nouveau

At the end of the nineteenth century and early twentieth century, artists and designers wanted a new art that reflected the new materials they were using. Under the term **art nouveau**, or "new art", artists, architects, and designers experimented with new materials and techniques. The style they created was ornamental and inspired by nature. It used long, flowing lines and natural curves.

The poster

Art nouveau and the poster went well together. The poster was a piece of art that could look beautiful in addition to being useful by advertising products or events. The poster had a big impact on history, too. During World War I it was the most important of all visual media. It could be printed quickly and put up where the public could see it, to have an immediate impact. A poster could also communicate with people who couldn't read (see pages 42–43).

Depending on where they lived, the public would have seen this art form all around them. Art nouveau was used for architecture, interior design, jewellery and glass design, posters, and illustration. In the United States, the art nouveau style appeared in the work of popular artist Louis Comfort Tiffany. By 1900, Tiffany was creating lamps, jewellery, and pottery as well as his celebrated glasswork. His work made him a leader of the art nouveau movement. In London, the shop Liberty & Company was very influential in promoting the style. Liberty sold carpets and furniture in the art nouveau style, and also designed art nouveau fabrics used for clothing and furnishings. This was the fashionable place to shop.

In France, Hector Guimard designed the signs for the Paris Metro in the art nouveau style.

Architecture and design

While art nouveau remained popular up until World War I, there was a group of architects who started a new way of thinking about design. Their style was called **modernism**. These architects wanted to clear away fussy style and ornament and look at design in terms of function. They wanted to strip a design back to the basics and consider, for example, what a building needed to do and what materials were needed to achieve this. The new approach of modernism was being used all over the world, but it was easiest in the United States because there weren't centuries of tradition to overcome. Architects began to question why they should build an exciting new skyscraper and then cover it with decorations from an old pattern book.

One of the most successful architects of this new approach was American Frank Lloyd Wright, who designed buildings such as 540 Fair Oaks Avenue in Oak Park, Illinois, in 1902. Wright was the leading figure in what became known as the Prairie School of architecture.[1] Wright's prairie-style houses revolutionized the design of American homes. These houses had long, low, horizontal lines and intercommunicating interior spaces appealing to the way people wanted to live at the time. Wright's concept of "organic architecture" influenced architects throughout the United States and the world.

Frank Lloyd Wright's Robie House in Chicago, Illinois, shown around 1915. You can see the strong horizontal lines that made his designs so striking.

The Bauhaus teachers. From left to right: Albers, Scheper, Muche, Moholy- Nagy, Bayer, Schmidt, Gropius, Breuer, Kandinsky, Klee, Feininger, Stolzl, and Schlemmer.

Bauhaus

Bauhaus is the name of a school of architecture in Dessau, Germany, that was founded by Walter Gropius in 1919.[2] The school wanted to prove that art and engineering could work together instead of separately as previously thought. The Bauhaus ideals involved machine production as part of the design. The Bauhaus philosophy was that a building or object should be designed around the technology of mass production. This would allow objects to be made for the masses, rather than just for wealthy individuals.

Before students were allowed entry to the school, they had to take a six-month course. They were taught by some of the most outstanding artists of the twentieth century, including Josef Albers, Laszlo Moholy-Nagy, Paul Klee, Wassily Kandinsky, and Ludwig Mies van der Rohe.[3] The students were involved in the design of a Bauhaus building and all its fixtures and fittings. The Bauhaus style has influenced design beyond architecture, such as furniture and other objects for the home.

Notable architecture of the decades

1904: Frank Lloyd Wright, Larkin Building
1907–1909: Frank Lloyd Wright, Robie House
1909–1912: Peter Behrens, AEG Factory
1911–1914: Walter Gropius & Adolf Meyer, Fagus Works

Photography

The first photograph was taken in 1826. By 1900, photography was no longer a new invention, and people were exploring the possibilities that photography offered them. Mass-market photography had been available since 1889, when the first Kodak camera with a flexible roll of film was launched with the slogan "You push the button, we do the rest".[4] Photography became a popular pastime.

Did you know?

Between 1900 and 1919 colour photography was still not available. The first colour film was introduced in 1935 by Eastman Kodak Company.[5]

Photography as an art form

Photographers were starting to compose their shots as an artist would compose a painting. Initially photography wasn't regarded as an art form in the way that a painting or drawing was. This was because the camera seemed to do the work. Some people argued that the photographer didn't require imagination, creativity, or the manual skills that an artist did. Despite this, the interest in photography grew, and the photo gradually became accepted as an art form. Art dealers and photographers, such as the American Alfred Stieglitz, started to promote photography as an art form and held exhibitions of photographers' work.[6]

Documentary photography

Photography could be more than just a hobby or a form of artwork. Starting in the late nineteenth century, many photographers were using photos to influence society and culture by highlighting social problems. Jacob A. Riis, a Danish immigrant to the United States, used his camera to document the poverty faced by the urban poor.[7] In the United Kingdom, the suffragette movement and social reform organizations used photographs of women, children, and families living in poverty to promote their ideas and gain support for their work.

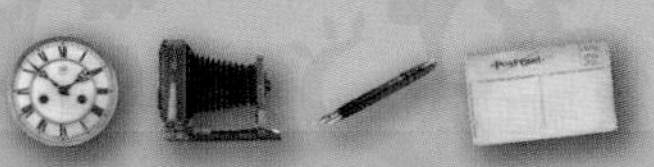

US photographer Lewis Hine took this photo of child labourers working in beet fields in Colorado in 1915.

Cameras on the front line

During World War I, the new, smaller, lightweight cameras were used by some soldiers to take photos of the fighting, even though they were ordered not to. The best of these shots from the front line were published in daily newspapers. The soldiers who took these photos were taking big risks to obtain the most spectacular or frightening photographs. They put themselves in physical danger on the battle scene and also risked facing a firing squad if they were caught taking the photos.[8]

Wartime propaganda

What is propaganda? Propaganda is an organized programme of publicity to promote particular beliefs. Before the twentieth century, the term had a neutral meaning. Since World War I, however, the term has a more sinister, manipulative implication. During World War I, governments needed a different way to influence the public. New military technology, such as machine guns, meant that soldiers were being killed in large numbers, and traditional forms of recruitment weren't enough. Governments needed to find a different way to sway public opinion. The answer was in the relatively new forms of mass communication. Cheap newspapers, posters, and movies meant that governments could communicate on a daily basis.

Propaganda posters and films

Governments made wartime propaganda look familiar by designing it like film posters and advertisements (see pages 36–37). They also made it look glamorous by exploiting the images of fantasy and desire created by mass entertainment. Propaganda movies were made like westerns or crime dramas, and used popular personalities from films, music, and sports. For example, Charlie Chaplin made *The Bond*, a propaganda film to promote US Liberty Bonds during World War I.[1] They even used cartoon characters to spread the official messages of the war effort.

The US Army's iconic 1917 recruitment poster uses the image of Uncle Sam to deliver the message, rather than a real solider or recognizable politician. This poster was designed by James Montgomery Flagg.

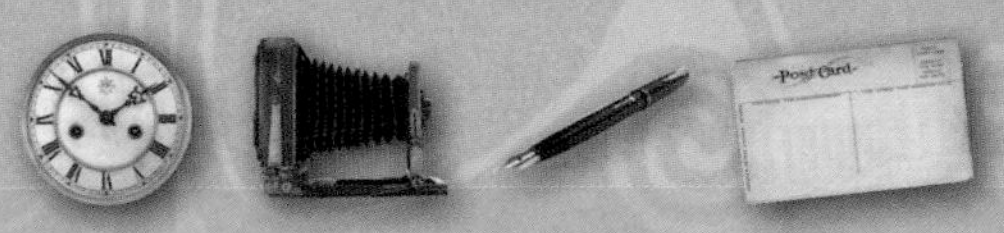

Recruitment posters were made to look like advertisements and film posters. Before World War I, few people would have considered joining the army. Posters with messages such as "I Want You for the U.S. Army" and "Your Country Needs You" brought world events to the general public's attention and encouraged people to become heroes.

This British recruitment poster was designed in 1914 by Alfred Leete. In this poster he made Secretary of State for War Lord Kitchener into an iconic image.

Newsreels

Newsreels were a common part of the cinema experience. They would be shown before the start of the feature film. During the war, newsreels were carefully censored by the government to ensure that only the information the government wanted the public to know would be shown. Some films even mixed genuine news footage with fictional sequences, such as D. W. Griffith's *Hearts of the World* (1918).[2]

Pathé Newsreels

The weekly Pathé newsreels dominated the world market in the early 1900s, and by 1908 Charles Pathé's company (see page 14) was the world's largest film producer. The French-based company was selling twice as many films in the United States as all the US film companies combined. The Pathé network collapsed with the outbreak of war, but the governments involved in the war quickly produced their own newsreels. These newsreels showed a biased version of world events.[3]

Fashion

There were many ways in which fashion influenced popular culture, and ways in which popular culture influenced fashion. People wanted to copy the glamour of the film stars that they saw at the cinema and in their magazines. These stars appeared with flawless make-up, and women wanted this look, too. The automobile craze influenced what people wore. The bicycle affected fashion, too – especially ladies' fashion, because women needed clothing they could pedal in safely. The increase in leisure time meant that sportswear and bathing suits were in demand. The women's rights movement influenced fashion as women fought for equality.

Fashion at the turn of the century

At the turn of the century it was common for women to wear uncomfortable and complicated clothes, such as corsets. Corsets are undergarments that pull in the waist and support the bosom. They were incredibly uncomfortable to wear and restricted the movement and breathing of the wearer. Corsets were used to give the body a different shape that was viewed as appealing by society at the time.

French designers Paul Poiret and Madeleine Vionnet are given the credit for liberating women from uncomfortable corsets.[1] Poiret's early dress designs were simple and straight. A corset would have changed the shape of these designs so he opted for the brassiere. Madeleine Vionnet created fluid, flowing designs that included new shapes such as cowl and halter necklines.

Menswear

Fashionable men wore trousers, a waistcoat, and a coat with a top hat. After 1880, the trend for beards passed and men were clean-shaven or wore just a moustache.[2]

Sportswear

The trend for sportswear was just beginning at the turn of the century, as clothing started to be made for the increasingly active women who took part in sports such as tennis, horse riding, sailing, and archery. Sportswear consisted of informal separates such as blouses, shirts, skirts, and shorts.

Women were expected to dress modestly, so their clothing had high necklines and skirts that reached the ground.

Swimsuits

The acceptance of more relaxed clothing for sports affected swimwear. Today we think of swimwear as being swim shorts or trunks for men, and swimsuits or bikinis for women. However, early swimsuits covered most of the body so the wearer maintained modesty. For people wanting to go for a dip in the water, bathing was strictly segregated. By the early twentieth century, men started to wear shorts without a top. In 1900,[3] Australian swimmer and film star Annette Kellerman introduced a loose one-piece swimsuit. It was made of wool! Just imagine how uncomfortable it must have been, especially when wet!

Bathers on the beach near Atlantic City in New Jersey, USA, show off the latest swimsuit fashions.

Did you know?

It became acceptable to wear lipstick in public around 1912.

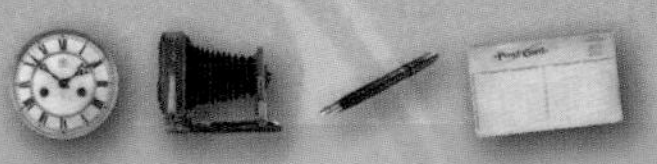

Hair and make-up

Women wanted to look like their favourite film stars, so the demand for cosmetics increased. Familiar names in the beauty industry include Max Factor, Maybelline, and L'Oréal. These companies all started out in the 1900s. Max Factor was a Polish immigrant who moved to Los Angeles and started to sell make-up that didn't crack or cake to film stars. In 1910, French chemist Eugene Schueller founded L'Oréal, which provided the first safe commercial hair dye. In 1914, T. J. Williams founded Maybelline, a cosmetics company that specialized in mascara. A year later, in 1915, Maurice Levy invented a metal container for lipstick.[4] Women were then able to easily carry their lipstick around with them in their handbags.

Did you know?

The zip was launched in 1914 by Swedish-born engineer Gideon Sundback.[5] Sundback's zip was used by the US Army on the clothing and gear of World War I troops.[6]

Bicycles and freedom

The development in the late 1880s of the safety bicycle, which looked more like today's standard bicycle, also affected women's fashion. Some women started to wear a kind of trouser to ride their bicycles. In the 1850s, American journalist Amelia Jenks Bloomer recommended wearing an outfit that consisted of a short jacket, a skirt, and loose trousers that gathered at the ankles. The look didn't take off and Bloomer was mocked. However, the name "bloomers" survived and was used to describe the divided skirts women used for cycling.[7]

In addition to changing women's fashion in the 1900s, the bicycle also helped with the fight for women's equality. The bicycle gave women more personal freedom. It was adopted as a symbol of freedom by the suffragette movement.[8] Susan B. Anthony, a leader of the US suffragette movement, declared that the bicycle did more than anything else did to **emancipate** women.[9]

Wartime fashion

World War I had an effect on every area of people's lives, even on fashion. Fashion became practical. The fashion for women's skirts before the war was ankle-length, but the hemline of skirts jumped to mid-calf by 1916.[10] The narrow hobble skirts that were introduced by Poiret were discarded in favour of more practical, wider skirts. Trousers for women had been thought ugly but were now seen as practical for war work. Short hair was seen as a sensible safety measure for women working in factories.

Uniforms

Women involved in the war effort and those who had joined military organizations wore uniforms. These military uniforms influenced the shape of fashionable dress.

CULTURE IN CONTEXT: War shortages

During the war there were shortages of many important things, such as food and building materials. There was also a shortage of fabric and fabric dye. This meant that fashions used less material than they did before the war. The shortage of dye meant that the colours available in the fashion world were limited.

Relaxation of rules

Up until World War I, there had been many rules for how men and women dressed. These rules had been in place since the more formal Victorian era.[11] The impact of war meant that these rules were relaxed. Ostentatious fashion didn't seem so important when families of all classes were losing sons and brothers in mud-filled trenches.

With their new shorter skirt lengths, women wore heeled shoes and skin-coloured stockings, not the high-button boots of earlier days. The war also spelled the end of the corset. With the practical work women were doing, such as nursing, factory work, and ambulance driving, corsets were too awkward and impractical. Women were discouraged from buying corsets made with steel, which would go to better use in war equipment. This saved 28,000 tons of steel in 1917 – enough to build two battleships![12]

After the war

After World War I ended in 1918, fashions changed again to a more informal look. There was a new enthusiasm for fashion. Underwear continued to be simplified once the corset was no longer worn. Women were trying to achieve a more girlish, straight silhouette. For relaxed, everyday clothing, sportswear was becoming very popular, especially in the United States. French designer Coco Chanel was having success with her "total look". She was the first designer to work skillfully with wool jersey fabric. This material was originally intended to make men's sports clothes, but she used it to make comfortable, chic clothes.[13]

During the war, fashions became simpler and more practical.

Changing times

The great technological advances made at the start of the twentieth century changed society. The affordable car had a huge impact on where people could live and gave them the freedom to travel where they wanted. Mass production of products such as cars, clothes, and magazines meant that they became more affordable. Time-saving devices such as the first electric washing machine meant people had more leisure time – more time for spending at the cinema or dancing the cakewalk!

The age of imperialism was at an end, and people were viewing the United States as the exciting place to be. All things American became popular.

The demand for equality for women and for people of colour was growing. Women finally got the right to vote in the United Kingdom in 1918 and in the United States in 1920.[1] The racial divide between blacks and whites continued from 1900 to 1919, but African American culture, especially in the United States, was influencing the trends of white society. For example, ragtime and jazz music and dances became more mainstream.

Overshadowed by war

The period from 1900 to 1919 was overshadowed by World War I. This war was supposed to be the war that ended all wars. Yet World War II began only 20 years later. The new technology that was so exciting in civilian life was devastating in the military world. The aeroplane, combined with the new machine guns and bombs, increased the fighting in the skies and over enemy territory. Technology changed the face of war and made it more brutal and deadly.

War also affected people on the home front. Everyone became part of the war effort and it changed their lives. Fashion seemed trivial compared with the realities of war. People wanted to know what was going on at the war front, so newspapers, newsreels, magazines, poetry, and fiction about the war were popular. But people also looked for escapism, and the new motion pictures were a great place to find this (see pages 14-19). A whole industry developed around the glamour of the film.

New technologies such as tanks and machine guns changed the nature of modern warfare.

What did the 1900s and 1910s do for us?

The 1900s and 1910s are influential in today's popular culture. The technology may have advanced, but motion pictures and photography still play a key role in today's leisure activities. Film production companies that were set up in the 1900s and 1910s, such as Universal Pictures and what became known as MGM, are still influential today. Although it is no longer the world's centre for film production, Hollywood is still associated with the greats of film, and many film stars live in neighbouring communities. The star system is still an established part of the film industry, and the public and media have an obsession with the latest film stars.

Jazz quickly developed and changed over the following decades, and still lives on in its many forms to delight audiences around the world. The technologies of sound recording have advanced to the degree that we are now able to hear original jazz recordings in a new, improved, digitally remastered form.

This postcard from 1911 shows the *Titanic* before setting off on its fateful journey across the Atlantic in April 1912.

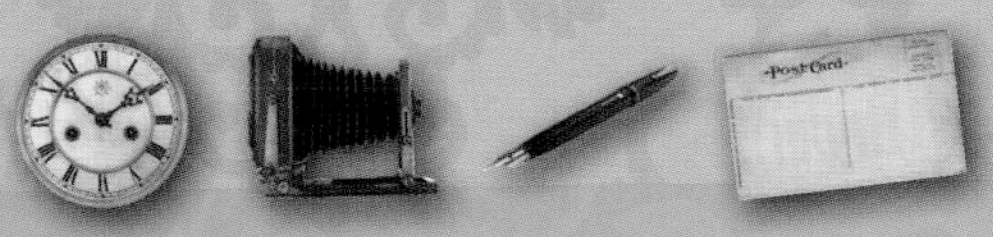

In 2009, an exhibition was held to celebrate the 90th anniversary of the Bauhaus movement, which influenced modern art, design, and architecture.

Today's fashion enthusiasts are still being instructed by *Vogue* as to what to wear, what exhibitions to attend, and how to live stylishly, although perhaps they are reading it all online. It's hard to imagine today's women and girls not having the choice of wearing trousers. And where would we be without the zip? Early twentieth century designers still influence today's fashions as designers continually recycle and reuse "vintage" looks. French designer Paul Poiret was the first designer to introduce the concept of "designer" perfume to complement the lifestyle created by his fashions. Nowadays it's rare to find a designer who doesn't have at least one perfume to offer customers.

Bauhaus design and architecture still look modern today, as does prairie style. It's hard to believe that some of it is nearly 100 years old. The art of this period is still fashionable, although it is more likely today's homes might have a poster or a print by an avant-garde artist such as Picasso or Matisse, who were unknown to the general public in the early 1900s. Today's shops stock furniture and other objects designed by some of the greats of this era, including modernist Mies van der Rohe. In cities around the world, the architecture of this period can still be seen. Mies van der Rohe, for example, was responsible for much of Chicago's skyline.

Even the disasters from this period still affect people today. The sinking of *Titanic*, and the stories and legends that surround it, fascinated the public at the time and continue to do so 100 years later. In May 2011, the cigar box of the captain of *Titanic* sold for £250,000[1] and the plans used to investigate the sinking of the *Titanic* reached £220,000[2].

Timeline

1901
Queen Victoria dies and is succeeded by Edward VII

September 1901
US President McKinley shot by an anarchist. Theodore Roosevelt becomes president.

1901
Australian Immigration Restriction Act of 1901 limits immigration to Australia to mostly Europeans. British emigrants are encouraged by the offer of land.

1902
Beatrix Potter's *The Tale of Peter Rabbit* is published

December 1903
The Wright brothers make the first successful flight

1904
London's first electric underground train is in service

1904
New York City's subway system is opened

1905
The first cinema opens in Pittsburgh, Pennsylvania

1905
Albert Einstein's Special Theory of Relativity is published

1906
First animated cartoon, *Humorous Phases of Funny Faces*, is produced

1907
Ziegfeld Follies begin performing

1907
First successful daily comic strip, *Mutt and Jeff*, is published

1908
Ford Model T car is released

1908
The tea bag is introduced

1908
The Boy Scout movement is founded

1909
General Electric (GE) patents and produces the electric toaster

1909
Vogue bought by Condé Nast and transformed into an influential women's magazine

1911
Fan magazines first appear

April 1912
Titanic sinks

1912
First blues record published

1913
Henry Ford opens the first moving assembly line in Michigan

28 June 1914
Archduke Franz Ferdinand is **assassinated**

9 August 1914
Britain declares war on Germany in response to the invasion of Belgium

1914
Vanity Fair is relaunched

1915
78 rpm record is available

15 September 1916
Tanks are used by the British for the first time at Flers, France

1917
First jazz recordings made

April 1917
United States enters World War I

7 November 1917
Communist revolution begins in Russia

11 November 1918
World War I ends

14–15 June 1919
First non-stop flight made across the Atlantic Ocean

1919
Felix the Cat is created

Best of the era

The best way to find out about the pop culture of the 1900s and 1910s is to experience it for yourself. Here are some suggestions for the best or most typical examples that will give you a sense of the time:

Films

Cinderella
The Great Train Robbery
The Life of an American Fireman
Quo Vadis
Voyage to the Moon

Music

King of Ragtime by Scott Joplin
King Oliver by Oliver's Creole Jazz Band
The Library of Congress Recordings by Jelly Roll Morton

Literature

Arthur Conan Doyle: *The Hound of the Baskervilles*
John Dos Passos: *Three Soldiers*
Robert Graves: *Over the Brazier* and *Fairies and Fusiliers*
Erich Maria Remarque: *All Quiet on the Western Front*
H. G. Wells: *The First Men in the Moon* and *The War of the Worlds*
Rebecca West: *The Return of the Soldier*
Oscar Wilde: *The Picture of Dorian Gray*

Drama & theatre

J. M. Barrie: *The Admirable Crichton* and *Peter Pan*
Oscar Wilde: *Lady Windermere's Fan* and *The Importance of Being Earnest*

Architecture

Behrens: AEG Factory
Gropius & Meyer: Fagus Works
Wright: Larkin Building and Robie House

Notes on sources

What is popular culture?

1. *The Oxford English Reference Dictionary*, Oxford University Press, 1996, 264.

2. "World War I," *Britannica Student Encyclopedia, Encyclopedia Britannica Online Library Edition, Encyclopædia Britannica*, 2011, http://library.eb.co.uk/all/comptons/article-9277797, Accessed June 2, 2011.

3. "woman suffrage," *Encyclopædia Britannica, Encyclopædia Britannica Online Library Edition, Encyclopædia Britannica*, 2011, http://library.eb.co.uk/eb/article-284442, Accessed April 19, 2011.

4. Joanna Hunter, *A Century in Photographs*, London: Times Newspapers, Ltd.,1999, 41.

5. http://www.localhistories.org/20thcent.html, Accessed July 17, 2011.

6. http://www.jazzistry.org/timeline.html, Accessed July 17, 2011.

7. "subway," *Encyclopædia Britannica, Encyclopedia Britannica Online Library Edition,*

Encyclopædia Britannica, 2011, http://library.eb.co.uk/eb/article-9070117, Accessed June 3, 2011.

8. Hunter, *A Century in Photographs*, 23.

9. "subway," *Encyclopædia Britannica.*

10. "airplane," *Britannica Student Encyclopedia, Encyclopedia Britannica Online Library Edition, Encyclopædia Britannica*, 2011, http://library.eb.co.uk/all/comptons/article-230877, Accessed June 3, 2011.

11. *The Oxford English Reference Dictionary*, 31.

12. Hunter, *A Century in Photographs*, 21.

13. Hunter, *A Century in Photographs*, 41.

14. "automobile," *Encyclopædia Britannica, Encyclopædia Britannica Online Library Edition, Encyclopædia Britannica*, 2011, http://library.eb.co.uk/eb/article-259068, Accessed July 18, 2011.

15. Hunter, *A Century in Photographs*, 41.

16. "United States." *Encyclopædia Britannica, Encyclopædia Britannica Online Library Edition, Encyclopædia Britannica*, Inc., 2011, http://library.eb.co.uk/eb/article-78004, Accessed July 18, 2011.

17. Immigration to United States, Video, *Encyclopedia Britannica Online Library Edition*, http://library.eb.co.uk/eb/art-71911, Accessed July 18, 2011.

Children's entertainment

1. "jigsaw puzzle," *Encyclopædia Britannica, Encyclopædia Britannica Online Library Edition, Encyclopædia Britannica*, 2011, http://library.eb.co.uk/eb/article-9043634, Accessed April 12, 2011.

2. "Roosevelt, Theodore," *Encyclopædia Britannica, Encyclopedia Britannica Online Library Edition, Encyclopædia Britannica*, 2011, http://library.eb.co.uk/eb/article-8428, Accessed June 2, 2011.

3. http://ezinearticles.com/?Toys-in-the-Early-1900s&id=2142431, Accessed April 12, 2011.

4. http://www.meccano.com/about/history/, Accessed June 1, 2011.

5. "child labor," *Britannica Student Encyclopedia, Encyclopedia Britannica Online Library Edition, Encyclopædia Britannica*, 2011, http://library.eb.co.uk/all/comptons/article-234147, Accessed June 1, 2011.

6. http://www.educationbug.org/a/compulsory-education.html, Accessed July 18, 2011.

Film and light entertainment

1. http://www.factmonster.com/ce6/ent/A0859791.html, Accessed April 12, 2011.

2. "motion picture, history of the," *Encyclopædia Britannica.*

3. "motion picture, history of the," Encyclopædia Britannica.

4. "Porter, Edwin S.," *Encyclopædia Britannica, Encyclopedia Britannica Online Library Edition, Encyclopædia Britannica*, 2011, http://library.eb.co.uk/eb/article-9060965, Accessed May 31, 2011.

5. "Birth of a Nation, The," *Encyclopædia Britannica, Encyclopedia Britannica Online Library Edition, Encyclopædia Britannica*, 2011, http://library.eb.co.uk/eb/article-9477268, Accessed May 31, 2011.

6. "Birth of a Nation, The," *Encyclopædia Britannica.*

7. "Griffith, D(avid) W(ark)," *Encyclopædia Britannica, Encyclopedia Britannica Online Library Edition, Encyclopædia Britannica*, 2011, http://library.eb.co.uk/eb/article-2869, Accessed May 31, 2011.

8. "Porter, Edwin S.," *Encyclopædia Britannica.*

9. http://www.parliament.uk/documents/commons/lib/research/rp99/rp99-111.pdf, Accessed June 3, 2011.

10. "Laemmle, Carl," *Encyclopædia Britannica, Encyclopedia Britannica Online Library Edition, Encyclopædia Britannica*, 2011, http://library.eb.co.uk/eb/article-9472708, Accessed May 31, 2011.

11. "Pickford, Mary," *Encyclopædia Britannica, Encyclopedia Britannica Online Library Edition, Encyclopædia Britannica*, 2011, http://library.eb.co.uk/eb/article-9059931, Accessed June 2, 2011.

12. "Messmer, Otto," *Encyclopædia Britannica, Encyclopedia Britannica Online Library Edition, Encyclopædia Britannica*, 2011, http://library.eb.co.uk/eb/article-9106439, Accessed May 31, 2011.

13. "Fields, W.C.," *Britannica Student Encyclopedia, Encyclopedia Britannica Online Library Edition, Encyclopædia Britannica*, 2011, http://library.eb.co.uk/all/comptons/article-9274306, Accessed June 1, 2011.

14. "Keaton, Buster," *Encyclopædia Britannica, Encyclopedia Britannica Online Library Edition, Encyclopædia Britannica*, 2011, http://library.eb.co.uk/eb/article-9044957, Accessed June 2, 2011.

15. "vaudeville," *Encyclopædia Britannica, Encyclopedia Britannica Online Library Edition, Encyclopædia Britannica*, 2011, http://library.eb.co.uk/eb/article-9074912, Accessed June 1, 2011.

16. "Ziegfeld, Florenz, Jr.," *Encyclopædia Britannica, Encyclopedia Britannica Online Library Edition, Encyclopædia Britannica*, 2011, http://library.eb.co.uk/eb/article-9078364, Accessed June 1, 2011.

17. "Muni, Paul," *Encyclopædia Britannica, Encyclopædia Britannica Online Library Edition, Encyclopædia Britannica*, 2011, http://library.eb.co.uk/eb/article-9054279, Accessed July 18, 2011.

18. "Metro-Goldwyn-Mayer, Inc.," *Britannica Student Encyclopedia, Encyclopædia Britannica Online Library Edition, Encyclopædia Britannica*, 2011, http://library.eb.co.uk/all/comptons/article-9312484, Accessed July 18, 2011.

Music

1. "ragtime," *Encyclopædia Britannica, Encyclopædia Britannica Online Library Edition, Encyclopædia Britannica*, 2011, 2011.http://library.eb.co.uk/eb/article-9062463, Accessed April 12, 2011.

2. Ian Carr, Digby Fairweather, and Brian Priestley, *The Rough Guide to Jazz*, London: Rough Guides Ltd., 1995, 742.

3. Carr, Fairweather, Priestley, *The Rough Guide to Jazz*, 742.

4. Carr, Fairweather, Priestley, *The Rough Guide to Jazz*, 345.

5. Carr, Fairweather, Priestley, *The Rough Guide to Jazz*, 344.

6. *The Oxford English Reference Dictionary*, 156.

7. "cakewalk," *Encyclopædia Britannica, Encyclopedia Britannica Online Library Edition, Encyclopædia Britannica*, 2011, http://library.eb.co.uk/eb/article-9018592, Accessed May 31, 2011.

8. "dance, Western," *Encyclopædia Britannica, Encyclopædia Britannica Online Library Edition, Encyclopædia Britannica*, 2011, http://library.eb.co.uk/eb/article-22138, Accessed July 18, 2011.

9. "phonograph," *Encyclopædia Britannica, Encyclopedia Britannica Online Library Edition, Encyclopædia Britannica*, 2011, http://library.eb.co.uk/eb/article-9059766, Accessed May 31, 2011.

10. "radio," *Britannica Student Encyclopedia, Encyclopedia Britannica Online Library Edition, Encyclopædia Britannica*, 2011, http://library.eb.co.uk/all/comptons/article-207095, Accessed June 1, 2011.

11. "radio," *Britannica Student Encyclopedia*, http://library.eb.co.uk/all/comptons/article-286019, Accessed June 1, 2011.

The printed word

1. "dime novel," *Encyclopædia Britannica, Encyclopædia Britannica Online Library Edition, Encyclopædia Britannica*, 2011, http://library.eb.co.uk/eb/article-9124824, Accessed July 18, 2011.

2. "Vanity Fair," *Encyclopædia Britannica, Encyclopedia Britannica Online Library Edition, Encyclopædia Britannica*, 2011, http://library.eb.co.uk/eb/article-9471681, Accessed May 31, 2011.

3. "Vanity Fair," *Encyclopædia Britannica*.

4. http://www.referenceforbusiness.com/history2/54/The-Cond-Nast-Publications-Inc.html, Accessed June 1, 2011.

5. "cartoons," *Britannica Student Encyclopedia, Encyclopædia Britannica Online Library Edition, Encyclopædia Britannica*, 2011, http://library.eb.co.uk/all/comptons/article-198337, Accessed July 18, 2011.

6. http://www.enotes.com/1900-media-american-decades/sunday-color-comics, Accessed June 2, 2011.

7. http://www.enotes.com/how-products-encyclopedia/comic-book, Accessed June 2, 2011.

8. http://www.enotes.com/how-products-encyclopedia/comic-book, Accessed June 2, 2011.

9. Lee Server, *Encyclopedia of Pulp Fiction Writers*, Facts on File, 2002.

10. "1000 Makers of the Twentieth Century," London *Sunday Times*, 1991; "Wells, H. G.," *Encyclopædia Britannica, Encyclopedia Britannica Online Library Edition, Encyclopædia Britannica*, 2011, http://library.eb.co.uk/eb/article-7863, Accessed June 2, 2011.

11. "Wells, H. G.," *Encyclopædia Britannica*.

12. *The Oxford English Reference Dictionary*, 784.

13. *The Oxford English Reference Dictionary*, 632.

14. http://www.ucalgary.ca/applied_history/tutor/popculture/, Accessed May 29, 2011.

15. http://www.ucalgary.ca/applied_history/tutor/popculture/.

16. *The Oxford English Reference Dictionary*, 1286.

17. *The Oxford English Reference Dictionary*, 1040.

18. "Barbusse, Henri," *Encyclopædia Britannica, Encyclopedia Britannica Online Library Edition, Encyclopædia Britannica*, 2011, http://library.eb.co.uk/eb/article-9013324, Accessed June 2, 2011.

19. "Graves, Robert," *Encyclopædia Britannica, Encyclopedia Britannica Online Library Edition, Encyclopædia Britannica*, 2011, http://library.eb.co.uk/eb/article-9037784, Accessed June 2, 2011.

20. "Remarque, Erich Maria," *Encyclopædia Britannica, Encyclopedia Britannica Online Library Edition, Encyclopædia Britannica*, 2011,http://library.eb.co.uk/eb/article-9063148, Accessed June 2, 2011.

21. "West, Dame Rebecca," *Encyclopædia Britannica, Encyclopedia Britannica Online Library Edition, Encyclopædia Britannica*, 2011, http://library eb.co.uk/eb/article-9076588, Accessed June 2, 2011.

Art and design

1. "Wright, Frank Lloyd," *Encyclopædia Britannica, Encyclopædia Britannica Online Library Edition, Encyclopædia Britannica*, 2011, http://library.eb.co.uk/eb/article-8019, Accessed April 18, 2011.

2. The Oxford English Reference Dictionary, 121.

3. "Bauhaus," *Encyclopædia Britannica, Encyclopædia Britannica Online Library Edition, Encyclopædia Britannica*, 2011, http://library.eb.co.uk/eb/article-647, Accessed April 18, 2011; E. H. Gombrich, *The Story of Art*, London: Phaidon, 1989, 444.

4. "photography," *Britannica Student Encyclopedia, Encyclopedia Britannica Online Library Edition, Encyclopædia Britannica*, 2011, http://library.eb.co.uk/all/comptons/article-229823, Accessed June 2, 2011.

5. *The Oxford English Reference Dictionary*, 1092.

6. "photography," *Britannica Student Encyclopedia, Encyclopædia Britannica Online Library Edition, Encyclopædia Britannica*, 2011, http://library.eb.co.uk/all/comptons/article-206481, Accessed July 18, 2011.

7. "photography," *Britannica Student Encyclopedia*, http://library.eb.co.uk/all/comptons/article-229823, Accessed July 18, 2011.

8. http://www.art-ww1.com/gb/present.html, Accessed June 2, 2011.

Wartime propaganda

1. http://www.imdb.com/title/tt0008907/, Accessed June 3, 2011.

2. Toby Clark, *Art and Propaganda*, London: George Weidenfeld and Nicolson, 1997, 104.

3. Clark, *Art and Propaganda*, 104.

Fashion

1. Bronwyn Cosgrave, *Costume and Fashion: A Complete History*, London: Hamlyn, 2003, 220.

2. "dress," *Encyclopædia Britannica, Encyclopædia Britannica Online Library Edition,*

Encyclopædia Britannica, 2011, http://library.eb.co.uk/eb/article-14028, Accessed July 19, 2011.

3. "swimsuit," *Encyclopædia Britannica, Encyclopedia Britannica Online Library Edition,*

Encyclopædia Britannica, 2011, http://library.eb.co.uk/eb/article-9070656, Accessed May 29, 2011.

4. http://www.digitalhistory.uh.edu/do_history/fashion/Cosmetics/cosmetics.html, Accessed July 19, 2011.

5. Hunter, *A Century in Photographs*, 43.

6. http://www.invent.org/hall_of_fame/302.html, Accessed July 19, 2011.

7. "bloomers," *Encyclopædia Britannica, Encyclopedia Britannica Online Library Edition, Encyclopædia Britannica*, 2011, http://library.eb.co.uk/eb/article-9015718, Accessed May 29, 2011.

8. "bicycle," *Encyclopædia Britannica, Encyclopedia Britannica Online Library Edition, Encyclopædia Britannica*, 2011, http://library.eb.co.uk/eb/article-230025, Accessed May 29, 2011.

9. Sue Macy, *Wheels of Change: How Women Rode the Bicycle to Freedom* (With a Few Flat Tires Along the Way), Washington, D.C., National Geographic, 2011.

10. http://www.costumes.org/classes/fashiondress/ww1toww2.htm, Accessed May 31, 2011.

11. http://www.costumes.org/classes/fashiondress/ww1toww2.htm.

12. http://muse.museum.montana.edu/sof/ww1.html, Accessed May 31, 2011.

13. "Chanel, Coco," *Encyclopædia Britannica, Encyclopædia Britannica Online Library Edition, Encyclopædia Britannica*, 2011, http://library.eb.co.uk/eb/article-9022401, Accessed April 19, 2011.

Changing times

1. "suffrage," *Encyclopædia Britannica, Encyclopedia Britannica Online Library Edition, Encyclopædia Britannica*, 2011, http://library.eb.co.uk/eb/article-9070175, Accessed June 3, 2011.

What did the 1900s and 1910s do for us?

1. http://www.bbc.co.uk/news/uk-england-merseyside-13450315, Accessed June 3, 2011.

2. http://www.bbc.co.uk/news/uk-england-wiltshire-13584306, Accessed June 3, 2011.

Find out more

Books

Great Inventions of the 20th Century, Peter Jedicke (Chelsea House Publishers, 2007)

Jazz (A History of American Music), Christopher Handyside (Heinemann Library, 2007)

Thomas Edison: The Man Who Lit Up the World, Martin Woodside (Sterling, 2007)

World War I (Facts At Your Fingertips), Alice Harman (Wayland, 2011)

World War I (Living Through...), Nicola Barber (Raintree, 2012)

Would You Believe ... two cyclists invented the aeroplane?!, Richard Platt (Oxford University Press, 2010)

Websites

www.channel4.com/history/microsites/H/history/guide20/part09b.html
Learn more about popular culture in the twentieth century.

kclibrary.lonestar.edu/decade00.html
Read more about American culture in the 1900s at this website.

www.vam.ac.uk/content/articles/c/corsets-early-20th-century
Find out more about corsets in the early twentieth century on this website.

www.ww1photos.com/WW1MusicIndex.html
Hear the songs of World War I being sung.

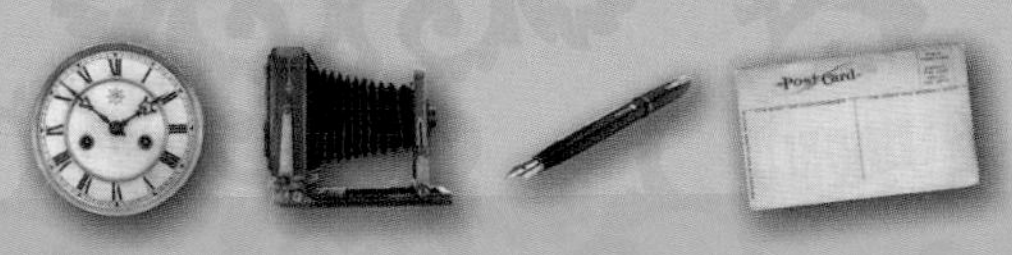

tirocchi.stg.brown.edu/514/story/fashion_earlycentury.html
This website has lots of information about the changing fashions of the 1900s.

tirocchi.stg.brown.edu/514/story/fashion_teens.html
This website has lots of information about the changing fashions of the 1910s.

http://www.iwm.org.uk/history/the-first-world-war
Find out more about World War I on this website.

Topics for further research

- Investigate the fight for women's votes around the world.
- Research World War I in more detail to discover what lessons the world should learn from it and why it wasn't the "war to end all wars".
- Explore the world of twentieth century art and design. Who influenced whom?

Glossary

animation drawing, such as a cartoon, made to move

anti-semitism against Jews

art nouveau popular, decorative style of design and art

assassinated killed

assembly line group of machines and workers to make (assemble) a product

axle centre pin a wheel spins around on

broadcasting radio signals being sent from one location to a widespread audience

child labour children made to work

circulation war battle between newspapers over who can sell the most copies

colony foreign country, or part of a foreign country, that has been taken over and controlled by another nation

colour supplement magazine printed in colour that comes with a newspaper

commercial flight flight that takes passengers for money

cubism art style utilizing geometric shapes and collages

dialogue conversation between two or more people

emancipate cause to be free

emigrant person who leaves one country to settle in another

empire number of countries ruled by one country

franchise right to vote in elections

genre style

home front people at home during a war

honky-tonk style of piano playing in ragtime music

immigrant person who settles in another country

imperialism policy of extending a country's military power or cultural influence to other countries or places

improvised music that is played without preparation, without written down notes

miscellany mixture

modernism art style that broke with traditional styles and forms

pageantry elaborate parade

publicity stills still photographs used to promote a film or actor

record flat disk used to capture sounds

revue light entertainment made up of sketches, songs, and dances

risqué slightly indecent and liable to shock

rpm (revolutions per minute) how fast a record spins

suffragette woman protesting to get the right to vote

surrealism art style utilizing strange and dreamlike images

synchronized made to occur at the same time

title card screen shown between scenes in a film with writing to explain what is happening or provide dialogue

variety show show that includes acts by musicians, dancers, singers, and comedians

vaudeville show that includes acts by musicians, dancers, singers, and comedians. Vaudeville is another name for a variety show or music hall.

Victorian era era of Queen Victoria's reign

work song song sung, usually by a group, in time to the actions of work to prevent boredom during a repetitive task

World War I war between 1914 and 1918 that started between Austria-Hungary and Serbia and ended up involving most of the nations of the world

Index

Happy birthday!

Alles Gute zum Geburtstag!

Text: Mary Risk
Illustrationen: Lucy Keijser
Ins Deutsche übertragen von Luz-Maria Linder

It's my birthday.

Ich habe Geburtstag.

Here are all my friends.
Hi! Hello! Come in, everyone!

Hier sind alle meine Freunde.
Hallo! Guten Tag!
Kommt alle herein!

All these presents for me?
What a brilliant mask!

Alle diese Geschenke für mich?
Was für eine tolle Maske!

And I love this dinosaur!

Und ich liebe diesen Dinosaurier!

Let's blow some bubbles.
Aren't they lovely?

Lasst uns ein paar Seifenblasen
machen. Sind sie nicht schön?

Whoosh!

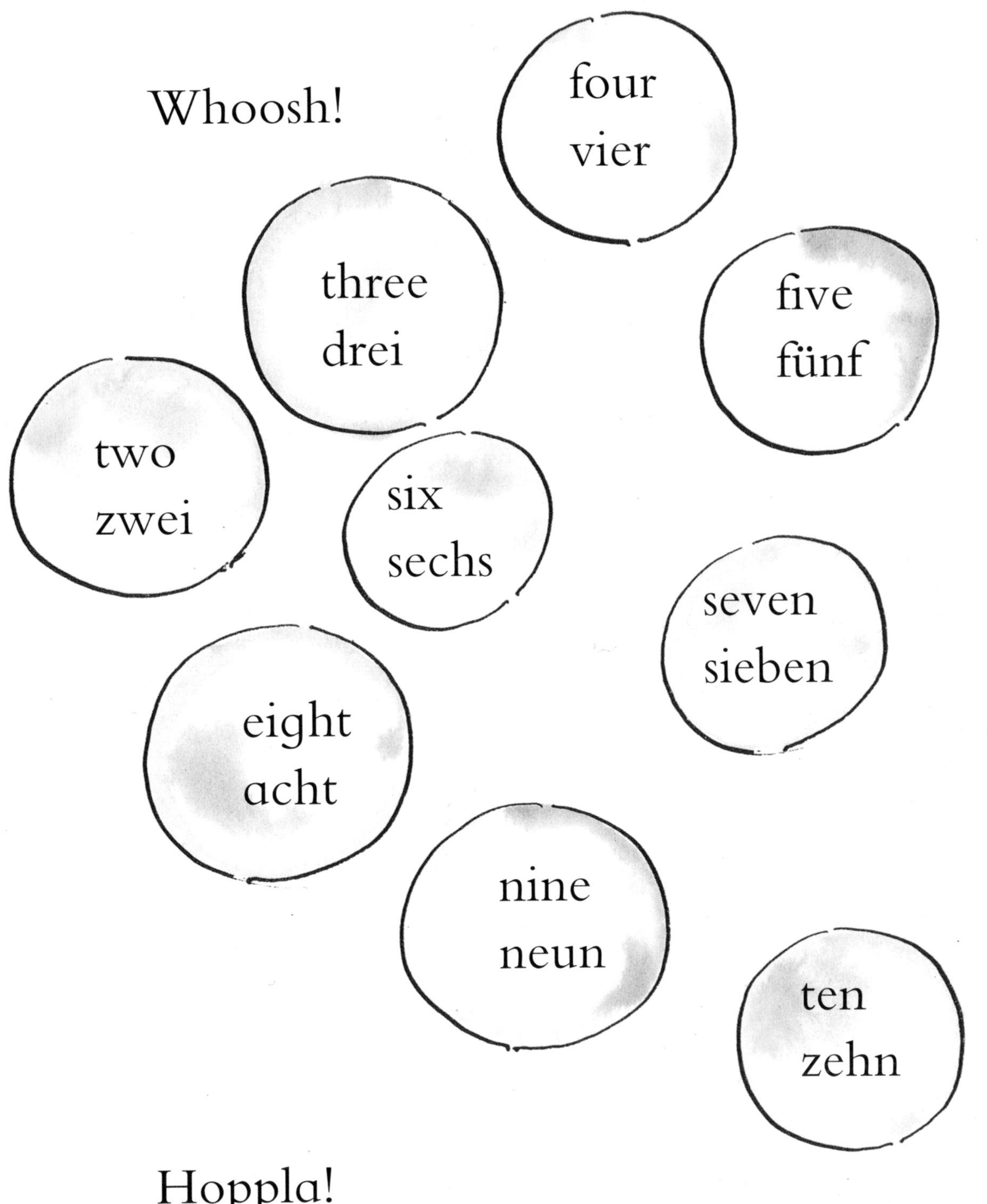

Hoppla!

Where have they all gone?

Wo sind sie alle hin?

Oh! Look at Sarah!

Oh! Schaut Sarah an!

Balloons!
Can I have one?

Ballons!
Kann ich einen haben?

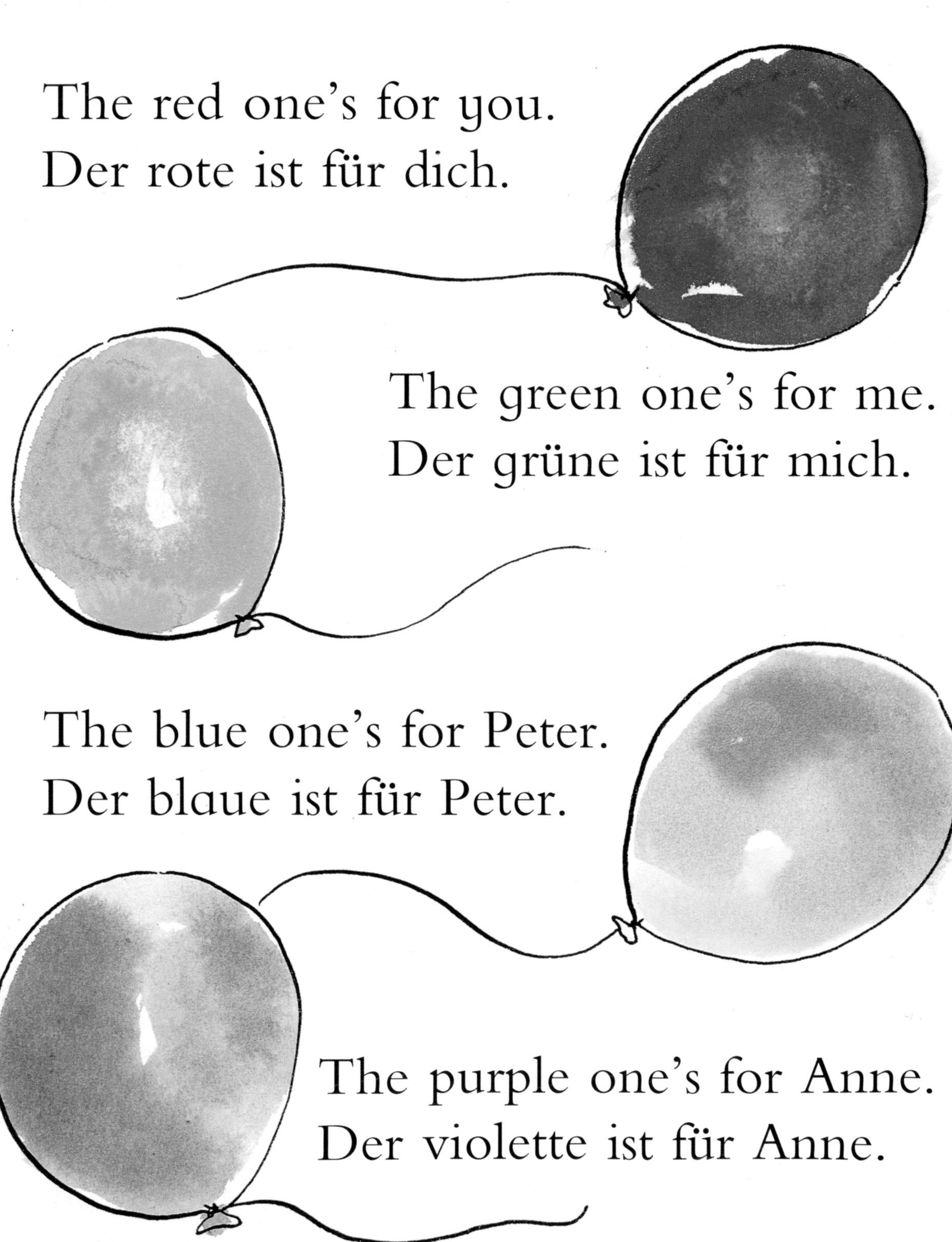

The red one's for you.
Der rote ist für dich.

The green one's for me.
Der grüne ist für mich.

The blue one's for Peter.
Der blaue ist für Peter.

The purple one's for Anne.
Der violette ist für Anne.

This is fantastic!
This is fun!

Das ist fantastisch!
Das macht Spaß!

Oh dear! Goodbye, balloons!

Oh je! Auf Wiedersehen, Ballons!

Have you lost your balloon?
Never mind, don't cry!

Hast du deinen Ballon verloren?
Das macht nichts, weine nicht!

Are you hungry?
Have some cake.

Hast du Hunger? Nimm dir Kuchen.

Are you thirsty?
Have a drink.

Hast du Durst? Nimm dir ein Getränk.

That was a lovely party.
Thank you for having us.

Das war eine schöne Party.
Danke für die Einladung.

Look! The balloons!

Schaut! Die Ballons!

Goodbye!

Auf Wiedersehen!

Das kleine Bilder-Wörterbuch

Damit du dir die englischen Wörter besser einprägen kannst, die du in der Geschichte gelesen hast, haben wir sie auf den folgenden Seiten für dich zusammengestellt. Du siehst das Wort zunächst auf Englisch, dann in der deutschen Übersetzung.

Falls du die ganze Geschichte im Zusammenhang lesen willst, findest du sie – und die Übersetzung – hinter dem Wortschatz.

Um die Aussprache zu üben, hörst du dir am besten die CD an oder bittest jemanden, dir die Geschichte einmal vorzulesen.

Viel Spaß beim Englischlernen!

Words Wörter

happy birthday!
alles Gute zum Geburtstag!

present
Geschenk

cake
Kuchen

balloon
Ballon

bubble
Seifenblase

mask
Maske

hi
hallo

hello
guten Tag

thank you
danke

dinosaur
Dinosaurier

goodbye
auf Wiedersehen

friend
Freund, Freundin

lovely
schön

brilliant
toll

fantastic
fantastisch

fun
Spaß

party
Party

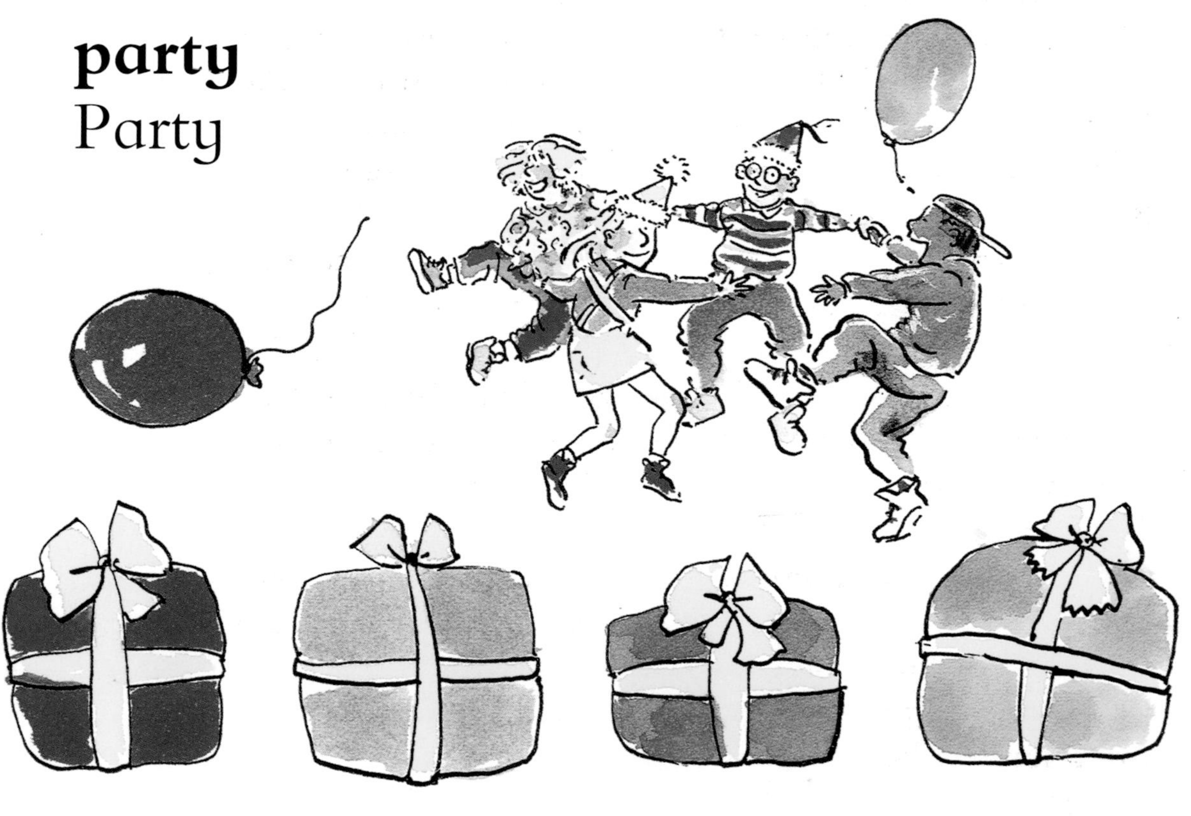

red
rot

purple
violett

blue
blau

green
grün

Hier kannst du die ganze Geschichte nochmal lesen:

It's my birthday.	Ich habe Geburtstag.
Here are all my friends.	Hier sind alle meine Freunde.
Hi! Hello! Come in, everyone!	Hallo! Guten Tag! Kommt alle herein.
All these presents for me?	Alle diese Geschenke für mich?
What a brilliant mask!	Was für eine tolle Maske!
And I love this dinosaur!	Und ich liebe diesen Dinosaurier!
Let's blow some bubbles.	Lasst uns ein paar Seifenblasen machen.
Aren't they lovely?	Sind sie nicht schön?
Whoosh! one, two, three, four, five, six, seven, eight, nine, ten	Hoppla! eins, zwei, drei, vier, fünf, sechs, sieben, acht, neun, zehn
Where have they all gone?	Wo sind sie alle hin?
Oh! Look at Sarah!	Oh! Schaut Sarah an!
Balloons!	Ballons!
Can I have one?	Kann ich einen haben?
The red one's for you.	Der rote ist für dich.
The green one's for me.	Der grüne ist für mich.
The blue one's for Peter.	Der blaue ist für Peter.
The purple one's for Anne.	Der violette ist für Anne.
This is fantastic!	Das ist fantastisch!
This is fun!	Das macht Spaß!
Oh dear! Goodbye, balloons!	Oh je! Auf Wiedersehen, Ballons!
Have you lost your balloon?	Hast du deinen Ballon verloren?
Never mind, don't cry!	Das macht nichts, weine nicht!
Are you hungry?	Hast du Hunger?
Have some cake.	Nimm dir Kuchen.
Are you thirsty?	Hast du Durst?
Have a drink.	Nimm dir ein Getränk.
That was a lovely party.	Das war eine schöne Party.
Thank you for having us.	Danke für die Einladung.
Look! The balloons!	Schaut! Die Ballons!
Goodbye!	Auf Wiedersehen!

ZIPPEL: THE LITTLE KEYHOLE GHOST

ZIPPEL: THE LITTLE KEYHOLE GHOST

Alex Rühle

Illustrated by

Axel Scheffler

Translated by Rachel Ward

ANDERSEN PRESS

First published in English in 2019 by
Andersen Press Limited
20 Vauxhall Bridge Road
London SW1V 2SA
www.andersenpress.co.uk

2 4 6 8 10 9 7 5 3 1

Originally published in German as Zippel, das wirklich wahre Schlossgespenst
in 2018 by dtv Verlagsgesellschaft mbH & Co. KG, Munich

The translation of this work was supported by a grant from the Goethe-Institut

British Library Cataloguing in Publication Data available.

ISBN 978 1 78344 905 7

Printed and bound in China by 1010

For Nica and Sophie

CHAPTER ONE

Paul was what used to be called a latch-key kid. Do you know what that is? It's a child who has their own front-door key even if they're quite young. Their parents work long hours so there's nobody there when they come home from school or after-school club. They have to unlock the door themselves. Paul was a child like that.

On the first day of term after the summer holidays, Paul was on his way home from school. He clattered his key along the bannisters as he went upstairs to his flat: *Clong-clong-cling. Clong-clong-clang.*

On the first floor, he met old Mrs Wilhelm, who had her flowery shopping bag with her. Mrs Wilhelm was rather strange. She could often be seen walking up and down the stairs or standing around outside somebody's door.

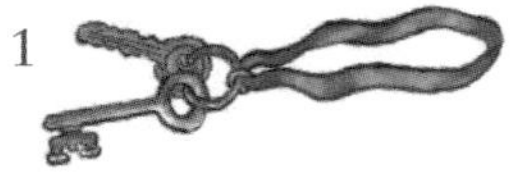

Sometimes when Mum or Dad opened the door in the morning, she was right there, as if she'd just been eavesdropping on them or looking through the keyhole.

'Hello, Mrs Wilhelm,' called Paul.

'Hello, Paul,' said Mrs Wilhelm. 'I haven't seen you around for a while.'

As she spoke, she was staring at him with her right eye. Her left eye was screwed up tight, the same as ever. This had made Paul very scared of her when he was younger. By now he was more or less used to her only looking at him with one eye, but it was still a bit creepy when she came right up close to him. He could see all the creases around her squinting eye.

'Yes,' said Paul, 'we only got back from our holiday last night.'

'And? Did you have a good time?' asked Mrs Wilhelm.

'Yes, very nice,' said Paul, 'but it was school again today.'

'Oh, no!' cried Mrs Wilhelm. 'Schooool! Is it bad?'

'Uh-huh,' said Paul, who really didn't like school. Not because of the lessons, or his teacher, Mr Ampermeier, who was actually very nice, but because of Tim and Tom, who picked on him every single day. So he generally ended up standing around alone in the playground. But he didn't want to tell Mrs Wilhelm all that now.

'I've got homework to do,' he exclaimed. 'Bye, Mrs Wilhelm!'

'Bye, Paul!' said Mrs Wilhelm.

Paul ran up another two flights of stairs, *clong-clong-cling, clong-clong-clang*, until he came to the flat with *Fellmann* on the door. That was where he lived. With his mum and dad. They were the Fellmanns.

Paul stuck his key in the lock and was about to turn it, when he heard a very quiet voice: 'Ow! Ow-ow-ow. Zippeldesticks, what's all this?'

Paul listened. Was somebody at home already? But the voice didn't sound the least bit like his parents. More like a child. He looked around. There was nobody on the stairs. He put his ear to the door. Nothing. So he moved the key in the lock again.

'Hey!' cried the voice. 'What's this stick doing in here?'

Paul pulled the key out, put his eye to the lock and looked into the flat. He saw the long, empty hallway. There were two half-unpacked suitcases standing there, and at the end of the hall, the parasol and lilo were leaning against the bookcase. It was all perfectly quiet. But hang on, wait a moment, what was that? Paul jumped. To the left. In the darkness. There was something moving. Something white. In the keyhole! Paul jerked his head back. He stood by the door, dead quiet, held his breath and listened.

He wasn't sure, but he thought he could hear someone breathing . . . in the door.

'Is there anyone there?' he asked.

'No-no,' said the voice. 'There's no one here. Nobody there.'

Paul ought to have been startled, but the voice sounded so small and scared that he wasn't afraid. Well, maybe only a little.

Cautiously, he asked: 'Really? Nobody there?'

'Yes-yes,' said the voice, 'no one at all. Really truly, nobody there.'

'So *nobody's* talking?' said Paul.

'Nobody's doing anything, it's just the wind.'

'The wind can't talk,' said Paul.

'Exactly, nor can I,' said the voice. 'I'm no one, no fear. There's nobody here.'

'Will you come out anyway?' asked Paul.

'No,' said the voice and then, a little more quietly: 'I'm scared.'

'I won't hurt you,' said Paul, 'cross my heart.'

It was as though a lamp went on in the lock. Then, for a moment, Paul thought that the lock was blowing

a little bubble of glowing gum. Because the thing that billowed from the keyhole was slowly getting bigger. At first it looked like a little white pea. But it grew from a pea to a ping-pong ball to the size of an orange, stretched lengthways, and gently eased itself away from the door, and floated over to Paul. Paul held his breath and stared at it in silence. Now the thing was as big as the water bottle he took to school. Or his cuddly tiger. It had big eyes and a mouth, and was gleaming white, and it said: 'Good morning.'

'Oh. Erm. Actually, it's getting late, it's five in the afternoon,' said Paul.

The white thing seemed to ponder. Then it said: 'But I've only just got up. Why's it late for you?'

'Because I get up in the mornings. When the sun comes up. And when it goes down, I go to bed.'

'Aha,' said the strange thing. 'The sun. Aha.' Then it sank slowly to the floor. 'Oh,' it went, 'oh-oh-oh.'

It seemed to have little arms. Or wings. At any rate, it was waggling some stumpy little things about in the air, but they weren't much help and the creature sank down lower and lower until it landed on the floor.

Paul crouched next to it. ‘Can I help you?’

‘No-no. I’m only just learning to float and fly properly. I’ll get there.’

‘But . . . What are you doing in our door?’ asked Paul, sitting down cross-legged on the floor.

‘Well, I live in there. Not in the door. I live in the keyhole.’

‘Oh, right, yes,’ said Paul. ‘Sorry. How long have you lived in the . . . in the keyhole?’

‘A little while,’ said the white creature.

‘Ah,’ said Paul. ‘Were you born there?’

'I'm not bored in my own lock. *You're* the bore. Everything was just right and very, very cosy in there till you came boring into my home with that stick.'

'Oh, I'm sorry,' said Paul. 'I didn't mean to. But why are you living there?'

'What do you mean, why? Where else should I live? I'm a keyhole ghost!'

The little thing said this with an air of pride. It even strutted and stretched a bit taller. Then it floated onto Paul's knee and said: 'That's where keyhole ghosts live.'

'Don't ghosts normally live in castles?' said Paul.

'*I* don't,' said the ghost. 'I live in keyholes. Really truly.' Then it looked questioningly at Paul. 'What sort of castles?'

'You know, big castles. The ones where kings live, and knights and princesses.'

'Are you a king?' asked the ghost.

'No, of course not, I'm Paul.'

'Oh, a Paul. Is that like a knight?'

'No, silly, that's my name. It's what I'm called. How about you?'

The ghost waved its right hand a bit and said: 'Not at all.'

'Your name's *Notatall?*'

'No. I mean I'm not at all cold. I think it's rather warm in here.'

Paul almost burst out laughing. 'No, not "are you cold", what are you *called*? Do you have a name?'

'Don't know,' said the keyhole ghost. 'Maybe . . . maybe Karaputzonogypolatusomow?'

'That's not a name,' said Paul.

'Why not? It sounds really big and dangerous,' said the ghost, spreading out its little arms as if it was trying to scare Paul. It floated to and fro on Paul's knee with a very serious face and a clenched fist. 'Oh, tremble, one and all! You kings and knights and Pauls and all, hear my name and tremble, here comes Karaputzo . . . Ah . . . what was my name again?'

'I don't know,' said Paul.

'Zippeldesticks,' said the ghost. 'Now I've forgotten my own name.'

'Zippel!' cried Paul.

'What?' said the ghost.

'Zippel,' said Paul, 'your name's Zippel.'

'Really truly? How do you know that?'

'I don't know it. I just think Zippel suits you.'

'Really?' The ghost thought. 'Zippel. Aha. Does it sound big and strong and dangerous?'

'Well,' said Paul, 'I think it sounds like a keyhole ghost. Like a . . . '

. . . A very small keyhole ghost, Paul had been going to say, but then he changed it to '. . . like a ghost in the keyhole of a front door.'

'Good. Very good. A ghost in the keyhole of a front door, that's just what I am. So—' Zippel suddenly stopped. 'Shh. Someone's coming.'

He was right. The light had gone on at the bottom of the stairwell. They could hear footsteps. Then the staircase creaked.

'Oh-oh-oh,' said Zippel. 'It must be a grow-nup.'

'A what?'

'A grow-nup.'

'Do you mean a grown-up?' laughed Paul.

'That's what I said. Aren't you listening?'

'And you're scared of them?'

'Oh yes, oh yes, oh yes. Grow-nups are nasty. All of them. Very nasty. One of them stuck a stick in my keyhole earlier, I tried to stop her, but she pushed and shoved and almost squashed me completely. I heard her say, "It will be tricky for a Paul if a grow-nup can't do it." So you won't give me away, will you?'

'I promise,' said Paul, trying not to laugh.

The little ghost flitted through the air towards the door like a ray of light. Then it seemed as though he was sucked in by the keyhole; Zippel grew smaller and smaller, and after two seconds, he was gone. There was a brief glow in the lock and then everything was dark again.

'Hello, Paul.'

Paul's dad had his suit on, as he always did when he came home from work. He looked tired.

'Oh, hi, Dad,' said Paul, who was still crouching in front of the door. 'Did you finish early today?'

It was still the afternoon. Dad didn't normally get home from work until the evening.

Instead of answering, Dad asked: 'Why are you sitting around on the landing?'

'I . . . er, I forgot my key this morning.'

'How many times have I told you?' said Paul's dad, pulling his keys from his pocket. 'Before you head out, always stop and think: Have I got everything? Key? Money and—'

'Yes, yes,' Paul interrupted, jumping up. 'I know. Key, money, school bag. But can I have your key please? I'd like to unlock the door.'

'Oh, right,' said Paul's dad, 'sure.' And he gave him the key.

Paul peered into the keyhole, whispered, 'Watch out,' and pushed the key in very slowly.

'What did you say?' asked Dad.

'Nothing, nothing,' said Paul. Then he whispered again: 'I need to turn it now, mind out.'

'Are you OK?' asked Dad, surprised at Paul muttering into the door.

'Yes, yes,' said Paul. 'Fine. How about you?'

He turned the key very carefully.

'Well,' said Dad, 'I'm not too bad.'

As the key turned in the lock, it wobbled a little.

'Oh,' whispered Paul, 'did I hurt you?'

'Are you talking to me?' asked Dad.

'Yes,' said Paul. 'How was work?'

'Work,' repeated Dad. 'Yes . . . well . . .' Dad seemed to hesitate. Then he said: 'Oh, just the same as ever. A bit boring.'

‘Oh,’ said Paul, not really listening. He’d turned the key right round now. The door opened.

‘How was your day?’ asked Dad.

‘Oh, quite boring too,’ Paul lied.

An hour later, over dinner, Paul’s mum gave him a terrible shock.

They were eating pasta. Or, to be perfectly honest, eating a pile of mush. Mum’s mind had been on other things while she’d been cooking: on her performance next week. Paul’s mum was a singer in the opera house. She sang in the chorus. But sometimes she was chosen to sing as a soloist. (Soloists are people who sing all on their own, so everyone can hear any mistakes they may make.) Paul’s mum was absolutely mad about singing, but she also got madly nervous if she had to sing by herself. So she was spending the whole time thinking about this upcoming performance and not about the pasta, and now they had to eat rather sticky, mushy spaghetti.

Paul still said that it was delicious, though. Dad said nothing, just ate his pasta in silence.

And then came the thing that gave Paul such a terrible shock. Mum asked Dad if he'd be able to get home from work a bit early on Friday.

'Er, what?' asked Dad, as if he hadn't been listening, 'Why?'

'I told you on the phone today,' said Mum. 'The lock's being changed.'

'Whaaaat?' asked Paul, dropping his fork with the claggy spaghetti. 'Which lock?'

'Uh, the one on the front door,' said Mum. 'We've been meaning to get it sorted out for ages.'

Paul yelled: 'But I love that lock!'

'Since when have you loved our door lock?!' asked Mum.

'It's my favourite lock,' cried Paul. 'Honest. There's no other lock like it. It's got such a great hole for looking through. And . . . and it sounds so lovely when you turn the key. And it smells nice.'

Mum and Dad looked at each other in astonishment.

Then Dad said: 'It's practically an antique. And it's technically very old-fashioned. Nowadays you can get security locks that—'

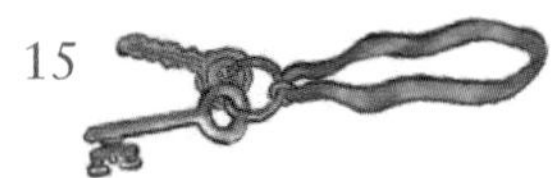

'But you normally love antiques, you love anything to do with history,' Paul interrupted. 'The brown chairs in the sitting room – you always say I have to be careful, they're special because they're antiques. And Mum's opera music is really old and you always say it's the most beautiful music of all.'

'Yes,' said Mum, 'but it doesn't matter whether a lock sounds nice if it doesn't work. And our lock's been sticking for a while when you turn the key. We've been wanting to change it for ages, and it was so bad this morning that I could hardly lock the door, so I went over to see Mr Nitzsche just now, and we're finally getting a new one.'

Mr Nitzsche was the caretaker, who always repaired everything.

'Oh,' said Paul. 'Aha. When will that be?'

'I just told you. On Friday. In three days.'

'Oh, really? On Friday?' asked Paul.

'Hmph, nobody listens to me around here!' Mum exclaimed in annoyance. 'Yes, this Friday!'

Paul looked at his plate of mushy spaghetti and the puddle of ketchup beside it and said nothing more.

The three of them ate in silence for a while, till Mum said: 'Oh, Paul – Dad and I just have to pop out to a tenants' committee meeting.'

'Oh, bother,' said Paul's dad. 'Is that tonight?'

'Yes! I told you that twice as well. What's wrong with you today?'

'Nothing, nothing,' said Paul's dad, attempting to sound light and unconcerned. It sounded pretty odd though. Something definitely wasn't right with him, but Paul didn't really consider it because he was thinking about Zippel, and Mum was cross because nobody was listening to her.

When she asked if Paul would mind them leaving him, he said: 'Oh, sure, no problem.'

'Are you sure?'

'Yes, honest,' said Paul. 'I can even put myself to bed.'

Mum had a moment's surprise, because she normally had to make Paul go to bed every evening, but she sighed with relief. 'Thank you, Paul. We'll be quick. You definitely won't have to go to bed by yourself.'

CHAPTER TWO

His parents had barely left the flat when Paul ran to the door.

'Hey, Zippel, can you hear me?'

'Yes, Zippel can hear, he's got good ears,' sang a voice from the lock.

'Come out a minute, I need to tell you something.'

The ghost just kept singing. 'Paul is there outside, but Zippel wants to hide.'

'Please,' said Paul nervously, 'it's really important.'

'Hey, Paul, don't worry, Zippel can hurry.' And plop, he popped out of the lock.

'What's the matter?' he asked.

'My parents want to change your lock.'

'Whaaat?' asked Zippel. 'Change it? How? When? Why?'

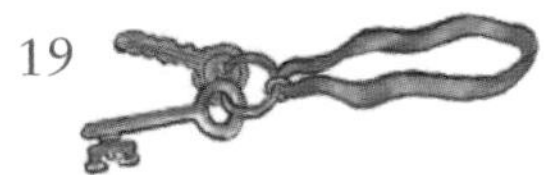

'They say the lock's ancient.'

'Zippeldesticks!' Zippel began floating restlessly to and fro. 'It's . . . it's not ancient at all, it's just the right age. That's not fair, it's my home!' He seemed to have an idea. 'I'll put a spell on your parents.'

'Can you do magic, then?'

Zippel stopped in the air and thought. 'No. But I'll learn. Have you got a book of spells? Get me a book of spells, quick!'

'Um,' said Paul, 'I don't think you'll have time. The locksmith's coming very soon.'

'The lock's myth? Are there stories about your lock?'

'No, the *locksmith*. That's the man who's going to change the lock. It's our caretaker, actually, but he's got a little workshop with tools in the cellar and does all kinds of jobs like that.'

'Oh,' cried Zippel. 'A caretaker. They're bad if they change locks. The baddest grow-nups in the whole world. I'll put a spell on him too! On him most of all!'

Zippel floated to and fro on the landing, waving his little arms around in the air. **'Hocus pocus, fiddle-de-dee, I'll turn the locksmith into a flea!'**

He was really very worked up and was glowing whiter than ever in the stairwell. 'No, wait, wait, I know something much, much worse: if he comes the day after tomorrow, I'll borrow his tools. When is he coming, this silly man?'

'In three days.'

All at once, Zippel dropped his arms and sank slowly to the floor like a balloon with the air gradually leaking out. Then he rubbed his eyes and cried bitterly, 'Boo-hoo-hoo-hooo. A keyhole ghost with no keyhole, it's all wrooong. Where will I liiiiiiive?'

'Yikes,' said Paul, 'where's all that dust coming from?'

You see, Zippel was suddenly wrapped from top to toe and back again in threads of dust.

'Oh,' he said, 'exscrews me, I was crying.'

Zippel wiped away the silvery threads, a bit like cobwebs, which trickled quietly to the floor as dust. He wasn't shining nearly as brightly as before, and now he looked more grey than white. Paul swept together the thin threads all around Zippel and picked them up.

'Look at that,' cried Zippel, pointing at the little heap of dusty tears in Paul's hand. 'Caaaan you seeee thaaaat?!'

He now sounded more angry than sad. ‘Keyhole ghosts hardly ever cry. Actually never. Sometimes at most. Rarely. But not often. Now and then, you know, but it’s very extremely rare.’

‘Ah, yes,’ said Paul, ‘that really isn’t often. But it’s not as bad as all that. We’ve got three days to find a new lock for you.’

‘It is as bad as all that!’ cried Zippel. ‘Good grief, that’s bad! It’s got to be an old lock, you know. With a keyhole that I fit into. A bit oily and a bit rusty and a bit dirty. You don’t know anything. Really truly.’

‘Oh, OK,’ said Paul. ‘So what will happen if you haven’t got a keyhole?’

‘First I’ll go grey and then get sick and then – boo-hoo-hoooo!’

The threads of dust started flying around again. And Zippel looked so grey that he reminded Paul more of a flying feather duster than a little, glowing keyhole ghost.

‘OK, OK,’ cried Paul, ‘we’ll look for a new old lock for you with lots of oil and rust and dirt. I’m sure we’ll find something suitable,’ he added, although he hadn’t the least idea how to get started. ‘But come with me for now.’

Paul went down the hallway to his room. Zippel floated beside him, looking curiously around the hall. Behind him, a last thread of dusty tears fell silently to the floor.

'So this is where you live?' he asked.

'Yes, this is our flat. I live here with Mum and Dad.'

'Wow-ow-ow,' said Zippel, sounding very impressed. 'Your flat is much bigger than my keyhole. Is your dad a king?'

'Oh no, he's a kind of teacher, called a trainer.'

'Really? Like a shoe? So is he hollow like me?'

'Are you hollow inside?' asked Paul in amazement.

'Zigackly. Ghosts are made of air and light and time and nothing else at all. Why are you laughing?'

'Because that's what Obelix says.'

'Is he a ghost made of air and light?'

'Oh no,' said Paul, 'he's a comic-book character. He's best friends with Asterix, and he's made of fat and meat and he's pretty much the opposite of you. But he often says "zigackly".'

'Oh right, oh yes,' said Zippel, who wasn't listening properly now, because by then they'd reached Paul's room. Zippel stopped in amazement in the air and asked in a whisper: 'Oh, oh, oh, what's this thing here?' He'd spotted Paul's train track, standing in the middle of the room.

'That's my train set,' said Paul, pushing the carriages along the track.

'Oooh!' whooped Zippel, who was glowing white again and bouncing up and down like a rubber ball in excitement. 'Ooh-hoo-hoo! That's amazing! Can I ride in it?'

'Yes, sure, of course,' said Paul.

Zippel floated to the last carriage, shrank to half his normal size and sank gently down onto the roof. Paul was amazed at the way Zippel could just change his size. He'd seen it twice before, when he'd come out of the lock, or vanished into it, but right in the middle of the room it was even more impressive.

Paul pushed the train off and Zippel let himself ride round in a circle.

'Can't it go any faster?' he asked after the first lap.

'Sure,' said Paul and pushed harder.

'Here comes the ghost train,' cried Zippel.

Paul had to laugh. 'Do you know what a ghost train is?'

'Uh, this, here,' cried Zippel. 'That's a train, I'm a ghost, so it's a ghost train.'

'Yes, but there are really big ghost trains too.'

'Oh,' said Zippel, looking excitedly round the room. 'Where are they?'

'Not here, they're much too big for my room. They have them at funfairs. They're so big even grown-ups can go on them. And get scared.'

'What are the grow-nups scared of? They scare *me*!'

'Well, of the ghosts.'

Zippel laughed and laughed: 'They don't need to be scared. I won't hurt them. Really truly.' He shook his head. 'Grow-nups are really daft sometimes.'

'The ghosts on a ghost train are very ugly,' said Paul. 'Gigantic, with blood round their mouths and their eyes hanging out and an axe in their heads, and they groan or suddenly scream.'

'Oh, are they all hurt?' asked Zippel. 'Is the ghost train a hospital for ghosts?'

'No, they're not real ghosts at all, just gruesome-looking puppets to give people a fright. We can go and see when it's Oktoberfest again.'

'Ooh, yes. Tomorrow?'

'No, Oktoberfest is in a few weeks.'

'Afeweeks?' asked Zippel. 'Is that a big city?'

'It's not a place. A week is seven days. Oktoberfest starts in two weeks, so you'll have to wait a while.'

'Oh, right,' said Zippel. 'I'll wait then. What shall we do in the meantime?' He looked expectantly around the room and suddenly shouted: 'Oh, stop-stop! Stop please.'

Paul caught hold of the train. Zippel floated away from the carriage, growing as he went.

‘That’s awesome,’ said Paul, ‘the way you can make yourself bigger and smaller.’

‘Yes-yes,’ said Zippel, not really listening. ‘But what’s this?’

‘My toy shop,’ said Paul. He’d had the little shop since he was very young. You could buy mini versions of all the things you get in a supermarket: fruit, milk, bread, washing powder.

Zippel floated behind the counter where there was a metal till. ‘No, I mean this here.’

‘That’s the till for the shop.’

‘Ah, and what do you do with it?’

‘You put the money in,’ explained Paul and opened the little drawer full of one, two and ten cent coins.

‘Oooooooooh!’ whooped Zippel, floating to and fro again. ‘Oo-hoo-hoo! You *are* a king!’

‘Me? No. Why d’you say that?’

‘You’ve got treasure. A huge, glittering treasure chest.’

‘That’s the change. If someone buys something from me, they give me money and I give them something back.’

‘Oh-oh-oh-oh, it’s so glittery! Who buys things here then?’

'Oh, I used to sell things to my friends, you know. Or Mum and Dad.'

'Don't your parents have their own things?'

'Of course, this is just pretend—'

'Shh,' Zippel interrupted him, listening intently. 'Someone's coming.'

Sure enough, the staircase was creaking with heavy footsteps.

Paul looked around his room. Where could he hide Zippel? He heard a key in the flat's door. Zippel shrank in the air to the size of a pea, flitted into the money drawer of the till and whispered: 'Quick, shut it.'

'Yes, good idea.' Paul closed the till.

At that moment, Paul's mum stuck her head round the door.

'Hello, Paul.'

'Hello.' Paul tried to smile.

'Oh, your shop,' said Mum. 'You haven't played with that for ages. Can I buy something?'

'Er, no, the shop's shut for the night, sorry.'

Mum laughed. 'Fair enough. Shall I read you a story?'

'No, that's OK, I'm really tired,' Paul lied.

‘Oh,’ said Paul’s mum, who normally read to him every evening. ‘OK.’

Paul quickly changed into his pyjamas and got into bed. ‘Good night. Can you shut the door? The light in the hall is so bright.’

‘Really?’ said Mum. Normally the door had to stay wide open because Paul was so scared of ghosts and monsters. ‘Fine, I’ll close it. Sleep well, love!’

‘You too,’ said Paul.

‘Me too,’ said Zippel. ‘I’m a lovely love.’

Paul’s mum had almost shut the door, but she popped her head back round. ‘What did you say?’

‘Love you,’ said Paul. ‘Good night!’

‘Good night, Paul.’

It was completely dark in the room now. Paul waited till he could hear the TV in the sitting room. Then he jumped out of bed and quietly opened the till again. ‘Phew,’ he said. ‘That was close.’

‘Yes,’ said Zippel, enthusiastically. ‘Very close, merry close, Mummy almost caught a ghost.’

‘But where will you stay tonight?’ asked Paul.

‘I’ll go into my keyhole.’

'I'm afraid it'll be a squeeze for you. My dad always sticks his key in the lock at night.'

'What? In my lock?' asked Zippel, outraged.

'He doesn't know that it's yours now. He always does that. He says that way he knows where his key is in the morning. But I think it's also to stop burglars getting in.'

'But why should he worry about burgers getting in?'

At first Paul didn't understand what Zippel meant. Then he laughed and said: 'Not burgers, burglars! Thieves. People breaking into the flat overnight and stealing stuff.'

'Let them come – I'd show them!' said Zippel, flailing around with his little arms. 'Come on, come on, come on. I've got to sleep in my keyhole. Can't you pull your dad's stupid key out?'

Paul thought. 'OK, I'll try.' Quietly, he opened his door and looked into the empty hall. He could hear voices in the sitting room. 'Quickly, come on,' Paul whispered, 'they're watching TV.' He ran on tiptoes to the front door.

Zippel overtook him, singing away to himself:

Your parents are watching TV,
Which means they can't hear you and me.

'Shh,' said Paul as he cautiously pulled out the key and set it down on the sideboard. 'OK, in you get.'

'Thank you,' said Zippel, as he floated towards his keyhole. He grew smaller and smaller till he was nothing but a glowing dot. Then even that vanished.

'Sleep well,' whispered Paul.

As he crept back to his bedroom, he could hear Zippel singing:

Sleepy Zippel says goodnight,
Today's been fun and now sleep tight.

CHAPTER THREE

When Paul woke up the next morning, he wondered whether he'd dreamt the whole Zippel business, but then he saw the toy till open, and the train still standing exactly where he'd left it yesterday. He jumped out of bed and got dressed as fast as possible. In the kitchen, he could hear his mother making breakfast. But when he reached the hallway, he got a shock: the key was back in the lock again. Last night, Dad must have noticed that Paul had taken the key out, and he'd stuck it back in again.

Paul ran to the door and whispered: 'Zippel?'

Nothing.

He put his ear to the lock and whispered: 'Hey, Zippel, can you hear me?' Still no sound.

'Morning, Paul.' Mum was standing in the kitchen

door, looking down the hallway. 'Everything OK?'

'Oh, hi, Mum,' said Paul. 'Yes, I just thought I heard a funny noise outside on the stairs. But I must have imagined it.'

'Maybe it was dear Mrs Wilhelm?' Mum said quietly. 'Are you coming for breakfast? It's getting pretty late.'

'Yes, sure,' said Paul. 'I'll just wash my face.'

He went into the bathroom, turned thc tap on full so that it sounded like he was washing, and then ran back to the front door. He tapped the wood quietly with his finger, just next to the lock. 'Zippel? Are you there? Zippel! Say something!'

Paul waited a moment, but nothing happened. Then he looked into the lock. It was all dark. Paul's heart lurched. Zippel couldn't have just gone.

Mum called from the kitchen: 'Paul, are you coming? It's nearly half past seven!'

'I'm coming, I'm coming,' mumbled Paul. He hastily turned off the bathroom tap, and went into the kitchen for breakfast with his mum. He was just scraping the burnt bits off his toast when she asked him if there was anything bothering him: 'You're so quiet this morning.'

‘Oh, er, no,’ said Paul, ‘I just don’t really want to go to school.’

‘I can understand that,’ said Mum. ‘It’s like my performance next week – I’m already so nervous because—’

‘Will you make me a sandwich?’ Paul interrupted her.

‘Yes, of course,’ said Mum.

‘Great, thanks,’ said Paul. ‘Can you put something in it this time? Yesterday you gave me two slices of dry bread.’

‘Oh, really?’ asked Paul’s mum. ‘I’m sorry, I’m so scatty just now. I’ve got such a hard role in this opera . . . ’

But Paul wasn’t even listening. He’d run back to his room, where he scribbled a little note and put it in the shop:

Dear Zippel, where are you? Sorry about Dad's key. I've got to go to school, but I'll be back this afternoon. Hope you will be too. Love, Paul

Then Paul went to school. Which was the same as ever. Tim and Tom picked on him at break time. They picked

on him at lunch. And they picked on him in between, whenever Mr Ampermeier wasn't paying attention. Tim was head-and-shoulders taller than Paul; Tom was twice as broad as Paul. And Paul had no chance against the two of them. At first, he used to hit back when they walked past him in the playground and whacked him or pinched him so quickly that none of the teachers saw. Or he'd run away. But then they used to run right after him. If he defended himself, they seemed to enjoy hassling him even more than normal. Which was why he'd eventually given up. Now he just let their teasing, their nastiness and their insults wash over him. It was like bad weather. If you see dark clouds on the horizon, you hope that the rain will blow over. When it rains, you just have to get wet, and then you wait until it dries up again. The difference between rain and hassle, though, is this: clothes really do get properly dry again, but your soul doesn't. There are words that are so mean they stay stuck in you like a splinter under your skin. Often Paul could still hear their insults in bed at night: *Paul's got no friends. Paul's lonely. Paul stinks. Paul's a stupid idiot.*

Today was particularly bad. Tim stole Paul's sandwich during break, and in art, Tom tipped some of the water from his brush pot down the back of Paul's neck. But even so, today bothered Paul less than normal. He was only thinking about Zippel, and hoping, hoping that he was still there, and that he'd see him again soon. He was just counting the hours until he was finally allowed to go home

again. Eventually, lunch was over. And when after-school club was finally, *finally* finished, Paul cycled home faster than ever before, and leaped up every second step on the stairs.

By the time he reached the top, he was out of breath. He stopped by the flat's door, waited for his heart to stop pounding and his breathing to calm. Then he listened. But there was nothing to hear. He screwed up his right eye and looked into the keyhole with his left. The suitcases were still standing around in the hall. But in the lock, it was still all dark.

He stood up again and said quietly: 'Zippel?'

Outside in the backyard, he could hear a scrubbing noise from a broom. *Sshsht, sshsht, sshsht.* Otherwise all was quiet.

Paul asked again: 'Zippel? Can you hear me?'

Nothing.

Very cautiously, he stuck his key in the lock and turned it slowly. The door creaked quietly open. Paul pulled the key out. He stood in the empty hallway and called out into the flat: 'Zippel? Are you there?'

When there was still no answer, he went into his room.

There was the train set. Just where he'd left it yesterday. The note he'd written that morning was still beside the till.

Paul let his school bag slip slowly from his shoulder and noticed the way the sadness was flooding through him. Zippel was gone. Dad had driven him away with his key. What a shame!

Paul looked out into the yard where Mr Nitzsche was sweeping up leaves and chatting to old Mrs Wilhelm. Mrs Wilhelm was holding her flowery shopping bag and squinting with her left eye, just the same as ever, and she was laughing about something while Mr Nitzsche carried on sweeping. *Sshsht, sshsht, sshsht.* Paul kept his forehead pressed against the cold window and watched the caretaker for at least five minutes, but he didn't even notice that he was looking out. He was just sad. But then he hesitated. And held his breath. Was that someone singing? A child? Quiet sounds. Very close by. Here in the flat somewhere. Paul went to the hall and listened. The noises were coming from Mum and Dad's bedroom. Paul tiptoed down the hall and peeped cautiously around the corner.

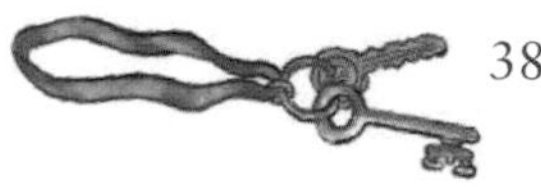

His parents' large wardrobe was open. Several drawers had been pulled out and there were socks and pants lying on the floor. Zippel must be hiding somewhere deep in one of the drawers. Paul could hear him singing and rummaging around. Whoops, there came a red sock flying out of the drawer. Followed by a blue one.

Paul's heart made a little jump for joy. 'What are you doing in there?' he asked.

There was a brief moment of quiet in the cupboard. Then there was movement in the sock mountain and, after a few seconds, Zippel emerged from the middle of it. He had a sock wrapped around him like a blanket.

'There are such lovely things in here,' said Zippel. 'Cloaks, blankets. All sorts of things to slip inside.' He sat his little ghostly bottom down on a pair of socks, swayed to and fro and said: 'And such fluffy-soft things to sit on.'

Then he wafted along to the end of the drawer and looked out over the edge. Several pairs of Dad's pants were lying on the floor. He pointed down. 'Hey, um, could I maybe have one of those lovely flags? Maybe that red one there?'

'They're my dad's pants,' said Paul. 'He has a pair for every day and he'd definitely be surprised if there was suddenly a pair missing. I bet I've got something else we could use as a flag.'

'Ha,' cried Zippel, but he suddenly sounded properly angry. 'Your dad! He's a bad man! He's a really horrible person. A real grow-nup. Yes-siree.'

'Why?' asked Paul.

'Why!' shouted Zippel, as if it ought to be entirely obvious why Paul's dad was the nastiest person in the whole world. 'I'll tell you why. Last night, he blocked up my keyhole with his key. I had no room at all and I was crushed and everything hurts and that's not fair and I didn't get a wink of sleep. Really truly.'

'Oh. I'm sorry. But Dad doesn't know that you live in the lock – he didn't do it on purpose.'

'But he did it and it's my lock and now I don't know where to sleep.'

'We'll find somewhere,' said Paul, starting to pick the pants up off the floor and tidy them back into the drawer. 'Promise. But help me tidy up now.'

'What's "tidy up"?' asked Zippel.

'It's when you put everything back in its place. My dad has this weird habit of sorting all his clothes strictly by colour. So I've got to put it all back like that again.'

While Paul sorted the black socks into a heap, and then the red ones, and then the green ones, Zippel sat on the edge of the drawer and sang a little tidying-up song:

Here's the red and there's the greeey,
Dad just loves his socks that waaaaay!

Meanwhile, Paul was doing the same with the pants, black pile, white pile, two blues, two reds. Zippel sang:

Black is dark and white is light,
Dad can find his pants all right.

Once he'd finished, Paul said: 'Come on, let's go into my room.'

'Hang on a minute,' said Zippel, 'can't I take this sleeping bag with me?' He held up a single blue and green sock.

Paul thought for a moment and said: 'OK, he won't notice that – he's got so many of those ones.'

Then he left the bedroom. Zippel floated after him, asking: 'Where were you, anyway? I woke up and you

were completely gone.'

'I went to school. I wrote you a note, you know.'

'I *don't* know. I can't read.'

'Oh,' said Paul. 'Really? I didn't know that. Shall I teach you?'

Zippel nodded enthusiastically. 'Ooh, yes!'

'OK, come on.' Paul went into his room, sat down at the desk, drew a big A on a sheet of paper and said: 'That's an A.'

'Well, really truly, that's not an A, that's a house,' the ghost contradicted him very patiently.

'Yes, it does look like a house,' said Paul, 'but we read it as an A.' Paul drew another letter. 'And that's an O.'

'No, it isn't,' said Zippel. 'I'll tell you what that is: it's a circle.'

'Yes, that too,' said Paul. 'As a picture it's a circle, but as a letter it's an O.'

Zippel laughed. 'You're very weird sometimes. OK, fine. House and circle. A and O. What else? Do I know everything now?'

'If only,' said Paul. 'There are lots of letters. 26.'

'26? That's more than a hundred! Really truly. And

they all look different? Nobody can learn all that!'

'Oh yes you can. Look: this is an E. E for Elephant.'

'Oh,' said Zippel, 'for elephant?' He was very excited: 'Yes! That's it! Write *elephant*.'

Paul wrote ELEPHANT.

'Hm,' Zippel sounded disappointed. 'Is that it?'

'Yes, why?'

'There's no trunk; I can't see a trunk at all.'

'I didn't draw an elephant, I only wrote it,' said Paul.

'And written elephants have no trunks at all? And no tusks or big ears?'

Paul looked at the word. 'That's not a real elephant, you know. That's just the letters.'

'And where's the real one?'

'In the zoo.'

'Ooh, then write zoo.'

Paul wrote ZOO.

'Finished?' asked Zippel. When Paul nodded, Zippel looked at the word from all sides. Then he picked up the paper that Paul had written on and said: 'I can't see an elephant.'

'Of course not. I just wrote ZOO.'

'But you said the elephant is in the zoo.'

'Well, the real elephant is in the real zoo. These are only the words here.'

Zippel stroked the word ELEPHANT: 'Don't be sad, unreal elephant, when you grow big, you'll get a trunk too.' Then he said to Paul: 'Hey, that was loads and loads of letters already. And really big ones, elephant-sized. I think that's enough for today.'

'I think so too.'

'But how do you know all that stuff?' asked Zippel.

'Our teacher taught us.'

'Oh, your dad?'

'No. My dad is a kind of teacher, but not at my school.'

'What? There can't be two schools?'

'Oh yes, there are lots of schools.'

'Aha, 26 then.'

'Why 26?'

'Because there are "lots" of letters too. "Lots" means 26. You said so yourself.'

'There are even more schools. My dad's a trainer for grown-ups. In a company. He trains people to do things on computers.'

'I don't understand all that. But if your dad's a teacher, why was he here at home this morning?'

'He wasn't,' said Paul. 'He always goes out very early in the mornings and doesn't get back till the evening.'

'Well this morning he did leave before you, but when you and your mum were gone, he came back very quietly.'

'What?' said Paul, and then asked in a whisper: 'Where is he then? He didn't hear us, did he?'

'No, don't worry,' said Zippel. 'Just before you came back from school, he went out again. But he spent the whole morning sitting around in your big room. He was talking quietly to himself and staring into a kind of silver box. There were lots of pictures in it and he was hammering on a lot of black buttons really crazy-fast.'

'Ah, the computer,' said Paul.

'Yeah, thanks, smarty-pants,' said Zippel, sounding as if he'd always known what a computer was. 'Then suddenly he looked up with a start at the thing with two little sticks, jumped up and went out again.'

'Which thing with two little sticks?' asked Paul.

'Oh, the sticks that turn slowly round in circles, and it goes ticker-tock all the time, even at night,' explained Zippel.

Paul laughed. 'Ah, the kitchen clock!'

'Yeah, thanks, smarty-pants,' said Zippel again. 'But your dad was so funny, you know. As if he was doing everything in secret. When he went, he opened and closed the flat's door really quietly. And then I went to play in the cupboard with the fluffy-soft things, and then suddenly you were there.'

Paul listened to Zippel and thought. Then he said: 'And Dad didn't see you?'

'Zigackly,' said Zippel. 'For one thing, he's a grow-nup and they're blind anyway. And for another, I hid really well. Look, like this.'

Zippel floated up to the ceiling. At first, Paul could see him climbing, but when Zippel was hovering right up under the white ceiling, Paul could barely make him out against the paint.

'I hovered directly above him,' said Zippel from somewhere up there. 'I even picked up a few little crumbs from the carpet and threw them at him. In revenge for the key in the lock. But he didn't notice a thing. Not a thing.'

'Hm,' said Paul, not really listening. What on earth was wrong with Dad? Paul had been wondering about him for days, because he'd been so distracted and so . . . so . . . As if he wasn't really there because he was thinking about something else all the time. And now he was secretly sitting around at home?

'Hey,' called Zippel, 'can't you hear me?' He was now floating right in front of Paul's face again.

'Er . . . what?' asked Paul.

'I asked if I can come with you to school tomorrow.'

'Better not,' said Paul, who didn't want Zippel to see how Tim and Tom teased him. 'First . . . first you need to know all the letters,' he said. 'Otherwise you won't understand what we're doing.'

'I know so many already,' said Zippel, starting to sing:

A. O. E. The elephant drinks tea.
E. A. O. To the zoo we go.
O. E. A. Now it's all OK.

'Another day maybe,' said Paul.

'Anuthaday, anuthaday, when purple pandas come to play,' said Zippel. He sounded pretty offended.

CHAPTER FOUR

So that night, Zippel slept in Paul's blue and green sock-sleeping-bag. Or, to put it another way, he tried to. Paul laid the sock on his shelf, well-hidden behind the books, and said: 'Here, this is your bed.'

Zippel looked really unhappy. 'A keyhole ghost always ought to sleep in his keyhole,' he said.

Paul nodded. 'Yes, I know. But for one thing, Dad'll stick his key in there again, and for another, we have to find you somewhere else anyway because of Mr Nitzsche.'

'Nitzsche, natzsche, nubble, I really am in trouble,' sighed Zippel. 'OK, fine, I'll sleep here. But it's far too soft. I need a hard bed. Can't we put something comfy and hard in there? With cuddly corners and edges?'

Paul looked round his room. He grabbed a handful of

marbles, two wooden blocks and a few Lego bricks, and stuffed them all into the sock. 'Better?'

Zippel vanished into the sock and, humming, rummaged around in there. The sock kept bulging out in all directions. In the end, Zippel appeared again and said: 'No oil and no rust and no dust, but at least it's nice and hard and narrow now.'

At that moment, they heard footsteps out in the corridor.

'Right,' said Mum as she walked into the room, 'you really do need to get into bed now. Oh, were you looking for a book for me to read you?' She joined Paul at the bookcase.

'Er, yes,' said Paul, 'right, this one here.' He hastily pulled out a book at random, pushed it into his mum's hand and dragged her towards the bed. 'I'm really tired.'

Mum sat down on the edge of the bed and said: 'Are you sure?'

'Why,' asked Paul, 'what do you mean?'

'Do you really want me to read you this? *Lexicon of Childhood Diseases*? I must have left it in your bookcase by mistake some time when you were ill. Come on, I'll find you a nice story instead.'

She was about to stand up and head back to the bookshelves but Paul grabbed her hand very tight: 'No-no-no, stay here, read me something about diseases – it's really interesting.'

Mum frowned.

'Please,' said Paul, 'there are some really cool diseases.'

Mum shrugged and said: 'All right then.' She flicked through the book a bit and said: 'Here, this bit's interesting: measles.'

'Oh yes, measles, very interesting,' agreed Paul.

So Mum read some things about measles, what they look like and how you tell them apart from chicken pox and rubella, and how long they itch for, and after three minutes, Paul yawned for the first time, and after five minutes he yawned a bit more conspicuously and Mum said, 'Well, you'd better get some sleep.' She stroked his head and turned the light out.

She'd barely left the room when Paul heard a quiet laugh from the bookcase.

'You people have such lovely bedtime stories,' giggled Zippel.

'Shh,' said Paul through the darkness.

But Zippel kept talking and now he sounded just like Mum when she read him a fairy tale: 'Once upon a time, a looong, looong time ago, there lived a teeny-weeny red spot, and its name was Measle. And it went running around someone's skin and met another spot. "O beautiful spot, what is your name?" "My name is Rubellina," said the other . . .'

'Hey, be quiet,' hissed Paul, 'Mum can hear us.'

'Exscrews me,' said Zippel, giggled again and was then finally quiet.

Paul asked: 'How do you do that?'

'Do what?' asked Zippel.

'Well, make yourself sound exactly like Mum?'

'Make yourself sound exactly like Mum,' said Zippel. But this time it sounded like Paul's own echo bouncing off the bookcase.

'Can we have a little quiet here, please?'

Paul jumped. That was Dad's voice. But the door was shut.

'Was that you too?' asked Paul.

'Was that me?' Paul's voice echoed from behind the books.

'Wow, that's mad!' cried Paul. 'Can you copy any voice?'

'Don't know about *any*,' said Zippel in his own voice. 'I only know you three so far, but I can do them pretty well.' He laughed quietly and then said in Dad's deeper voice: 'But we really need to get some sleep now. Zippeldesticks with bells on.'

CHAPTER FIVE

As soon as he woke up the next morning, Paul leaped over to the bookcase, looked behind the books and got a fright: the sock was still there, but Zippel was gone. Paul stuck his head deeper into the shelf, looked left, looked right, but there was no Zippel. He checked behind the books on the other shelves. Nothing. There was a lot of dust everywhere. And behind one of the books was a red marble. Zippel, however, was nowhere to be seen.

Once dressed, Paul looked around his room. There was his unmade bed. The train set. No Zippel. His heap of clothes on the chair. His desk. His school bag. No Zippel. The windowsill. The curtains. The radiator. No Zippel. The play shop. The till. Ah. The toy till. It was open.

Paul ran over to the shop and saw at once that the

coins were gone. All of them. Hmm? Paul kept on looking round his room, but he didn't notice anything obvious. He could hear a quiet sound, though. It sounded like a purring cat, and a bit like a saucepan lid when the steam hisses out of it: *rrrrrrr-pheeew.* The noise was coming from his desk. And on his desk was his piggybank. Was it grunting? *Rrrrrrr-pheeew.* The piggybank looked the same as ever: big eyes, open mouth, and the mouth seemed to be making the sound: *rrrrrrr-pheeew.*

Paul cautiously knocked on the porcelain with his fingernail and instantly, Zippel shot out of the slit on the pig's back, shouting: 'Help, I'm under attack!'

Paul jumped, and Zippel must have got a shock too. He stopped in mid-air and it was only then that he opened his eyes. 'Oh, ah, where am I?'

'Above my piggy bank,' said Paul. He saw that Zippel was a lot greyer than the evening before. 'Did you make yourself a camp in there with all the coins from the shop?' he asked.

Zippel couldn't help yawning massively but still managed to complain, even in mid-yawn. 'Everything's absolutely awful,' he moaned. 'Your dad's sock was faaaaaaaaar too soft.'

'What about the piggy bank?' asked Paul. 'Wasn't that any good either?'

'It's not rusty,' said Zippel. 'And, I'm not a piggybank ghost, if you don't mind – I'm a keyhole ghost. I need a lock with metal and oil and dust and it has to be narrow and dark and old. It has to be like that. And I can't sleep and tomorrow the lock's being changed and then I won't have a home at all.'

'Hmm,' said Paul, thinking frantically. 'Perhaps . . . perhaps I've got an idea.'

'You and your ideas,' said Zippel, who looked really

pretty grey. 'What is it this time?'

'We can look all around the building and see if any of our neighbours have an old keyhole that you could live in.'

'Oh, do other people live here too?'

'Of course,' said Paul. 'There are lots of flats here.'

'But then I won't live with you,' said Zippel.

Paul was stumped but tried to hide it by saying: 'Well then, you'll just have to go and sleep in the other keyhole and the rest of the time you can live here.'

'Boo-hoo-hooo,' cried Zippel and the cobwebs flipped and flapped all around him. 'You don't liiiiiiiike me any more.'

'Hey, course I do, I like you a lot,' whispered Paul, raising his hands to comfort Zippel. 'I think you might be my best friend.'

'Boo-hooooo-hoo,' Zippel was still crying:

No one likes me, not a sooouI.
I'm so lonely, so aloooone,
That I weep and wail and groooooooan.
And even in my rhymes I moooooan.

'Paul?' Mum called from the kitchen where she was making breakfast. 'Are you OK?'

'Yes, yes, fine,' Paul called back.

'Have you hurt yourself?'

'No, I'm just listening to a CD. A ghost story. With rhymes!'

'Oh, that's nice,' called Mum. 'Sounds really realistic. Hurry up, though, breakfast's in two minutes.'

'Yes, I'm nearly ready.' Then he said quietly, while carefully picking up the dusty cobwebs from all around Zippel: 'Now, listen, Zippel, this afternoon we'll look for another keyhole for you, and if you like it, you can sleep there, just to try it out, and if not, you don't have to.'

'OK, then,' said Zippel. 'But hurry up with school, it's terribly boring here without you.'

'I will.' Then he went for breakfast.

CHAPTER SIX

When Paul came home that afternoon, he stood in the hallway to listen. Everything was quiet. Well, almost everything. There was an audible, and already familiar, sound coming from the kitchen. Paul crept down the hall towards the quiet *rrrrrrr-pheeew.*

Zippel was lying in the middle of the kitchen floor. In an enormous heap of flour. He'd piled it into a mountain right in the middle of the room, and made a little hollow at the top, in which he was curled up like a sleeping cat. '*Rrrrrrr-pheeew,*' he went, very quietly, '*rrrrrrr-pheeew,*' and every time he breathed out, he blew a tiny cloud of flour off the peak of his little mountain. It looked a bit like the volcano Paul had seen with Mum and Dad last year in Italy, where little clouds of steam puffed away from its summit all day long.

Paul walked softly to the sink to get himself a glass of water. He crept really cautiously around Mount Flour, but Zippel must have heard him anyway. He opened his eyes. Then he stretched, in a very similar way to people when we wake up. But when he did it . . . ! First, he stretched his right arm to the right, and it grew longer and longer and longer, almost like a rubber band. Then he stretched his left arm to the left and his right arm shrank again while the left arm extended way beyond the flour mountain. He yawned, elongating his head, which stretched very long and thin and tall. Finally, he shook his whole body like a dog or a cat shaking its wet fur once through from top to bottom. Now he looked just the same as ever, except that he was proudly sitting at the summit of his little mountain.

'Just look at this! Such gorgeous dust! The loveliest I've ever seen.'

'That isn't dust though,' said Paul.

'Oh, yes, it is. It's sleeping dust. Dust that I can finally get a really lovely sleep in.'

Paul shook his head. 'That's flour. You cook with it.'

‘Look with it?’ Zippel blew out his cheeks.

‘Cook,’ said Paul. ‘Bake cakes. Or bread. Things to eat. And that’s why I’ve got to clear it off the floor. If my parents see a heap of flour on the floor, they’ll be cross.’

Paul was just about to get the dustpan from under the sink when Zippel asked: ‘What’s eating?’

Paul stopped and stared at him in amazement: ‘You really don’t know what eating is?’

‘Don’t think so,’ said Zippel.

‘Wow,’ said Paul, and thought for a moment. Then he said: ‘Eating’s like this,’ and he took a roll from the bread bin.

‘What’s that?’ asked Zippel.

‘A bread roll,’ said Paul. He tore off a piece, held it between two fingers, opened his mouth, popped it in, chewed a few times and swallowed it down.

Zippel watched him, aghast. ‘Where . . . where’s it gone?’ he asked.

‘Uh, in my tummy.’

‘Open your mouth,’ said Zippel agitatedly, ‘open your mouth right now.’

Paul sat on one of the kitchen chairs and obediently

opened his mouth. Zippel flew right up to it and looked in curiously.

'Tongue up!'

Paul rolled up his tongue.

Zippel looked in every corner of Paul's mouth.

'Where's the roll?'

'Uh, swallowed down,' said Paul.

'Stand up a minute.' Zippel fidgeted. 'Go on, go on, go on, get up.'

Paul stood up. Zippel looked first at the chair and then at Paul: 'I don't believe it. How do you *do* that? Pull up your jumper.'

Paul pulled up his jumper and his T-shirt. Zippel flew right up to his tummy. He pressed his ear against it and said quietly: 'Hello? Roll? Hello? Are you in there?'

Then he floated right round Paul, once, twice. 'Own up,' he said. 'You've hidden it somewhere. You haven't really thrown it inside yourself at all.'

'Yes, I have,' said Paul.

'Zippeldesticks!' Zippel cried with delight, clapping his hands. 'You can do magic!'

'No, no, I just ate it.'

'Yes, but where did it go then?'

'In my tummy.'

Zippel looked enthusiastically at Paul's tummy and said: 'Can I eat something too? A piece of roll?'

'I think that would be too big for you,' said Paul. 'Wait a bit.'

He pulled a bag of raisins out of the cupboard and held it out to Zippel.

Zippel looked very disappointedly at the raisins. 'What's that brown, wrinkly stuff?'

'They're raisins. They're yummy.' Paul popped three raisins in his mouth, chewed for a while and then swallowed them down.

Zippel took a raisin, opened his mouth really wide, cautiously slipped it in and hastily shut his mouth again.

A gentle plop. The raisin lay on the kitchen floor, directly below Zippel.

'Oh,' said Zippel.

'Oh,' said Paul.

They both looked at the raisin lying next to the flour.

'Maybe I need to keep it in my mouth for longer,' said Zippel.

He took another one, popped it in his mouth – plop. The second raisin was lying next to the first one.

'Hmm,' said Paul, 'they just fall right through you.'

'Pity,' said Zippel.

'Oh well, at least you can't get a tummy ache. But I really have to sweep up the flour now,' said Paul.

'Can you eat the flour too?' asked Zippel.

'Well, that's too dry. But here, look,' Paul opened the fridge. 'You can eat pretty much everything in here.'

Zippel floated into the fridge.

'Oh, it's icy cold in here. What's this hard lump?'

'Butter,' said Paul.

'Butter's for nutters,' sang Zippel, still floating there. 'And the red jar?'

'Jam,' said Paul.

'Jam, wham, bam. Oh, and this here, these yellow strings?'

'That's a pot of spaghetti. It's pasta. Mum burnt it yesterday evening.'

'They're so pretty,' cried Zippel. 'Like really, really long hair. So golden and brown and black underneath.'

Paul took out the little pot of spaghetti.

Zippel grabbed two strands and wrapped them several times round his neck. Then he floated around the kitchen, holding the spaghetti necklace daintily in his fingers like an elegant lady and sang:

Spaghetti-neckletti, long and smart
Spaghetti-neckletti looks the part.

Suddenly he stopped in mid-air, looked at the spaghetti in the pan and said: 'But you can't eat anything as big and long as that, can you?'

'Of course I can,' said Paul. He took a fork, wound up a few strands of spaghetti from the pan, stuck it in his mouth and gulped.

'But,' said Zippel. 'But, but, but . . . There's no room left in your tummy! Isn't the roll still in there?'

'Oh, you can fit quite a lot in,' said Paul.

'And then it stays in there forever?'

'No, it starts off in my stomach, then it gets digested, and eventually I go to the loo and do a poo.'

'Poo?' asked Zippel eagerly.

'Yes. And wee.' Paul explained to him what they were.

'Wee?!' Zippel sounded even more enthusiastic.

'Poo and wee? Those are really good words. Poo and wee! They sound like two best friends.'

He sang:

Poo-Poo and Wee-Wee were two friendly fellows.
Poo was the brown one and Wee was all yellow.
Wee was a liquid and Poo was rather harder,
And both were what's left of the food from your larder.

'Aah, I understand now,' said Zippel. 'The round thing's called a roll because it rolls through you. And the pasta gets passed through your tummy until it comes out again.'

'Maybe,' said Paul. 'But anyway, I need to clean up the flour now.'

'No problem; I'll help.' Zippel used both hands to lift the glass of water from beside the sink, and then he poured it on the floor.

'Hey, what on earth are you doing?'

'Water's great for washing things away,' said Zippel.

Paul hastily grabbed a handful of tissues and threw them into the huge puddle. The tissues sucked up the water. 'Whoa, Zippel, you can't just pour water around in the flat. You have to sweep the flour up with a broom.'

'Exscrews me,' said Zippel, 'I didn't know that.'

Paul threw away the soggy tissues and swept up the flour. Then he said: 'There. I'll just go to the loo. And then we've really got to go out onto the stairs to look for a keyhole for you.'

'Oh,' said Zippel, 'can I come to the loo too? I want to see it.'

Paul shrugged. 'If you really want to.'

CHAPTER SEVEN

Paul walked to the bathroom with Zippel floating along behind him.

'Hey, look at that,' he said when he saw the toilet bowl, 'a white chair.'

'That's the loo,' said Paul. He lifted the lid.

'Oh,' cried Zippel, anxiously, 'mind out, mind out, mind out.' He ripped the fat toilet roll out of its holder and threw it into the loo. There was a splash, then the whole roll soaked full of water.

'Hey! What are you doing now?' yelled Paul.

'Cleaning,' cried Zippel. 'There was water. Right in the middle of the loo. That's not right! That's not allowed! You said so yourself. Water needs clearing up right away. Really truly.'

'But, Zippel, there's meant to be water in the loo,' said Paul, pulling the dripping wet toilet roll out of the bowl and throwing it in the bin.

'Oh, right,' sighed Zippel. 'Exscrews me. I didn't know that either.'

'*Excuse* me,' said Paul, pulling down his trousers and sitting down to wee.

'Don't mention it,' said Zippel, sounding very generous.

‘No, I mean, you always say “exscrews me”. But it should be *excuse* me.’

‘Well I say *exscrews* me. It sounds much better. You screw up and then you say exscrews me.’

‘Have it your own way,’ said Paul, as he started to wee.

‘Oh, that’s such a nice noise,’ cried Zippel. ‘Listen to it tinkling. Beautiful.’

Paul stood up, pulled up his trousers and pressed the flush.

‘Help!’ shouted Zippel. ‘Watch out! Stop!’ He stared at the rushing water. Then he looked at the floor. Then back to the water, rushing through the toilet bowl. And then back to the floor in front of it. ‘Fancy that,’ he said. ‘The floor didn’t even get wet.’

‘No, it all goes down the drain here,’ said Paul.

Zippel was watching the rushing water in fascination.

‘So you’ve got a waterfall right in your flat? That’s so . . . so . . . Can I fall some water too?’

‘Flush it, you mean?’

‘Yes. Please-please-please. I want to flash it.’

‘Flush,’ Paul corrected him. ‘Sure. But you’ll have to

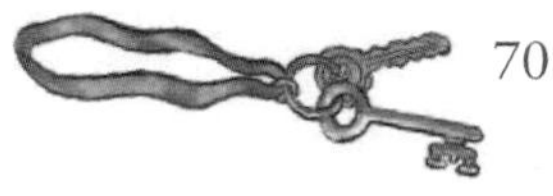

wait till the tank's filled up again. And then you press down on this lever here.'

Zippel jiggled up and down by the tank, waiting for the water to refill. He stroked the cistern gently and said: 'Nice water tank, kind water tank, be good and fill up with lots of lovely water, yes?' Then he pressed the flush and yelled: 'Waterfall! Waterfaaall! Look out, look out! A thousand hundred litres, ta-ran-ta-raaaa!'

He floated excitedly over the bowl, flailing his little arms around as if he were conducting the water. Once it had all gurgled away, he looked enthusiastically at Paul and said: 'Again.'

'Go on, then,' said Paul. 'But then we need to go. Mum and Dad will be back at some point.'

'Soon-soon-soon,' said Zippel as the flush roared again. 'Waterfall! Waaaterfall!' Zippel was bobbing up and down faster than ever, laughing and clapping and singing a little flushing and roaring song, but you couldn't hear it over the flushing and roaring water.

Paul went back into the hallway and fetched his key. He waited a while, but after Zippel had flushed a fifth time, he said: 'Come on, that's enough now.'

'OK,' said Zippel, 'fine, but I'll carry on later. Oh boy, that's sooooooo cool. A waterfall! In the middle of the flat. Really truly.'

'Yes, yes,' said Paul, 'but be quiet now and come *on*.'

CHAPTER EIGHT

Paul took his key, opened the flat door a crack and listened for anyone coming. He couldn't hear a thing.

'Come on, then,' he whispered. He peeked quickly over the bannisters to see if he could see anyone. Nothing.

Zippel, who was floating beside him, also looked down the three storeys. 'Hoo-hoo-hoooo!' he yelled excitedly. 'What a lovely long way down. And what's this pipe?'

'Do you mean the handrail?' asked Paul.

'Dunno if I mean the randhail. I mean this wooden slide that goes whee-whee-whee all the way down.'

'Yes, that's the handrail.'

Zippel floated onto it and then slid down one storey at a time into the depths.

He sang:

Oh yes, the shiny hand-and-rail
Goes down and down and round the trail:
Handrail, doornail, tell-tale, derail.

Zippel grew quieter and quieter and smaller and smaller. When he was right downstairs, he called up: 'Come on, your turn!'

Paul shook his head: 'I'm scared.'

Whoosh, Zippel popped right up the middle of the stairwell. 'Why?'

'If I fell, I'd be dead.'

'Oh. Dead? What's dead?' asked Zippel.

'Um, if you're dead, you're not here any more,' said Paul.

'What? Not here any more? Would you be hiding down there, then?' asked Zippel. 'Ooh, go on! Jump down!'

'No, if you're dead, you stop living,' said Paul.

'How can you stop living? You just keep on all the time.'

Paul looked at Zippel in surprise: 'Can't ghosts die at all then?'

Zippel thought for a moment: 'Don't think so. At any rate, I've never died. Have you?'

'No, I haven't. Otherwise I wouldn't be here. But my grandma died two years ago. And Mr Wilhelm died here in the house not long ago. Old Mrs Wilhelm's husband.'

'And where are your grandma and Mr Wilhelm now?'

'In heaven, maybe,' said Paul.

'That's a very long way up,' said Zippel. 'How did they get up there? Can you people fly after all?'

'Their bodies aren't up there,' said Paul, 'they're in the cemetery. But their souls are.'

'What on earth is that?' asked Zippel.

'A soul? I don't really know,' said Paul. 'Really, I've always imagined a soul as a bit like you, something small and shining, all light and white, and it can fly.'

'Oh, how nice! Do people all have a keyhole ghost hidden inside them?' Zippel flew right up to Paul's eyes, looked deep into his pupils and said: 'Little Paul-ghost, will you come out from Paul and see me?'

'My soul can't come out,' said Paul, 'it always stays inside me.'

'You just said it could fly,' said Zippel. 'You people are

really weird. You've got all that food inside you. And now there's a soul too. You must be really full up. Rolls. Flying souls. Pasta. But Paul, where are all the keyholes I can live in?'

'Exactly,' said Paul. 'We need to go round all the doors in the house.'

So they went down to the ground floor – that is, Paul ran down, in which time, Zippel slid right down the whole 'hand-and-rail' six times. Then they ran up one flight of stairs at a time, but all the other flats in the building had very modern locks: all narrow with a tiny slit instead of a proper keyhole to look into.

'I'm not a slit ghost,' moaned Zippel, 'I'm a keyhole ghost. What are they all thinking of?'

'Yeah, it's silly,' said Paul, once they'd reached the sixth floor. He glanced quickly at the last few front doors and was just thinking that that was it when, right at the end of the dark corridor, he saw Mrs Wilhelm's door.

Her door was very different. Much older. And the keyhole was really big, even bigger than the one at Paul's home.

'Ooooh,' said Zippel in delight, 'what a lovely keyhole.'

Even as he spoke, he was shrinking, and then *whoosh*, he was gone.

'Ooh-oo-ooh!' Paul could just hear him from outside. 'Hoo-hoo.' Then he heard Zippel rummaging and rustling around inside the door.

'Zippel?' asked Paul.

It was silent for a moment, and then the little ghost reappeared and grew large. He was shining brighter than normal and sounded really thrilled. 'Oh, Paul, if only you could see that!'

'Why? What's up?'

'That's what I call a *lock*! Just how a lock ought to be. With very ancient springs. And there's lots of space and it smells great. And it's all so nice and rusty and oily. Oh, Paul, I've got to go back in. It's the perfect keyhole-ghost keyhole.'

Before Paul could say a word, Zippel had gone again. This time he stayed away for longer. Paul could hear two pigeons cooing outside in the gutter. But it was very quiet in the keyhole now.

'Zippel?' Paul whispered after a while. 'What are you doing?'

No answer. Had he fallen asleep in there?

'Hey, Zippel, come out, I don't want to stand around here alone.'

Silence. Paul was just about to sit down on the stairs to wait when the door to Mrs Wilhelm's flat popped quietly open.

Zippel appeared in the doorframe. 'Come on in,' he whispered excitedly.

'You can't do that,' Paul hissed. 'What if Mrs Wilhelm sees us?'

'She's not even here,' said Zippel.

'All the same. It's breaking in.'

Zippel zipped around. 'Oh, break it in, break it out, break a leg. I just want to show you something. Really quickly. Hurry up.'

'This really isn't right,' said Paul, hurriedly glancing over the bannister to check if anyone was coming.

'It is so right,' said Zippel. 'I've found something you need to see.' He vanished into the flat again.

Paul felt very uneasy as he pushed the heavy old door open. It squeaked so loudly that he jumped and looked round in case anyone could see him.

A long, empty hall. On the walls were old picture frames. Paul stepped nervously through the door.

'Hello?' he asked cautiously. 'Mrs Wilhelm?'

Silence.

He walked slowly down the hall. The floorboards creaked under his feet. He stirred up dust that danced in the slanting beams of afternoon sunlight.

'Zippel?' asked Paul quietly. 'Where are you?'

'Here,' Zippel yelled enthusiastically from the very far end. 'Ooh-ooooh! In the sitting room. Hurry up. You've got to see this.'

Paul walked on down the hall, past the picture frames. To his surprise, they were all empty. There were no pictures in them. 'Weird,' he said. 'Did you see that, Zippel? The fra—' Then he stopped. Open-mouthed. In the sitting room doorway.

The room was quite large. In the middle were two beautiful old upholstered armchairs. Between them was a small table. Opposite the chairs was a wide bookcase. Really wide. And as high as the ceiling. And on the shelves were nothing but locks. Nothing else. Old door locks. Side by side. Large iron locks. Small ones that looked gilded.

Fat locks, thin locks. But all with big keyholes. Lying next to some of the locks were their keys.

Zippel hovered by the bookcase, whooping quietly. 'Can you see that?' he cried, positively glittering with happiness. 'See that? Canyouseeeeeethat?'

Paul nodded. 'Yes,' he said, quietly, but Zippel had already vanished into a fat, round lock. 'Oo-hoo, what a smell,' he called from inside, 'smells of twenty-two-hundred-year-old oil.'

Then he came out again – and vanished into the next lock, a square one that even had its gilded door handle still attached. Paul sat in one of the two armchairs, which were positioned so as to look straight at the shelves of locks.

'And there's loads of rust in here, glorious,' enthused Zippel from a highly-decorated lock. 'And dust – just right, just exactly right! I really like this Mrs Wilhelm.'

Little clouds of dust and rust flew out of the lock.

Why would someone collect old locks? Paul wondered. Where had Mrs Wilhelm got them all from? And why had she displayed them like valuable paintings and cleaned them like precious treasure?

'What a cheek,' said a sudden voice behind Paul. Paul jumped. Mrs Wilhelm was standing in the half-darkness of the hallway. She had her left eye screwed up more tightly than ever. 'What are you doing in here?'

Paul leaped up. 'Oh, sorry,' he said. 'I . . . Um . . . '

Mrs Wilhelm put her head on one side. There was a deep frown on her brow. She was looking at Paul with her large right eye and waiting for him to carry on.

'Your door,' said Paul. 'Well . . . It was open. I was just going to the attic when I saw the open door and I called out to you and then I accidentally went in and—'

Mrs Wilhelm listened to his stammering. She seemed to be growing angrier – the frown was getting deeper and deeper, and she interrupted him crossly: 'You don't

go into other people's flats. Not even accidentally.'

'Yes, I know, I agree,' said Paul. 'That's what I said. Er, to myself.'

'But you walked in anyway?'

Paul stared at the floor. 'Sorry, Mrs Wilhelm,' he said quietly.

'I thought better of you, Paul,' said Mrs Wilhelm. 'Go home, now, please.'

'Yes,' said Paul and nodded, without looking up, 'I was just about to.'

He walked past Mrs Wilhelm in the hallway, muttered 'Bye' without turning round, and stumbled out to the stairs. He ran down the first flight. Then he waited for Zippel. But Zippel didn't come.

'Bother,' Paul whispered to the empty stairwell. What should he do now? He couldn't exactly ring Mrs Wilhelm's doorbell and ask if his ghost was still there. He waited another minute and then went down to the flat and into his room.

Zippel was already there, sitting on the edge of the play shop.

'There you are!' said Paul and Zippel at the same time.

'I was waiting for you,' said Paul.

'Me too,' said Zippel. 'Well, not for me, but for you.'

Paul sat on his bed.

'That Mrs Wilhelm is super-duper,' gushed Zippel, 'a really good grow-nup at last.'

'Wow,' said Paul. 'She's hopping mad.'

'Yes, but she's got great taste – those were amazing keyholes.'

'Maybe, but I'm scared that she'll ring the doorbell tonight and tell my parents that I was sneaking around in her flat. And then I'll be in trouble with Dad again.'

'I don't think so,' said Zippel.

'What don't you think?'

'That your dad will tell you off.'

'What makes you think that?' asked Paul.

'Well,' said Zippel, 'he's sneaking around in a flat every day himself.'

'What do you mean?'

'Well, this morning. When you and your mum had gone. He came creeping back in here again.'

'What?' shouted Paul. 'Really? Why didn't you tell me earlier?'

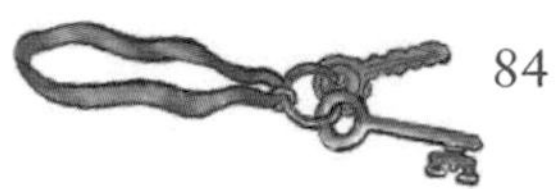

'There was so much going on,' said Zippel. 'First the kitchen, then the amazing waterfall in the loo and then Mrs Wilhelm. Anyway, that Mrs Wilhelm, she—'

'And what was Dad doing here?' Paul interrupted the torrent of words.

'Nothing. He sat around for hours, stared into the computer for ages and bashed about on the buttons and eventually he ran out again. I'm not a human, so I might be wrong, but if you ask me, he didn't look very cheerful.'

Paul was completely confused. Who could his dad be hiding from? And why was he acting so oddly? Or was Zippel making it all up?

'Anyway,' Zippel said, 'all I wanted to say was that your dad can't exactly tell you off if Mrs Wilhelm comes. He's sitting around in secret in a flat too.'

'That's different though,' said Paul. 'This is *his* flat.'

CHAPTER NINE

The next morning, Paul cycled to school, just as he did every day. He had to ride down Three Mill Street and then along the stream. He was just looking up into the trees, where two squirrels were playing chase, when he heard a quiet voice singing:

School's not very far away
Zippel's going to learn today.
How to count and read and draw,
And all one hundred numbers, for
Zippel's got a plan to be
The brainiest ghost you'll ever see.

Paul braked suddenly. He stood right in the middle of the cycle path and twisted round to peer at his school bag.

'Oh, no, Zippel.'

'No-no,' said Zippel, 'I'm not here. Not at all. That was just a sort of little song floating about by itself.'

'Of course you're here,' groaned Paul. 'But I told you: I can't take you today.'

'You aren't taking me at all,' said Zippel. 'I just float into your school bag all by myself, and your school bag gets taken to school, and then I just happen to be at school too. You ride on and don't worry about it.'

Paul wondered whether he should take Zippel back home. But then he'd be late.

'OK, I'll bring you,' he decided. 'But school is heaving with grown-ups. What if they see you? You have to be really quiet. Promise?'

'Yes-yes-yes,' said Zippel. 'You have my solemn premise.'

Paul rode on. Zippel was quiet for a while. Then he said: 'Hey, Paul.'

'What's up?' asked Paul, without stopping.

'There's some kind of jar in here next to me. It wobbles to and fro all the time. I'm afraid it'll fall over. Can you take it out?'

That must be the strawberry yoghurt Mum had given him for a snack. 'Yeah,' said Paul. 'I will when we get there.'

Five minutes later, they arrived outside the school and Paul parked his bike. He looked all around to check that

nobody was watching him. Then he quickly put his bag on the ground and opened it.

Zippel was sitting on the books, grinning at him. 'By the time we get home this afternoon, I'll be able to read all that,' he said, rubbing his hands. 'Then you can pick a book and I'll read it to you, OK?'

Paul took out the jar of strawberry yoghurt. At that moment, Tim and Tom came round the corner. 'Oh no,' muttered Paul.

'What's wrong?' asked Zippel. He was about to peek over the edge of the bag.

'Shut up,' hissed Paul, hurriedly closing the bag. He was holding the yoghurt in his hand, which meant it took longer than usual to do up the two straps. Just as he was about to put the bag on, Tim and Tom looked over his shoulder.

'Oh, this looks nice,' said Tim. He took the jar from Paul's hand. 'Strawberry yoghurt! Yum! My favourite. Thanks!' Tim kept hold of the jar and just walked away without looking round.

Paul stood there, empty-handed. Tom laughed. 'Paul's self-service shop. We'll come here for all our morning snacks from now on.' Then he ran off after Tim.

The whole scene had taken just a couple of seconds. Tim had taken Paul's snack as if it was the most ordinary thing in the world. As if it actually belonged to him.

Paul had a salty taste in the back of his throat from biting back the tears that were rising up inside him. Just don't cry now. That was what they were waiting for. He picked up his bag and went on towards the school. Ten metres ahead of him, he could hear Tim and Tom laughing.

And directly behind him, in his school bag, he could hear a small, angry voice. 'Revenge!' huffed the voice. 'That was the very meanest meaniness in all the world! Just wait till I get hold of you two – I'll squish you into a ghostly mush!'

'Shh,' whispered Paul, trotting quietly into the classroom.

Tim and Tom had already hung their jackets over their chairs and were sitting in their places. 'Hey, here's Paul,' cried Tim, as if he were really pleased to see him. 'Good morning. How are you?'

Paul walked in silence past the two of them and sat down in the back row.

CHAPTER TEN

First, they had science. Mr Ampermeier had brought lots of little plastic trees and the children had to tell him their names: birch, fir, spruce, beech . . . Once he asked Paul what type of tree had a white trunk. Paul hadn't been listening because he was still so furious. Because of the stolen yoghurt, obviously, but also because he knew that Zippel had seen Tim and Tom being so nasty to him. His heart was pounding and he was still having to hold back the tears that were welling up behind his eyes like water behind a dam. That made him even more furious. The fact that those two kept making him cry was the nastiest thing of all. So now, when Mr Ampermeier asked him what that tree was called, the one with the white trunk, Paul just shrugged his shoulders. 'Don't know.'

'Come on now,' said Mr Ampermeier. 'You know this. White trunk. Green leaves.'

'I don't care,' said Paul.

Mr Ampermeier frowned: 'Is something wrong?'

Paul almost said: 'Yes, there is! They stole my strawberry yoghurt.' But he just muttered: 'No, no, it's fine.'

Mr Ampermeier gave him another searching look and then shrugged too, saying: 'OK, fine, who can answer my question?'

Lots of hands went up and Tim shouted: 'You must mean a birch, Mr Ampermeier!'

'Yes,' said Mr Ampermeier, 'but don't just shout out, Tim.'

'Sorry, Mr Ampermeier,' said Tim, as if he were an absolute model pupil.

Then they carried on with other trees, and twenty minutes later, Mr Ampermeier said: 'So, now let's all go out into the playground and see what kinds of trees we can find there.'

Most of the children jumped up immediately from their chairs. Paul took his time – he didn't want to speak to anyone. As he walked out, he saw Tim and Tom trying to hide in the classroom. But Mr Ampermeier spotted them too and called out: 'Go on, you two, out you go!' Tim and

Tom shuffled, grumbling, into the corridor.

Outside, they were all standing around while Mr Ampermeier pointed to an evergreen tree on the edge of the playground and asked what it was. Someone said: 'fir'. Mr Ampermeier said: 'correct' and asked about the next tree.

Fifteen minutes later, when they walked back into the school, there was a rather sickly-sweet smell in the classroom. Lotti, who sat two rows in front of Paul, said: 'Smells of chewing gum in here.'

'Nah,' said Johanna next to her, 'more like fruit muesli.'

But Mr Ampermeier said it must be coming from outside and carried on with the lesson.

When the bell went for break time, everyone jumped up. Tim and Tom hastily pulled on their jackets. Tim was just walking through the classroom door when he shoved both hands into his jacket pockets – and froze. His eyes grew bigger and bigger. He was standing in the doorframe with a cluster of other children behind him, who all wanted to get past and were now staring to see why Tim had stopped. He slowly pulled his hands from his pocket. Pink slime dripped from his fingers.

'Eww,' screeched some of the girls behind him.

Now Tom, who was standing by the board, also pulled his hands from his pockets. Same thing: big eyes. Astonishment. Pink hands, dripping onto the floor.

'Oh, that's what the smell was,' giggled Selina. 'Strawberry yoghurt.'

Tim and Tom looked at each other. Then they both glared with hatred at Paul. 'Did you do this?' asked Tim.

'N . . . n . . . no,' stammered Paul. 'How could I? When?'

'What's all that yoghurt?' asked Mr Ampermeier.

'It's Paul's,' said Tim and Tom in one voice.

'Oh,' said Mr Ampermeier, 'so how did it get into your jacket pockets?'

'Don't know,' said Tim.

'No idea,' said Tom.

Little pink lakes were forming around the two of them as the yoghurt carried on dripping from their hands. And it was oozing from their jackets too.

'Can you explain this?' asked Mr Ampermeier, looking at Paul as he spoke.

'Um, well,' said Paul with a shrug, 'They took it off me this morning outside school.'

‘Why did you take Paul’s yoghurt?’ Mr Ampermeier asked.

‘Because . . .’ Tim shrugged. ‘It tastes nice, I guess.’

Tom said nothing.

‘You two, go to the toilets, wash your hands and clean your jackets,’ ordered Mr Ampermeier. Then he pointed to the pink puddles on the floor. ‘After that, you will wipe up this mess, and we’ll talk.’

Paul went out to the playground. Max stood beside him. ‘Those two are real idiots,’ he said. ‘Would you like some of my snack?’ He held out a pot of grapes to Paul.

‘Oh,’ said Paul, ‘thanks.’

Max was a new boy in their class. He’d moved here over the summer holidays. Paul took a couple of grapes from Max’s pot and they looked around for Tim and Tom. But those two hadn’t finished cleaning up yet.

Max asked: ‘Are they always that stupid?’

Paul nodded. ‘To me, at any rate. I’d better hide.’

He ran across the whole playground and then the sports field, to the gorse bushes right at the far end. There he crouched behind the largest bush and looked towards the school. Max was watching him the whole time, and Paul signalled to him not to look over at him so obviously. He was so scared. Tim and Tom would be bound to get revenge once they'd finished clearing up. His heart was thumping in his throat. But he was secretly happy too. Finally. Proper vengeance at last. Thanks, Zippel, he thought.

Then he saw them. Tim and Tom were coming out of school. They were both searching, turning their heads. Tim gestured to Tom: *You go round to the left, I'll go right.* They ran slowly through the bustling playground, looking out for him. Three girls from their class laughed when they saw Tim. They turned their noses towards him and closed their eyes, sniffing as if he smelled particularly delicious. Tim took no notice but just kept scanning the playground with narrowed eyes. Paul's heart was in his mouth. At that moment, Tim pointed across the sports field towards him. Tom looked towards the bushes too, and nodded. They were both about to set off when, luckily, the bell rang. Tim and Tom looked at each other. They seemed to be considering whether they should run over to him anyway. But then they went back into the school. Max was the last at the glass door, and waved briefly to show Paul that the coast was clear. But Paul still waited another minute before running back.

He just managed to slip back into the classroom on time so as not to miss the beginning of the next lesson. It was maths. Mr Ampermeier turned to the board.

'Righty-ho,' he said, writing up *17 + 25 + 6*. 'Let's see who's any good at mental arithmetic.'

He'd only just finished writing up the sum when Tim's voice shouted from the back: 'Mr Amplifier! Mr Amplifier! I know the answer, Mr Amplifier.'

Mr Ampermeier turned round, narrowed his eyes and looked sharply at Tim: 'I beg your pardon?' Mr Ampermeier always spoke extra quietly when he was angry.

Tim gulped. 'That wasn't me,' he said, 'I didn't say anything.'

Mr Ampermeier asked in that thin, cutting voice: 'Did you just call me Mr Amplifier?'

'No,' said Tim. 'Honest.'

Mr Ampermeier stood stock-still. His face flushed red and the veins in his neck were throbbing. Slowly, he turned back to the board.

At once, everyone could hear Tim's voice again: 'Mr

Amplifier, Mr Amplifier, I know what you get. Eleventy-hundred, seven thousand and twelvety lots of five.'

Tim shouted, even before Mr Ampermeier had finished turning round: 'Someone's copying my voice, Mr Ampli— sorry, Mr Ampermeier.'

'Oh really,' said Mr Ampermeier. 'And who can imitate your voice that well?'

'I . . . I . . . don't know,' stuttered Tim, looking questioningly at Tom, who looked equally baffled and was shaking his head frantically.

Out of the corner of his eye, Paul, who was desperately trying not to laugh, saw something white flitting over the ceiling.

Mr Ampermeier turned back to the board and was about to carry on writing.

'Hey, Mr Ampleliar, it was me.' This time it sounded as though Tom had called out.

Mr Ampermeier's hand stopped in mid-air, holding the chalk. For several long seconds. He looked like a waxwork except that the vein in his neck was so swollen you could see the blood throbbing through it. His whole face was red with fury.

'Ho ho,' said the voice, 'Ampleliar's angry head is such a pretty shade of red!'

Mr Ampermeier's whole body was trembling now. The chalk snapped in his fingers and he spoke extremely quietly: 'Get out, Tom! Now!'

Tom muttered that it hadn't been him, but Mr Ampermeier looked so formidable in his rage that he immediately stood up and walked out.

Mr Ampermeier was trying to calm down. He took several deep breaths, in and out, undid the top button of his shirt, looked briefly out of the window, then turned back to the board and said: 'Well, where was I? Oh, yes, *17 plus 25 plus 6*, what does that come to?'

He had just written the equals sign on the board when Tim's voice called out again: 'But Mr Campfire, what did you go and throw Tom out for?'

Mr Ampermeier froze. His right hand hovered by the board as the voice trilled:

A campfire can cook something yummy
To fill up your great big, fat tummy!

17+25+6=

Mr Ampermeier turned as if in slow motion. His face was now lobster-pink, his neck was at full stretch, his eyes were almost bulging right out of his head. 'OUT!' he yelled. 'NOW!'

Tim ran in panic from the classroom.

After school, Paul rushed straight to the bike-shed in the car park. He was looking around nervously for Tim and Tom, but he couldn't see them in the crush. He kneeled down to unlock his bike, and when he looked up again, he saw the two of them by the school gate. Standing next to them were Mr Ampermeier and the head teacher who were both talking crossly to them. The boys looked much smaller than usual.

Paul jumped onto his bike and cycled slowly away. But he felt as though someone were pushing him along. As if he had the wind behind him. As if his bike were freewheeling all by itself. He pedalled and heard a very quiet voice singing in his school bag:

Eleventy-hundred, seven thousand, twelvety lots of three,

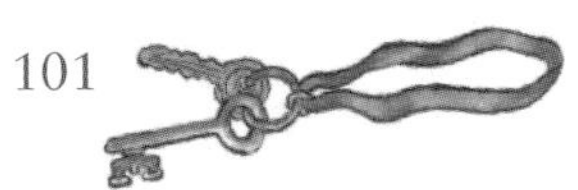

School is very boring, but it's over now, whoopee.
Eleventy-hundred, seven thousand, twelvety lots of four,
Timmy, Tommy, popple-pommy, they got shown the door.
Eleventy-hundred, seven thousand, twelvety lots of ten,
Tommy, Timmy, pipple-pimmy, daren't show up again.

Paul felt as though the voice was singing inside him. When he got to the stream, he stopped and just let his bike drop into the meadow. There was nobody in sight. Even before he'd taken his school bag off, Zippel came floating out.

'Whew,' grinned Paul, as he sat down in the grass.

'Whee-whew!' cried Zippel, doing a somersault in the air.

Paul beamed. 'That was so cool. I reckon they'll leave me alone now.'

'I should hope so,' said Zippel. 'Cos, well, school . . . Who on earth came up with an idea like that? Seventeen

and four, sixteen and five, and what's that tree called? I thought people played at school, like we do at home, only all together.'

'Nah, you have to sit quietly and learn stuff.'

'Oh,' said Zippel. 'I know lots already. Of course I'll come if you need me again, but if not, I think I'd rather stay at home and play waterfalls.'

At home. The words suddenly made Paul's whole body tense up. What if the lock had already been changed? After all, today was Friday. Paul gulped. He felt as though there was a cold, heavy lump in his stomach. He didn't want to spoil the happy mood, though, so he said nothing. Well. He said one thing: 'Hey, Zippel, thanks. You really did help me a lot.'

'Zigackly,' said Zippel. 'That's what I'm here for. Oh. What's the matter?'

Paul had suddenly fallen silent. No wonder. He'd spotted Tim. There he was, coming over the meadow on his orange bike. He wheeled very slowly over to the two of them, looking at Paul all the time. Paul stood up and wiped the grass off his hands. Zippel vanished behind the little tree that was right beside the stream. Tim parked his bike near the tree. His school bag was strapped to the rack on the back. He came towards Paul without a word. Paul swallowed and forced himself not to run away. When Tim was a metre away, he said: 'You did that.'

'What?' asked Paul.

'With the yoghurt,' said Tim. 'And disguising your voice. I don't know how you did it, but it was all you.'

'Maybe,' said Paul, gulping again. 'But maybe it was someone else.'

'Oh, yeah?' scoffed Tim. 'And who would that be?'

'None of your business,' said Paul.

'Well,' said Tim. 'Do you know what's going to happen now?'

'Not a clue,' said Paul.

'Your school bag,' said Tim, pointing to Paul's school bag which lay on the grass between the two of them, 'is about to go for a swim down the stream. With all your books and pens and stuff. And doing funny voices won't help you then.'

'We'll see,' said Paul.

Tim hesitated. Paul was so different today. Normally, he was dead scared and stared at the ground as soon as

Tim spoke to him. But this time, Paul was facing him and just looking straight back. And because Paul was looking at him all the time, Tim didn't notice something small and white flitting rapidly beneath the saddle of his bike.

'Well,' said Paul. 'Do *you* know what's going to happen now?'

'You're just repeating what I said,' scoffed Tim. But he didn't sound as arrogant as usual, and he added: 'Why? What?'

'Your school bag,' said Paul, pointing over Tim's shoulder. 'And your bike. And the stream.'

Tim was really trying not to turn round, because that would be lame, obviously, but then he saw Paul smiling, and he heard a sound. Tyres, rolling through the grass. And when Tim *did* turn round, he saw his bike, ten metres away, gliding past him towards the stream. 'But . . .' he stammered, 'But . . . Stop!'

The bike kept rolling slowly on. Two ducks fluttered up in shock as it passed them. The bike was right on the edge now, another half metre and it would fall over the bank into the water.

'Stop!' called Paul. 'That's enough.'

The bike stopped, its front wheel dangling in the stream, its back wheel still on the meadow.

Tim stared wide-eyed at Paul. Then he slowly drew back. One step, two steps.

Paul stared calmly back. 'Just leave me in peace,' he said. 'OK?'

Tim ran to his bike. He grabbed it out of the stream, still staring at Paul, wrenched it round, leaped on and pedalled away so frantically, he almost fell off.

CHAPTER ELEVEN

Half an hour later, Paul was sitting in his bedroom when the doorbell rang. That must be Mr Nitzsche.

Paul's mum called from the kitchen: 'Paul? Can you get the door? I'm just in the middle of cooking.'

'OK.'

Zippel floated restlessly up and down in front of Paul. 'No!' he whispered. 'No-no-no. Let's just not open the door. Then the silly man will go away again. Or wait, I've got a better idea: I'll put a spell on him!' He hovered in the middle of the room, waved his arms around in the air and muttered:

Nasty Nitzsche, here's my spell:
You'll never-ever ring the bell.

It rang again.

'Paul?!' The voice from the kitchen was sounding impatient, although that might have something to do with a slight burning smell.

'Yes, yes, I'm coming,' said Paul.

Paul walked slowly down the hall and opened the door.

Standing in front of him was Mr Nitzsche with his enormous toolkit.

'Hi, Paul. I've come to . . . Oh, there's smoke coming from your kitchen. Is there a fire?'

'No, no, that's just Mum cooking,' said Paul.

'Oh, right,' said Mr Nitzsche. 'Anyway, I've come to change your lock.'

'Do you have to right now?' asked Paul. 'The old lock is still fine, actually.'

His mother appeared briefly in the kitchen doorway. 'Hello, Mr Nitzsche, good to see you.' There were little clouds of smoke following her. 'I need to start again; the spinach got a teeny-tiny bit burnt. Will you be all right getting on with it?'

'No problem,' said Mr Nitzsche.

He kneeled down by the open door and took a closer look at the lock, the screws, the door handle and the big keyhole. Finally, he shut his left eye and looked into it with his right. Suddenly he jerked his head back from the door and sucked air through his teeth, the way adults often do when something hurts and they don't want to say *ow*. 'Sugar! What the heck was that?' He was holding one hand over his right eye.

'What's the matter?' asked Paul.

'I don't know, said Mr Nitzsche. 'There was a cloud of dust. Could I wash my eye out, please?'

'Yes, of course,' said Paul, 'follow me.'

Paul opened the bathroom door, Mr Nitzsche bent over the washbasin and started carefully rinsing his eye with cold water.

At that very same moment, they heard an enormous noise that clattered and crashed right down the stairwell. Mr Nitzsche straightened up. Then there was another crash. Paul could see Mr Nitzsche's astonished expression in the mirror over the basin. They both listened. *Ding! Bang! Pow! Dong!* Mr Nitzsche ran out of the bathroom to the stairs with a dripping wet face. His toolbox was no longer outside the door – it was up on the bannisters. And it was wide open. 'But . . .' he yelled, baffled. 'What on earth . . . ?'

He looked in the box. 'Where are my tools?' Then he leaned over the bannisters and looked down in disbelief.

'Holy moly . . . Who did that?' He looked up and down the stairs, then glared at Paul.

'It wasn't me,' said Paul, 'honest!'

Paul's mother appeared. 'What happened?'

'Somebody threw my tools down the stairs.'

'What? Paul, was it you?'

'No, honestly it wasn't, I'd never do anything like that, and anyway, I was showing you the bathroom.'

'Yes, that's true,' said Mr Nitzsche.

'Ouch! What happened to your eye?' asked Paul's mother in horror.

The eye was looking pretty bad – it was red and watering, as if Mr Nitzsche had rubbed onion juice into it.

'No idea,' he said. 'I was just looking into your lock when all this dust blew into my eye. I think I'll pop to the

doctor's. It stings a bit. Is it OK if I change your lock on Monday instead?'

'Yes, of course,' said Paul's mum.

'I'll help you pick up your tools,' offered Paul, slowly following Mr Nitzsche down the stairs.

CHAPTER TWELVE

Over tea, Paul's mum asked: 'How on earth did all those tools tumble down like that?'

'No idea,' said Paul.

'There really wasn't anyone on the stairs?'

'Well, I guess there must have been,' said Paul. He pushed the bone-dry cauliflower around his plate a bit.

'Who, though?' said his mum.

Instead of answering, Paul asked: 'Anyway, what are we doing at the weekend?'

'Oh, no idea, how about a trip somewhere?'

'Ooh, yes!' cried Paul.

'Hmm,' said Mum. 'What's up with you?'

'Why?'

'Well, normally if I say "Let's go on a trip," you react

as if I've told you to tidy your room.' She screwed her face up until she looked all frowny and grumpy, and put on a sulky voice: "Do we have to? I don't want to. I'd rather stay here."'

'Yeah. Uh, no. Um . . .' Paul thought for a moment and then said: 'I really urgently need to look at a castle.'

'A castle?'

'Yes. A castle. You know, where kings and knights used to live. Like last year in Italy, where there was even still that drawbridge.'

'Oh, you mean the *Castello di Uviglie*,' sighed Mum, with the strange look on her face that she always got when she was remembering something nice.

'Don't remember the name,' said Paul.

'Ah, that was suuuch a beautiful place,' gushed Mum. 'The gardens. The paintings. And do you remember, in the evening we sat in the piazza in that little village and—'

'Exactly,' Paul interrupted. 'There must be a castle like that somewhere round here too.'

'Yes, of course,' said Paul's mum. 'Castle Grafenburg. We went there once with you, when you were two.' She got that look on her face again. 'You stomped down all the long corridors on your little legs and said: "I want to live here." Do you remember?' She looked fondly at Paul.

'No, not at all, but it's even better that way. Can we go there, please? Please!'

'Of course,' said his mum.

'Tomorrow?' Paul asked at once.

'Fine by me,' said Mum.

'Promise?' asked Paul.

'Yes, sure,' said Mum. 'Promise. But why's it so urgent?'

'For school,' he lied. 'Because we're reading something about knights and castles. But I've got homework to do now.'

He went to his room, but then turned back again: 'It's really hard stuff, Mum, I really need to contemplate, so I'm shutting the door, OK?'

Mum laughed quietly and said: 'It is important to *concentrate*, so you just shut your door.'

Paul shut his door behind him and ran over to the toy shop.

'Hey, come out,' he whispered into the till.

No reaction.

Paul looked in the bookcase. Nothing. He looked at

the train set, he looked under his bed, he looked in his wardrobe drawers, but Zippel was nowhere. Paul went into the hallway, crept past the kitchen door and looked into the keyhole of the flat door. Nothing to be seen.

'Hey, are you in here?' he whispered, and pressed his ear to the door, but it was perfectly silent. In the end, he went to his parents' bedroom and glanced into all the drawers in their wardrobe. But Zippel remained missing.

'What are you doing in here?' His mother was standing in the bedroom doorway.

'Oh,' said Paul, 'nothing, I was just looking for my green jumper.'

'The green jumper you're wearing?' Mum crossed her arms.

Paul looked down at himself. Rats.

His mother frowned at him. 'Weren't you going to do your homework?'

'Oh, yes, bother, so I was,' said Paul as if he'd only forgotten for a moment, and he went back to his room and closed the door.

CHAPTER THIRTEEN

A little later, the doorbell rang. Paul ran straight to the hallway to open the door, but his mother beat him to it. Standing in the stairwell was Mr Nitzsche. There was a kind of bandage over his right eye, white and thick.

'Oh dear, how's your eye?' asked Paul's mum.

'Oh, that,' said Mr Nitzsche, carefully touching the bandage. 'Not so bad. One of the little veins burst. I have to wear this plaster for a couple of days, then it'll all be fine. But . . .' Mr Nitzsche stood there, looking properly confused.

'What's wrong?' asked Paul's mum.

'I don't know myself,' said Mr Nitzsche, scratching his head. 'Well . . . In my flat . . . '

Paul's mother frowned. 'What's the matter?'

'You'll have to see for yourself,' said Mr Nitzsche as he hurried down the stairs again.

'Can I come too?' asked Paul.

'Fine by me,' called Mr Nitzsche from the half-landing.

Mum picked up her door key and pulled the door shut behind her and they both followed Mr Nitzsche down the stairs, across the yard and up to the second floor again on the other side. Mr Nitzsche was muttering away to himself all the time as he climbed the stairs ahead of them. His door was open. He took a step back, stretched out his arm in welcome and said: 'Please, after you.'

Paul and his mum walked down the hall into the little living room. There was a large bookcase there.

'Oh,' said Mum, 'what a fun idea.' She pointed at the books, which were all sorted by colour. Right at the top were the ones with a white spine, then a few shelves of red ones, then green, a few blues, and so on.

'Do you think so?' said Mr Nitzsche, looking at the books. 'Well, maybe it is fun – but it wasn't my idea.'

'What do you mean?' asked Paul's mum.

'Before I went to the doctor's earlier, the books were all jumbled up. When I came back, they were sorted by colour.'

'Oh, really?' said Paul's mum. 'Does anyone else live here?'

'Not that I know of!' said Mr Nitzsche. 'And the bookcase is just the start.' He went into his bedroom and opened his wardrobe. In one pile were red jumpers, T-shirts and socks. In another pile were blue jeans and a few blue shirts and T-shirts.

Paul's mum couldn't help laughing quietly.

'You laugh,' said Mr Nitzsche, 'but coming home to your own flat and finding everything different is pretty creepy.'

'Everything?' asked Paul. 'Is *everything* sorted so weirdly?'

Mr Nitzsche nodded. 'The towels in the bathroom. My store cupboard . . . I like making jam, you know – everything's sorted strictly by colour. You've seen the wardrobe – now come and have a look in the kitchen.'

Paul ran to the kitchen. Everything looked pretty normal. Until Mr Nitzsche opened the crockery cupboard. There were the white plates and cups – and next to them was white yoghurt, a piece of white feta cheese, milk, hankies, white candles. The mug cupboard had a couple

of red cups beside the tomatoes, and there were two oranges and some orange napkins in an orange bowl.

'Someone wanted to tidy up for you,' said Paul's mum.

'Yes, but who?' asked Mr Nitzsche. 'I live alone here. And nobody but me has a key. I think I ought to call the police.'

'The police?!' cried Paul, immediately realising that he'd shouted far too loudly.

Mr Nitzsche looked at him. 'Well, yes, there's been a break-in here.'

Paul's mum nodded. 'True. But nothing's gone missing, has it? Couldn't it have been children, playing a trick on you?'

'Or . . . or wanting to say sorry for something?' said Paul.

'I tell you what,' said Paul's mum. 'How about I just help you put things straight again?'

'And I'll get back to my homework,' said Paul. 'Bye, Mr Nitzsche.'

He just heard Mr Nitzsche saying to Mum: 'When I change your lock on Monday, I'll change mine too.

This one's really old as well. And I'll look round the whole house to see who else has a lock like this that's easy to pick.'

Paul ran quickly back to the main house. He'd hardly got the flat door open before he called out: 'Zippel! Come out at once! Where are you?'

Zippel seemed to be waiting for him. He was floating above the carpet in the middle of the room, beaming. 'Well, was he pleased?'

'You must be kidding!' cried Paul.

Zippel paused for a moment, then he said: 'No, you're the kid around here, not me.'

'I mean: you're nuts!'

'No, I'm not,' said the ghost, still smiling. 'I share my lock, I mean your door, with a really teeny-weeny spider called Alan, but I definitely haven't got any nuts in there—'

'Hey,' Paul interrupted him. 'You went into Mr Nitzsche's flat.'

'Yes, zigackly, I did,' said Zippel proudly. 'And I tidied up sooooo neatly! Really truly.' Zippel flitted excitedly to

and fro, waggling his little arms in the air and singing:

When everything is in a mess,
Mr Nitzsche's in a stress.
When everything is in its place,
Mr Nitzsche's feeling ace.

'Oh no, he's not,' cried Paul. 'Mr Nitzsche almost called the police because of you. He thinks it was burglars. On Monday he'll definitely change your lock. And all the other old locks in the house along with it.'

Zippel sank down to the carpet. 'What? Why? Oh no. Oh nooooo. I didn't want that.'

He started to sob.

'Boohoohoohoo, I wanted to exscreeeeeews myself. For hurting his eye. And now . . . I get everything wrong.'

Paul sighed. His whole carpet was covered in cobwebs of dusty tears again. And he was almost in tears himself when he said: 'Guess what, tomorrow we're going to a proper castle.'

'What's a proper castle?' sniffed Zippel, wiping a few teary threads from his face.

'Um, one for kings and princesses.'

'Oh,' said Zippel. 'Aha. But . . . but you're going too?'

'Yes, of course,' said Paul, trying to smile. 'Don't worry. I'll take you there.'

'You'll take me there? What do you mean? Are you going away again?'

'We'll look at it. And if you like it, you can stay there.'

The ghost started to cry again. 'Boohoohoohoooo. You're leeeeeeeaving me! I'm a baaad ghost.'

When Paul saw him like that, he didn't know whether to laugh or to cry too. Dear, dear Zippel, he thought. He was so fond of him. He'd probably never liked anybody as much as this little white creature that was currently spreading cobweb tears around the whole room.

'Oh, Zippel,' he said, 'you're a super ghost. But you're a keyhole ghost. I think you'd be better off in an old castle lock. Not just the door to a little flat. A lock in a big, old castle with towers and spiral staircases and treasure chests and suits of armour. Where there are other ghosts haunting the corridors at night.'

'Hunting?' asked Zippel, wiping away more dusty tears from his face. 'What do they hunt? Doesn't it mess up the corridors?'

'Haunting,' said Paul. 'They float through the corridors at night, making spooky noises.'

'How do you know all that stuff?' asked Zippel.

'It's in all the ghost stories.' Paul went to his bookcase and pulled three books off the shelves. They all showed a small ghost hovering over a castle. 'Look,' said Paul. 'They all live in big, old-fashioned knightly castles.'

'Uh-huh,' said Zippel, not really convinced. 'And who wrote them?'

‘Um, lots of authors.’

‘What does that mean? Are they ghosts?’

‘No, authors are people. They’re grown-ups who write books.’

‘Grow-nups!’ yelled Zippel, outraged. ‘Grow-nups! What do grow-nups know about ghosts? They know nothing! Nothing! Grow-nups are all stupid and big and stick keys in my lock and take lovely old locks out of doors and put ugly new locks in and complain and make things silly and tidy with colours while other grow-nups make things tidy with no colours and they’re all cross all the time! Really truly!’

‘Yes, but do you know the good thing about a castle?’ said Paul. ‘A proper castle? There are no grown-ups in the evenings and at night.’

‘Oh,’ said Zippel. ‘Really? Not even one?’

‘Not one. At night you can be as noisy as you like. And there’s lots of dirt and dust and antique doors with even antiquer locks in them.’

‘Oh,’ said Zippel. ‘Where’s this castle with no grow-nups then?’

‘You’ll see. We’ll go tomorrow.’

'Mm. And these authors, what do they write about ghosts?'

'That they rattle their chains. And float down corridors going *wooo* and *boo!* and live in armour and spend the nights in treasure chests.'

'There, you see,' said Zippel. 'Your authors haven't a clue. I'm a real ghost. And the ones in your books are only drawings. But, fine, let's go and have a look. Really truly. Sometimes you're almost as strange as a grow-nup.'

CHAPTER FOURTEEN

When Paul and his parents left the house the next morning, they paused by the letter boxes. A large sheet of paper had been stuck up. In rather scribbly writing, it said:

Dear Mr Nitsha
Ime very sory, very, very.
Your the bestest bestest caretaker Ive ever met.
And I hope your eye gets better soon.
Ime very sory about that to. Reely truly.
I did it all rong.
But now Ime going away and it will all be good.
Hopefuly. An it wasnt Pauls fault. Promiss!
Yours sinceerly,
A stranger hoo you dont no

Paul's mum laughed. 'Someone seems to have a guilty conscience.'

'And very bad spelling,' said Paul's dad.

Paul said nothing.

Then they set off. Mum told them that she'd booked a tour online for ten o'clock, and how happy she was that they were all going out together, and how nervous she was about her opera performance. Dad hardly said a word, again.

Paul was very quiet too. He'd brought his little rucksack, which he held tightly with both hands, keeping it in his lap all the way. He spent most of the time looking out of the window, and swallowing down the sadness that rose up inside him whenever he thought about what would happen with Zippel and the castle.

They arrived at the castle just before ten. When Mum saw that Paul was bringing his rucksack, she said: 'You can leave that in the car if you like.'

'No,' said Paul, 'I'm bringing it with me.'

'But why?'

'Because,' said Paul, hugging the rucksack tight. There

would normally have been a long discussion, but Mum was determined not to miss the tour. So she shrugged and said: 'Fine, bring it then.'

When they got to the entrance, Paul had quite a shock: there was a security guard in a grey uniform, checking all the bags.

The man gave Paul a fierce look and said: 'Open that up!'

'The rucksack?' asked Paul.

'Yes, obviously the rucksack, what else?'

'It's only got a snack in it,' said Paul.

'Doesn't matter. The mayor's visiting today so we have to check every bag and every visitor,' said the guard.

He took the rucksack from Paul, took out the flask without a word, and shook it. Then he held it to his ear and shook it more violently.

'Not so hard!' cried Paul.

'There's no tea in it,' said the guard.

'I drank it on the way because it was such a long journey,' mumbled Paul.

'Hmm,' said the guard, tipping it from side to side again.

Then he said: 'OK.'

Paul shoved the flask back into the bag and ran after his parents.

A big man in a black suit was standing on the wide castle staircase. A group of people were waiting around him. That must be the tour.

'I need to go to the loo,' cried Paul, heading for the gents. 'You go on, I'll find you.'

As soon as he reached the toilets, he opened the rucksack, took out the flask and unscrewed the lid.

'Phew,' he said, 'that was close.'

'Pheeew,' groaned Zippel, deep inside the flask. 'That wasn't close. That was an earthquake. Or the cola-roaster at the Novemberfest.'

'Roller-coaster,' said Paul. 'Oktoberfest. Come on, quickly, we're here.'

Zippel floated out, but he swayed to and fro, to and fro, over the flask, like steam snaking up from a cup of hot tea. 'I'm still all wibble-wobble-wibbly dizzy,' he groaned.

'I'm sorry,' said Paul. 'But I've got to go on this tour. Are you coming? You'll be able to see the castle then.'

'Fine by me,' said Zippel.

'Just make sure nobody sees you,' Paul called as he ran off. But Zippel had long since floated up to the ceiling and, very handily, he was exactly the same shade of white as most of the walls, so he was pretty much invisible floating along up there.

When Paul got back to the entrance hall, the group was still standing on the stairs. The man in the black suit had a name badge on his jacket. It said: Dr Schlomm. He had a very loud voice and an even louder laugh, and he kept glancing over to a woman in a green skirt. Paul asked his mother what was going on.

'Oh,' sighed Mum, 'the woman over there, the one in the green skirt, is the mayor of Grafenburg. She is going to join the tour. And the castle manager keeps on telling her how efficient and brilliant he is.'

At that moment, Dr Schlomm clapped his big hands and said: 'Okaaay. Wonderful, all good, let's get going then.'

He took the group down a long corridor, staying by the mayor's side all the time, and explained that the whole castle used to look dreadful. 'When I started as manager here, it was practically derelict,' he said, 'but I've had every room renovated over the past five years. And now – it's wonderful, all improved. You won't find a single speck of dust or rust anywhere in the castle any more. All spotless.'

Dr. Schlomm.

He was just saying that the building works had cost six million euros when a little girl with red plaits and black glasses interrupted: 'Are there any ghosts here in the castle?'

Dr Schlomm was apparently not used to being interrupted. He stood there for a moment, staring at the girl open-mouthed. Then he said: 'Of course not. There are no such things as ghosts. Not here and not anywhere else.'

He shook his head in annoyance. Then he walked on, telling the mayor that he'd had all the old doors and locks changed for ultra-modern fire doors and that that had also been very expensive. 'But now – security locks everywhere, wonderful, all good.'

Paul groaned quietly when he heard that about the security locks.

The girl with the red plaits interrupted again. 'Excuse me, Dr Schlomm, but how do you know there's no such thing as ghosts?'

The manager stopped in the middle of the corridor, as if frozen to the spot. Then he said, rather loudly: 'Let's keep things nice and polite, shall we? If you children have

any questions, kindly put up your hands.'

Bang. At the same moment, a suit of armour fell over at the end of the corridor; the helmet rolled slowly across the wooden floor. It looked as though someone had chopped the armour's head off.

Dr Schlomm ran off anxiously down the corridor. 'Oh, my goodness. That's from the fourteenth century. A particularly valuable piece from our collection. Could someone help me, please?'

The mayor kneeled down, she and Dr Schlomm grabbed the suit of armour and put it back upright again. Paul, who had run over with them, was about to pick up the helmet when the manager bent down beside him and hissed: 'Hands off. I'll do that myself.'

As Dr Schlomm picked up the helmet with both hands and straightened up with it, his own voice spoke quietly from the helmet: 'Let's keep things nice and polite, shall we?'

Dr Schlomm was so startled that he accidentally stood on the mayor's foot.

'Oh, excuse me,' he said, 'I'm terribly sorry.'

'Oh, exscrews me,' whispered the helmet, 'me too, most

tebberly sorry,' but nobody heard it except Dr Schlomm, and Paul, who was standing beside him.

Paul had to laugh. Dr Schlomm looked in confusion from the helmet to Paul and back again. Paul could tell that Dr Schlomm would have dearly loved to yell at him, but for one thing, Paul hadn't done anything and, for another, the whole group had gathered around him and the armour again.

So Dr Schlomm set the helmet cautiously onto the suit of armour, smoothed his tie and said: 'Well, that went well. Wonderful, all good. So, let's go to the ceremonial hall. Mrs Mayor, if you'd kindly follow me.'

The mayor rolled her eyes slightly as the manager fluttered so anxiously around her again.

Paul's mum, who was standing right next to her, whispered to the mayor: 'It seems to me that the manager's doing the whole tour just for you.'

The mayor whispered back: 'I get that impression too. It's terribly embarrassing. It must be because he wants more money for building work. He's always writing me letters about how he needs more and more.'

Dr Schlomm hurried along at the head of the group.

Paul was now walking beside the red-haired girl who had asked about ghosts. They smiled at each other.

'This Schlomm has no idea,' the girl said quietly.

Dr Schlomm was just stopping in a smaller room with all kinds of golden plates, from large serving platters to small saucers, on the walls. He rubbed his hands enthusiastically: 'So, ladies and gentlemen, Mrs Mayor, this is the royal dining room. I have had our extraordinarily valuable collection of plates displayed here.'

The girl put up her hand. Dr Schlomm pretended at first that he hadn't seen her, and he just kept talking until the mayor said: 'I think this young lady has a question.'

Dr Schlomm put on a wry smile and said: 'Weeell, my dear, what would you like to know?'

'I wanted to ask again about the gho—'

'Little girl!' Dr Schlomm interrupted her, 'there are no flying saucers, no unicorns and there are certainly no gho—'

He was obviously about to say 'ghosts', but at that very moment he saw, behind the group of visitors, one of the golden saucers detach itself very gently from the wall and float slowly across the room towards the door.

Paul, his parents, the mayor and all the other visitors had their backs to the plates. They just saw Dr Schlomm turn as white as chalk. His mouth opened and closed in slow motion. And then he stammered: 'A flying . . . a flying . . . the saucer, um, it really is highly, highly valuable.'

By the time the group turned round, the small golden plate had already floated out of the room into the hallway and there was nothing to be seen but a wall of large and small plates.

'What do you mean?' asked the mayor. 'What's the matter with you?'

Dr Schlomm sank down onto a golden throne, staring silently into space. The visitors looked at him in concern. But Paul and the girl ran out of the room into the corridor. The only thing there was a table. On it stood a single plate. Paul spotted Zippel flitting round the corner at the far end of the hallway as the girl asked him: 'Do you believe in ghosts too?'

Paul said: 'Hm, well, maybe, but I can't imagine any ghosts living in a castle like this one.'

CHAPTER FIFTEEN

When Paul and the girl returned to the hall, Dr Schlomm was standing in the middle of the group once more, saying: 'Wonderful, all good. I just needed to catch my breath for a moment. Now I'd like to show you, Mrs Mayor, the three most beautiful rooms in the castle.'

So he walked through the halls, telling them how great they were now and how dreadfully expensive the repairs had been, by which time, some of the adults were shaking their heads at his stupid tour.

Meanwhile, Zippel had discovered something much, much more exciting. After hiding behind the plate and floating out of the dining hall with it, he had flown all alone down the long corridor and disappeared round the nearest corner into a little side passage. There, he stopped for a moment in mid-air, whispering: 'Oooooohh . . .'

Until then, Zippel had found everything in the castle so ugly – no rust, no dust, no oil, and all the locks were brand-new and tiny. But this passage, now, this was something else! There was the bright-red barrier tape for a start. That looked really interesting. The tape had big shouty warning letters on it. To Zippel, that looked even more interesting.

He hovered cautiously in the semi-darkness. Cobwebs everywhere. And dust. Lots of dust. On the floor. On the walls. On the ceiling. There were a few planks lying around, tools, spades and bricks, all higgledy-piggledy. But best of all, Zippel thought, it was lovely and dark. The old window shutters were almost completely closed so only a few milky-white strips of light could find their way in. After a few metres, there was another corner. Round it stood a wonky throne with its left armrest missing. A little further on, there were picture frames on the wall. Zippel floated deeper into the darkness, past a rusty suit of armour and a few lances and swords.

And then he saw the clock. An old, heavy grandfather clock with a long, chunky pendulum chain. Zippel immediately started to swing the chain to and fro. Unfortunately, it was so rusty it snapped in the middle. By now, Zippel was really excited. It looked just like the chains that Paul had told him about, the ones in his castle-ghost-books. The chains that the ghosts rattled when they haunted corridors. He picked up the chain, wrapped it around himself once, twice, like a scarf, and flew down the dark corridor with it.

'Hoo-boo, boo-hoo!' he cried. Then he swung the chain with both hands, shouting in a deep voice: 'Rattle, rattle, rattle.' He chased little clouds of dust to his left and to his right, crying: 'I'm a hunting ghost!', and hunted, rattled and woohoo-booed his way down the passage. He was having such a good time that he made up a little hunting and haunting song:

Rattle, rattle, boo-di-hoo.
I'm so scary, shoo-bi-doo.
Boo-di-hoo and rattle-run,
Hunting is enormous fun!

CHAPTER SIXTEEN

There was something that Zippel couldn't know, however: the dark passageway he was enjoying so much led directly to the coronation hall. The very same coronation hall where Dr Schlomm, the mayor and the group of visitors had just arrived. Dr Schlomm was in the middle of telling them that all the lamps had been replaced the month before, and how exceptionally expensive that had been, when a sudden series of very strange noises could be heard in one corner of the hall.

Paul noticed a door marked: 'Strictly no entry! Building site!' The noise seemed to be coming from behind that door. It sounded as though someone was bashing on the strings of a guitar with a hammer, as an accompaniment to a very peculiar song. Or was that just the wind, howling in through a gutter?

Dr Schlomm froze. 'Please wait for me here, I'd better take a look.' He opened the door and vanished behind it.

Before he could close it again, however, Paul slipped through with him. Dr Schlomm was about to tell him off, but his mouth just hung open. Floating right in front of him was a ghost. As clear as day. A glowing, white ghost with a rattling chain, rocking to and fro in the middle of the room, tossing its head furiously and, even worse, singing hideously off-key.

In the meantime, you see, Zippel had found an old and very out-of-tune harp, standing between a couple of tables.

He was clattering up and down the strings with his rattly chain, running it back and forth, forth and back, *ker-plong-plonk-plonk*, *ker-pling-ling-ling*, and it all sounded seriously skewed and distorted, even without his little song, which he was still singing. It had been adapted from a haunting and hunting song into a haunting and taunting song, though, and it went like this:

Rattle-rittle-ruttle-rastle,
Someone's spoilt this lovely castle.
Boo-di-hoo and hoo-di-bom,
You're the fool, old Dr Schlomm.

'WHAT A CHEEK!' a voice suddenly screamed from behind Zippel. The ghost jumped so violently that he dropped the chain right onto the harp strings, and the noise was awful. But even worse, there was an enormous grow-nup standing there: the horrible Dr Schlomm.

Dr Schlomm's face was red with rage and he began roaring: 'Security! Cleaners! Police! All hands on deck! What a messss!!'

Zippel was panicking and looking around the corridor for somewhere to hide when he spotted Paul behind

Dr Schlomm's back. Paul whipped his flask out of his rucksack, unscrewed the lid, and waved it invitingly.

Dr Schlomm had his eyes shut as he screamed: 'Clean this up at once! Everything out! Get rid of the dust and dirt! I want every last scrap gone by tomorrow morning.'

Dr Schlomm was roaring so blindly he didn't even see Zippel whoosh past him and vanish into Paul's flask.

By this time, the tour party had opened the door from the hall. For a while, they all looked on in amazement as Dr Schlomm stood in the cluttered passageway, yelling at chairs and tables.

Eventually, the mayor said: 'Excuse me, Dr Schlomm, but all these people have made rather long journeys to come on your tour. Would you kindly now tell us something interesting about this castle for a change, instead of either showing off or having tantrums?'

'No,' said Dr Schlomm, still bright red in the face. 'This tour is over. Goodbye.' And with that, he vanished down the dark hallway towards his office.

The group stood flabbergasted around the door, watching him go.

Only Paul heard the red-haired girl whisper: 'They so do exist.'

The first visitors were about to head out of the coronation hall towards the exit when somebody suddenly spoke: 'Uh, if you like . . . '

Paul turned towards the voice. It was his dad. He was standing in the middle of the group and saying: 'I know quite a lot about history, and I could give you a bit of a tour – it would be a shame if you all just had to go home now.'

The others looked at each other in amazement. A few hesitated for a moment, but Paul's dad rubbed his hands, coughed twice and began: 'OK, so. It was like this: King Kunibert the Proud died here, in this hall where we're standing, after the Battle of Waldofing. He died of a terrible sword injury that he'd suffered while fighting Bertram the Most Abominable . . . '

And Dad told stories: about Kunibert and his golden sword. About the terrible Battle of Waldofing. And about Kunibert's great golden treasure that is said to lie hidden somewhere beneath the castle to this day. Now things were properly interesting, and people listened in fascination.

Paul was amazed at how much his dad knew, and by the time they reached the entrance again, an hour had passed and everyone was clapping.

Once the applause had died down, the mayor stepped out of the tour party and said: 'Thank you very much – you saved the day for us all. As mayor, I'm in overall charge of everyone who works here at the castle. I'm sure you have enough to do with your work and your family, but if you ever wanted to lead tours here again, I'd be very pleased to welcome you.'

'Really?!' cried Dad, grabbing the mayor's hand. 'When can I start?'

Mum looked at him in surprise. The mayor looked at him in surprise, and Paul looked at him in surprise.

'Uh, well, tomorrow, if you like,' said the mayor.

'Done,' said Dad, shaking the mayor's hand so vigorously that the sleeves of her blouse fluttered madly.

'But . . .' said Mum.

'I'll be here at ten o'clock tomorrow,' cried Dad.

'But . . .' said Paul.

Dad looked at him and Mum and said: 'The three of

us should head to the café; there's something I should have told you a long time ago.'

And so, five minutes later, they were sitting on the terrace outside the museum café. At first, Dad stared at the car park because he didn't know where to start. And actually the car park was really very interesting, just then. Dr Schlomm was standing there, still bright red in the face, ordering the two police officers who'd answered his call to kindly get on with arresting the ghost in his castle. The two police officers looked at each other, and then enquired politely if Dr Schlomm might not be feeling a little feverish.

And just as Paul's dad was finally about to say something, an ambulance drove up. A doctor got out and talked soothingly to Dr Schlomm.

Eventually, Paul's mum said: 'Come on, spit it out – what's bothering you?'

So Paul's dad looked at them both, gulped twice and said: 'I lost my job a few days ago.'

Paul's mum lowered her cake fork and stopped chewing so that you could see the crumbs of chocolate cake in her mouth.

Dad told them that since the beginning of the week, a computer had been doing his job, so that he wasn't needed any more, and that he'd only be paid for another month.

'But you're a teacher,' said Paul.

'Well,' said Paul's dad. 'I'm a bit like a teacher. I teach new recruits in our company how to write computer programs, but they're all meant to teach themselves now.'

'But why didn't you say anything?' asked Paul's mum.

'I wanted to, all the time,' said Paul's dad. 'But I didn't know how. And you've got your performance next week so I didn't want to add to your worries.'

'And you've spent a lot of time sitting around at home, haven't you?' asked Paul.

'How do you know that?' asked Paul's dad.

'Oh, just because,' said Paul mysteriously.

'Yes . . . every day,' Dad went on. 'I've been searching for new jobs on the internet.' Then he smiled and said: 'And instead, I've found one here, by chance. A little one, at any rate. For the time being. And history, knights, the

Middle Ages, castles – all that stuff was always far more interesting than stupid computers.' Only dad used a ruder word than 'stupid'.

'Language!' said Paul and his mum at the same time, and laughed.

CHAPTER SEVENTEEN

When they got home two hours later, Paul went straight to his room. He'd barely opened the flask when Zippel came shooting out like a ping-pong ball.

He shook himself out in the air to his proper size and immediately starting complaining: 'Awful. Aaaaaawful!'

'What is?' asked Paul.

'Everything!' shouted Zippel, so loudly that Paul hissed at him to talk more quietly.

'Everything,' repeated Zippel in a whisper. 'That pitch-black flask. Driving around in that pitch-black flask. Sitting around for ever in the café in that pitch-black flask.'

'Sorry,' said Paul, 'but I had to get you to the castle and back somehow, didn't I?'

'Zigackly!' shouted Zippel furiously. 'The castle.

That was the awfulest thing of all. What grow-nup had the idea that ghosts could live in stone boxes like that? Total nonsense. Keyhole ghosts need a cosy little lock, not a massive, clean and tidy box. Dr Screamy-Schlomm. Bah! I'm never going there again. Never! Do you hear me?'

'Yes,' said Paul quietly. 'I'm not deaf. It was probably a stupid idea of mine. But now I really don't know what we're going to do.'

Paul looked very sad, sitting there hunched and puzzled on his bed.

Zippel immediately floated over and patted his knee.

'Oh, it'll work out,' he said. 'Don't worry. Really truly.'

'Yeah?' asked Paul.

'Course,' said Zippel. 'If you don't know what to do, a friendly ghost will help you too. Old ghostly saying, just invented by Zippel the Very First.'

At that moment, there was a knock on Paul's door. Zippel whizzed up to the ceiling. Paul's mum opened the door. She was holding the phone and looking rather confused. 'Mrs Wilhelm would like to speak to you.'

Paul gulped. Mrs Wilhelm. Why could she be phoning? Had she just told his parents that he'd broken into her flat? Paul took the telephone and said quietly: 'Hello?'

'Is that Paul?' asked Mrs Wilhelm.

'Yes,' said Paul.

'Hello, Paul, this is Mrs Wilhelm speaking. Would you pop up and see me, please?'

'Uh, now?' asked Paul.

'Yes, if you have time.'

Paul tried to answer as calmly as possible. 'That's fine,' he said, hanging up.

'What does Mrs Wilhelm want?' asked Mum.

'No idea,' said Paul, putting on his shoes. He was trembling so much, he could hardly tie the laces. Without looking round, he called, 'Back in a bit,' and went out. Boy, oh boy. What on earth did she want? But it was still better for her to scold him than to come down and tell his parents. He walked slowly up the stairs. They creaked with every step. Three floors is quite a lot of steps when you're afraid of what's waiting for you up above. He'd got to the top and was about to ring the bell when he saw that Mrs Wilhelm's door was open a crack.

'Come in,' she called from inside when he knocked cautiously.

Paul pushed open the creaky door. The hall was empty. There was a light on, down in the sitting room. Everywhere else was dark. Hesitantly, he walked down the narrow passage. In the dark, the empty picture frames looked even creepier than they did in the daytime.

'Hellooo?' he enquired in the darkness.

'I'm in the sitting room,' called Mrs Wilhelm's croaky voice.

Paul gulped. The old wooden floorboards creaked. In the kitchen, the tap was dripping, drop, drop, drop. Three more steps, and he was standing at the sitting room door. Mrs Wilhelm was sitting in the armchair where he'd sat last time. She was looking at the shelves with all the locks, although Paul couldn't see if she was really looking at the bookcase. From the side like this, he could only see her strangely-squinting left eye, which seemed even more wrinkled than normal.

'Come in,' she said, pointing at the second chair, 'and sit here with me.'

Paul walked round Mrs Wilhelm and sat in the old

armchair. Now she turned her head slowly towards him, stared at him with her one large eye and asked: 'Well? Did you come alone?'

'Er, yes,' said Paul with a gulp. 'Why? Should I have brought my parents?'

Suddenly the idea of his parents being here seemed very attractive. 'Shall I run and fetch them?' he asked, on the point of jumping up.

Mrs Wilhelm laughed quietly. 'Certainly not! Stay where you are.' She reached out her bony hand to stop him standing up. 'The two of us need to talk alone.'

Paul sat stiff as a board. Mrs Wilhelm pointed to the little table between the two chairs. There was a small bowl filled with black balls. 'Would you like one?' she asked.

'No, thank you,' said Paul. Was she trying to poison him? Mrs Wilhelm took one of the balls herself and bit it in half. 'I always used to eat these chocolates with my husband,' she said.

'Thanks,' said Paul, 'but we'll be having dinner soon.'

Mrs Wilhelm looked at him again. Perhaps her eye only looked so big because the other one was always squinting. She fixed her healthy blue eye on him, said nothing at all for what must have been ten seconds, and then asked: 'What's its name, then?'

'What?' asked Paul. 'Who?'

'Come on,' said Mrs Wilhelm, 'I may be *really* old, but I'm not *really* stupid.'

Paul gulped. He felt trapped. To win a bit of time, he asked: 'What actually happened to your eye?'

'Well,' Mrs Wilhelm asked in return, 'what happened to Mr Nitzsche's eye?'

'Oh, that,' said Paul, 'that's different. He hurt it when he was looking into our lock yesterday.'

'Yes, exactly,' said Mrs Wilhelm, 'that's what he told me. And whether you believe it or not, something very similar happened to me. Except that it was seventy-five years ago. On the 10th of August. I'll never forget that because it was the worst day of my life. And the best.'

'Why?' asked Paul. 'What happened?'

'I was about your age,' said Mrs Wilhelm. 'Eight years old. And I lived with my parents in the ground-floor flat.'

'Really?' said Paul, who didn't know himself which he found more surprising: that Mrs Wilhelm had once been as young as he was, or that she'd lived in this building since she was a child.

As if she'd heard his thoughts, Mrs Wilhelm said: 'I was even born here. But that's another story. At any rate, I had my own door key. Just like you. My parents had a little shop. We sold buttons and braces, sewing things and fabric. My parents worked all day, but we still had hardly any money. Sometimes there was only milk for supper, and nothing to eat. But that's another story too.'

She popped the second half of the chocolate into her mouth, closed her good eye and chewed it slowly and lingeringly, without saying a word. She seemed to be really savouring it. Then she rubbed her hands together and said: 'Anyway, I came home from school one afternoon and heard a funny noise as I was about to unlock the door. It sounded as though someone was talking inside the door. When I looked into the keyhole, there was a sudden cloud of dust and rust. And there must have been a little piece of metal in there too. I didn't pull my head away quickly enough. There weren't such good doctors in those days as there are now and so I lost my left eye. But I gained a friend in return. Maybe the best friend I ever had.'

She looked at Paul with her blue eye and said quietly, as if she were telling him a secret: 'His name was Quockle.'

'Quockle?' asked Paul. 'Quockle? What kind of a name is that?'

'Well, when he was rattling around in the lock, rabbiting on to himself, it sounded like "quockle-quackle-quockle-quackle".' She laughed quietly as she imitated the ghost's chatter. Then she said: 'He lived with me for almost a year. It was so much fun with him. So lovely. My Quockle really loved singing. And he was always getting

up to mischief. Once, we were in the attic, right above my flat here. There's that little window with the bars on that reaches down to the floor, do you know the one? We sat high above the town and threw porridge oats down on everyone who walked past. It was the middle of summer, I was barefoot, and every time Quockle let the oats trickle down, he cried out: "It's snowing! It's snowing!"' Mrs Wilhelm's shoulders shook as she laughed soundlessly.

Paul looked at the frail old Mrs Wilhelm who had apparently once sat barefoot up in the attic, dangling her little legs in the air and laughing as she threw porridge oats down into the street.

'And Quockle loved coal,' said Mrs Wilhelm.

'Coal?' asked Paul.

'There was no central heating then,' explained Mrs Wilhelm. 'We had a stove in the kitchen and a fireplace in the sitting room. They were both heated with coal briquettes, sort of black lumps of coal. Quockle used to rub himself on them until he was all covered in coal dust, and he loved it because he thought it made him look scarier.'

'And how did you lose Quockle?' asked Paul.

'He was discovered one day. By a neighbour. While I was at school. It was probably his singing that gave him away. At any rate, a neighbour heard a voice in our flat and called the police because he thought it was burglars. The police broke down our door and took Quockle away. When I came home, the flat was wrecked. It must have been a pretty long chase. There were black marks on the walls; I think he must have just rubbed himself with coal dust and that was why he couldn't hide on the ceiling. The police took him to a top secret research institute and I never saw him again.' Mrs Wilhelm shook her head sadly.

'But . . .' said Paul. 'If it was such a top secret institute, how do you know about it?'

'I went to the police the next day and asked about Quockle. Two of the police officers just looked sternly at me and said there were no such things as ghosts and I should go home and never talk such rubbish again. But the third one was nice. He ran after me as I left in tears and told me about the institute. I even tried to break in to the place, but of course a security guard caught me and took me home. After that, I always hoped that Quockle would come back. Or another of his kind.'

Mrs Wilhelm fell silent and stared at her collection of locks for a long time. In the kitchen, you could hear the tap dripping to itself, but otherwise there wasn't a sound.

'Zippel,' said Paul.

'Sorry?' said Mrs Wilhelm.

'Mine's called Zippel.'

Mrs Wilhelm clapped her hands and threw back her head: 'Ziiippel!' she cried in delight. 'Wonderful! Tell me, does he say "Zippeldesticks" whenever he's annoyed?'

'Yes,' said Paul.

'Zippeldesticks,' repeated Mrs Wilhelm. 'Just like Quockle used to say.'

'Really?' mused Paul. 'Are they related?'

'I don't know,' said Mrs Wilhelm. 'But I do know one thing: they're quite right to be afraid of grown-ups.'

'Grow-nups,' said Paul, just the way Zippel always said it.

Mrs Wilhelm chuckled: 'Grow-nups, exactly.' Then she grew serious again: 'My parents glued up all the locks after that. They were very shocked that I had had a secret friend living with us for a year. And they were determined to stop any more keyhole ghosts joining us. I tried to explain to them that Quockle was my best friend. They just nodded and said yes-yes, and then they still glued up all the locks.'

'So is it really true that keyhole ghosts always live in front doors?'

'Of course it's true.'

'Is that why you collect locks?'

'Yes. All my life, I hoped that another keyhole ghost would make his home with me. But instead one came to you. It's better that way. Your Zippel would just be bored with an old biddy like me. That's why . . .' She leaned on the arm of her chair, stood up slowly and walked over to the bookcase. 'That's why I'm giving you one of my locks. If I've understood correctly, your Zippel is in urgent need of a new home.' She looked at her collection. Then she pointed to an ornate, rectangular metal lock and said: 'He seems to have particularly liked this one. He must have been doing loop-the-loops in there, given how much dust whirled out of it.'

Paul saw that there was a little heap of rust and dust in front of the lock.

'Oh,' he said. 'Is that how you guessed that I've got a ghost too?'

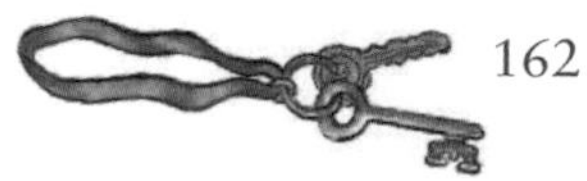

‘Well, it really wasn’t very hard,’ said Mrs Wilhelm, carefully lifting the large, angular lock down from the shelf. ‘First, you were sitting here, staring at my bookcase. After you left, there were little piles of dust by all the locks. Then Mr Nitzsche hurt his eye. And shortly after that, there was that letter to Mr Nitzsche downstairs. When I asked Mr Nitzsche about it, he told me the strange thing that had happened to his flat. All in all, I didn’t exactly need to be a great detective.’

She looked at Paul and said: ‘I’m a hundred per cent on your side. But be more careful in future, do you hear? Both of you. I want Zippel to stay with you for ever.’

Paul nodded.

Mrs Wilhelm held the lock in both hands and passed it to Paul.

‘Oh,’ said Paul. ‘It’s pretty heavy.’

‘Yes,’ said Mrs Wilhelm. ‘But very homelike, I think.’

‘Thanks a lot,’ said Paul. ‘Really truly.’

‘Please,’ said Mrs Wilhelm, ‘say hello to Zippel for me. You two can come up here any time.’ She pointed to her lock collection. ‘I’d be really very pleased if he used my playground now and again. And I’d like to tell him about

Quockle. It would be good for him to know that there are a few of his kind. But you should probably go now, or your parents will be wondering what's going on. Besides, I'm tired. But would you like to come back tomorrow?'

'Yes, please,' said Paul. 'Bye, Mrs Wilhelm.'

'Bye, Paul.'

Now, when she smiled at him, Paul found her face beautiful. All the lines around her damaged left eye looked like the wrinkles on a round, shrunken apple.

CHAPTER EIGHTEEN

That's almost the whole story. When Paul got back to his flat, there was a note on the kitchen table:

Dear Paul,
We've gone to the café for an ice cream to celebrate Dad's new job.
Come and join us if you like.
Love,
Mum and Dad

But Paul wanted to celebrate something else entirely. He called out to Zippel, who had been hiding in his bedroom and now came floating out into the hall. When he saw the lock, he did such wild loop-the-loops down the whole

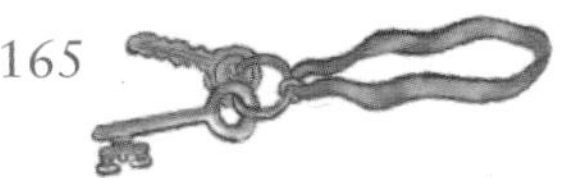

corridor that Paul was afraid he'd crash into a wall.

Then, together, they placed the lock in Paul's bookcase.

Zippel has slept there ever since. Every morning he says that he's never slept so well in all his life as in Mrs Wilhelm's lock, really truly. And that Mrs Wilhelm is the nicest grow-nup there is in the whole wide world.

When Mr Nitzsche came on Monday to change the lock, Paul even helped him, and not a single tool fell down the stairs, and no dust clouds came out of the lock either. But afterwards, all the tools in his toolbox were sorted by colour, and Zippel said that Mr Nitzsche is actually quite nice for a grow-nup too. And on Tuesday, Paul's mum had her opera performance, and she sang really beautifully. And Dad did more of the cooking after that, so there was less burnt pasta.

But on the evening that Paul's parents went out for ice cream, Zippel had to start settling in to his new home, and dust and rust flew all over the place while he sang a little keyhole-ghost-moving-in song. Once he had finally finished, Paul said that he wanted to try something out. And Zippel said that trying things out was always very good and what were they going to try out, then?

'Come on,' said Paul. And they went out onto the stairs, and right up to the sixth floor. And Zippel thought that they were visiting Mrs Wilhelm because he now liked her even better than he'd done before – *that Mrs Wilhelm, wow, super-duper, really truly.* But instead Paul climbed the narrow stairs up to the attic, where he'd never dared go alone before because it was all dark and empty and dusty up there. But with Zippel alongside him he didn't mind, and Zippel felt right at home in the dark and dust anyway. Paul saw that Mrs Wilhelm had been right – at the end of the attic there really was an ancient, barred window that reached down to the floor. When Paul opened the window, it creaked so horribly that Zippel said, 'Wow, that's a really good window.' Outside, the golden September sun was gilding all the rooftops and you could see the whole town, and Paul sat on the floor and dangled his legs through the iron bars, and Zippel sat very smartly beside him. He looked cautiously down the seven floors and said: 'Hoo-oo-oo, even for me that's very high.'

Paul pulled a bag that he'd brought from the kitchen out of his pocket, flung a pinch of flour into the air and said to Zippel: 'Look, snow in summer.'

Of course, Zippel loved it. Paul held the open bag out to him, Zippel dived into it, head first, flailed around wildly with his arms and cried: 'Warning, snowstorm! Warning, snowstorm!'

And so first there was a very quiet shower of flour-snow, and then a brief Zippelish flourstorm. Paul held onto the bag that was raising dust like a volcano, and looked out over the golden rooftops and he knew, he knew for absolute certain, that life with Zippel was going to be exciting and bold and beautiful. And in the distance, he could see the first cranes, which were already setting up the ghost train for Oktoberfest.

The Economic Analysis of Accounting Profitability

The Economic Analysis of Accounting Profitability

Jeremy Edwards
John Kay
Colin Mayer

CLARENDON PRESS · OXFORD
1987

Oxford University Press, Walton Street, Oxford OX2 6DP
Oxford New York Toronto
Delhi Bombay Calcutta Madras Karachi
Petaling Jaya Singapore Hong Kong Tokyo
Nairobi Dar es Salaam Cape Town
Melbourne Auckland
and associated companies in
Beirut Berlin Ibadan Nicosia

Oxford is a trade mark of Oxford University Press

Published in the United States
by Oxford University Press, New York

British Library Cataloguing in Publication Data
Edwards, Jeremy
The economic analysis of accounting profitability.
1. Accounting
I. Title II. Kay, J. A. III. Mayer, Colin
657'.48 HF5635
ISBN 0-19-877241-6
ISBN 0-19-877240-8 Pbk

Library of Congress Cataloging in Publication Data
Edwards, J. S. S. (Jeremy S. S.)
The economic analysis of accounting profitability.
Bibliography: p.
Includes index.
1. Corporations—Accounting. 2. Accounting—Effect of inflation on. 3. Deferred tax. I. Kay, J. A. (John Anderson) II. Mayer, C. P. (Colin P.) III. Title.
HF5686.C7E34 1987 657'.95 87-5575
ISBN 0-19-877241-6
ISBN 0-19-877240-8 (pbk.)

Typeset by Cotswold Typesetting Ltd, Gloucester
Printed and bound in Great Britain by
Biddles Ltd, Guildford and King's Lynn

Preface

THIS book has its origins in the Institute for Fiscal Studies (IFS) project on Fiscal Policy in the Corporate Sector. This project made considerable use of company accounting data in analysing the effects of corporate taxation on firm behaviour. In the course of the project careful attention was given to the question of how company accounts could be best applied to economic analyses. This book is the outcome of that assessment.

We have incurred a number of debts to both individuals and organizations while carrying out the work for this book. The Economic and Social Research Council and the Esmee Fairbairn Charitable Trust provided financial support for the IFS project. The Association of Certified Accountants also supported the work reported in Chapter 6 of the book. We are very grateful to these organizations for their help, as we are to Dr Geoffrey Meeks of the Department of Applied Economics of the University of Cambridge, and to Datastream Limited, for providing us with the data on which some of the analysis in the book is based.

Shirley Meadowcroft is owed a particular debt for patiently and efficiently carrying out a great deal of computational work to produce the empirical estimates in Chapters 6 and 7. We have also received a lot of help from a number of other members of the IFS staff for which we are most grateful. An early draft of the entire manuscript was read through and commented upon by Dr Geoffrey Harcourt of the University of Cambridge and Professor Geoffrey Whittington of the University of Bristol, and their suggestions have materially improved the book. We are extremely grateful to these two individuals for their assistance. We must also acknowledge the help that Geoff Whittington's two books on inflation accounting (one written jointly with David Tweedie) gave us in understanding the history and development of the debate on inflation accounting. Needless to say none of the above can be held responsible for any errors in this book.

Finally we would like to thank Indira Dholakia, Christine Molton, Judith Parry, and Nguyet Thu Luu for typing a never-ending series of drafts of the manuscript. Their patience is much appreciated. We are also grateful to Judith Payne for proof-reading the entire manuscript.

Contents

I
Introduction

ACCOUNTING can be defined in general terms as the provision of information relating to economic transactions. Financial accounts are probably the best-known form of accounting: these are the financial statements which are drawn up periodically, primarily for the benefit of the providers of finance for the firm (the shareholders and creditors), reflecting the traditional stewardship role of financial accounting. But the range of users of financial accounts extends well beyond the suppliers of finance to the company, and includes financial analysts, governments, and economists. Examples of the decisions for which the information contained in financial accounts is potentially relevant are the decision by an investor to buy or sell shares in a company; the decision by a company's directors about appropriate dividend distributions; the decision by a creditor to lend to a firm; the decision by regulators as to whether a firm is making excessive profits; and the decision as to whether a particular activity yields a sufficient return to justify its undertaking.

The traditional financial accounts of a company comprise a balance sheet and a profit and loss account. The system of double entry book-keeping is such as to ensure that, in the absence of capital injections or withdrawals by the proprietors, the change in the book value of capital employed is exactly equal to the profit or loss for a period.

It is conventional for accounts to be constructed in historic cost terms. Historic cost accounts value the resources used in the production process at the cost at which they were originally purchased. Likewise the amount that has to be set aside to maintain physical capital intact is calculated in relation to the original purchase cost of the physical assets. Profit is then measured as the surplus accruing during a period over the historic cost of resources employed. The use of historic cost accounts is justified on the grounds of their objectivity (historic costs can be readily ascertained and verified) and the fact that they naturally arise out of the physical transactions of the company. They are frequently described as performing a stewardship role by providing a check on the application of the capital raised by a firm.

This stewardship role is, however, a very limited one, merely recording how funds currently or previously employed are yielding returns. Historic cost accounts provide no indication of the efficiency with which a firm is undertaking its activities since they give no guidance as to the current value of the resources that the firm is employing. Thus a profit in historic cost terms may be the outcome of a change in the value of resources that are being employed in the production process since the date at which they were acquired. Alternatively the firm may indeed be earning a profit on and above the amount that could be raised from employing the assets in their next best alternative. Historic cost accounts are not able to distinguish between these two possible explanations. For this purpose the current value of the company's assets is required.

There are three current valuation bases for assets which represent the value of currently available opportunities: replacement cost, net realizable value, and present discounted value of future net cash flows. All three have their supporters (see Whittington (1983) ch. 5). Following Hicks' classic analysis of income concepts (Hicks (1946)) there is now virtually universal acceptance in the academic literature of the view that income measures should be based on the present value of the earning power of an individual or a firm. Hicks defined income as 'the maximum value which [a man] can consume during a week, and still expect to be as well off at the end of the week as he was at the beginning' (Hicks (1946)). The analogous definition of a company's profit is the maximum value which a company can distribute during a period, and still expect to be as well off at the end of the period as it was at the beginning. If 'as well off' in the above definition is interpreted to mean owning assets with the same present value, then the profit figure which results from accounts using present value as the valuation base corresponds to Hicksian income for the company (assuming that expectations were fully realized during the period in question). Hicksian or economic profit for a period under this approach is given by the present value of future net cash flows at the end of the period less the present value of future net cash flows at the beginning of the period plus the net cash flow arising within the period after adjusting for the introduction of new capital during the period.

There are two major problems that are encountered in trying to apply the Hicksian definition of profit to an accounting concept. First, the accountant is being asked to provide an estimate of the present value of future cash flows. This prediction is clearly going to be highly subjective and open to contentious disagreement. It certainly does not enjoy the advantage possessed by historic cost accounts of being readily verifiable. Furthermore it could be argued that accountants' estimates of present value are likely to be inferior to those generated on the stock market. According to one body of theory, the stock market impounds most, if not all, relevant information about the firm's future prospects (see Fama (1970), Grossman and Stiglitz (1980)).

Secondly the profit concept described above as the difference between opening and closing present values plus net cash flows during the intervening period is an *ex post* one. It only provides a guide to the profit distribution of a firm if it is expected that this profit will be maintained in the future. In other words what happened *ex post* may be affected by unanticipated events, luck or misfortune, which will not be indicative of likely future performance. If expectations were not fulfilled during the period then it would be inappropriate to base distribution decisions (in the case of a firm) or consumption decisions (in the case of an individual) on actual out-turns. Instead, unanticipated components will have to be excluded from the backward-looking income and profit measures if they are to be relevant indicators of sustainable earnings.

The measurement of Hicksian or economic profit of a company thus presents severe practical difficulties for accountants. So much so that some have argued that accountants should not try to calculate economic profit (Treynor (1972)) and that accountants should not try to estimate present value but should concentrate on supplying relevant information to users of accounts who will form their own estimates of present value (Bromwich (1977), Peasnell (1977)). Indeed it is clear that it is this latter role of accounting information which is its major one: in general investors, regulators, economists, and other users of financial accounts are attempting to assess the performance of firms, either prospectively or retrospectively, rather than looking to the accounts for an estimate of the maximum sustainable distribution that the company can make. This information is then impounded in the company's stock market value, and if the firm's stock market value is taken as the best available estimate of its present value, then economic profit for a period can be straightforwardly estimated as present value at the beginning of the period multiplied by the real discount rate.[1]

Thus the Hicksian definition of profit can be directly ascertained from market valuations and the real discount rate. Accounts would appear to serve no independent function except in so far as they contributed to the determination of appropriate stock market valuations.

Against this background, it is perhaps curious to note that there is a substantial economics literature that has used the profit estimate from company accounts directly. Many examples of the use of accounting information can be given. Rates of profit have been calculated at an aggregate level, either for manufacturing industry as a whole or for particular industrial sectors, using national accounts data for individual countries. Underlying such calculations is the view that changes in these aggregate accounting rates of profit are indicative of changes in the incentive to invest in particular economies. Studies of this type include the regular estimates of company profitability in the UK produced by the Bank of England (in the June issue of the Bank of England Quarterly Bulletin) following the original work by Flemming *et al.* (1976) (see also Williams (1981)); those by Feldstein and Summers (1977) and Holland and Myers (1979) in the USA, and the comparative study of profitability in seven countries by Hill (1979).

Accounting rates of profit are also widely used in industrial economics. There are a number of well-known hypotheses concerning the relationship of the profits earned by a firm or in an industry as a whole to the number and size of firms in an industry (the concentration of the industry) and the degree of potential competition from firms outside the industry, which in turn is affected by the presence of economies of scale, sunk costs, product differentiation, brand loyalty, and so on (i.e. barriers to entry). These hypotheses have been subjected to extensive empirical testing, and in many of the empirical studies rates of profit obtained from company accounts have been used to measure firm or industry profitability (see Hay and Morris (1979) chapter 7 for a review of the relevant empirical work).

A related area in which accounting rates of profit are used is in competition policy. In the UK, investigations into the competitive structure of an industry are undertaken by the Monopolies and Mergers Commission. According to Fairburn (1985), the typical use of profitability figures by the Commission comes at the stage after the market power of the firm under investigation has already been established to some degree by other forms of analysis (and indeed further analysis may follow, to check that high profits are the result of the company's market position). The accounting rates of profit are not used to assess the degree of market power but rather to derive conclusions as to whether a situation is against the public interest. Generally this is done by comparing the company's accounting rate of profit with the average accounting profitability of manufacturing industry as a whole, or perhaps the average for the particular industry in which the company operates. The Commission tends to make an adverse finding only if the company's accounting rate of profit greatly exceeds the average—i.e. is three or four times as high, or more. It is clear therefore that accounting rates of profit play a significant role in UK competition policy. Accounting rates of profit are also important in anti-trust policy in the USA,[2] where they are used as a means of regulating potentially monopolistic utilities in the private sector: a minimum rate of profit on capital is specified for the utility.

Accounting rates of profit are thus widely used, by economists and others, to assess the performance of activities such as firms, industries and entire sectors. The theoretical basis for this use of accounting rates of profit is, however, far from clear. The activities whose performance is being assessed all have the general characteristics of investments, in that they involve forgoing potential consumption in the prospect of generating future returns. Therefore the natural way in which to attempt to give a firm grounding to the use of accounting rates of profit in the assessment of the performance of these activities is in terms of the theory of optimal investment decisions. But this theory suggests that in general the way to appraise investments is by discounting the net cash flows generated by an investment using as discount rate a measure of the opportunity cost of the funds tied up in the project, and comparing the resulting figure with the initial cost of the investment—the net present value approach. In some cases it is possible to make optimal investment decisions by calculating the discount rate at which an investment has a zero net present value—which is known as the internal rate of return—and comparing it with a measure of the opportunity cost of funds. If the accounting rate of profit of an activity corresponded to its internal rate of return, then the use of accounting rates of profit as summary indicators of performance, to be compared with the opportunity cost of capital, could be justified.[3] But unfortunately matters are not that simple.

First, investment appraisal using the internal rate of return will not always yield correct results, so that this method of assessing investments is inferior to the net present value one. In particular, as we discuss in Chapter 2, the internal rate of return method may not yield a single solution, and interpretation of multiple solutions is difficult. Second, even putting aside the drawbacks of the internal rate of return as a method of investment appraisal, the accounting rate of profit, which is measured at a point of time as the ratio of accounting profit to book value of capital employed, is a different concept from the internal rate of return, which is the discount rate that makes the present value of the flow of receipts and expenditures attributable to an investment over its lifetime zero. There have been a number of analyses of the relationship between these two concepts, the conclusions of which make depressing reading: accounting rates of profit do not in general coincide, even on average, with the corresponding internal rates of return. The following quotation from Turvey (1971) is probably representative of currently prevailing opinion: 'the accounting rate of return on total assets . . . means little. In particular it does not approximate the average of the d.c.f. [i.e. internal] rates of return on past investments and so does not indicate whether these past investments were, on average, reasonably successful'.

These deficiencies of accounting rates of profit as summary indicators of the performance of investments are quite widely appreciated, at least among economists. Thus both Feldstein and Summers, and Hill in the studies mentioned above state that their measures of profit rates are exact measures of the internal rates of return on investments only under particular assumptions about depreciation and in general can only be taken as approximations to internal rates of return. In the industrial economics literature, however, other measures of profitability have been used in order to avoid the problems with accounting rates of profit—examples are the ratio of profits to sales revenue, which under constant returns to scale is equivalent to Lerner's index of monopoly power (price minus marginal cost divided by price), and Tobin's *q* (the ratio of the firm's market value to its replacement cost), as recently used by Lindenberg and Ross (1981), Salinger (1984), and Smirlock *et al.* (1984).

Nevertheless, accounting rates of profit continue to be widely used to assess performance, both by economists and others. This can in large part be explained by the ready availability of accounting profitability data, and the fact that a rate of profit or rate of return concept has considerable intuitive appeal as a potential method of assessing the performance of investment activities.

Our objective in this book is to try and justify the use of accounting rates of profit in the assessment of the performance of activities, developing arguments put forward in Kay (1976) and Kay and Mayer (1986). We contend that the

Hicksian definition of income is not in fact the one that is most relevant to establishing the profit of a firm or industry. Income and profits are different concepts, and while that distribution which leaves future earning power unchanged is of some interest, it is not the one that is most relevant to answering the questions in which investors, financial analysts, regulators, and economists are most interested. Instead what is required is a measure that tells us the benefits from undertaking one activity rather than another. What is the gain to be derived from additional investments in an activity as against investments elsewhere? To what extent has a firm operating in a particular industry derived benefits from that industry as against another?

In this book we argue that the internal rate of return is the correct approach to answering these types of questions only under certain circumstances. In particular, for a project whose net earning stream over its entire life is known, the internal rate of return should be compared with the cost of capital along the lines mentioned above. Furthermore, as demonstrated in Chapter 2, the internal rate of return of such a complete set of cash flows can be derived precisely from any accounting rate of profit concept. Thus accounting numbers are relevant in this case, but only to the extent that they can be used to replicate cash flows and thereby generate internal rates of return.

While of some value, this result is not of very profound interest. More pertinent is the question of what is the appropriate measure of profit for any activity whose performance can only be monitored over a limited segment of its life. It is the central purpose of the book to demonstrate that there is a set of accounting rules which are appropriate for answering questions about investment or disinvestment, or entry into or exit from an industry over a finite segment of a firm or industry's life. Furthermore this set of accounting rules has received a wide measure of support from the accounting profession. Many of the conventions that are currently employed approximate these rules and what this book does, in particular in Chapter 4, is to provide a strong theoretical justification for a set of rules that many regard as intuitively appealing.

The reason why the conclusions of this book are so very much more positive about the role of accounting information in economic analysis than previous studies is that, in our view, previous studies have been applying the wrong standards against which to judge accounts. The appropriate criterion is *not* whether accounting rates of profit equal internal rates of return—nor is it whether accounting profit equals Hicksian profit. The latter is relevant to establishing the level of distribution that can be maintained i.e. permanent income streams. It is not relevant to answering questions about expansion or contraction of a firm or industry or about the relationship between returns being earned in different sectors. That is what will concern us in this book and it is our view that it is this set of issues that has been at the heart of many previous economic studies which have used accounting profitability data. The internal rate of return concept is designed to address these questions but it has little to say about how evaluation over a finite segment of a firm's life should be made.

Our concern then in this book is to establish the set of accounting rules under which the answers to economically interesting questions can be derived. As we demonstrate in Chapter 4, these rules are really most straightforward and could in practice be implemented without undue measurement difficulties being encountered. If these rules were implemented then this book suggests that accounts would be of real practical value to a wide body of individuals: investors, regulators, managers, and economists. Furthermore, once these rules are appreciated, then the resolution of some major controversies that have bedevilled the accounting profession for so long would be immediately apparent. Neither inflation nor deferred taxation present particular difficulties for implementing the set of rules that we and many others have advocated. Inflation corrections are readily and conveniently computed and the extent to which provision for deferred taxation should be made follows immediately.

The plan of the book is as follows: in Chapter 2 we set out the essentials of the standard theory of optimal investment decisions, comparing the net present value and internal rate of return approaches, and then discuss the relationship between the accounting rate of profit and the internal rate of return in some detail. The various analyses of this relationship which have led to the view represented by the above quotation from Turvey are surveyed briefly. However, it is then shown that a number of general results relating the accounting rate of profit to the internal rate of return are available if the accounting profitability data cover the entire lifetime of the investment: in particular in this case it is always possible to deduce the internal rate of return from accounting profitability data so long as the accounts are fully articulated.

In Chapter 3 however, we consider the point that in many, perhaps most, cases the available accounting data will cover only a segment of the lifetime of an investment, and when this segment is short relative to the complete life of the investment, accounting data provide little useful information about the investment's internal rate of return. But in such cases it is not clear that calculation of an investment's internal rate of return is the appropriate way to assess its performance over a segment of its lifetime, because the internal rate of return is defined as a single figure irrespective of the duration of the investment. In Chapter 3 we define an alternative rate of return concept for summarizing the performance of an activity over a finite segment of its life—the accounting rate of return. As its name suggests this is based on accounting data, and the basis on which book value of capital employed is determined becomes crucial for giving any economic interpretation to this rate of return concept. We argue in Chapter 3 that assets should be valued on the basis of the value-to-the-owner rules, and we consider some of the practical problems involved in implementing these valuation rules.

In Chapter 4 we show that the accounting rate of return computed over a segment of an activity's lifetime, using value-to-the-owner rules for book value of capital employed, can provide economically relevant information, in the sense that it can be compared meaningfully with a measure of the opportunity cost of capital over the segment. Thus investors, financial analysts, regulators, and economists can, in certain circumstances, use accounting profitability data in order to give relevant answers to a range of different questions.

Chapter 5 considers the implications of the analysis in Chapters 3 and 4 for the debate on inflation accounting. On the basis of that analysis we argue in favour of the approach to inflation accounting known as Real Terms accounting, in which a current valuation base for capital employed (the value-to-the-owner rule) is combined with a general index adjustment for the effects of inflation. We argue that this form of inflation accounting, which has a distinguished intellectual history, is superior to the two better-known methods of inflation accounting, Constant Purchasing Power and Current Cost accounting.

In Chapter 6 we illustrate the quantitative significance of the differences between Real Terms, Constant Purchasing Power, Current Cost accounting, and Historic Cost accounting profitability measures. We do this in two ways: first by examining the profitability figures that the different approaches produce under various hypothetical situations and second by estimating profitability figures on the different bases for a sample of British companies over the period 1966–81.

Chapter 7 considers the implications of the analysis in Chapters 3 and 4 for the issues involved in accounting for deferred taxation. The various ways in which deferred tax has been accounted for are described, and it is shown that, in the case where accounting data over the complete lifetime of an investment are available, any method of accounting for deferred taxation which is fully articulated and takes deferred tax balances from an initial value of zero to a corresponding final value of zero will permit the post-tax internal rate of return to be calculated from post-tax accounting profitability data. This result is of limited value however: interest is more likely to be focused on performance over a segment of an activity's lifetime. We show that the analysis of Chapter 4 can be straightforwardly adapted to cover the case where companies are subject to taxation. If the accounting rate of return over a segment of an activity's life calculated from post-tax accounting profitability data and initial and final valuations of capital employed is to be relevant for economic analysis then the deferred tax balance in any period must be such as to translate the book value of capital employed from value to the owner before tax to value to the owner after tax, and all changes in the deferred tax balance from period to period must flow through the profit and loss account via the transfer to or from the deferred tax account. We then illustrate how these principles for deferred tax accounting can be applied by calculating a post-tax accounting profitability measure for a sample of UK companies.

Finally, Chapter 8 draws together the main themes of the book.

There are some general features of the argument in the book which it is useful to set out at the start. Our aim is to argue that a rate of return which is relevant for economic analysis can be defined over a segment of an activity's lifetime and, under certain conditions, this rate of return can be measured using accounting profitability information. The justification for the claim that this rate of return is relevant for economic analysis comes from the fact that a comparison of this rate of return with a measure of the opportunity cost of capital allows relationships between the present value, replacement cost, and net realizable value of the activity at the start of the segment to be inferred. Thus the aim of this part of our argument is to give the intuitively appealing use of a rate of return measure to assess the performance of an activity (by comparing it with the opportunity cost of capital) a solid grounding in terms of the net present value method of investment appraisal—the method supported by the theory of optimal investment decisions. A critical assumption in deriving the net present value rule for investment appraisal is that capital markets should be perfect and complete: without this assumption it is very difficult to have any general theory of optimal investment decisions. The extent to which this assumption is not satisfied in practice is difficult to judge: our analysis, which argues for particular measures of accounting profit and book value of capital to be adopted so that the resulting accounting rate of profit can be justified as a summary performance indicator in terms of the theory of optimal investment decisions, rests on the view that departures from the ideal of complete and perfect capital markets in reality are not that significant. Such an assumption is, however, implicit in most other uses of accounting data.

Our analysis, arguing as it does for a particular way of measuring accounting profit and book value of capital, may seem to be in conflict with a view that has developed in the academic accounting literature according to which emphasis on a single profit measure, or a single summary measure of economic performance, is misplaced. This approach argues that in a world of uncertainty, with imperfect and incomplete markets, it is not possible to define a single unambiguous measure of the 'true' value of the firm's assets or its 'true' profit for the period, and hence accounts should report a variety of measures of these concepts, which can be used by different users for different purposes, and are all potentially useful sources of information for the estimation of the firm's future uncertain cash flows. This view (an example of which is Beaver (1981)) is largely concerned to argue against accounts trying to report a single measure of economic profit, because it regards the purpose of accounts to be the provision of information which is useful for the estimation of economic profit. It will be clear from the earlier discussion that there is in fact no conflict between this approach and our argument: we do not regard the reporting of economic profit to be a suitable function of accounts, and agree that accounts should rather provide information which will be useful for estimates of economic profit and present value. But, as we have argued, accounting information is widely used to assess performance, and this is commonly done by means of the accounting rate of profit. It must be recognized that this function of accounts is distinct from that of general provision of information relevant to the assessment of future net cash flows, and our purpose is to argue that there is a correct way to measure accounting profit and book value of capital if the objective is to calculate an accounting rate of profit which will be compared with the opportunity cost of capital in order to assess performance. Our concentration on the single correct way of measuring profit and capital for this purpose does not mean that we exclude other measures of profit and capital for other purposes. We are broadly sympathetic to the view that accounts should report a wide range of potentially relevant information.

One other general point which should be made at the outset is that accounting profitability data can, by their very nature, only provide information about the *financial* rather than *social* appraisal of investments. The latter differs from the former, of course, by taking account of certain social costs or benefits which do not appear as private costs or benefits in the financial accounts. It is well known that the private profitability of an action is not always the same as its social desirability, and this should be borne in mind in what follows. Statements of the form that an accounting rate of return less than the cost of capital indicates that exit from an industry is appropriate are to be interpreted as referring to the appraisal of this action on a financial rather than a social basis.

Notes

1. This can be seen as follows. Let D_t^e denote the distribution in period t expected at the start of period 1, ρ the one-period discount rate (assumed constant), PV_0 the present value at the beginning of period 1 (end of period 0) and PV_1^e the present value at the end of period 1 (beginning of period 2) which is expected at the start of period 1. By definition

$$\mathrm{PV}_0 = \sum_{t=1}^{\infty} \frac{D_t^e}{(1+\rho)^t} = \frac{D_1^e}{1+\rho} + \frac{\mathrm{PV}_1^e}{1+\rho}. \tag{1}$$

The company's Hicksian or economic profit in period 1 is the maximum distribution it can make during period 1 and still expect to have the same present value at the end of the period as it does at the beginning. Using equation (1) we find that

$$\mathrm{PV}_1^e - \mathrm{PV}_0 = \rho \mathrm{PV}_0 - D_1^e$$

so that the maximum distribution it can plan to make in period 1 while expecting to have an unchanged present value at the end of the period is $\rho \mathrm{PV}_0$.

Note that, in order to take account of Scott's point that changes in value due to expected changes in (one-period) discount rates must be excluded in order to estimate the maximum sustainable distribution in this way (Scott (1976)), the discount rate which should be used in practice to estimate economic profit from stock market values should be based on long-term real interest rates.

2. It was the recent US versus IBM anti-trust case which inspired the particularly virulent denunciation of the relevance of accounting profitability measures as indicators of the economic rate of return by Fisher and McGowan (1983) which is discussed in Chapter 2.
3. In terms of the notation in note 1, this can be seen as follows. If accounting profit in period 1 equals economic profit it is ρPV_0 and if book value of capital at the start of the period is PV_0, the accounting rate of profit in period 1, defined as accounting profit divided by book value of capital employed at the start of the period, is ρ.

2

The Assessment of Complete Activities using Accounting Profitability Data

THE purpose of calculating a rate of profit on capital is usually to assess the performance of the investment involved in using a sum of capital in a particular way. The assessment may be *ex ante*, in which case its purpose is to decide whether a particular investment project should be undertaken, or *ex post*, in which case the object is to determine how well an investment which has already been made has performed. The investment in question may be a single project, such as the building of a new factory or the purchase of a new lorry, or it may be the operation of an entire firm or industry. Both single projects and the operation of an entire firm or industry have the characteristics of investment in that they involve a sacrifice in one period and gains (which may turn out to be negative) in subsequent periods. The initial sacrifice in the case of a single project is obvious: in the case of an existing firm the sacrifice is the value (appropriately defined) of the firm's assets at the start of the interval over which its performance is assessed. We shall use the term 'activity' throughout the book to refer both to single projects and to the operation of firms or industries. The assessment of the activity may be from the point of view of an individual firm or it may be from the point of view of the efficient use of an economy's overall resources. In all these cases the aim of calculating the rate of profit on capital employed is to compare it with a measure of the opportunity cost of the capital employed and, on the basis of this comparison, assess the desirability of the activity. Thus one would like to be able to say that if the expected rate of profit on a new factory exceeded the opportunity cost of capital then the factory should be built, or that if the rate of profit earned in a particular industry exceeded the opportunity cost of capital then that industry should expand.

The extensive literature on the theory of optimal investment decisions[1] has, however, shown that great care must be exercised in assessing investments by comparing their rates of profit with a measure of the opportunity cost of capital. Indeed it is now generally accepted that if capital markets are perfect, a firm acting in its shareholders' interests should assess investments on the basis of their net present value rather than by any rate of profit measure. Section 2.1 of this chapter illustrates the use of net present value and discusses the difficulties involved in appraising investments on the basis of the alternative internal rate of return approach.

The conceptual problems encountered in Section 2.1 arise even before any questions of measurement are addressed. A widely used source of information on performance is that available from company accounts. In particular statements about company profits would appear to provide data relevant to investment analysis. But, as Section 2.2 describes, the purposes for which accounts are constructed are by no means restricted to investment analysis and the conventions that are followed in devising accounts are not, as a consequence, the ones that are most suitable for investment appraisal. Indeed it has been suggested by several authors that accounting statements of rates of profit provide no guidance whatsoever regarding the underlying economic performance. These criticisms of accounts have received widespread attention, and Section 2.3 thus devotes some time to a careful presentation of these arguments.

There is one set of circumstances in which the criticisms of Section 2.3 are unduly pessimistic. Where complete data over the entire lifetime of a project are available, then precisely relevant economic information can be obtained from accounting profitability figures. Indeed there are a number of important results that can be derived for self-contained data on an activity, and Section 2.4 is devoted to a description of these results. Section 2.5 thus concludes by noting that although caution is needed in the use of accounting profitability data, it is not the case that accounting information can be rejected out of hand as irrelevant.

2.1 Investment appraisal

The present value of an investment is given by discounting all the net cash flows it generates over its life at a rate given by the appropriate opportunity cost of capital. The opportunity cost of capital should reflect both the time value of money and the risk involved in the investment. Subtracting the initial cost of the investment from its present value gives net present value. If capital markets are perfect then firms acting in their shareholders' interests should undertake investments with net present values greater than zero, and should reject investment projects with net present values less than zero.

The discount rate used in the net present value calculation represents the opportunity cost of investing in the activity rather than on the capital market. The opportunity cost of capital is the highest return that shareholders could have earned elsewhere on the equity capital that is invested in the firm. Although the basic idea of the opportunity cost of capital is straightforward, measuring it in practice is less clear-cut, as it is necessary to allow for risk (so that the assets which shareholders could invest in directly must be ones with risks equivalent to the activity under consideration) as well as the influence of taxes and the fact that investment funds come from several different sources. There is an extensive literature on the measurement of the cost of capital to a firm which we shall simply note: Brealey and Myers (1981, chs. 16–19) provide an excellent introduction to the issues involved. We shall simply assume that the appropriate cost of capital is known.[2]

It is useful to consider a simple example of the net present value of an investment project. Consider an investment project involving the purchase of an asset for £100 at the end of period 0 which generates positive cash flows at the end of each of the next four periods. It is assumed that there is perfect certainty, so that no distinction need be made between the *ex ante* and *ex post* assessment of a project. The net cash flows associated with the project are shown in Table 2.1, together with its net present value for various different discount rates. The general expression for net present value can be written as

$$\mathrm{NPV} = \sum_{i=1}^{n} \frac{C_i}{\prod_{s=1}^{i} (1+\rho_s)} + C_0 \tag{2.1}$$

where C_i denotes net cash flow in period i, ρ_s denotes the one-period discount rate (or cost of capital) between periods $(s-1)$ and s, and the project lasts from period 0 to period n. In the case where these one-period discount rates are all constant over the life of the investment, equation 2.1 simplifies to

$$\mathrm{NPV} = \sum_{i=1}^{n} \frac{C_i}{(1+\rho)^i} + C_0 \tag{2.2}$$

where the time-period subscript on ρ has been dropped as it is now constant. If the one-period discount rate (or cost of capital) is constant at 10 per cent, the net present value of the investment shown in Table 2.1 is 26.87, so that it should be undertaken. If the one-period discount rate is constant at 20 per cent, the project has a zero net present value, and so is just acceptable, while if

Table 2.1. Net cash flows and net present value (NPV) of a project

	Period				
	0	1	2	3	4
Net cash flow	−100	12	43.2	69.12	41.47
NPV (constant 10 per cent discount rate)			26.87		
NPV (constant 20 per cent discount rate)			0.00		
NPV (constant 30 per cent discount rate)			−19.23		
NPV (varying discount rate)[a]			11.07		

[a] See text for details.

the one-period discount rate is constant at 30 per cent, the project's net present value is −19.23 and so it should not be undertaken. The case of a constant one-period discount rate is special, and in general the one-period discount rate is likely to vary over time. There is no difficulty in using the net present value rule in such circumstances: if the one-period discount rate was 10 per cent between periods 0 and 1, 20 per cent between periods 1 and 2 and periods 2 and 3, and 10 per cent between periods 3 and 4, the net present value of the project shown in Table 2.1 would be 11.07, so that it should be undertaken.

If the consensus of the theoretical literature on optimal investment decisions is that the net present value rule is the appropriate one to use for investment appraisal in most cases,[3] does this mean that investments cannot be assessed by comparing their rate of profit with the cost of capital? The answer is no: in certain circumstances optimal investment decisions can also be made by accepting activities whose rate of profit exceeds the cost of capital. It is, however, necessary to define the rate of profit carefully if optimal investment decisions are to be made in this way, and to emphasize this point the correctly defined rate of profit is usually referred to as the internal rate of return of the activity.

The internal rate of return (henceforth IRR) is that constant one-period discount rate which makes the net present value of an investment zero. Formally the IRR is defined as r such that

$$\sum_{i=1}^{n} \frac{C_i}{(1+r)^i} + C_0 = 0. \tag{2.3}$$

In the example of Table 2.1 above, the IRR of the project is 20 per cent. So, in that example, optimal investment decisions could be made by comparing the project's IRR with the cost of capital in the case where the one-period cost of capital was constant over the life of the project: so long as the cost of capital was less than 20 per cent, the project should have been accepted. Matters are a little more complicated when the one-period cost of capital is not constant: in such circumstances the IRR must be compared with a constant cost of capital obtained either from a comparable financial asset which pays a fixed return over the same period of time as the lifetime of the project or from an appropriately weighted average of the one-period costs of capital.

Decisions simply to accept or reject an investment which are based on a comparison of the IRR with the cost of capital will be exactly equivalent to those based on the net present value rule whenever the net present value of an activity is a steadily declining function of the discount rate as in Fig. 2.1. In that diagram the net present value of the activity is zero at a discount rate r, which is therefore the activity's IRR. It is clear that, given the smooth decline of the activity's net present value as a function of the constant discount rate, the net present value of the activity is positive whenever the IRR exceeds the cost of capital, and negative when the IRR is less than the cost of capital.

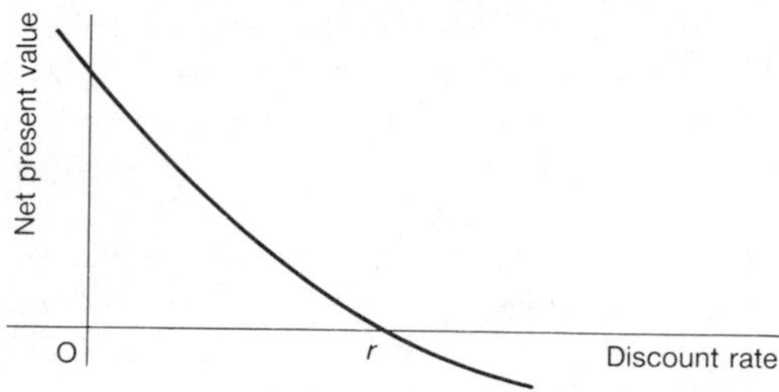

Fig. 2.1. The net present value of an activity as a function of the constant discount rate, with a unique internal rate of return

However, net present value cannot be guaranteed to be a steadily declining function of the discount rate. It is quite possible for the relationship to take the form shown in Fig. 2.2. Now there are two IRRs, r_1 and r_2. Net present value is positive at discount rates between r_1 and r_2, but negative otherwise. Hence if the cost of capital is less than r_1, the activity should not be undertaken, and thus investment decisions cannot be made simply by comparing the IRR and the cost of capital in this case. A situation like that depicted in Fig. 2.2 can arise when there is more than one change in the sign of the stream of net cash flows associated with an activity, as for example is the case whenever there are costs involved in shutting down a project so that both the initial net cash flow (the original cost of the investment) and the final one (the shut-down costs) are negative. If there is only one change of sign in the stream of net cash flows, with all negative ones preceding all positive ones, then the activity's net present value will be a steadily declining function of the constant discount rate and its IRR is guaranteed to be unique, so that investment decisions can be made using either the IRR or the net present value rule. We will assume henceforth that a unique IRR exists, although, for individual projects at least, this is rather restrictive.[4] As we shall see it is not a particularly restrictive assumption when applied to an evaluation of the performance of a firm or industry over a relatively short period.

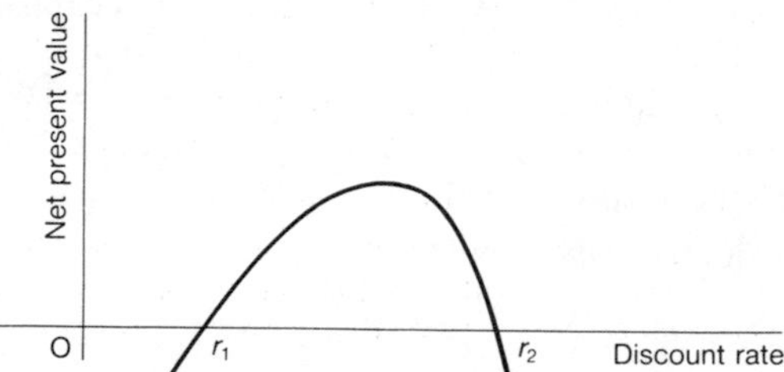

Fig. 2.2. The net present value of an activity as a function of the constant discount rate, with two internal rates of return

Even when the IRR is unique there is another complication which must be considered, and this is that the ranking of activities by IRR may differ from that given by net present value. Consider the example shown in Table 2.2. There are two activities, both of which require an initial investment of 100 at the end of period 0 and then generate positive net cash flows at the end of each of the next three periods. Activity 1 has the higher IRR, because it generates a large amount of cash at the end of period 1. But if the constant discount rate is 10 per cent then activity 2 has the higher net present value. If the interest in assessing activities is simply whether or not they should be undertaken then this problem does not matter: activities should be accepted if they have a positive net present value or, equivalently, if their IRR exceeds the cost of capital, and the ranking of activities which are going to be undertaken anyway is not relevant. But if activities are being assessed in order to see which is the most profitable (as is often the case in the comparison of firms or industries) then this problem does matter. If the activities are being assessed from an investor's point of view when credit is rationed and only a portion of desired investment can be undertaken, so that the issue is whether one project or firm yields higher returns than another, then the correct ranking is in terms of net present values (an activity with a higher net present value implies a larger increase in shareholder wealth), or, if the activities have different initial costs, in terms of net present value per unit of initial capital cost. If the activities are being assessed from a regulator's point of view then it is not clear what the correct ranking is; the regulator may be more concerned with the absolute size of the net present value generated by the activity than with net present value as a proportion of capital cost. Hence our discussion here is confined to the case where activities are assessed from an investor's viewpoint. So long as the returns to an investment accrue over several time periods, then the ranking by IRR can differ from the correct one. It is only if there is a single pay-off that the ranking by IRR will correspond with that by net present value, as can easily be checked from the definitions of net present value and IRR in equations 2.1 and 2.3. But physical investments which yield a single pay-off would appear to be rather rare, which implies that, in general, the IRR can be used only to indicate whether or not an activity should be undertaken (in conjunction with the cost

Table 2.2. Net cash flows, net present values (NPV), and internal rates of return (IRR) of two activities

	Net cash flow by period					
	0	1	2	3	IRR (%)	NPV at 10%
Activity 1	−100	102	14.4	8.64	20	11.12
Activity 2	−100	5.75	13.225	129.27	15	13.28

of capital) and not to indicate the relative profitability of different activities. We will return to this difficulty with the IRR in Chapter 3. It reflects the general problems of using the IRR to make correct investment decisions when the choices involve mutually exclusive activities.

Thus, if the stream of net cash flows associated with an investment changes sign only once, the decision as to whether or not an investment is (or was) justifiable can be made by comparing its IRR with the cost of capital. But unless the investment lasts for only one period, generating a single pay-off after the initial investment, the IRR cannot be used to compare the profitability of investment, as there is no guarantee that the ranking of investments which generate cash flows over several periods by IRR will correspond to that by net present value, which is the correct ranking. In general therefore the IRR of an investment, even when unique, can only be used to assess whether or not the investment should be (or should have been) undertaken.

2.2 Accounting profit rates

In many cases the data which are available for assessment of the performance of activities are accounting data which have been produced for rather different purposes. The traditional function of financial accounts is that of stewardship, and this role of accounts means that accounting data are primarily concerned with providing an objective picture of the way in which a firm has been run, for the benefit of the shareholders. The traditional accountant's view is that profitability is concerned with the assessment of the surplus of revenue over costs over some past period, usually the accounting year. Although accounting profits are primarily a historical statement of a company's record, the conventions which have developed in measuring accounting profits also affect forward-looking decisions: the decision as to whether or not to undertake an investment project is sometimes based on forecast accounting data.

The basic inputs into the computation of accounting profits are the net cash flows which, as we have seen, form the basis of optimal investment decisions. But a number of adjustments are made to these net cash flows to arrive at accounting profits, and these raise serious questions about the usefulness of such accounting data for assessing the performance of activities. One adjustment results from the accountant's desire to show profit as it is earned rather than when net cash flows are actually generated, so that the timing of actual net cash flows may differ from that of accounting profit figures. Secondly, an adjustment has to be made for costs that may not be directly associated with an individual project. Most obviously overhead costs may be allocated on an approximate pro rata basis across projects. However, the incremental overhead charge associated with a particular project may be very different from this allocation. The difference is that between marginal and average costs. In the case where the overhead is a fixed cost which a particular project does not augment, then no overhead should be attributed to the project in evaluating its incremental contribution to company performance. The most significant adjustment made by accountants to the net cash flow figures is that of depreciation charges. Accounts distinguish two sorts of cash outflows: current expenses and capital expenses. The former are deducted from cash inflows when accounting profits are computed but the latter are not. Instead, capital expenses are depreciated according to some more or less arbitrary rule[5] over a number of years, and the resulting annual depreciation charge is deducted from subsequent cash inflows in computing subsequent accounting profits. These depreciation decisions do not, of course, have any effect on cash flows,[6] and as a result accounting profit figures exclude some cash inflows.

The performance of an activity is often assessed on the basis of accounting data by means of the accounting rate of profit (ARP henceforth). This is defined as the ratio of the accounting profits earned in a particular period to the book value of the capital employed in the period. The book value of capital employed by an activity in a particular period is calculated by cumulating all the capital expenditures associated with the activity up to that period and subtracting all the depreciation charges up to that period from them. The ARP of an activity is thus computed on a very different basis from the IRR, not least in that it is calculated at a point in time rather than over the lifetime of the activity. The question naturally arises of what is the relationship between assessments of activities based on the comparison of the ARP with the cost of capital with those based on the comparison of the IRR with the cost of capital. An extensive literature has developed on the relationship between the ARP and the IRR, the conclusions of which are largely pessimistic and hence imply that the assessment of activities using the ARP may be highly misleading. Before considering this literature it will be useful to assess the investment project whose net cash flows were shown in Table 2.1 above on the basis of the ARP in order to illustrate the problems involved.

Table 2.3 shows the net cash flows of the project together with various

Table 2.3. Net cash flows and accounting profitability measures of a project

	Period				
	0	1	2	3	4
Net cash flow	−100	12	43.2	69.12	41.47
Accounting depreciation	—	25	25	25	25
Accounting profit	—	−13	18.2	44.12	16.47
Book value of capital at beginning of period	—	100	75	50	25
Accounting rate of profit (%)	—	−13	24.27	88.24	65.88

accounting measures. The project requires an initial cash outflow of £100 at the end of period 0, which is taken as equivalent to the beginning of period 1, and generates cash inflows at the end of each of the next four periods. The book value of capital employed in this project at the start of each period is given by the initial capital expenditure of £100 less cumulative depreciation charges up to that period. The depreciation charges are computed on a straight-line basis over the four periods, and the accounting profit figure in each period is given by subtracting the depreciation charge for the period from the cash inflow generated at the end of each period. The ARP in a period is measured as accounting profit in that period divided by the book value of capital employed at the beginning of the period.[7] As we know from the earlier discussion, this project has an IRR of 20 per cent, so that if the cost of capital per period is constant over time and less than 20 per cent the project is (or was) worth undertaking, while if the cost of capital per period is constant and greater than 20 per cent then the project is not (or was not) worth undertaking. However, it is not easy to see how an assessment of the project based on the ARPs in individual periods would reach the same conclusion as that based on its IRR. The ARP in period 1 is negative, and although in period 2 the ARP is relatively close to the IRR the ARPs in periods 3 and 4 vastly exceed the IRR. Faced with such variation in the project's ARPs it is not obvious what should be done in an attempt to measure its overall profitability: the natural first step of taking a simple average of the ARPs yields a figure of 41.35 per cent which is more than double the IRR. Clearly any assessment of the project based on the comparison of this simple average of the ARPs with the cost of capital will be very misleading: the project will appear to be (have been) worthwhile at (constant) costs of capital of up to 40 per cent per period, which we know to be incorrect. If the project's accounting profits over its lifetime are averaged and expressed as a ratio of the average book value of capital employed, the resulting profitability figure is 26.32 per cent: this is clearly closer to the IRR, but is still significantly above it.

It is important to note that the problems involved in using the ARP to assess the performance of an investment illustrated in Table 2.3 arise from one particular feature of the accountant's method of measuring profitability, namely the use of more or less arbitrary depreciation charges in arriving at accounting profits and book value of capital employed. As we shall see it is this aspect of accounting practice which has been regarded as crucial in the literature on the relationship between the ARP and the IRR, to which we now turn.

2.3 Does the ARP provide any information about the IRR?

There have been many analyses of the relationship between the ARP and the IRR, and the conclusions of most of this work have resulted in a widely-held view that the ARP of a project or firm is a very bad indicator of its IRR.

According to this view, the failings of the ARP are not due to the measurement problems which arise in using accounting information to measure profitability, such as the absence of inflation adjustments or the failure to capitalize activities such as research and development and advertising in the accountant's definition of assets employed. Rather, the view is that there is a fundamental conceptual problem: the ARP, even in ideal conditions, will in general bear little relation to the IRR, as illustrated in Table 2.3 above.

The two pioneering analyses were those of Harcourt (1965) and Solomon (1966), which investigated the relationship between the ARP and the IRR for individual projects and balanced stocks of projects under alternative assumptions about depreciation policy, asset life and the growth of the asset stock. Harcourt concluded that 'as an indication of the realised rate of return, the accountant's rate of profit is greatly influenced by irrelevant factors, even under ideal conditions', while Solomon's view was that 'book yield [i.e. ARP] is not an accurate measure of true yield [i.e. IRR]; the error in book yield is neither constant nor consistent'. A number of subsequent papers (Livingstone and Salamon (1970), Solomon (1970), Stauffer (1971)) reinforced the conclusions that the ARP was not an accurate measure of the IRR and that there was no systematic pattern in the discrepancies between the two which might have permitted corrections to be made to the ARP in order to arrive at a better indicator of the IRR. The view that the ARP provides no information about the IRR is now found in finance textbooks: for example Brealey and Myers (1981) state that 'book income [i.e. accounting profits] and ROI [i.e. ARP] are often seriously biased measures of true profitability and thus should not be directly compared to the opportunity cost of capital', and argue that managers should concentrate less on accounting measures of profitability and more on the net present value of projects or activities.

A paper by Fisher and McGowan (1983) provides a clear statement of the conventional scepticism as to the relevance of the ARP as a measure of the IRR. They prove a number of theoretical results (some of which were already known), applying to both pre- and post-tax ARPs, which we now list in summary form:

1. Unless the book value of capital employed by an investment is calculated as the present value of the remaining stream of cash flows associated with it discounted at the investment's IRR (note that the discount rate in this present value calculation is not in general the cost of capital), so that the depreciation charge in each period is the change in the present value so calculated, the ARP on a single investment will differ from period to period and will not in general equal the IRR in any period. If the ARP is constant over the project's lifetime then it equals the IRR. Thus the example in Table 2.3 illustrates a general point: unless a very special depreciation schedule is used (and one which is highly unlikely to occur in practice) the ARP will vary between periods and not in general equal the IRR in any one. Table 2.4 shows that if the

Table 2.4. Net cash flows and accounting profitability measures of a project when Hotelling depreciation is used

	Period				
	0	1	2	3	4
Net cash flows	−100	12	43.2	69.12	41.47
Hotelling depreciation		−8	21.6	51.84	34.56
Accounting profit (using Hotelling depreciation)		20	21.6	17.28	6.91
Book value of capital at beginning of period (using Hotelling depreciation)		100	108	86.4	34.56
Accounting rate of profit (%)		20	20	20	20

depreciation schedule used for the project we have been taking as an example calculates the depreciation charge in each period as the change in the present value of the project's remaining net cash flows discounted at its IRR of 20 per cent, a depreciation charge we call Hotelling depreciation (see Hotelling (1925)), the ARP in each period is constant and equal to the IRR. But Table 2.4 shows the exception rather than the rule: all other depreciation schedules will produce ARPs which vary and will not equal the IRR in any one period except by chance. In particular it should be noted that calculating the depreciation charge as the change in the present value of the project's remaining net cash flows discounted at the cost of capital, which is sometimes known as economic depreciation, will not in general produce a constant ARP equal to the IRR. The project's IRR must be known to calculate the depreciation schedule which makes its ARP constant and equal to the IRR.
2. The ARP for the firm as a whole is a weighted average of the ARPs for individual investments made in the past, with the weights being the book value of these past investments which depend on the depreciation schedule adopted and the amount and timing of such investments. It follows that the ARP for the firm as a whole will be constant only if one of two very special conditions holds: either the ARP on the firm's individual investments must be constant both over the lifetime of the investments and between investments, or the relative weights in the average must be constant over time. This latter condition in general requires that there should be a fixed proportion of investments with a given time pattern of returns in each year and that the firm should grow exponentially, increasing investment in each different type of asset by the same proportion each year. If the firm grows in this way it is said to be in steady-state growth.
3. Even when the firm does operate in the unrealistic manner of steady-state growth, so that its ARP is constant, the ARP varies with the rate of growth of the firm and will not generally equal the IRR. The only reliable inference that

can be made in the case of steady-state growth rate is that the ARP and the IRR will both be on the same side of the firm's steady-state growth rate: in particular this means that if the ARP equals the steady-state growth rate then it also equals the IRR. It is not true in general that the IRR for the firm must lie between the ARP and the steady-state growth rate, nor that the ARP of firms with high steady-state growth rates tends to understate their IRR while the ARP of firms with low steady-state growth rates tends to overstate their IRR.

On the basis of these theoretical results, together with some examples which show that the theoretical effects involved are far from being so small that they can be ignored in practice, Fisher and McGowan conclude that

> there is no way in which one can look at accounting rates of return [i.e. ARPs] and infer anything about relative economic profitability or, *a fortiori*, about the presence or absence of monopoly . . . . The literature which supposedly relates concentration and economic profit rates [i.e. IRRs] does no such thing, and examination of absolute or relative accounting rates of return to draw conclusions about monopoly profits is a totally misleading enterprise.

This view reinforces Harcourt's original conclusion that

> any 'man of words' who compares rates of profit of different industries, or of the same industry in different countries, and draws inferences from their magnitudes as to the relative profitability of investments in different uses or countries, does so at his own peril.

Put bluntly, the overall conclusion to be drawn from these studies would appear to be that the ARP provides no useful information for the purposes of economic analysis. It is such a bad indicator of the IRR that its use in any form of economic analysis is very questionable. The use of the ARP for any of the purposes discussed in Chapter 1—in empirical studies of industrial organization, for regulation of utilities and public enterprises, for investment appraisal, in competition policy, and in macroeconomic studies of profitability—would seem to be almost completely undermined. Before accepting this conclusion, however, it is necessary to analyse some aspects of the relationship between the ARP and the IRR in more detail.

2.4 The relationship between the ARP and the IRR over the complete lifetime of an activity

The impression conveyed by most of the existing literature on the relationship between the ARP and the IRR, as indicated in the previous section, is that very little can be said in general about this relationship. However, it is not true that there are no general results linking the ARP and IRR, and in this section we discuss those that are available for the case when the accounting profitability data cover the entire lifetime of the activity, in the sense that the data start and finish with a value of zero for the book value of capital employed. These results apply to both *ex ante* and *ex post* assessment of the activity, so to simplify the discussion and avoid the need to distinguish these two forms of assessment we shall again assume perfect certainty.

The relationship between the accountant's definition of profit in a period and the change in the book value of capital employed over the period is crucial in establishing general results linking the ARP and IRR, as has been emphasized by Peasnell (1982) and Franks and Hodges (1983). In the examples shown in Tables 2.3 and 2.4 above, accounting profit in a period was obtained from net cash flow in that period by deducting a depreciation charge, and the depreciation charge was equal to the difference between the book value of capital employed at the beginning of the period and the book value of capital at the end of the period. It will be assumed that this relationship between accounting profit, net cash flow, depreciation, and book value of capital employed always holds: formally we assume that

$$Y_t = F_t - K_t + (V_t - V_{t-1}) \tag{2.4}$$

where Y_t is accounting profit in period t, F_t is revenue generated in t, K_t is new capital required in t, V_{t-1} is the book value of capital employed at the end of period $t-1$ (i.e. at the start of period t), and V_t is the book value of capital at the end of period t. Note that V_t, the book value of capital employed at the end of period t (or start of period $t+1$), is defined to include K_t, the new capital injected into the activity in period t. Accounting profit is obtained by subtracting a depreciation charge from revenue generated in t: equation 2.4 therefore implies that the depreciation charge in t, D_t, must be defined as

$$D_t = V_{t-1} - (V_t - K_t)$$

i.e. depreciation in t equals the change in the book value of capital employed between the beginning of t and the beginning of $t+1$, adjusted for any new capital required during t. The crucial feature of the relationship shown in equation 2.4 is that it requires *all* changes in the book value of capital employed to flow through the profit and loss account: the balance sheet and the profit and loss account are thus fully articulated. Given this assumption the following results linking the IRR of an investment and its ARP in each of the individual periods of its life can be obtained (the results are derived formally in the appendix to this chapter):

1. If the ARP over the investment's lifetime is constant then it equals the IRR, as we already know from the discussion of Fisher and McGowan's results. We also know from that discussion that the ARP will be constant over the lifetime of an investment only if the accounting depreciation schedule calculates depreciation in any period as the change over the period in the present value of the investment's subsequent net cash flows discounted at the investment's IRR, so that in practice it is most unlikely that an investment will have a constant ARP over its lifetime. This result is nevertheless of some practical

value. First it shows that the common practice in the case of non-competitive government contracts of paying the firm a constant ARP on the book value of the capital employed on government work will ensure that the IRR earned on such a project equals the constant ARP. This follows whatever depreciation scheme the firm employs: it can over-depreciate relative to Hotelling depreciation, but the consequence is that its capital base is reduced for the purpose of subsequent calculations by an exactly offsetting amount. Secondly it shows that if regulatory agencies use a constant ARP to assess the fair rate of return for regulated utilities, then a regulated firm earning accounting profits in line with the fair rate of return so determined will have an IRR equal to the constant ARP. These arguments can be generalized to the case where the ARP on government contracts, or used to determine the fair rate of return for a regulated utility, is varied over time in order to keep it in line with prevailing yields being earned in other activities. In this situation the firms involved will receive payments such that the present value of all receipts and expenditures, discounted at rates which are appropriate given the yields being earned elsewhere at the time, will be zero, and this will be true whatever depreciation scheme the firms use.

2. Consider two activities with different sequences of ARPs over their lifetimes. Suppose that it is possible to find some constant such that one activity always has ARPs greater than this constant while the other activity always has ARPs less than it. If this is the case then it follows that the activity which always has ARPs in excess of the constant has an IRR which is greater than that of the activity with ARPs consistently less than this constant. In particular if this constant is the cost of capital then an activity which always has ARPs in excess of the cost of capital has an IRR greater than the cost of capital, and conversely if the ARPs are always less than the cost of capital.

3. If the average accounting rate of profit over the life of an activity is defined as a weighted average of the individual ARPs with the weights being the book value of capital employed discounted at the cost of capital, then this average ARP will be greater than, equal to, or less than the cost of capital according as the IRR is greater than, equal to, or less than the cost of capital. A particular case of this result is that the IRR is equal to the average ARP of an activity weighted by the book value of capital employed discounted at the IRR, thus enabling the IRR of an activity to be derived iteratively from the ARPs and book values of capital employed over the activity's lifetime. Although proofs of all these results are contained in the appendix, it is useful to derive this final one in the attractively simple manner of Franks and Hodges (1983). Suppose that all cash flows occur at the ends of accounting periods. The IRR of an activity, r, is defined by the equation

$$-K_0+\frac{F_1-K_1}{(1+r)}+\frac{F_2-K_2}{(1+r)^2}+\ldots+\frac{F_T-K_T}{(1+r)^T}=0 \qquad (2.5)$$

If the initial book value V_0 is equal to K_0 and the ARP in the period ending at t,

a_t, is defined by

$$a_t = Y_t / V_{t-1} \tag{2.6}$$

then equations 2.4 and 2.6 can be substituted into 2.5 and the resulting equation rearranged to give

$$\sum_{t=1}^{T} \left[\frac{a_t V_{t-1}}{(1+r)^t} - \frac{r V_{t-1}}{(1+r)^t} \right] = 0$$

so that

$$r = \frac{\sum_{t=1}^{T} \frac{a_t V_{t-1}}{(1+r)^t}}{\sum_{t=1}^{T} \frac{V_{t-1}}{(1+r)^t}} \tag{2.7}$$

Equation 2.7 shows how the IRR can be computed iteratively from ARPs and book values of capital over an activity's lifetime.[8] The application of this technique to the project which has been used as an example throughout this chapter is illustrated in Table 2.5. If straight line depreciation is used in calculating accounting profit, the book value of capital employed and ARPs are as in Table 2.3, and suitably weighting these does indeed produce a figure of 20 per cent for the IRR.

Thus the IRR of an operation can always be found from accounting data if details of the ARP and book value of capital employed are available for every period of the operation's life. But although these results make it clear that general relationships between the IRR and the ARP do exist, their importance should not be overstated. One reason for this is that if book values and ARPs

Table 2.5. Example of calculation of a project's IRR from its suitably weighted ARPs and book values of capital

	Period			
	1	2	3	4
ARP (a_t)	−0.13	0.2427	0.8824	0.6588
Book value of capital employed at the beginning of the period (V_{t-1})	100	75	50	25
$a_t V_{t-1}/(1+r)^t$ ($r=0.2$)	−10.83	12.64	25.53	7.94
$V_{t-1}/(1+r)^t$ ($r=0.2$)	83.33	52.08	28.94	12.06

$\sum_{t=1}^{4} a_t V_{t-1}/(1+r)^t = 35.28$ $\sum_{t=1}^{4} V_{t-1}/(1+r)^t = 176.41$ $35.28/176.41 = 0.20$

are known for the entire lifetime of an operation and the depreciation schedule is such that all changes in book value flow through the profit and loss account, then sufficient information is available for the net cash flows of the operation to be calculated, and hence it is possible to measure the operation's IRR directly. Substituting equation 2.6 into equation 2.4 shows that:

$$a_t V_{t-1} - (V_t - V_{t-1}) = F_t - K_t$$

Thus the conditions under which the IRR can be calculated from a weighted average of the operation's ARPs are also the conditions under which the ARPs and book values can be unscrambled to reveal the operation's net cash flows. This observation is, of course, merely a restatement of the fact that appropriately defined accounting rates of profit do provide economically relevant information in the single project case. It does not therefore detract from the contention that accounting profitability data can be of direct economic significance.

Another, more important, reason for caution in interpreting these results is that they apply only to sequences of accounting data which begin and end with values of zero for the book value of capital employed and cover a complete self-contained set of cash flows. The results are therefore useful for the assessment of the performance of a single investment project, but are much less so for evaluating the performance of firms or industries, as pointed out by Wright (1978). The results described above show that the IRR of a now defunct firm or industry can be calculated from accounting data, but this is an exercise of rather limited interest. It may be possible to apply the results to a continuing firm or industry by forecasting all its future ARPs and book values, but one then has to face the fact that firms and industries are generally rather long-lived investments, while the IRR is defined as a single figure irrespective of the duration of the investment. The relevance for any present purpose of a single rate of profit representing the overall performance of a currently operating firm which was founded in, say, 1900 is not obvious. In many cases interest focuses on the performance of a continuing firm or industry over a relatively short period of time, and in such circumstances the results described in this section are not directly applicable. It is to this more substantial issue that the next chapter therefore turns.

2.5 Conclusion

This chapter has provided the setting for an economic evaluation of accounting profitability figures. At the heart of the discussion lies the proposition that information on performance is of relevance in assessing investment decisions—either in an *ex ante* sense of whether the investment should be undertaken or in an *ex post* context of whether past investment decisions have been successful.

Two alternative techniques for evaluating investments have been suggested:

net present value and internal rates of return. The latter suffers from the difficulty that the IRR may not be uniquely defined. Furthermore if it is necessary to rank projects, perhaps because investment funds are limited, then NPV and IRR do not necessarily produce equivalent rankings. For most purposes NPV (perhaps defined as a proportion of initial capital costs) is the appropriate basis of assessment.

Even dismissing these problems associated with IRRs, a more fundamental difficulty arises in using accounting data for investment appraisal. A number of authors have noted that it is only in an exceptional circumstance that the ARP will equal the IRR. The exception is when the accounting depreciation charge used in the calculation of accounting profit is computed along the lines described by Hotelling as the change in the present value of remaining net cash flows discounted at the IRR. But in this case the IRR must already be known! Even the change in economic valuation, defined by using the cost of capital instead of the IRR to discount remaining net cash flows, will not yield a depreciation figure such that the ARP equals the IRR.

Much of the economics literature is therefore very pessimistic about the applicability of accounting information to economic analysis. The last section of this chapter demonstrated that this pessimism is exaggerated. At least in the single project case in which a complete set of accounting data is available for the entire life of the project then a number of valuable results are readily available:

1. If the ARP is constant for a single project then it equals the IRR.
2. If the ARP of one project is always in excess of the ARP of another then the IRR of the former is also in excess of the IRR of the latter.
3. If the ARP of a project is in excess of the cost of capital then so too is its IRR.
4. A weighted average ARP can be defined such that the IRR of the project is exactly equal to this average ARP.

Thus the IRR can be precisely derived from accounting information for a single project—a result that stands in marked contrast to the pessimism described in Section 2.3. However, for the very reason that the single project requires complete data over the entire life of the project, these results are only of limited interest. Of much more fundamental concern is the performance of a firm over a limited segment of its life. We pursue this line of argument in detail in the next chapter.

Notes

1. Hirshleifer (1958) is the classic reference, but there are also numerous textbook treatments, for example those by Brealey and Myers (1981) and (at a more rigorous level) Fama and Miller (1972).
2. Throughout this discussion we abstract from the difficulties associated with

disagreements amongst shareholders about the appropriate policy for the firm to follow. These can arise in the presence of uncertainty when the set of returns on an investment is not spanned by existing securities.

3. The major exceptions occur when a choice has to be made between mutually exclusive projects: even in this case the appropriate rule is to select projects in order of their net present value per unit of initial cost if capital is rationed in only one period.
4. For a more extensive discussion of this point see Flemming and Wright (1971).
5. There are a number of standard accounting depreciation methods: for example the straight-line method, where each year a constant proportion of the asset's depreciable value is deducted, the declining balance method, and the sum of the year's digits method.
6. Except in those cases where the accounting depreciation method used has consequences for tax and hence cash flows.
7. Other definitions of the ARP are clearly possible, for example accounting profit in a period could be divided by a simple average of the beginning- and end-period book values of capital employed, but the general features of the example do not depend on the precise definition of the ARP.
8. Computing the IRR iteratively using equation 2.7 involves picking a value for r, calculating the numerator and denominator of the ratio on the right-hand side of 2.7 from the accounting profitability data for the project's lifetime, evaluating the ratio and hence the implied value of r, recalculating the numerator and denominator of the ratio on the right-hand side of 2.7 with a new value of r, and continuing until the value of r implied by the ratio in equation 2.7 is consistent with the value of r used to calculate numerator and denominator of the ratio.

APPENDIX

In this appendix a number of propositions discussed in the text concerning the relationship between the ARP and IRR for a complete self-contained set of cash flows are proved using a continuous time framework.

Define $F(t)$ as the revenue generated by an activity at time t and $K(t)$ as the new capital required at that date. Accounting depreciation at t is an arbitrary amount $D(t)$ which yields a book value of capital employed $V(t)$ defined by

$$\dot{V}(t) = K(t) - D(t) \tag{A2.1}$$

with $V(0)$ and $V(\infty)$ conventionally set at zero so that the whole life of the activity is covered ($\dot{V}(t)$ is the derivative of $V(t)$ with respect to time). The ARP at t is then defined as

$$a(t) = \frac{F(t) - D(t)}{V(t)} \tag{A2.2}$$

and the IRR of the activity by r such that

$$\int_0^\infty \{F(t)-K(t)\}e^{-rt}\,dt=0.$$

Attention is confined to activities with unique IRRs, so that

$$\frac{d}{di}\int_0^\infty \{F(t)-K(t)\}e^{-it}\,dt<0\ \forall\, i>0. \tag{A2.3}$$

From equations A2.1 and A2.2

$$\dot{V}(t)-a(t)V(t)+F(t)-K(t)=0 \tag{A2.4}$$

and hence

$$\int_0^\infty \{\dot{V}(t)-a(t)V(t)\}e^{-it}\,dt+\int_0^\infty \{F(t)-K(t)\}e^{-it}\,dt=0.$$

Integrating this by parts gives

$$\int_0^\infty \{(i-a(t))V(t)\}e^{-it}\,dt+\int_0^\infty \{F(t)-K(t)\}e^{-it}\,dt=0 \tag{A2.5}$$

which holds for any arbitrary value of i.

The following propositions can all be obtained by immediate application of equations A2.3 and A2.5:

Proposition 1: If a is constant then $r=a$

Proposition 2: Consider two activities with ARP profiles $a_1(t)$ and $a_2(t)$ respectively. Then if there exists some i such that $a_1>i\,\forall\, t$ and $a_2<i\,\forall\, t$, $r_1>r_2$

One value of i which is of particular interest is the cost of capital ρ.

Proposition 3: If $a(t)\gtreqless\rho\,\forall\, t$ then $r\gtreqless\rho$.

Defining the average ARP over the life of the activity ($\bar{a}$) as

$$\bar{a}=\frac{\int_0^\infty a(t)V(t)e^{-\rho t}\,dt}{\int_0^\infty V(t)e^{-\rho t}\,dt}$$

then

Proposition 4: $\bar{a}\gtreqless\rho$ as $r\gtreqless\rho$.

The relationship between the activity's IRR and accounting data is given by

Proposition 5:

$$r=\frac{\int_0^\infty a(t)V(t)e^{-rt}\,dt}{\int_0^\infty V(t)e^{-rt}\,dt}$$

Proposition 1 can be generalized to the case where the ARP varies over time. The concept of the IRR can be generalized by noting that there are infinitely many valuation functions $q(t)$ such that

$$\int_0^\infty F(t)q(t)\,dt=\int_0^\infty K(t)q(t)\,dt.$$

Any such function is defined by a sequence of rates of return $r(t)$ and the conditions

$$q(0)=1,\ \dot{q}(t)=-r(t)q(t).$$

The IRR describes that particular valuation function for which $r(t)$ is constant. In general we can derive

Proposition 6: Every sequence of ARPs defines a valuation function under which the present value of the activity's cash flows is zero.

From (A2.4)

$$\int_0^\infty F(t)\exp\left[-\int_0^t a(x)\,dx\right]dt=\int_0^\infty a(t)V(t)\exp\left[-\int_0^t a(x)\,dx\right]dt$$
$$-\int_0^\infty \dot{V}(t)\exp\left[-\int_0^t a(x)\,dx\right]dt$$
$$+\int_0^\infty K(t)\exp\left[-\int_0^t a(x)\,dx\right]dt.$$

Integrating by parts gives

$$\int_0^\infty F(t)\exp\left[-\int_0^t a(x)\,dx\right]dt=\int_0^\infty K(t)\exp\left[-\int_0^t a(x)\,dx\right]dt$$

and $q(t)=\exp[-\int_0^t a(x)\,dx]$ has the properties $q(0)=1$ and $\dot{q}(t)=-a(t)q(t)$; hence $a(t)$ defines an appropriate valuation function.

3

The Value-to-the-Owner Rules for Capital Valuation

3.1 Introduction

THE analysis in the previous chapter showed that if the accounting data for an activity satisfied the condition that all changes in the book value of capital employed from period to period flowed through the profit and loss account then the activity's internal rate of return (IRR)—the measure of the rate of profit which is generally regarded as the economically relevant one—could be deduced from accounting rates of profit (ARP) and book values of capital employed covering the entire life of the activity. This proposition is true irrespective of the type of depreciation scheme employed. However, in many cases a complete set of accounting profitability data for an activity will not be available, particularly where long-lived activities such as continuing firms and industries are being assessed. The question naturally arises, therefore, of whether accounting profitability data covering only a relatively short segment of an activity's lifetime can provide any information about its IRR.

As Section 3.2 of this chapter demonstrates, the problem of relating ARPs to IRRs over a short segment is that opening and closing book values of the capital stock differ from those obtained by discounting subsequent cash flows at the IRR—the Hotelling valuation of capital. To be able to infer an activity's IRR from an isolated segment of its life, the excluded portions must be summarized in measures that value cash flows at the appropriate discount rate—namely the IRR. As Section 3.2 shows, certain relations between the ARP and IRR can be derived in the special case in which the activity is in steady state growth. But it is not possible to derive general relations between the ARP and IRR. Indeed it is not usually possible even to establish that the ARP will be greater than, less than, or equal to the IRR.

Of course this is really a restatement of the pessimism expressed in Section 2.3 of the previous chapter. But by focusing attention on the opening and closing valuations of capital employed, Section 3.2 serves to emphasize the issue that lies at the heart of the debate on the relevance of accounting profitability. If the book value of capital employed differs from the Hotelling valuation then the ARP will not equal the IRR. The importance of this result depends, however, on whether knowledge of an activity's IRR is useful. Clearly if the activity in question is a single investment project, then its IRR does provide useful information (subject to the qualifications discussed in

Section 2.1 of the previous chapter). But if the activity in question has a very long life (for example a continuing firm) then it is not obvious what meaningful information is provided by the IRR. The point here is that the IRR is defined as a single figure irrespective of the lifetime of an activity, so that it cannot be used to evaluate performance over a portion of an activity's life. For a firm which began life in 1930 and will continue until well into the next century, accounting data over the period 1970–86 will almost certainly not be useful in calculating its IRR, which depends on its lifetime net cash flows. But it is not clear what we could do with this figure even if we could deduce it from accounting data for 1970–86: our interest in the accounting data for this period is far more likely to stem from a desire to know whether the firm had performed well or badly over this period, and for this purpose the firm's IRR, which of course depends on its operations over a much longer time-span, is of questionable relevance. All of the criticisms of the usefulness of accounting profitability for economic analysis described in Section 2.3 of the previous chapter take it for granted that the ultimate test of the relevance of accounting data is whether an activity's IRR can be obtained from them. But if the IRR does not provide any meaningful information then the relevance of accounting measures of performance is being judged by the wrong yardstick.

What are the questions to which investors, economists, regulators, and others are seeking answers when they turn to accounts and other measures of performance? The previous chapter suggested one group of questions concerned with investment appraisal. Should a particular investment project or group of projects be undertaken? Another set of questions is concerned with retrospective evaluation. How well has the management of a firm done? In most of these cases interest centres on the evaluation of performance over a limited period, and hence the IRR cannot help with such an evaluation. Consequently the widespread pessimism about the relevance of accounting profitability information for economic analysis seems to us to be based on a misplaced view as to the usefulness of the IRR for evaluating an activity's performance.

In this and the following chapter we therefore explore the question of whether there exists an accounting profitability measure and an associated set of accounting valuation conventions that permit these economically relevant issues relating to an activity's performance over a segment of its lifetime to be addressed. We begin in Section 3.3 of this chapter by defining an accounting profitability measure over a finite segment of the life of an activity. This accounting rate of return (ARR) is the rate of return that discounts cash flows, including the terminal book value of capital employed, back to the initial book value of capital. It is the obvious counterpart to the IRR for a segment of an activity's life.

The value of the ARR will be crucially dependent on the opening and closing valuations of the capital stock. In Section 3.4 we discuss some accounting valuation concepts which have been widely advocated. 'Value-to-the-owner' rules have received a strong measure of support from both the accounting and academic professions, although a number of practical objections have been raised, as described in Section 3.5. While these valuation conventions are intuitively attractive, a theoretical rationale for their application has not yet been forthcoming. Chapter 4 and the remainder of the book is devoted to providing just such a rationale by demonstrating that if these valuation rules are adhered to, then the ARR computed using them provides meaningful answers to the various questions listed above.

3.2 The relationship between the ARP and the IRR over a segment of the lifetime of an activity

We begin the analysis of accounting profitability data which do not cover the complete lifetime of an activity by continuing the approach of the previous chapter, in which the relationship of ARPs to an activity's IRR was examined. Thus we are concerned with the question of whether accounting data covering only part of the activity's lifetime, and hence having at least one, and generally both, of the initial and final book values of capital employed different from zero, provide any information about the activity's IRR over its lifetime.

Maintaining the assumption that all cash flows occur at the end of a period, the IRR over an activity's lifetime can be defined in terms of a segment of its life lasting from the end of period 0 to the end of period T as

$$-M_0+\frac{F_1-K_1}{(1+r)}+\frac{F_2-K_2}{(1+r)^2}+\ldots+\frac{F_T-K_T+M_T}{(1+r)^T}=0 \tag{3.1}$$

where M_0 denotes the value of the activity at the end of period 0 (equivalent to the beginning of period 1) obtained by discounting all subsequent net cash flows back to the end of period 0 at the activity's IRR, and similarly for M_T, F_t is revenue generated in t, and K_t is new capital required in t. Substituting equations 2.4 and 2.6 into equation 3.1, adding and subtracting V_0 (the book value of capital employed at the end of period 0), and rearranging gives the following expression for the IRR (r):

$$r=\frac{\sum_{t=1}^{T}\frac{a_t V_{t-1}}{(1+r)^t}+(V_0-M_0)-\frac{[V_T-M_T]}{(1+r)^T}}{\sum_{t=1}^{T}\frac{V_{t-1}}{(1+r)^t}} \tag{3.2}$$

where V_{t-1} denotes the book value of capital employed at the end of period $t-1$ (i.e. at the start of period t). Equation 3.2 makes it clear that if accounting data covering a segment of a continuing activity's life are to be used to deduce the activity's lifetime IRR, then it is necessary to make corrections for possible differences between book values of capital employed at the beginning and end of the segment under consideration and the corresponding values given by discounting subsequent net cash flows at the activity's IRR. Valuation errors of this sort over the intermediate period are irrelevant so long as all changes in book values flow through the profit and loss account in the manner of equation 2.4.

It is useful to examine the bias in the ARP as a measure of an activity's lifetime IRR when the available accounting data cover only a single period, and to do this we draw on the analysis of Franks and Hodges (1983). Consider the single time period from $t=0$ to $t=1$ and again assume that cash flows occur at the end of the period. The IRR of an activity over its lifetime is defined in terms of this single time period as

$$-M_0+\frac{F_1-K_1+M_1}{1+r}=0$$

and this equation can be rearranged to give

$$r=\frac{F_1-K_1}{M_0}+g_m \tag{3.3}$$

where $g_m=(M_1-M_0)/M_0$ and is the rate of growth over the period of the value of the activity obtained by discounting subsequent net cash flows at the activity's IRR. Recalling equation 2.6, equation 2.4 becomes for this period

$$a_1 V_0=F_1-K_1+V_1-V_0$$

which gives on rearrangement

$$a_1=\frac{F_1-K_1}{V_0}+g_v \tag{3.4}$$

where $g_v=(V_1-V_0)/V_0$ and is the rate of growth of book value over the period. Subtracting equation 3.3 from 3.4 gives an expression for the bias between the activity's ARP in this period and its IRR:

$$a_1-r=(g_v-g_m)+\frac{F_1-K_1}{M_0}\left[\frac{M_0}{V_0}-1\right]. \tag{3.5}$$

It is clear from equation 3.5 that the ARP can either exceed or fall short of the IRR, which is of course unsurprising in the light of the discussion in Section 2.3. Even if we suppose that the net cash flow at the end of period 1 is positive and the accountant's principle of conservatism implies that $M_0>V_0$ so that the second term on the right-hand side of equation 3.5 is positive, it is quite possible for further over-depreciation during the period to result in g_v being less than g_m so that the first term on the right-hand side is negative and hence the sign of the bias is ambiguous.

Thus in order to deduce an activity's IRR from accounting data covering a short segment of its life, it is necessary to know how the activity's book value at the beginning and end of this segment relates to its value given by discounting subsequent net cash flows at its IRR. As knowledge of the activity's IRR is therefore essential in order to deduce the IRR from the ARP over short segments, there is obviously little point in performing this exercise. Accounting data covering a short segment of an activity's life cannot therefore provide any useful information about that activity's IRR. It is important to realize that the values that are required for comparison with book values will not in general be given by market values. Market values are given by discounting subsequent net cash flows at the cost of capital, not at the activity's IRR, and it is only when the activity's IRR equals the cost of capital that market values will be appropriate.

Using equation 3.3, equation 3.5 can be rearranged to express the relationship between the ARP in a single period and the IRR in a different way as follows:

$$a_1 - g_v = \frac{M_0}{V_0}(r - g_m).$$

If the activity is in a state of steady growth at the rate g then the ratio M/V and the ARP will both be constant over time, so that we have

$$a - g = \frac{M}{V}(r - g). \qquad (3.6)$$

Equation 3.6 shows that in steady-state growth the ARP will equal the IRR only if $M = V$ or if $g = r$, and so confirms the claim made by Fisher and McGowan discussed in Section 2.3 that, if $M \neq V$, there is very little that can be said in general about the relationship between the ARP and the firm's steady-state growth rate of a given IRR. It is however clear from equation 3.6 that if the accountant's principle of conservatism succeeds in making M/V greater than one, then the IRR will lie between the ARP and the steady-state growth rate and the ARP of rapidly growing firms will understate their IRR (and conversely for slow growing firms).

3.3 The definition and measurement of the accounting rate of return

The discussion in the previous section was restricted to a single period analysis. Before we can make any further progress we have to define what is meant by an accounting measure of performance over a finite segment that spans a number of periods of cash flow. In examining a segment in the life of an activity we are concerned with the cash flows during that segment, but we must also take account of events which precede and succeed it. By treating the capital stock at the start of the segment as a purchase at that date, and the terminal capital stock as a sale, we can derive a complete series of cash flows from which a rate of return for the period taken as a whole can be calculated. Clearly such a rate of return will depend on the basis used for computing the values of the initial and terminal capital stocks, and we are interested in the interpretation of the rate of return which is obtained by using the book value of the firm's capital as a measure of capital input and output at the beginning and end of the segment respectively. We shall define this measure as the accounting rate of return (ARR). The ARR over a segment is that discount rate which makes the discounted value of the net cash flows over the segment plus the discounted book value of capital employed at the end of the segment equal to the book value of capital employed at the beginning of the segment. In formal terms the ARR over the segment from the end of period 0 to the end of period T is given by $\alpha_{0,T}$ such that

$$V_0 = \sum_{t=1}^{T} \frac{(F_t - K_t)}{(1+\alpha_{0,T})^t} + \frac{V_T}{(1+\alpha_{0,T})^T} \tag{3.7}$$

where V_0 is the book value of capital employed at the end of period 0 (which is taken to be the same as the start of period 1), V_T is the book value of capital employed at the end of period T, F_t is revenue generated in t, K_t is new capital required in t, and all cash flows are assumed to occur at the end of the period.

Although the ARR over a segment is defined in terms of initial and terminal book values of capital and cash flows during the segment, the results of the previous chapter suggest that it can be deduced from accounting data provided that all changes in the book value of capital employed flow through the profit and loss account. This is indeed the case. If the accounting profit of the activity in period t, Y_t, is defined as

$$Y_t = F_t - K_t + V_t - V_{t-1} \tag{3.8}$$

(which implies that depreciation in period t, D_t, equals $-[(V_t - K_t) - V_{t-1}]$) and the activity's accounting rate of profit in period t is

$$a_t = \frac{Y_t}{V_{t-1}} \tag{3.9}$$

then, substituting equations 3.8 and 3.9 in 3.7 and rearranging, we find that

$$\alpha_{0,T} = \frac{\displaystyle\sum_{t=1}^{T} \frac{a_t V_{t-1}}{(1+\alpha_{0,T})^t}}{\displaystyle\sum_{t=1}^{T} \frac{V_{t-1}}{(1+\alpha_{0,T})^t}}. \tag{3.10}$$

Equation 3.10 shows that, just as in the case discussed in the previous chapter where accounting data for the entire lifetime of an activity were available, the ARR over a segment of an activity's life can be calculated as a weighted average of the ARPs of the activity in the individual periods of the segment, where the weights are the book values of capital employed in each period discounted at the ARR. Hence if data on the activity's ARP and book value of capital employed are available for a number of periods the activity's ARR over that segment of its life can be calculated from the data iteratively. Notice that, if equation 3.8 holds, the ARP for period t (a_t) equals the ARR over the one-period segment from period $t-1$ to period t ($\alpha_{t-1,t}$). There are a number of advantages in focusing attention on the ARR over a one-period segment, apart from the computational one of not having to calculate the ARR iteratively on the basis of equation 3.10. One is that it is most straightforward to obtain costs of capital required for comparison with the ARR on a one year basis. Another is that the problem of possible non-uniqueness of the ARR (which arises for the same reasons as the non-uniqueness of the internal rate of return discussed in the previous chapter) is minimized by looking at a single year at a time, for then the opportunity for multiple sign changes in the stream of initial book value, cash flows, and final book value does not arise (assuming that both initial and final book value of capital employed are positive).

These ideas are illustrated by the simple numerical example in Table 3.1, which shows a three-period segment of the life of an activity with an initial book value of capital employed of 1,000 and a terminal book value of capital of 931.7. The activity's ARR over this segment is 10 per cent, as can be checked from the cash flows and initial and terminal book values of capital:

$$-1000+\frac{150-40}{1.1}+\frac{161-40}{(1.1)^2}+\frac{133.1+931.7}{(1.1)^3}=0.$$

Information about the activity's cash flows is of course unlikely to be available, but if the ARPs and book values of capital employed in individual periods are available this is enough to deduce the ARR. In the example,

$$\sum_{t=1}^{3}\frac{a_t V_{t-1}}{(1.1)^t}=240.87 \text{ and } \sum_{t=1}^{3}\frac{V_{t-1}}{(1.1)^t}=2408.7,$$

confirming that a suitably weighted average of the individual ARPs will reveal the ARR to be 10 per cent.

3.4 Accounting valuation conventions

It is clear that the interpretation of the ARR will depend on the accounting conventions used to establish the initial and terminal book values of capital

Table 3.1. A segment of the life of an activity

Period	V_{t-1}	V_t	Depreciation $(=-[(V_t-K_t)-V_{t-1}])$	F_t	K_t	$Y_t(=a_tV_{t-1})$	a_t
1	1000	960	80	150	40	70	0.07
2	960	940	40	161	40	101	0.1052
3	940	931.7	58.3	183.1	50	124.8	0.1328

employed. Accounting theory offers a number of different valuation concepts, and we do not intend to discuss them in any detail (Whittington (1983) gives an excellent discussion of the relative merits of each of the major valuation bases). The valuation base of traditional accounting is historic cost, which is the depreciated original cost of assets. Accounts based on historic cost values are of some use, as records of past events, in fulfilling the traditional stewardship role of accounting. But if accounts are to provide information relevant to current decisions then it is current values, which represent the value of opportunities currently available, rather than historic cost ones, that are more likely to be useful.

As there are a number of opportunities open to a business at any moment there are correspondingly a number of current value bases available. One opportunity currently available is to replace assets, and this leads to the replacement cost valuation base (RC)—the current cost of purchasing similar assets.[1] Another is to sell assets, and this leads to the net realizable value base (NRV)—the disposal value of assets. A third opportunity is to continue to use assets, and this leads to the present value base (PV)—the present value of future net cash flows associated with current assets discounted at the cost of capital. The fact that several current value bases are available raises the problem of whether any single current valuation method should be chosen and, if so, which one. The case for each of these three broad bases has been made by a number of authors, and Whittington (1983) has given a comprehensive survey of the arguments for and against them. Whittington concludes that 'each is of potential relevance in particular circumstances', and hence it is natural to consider an approach to valuation which makes use of all three 'pure' current valuation bases, selecting according to their relative values for the assets concerned. This is the basis known variously as 'value-to-the-owner', 'opportunity value', or 'deprival value', which we shall refer to by the first of these names.

The basic method of the value-to-the-owner valuation technique is to choose one of RC, NRV, or PV as the value of an asset by establishing the minimum loss that a firm would suffer if it were deprived of an asset. The idea seems to originate from the USA in the 1920s. Canning (1929) devised rules of the value-to-the-owner type, and his work influenced that of Wright (1964 and 1970). Bonbright (1937) also devised rules of this form, and his work was explicitly acknowledged by Baxter (1967, 1971, and 1975), Edey (1974), Parker and Harcourt (1969), Solomons (1966) and Stamp (1971). In the UK, in 1975 the Sandilands Committee adopted value-to-the-owner (which it referred to as 'value to the business') as the appropriate valuation base in its report on inflation accounting. In the USA, value-to-the-owner rules for asset valuation were incorporated into the Financial Accounting Standards Board's 1978 Exposure Draft 'Financial Reporting and Changing Prices' and the subsequent 1979 Financial Accounting Standard of the same title. They were similarly incorporated in the 1979 Canadian Exposure Draft 'Current Cost

Accounting' and the 1982 Canadian Standard 'Reporting the Effects of Changing Prices'. In Australia a simplified version of the value-to-the-owner rules, in which the amount of replacement cost recoverable from the further use of the asset ('recoverable amount') is substituted for present value,[2] was introduced in the 1976 Provisional Accounting Standard 'Current Cost Accounting' and eventually incorporated into the 1983 Statement of Accounting Practice No. 1 of the same title. This simplification was also incorporated both in the UK Exposure Draft 24 of 1979 (see Gibbs and Seward (1979)) and the subsequent Statement of Standard Accounting Practice 16 'Current Cost Accounting' of 1980, and in the New Zealand Exposure Draft 'Current Cost Accounting' of 1981 and the subsequent 'Current Cost Accounting Standard No. 1' of 1982.

The value-to-the-owner rules are commonly set out in inequality form, as in Table 3.2. There are six logically possible relationships between RC, NRV, and PV, and for each possible case there is a particular value which is the minimum loss that a firm would suffer if it were deprived of an asset: this is the value to the owner in that particular case. In each of cases 1, 2, 5, and 6 it would be worthwhile to replace the asset if the firm were deprived of it, so that in these cases replacement cost sets a ceiling on the loss that would be suffered. In cases 3 and 4 replacement is not worthwhile, and the value to the owner in these cases depends on which of two opportunities available, given that the asset is already owned by the firm, is more profitable—continued use (case 3) or disposal (case 4).

However although there are six logically possible relationships between RC, NRV, and PV, in practice 'for fixed assets, cases in which the asset's selling price (NRV) exceeds its buying price (RC) *are all likely to be extremely rare*' (Gee and Peasnell (1976)—emphasis in original). A situation in which NRV is greater than RC is unlikely to persist for long, for in these circumstances firms will be able to make a sure profit by selling the assets they possess and buying new ones which will lower selling price and raise buying price, and this process will continue until RC is no longer less than NRV. If it is assumed that RC is never less than NRV, then only cases 1, 3, and 4 in Table 3.2 need be considered. Under the assumption that $RC \geqslant NRV$, the value-to-the-owner

Table 3.2. Value-to-the-owner rules

Case	Relationship between RC, NRV, and PV	Value to the owner
1	$PV_t > RC_t > NRV_t$	RC_t
2	$PV_t > NRV_t > RC_t$	RC_t
3	$RC_t > PV_t > NRV_t$	PV_t
4	$RC_t > NRV_t > PV_t$	NRV_t
5	$NRV_t > PV_t > RC_t$	RC_t
6	$NRV_t > RC_t > PV_t$	RC_t

rules for asset valuation can be written as

$$V_t = \left.\begin{matrix} RC_t \\ PV_t \\ NRV_t \end{matrix}\right\} \text{ if } \left\{\begin{matrix} PV_t > RC_t > NRV_t \\ RC_t \geqslant PV_t \geqslant NRV_t \\ RC_t > NRV_t > PV_t . \end{matrix}\right. \tag{3.11}$$

An equivalent way of formulating the value-to-the-owner rules is to define the economic value of an asset (EV) as the higher of PV or NRV—clearly if the value of an asset in current use (PV) is less than its disposal value (NRV) it is in the interests of a firm's shareholders for that asset to be sold, so that its economic value is NRV, while if PV > NRV it is in the shareholders' interests for the asset to be retained in use, making economic value equal to PV—and then say that value to the owner is given by the lower of replacement cost and economic value. Formally

$$V_t = \min\{RC_t, EV_t\} \text{ where } EV_t = \max\{PV_t, NRV_t\}. \tag{3.12}$$

3.5 Objections to 'value-to-the-owner' rules

There are a number of difficulties involved in using the value-to-the-owner basis for valuation. At a conceptual level several authors have objected that there is no theoretical underpinning to the value-to-the-owner rules. Whittington (1983) concludes his discussion of the value-to-the-owner concept by saying that 'it is to some extent still a practical technique in search of a theoretical justification' and that it is necessary to know more about the properties of the income measure to which it gives rise. He regards the most fundamental problem with the concept as being that 'value to the owner has never been demonstrated to arise out of a particular information requirement of a potential user of financial reports, other than that of an insurer'. This criticism has also been made by one of the present authors in earlier work: Kay (1977) states that 'there are few . . . purposes [other than insurance] for which it is useful to know the loss which you would suffer if deprived of an asset'.

Chapter 4 is primarily devoted to providing the theoretical rationale for the value-to-the-owner rules. But in addition a number of practical objections have been raised, which can be classified under four headings: subjectivity, aggregation, intangibles, and capitalization. In considering these objections we can for the most part do no more than restate well documented practical difficulties, although in some cases the theoretical analysis of Chapter 4 sheds light on how these problems should be addressed. Hence at this stage we largely reserve comment on these issues until the next chapter, and merely document objections for future reference.

Subjectivity. The main practical objection which is raised against any form of current valuation is the subjectivity involved, in contrast to the objectivity of historic cost values which results from historic cost being based on the recording of events which have actually occurred (although it must be noted that the objectivity of the depreciation schemes used to establish historic cost values is open to question). As the value-to-the-owner rules combine each of the three pure valuation bases they unfortunately involve the subjectivity problems of all. Present value is the valuation base which suffers most severely from the difficulties of subjectivity, as it depends entirely upon estimates of future cash flows and discount rates. But replacement cost and net realizable value have similar, though less severe, problems. It is by no means straightforward to establish the net realizable value of a partly used asset which has a highly specialized function, although it is clear that for many assets difficulties of this sort will not arise. As for replacement cost it is necessary to specify what concept of replacement is involved: when technical progress or changes in relative prices have occurred there is a divergence between the cost of physical replacement of an asset and the cost of replacing the services yielded by the asset. When the two concepts of replacement cost differ this means that the assets currently used by the firm are not the best current practice ones: if it were to purchase the services yielded by its assets at their lowest current market price it would not buy those it is currently using. In our view the appropriate concept of replacement cost is the minimum cost of replacing the services yielded by the firm's existing assets: replacement cost valuation means valuing assets at the cost of replacing the services embodied in them. In assessing the cost of replacement of the service, an appropriate allowance must be made for any changes in the costs of other factors of production which are associated with replacement of the service by a physically different asset, which requires the estimated present value of these cost changes to be added to or subtracted from the cost of the new asset in calculating the replacement cost of existing assets. All three valuation bases thus have subjectivity problems, and value-to-the-owner has all of them. We do not have any simple solutions to these difficulties, and can only make the usual response in this situation that 'it is better to be roughly right than precisely wrong'. Current values are less precise than historic cost ones, but they are far more useful, as we shall demonstrate in what follows.

Aggregation. Another problem in applying the value-to-the-owner rules concerns aggregation. These rules have their roots in the valuation of individual assets, but the sum of the values to the owner of individual assets may, when the assets are interdependent, fail to indicate the value to the owner of the group of assets taken as a whole. Consider the example given by Edey (1974) where an electricity generating system comprises a number of coal-fired stations with a large-scale interconnected grid. The system as a whole is semi-obsolescent, but hypothetical replacement of one coal-fired station alone would not allow the complete reconstruction of the system as a whole, so that the replacement cost of a coal-fired station would be the cost of a similar station which would fit in with the rest of the system. The sum of the replacement costs of the components of this system would be much larger than the replacement cost of the system as a whole.

The above example of aggregation difficulties concerned technical progress, but aggregation problems can arise in other circumstances. In the presence of economies of scale or scope the sum of the replacement costs of the components of the system taken one by one can fall below the cost of replacing the system as a whole. If the replacement cost of a component is defined as the replacement cost of the whole less the replacement cost of all other components, then the marginal cost of the last component will fall below the average cost of the system. Likewise, economies of scale or scope cause the sum of economic values of components to exceed the economic value of the system. Here we define economic value of a component as the economic value of the system less the economic value of all other components. In the case of the electricity generating system, the presence of the fixed cost of the network and overhead charges of managing the system will cause the sum of replacement costs to fall short of the replacement cost of the system and the sum of economic values to exceed the economic value of the system. Thus if

$$\mathrm{RC}(i) = \mathrm{RC}\left(\sum_j j\right) - \mathrm{RC}\left(\sum_{j \neq i} j\right) \tag{3.13}$$

and

$$\mathrm{EV}(i) = \mathrm{EV}\left(\sum_j j\right) - \mathrm{EV}\left(\sum_{j \neq i} j\right) \tag{3.14}$$

where $\mathrm{RC}(i)$ = replacement cost of asset i

$\mathrm{RC}\left(\sum_j j\right)$ = replacement cost of the system

$\mathrm{EV}(i)$ = economic value of asset i

$\mathrm{EV}\left(\sum_j j\right)$ = economic value of the system

then in the presence of economies of scale or scope

$$\sum_i \mathrm{RC}(i) < \mathrm{RC}\left(\sum_j j\right) \text{ and } \sum_i \mathrm{EV}(i) > \mathrm{EV}\left(\sum_j j\right).$$

By itself the above does not raise particular difficulties. If the replacement of the electricity generating system as a whole is being considered then the relevant degree of aggregation is the system as a whole for replacement cost and economic value measurement. Thus $\mathrm{EV}\left(\sum_j j\right)$ should be assessed in relation to $\mathrm{RC}\left(\sum_j j\right)$ taking account of technological advances if replacement of the system as a whole permits their exploitation. If investment in a component is at issue then $\mathrm{RC}(i)$ and $\mathrm{EV}(i)$ are the relevant measures. Similarly we may be interested in evaluating performance either at the aggregate or at the individual component level. Accounting statements for firm groups provide information on performance at the aggregate level. However, managerial monitoring may require performance evaluation at subsidiary, plant or asset level.

The more troublesome question comes at the stage of asking whether the value-to-the-owner rules should be applied at the level of a group of assets or at individual component level. Thus abstracting for the moment from economies of scale or scope, is the value of the group of assets appropriately obtained as

$$\min\left(\sum_i \mathrm{RC}(i), \sum_i \mathrm{EV}(i)\right) \tag{3.15}$$

or

$$\sum_i \min(\mathrm{RC}(i), \mathrm{EV}(i))? \tag{3.16}$$

To take an example, one of the stations in the electricity generating system discussed above may, through being favourably located, have lower operating costs than the remainder. Its economic value may therefore exceed its replacement cost while economic value falls short of replacement cost for the other stations. Since equation 3.16 is always less than, or equal to equation 3.15, applying the value-to-the-owner rules at the individual asset level usually yields a lower accounting valuation of the capital stock. The accounting valuation is lower because in constructing its bundle of assets the firm is assumed to be able to combine judiciously assets already in place with opportunity costs EV(i) and assets external to the firm with costs of employment of RC(i). In equation 3.15 the firm is required to choose from a set of assets either external to the firm (with opportunity cost $\sum_i \mathrm{RC}(i)$) or internal to the firm (with opportunity cost $\sum_i \mathrm{EV}(i)$). In general, the cost of a set of assets assembled in the former way will be lower than the cost of a set obtained in the latter manner. In the presence of economies or diseconomies of scale or scope, the analysis is complicated by the interaction between assets in place in the firm and assets purchased externally. A simple minimum condition does not therefore apply. But the principle remains the same and the difference between applying the value-to-the-owner rules at the individual and aggregate level boils down to a question of whether components external and internal to the firm can be aggregated together, or whether the firm is faced with a choice of buying the system externally or retaining existing assets. We will see in the next chapter that the answer to the question depends on whether an *ex ante* investment appraisal or an *ex post* performance evaluation is being undertaken. In the case of an investment analysis, an expansion of operations by the purchase of additional assets is being contemplated. In a performance evaluation, the question of whether existing assets could be better organized is being addressed. In the former case, equation 3.15 is relevant and in the latter 3.16 applies. Accounting statements are *ex post* records so that equation 3.16 applies in practice. But it then has to be borne in mind that one of the reasons why adjustments have to be made in undertaking investment appraisals is that the opportunity set presented to the firm *ex ante* is not that which has been used in the *ex post* evaluation. This gives rise to an interesting distinction between performance and investment evaluations which differs from the normal marginal/average distinction i.e. equations 3.15 and 3.16 differ even in the absence of economies of scale and scope. We return to this in the next chapter.

Intangibles. One of the items that accountants have found most troublesome to evaluate has been intangible assets. Goodwill is usually considered under three headings:

(i) premia arising on consolidation of subsidiaries representing the excess of the cost of an acquisition over its book value,
(ii) rights or facilities such as production rights, processes or 'know-how' and premia paid for tangible assets in excess of their book value,
(iii) assets such as patents, trade-marks and copyrights.

The conflict between recording the historic cost of acquiring an asset and the current value to owners of assets in possession becomes most blatant in the case of assets for which no simple mechanical correction to the former permits the approximate derivation of the latter. It is therefore tempting to go to the other extreme of saying that goodwill is essentially the residual item that reconciles a market valuation of the firm with the book value of tangible items. According to this approach then, goodwill equals the market value of the firm less its book value of tangible items. The premia on consolidation of acquired assets is an example of an application of this latter approach. The other components of goodwill referred to above are frequently recorded on a cost basis and written off over a variety of periods thereby yielding a valuation that bears little relation to a market value.

The treatment of goodwill as the difference between market and book value may or may not be appropriate. Consider first the case of a proposed investment by an existing firm of high repute. Suppose that its reputation extends into the new market. In that case an important reason why the economic value of the investment may exceed its cost is that the cost of acquiring one of its constituent inputs, namely goodwill, is zero. For example, when Mercedes–Benz diversified into the smaller/medium sized saloon range its performance in that market reflected a reputation established elsewhere. Valuing the goodwill at its economic value would clearly be inappropriate and would erroneously eliminate the apparent desirability of the investment. The reason that it is profitable for Mercedes to diversify is that its cost of establishing a reputation in the new market is below that of other firms, i.e. there is an economy of scope. The value-to-the-owner rule of valuing goodwill at the minimum of replacement cost and economic value is again directly appropriate here.

What happens when at some future date we come to evaluate the performance of this investment? There are a number of questions that might be of interest in an *ex post* assessment and the next chapter discusses the differences in approach required to answer them. One issue that is of concern to investors is the performance of management. Here we are interested in whether another management (or, to be precise, the best alternative management) could have surpassed the performance of the existing management. Suppose that the new management could have replicated consumers' perceptions of the firm's reputation at some cost through the use of, for example, guarantees or advertising promotion.[3] Then we would expect that the economic value which the existing management could extract from its goodwill is this cost of replicating reputation. If economic value exceeds the replacement cost then the existing management can generate the stream of benefits associated with the goodwill at lower cost than the best alternative management. The current management is exploiting the asset goodwill to better advantage than others could and this is reflected in an economic value in excess of replacement cost. If the replacement cost of goodwill exceeds its economic value then goodwill is valued at economic value where this is, as before, determined as the difference between the economic value of the firm in the presence and absence of this asset. In that case, the cost of substituting an alternative management is not a replication cost (since this is too expensive to be worthwhile) but the economic value of the existing management's reputation itself. But even in this case in which goodwill is recorded at economic value, goodwill does not, in general, equal the difference between economic and book value. It is only if all component assets are valued at economic value and goodwill is determined likewise that this will be appropriate.

Capitalization. Separate from the question of the valuation of assets is the issue of which assets should be included in a measure of the firm's capital stock. By the replacement cost of the firm's capital it will be recalled that we mean the cost of acquiring capital assets that yield the stream of services that the firm is producing. Some of the services will only be produced in the future so that the issue of what items should be capitalized in the firm's assets and liabilities centres around a description of the future stream of services that we are attempting to replicate. At one extreme, market valuations capitalize the stream of all predictable future services, attribute certain probabilities to the realization of these services, and discount them at some appropriate risk-adjusted rate. At the other, accounts tend in the direction of only capitalizing services to which the firm (or its owners) has a property right or legal liability—assets in place. Definitions of goodwill referred to above included patents, trademarks, copyrights, selling or production rights but did not include promotion expenditure or measures of reputation. The 1981 Companies Act requires that research costs be written off as incurred.

Deferred taxation is designed to reconcile tax and accounting treatments of assets in place but not anticipated future investments. Marketable financial investments are valued at acquisition cost or market value and thus indirectly or directly refer to anticipated future investments while only current and past investments are recorded for consolidated subsidiaries. Dividends announced but not yet paid are capitalized but future anticipated dividends are not. Pension provisions are made for existing or past but not future services by employees. Work in progress but not in prospect is capitalized. Accounting valuation procedures display considerable variation across items but the principle of restricting accruals to current or past activities and future services to which a company has already established property rights is well established.

The distinction between forward-looking market valuations and backward-looking accounting valuations is an important one. The exclusion of future services over which a company has not yet established property rights is a useful benchmark for distinguishing *ex post* out-turns from *ex ante* prospects. Measuring performance in relation to market valuation will only reveal abnormal returns if *ex ante* expectations were not fulfilled. Measuring performance in terms of accounting valuations (even if stated at economic value and not replacement cost) will reveal abnormal returns if subsequent activities contribute to property claims at a rate that differs from the cost of capital. Irrespective of whether the earnings or liability was anticipated, if a claim materializes in a particular period, then accounting performance will be affected.

The property right concept would appear to be the appropriate one for distinguishing between assets and liabilities in place, and future opportunities. An accounting measure of performance should be able to provide information about the returns to investment decisions that may have been entirely predictable but are only currently being implemented as reflected in the receipt of a payment or the signing of a contract. Where a correct application of value-to-the-owner rules differs from the practices described above is in its valuation of assets in place. An expenditure on research and development or the training of the labour force may not yet have yielded a patent or a return on skills acquired but the expenditure has been made and if there is any prospect of a return being earned then that expenditure should not be capitalized at less than its economic value. If there is a strong possibility of a high profit accruing then the expenditure should not be valued at more than its current replacement cost. In other words, a consistent application of the rule that assets be valued at the minimum of replacement cost and economic value implies that an immediate write-off of such an expenditure is rarely appropriate.

Likewise a range of activities that are currently treated as 'off balance sheet' items should in general be accounted for. An option to purchase or sell an asset will have an economic value. Transaction costs will in general cause replacement cost and realizable value on disposal to lie on opposite sides of present value. Occasionally an informed assessment of present value will cause market values as reflected in replacement cost and disposal value to lie on one or other side of present value. Irrespective of whether such options are valued at replacement cost or economic value the fact that a contract has been signed giving the firm a future option means that this service should be capitalized. However, options that a firm is likely to sign in the future (which will be reflected in the firm's market value) are excluded from accounting valuations. Research and development expenditures that may follow naturally on from past expenditure will be captured in market but not accounting valuations. Where past operations and expenditures have given a firm a right to future services or an obligation to provide future services, then these should be valued. Existing conventions correctly attempt to distinguish between past and future activities but confuse these with the past and future earnings to which their activities are likely to give rise. It is appropriate to exclude future activities to which a firm is not yet obligated but incorrect to exclude the earnings and costs associated with future services deriving from past activities to which the firm is obligated.

3.6 Conclusion

The chapter began by arguing that in most circumstances the economist, investor, or regulator is interested in the performance of a firm over a limited segment of its life. The results of the previous chapter are not generally applicable to this type of analysis. Section 3.2, however, demonstrated that in steady state growth relations between the ARP and IRR can be derived. In particular if the accountant's principle of conservatism keeps the accounting valuation of assets below the value given by discounting future net cash flows at the IRR then the IRR will lie between the ARP and the steady-state growth rate and the ARPs of rapidly growing firms will understate their IRR.

Generally, for a limited segment of the life of a firm, accounting measures of performance will be affected by the conventions that are employed in valuing the opening and closing capital stock. Several accounting conventions have been suggested. The one that is discussed in some detail in this chapter is the value-to-the-owner rule by which the accounting valuation of the capital stock is equated to the lower of economic value and replacement cost. Economic value is in turn defined as the maximum of the present value of the expected future earnings of an asset and its net realizable value on disposal. Thus the value-to-the-owner rules set upper and lower bounds at replacement cost and disposal value around an asset's present value. The next chapter demonstrates that an application of value-to-the-owner rules permits a range of economically interesting questions about company and investment performance to be answered.

But before these questions can be considered, some of the practical difficulties associated with the implementation of these rules have to be addressed. Section 3.5 considered four of these: the subjectivity of replacement cost and economic valuations; the question of how the rules should be applied at the aggregate level of the plant, firm, or industry; the measurement of intangibles; and the issue of what should be included in the capital stock. On subjectivity, we argued that the difficulties inherent in establishing valuations do not undermine the validity of recording best estimates. On aggregation, it was suggested that in the *ex ante* appraisal of investment the value-to-the-owner rules should be applied at the aggregate level. In an *ex post* assessment of performance it may be appropriate to apply the rules at the individual asset level. Goodwill, it was argued, should be treated like any other asset and valued at the minimum of its replacement cost and economic value. Finally, the appropriate criterion by which assets should or should not be capitalized is not the degree of uncertainty attaching to future earnings and liabilities, but whether actions and decisions in the relevant time period establish legal claims to future services. Irrespective of the degree of uncertainty surrounding the value of these services, they should be capitalized at the minimum of replacement cost and economic value.

Notes

1. Exactly what is meant by 'similar assets' in the context of replacement is discussed below.
2. Recoverable amount requires the estimation of future cash flows, and so differs from present value only in that a discount rate is not applied to future cash flows.
3. Deferred managerial compensation (e.g. generous pension provisions, or a rising lifetime remuneration scheme) is one means by which a management could signal quality.

4
The Assessment of Activities over Limited Segments using Accounting Profitability Data

4.1 Introduction

CHAPTER 3 described a set of accounting valuation conventions, the value-to-the-owner rules, which have been suggested by several commentators to be an intuitively appealing compromise between the three current valuation bases, but for which no theoretical rationale has as yet been forthcoming. The purpose of this chapter is to demonstrate that the value-to-the-owner rules can be used to investigate economically interesting questions.

One set of questions concerns the desirability of undertaking a particular investment project. Section 4.2 of this chapter demonstrates that accounting profitability figures obtained using value-to-the-owner rules as the valuation convention can assist in an investment appraisal and in particular can indicate the desirability of undertaking, postponing, or not implementing an investment. Section 4.3 returns to the practical issue raised in Chapter 3 of the way in which assets should be aggregated for the purpose of making *ex ante* investment decisions.

Section 4.4 considers the *ex post* performance of assets in place. Accounts are used for a variety of *ex post* assessments. Investors are interested in the return that has been earned on equity funds invested in comparison with what could have been earned had a different management been in charge or different investment decisions been made. Regulators are interested in whether barriers to entry into or exit from an industry are indicated. Economists are concerned about how market structure has affected performance.

As Section 4.5 of this chapter shows, the *ex post* analysis of performance raises different problems of aggregation from the *ex ante* one. The difference arises from the wider range of opportunities presented by replication in the *ex post* case than in the *ex ante* one. Section 4.6 concludes this chapter.

4.2 The use of the ARR in making investment decisions

To demonstrate that if the book values of initial and terminal capital stocks are valued on value-to-the-owner conventions, the accounting rate of return (ARR) defined in the previous chapter is directly relevant to economic analysis, we first consider the use of the ARR in investment decisions. We wish to establish that if, at the beginning of a segment of the life of an activity, the expected ARR over the segment exceeds the cost of capital, then the activity should be undertaken at the start of the segment. On the other hand, if the expected ARR over the segment is less than the cost of capital, then the activity should not be undertaken at the start of the segment. The analysis is perfectly general, in that the activity in question might be a particular investment project or an entire firm, and hence the decision involved might be whether or not to undertake a particular project or whether to enter or leave a particular industry.

We use the simplest possible example to show that investment decisions can be correctly made by comparing the expected ARR of an activity with the cost of capital. It is assumed that the decision is being made at the end of period 0 (which we take to be equivalent to the beginning of period 1) and that the segment in question lasts for just one period, until the end of period 1. The cash flows in period 1 occur at the end of the period. We show in the appendix to this chapter that our conclusions about the relevance of the ARR based on value-to-the-owner conventions do not depend on the simple one-period nature of this example. The cash flows and the book value of capital at the end of period 1 are of course not known at the beginning of period 1. We use an asterisk to indicate the cash flows and book value of capital which, at the start of period 1, are expected to occur at the end of period 1. The expectations held at the beginning of period 1 are single-valued and held with certainty: under appropriate conditions they can be regarded as certainty equivalents.[1]

The expected ARR on value-to-the-owner conventions over period 1 is given by α^* where

$$V_0 = \frac{F_1^* - K_1^*}{1+\alpha^*} + \frac{V_1^*}{1+\alpha^*} \tag{4.1}$$

and, for simplicity, the subscripts indicating the segment over which α^* is measured have been suppressed. In this equation F_1^* is the revenue generated at the end of period 1 which is expected at the end of period 0; K_1^* is the new capital required at the end of period 1 which is expected at the end of period 0; V_0 is the book value of capital employed at the end of period 0; V_1^* is the book value of capital employed at the end of period 1 which is expected at the end of period 0. Both book values are determined on the basis of the value-to-the-owner rules under the assumption that net realizable value never exceeds replacement cost. Hence equations 3.11 and 3.12 are used to establish actual and expected book values of capital employed. It should be noted that the ARR is defined in terms of net cash flows and initial and terminal book values of capital: in practice, of course, the net cash flows are unlikely to be known and the ARR will probably have to be deduced from ARPs and book values of capital in the manner discussed in Section 3.3.

The present value of the activity at the end of period 0 is given by

$$\mathrm{PV}_0 = \frac{F_1^* - K_1^*}{1+\rho} + \frac{\mathrm{EV}_1^*}{1+\rho} \tag{4.2}$$

where PV_0 is present value at the end of period 0, EV_1^* is the economic value of the activity at the end of period 1 which is expected at the end of period 0, and ρ is the cost of capital. Note that present value is defined in terms of the expected cash flows which occur at the end of period 1 and the expected economic value of the activity at the end of period 1. This allows for the possibility that at the end of period 1 the net realizable value of the activity exceeds its present value at that time: in such circumstances it is more profitable to end the activity at the end of period 1 rather than to continue it into subsequent periods, and hence the present value of the activity at the end of period 0 would be based on expected NRV at the end of period 1. Of course if expected PV at the end of period 1 exceeds expected NRV, then it is more profitable to continue the activity into period 2 than to end it, and then PV at the end of period 0 would be based on expected PV at the end of period 1.

We wish to show that if the expected ARR over period 1 exceeds the cost of capital then the activity should be undertaken at the start of period 1, while if the expected ARR is less than the cost of capital then the activity should not be undertaken at that time. To do this we must examine the implications for the relationship between present value, net realizable value, and replacement cost at the end of period 0 of different expected book values of capital at the end of period 1 and different relationships between the expected ARR and the cost of capital.

Subtracting equation 4.1 from 4.2 and rearranging, we find that

$$\mathrm{PV}_0 - V_0 = \frac{\mathrm{EV}_1^* - V_1^*}{1+\rho} + \frac{V_0(\alpha^* - \rho)}{1+\rho} \tag{4.3}$$

Equation 4.3, together with equations 3.11 and 3.12 which represent the value-to-the-owner rules when replacement cost is assumed to be never less than net realizable value, forms the cornerstone of our analysis.

We begin with the case where the expected ARR over period 1 exceeds the cost of capital, i.e. $\alpha^* > \rho$. We know from equation 3.12 that if book values of capital employed are determined on the basis of value-to-the-owner conventions, then economic value can never be less than book value: it follows that $\mathrm{EV}_1^* - V_1^*$ in equation 4.3 must be non-negative. It is therefore clear from equation 4.3 that $\alpha^* > \rho$ implies that $\mathrm{PV}_0 > V_0$, whatever the basis of expected book value at the end of period 1. From equation 3.11 we see that the present value of an activity exceeds its book value if and only if present value is greater than replacement cost, so we can conclude that $\alpha^* > \rho$ implies that $\mathrm{PV}_0 > \mathrm{RC}_0$. However this is not sufficient on its own to justify undertaking the activity at the end of period 0: even if $\mathrm{PV}_0 > \mathrm{RC}_0$ it is possible that PV_1^* exceeds RC_1^* by more, so making it worthwhile to defer undertaking the activity until the end of period 1. It is clear that deferral is not worthwhile if $V_1^* = \mathrm{EV}_1^*$, for then

$RC_1^* \geqslant EV_1^*$ (from equation 3.12). Deferral can only be profitable when $EV_1^* > V_1^*$; in this case $PV_1^* > V_1^*$ and $V_1^* = RC_1^*$, but we can see from the second term on the right-hand side of equation 4.3 that when $\alpha^* > \rho$ PV_0 exceeds $RC_0 (= V_0)$ by more than the value of the difference between PV_1^* and RC_1^* discounted at the cost of capital. Thus the value of undertaking the activity at the end of period 0 is greater than the value of waiting until the end of period 1: the returns accruing at the end of period 1 justify commencing the activity at the end of period 0.

Thus we see that an expected ARR over period 1 computed on the basis of the value-to-the-owner rules set out in equations 3.11 and 3.12 which exceeds the cost of capital unambiguously implies that the activity should be undertaken at the end of period 0. The analysis can be extended straightforwardly to the many-period case (as is done in the appendix to this chapter), so that the conclusion that an expected ARR in excess of the cost of capital is appropriately interpreted as a signal to undertake the activity is quite general.

We next consider the case where the expected ARR over period 1 is less than the cost of capital, i.e. $\alpha^* < \rho$. In these circumstances it follows from equation 4.3 that

$$PV_0 - V_0 < \frac{EV_1^* - V_1^*}{1 + \rho} \tag{4.4}$$

and hence a new activity should not be started at the end of period 0. This is obvious when $EV_1^* = V_1^*$, for then $PV_0 < V_0$ and we see from equation 3.11 that present value is less than book value if and only if $PV_0 < NRV_0$, so that not only is it not worthwhile to start a new activity but it is also profitable to stop undertaking an existing one. If $EV_1^* > V_1^*$ then it is not possible to conclude anything about the relationship between PV_0, RC_0 and NRV_0 from $\alpha^* < \rho$. But even if $PV_0 > RC_0$, $\alpha^* < \rho$ indicates that a new activity should not be started at the end of period 0: substituting PV_1^* for EV_1^* and RC_1^* for V_1^* in equation 4.4 we see that

$$PV_0 - RC_0 < \frac{PV_1^* - RC_1^*}{1 + \rho}$$

so that the expected excess of present value over replacement cost at the end of period 1 discounted at the cost of capital is greater than the excess of present value over replacement cost at the end of period 0, and hence it is profitable to defer starting the activity until the end of period 1. This is because the activity does not yield returns at the end of period 1 that compensate adequately for the opportunity cost of financing the activity at the end of period 0.

Thus an expected ARR over period 1 (computed on value-to-the-owner conventions) which is less than the cost of capital is an unambiguous indication that a new activity should not be undertaken at the end of period 0. However it is not clear, in such circumstances, whether or not an existing activity should be discontinued. As we have noted, if $EV_1^* = V_1^*$ then $\alpha^* < \rho$

indicates that termination of an existing activity is desirable, but if $EV_1^* > V_1^*$, $\alpha^* < \rho$ is quite compatible with $PV_0 > NRV_0$ in which case an existing activity should be continued. The ambiguity here can be resolved by calculating an expected ARR using net realizable value at the end of period 0 as the initial book value of capital: if this is less than the cost of capital the existing activity should unambiguously be terminated at the end of period 0, and possibly recommenced at the end of period 1 (if the expected ARR computed on value-to-the-owner conventions at the end of period 1 exceeds the cost of capital). These conclusions extend to the many-period case, as is shown in the appendix to this chapter.

Finally we consider the case where the expected ARR over period 1 equals the cost of capital, i.e. $\alpha^* = \rho$. Equation 4.3 now becomes

$$PV_0 - V_0 = \frac{EV_1^* - V_1^*}{1+\rho} \tag{4.5}$$

If $EV_1^* = V_1^*$ then $\alpha^* = \rho$ implies that $PV_0 = V_0$, and from equation 3.11 we see that this implies that $NRV_0 \leqslant PV_0 \leqslant RC_0$. An existing activity should therefore be continued, but a new one should almost certainly not be started: at best the returns from starting a new activity at the end of period 0 just cover the costs of doing so. If $EV_1^* > V_1^*$ (so that $PV_1^* > RC_1^*$) then $PV_0 > V_0$ and hence $PV_0 > RC_0$. An existing activity should definitely be continued, while so far as a new activity is concerned it can be seen that the excess of present value over replacement cost at the end of period 0 is exactly equal to the expected excess of present value over replacement cost at the end of period 1 discounted at the cost of capital, so that starting a new activity at the end of period 0 is just as profitable as doing so at the end of period 1.

Thus when the expected ARR over period 1 (computed on value-to-the-owner conventions) equals the cost of capital, an existing activity should unambiguously be continued, while new activities should almost certainly not be started. The slight ambiguity in the conclusion for new activities arises because it is possible that an expected ARR over period 1 equal to the cost of capital indicates that the returns from starting a new activity at the end of period 0 just cover the cost of doing so. As in the other two cases these conclusions extend to the multi-period case.

To summarize the discussion in this section, we have seen that the comparison of the expected ARR over a segment of an activity's lifetime (computed using value-to-the-owner rules and assuming that replacement cost is never less than net realizable value) with the cost of capital provides a great deal of relevant information. If the expected ARR exceeds the cost of capital, starting a new activity is worthwhile, as is (*a fortiori*) the continuation of an existing one. If the expected ARR equals the cost of capital, then starting a new activity is almost certainly not worthwhile (although doing so may yield returns which just cover costs), but continuing an existing activity is worthwhile. If the expected ARR is less than the cost of capital then starting a new activity is not worthwhile, but the signal for existing activities is ambiguous, and needs to be clarified by computing an expected ARR in which terminal book value is determined on the basis of value-to-the-owner rules while initial book value is given by net realizable value.

4.3. Valuing assets in the *ex ante* analysis

An application of the value-to-the-owner rules at the level of the individual asset therefore indicates whether an investment should be undertaken, not undertaken, or postponed, and whether an existing asset should be sold.

In many cases, however, we will be concerned with whether a group of assets should be purchased, whether a firm should expand its activities in general, or whether there should be entry into an industry. In that case we wish to evaluate investment in a set of assets. Application of the value-to-the-owner rules presents no special difficulties here because we are considering replication or disposal of a group of assets or a firm. If expansion is being considered then the cost of expansion will be the replacement cost of replicating the entire group of assets or the firm. If disposal is at issue then we are assessing the value that can be realized from selling the group of assets or ceasing the firm's operations. In both cases then the correct procedure is to apply the value-to-the-owner rules at the aggregate level of the group of assets and define the accounting value of the capital stock as

$$\min\left\{\mathrm{RC}\left(\sum_j j\right), \max\left[\mathrm{PV}\left(\sum_j j\right), \mathrm{NRV}\left(\sum_j j\right)\right]\right\}. \tag{4.6}$$

For the *ex ante* analysis, the replacement cost, present value, and net realizable value of the group of assets under consideration are evaluated and the value-to-the-owner rules are then applied to these aggregates as described in Section 3.4.

4.4 The use of the ARR in assessing performance

We now consider the use of the *ex post* accounting rate of return, calculated on the basis of value-to-the-owner conventions but using actual (out-turn) data, in assessing the performance of activities. As in Section 4.2 we use a simple one-period example to illustrate our arguments. At the end of period 1, *ex post* accounting data covering the period will be available. The analysis of *ex post* accounting data is not equivalent to *ex ante* analysis with correct information, because when expectations are not fulfilled, accountants do not go back to reassess previous valuations with the benefit of hindsight. Thus the *ex post* ARR is calculated using the book value which was attributed to capital employed at the end of period 0 on the basis of the expectations which were held at that time. Hence the *ex post* ARR computed using value-to-the-owner rules is given by

$$V_0 = \frac{F_1 - K_1}{1+\alpha} + \frac{V_1}{1+\alpha} \tag{4.7}$$

where, as in the previous section, the subscripts on α have been suppressed for simplicity. The absence of stars on F_1, K_1, and V_1 indicates that these are now actual rather than expected values, and V_0 and V_1 are determined according to equations 3.11 and 3.12.

The correct (i.e. with the benefit of hindsight) estimate of present value at the end of period 0 is $\overline{\text{PV}}_0$ where

$$\overline{\text{PV}}_0 = \frac{F_1 - K_1}{1+\rho} + \frac{\text{EV}_1}{1+\rho} \tag{4.8}$$

We define the difference between the actual estimate of present value which was made at the end of period 0 and the correct estimate as the error in present value expectations at the end of period 0, ε_0, so that

$$\overline{\text{PV}}_0 = \text{PV}_0 + \varepsilon_0. \tag{4.9}$$

As in the previous section we consider what can be inferred from a comparison of the *ex post* ARR using value-to-the-owner rules with the cost of capital. The results, although derived in a one-period example, all extend to the many-period case, as is shown in the appendix to this chapter. Subtracting equation 4.7 from 4.8 and rearranging gives the following equation, which is central to our analysis in this section:

$$\overline{\text{PV}}_0 - V_0 = \frac{\text{EV}_1 - V_1}{1+\rho} + \frac{V_0(\alpha - \rho)}{1+\rho}. \tag{4.10}$$

We begin with the case where the *ex post* ARR exceeds the cost of capital, i.e. $\alpha > \rho$. We know that under the value-to-the-owner rules, economic value can never be less than book value (see equation 3.12), so that $\text{EV}_1 - V_1$ is non-negative. Hence, from equation 4.10, if $\alpha > \rho$ then $\overline{\text{PV}}_0 > V_0$: the correct estimate of present value at the end of period 0 was greater than the book value of capital employed at that time. Substituting for $\overline{\text{PV}}_0$ from equation 4.9 we find that if $\alpha > \rho$, then

$$\text{PV}_0 + \varepsilon_0 > V_0$$

so that one of two possibilities must be true. Either $\varepsilon_0 > 0$, so that expectations were more than fulfilled during period 1, or $\text{PV}_0 > V_0$, which implies (from the value-to-the-owner rules expressed in equation 3.11) that $\text{PV}_0 > \text{RC}_0$. In this latter case, when the present value of a firm based on expectations held at the end of period 0 exceeds the replacement cost of its assets at that time, then it was certainly worthwhile to undertake the activity at the end of period 0. When the activity in question is a firm, a situation where present value based on expectations held at the end of period 0 exceeds replacement cost, where the latter is measured as the cost to a hypothetical competitor of creating a similar organization, provides evidence of barriers to entry sustaining monopoly power on the part of the firm. The qualifications which have to be borne in mind in practice when interpreting $PV_0 > RC_0$ as prima-facie evidence of monopoly power relate to the difficulties of measuring replacement cost correctly, as were discussed in Section 3.5, and these will be considered shortly.

We now consider the case where the *ex post* ARR is less than the cost of capital, i.e. $\alpha < \rho$. If the book value of capital at the end of period 1 equals economic value at the end of period 1 then we can see from equation 4.10 that $\alpha < \rho$ implies that $\overline{PV}_0 < V_0$. Substituting for $\overline{PV}_0$ in equation 4.9 we have

$$PV_0 + \varepsilon_0 < V_0$$

and so if $\alpha < \rho$, either $\varepsilon_0 < 0$ so that expectations were disappointed during period 1, or $PV_0 < V_0$, which (from equation 3.11) implies that $PV_0 < NRV_0$, and hence provides evidence that the continuation of the activity was not worthwhile at the end of period 0. Unfortunately matters are more complicated if economic value at the end of period 1 exceeds book value: in such circumstances it is clear from equation 4.10 that when $\alpha < \rho$, the relationship between PV_0 and V_0 is ambiguous, which means that it is not possible to deduce anything about the relationship of present value based on expectations held at the end of period 0 to either replacement cost or net realizable value at that time. Thus the overall conclusion is that it is necessary to know the basis on which the book value of capital employed at the end of period 1 is established before it is possible to infer anything from the *ex post* ARR being less than the cost of capital. If the terminal book value equals economic value then we can say that $\alpha < \rho$ implies either that expectations were disappointed or that the expected returns to the activity over the period did not justify its continued operation (which in the case of a firm provides prima-facie evidence of barriers to exit), but if terminal book value equals replacement cost nothing can be said.

Finally we consider the case where the *ex post* ARR equals the cost of capital, i.e. $\alpha = \rho$. From equation 4.10 we see that if $EV_1 = V_1$, $\alpha = \rho$ implies that $\overline{PV}_0 = V_0$. It is difficult to conclude anything very definite from this equality: expectations may have been exceeded or disappointed during the period, while present value based on expectations held at the end of period 0 may have been greater or less than book value at that time, so that it is not possible to say anything about its relationship to replacement cost or net realizable value at the end of period 0. However if $EV_1 > V_1$, then we see from equation 4.10 that $\alpha = \rho$ implies that $\overline{PV}_0 > V_0$, and the same argument as was used above in the case where $\alpha > \rho$ shows that this inequality implies that either expectations were exceeded during period 1, or $PV_0 > RC_0$, with the same implications for the assessment of the activity's performance.

Bringing these results together we see that if the *ex post* ARR exceeds the cost of capital, then this implies either that expectations were more than fulfilled during the period in question, or that present value at the start of the period, based on expectations held at that time, exceeded replacement cost. Therefore it was certainly worthwhile to undertake the activity, and, if possible, the activity should have been expanded. The interpretation of the situation where the *ex post* ARR is less than or equal to the cost of capital is more complicated, and it is necessary to know the relationship of the book value of capital employed at the end of the period to economic value and replacement cost before anything definite can be said about these cases. The appendix to this chapter shows that these results all generalize to the many-period case.

The result concerning the interpretation of the *ex post* ARR computed on value-to-the-owner conventions exceeding the cost of capital is one of great value in attempting to assess the performance of activities. An application which is of particular interest to economists and regulators involves the use of ARRs in excess of the cost of capital as indicators of monopoly power. As has been noted, however, there are a number of practical difficulties in using the above theoretical results in this way. It is far from straightforward to measure the cost to a hypothetical competitor of creating a similar organization, which is the correct concept of replacement cost for a firm as a whole, because of the need to include in this measure the cost of intangibles such as goodwill, advertising, research and development, and so on, and to distinguish how much expenditure on these would be actually necessary to create a similar organization as opposed to creating barriers to entry. So it must be realized that an ARR above the cost of capital, even when it is known that expectations have been fulfilled, is not in practice an unambiguous sign of monopoly power (nor for that matter is an ARR equal to the cost of capital a definite signal of the absence of monopoly power). Detailed investigations will still be required to supplement the evidence provided by ARRs before competition policy is brought to bear on a firm. But it must also be realized that the estimation of the replacement cost of a firm by accountants, though inevitably subject to a high degree of uncertainty, is likely to be as good an estimate as can be hoped for, and hence it is not unreasonable to regard an *ex post* ARR in excess of the cost of capital as a prima-facie indication of monopoly power if it is known that expectations have been fulfilled.

Another difficulty in the practical application of these results, which is relevant for all uses of the *ex post* ARR, is of course to distinguish cases of unfulfilled expectations from those where expected returns did or did not justify the operation of the activity. We discuss this problem in the context of identifying potential monopoly power, but the general principles apply to all uses of the *ex post* ARR. The test that must be applied by any investigator is that of persistence. An *ex post* ARR which is calculated for each of a number of successive years and is persistently above the cost of capital suggests that the high ARR is a prima-facie indicator of monopoly power, as systematic over-fulfilment of expectations over a number of years is rather implausible. An investigator will often be assisted in trying to distinguish unfulfilled expectations from potential barriers to entry as explanations of high *ex post* ARRs by the existence of alternative data sources. If actual (*ex ante*) present values (PV_0 in the notation above) are observable, then a comparison with the *ex post* present value based on hindsight ($\overline{PV_0}$) immediately provides evidence of incorrect expectations. The stock market value of a company's shares does provide a market assessment of the present value of expected returns to shareholders, and so can be used for the purpose of identifying mistaken expectations. Stock market data can be used to analyse *ex post* whether the return on a company's shares was above or below the return on the market as a whole (appropriately adjusted for risk): if the return is above that of the market as a whole, then this is evidence of performance having exceeded expectations, and conversely if the company return is less than that of the market. It should be noted that studies which employ market valuations in analyses of rates of return are no more and no less than assessments of unfulfilled expectations. They can provide no evidence on whether or not rates of return on invested assets exceeded the cost of capital, because, if assets are valued at the present value of the expected future net cash flows to which they give rise discounted at the cost of capital, then the rate of return on those assets will equal the cost of capital if expectations are fulfilled and differ from it if expectations are not fulfilled. The *ex post* analysis of stock market rates of return does, however, provide just the information that is required to identify whether or not expectations were fulfilled over a period. The conclusion we reach is thus that a combination of *ex post* analyses of the ARR (using the value-to-the-owner rules) and the stock market rate of return is relevant in attempting to assess whether firms possess monopoly power.

One final problem concerning the use of the *ex post* ARR to assess performance needs to be mentioned, and this arises when the *ex post* ARR equals the cost of capital. As we have seen, if the terminal book value of capital employed equals economic value it is difficult to conclude anything definite from the equality of the *ex post* ARR and the cost of capital. But suppose that terminal book value was equal to economic value and we were sure that expectations had been fulfilled over the period for which the *ex post* ARR was measured: then $\alpha = \rho$ would imply that $PV_0 = V_0$; the initial book value of capital employed was equal to present value. Under the value-to-the-owner rules, this situation arises when $RC_0 \geqslant PV_0 \geqslant NRV_0$ (see equation 3.11 above). It is clear that if there is a significant difference between replacement cost and net realizable value the equality of the *ex post* ARR and the cost of capital can conceal substantial variations in the performance of an activity: for example a firm with PV_0 fractionally below RC_0 would have an *ex post* ARR equal to the cost of capital (if expectations were fulfilled) as would another firm with PV_0 only just above NRV_0, but the performance of these two firms is clearly rather different, with the first being virtually in a sustainable long-run position while the returns to the second are only just sufficient to avoid immediate liquidation.

4.5 Valuing assets in the *ex post* analysis

The valuation of assets in the *ex ante* analysis was seen to be conceptually straightforward: value all component assets at one of replacement cost, present value, or net realizable value. Valuation in the *ex post* case is somewhat different because here we are concerned with a rather different set of questions. We are now looking back and saying how well a single project or group of projects has actually performed. As far as possible we then wish to attribute this performance to one of three possible explanations: luck (mistaken expectations), skill (superior management), and inherent advantages (barriers to entry).

We have already considered mistaken expectations and concluded that persistence is the best way in practice of establishing systematic factors. The rest of the discussion will therefore abstract from the problem of determining whether expectations were fulfilled. Evidence for superior performance in one of the other two senses comes from a present value of net earnings in excess of the cost of replicating the activity of a firm. If the firm is earning a net revenue stream whose present value (over the relevant period being examined) is greater than the cost of replicating the firm's assets, then the only explanation for why others have not actually replicated is that they do not possess either the ability or the opportunity. Likewise if the firm is earning a return below that required to produce a normal return on its disposal value, then it is either being badly managed or constrained in the actions that it can pursue.

But notice what is involved in the act of replication as against investment. If a firm comprises a number of assets (whose costs and values are determined on the basis described previously) then it is likely that for some of the component assets economic value at the beginning and end of the period is in excess of replacement cost and for some economic value is below replacement cost. For the former the firm, if deprived of these assets, would choose to replace them; for the latter it would not. Replication at minimum cost therefore involves replacing the former assets at replacement cost and the latter at economic value. In the *ex post* analysis, replacement cost is thus defined as,

$$\sum_{i=1}^{N} \min(\mathrm{RC}_i, \mathrm{EV}_i) \qquad (4.11)$$

(provided $\mathrm{EV}_i \geqslant \mathrm{RC}_i$ for at least one i) where the firm is assumed to possess N assets $i = 1 \ldots N$. But the replacement cost of the firm as a whole may be less than this summation of the replacement cost of the individual assets so that the aggregate replacement cost has to be defined as,

$$\min\left\{\sum_{i=1}^{N} \min(\mathrm{RC}_i, \mathrm{EV}_i), \mathrm{RC}\right\} \qquad (4.12)$$

where RC is the cost of replacing the total of the firm's assets.

The difference between aggregation across assets in the *ex ante* and *ex post* analyses comes from the fact that in the former, the firm is by definition purchasing new assets. In the latter, however, the replication of the firm may involve the employment of assets that are currently under the possession of the firm. An outside replacement cost is thus not relevant to a replication decision in this particular case.

Having defined exact replication we are now in a position to establish the cause of excess returns. We relax the assumption of exact replication by assuming either that any management other than the present management has access to the firm's resources, or that the existing management only has access to the opportunities available to outside firms. If excess returns persist in the former case then they are at least in part attributable to barriers to entry. If they persist in the latter case then they are at least in part attributable to superior management.

The replacement cost of a new firm attempting to replicate the activities of an existing firm will differ on a number of counts. First, there may be economies or diseconomies of scale or scope associated with the combination of the activities in question with existing assets. Recall from Section 3.5 that the replacement cost of a particular asset is established as the replacement cost of the firm as a whole less the replacement cost of the firm excluding this asset. The relationship between the stand-alone replacement cost and that incurred by a firm is dependent on how new assets can be integrated with existing ones. Secondly, the firm whose assets are being replicated may have access to resources on superior terms. It may receive preferential contracts that confer economic advantages on the firm. More interestingly, we have noted above that some component assets may have an economic value below replacement cost. If we value these at the cost of replacing them as against their economic value then the capital cost of entry will be correspondingly higher. Thus a competitor faces a cost disadvantage in replicating an existing firm in so far as it would not choose to acquire some of the assets that are already in the possession of the existing firm. These assets will be maintained in operation but would not be replaced were the firm to be deprived of them. If these three cost disadvantages of a potential rival (economies of scale or scope, cost advantages, or assets in place) are sufficient to explain a decision not to enter then the abnormal return of the existing firm can be attributed to a barrier to entry.

However, if the existing firm's replacement costs are equal to those of a potential rival (i.e. all assets are valued at replacement costs not economic value and outside firms can attain similar replacement costs for component assets) then the abnormal return of the existing firm must be attributable to superior management. This follows since we are saying that even if the firm has access to resources on the same terms as outside firms then it still can earn an abnormal return. The ability of a management to earn excess returns on an opportunity open to others must be evidence of superior skill.

We can illustrate this in relation to the most important class of assets for which replacement cost is in excess of economic value—goodwill. If goodwill reflects the past investments that a firm has made in building up a reputation then it may be close to impossible for a new firm to attempt to replicate instantaneously the reputation of the existing firm. Reputations can by definition only be acquired over time so that it will often be the case that the replacement cost of this type of goodwill will be well in excess of its economic value. If we wish to compute replacement cost assuming exact replication then we would include goodwill at economic value. The return earned on the firm's goodwill is a normal one unless during the period in question the firm built on its reputation and increased its economic value over and above that which was anticipated at the start. From the point of view of measuring the performance of the firm this is entirely appropriate. The minimum cost at which the assets of the firm could be replicated is either the cost of purchasing from outside, or in the case of the goodwill, its economic value at the start of the period. But from the point of view of a firm contemplating entering the market, the cost of attempting to replicate its goodwill will be well in excess of its economic value. Thus exact replication will not be attempted and subsequent excess returns may be attributable to this competitive advantage.

But notice that one of the primary objectives of the analysis is to associate abnormal returns with specific time periods and actions. Quite rightly the firm only earns a normal return if actions taken after the opening period do not further augment the goodwill of the firm. To put this another way the opening and closing valuations and the costs should discount the value of actions taken up to the two periods. If a firm has gained a strong reputation in the past, then that is included in its economic valuation, and the replacement cost of this is the present value of the cost of replicating this reputation at the opening period. Subsequently actions will be taken that will augment or diminish this valuation and these are appropriately attributed to the time period under study. Thus to return to the example of goodwill described above, if we want to determine the contribution of management decisions taken to performance between T_1 and T_2 then we should value the goodwill in relation to decisions taken to T_1 (assuming that decisions are taken that yield normal returns thereafter) and then value the goodwill in relation to decisions taken to T_2. Only if decisions taken between T_1 and T_2 augment economic value over and above a normal return will management performance between T_1 and T_2 have been abnormal.

We thus emerge with some precise criteria on which to establish valuation. If the principles described in equations 4.11 and 4.12 are followed, the abnormal returns are either due to good management or opportunities that were not open to others. We can establish which is the contributory factor by undertaking valuations of assets on the basis of opportunities open to competitors. If when valuing assets on the basis of opportunities available to competitors, abnormal returns persist, then superior managerial performance is suggested. Furthermore we can attribute managerial performance to particular time periods by valuing assets on the basis of actions taken to the opening and closing periods.

Consider, for example, the question considered in Chapter 3 as to whether the expenditures made by a firm on a research and development programme should be capitalized or treated as a current expenditure. The above discussion suggests that the value of the activities undertaken to periods T_1 and T_2 should be recorded as opening and closing valuations if less than the current cost of replicating these activities. Otherwise replacement costs should be used. Then abnormal returns will be earned between T_1 and T_2 if actions taken between these two periods alter the probability of successful outcomes and the returns associated with these outcomes.

4.6 Conclusion

The analysis of this chapter has shown that if book values of capital employed are determined on the basis of value-to-the-owner conventions, and all changes in book values flow through the profit and loss account, then the accounting rate of return over a segment (of whatever size) of an activity's lifetime provides information which, in a great many cases, is directly relevant for economists, investors, regulators, and others who are concerned to assess the performance of activities. Contrary to what is often supposed, therefore, appropriately defined accounting profitability measures can be extremely useful for economic analysis. Our arguments in this chapter provide theoretical support for an accounting valuation convention which has been widely adopted in the past decade during the course of the debate on inflation accounting, but which has usually been regarded as a pragmatic compromise between competing pure valuation bases with little theoretical justification. The justification we offer is that the ARR which is computed from accounting profitability measures based on value-to-the-owner conventions can in many cases (sometimes in conjunction with additional information) be given a straightforward economic interpretation. In fact the annual accounting rate of profit given by value-to-the-owner conventions and fully articulated accounts is the ARR for a one-year segment of an activity's life, and there is much to be said for using this ARR for economic analysis. Not only does it avoid the need for iterative calculations based on equation 3.10 above, it also provides a large number of ARRs over time so facilitating the persistence test required to distinguish expected from unexpectedly good or bad performance when *ex post* ARRs are being used. Table 4.1 summarizes the results that we have derived in this chapter.

Our analysis in this chapter does not mean that economists should make uncritical use of accounting profitability data. First, we have noted in Sections 4.3 and 4.5 that care is required in applying the value-to-the-owner rules at the aggregate level of a group of assets, firm or industry. The

Table 4.1. Accounting rate of return signals

	Summary of ex ante Results (α^* = *ex ante* ARR; ρ = Cost of capital)
$\alpha^* > \rho$	New activity should be undertaken at beginning of period
$\alpha^* = \rho$	New activity should not commence. Existing activities should continue
$\alpha^* < \rho$	New activity should not be undertaken at beginning of period. Existing activity should cease if initial accounting valuation is on net realizable basis (with possible recommencement at a later date)
	Summary of ex post Results (α = *ex post* ARR; ρ = Cost of capital)
$\alpha > \rho$	Expectations were more than fulfilled or prima-facie evidence of a barrier to entry
$\alpha < \rho$	If closing book value of capital is economic value, then either expectations were disappointed or prima-facie evidence of a barrier to exit

procedures that are required to aggregate for the *ex ante* and *ex post* analyses are different: in the former the rules should be applied at the aggregate level of the group of assets and in the latter in certain cases they should be applied at the level of the individual asset. Secondly, care is required in interpreting rankings of ARRs. We noted that in the single period case where $\alpha^* > \rho$, the acceleration of a project from the end to the beginning of the period may be signalled. Likewise, in those cases in which terminal book value is measured at replacement cost, the ranking of activities with $\alpha^* > \rho$ reflects the relative desirability of *accelerating* implementation.[2] A third reason for caution in the use of accounting profitability figures computed on the basis of value to the owner is the inevitable uncertainty involved in estimating the current values of the activities in question which form the basis of the value-to-the-owner rules, especially when these are calculated for a concern as a whole. Finally, although the value-to-the-owner rules have received widespread support from accounting bodies throughout the world over the past decade, historic cost valuation conventions were dominant previously, and still exert enormous influence on accounting practice. We would not derive the results of this chapter for book values based on historic cost, and the use of historic cost profitability figures for economic analysis cannot be justified within our framework. But this means that our analysis has important implications for accounting criteria themselves: it provides a basis on which accountants can discriminate between the alternative rules and standards available to them by reference to their relevance to the information required by investors and regulators. We pursue this theme in the following chapters which consider two controversial areas in accounting—inflation accounting and the appropriate treatment of deferred taxation.

Notes

1. For example Fama (1972) discusses the conditions under which the Capital Asset Pricing Model is applicable in a multiperiod context.
2. This can be seen as follows. Assuming perfect certainty, as the point at issue does not depend on the existence of uncertainty, and dividing equation 4.3 by V_0, we have

$$\frac{\mathrm{PV}_0 - V_0}{V_0} = \frac{\mathrm{EV}_1 - V_1}{V_0(1+\rho)} + \frac{\alpha - \rho}{1+\rho}$$

If $\alpha > \rho$ and $\mathrm{EV}_1 \geqslant \mathrm{RC}_1$ then this equation can be written as

$$\frac{\mathrm{PV}_0 - \mathrm{RC}_0}{\mathrm{RC}_0} - \frac{\mathrm{PV}_1 - \mathrm{RC}_1}{\mathrm{RC}_0(1+\rho)} = \frac{\alpha - \rho}{1+\rho}$$

in which case rankings of α relate to benefits of accelerating implementation.

Appendix

In this appendix a number of results which were derived using a very simple example in Sections 4.2 and 4.4 of Chapter 4 are shown to hold much more generally. Using a continuous time framework, the analysis in this appendix shows that all the results discussed in the main text extend to the many-period case.

We begin with some definitions. Let $F(t)$ denote the revenue generated at t, $K(t)$ the new capital required at t, $V(t)$ the book value of capital employed at t, and ρ the instantaneous cost of capital (which is taken to be constant for simplicity). We consider a segment in the life of a continuing activity, extending from time T_1 to time T_2. We start with the problem of evaluating returns during the segment (T_1, T_2) from the viewpoint of expectations held at T_1, which are assumed to be single-valued and held with certainty: this corresponds to the analysis in Section 4.2 of the main text.

The present value of the activity at T_1 is

$$\mathrm{PV}(T_1) = \int_{T_1}^{T_2} (F^*(t) - K^*(t))e^{-\rho(t-T_1)}\,\mathrm{d}t + \mathrm{e}^{-\rho(T_2-T_1)}\mathrm{EV}^*(T_2) \qquad \text{(A4.1)}$$

where an asterisk indicates the value of a variable which is expected at time T_1 and

$$\mathrm{EV}(t) = \max(\mathrm{PV}(t), \mathrm{NRV}(t)) \qquad \text{(A4.2)}$$

denotes the economic value of an activity at t, which is the maximum of its present value at t ($\mathrm{PV}(t)$) or its net realizable value at t ($\mathrm{NRV}(t)$).

The expected accounting rate of return (ARR) of the activity over the segment (T_1, T_2), computed using value-to-the-owner rules for the book value of capital employed, is defined by α^* such that

$$V(T_1) = \int_{T_1}^{T_2} (F^*(t) - K^*(t))e^{-\alpha^*(t-T_1)}\,dt + e^{-\alpha^*(T_2-T_1)}V^*(T_2) \quad \text{(A4.3)}$$

where

$$V(t) = \min(\text{RC}(t), \text{EV}(t)) \quad \text{(A4.4)}$$

where RC(t) denotes the replacement cost of the activity at t. We make the important assumption throughout the analysis that

$$\text{RC}(t) \geqslant \text{NRV}(t)\ \forall\, t. \quad \text{(A4.5)}$$

The justification for this assumption is discussed in the main text.

First consider the case where $V(T_2) = \text{EV}(T_2)$. Then, from equations A4.1 and A4.3, we have that

$$\alpha^* \gtreqless \rho \text{ as } V(T_1) \lesseqgtr \text{PV}(T_1)$$

and hence, using equations A4.2, A4.4, and A4.5

$$\alpha^* \gtreqless \rho \text{ as } V(T_1) \begin{cases} = \text{RC}(T_1) < \text{PV}(T_1) \\ = \text{PV}(T_1) \\ = \text{NRV}(T_1) > \text{PV}(T_1). \end{cases} \quad \text{(A4.6)}$$

Equation A4.6 shows that when $V^*(T_2) = \text{EV}^*(T_2)$, decisions as to whether a new activity should be undertaken or an existing activity should be discontinued can be correctly made by comparing the forecast ARR computed using value-to-the-owner rules with the cost of capital.

Now consider the case where $\text{EV}^*(T_2) > V^*(T_2)$, so that $V^*(T_2) = \text{RC}^*(T_2)$. Subtracting equation A4.3 from A4.1 we have that

$$\alpha^* \gtreqless \rho \text{ as } \text{PV}(T_1) - V(T_1) \gtreqless (\text{PV}^*(T_2) - \text{RC}^*(T_2))e^{-\rho(T_2-T_1)}. \quad \text{(A4.7)}$$

Using equation A4.4 and the fact that the right-hand side of equation A4.7 is positive by assumption gives

$$\alpha^* \geqq \rho \text{ as } \text{PV}(T_1) - \text{RC}(T_1) \geqq (\text{PV}^*(T_2) - \text{RC}^*(T_2))e^{-\rho(T_2-T_1)} \quad \text{(A4.8)}$$

so that an expected ARR in excess of the cost of capital unambiguously indicates that an activity should be undertaken. If $\alpha^* < \rho$ then, from equation A4.7, one of the following three conditions must hold depending on the basis of the book value of capital at T_1:

$$V(T_1) = \text{RC}(T_1)\text{: } \text{PV}(T_1) - \text{RC}(T_1) < (\text{PV}^*(T_2) - \text{RC}^*(T_2))e^{-\rho(T_2-T_1)} \quad \text{(A4.9)}$$

$$V(T_1) = \text{PV}(T_1)\text{: } 0 < (\text{PV}^*(T_2) - \text{RC}^*(T_2))e^{-\rho(T_2-T_1)} \quad \text{(A4.10)}$$

$$V(T_1)=\text{NRV}(T_1)\text{: PV}(T_1)<\text{NRV}(T_1)+(\text{PV}^*(T_2)-\text{RC}^*(T_2))e^{-\rho(T_2-T_1)} \tag{A4.11}$$

It is clear from these three conditions that if $\alpha^*<\rho$, a new activity should not be undertaken at T_1, even if $\text{PV}^*(T_2)>\text{RC}^*(T_2)$. But the signal for an existing activity when $\text{PV}^*(T_2)>\text{RC}^*(T_2)$ and $\alpha^*<\rho$ is ambiguous: only if equation A4.11 holds should the activity be terminated at T_1 and possibly resumed at T_2.

Drawing equations A4.6, A4.8, and A4.9–11 together, it is clear that the results discussed in Section 4.2 of the main text continue to hold in the many-period context.

We now turn to the issue of evaluating the performance of activities *ex post*, using actual accounting data. This corresponds to Section 4.4 of Chapter 4. The *ex post* ARR over the segment (T_1, T_2) is defined by α such that

$$V(T_1)=\int_{T_1}^{T_2}(F(t)-K(t))e^{-\alpha(t-T_1)}\,dt+e^{-\alpha(T_2-T_1)}V(T_2). \tag{A4.12}$$

The correct (i.e. with the benefit of hindsight) estimate of the present value of the activity at T_1 is

$$\overline{\text{PV}}(T_1)=\int_{T_1}^{T_2}(F(t)-K(t))e^{-\rho(t-T_1)}\,dt+e^{-\rho(T_2-T_1)}\text{EV}(T_2). \tag{A4.13}$$

The error in present value expectations at T_1 is defined as $\varepsilon(T_1)$ such that

$$\overline{\text{PV}}(T_1)=\text{PV}(T_1)+\varepsilon(T_1). \tag{A4.14}$$

First, suppose that $\text{EV}(T_2)=V(T_2)$. Then from equations A4.12 and A4.13

$$\alpha\gtreqless\rho \text{ as } V(T_1)\lesseqgtr\overline{\text{PV}}(T_1). \tag{A4.15}$$

Using equations A4.2, A4.4, A4.5, and A4.14 it follows that:

(i) if $\alpha>\rho$, then either $\text{PV}(T_1)>\text{RC}(T_1)$, so that expansion of the activity was desirable at T_1, or $\varepsilon(T_1)>0$, so that expectations were more than fulfilled during (T_1, T_2),

(ii) if $\alpha<\rho$, then either $\text{NRV}(T_1)>\text{PV}(T_1)$, so that contraction of the activity was desirable at T_1, or $\varepsilon(T_1)<0$, so that expectations were disappointed during (T_1, T_2).

Now suppose that $\text{EV}(T_2)>V(T_2)$ so that $V(T_2)=\text{RC}(T_2)$. Using equations A4.12 and A4.13 we have

$$\alpha\gtreqless\rho \text{ as } \overline{\text{PV}}(T_1)-V(T_1)\gtreqless(\text{PV}(T_2)-\text{RC}(T_2))e^{-\rho(T_2-T_1)}. \tag{A4.16}$$

Thus $\alpha>\rho$ implies that $\overline{\text{PV}}(T_1)>\text{RC}(T_1)$ by more than the discounted excess of $PV(T_2)$ over $RC(T_2)$, and hence either $PV(T_1)$ exceeded $RC(T_1)$ by enough to justify expansion of the activity at T_1 or $\varepsilon(T_1)>0$, so that expectations were more than fulfilled. However there is no obvious interpretation of $\alpha \leqslant \rho$ in this case.

Drawing equations A4.15 and A4.16 together again confirms that the results discussed in Section 4.4 of the main text continue to hold in the many-period framework.

5
Inflation Accounting I
The Case for Real Terms Accounts

5.1 Introduction

THE analysis of the previous chapter showed that accounting profitability data would be directly relevant for economic analysis, providing investors and regulators with appropriate signals about the performance of activities, if two basic principles were adhered to in the construction of the accounting data, and one rather weak assumption is made. The assumption is that the replacement cost (RC) of an asset should not be less than its net realizable value (NRV). While there is nothing in logic to rule out the possibility that the net realizable value of an asset exceeds its replacement cost, such a situation is unlikely to persist for long, for if NRV is greater than RC, firms will be able to make a sure profit by selling the assets they possess and buying new ones, and the resulting price changes will soon ensure that $RC \geqslant NRV$. The two basic principles which must apply in constructing the accounting data are, first, that capital employed should be valued using the value-to-the-owner rules, according to which book value is given by the minimum of replacement cost and the maximum of present value and net realizable value, and, second, that the accounts should be fully articulated, with the whole of any change over time in the book value of capital employed flowing through the profit and loss account during the intervening period.

As we saw in Chapter 3, the value-to-the-owner rules for the valuation of capital employed have become a common feature of inflation accounting standards in the English-speaking world over the past decade (sometimes in a modified form in which 'recoverable amount' is substituted for present value: see Tweedie and Whittington (1984) chapter 10 pp. 248–51). However, accountants are traditionally reluctant to recognize gains on holding assets as profits until they are realized, so that the second of our basic principles for the construction of accounting profitability data is far less widely accepted than is the first. Nevertheless, the view that accounting profits should include all gains on holding assets, whether realized or unrealized, has a distinguished pedigree in the academic accounting literature. Sweeney (1936) divided the profit and loss account into realized and unrealized sections, but showed at the bottom of the profit and loss statement the total of realized and unrealized income, which he called 'final net income for the period'. Edwards and Bell (1961) proposed a measure of 'realized profit' which included realized holding gains and a measure of 'business profit' which included unrealized holding gains as well. In arguing for this second basic principle to be employed in the construction of accounting profitability data, we do not wish to suggest that the division of holding gains into realized and unrealized gains may not provide much useful information for the users of accounts. However, the accounting measure of profit must include *all* changes in the value of capital employed, whatever their source, if the resulting accounting profitability figures are to be useful for economic analysis.

The purpose of the present chapter is to consider the issues involved in inflation accounting in the light of the principles which have emerged from the preceding theoretical discussion. In particular we wish to argue in favour of the Real Terms approach to inflation accounting, which combines current values for assets with general index adjustment of capital for the effects of inflation.

5.2 The measurement of inflation-adjusted profitability

Perhaps the first point to make in discussing inflation-adjusted accounting profitability measures is that it is not obvious that such adjustments are absolutely necessary. If an accounting rate of return is to be constructed from accounting profitability data for comparison with a measure of the cost of capital in order to judge the performance of an activity, then a case can be made for this accounting rate of return to be in nominal terms. The reason is simply that the measure of the cost of capital will usually be based on market interest rates and security yields, and these are generally in nominal terms, so that comparison with the accounting rate of return will be much simpler if the latter is also in nominal terms. In this case no inflation adjustments are required: at any date assets are valued according to the value-to-the-owner rules in terms of the prices appropriate to that date, and cash inflows and outflows are also measured in current price terms. Of course, if the accounting rate of return is to be interpreted in the manner discussed in the previous chapter then it is necessary for all changes in the book value of capital employed between any two periods to flow through the profit and loss account, and this implies that increases in the book value of capital due to a general rise in prices must be reflected in the depreciation charge. We require the following relationship between accounting profit in period t, Y_t, revenue generated in t, F_t, new capital required in t, K_t, and book value of capital employed at the end of period $t-1$, V_{t-1}, and period t, V_t, to hold:

$$Y_t = F_t - K_t + V_t - V_{t-1}. \tag{5.1}$$

Depreciation, D_t, is defined by

$$Y_t = F_t - D_t \tag{5.2}$$

and therefore must satisfy the following equation:

$$D_t = K_t + V_{t-1} - V_t. \tag{5.3}$$

If all variables are measured in current prices, it is clear from equation 5.3 that increases in the book value of capital employed due to a rise in the general price level must reduce the depreciation charge and hence boost accounting profits in period t in order for the resulting nominal accounting rate of return to be compared meaningfully with a nominal measure of the cost of capital.

The introduction to this book and the previous two chapters have emphasized that a profit concept is best described in relation to alternative opportunities—investment, disinvestment, entry, exit—or alternative scenarios—replacement of a management, changing the set of investments open to a firm. Associated with each of these alternative opportunities or scenarios is a book value of capital which yields a particular earnings figure. If these earnings are in nominal terms, then a comparison with the nominal earnings of the investment, firm or industry in question provides appropriate answers to the issues considered above. This comparison is summarized in the relation of nominal accounting rates of return to nominal costs of capital. The value-to-the-owner rules therefore serve to emphasize that inflation adjustments are irrelevant to a broad range of economically interesting questions. Once the appropriate opportunity cost of capital can be identified then provided that all assets are valued at current prices, be they at net realizable value, present value, or replacement cost, problems associated with identifying price indices for inflation adjustments do not arise.

Where they are of concern, however, is in trying to answer the other set of questions discussed in the introduction, namely those associated with distribution. If profit is to be used to determine the income accruing to shareholders in the Hicksian sense of feasible consumption while maintaining capital intact, then the real earnings potential of capital has to be established. For this purpose a price index to revalue closing capital measures in terms of opening ones is required.

There are two central concepts of capital maintenance: the proprietary approach and the entity approach.[1] The former views the firm's capital as a fund of wealth attributable to the proprietors—the equity shareholders. If the general price level is constant then it is the money value of opening capital which must be maintained before a profit is recognized. However, if the general price level changes, the real purchasing power of capital must be maintained, and this is derived by applying a general price index to yield a measure of capital which maintains its command over goods and services in general. In contrast the entity approach aims to preserve intact the operating capacity of the business—its ability to provide goods and services. This also leads to money capital maintenance if all prices are constant, but if there are relative price changes it requires opening money capital to be adjusted by changes in the prices of specific assets of the firm, so that the cost of maintaining the assets necessary to preserve productive capacity is deducted from revenue before a profit is recognized.

If accounting profitability data are to be useful for economic analysis, enabling assessments of the performance of activities to be made, then it seems clear that the appropriate concept of capital to be maintained is the proprietary one. The general approach that we have adopted in our discussion of accounting profitability data is to ask whether it provides information which enables one to assess how worthwhile a particular use of capital is. In particular, we want to be able to use these data in order to determine whether the present operating capacity of a firm *should* be maintained, rather than being committed to the maintenance of the existing form of a business as under the entity approach to capital maintenance. If accounting profitability data are to provide information enabling investors to make decisions about the allocation of their wealth between different uses then it is necessary to regard each individual firm as a stock of resources to be applied in whatever use is of most benefit to the shareholders. This means that the appropriate concept of capital to be maintained is a fund of general purchasing power which, under inflationary conditions, is adjusted by a general price index. It is difficult to see how efficient allocation decisions can be made on the basis of accounting profitability data if the latter are based on a concept of capital maintenance which regards each individual firm as a going concern that must preserve, at all costs, its ability to continue producing its goods and services.

We regard the above argument as being sufficient on its own for the use of a proprietary concept of capital maintenance rather than an entity one, but it is worth noting two others. One is that it is very difficult indeed to provide a measure of operating capacity as the basis of an entity capital maintenance concept. After an extensive discussion of the issues involved in defining operating capacity, Tweedie and Whittington (1984) state that 'it is tempting to conclude that the concept of operating capacity should be abandoned entirely' because of the complications involved in trying to measure it. In contrast, the proprietary concept of capital is relatively simple and objective. The other argument against the use of an entity capital maintenance concept is that because it is designed to compensate for changes in the prices of the specific assets of the firm holding gains on assets are never recognized as part of profit. As we have constantly emphasized, a basic principle which must apply in the construction of accounting profitability data if it is to be directly relevant for economic analysis is that all changes in the book value of capital employed must flow through the profit and loss account. A concept of capital maintenance which excludes increases in the current value of assets owned by the firm from profit obviously fails to satisfy this basic principle, and hence the entity concept of capital must be rejected.

Our rejection of the entity concept of capital maintenance means that we also reject the use of specific price indices in adjusting the value of capital which has to be maintained before a profit is recognized. It is clear that an index of the prices of the specific assets used by the firm will not be an appropriate index with which to measure whether the proprietors' interest has been maintained in terms of command over a basket of goods representative of that purchased by the average shareholder. The use of a general price index to adjust the value of the capital which is to be maintained will result in constant real capital representing approximately constant command over goods and services in the economy. It has to be recognized that a perfect price index does not exist, for shareholders will have differing tastes and consumption patterns and it is impossible for any one price index to ensure that constant real capital maintains a constant command over goods and services consumed by all shareholders. The important point is that some general index should be used in order to take account of changes in the general purchasing power of the monetary unit. Economists generally advocate the use of a consumer price index on the grounds that what matters to shareholders is the amount of real consumption a company affords them, not the quantities of goods a company buys or sells, except in so far as the latter are a means to that end. However, given that no perfect price index exists, it is also possible to make a case for using other general price indices. The essential point to note is that a general price index must be used to express capital and profit in terms of constant purchasing power.

To summarize the discussion in this section, our theoretical analysis suggests that the appropriate way in which to take account of inflation in the construction of accounting profitability data which will be relevant for economic analysis is to combine a current valuation base for capital employed—the value-to-the-owner rules—with general index adjustment of capital for the effects of inflation. The appropriate way to measure inflation-adjusted profit then emerges naturally from the requirement that all changes in the book value of capital employed should flow through the profit and loss account. This approach to inflation accounting, in which general index adjustment is superimposed on a current valuation basis, is known as Real Terms accounting and it has a distinguished intellectual history, which we consider in the next section, together with what we believe to be the advantages of our particular version of it.

5.3 Real Terms accounting

The Real Terms (RT) approach to inflation accounting can be traced back to the work of Sweeney (1936), who argued in favour of adjusting capital by a general price index for profit measurement purposes while valuing real assets at replacement cost. Sweeney distinguished between realized and unrealized gains in his treatment of appreciation, although proposing that both should be included in 'final net income'. Edwards and Bell (1961) also advocated the use of replacement cost values together with a general index adjustment of capital, but they proposed a far more detailed presentation of the profit and loss statement, in which a distinction was made between operating and holding gains, money gains and real gains, and realized and unrealized gains. Edwards and Bell's final measure of 'business profit' included all these items, but their approach provides a broad set of information about the effects of general and specific price changes. Chambers (1966) also proposed a RT approach, but in his view, general price index adjustment of capital was appropriately combined with net realizable value as the current valuation base. In contrast, Baxter (1975) suggested value to the owner as the appropriate current value base of a RT system, although he excluded unrealized gains from the definition of profit, reporting them only in the shareholders' equity interest in the balance sheet. An adaptation of the value-to-the-owner base has also been proposed by Edwards and Bell in their more recent work (Edwards, Bell and Johnson (1979)). They advocate a mixture of 'entry values' (replacement cost) and 'exit values' (net realizable value) together with general index adjustment of capital and a number of distinctions between the component parts of 'business profit' as in their earlier work.

It is clear from this summary of the history of RT accounting proposals that the general approach is not new, and the version of it that we support, with the current valuation base being value to the owner, and all changes in the value of capital employed, whether realized or unrealized, flowing through the profit and loss account, is similar, although not identical, to the proposals of Baxter (1975) and Edwards, Bell and Johnson (1979). Our claim, however, is not that we have discovered a new system of inflation accounting—clearly we have not—but rather that our theoretical analysis of the conditions under which accounting profitability data would provide relevant information to investors, regulators, and economists about the performance of activities establishes a set of criteria by which the merits of alternative proposals can be assessed.

The intense debate on inflation accounting which took place in the 1970s and early 1980s did not result in RT accounting being adopted in practice, although some more recent signs of a move towards RT accounting can be discerned (see Tweedie and Whittington (1984) for a comprehensive review of developments in inflation accounting). Tweedie and Whittington characterize the course of the inflation accounting debate at the professional level in the English-speaking world as follows. Initially there was widespread support for conventional Constant Purchasing Power (CPP) accounting, in which the historical cost valuation base is adjusted by a general price index.[2] Between 1973 and 1975, CPP proposals appeared in the USA, the UK, Australia, Canada, and New Zealand. But CPP became standard practice in none of these countries—the closest being a Provisional Standard (PSSAP7) in the UK in 1974. The initial support for CPP was followed, in 1975 and 1976, by a 'Current Cost Revolution' in which official bodies in several English-speaking countries moved towards Current Cost accounting (CCA), partly as a result of government influence.[3] Tweedie and Whittington (1984) distinguish two major reasons for this sudden change. One was anxiety by governments concerning the possible destabilising effects of any form of general indexation such as that involved in CPP. The other was anxiety on the part of firms that CPP did not show the true state of affairs as reflected by the specific prices which they faced. The period was one of important relative price changes which CPP, by valuing assets at historic cost adjusted by a general price index, failed to capture.

CCA uses current values for asset valuation and, in its pure form, involves an entity capital maintenance concept which means that capital is adjusted by the specific prices of the assets held by the firm. However, there was considerable controversy over CCA in its pure form, and the professional bodies which were asked to implement it were reluctant to do so. The resulting discussion led to some variant of value to the owner being widely adopted as the current valuation base, and in an attempt to fill the gap left by pure CCA, which takes no account of the losses on holding assets fixed in money value and gains on liabilities fixed in money terms, there were experiments in the UK, New Zealand, and Canada with monetary working capital adjustments (to deal with the former) and gearing adjustments (to deal with the latter) based on changes in the prices of the specific assets held by the firm. The monetary working capital adjustment attempts to extend the concept of the entity beyond its physical assets to its monetary working capital, and applies to initial monetary working capital a specific index which is intended to reflect the change in the firm's need for monetary working capital (in order to maintain its operating capacity) arising from price changes during the period. The gearing adjustment involves the entity approach to maintaining equity capital but a proprietary approach (using money rather than general purchasing power) to long-term borrowing, crediting equity shareholders with an additional profit during a period of inflation as a result of the ownership of the firm shifting from providers of long-term fixed money capital (gearing) to the shareholders. In the form advocated by Godley and Cripps (1975) and Gibbs (1976) the gearing adjustment credits a proportion, equal to the firm's gearing ratio, of all real holding gains to profits. Holding gains on equity-financed assets are not included because the equity capital to be maintained is updated by an index appropriate to the specific assets of the firm. These experiments by no means resolved the controversy, and as a result only the UK has issued a CCA standard (incorporating the two adjustments discussed above)—SSAP16 in 1980. The version of the gearing adjustment adopted in SSAP16 is restricted to apply only to realized holding gains, a development which has been condemned by proponents of the gearing adjustment such as Kennedy (1978) and Gibbs and Seward (1979).

A natural way to reconcile the differences between conventional CPP and pure CCA is to adopt RT accounting, and this was proposed in the UK by the Consultative Committee of Accountancy Bodies (CCAB) in its *Initial Reactions* to the Sandilands Report (1975). But most of the English-speaking world, including the UK, attempted to resolve these differences along the lines of the monetary working capital adjustment and the gearing adjustment. Only in the USA has there been some move towards RT in practice: in 1979 FAS33, issued by the Financial Accounting Standards Board, required companies to report both CCA and CPP profit data, with an element of RT in the reporting of real holding gains and losses. There have also been some limited steps towards RT in more recent proposals for Australia, New Zealand, and Canada, and RT systems were also proposed in the Netherlands in 1976 and Sweden in 1980. But despite these signs of moves towards RT in practice it is clear that this system of accounting has not yet had a significant impact on inflation accounting at the professional level. The most recent official pronouncement on inflation accounting in the UK, the 1984 ED35 'Accounting for Effects of Changing Prices', retains the basic concepts of SSAP16: the changes proposed relate principally to the disclosure requirements of the standard and the companies to which they apply. The only significant change at the level of basic concepts is that a choice of three methods for calculating the gearing adjustment is proposed in ED35: these are the SSAP16 gearing adjustment, which is restricted to realized holding gains only; the Godley–Cripps–Gibbs one, which applies to all holding gains; and a restricted version of what we would regard as the proper gain on borrowing measure, in which a general price index is applied to monetary items not included in monetary working capital.

The superiority of RT over CPP or CCA seems to us to be clear-cut. CPP as conventionally interpreted applies general index adjustment to a historic cost base, and we have argued in detail in the previous chapter that current values, of the value-to-the-owner type, rather than historic costs must be used for assets if information on accounting profitability is to be relevant for economic analysis. Consequently CPP is not a satisfactory system of inflation accounting because of its inappropriate balance sheet conventions. In contrast, CCA, to the extent that it uses value-to-the-owner rules for asset valuation, has precisely those balance sheet conventions which are appropriate for economic interpretations of the accounting rate of return on capital. But the rules applied to the profit and loss account by CCA are inappropriate for such interpretations, because they do not satisfy the basic principle that the whole of any change in the book value of capital should flow through the profit and loss account. CCA in its pure form excludes the holding gain on liabilities and the holding loss on assets fixed in money terms: in the version of CCA that developed subsequently the holding loss on monetary working capital was recognized (albeit via a specific index, reflecting the entity capital maintenance concept of CCA), and some part of the gain on borrowing was incorporated into profit via the gearing adjustment. But the gearing adjustment only recognizes real holding gains as profit to the extent that they are debt-financed (and indeed the UK version in SSAP16 applied the gearing adjustment only to realized holding gains), and it fails to separate the gain on borrowing from holding gains on assets, involving a serious loss of information. The gearing adjustment seems to us to be a confused mixture of entity and proprietary concepts of capital maintenance. We have argued above that the appropriate concept of capital maintenance is a proprietary one, and for this reason, together with its failure to include all changes in the book value of capital in profit, we regard CCA too as an unsatisfactory system of inflation accounting. Both CPP and CCA have certain appealing features, however, and it is quite straightforward to combine them in a CPP adjustment of the CCA value-to-the-owner asset valuation base, with all changes in the book value of capital employed, realized and unrealized, flowing through the profit and loss account. This is the version of RT accounting that we regard as the appropriate system of inflation accounting.

It is useful to spell out the form that this version of inflation accounting would take. Our objective is to use accounting profitability data to derive a real accounting rate of return which can be meaningfully compared with a real cost of capital to give signals to investors and regulators. To show the adjustments to nominal accounting data that are required to allow for inflation we use a simple algebraic example. As the issues involved here do not depend on uncertainty we assume that there is perfect certainty so that no distinction need be made between the *ex ante* and *ex post* accounting rate of return. The nominal accounting rate of return (ARR) on value-to-the-owner conventions over period 1 is given by α where

$$V_0 = \frac{F_1 - K_1 + V_1}{1+\alpha}. \tag{5.4}$$

Here V_0 is the book value of capital employed at the end of period 0 and V_1 is the book value of capital employed at the end of period 1, both being determined on the basis of the value-to-the-owner rules. F_1 denotes revenue generated during period 1 and K_1 new capital required in period 1. For simplicity all cash flows are assumed to occur at the end of the period. All variables are in nominal terms, i.e. in the current prices of the period by which they are dated. The definition of the ARR in equation 5.4 is directly in terms of net cash flows and initial and final book values of capital: in practice, however, the ARR will probably have to be deduced from accounting profitability data in the manner described in Chapter 3, and we know that this requires accounting profit in period 1 (Y_1) to be defined as

$$Y_1 = F_1 - K_1 + V_1 - V_0 \tag{5.5}$$

while accounting depreciation (D_1) has to satisfy

$$D_1 = K_1 - (V_1 - V_0) \tag{5.6}$$

so that accounting profit can also be written as

$$Y_1 = F_1 - D_1. \tag{5.7}$$

From equation 5.4 the nominal ARR is given as

$$\alpha = \frac{F_1 - K_1 + V_1 - V_0}{V_0} \tag{5.8}$$

which can, using equations 5.5 and 5.7, also be expressed as

$$\alpha = \frac{Y_1}{V_0} \tag{5.9}$$

or

$$\alpha = \frac{F_1 - D_1}{V_0}. \tag{5.10}$$

We know from the analysis of Chapter 4 that a comparison of the nominal ARR obtained in this way with the nominal cost of capital, ρ, is a valid way of assessing the performance of the activity in question.

How can a real ARR be measured in order for comparisons with the real cost of capital, r, to be made? The relationship between the nominal and real costs of capital is given by

$$(1+\rho) = (1+r)(1+\pi)$$

where π is the rate of inflation over a period, measured by the increase in some general price index over the period, so that

$$\rho = r(1+\pi) + \pi. \tag{5.11}$$

It follows that the nominal ARR is related to the real ARR, a, as follows

$$\alpha = a(1+\pi) + \pi. \tag{5.12}$$

Substituting for α in equation 5.8 from 5.12 and rearranging, we find that

$$a = \frac{F_1 - K_1 + V_1 - (1+\pi)V_0}{(1+\pi)V_0}. \tag{5.13}$$

Alternatively, substituting in equation 5.10 from 5.12,

$$a = \frac{F_1 - D_1 - \pi V_0}{(1+\pi)V_0}. \tag{5.14}$$

The numerators of the right-hand side of equations 5.13 and 5.14 are two alternative ways of writing the same inflation-adjusted profit figure. The required adjustment to nominal accounting profits is simply the subtraction of πV_0, the inflation rate times the initial book value of capital employed, from nominal accounting profit. Equations 5.13 and 5.14 show that in order to derive the real ARR, real (inflation-adjusted) accounting profits must be divided by the initial book value of capital employed expressed in constant (end-period) prices, $(1+\pi)V_0$.

The various inflation adjustments which are required to be made to nominal accounting profits can be seen more easily if we write the book value of capital employed in terms of its constituent parts: at any date t

$$V_t = G_t + S_t + M_t - L_t \tag{5.15}$$

where G_t is the value of fixed assets at t, S_t the value of stocks, M_t the value of net monetary assets held, and L_t the value of outstanding liabilities at t. In each case the value of these items in the balance sheet is established using the value-to-the-owner base. This raises the question of how the value-to-the-owner rules apply to these different assets and liabilities. Clearly there is no distinction to be made between present value (PV), replacement cost (RC), and net realizable value (NRV) for net monetary assets which have a clearly defined money value. It is also probable that for many types of stocks, buying and selling prices will not differ and hence the current market price of stocks can be used to obtain the value to the owner, although this is unlikely to be the case for work in progress, in which market dealings are rare so that neither a buying nor a selling price exists and hence a choice between PV, RC, and NRV has to be made in the same way as for fixed assets. As far as liabilities are concerned, these can be valued by a straightforward adaptation of the rules used to value assets, as suggested by Baxter (1975).[4] The value of a liability under value-to-the-owner rules is given by

Value of the liability = max {Replacement loan, Net payments to meet the liability}

where

Net payments to meet the liability = min {PV of future payments, Current repurchase price}

For long-term fixed interest loans, for example, the current repurchase price is the call price, and the replacement cost is the amount borrowed inclusive of transactions costs. The PV of future payments is then computed at the cost of capital associated with the replacement loan.

We can now give a simple analysis of the inflation adjustments that must be made to nominal accounting profits in order to arrive at real accounting profits. Suppose that at time t, a firm's assets and liabilities comprise:

(a) g_t units of a single fixed asset which decays at the rate δ per period, so that if the firm does not purchase any new units of this asset in the subsequent period it will hold only $(1-\delta)g_t$ units at time $t+1$. We assume that the market price at which units of the asset can be bought at t is p_t, and that the value-to-the-owner rules lead to replacement cost valuation of the fixed asset so that p_t is the price used to value the firm's holding of this asset.

(b) s_t units of a single type of stock which can be bought or sold at a market price q_t, and hence are valued at this price. The entire stock held at time t is assumed to be used up during the subsequent period.

(c) net monetary assets with a money value m_t.

(d) l_t outstanding bonds each with a current market price b_t which is therefore used to value this liability.

The book value of capital at the end of period t (equivalent to the beginning of period $t+1$) is therefore

$$V_t = p_t g_t + q_t s_t + m_t - b_t l_t. \tag{5.16}$$

Inflation-adjusted profit $\bar{Y}_t$ is

$$\bar{Y}_t = F_t - K_t + V_t - (1+\pi)V_{t-1}. \tag{5.17}$$

Consider period 1 (which lasts from $t=0$ to $t=1$), and assume that all transactions and cash flows occur at the end of the period. In terms of the assets and liabilities held by the firm, K_1 can be written as

$$K_1 = p_1(g_1 - (1-\delta)g_0) + q_1 s_1 + (m_1 - m_0) - b_1(l_1 - l_0). \tag{5.18}$$

Substituting equations 5.16 and 5.18 into 5.17 and rearranging yields the following expression for inflation-adjusted profit:

$$\begin{aligned} \bar{Y}_1 = F_1 - p_1\delta g_0 + (p_1 - (1+\pi)p_0)g_0 - (1+\pi)q_0 s_0 - \pi m_0 \\ - (b_1 - (1+\pi)b_0)l_0. \end{aligned} \tag{5.19}$$

Equation 5.19 shows clearly the various steps that are involved in obtaining the real terms accounting profit figure which we regard as the appropriate one if inflation-adjusted accounting profitability data is to be useful for economic analysis. Revenues received, F_1, are adjusted as follows:

(i) a term $p_1\delta g_0$ is subtracted, reflecting the current (replacement cost) value of the decay of the stock of the fixed asset over the period.

(ii) a term $(p_1 - (1+\pi)p_0)g_0$ is added, reflecting real holding gains or losses on the stock of fixed asset held at the start of the period. There is a real holding gain if $p_1 > (1+\pi)p_0$, so that the buying price of the fixed asset has risen by more than the rate of inflation over the period, and a real holding loss if $p_1 < (1+\pi)p_0$, so that the buying price of the fixed asset has increased by less than the inflation rate. If $p_1 = (1+\pi)p_0$ there is no adjustment as there is neither a real holding gain nor a loss. It should be emphasized that the particular forms taken by both the adjustment for the decay in the stock of the fixed asset and the adjustment for real holding gains or losses on fixed assets in equation 5.19 are a result of the assumption made for this illustration that the value-to-the-owner rules lead to replacement cost valuation at time 0 and time 1. Although it has been argued that the value-to-the-owner base is likely to be replacement cost in most circumstances (Gee and Peasnell (1976)), it cannot be assumed that the value-to-the-owner rules will always result in RC valuations. If the stock of the fixed asset were to be valued at replacement cost at time 0 and at net realizable value at time 1, and the selling price of the fixed asset at time 1 were to be d_1, the adjustment for decay would become

$d_1\delta g_0$—the value of the decay would be given by current sale (NRV) prices—and the real holding gain or loss adjustment would be $(d_1-(1+\pi)p_0)g_0$—there would be a real holding loss if $d_1<(1+\pi)p_0$, and conversely a gain if $d_1>(1+\pi)p_0$.

(iii) a term $(1+\pi)q_0s_0$ is subtracted, reflecting stock appreciation over the period. The caveats mentioned above with respect to the precise form of the adjustment shown in equation 5.19 also apply to the stock appreciation adjustment, but in general there is less scope for PV, RC, and NRV valuations of stocks to differ than is the case with fixed assets.

(iv) a term πm_0 is subtracted, reflecting the real holding loss on net monetary assets held at the start of the period.

(v) a term $(b_1-(1+\pi)b_0)l_0$ is subtracted, reflecting the change over the period in the real value of the firm's liabilities. If $b_1=b_0$, so that the current market price of the firm's bonds is unchanged over the period, this adjustment reduces to the addition of $\pi b_0 l_0$, the gain on borrowing as it is conventionally called. Note that this case of constancy in the market price includes the one where the firm's liabilities are fixed in money terms. But in general this adjustment will take a more complex form because there will be gains or losses due to changes in the market price of bonds as well as the gain resulting from inflationary erosion of the real value of outstanding debt.

The above analysis has shown, by means of a simple algebraic example, how a real accounting rate of return is measured and the adjustments which have to be made in order to arrive at a real terms profit figure using value to the owner as the current valuation base. We must emphasize that the particular valuations used in the example are not to be interpreted as the universally appropriate ones. The purpose of the example was to illustrate the inflation adjustments implied by our version of Real Terms accounting, and to that end it was based on the specific assumption that the value-to-the-owner rules resulted in RC values for the fixed asset and market price valuation for stocks and liabilities.

5.4 Conclusion

In this chapter we have argued in favour of a particular version of a form of inflation accounting which has a distinguished intellectual history—Real Terms accounting. This form of inflation accounting combines a current valuation basis for capital employed with general index adjustment of capital for the effects of inflation. The specific version of RT accounting that we advocate uses value to the owner as the current valuation basis, and also requires all changes in the book value of capital employed between any two dates, reflecting both relative price changes and general inflation, to flow through the profit and loss account for the intervening period. Our reason for advocating this particular version of RT accounting is that it emerges naturally from our discussion in the previous chapter as the appropriate way in which to measure real accounting profitability if the resulting information is to provide economists, investors, regulators, and others with appropriate signals about the performance of activities.

The discussion in this chapter has, together with much of the whole debate on inflation accounting, been conducted at a theoretical level, and it is natural to ask whether the different methods of inflation accounting lead to significant differences in accounting profitability in practice. In the next chapter we turn to an investigation of the quantitative significance of the differences between accounting profitability measures based on CPP, CCA, and RT approaches, which will help to bring out the importance of some of the theoretical points discussed in this chapter.

Notes

1. See Whittington (1983) ch. 6 for a full discussion of these capital maintenance concepts.
2. The conventional interpretation of CPP as applying a general index adjustment to the historical cost base is a rather narrow interpretation of CPP, which can be applied to current value bases, and this is, of course, what RT accounting does. CPP is, however, generally interpreted in this narrow sense.
3. These were the Securities and Exchange Commission in the USA with its ASR190 replacement cost disclosures (announced in 1975); the Mathews Report in the Committee of Inquiry into Inflation and Taxation (1975) in Australia; the Sandilands Report (1975) in the UK; and the Richardson Report (1976) in New Zealand.
4. Baxter suggests that, symmetrically with the idea that the value-to-the-owner rules give the minimum loss that a firm would suffer if deprived of an asset, the value-to-the-owner rules should, when applied to liabilities, give the maximum gain that a firm would receive if it were relieved of the liability.

6

Inflation Accounting II
Alternative Profitability Measures

6.1 Introduction

In this chapter we illustrate the quantitative significance of the differences between CPP, CCA, and RT measures of accounting profitability, firstly by examining the profitability figures that the three approaches produce under various hypothetical situations, and secondly by estimating CPP, CCA, and RT profitability figures for a sample of British companies over the period 1966–81. We also include historic cost (HC) profitability figures in these illustrations in order to compare the various inflation-adjusted measures with what remains the most widely used accounting profit measure. In these illustrations the version of CCA that we use is that introduced in the UK as a statement of standard accounting practice in 1980—SSAP16, Current Cost Accounting—modified by the use of replacement cost as the asset valuation method instead of value to the owner as prescribed in SSAP16. Similarly the version of RT accounting used in the following illustrations is not exactly the one we recommend as it too uses replacement cost rather than value to the owner as the asset valuation base. This substitution of replacement cost for value to the owner as the current valuation basis is made necessary by the fact that we simply do not possess the information to establish asset values on the value-to-the-owner rules. It can be argued that the value-to-the-owner rules will result in the use of replacement cost in many circumstances, so that the RT profitability figures reported below might be justified as a good approximation to the inflation-adjusted accounting profitability measure which we regard as being relevant for economic analysis, but the purpose of the exercise in this chapter is not to produce 'correct' accounting profitability figures—indeed we wish to make clear that the following measures are not to be interpreted in this way—rather it is to *illustrate* the differences between various approaches, and for this purpose it does not matter that replacement cost is used instead of value to the owner as the asset valuation base.

A crucial part in the following illustrations is played by the Institute for Fiscal Studies inflation accounting model, which uses a company's published historic cost accounting data to estimate its inflation-adjusted accounts. This model is described in detail by Mayer (1982) and Meadowcroft (1983). The major practical difficulty in using historic cost information to produce inflation-adjusted accounts arises from the need to estimate the length of life of a firm's capital stock and to have a historical record of past investments over this lifetime in order to revalue depreciation and capital employed from historic cost to current prices. Indeed if, as is highly probable, firms have heterogeneous capital stocks then different life-times and depreciation rates have to be established and appropriate price indices have to be applied to the various components of past investments: the paucity of information on the composition of company investments, however, means that this complication has not been considered, and is another reason why the figures to be reported should only be regarded as illustrative. The average length of life of fixed assets (buildings, plant and machinery, and vehicles) obtained from company accounts and used by the model in its computation of inflation adjustments is seventeen years: this is substantially less than the service times employed by the Central Statistical Office in the determination of National Accounts valuations of capital consumption and replacement cost capital stocks (the average CSO length of life of fixed assets for the entire corporate sector is just under forty years). The reasons for preferring the shorter estimate, and possible explanations for the difference between the two, are discussed in Mayer and Meadowcroft (1984). A number of other technical issues are raised in inflation-adjusting historic cost accounts: takeovers, for example, seriously distort the time profile of a company's gross investment, while revaluations of past investments already included in reported statements threaten to introduce an element of double counting. The way in which the model corrects for these complications is discussed in Meadowcroft (1983); inevitably a number of heroic assumptions have to be made, but the model attempts to incorporate available information in as systematic a fashion as possible.

The inflation accounting model produces estimates of CPP profit and loss statements and balance sheets by applying movements in the Retail Price Index (RPI) to the average of opening and closing stocks and net monetary assets (defined as cash, marketable securities, and net trade debtors less bank overdrafts and loans, long-term liabilities, and dividend, interest and tax liabilities) and revaluing historic cost investments by the RPI to give CPP depreciation and capital employed. Estimates of accounts on a CCA basis are given by revaluing historic cost investments by the plant and machinery and building price deflators implicit in the National Accounts 'Blue Book' capital expenditure figures, weighted together by the investment proportions of the main industry in which the firm in question is operating. This enables current depreciation and capital employed to be stated on a replacement cost basis. The adjustments for stock appreciation (called the 'cost of sales adjustment' in CCA terminology) and monetary working capital are made by applying the Wholesale Price Index (WPI) of materials and fuel and output of manufactured products weighted together by aggregate stock proportions to the average of opening and closing stocks and monetary working capital (defined as cash plus net trade debtors) respectively. The gearing adjustment then abates the other corrections (for depreciation, stock appreciation, and monetary working capital) by the proportion of capital employed which takes the form of debt (essentially all net monetary liabilities that have not been included in monetary working capital). Finally, estimates of RT accounts are produced by making a monetary adjustment which is identical to the CPP correction, a depreciation adjustment which is identical to the CCA correction, revaluing depreciation to current replacement cost, and recording fixed assets on the balance sheet at replacement cost. But the real value of capital which has to be maintained before a profit is recognized is given by applying the increase in the RPI to initial capital at replacement cost, so that RT profit includes real holding gains and losses on fixed assets to the extent that the change in the weighted implicit deflators for plant and machinery and buildings differs from that in the RPI. Similarly stocks are revalued to current replacement cost on the balance sheet, as in CCA, but the stock appreciation adjustment is given by applying the change in the RPI over the accounting year to the average of opening and closing replacement cost stocks.[1] Assets are thus shown at replacement cost but the inflationary erosion of their value is related to the RPI rather than to a specific price index. A feature of these RT accounts that should be noted is that long-term liabilities are treated as having a fixed monetary value: as was made clear in Section 5.3 of the previous chapter, however, we regard the appropriate valuation of such liabilities as being in terms of market prices. Data limitations prevent us adopting this valuation method in the RT estimates presented.

6.2 Simple examples of the differences between various approaches to inflation accounting

In this section we consider the differences between the various methods of accounting in a number of highly simplified examples. We begin with that shown in Table 6.1, the first column of which gives the historic cost accounts of an 'average' quoted firm operating in the first half of the 1970s. It has been derived from the aggregate profit and loss statements and balance sheets shown in *Business Monitor* for the years 1970–4, but has been altered in one fundamental respect for reasons which will become self-evident—dividends have been increased to the full level of profits so that retentions are assumed to be equal to zero. These accounts will be associated with 1972, and it is assumed that there has been no inflation before 1972 and that this company has been in a stationary state, with constant real gross profit, real depreciation, real assets and liabilities, etc., for a long time. In these circumstances the HC accounts correctly measure capital employed, capital expenditure required to maintain the constancy of the physical assets employed, etc.; measured on end-year shareholders' capital and reserves the company earned an impressive real rate of return in 1972 of 4162/19500 = 21.3 per cent.

Now suppose that in 1973 the activities of the firm remain unchanged, but all prices are 10 per cent higher as is the return on all monetary assets and

Table 6.1. Inflation adjustments for a set of accounts for a firm with unchanged real behaviour and a 10 per cent rise in prices between 1972 and 1973

	Accounts (£000)			
	1972	1973 HC	1973 CPP/RT	1973 CCA
Gross income (net of interest and taxes)	5 631	6 403	6 403	6 403
Current depreciation	1 469	1 469	1 469	1 469
Dividends	4 162	4 578	4 578	4 578
Inflation corrections	—	—	−356	−938
Retained profit	0	356	0	−582
Assets				
Trade debtors and cash	13 001	14 301	14 301	14 301
Marketable securities	2 348	2 583	2 583	2 583
Stocks	11 341	12 475	12 475	12 475
Net fixed assets	17 411	17 558†	19 152	19 152
TOTAL ASSETS	44 101	46 917	48 511	48 511
Liabilities				
Trade creditors	11 043	12 147	12 147	12 147
Other liabilities	13 558	14 914	14 914	14 914
Shareholder capital and reserves	19 500	19 856	21 450	21 450††
TOTAL LIABILITIES	44 101	46 917	48 511	48 511
Adjustments to HC profits required by different inflation accounting methods				
Stock appreciation	—	—	1 134	1 134
Depreciation adjustment	—	—	147	147
Monetary loss	—	—	−925	—
Monetary working capital adjustment	—	—	—	196
Gearing adjustment	—	—	—	539
TOTAL INFLATION ADJUSTMENT	—	—	356	938

† This increase of 147 over the 1972 figure reflects the HC provision of 1469 against investment of 1616 which is made to maintain the physical assets employed constant.
†† Including CCA reserves.

liabilities. For simplicity it is assumed that the HC values of all monetary assets and liabilities correspond to the current ones: this can be rationalized by thinking of the firm acquiring a completely new set of such assets and liabilities in 1973. Column 2 of Table 6.1 shows that HC earnings rise in consequence by 18.5 per cent (as the HC depreciation provision is unchanged), so that if real dividends are maintained, the firm reports HC retained profits of £356 000 and

HC shareholders' capital and reserves of £19 856 000—a rise in nominal terms but a fall in real terms. The HC rate of return is 24.8 per cent.

In this example, with just a general rise in prices, there is no difference between CPP and RT accounts, which are shown in column 3 of Table 6.1. The adjustments which have to be made to the HC accounts are as follows: first, fixed assets are revalued to 1973 prices in the balance sheet; second, the HC depreciation provision has to be augmented by £147 000 to reflect the investment of £1 616 000 (=£1 469 000 × 1.1) which is required to maintain the physical assets employed constant; third, a provision of £1 134 000 (=£11 341 000 × 0.1) for stock appreciation has to be subtracted; and fourthly an overall gain on monetary assets (shown as a negative loss in the table) of £925 000 (=£(11 043 000 + 13 558 000 − 13 001 000 − 2 348 000) × 0.1) has to be added. The overall correction reduces CPP/RT profits to £4 578 000 and the rate of return is correctly measured as 21.3 per cent on an unchanged real shareholders' capital of £21 450 000.

Column 4 of Table 6.1 shows the CCA accounts for 1973. The revaluation of fixed assets, stock appreciation adjustment, and depreciation adjustment are the same as for CPP and RT. The differences lie in the monetary working capital adjustment (MWCA) of £196 000 (=£(13 001 000 − 11 043 000) × 0.1) and the gearing adjustment of £539 000 (=£(1 134 000 + 147 000 + 196 000) × ([14 914 − 2 583]/[14 914 − 2 583 + 21 450])) which produce a total CCA monetary adjustment of −£343 000. As a result CCA profits are some 13 per cent lower than CPP/RT ones, at £3 996 000, so that if an unchanged real dividend is paid retentions are −£582 000 thus reducing shareholders' capital (excluding CCA reserves) to £20 868 000 and the CCA rate of return is 3 996/20 868 = 19.1 per cent. CCA profits and profitability differ from the correct CPP/RT figures even in this simple case where there is no history of inflation, merely a step change in prices.

The reason for this discrepancy is simply that the gearing adjustment and the MWCA do not incorporate all monetary adjustments in a systematic fashion. Those items not covered by the MWCA are included in the gearing adjustment but only with reference to the inflation adjustments made elsewhere. In particular, the gearing adjustment is related to the depreciation adjustment which is in turn dependent on a long past history of inflation rates. If inflation has historically been low in relation to its current level then the gearing adjustment will be small on account of the relatively low depreciation correction, and inflation adjusted profits will be understated. This is precisely the situation that is being described in Table 6.1 where inflation was historically zero and suddenly rose to 10 per cent. Similarly if inflation is currently lower than it has been in the recent past then the gearing adjustment will be large due to the relatively large depreciation correction and inflation adjusted profits will be overstated.

We provide a further illustration of this point by assuming that our hypothetical 'average' company's accounts had remained constant in nominal terms at their 1972 level from 1948 onwards and will continue to do so indefinitely subsequent to 1972, while all prices rose at a constant rate of 5 per cent per annum until 1972 and 20 per cent thereafter. The resulting rates of return under HC, CPP/RT (as in the previous example these two methods give the same answer) and CCA are shown in Table 6.2. The HC rate of return is constant at 21.3 per cent throughout, but this is now a nominal return on an undervalued shareholders' equity capital. Following the rise in the inflation rate in 1972 the CPP/RT rate of return falls smoothly to its new steady-state value of −8.5 per cent (column 2 in Table 6.2). But, since the gearing adjustment in CCA is based on depreciation adjustments which depend on inflation over the previous seventeen years (the assumed average length of life of the capital stock), when the increase in inflation occurs the gearing adjustment is in large part determined by the previous 5 per cent inflation rate. Hence the gearing adjustment is understated and CCA profitability lies substantially below CPP/RT profitability immediately after the increase. But as the influence of the 5 per cent inflation rate on the depreciation adjustment fades so too does the discrepancy between CCA and CPP/RT profitability, and the CCA rate of return eventually tends to a steady-state value of −9.1 per cent. The short-run transition of CCA profitability is thus seriously distorted by the gearing adjustment's dependence on past inflation rates, and even in the long-run there remains a small discrepancy which depends on the relationship between the depreciation adjustment and the decline in the real value of physical assets as a consequence of inflation.[2]

Table 6.2. Constant nominal accounts, 5 per cent inflation to 1972, 20 per cent inflation thereafter

	HC (%)	CPP/RT (%)	CCA (%)
1970	21.3	12.9	12.6
1971	21.3	12.9	12.6
1972	21.3	13.0	12.7
1973	21.3	9.3	5.9
1974	21.3	6.8	3.9
1975	21.3	5.0	2.4
1976	21.3	3.4	1.1
1977	21.3	2.0	−0.1
1978	21.3	0.7	−1.1
1979	21.3	−0.5	−2.1
1980	21.3	−1.6	−3.1
1981	21.3	−2.6	−4.0

Note: The slight rise in 1972 for CPP/RT and CCA profitability figures is due to a timing difference between the revaluations of end of year balance sheet entries and mid-year profit and loss items.

While the gearing adjustment is an important reason for the differences between CCA, CPP, and RT profit measures it is not the only one. CCA employs a specific price index in the determination of monetary adjustments while CPP and RT use a general consumer price index. To illustrate the significance of this we return to our original example of constant real accounts and suppose that between 1972 and 1973 there had been a 10 per cent rise in the price of stocks and fixed assets (and the costs of producing them) but that other prices remained unchanged so that these increases were real ones relative to consumer prices. Table 6.3 shows the accounts for this situation under the various approaches. Column 1 gives HC accounts for 1973: there is no change in HC profit but in the balance sheet end-year stocks are valued at £12 475 000 reflecting their higher cost of purchase, while there is also a small increase in the HC value of fixed assets reflecting the difference between the depreciation provision and the cost of maintaining fixed assets employed constant. The HC value of shareholders' capital therefore rises and HC profitability falls to 4 162/20 781 = 20.0 per cent. The expenditure on new capital goods which is needed to maintain fixed assets constant exceeds the HC depreciation provision by £147 000: a correct depreciation charge requires the restatement of the accounts on a RT basis (column 2) with depreciation raised by £147 000 to reflect the 10 per cent increase in the price of capital goods. It is also necessary to allow for the higher cost of replacing stocks with a stock appreciation provision of £1 134 000. But set against these are the real holding gains on the fixed assets and stocks already in the possession of the firm, so that RT profit is £5 756 000. In the balance sheet both stocks and fixed assets are valued at current (1973) prices, so shareholders' capital is £22 375 000 and RT profitability is 5 756/22 375 = 25.7 per cent. It should be noted that the adjustments made to HC accounts to reach RT ones have nothing to do with inflation—they are merely the appropriate responses to the relative price changes. There is no general inflation in this example. As a result the accounts in this example given by CPP, which simply adjusts HC accounts by the movements in a general price index, are identical to the HC ones: CPP fails to take account of the rise in the price of stocks and fixed assets in either the profit and loss account or the balance sheet.

The CCA accounts for this example (column 4 of Table 6.3) are, however, radically different not only from the HC ones but also from the RT accounts. CCA makes the same balance sheet, stock appreciation and depreciation adjustments as RT, but it also makes a MWCA of £196 000 by applying the 10 per cent rise in stock prices to net trade debtors and cash, and it then abates the stock appreciation, depreciation and MWCA corrections by a gearing adjustment of £493 000. The result is that CCA profits are £3 178 000 and CCA profitability is 3 178/22 375 = 14.2 per cent, both substantially below the RT figures.

The reasons for this understatement of profitability by CCA are clear. While it is correctly revaluing fixed assets and the depreciation adjustment to current

Table 6.3. Adjustments for a set of accounts reflecting constant real activities and a 10 per cent rise in the price of stocks and fixed assets between 1972 and 1973

	Accounts (£000)			
	1973 HC	1973 RT	1973 CPP	1973 CCA
Gross income (net of interest and taxes)	5 631	5 631	5 631	5 631
Current depreciation	1 469	1 469	1 469	1 469
Dividends	4 162	4 162	4 162	4 162
Price-change corrections	—	1 594	—	−984
Retained profit	0	1 594	0	−984
Assets				
Trade debtors and cash	13 001	13 001	13 001	13 001
Marketable securities	2 348	2 348	2 348	2 348
Stocks	12 475	12 475	12 475	12 475
Net fixed assets	17 558	19 152	17 558	19 152
TOTAL ASSETS	45 382	46 976	45 382	46 976
Liabilities				
Trade creditors	11 043	11 043	11 043	11 043
Other liabilities	13 558	13 558	13 558	13 558
Shareholder capital and reserves	20 781	22 375	20 781	22 375
TOTAL LIABILITIES	45 382	46 976	45 382	46 976
Price-change adjustments				
Stock appreciation	—	1 134	—	1 134
Depreciation adjustments	—	147	—	147
Monetary working capital adjustment	—	—	—	196
Gearing adjustment	—	—	—	−493
Holding gain on stocks	—	−1 134	—	—
Holding gain on fixed assets	—	−1 741	—	—
TOTAL PRICE-CHANGE ADJUSTMENT	—	−1 594	—	984

cost and adjusting for stock appreciation, CCA is failing to recognize the holding gain on fixed assets and stocks. It is therefore suggesting that a rise in the price of assets under the possession of investors in the firm does not make them better off. This is both counterintuitive and wrong. Capital gains are earnings analogous to the trading profits that the firm is generating, and whilst the gains might be more volatile than normal trading returns this in no way undermines their inclusion in the profit and loss account. It may be appropriate to draw investors' attention to the volatility of earnings in the form of capital gains (or losses) on assets owned by the firm, but it is not appropriate to exclude them.

This confusion, which results from the entity concept of capital maintenance on which CCA is based, also pervades the monetary adjustments. It is quite inappropriate for the MWCA to be based on specific stock prices. Why should £100 cash in the possession of the firm in 1972 be worth £90 in 1973 prices when all that has changed is the price of stocks and fixed assets? Since not many shareholders regularly purchase such goods their prices would appear to be of little relevance in computing the value of cash retained in the firm. Exactly the same objections apply to the gearing adjustment, which attempts to reflect shareholders' gain on borrowing but does so by abating the adjustments for stock appreciation, depreciation, and monetary working capital and hence relates the gain to movements in specific prices. The gain on borrowing in money terms to shareholders as a result of a rise in the price of bulldozers is not easy to discern. In the example of Table 6.3 the error resulting from the gearing adjustment attributing borrowing gains as a result of the rise in the relative price of stocks and fixed assets partially offsets the errors from excluding holding gains and including a loss on monetary working capital due to the relative price increase, but the overall conclusion to be drawn from this example is that CCA creates a great deal of confusion even in the absence of general inflation.

The differences between CCA, CPP, and RT can be illustrated in a different way by computing the annual adjustment to accounts that relative price movements would have created in the absence of general inflation had profit and loss and balance sheet statements remained at their 1972 level in nominal terms from 1948 onwards. This time we have taken the actual relative price changes of stocks and capital goods between 1966 and 1981 but have assumed that there was no underlying inflation so that consumer prices remained constant. Thus, as explained above, there is no CPP correction and CPP rates of return in Table 6.4 (column 2) are identical to the HC return of 21.3 per cent (column 1). In contrast CCA profitability displays some dramatic movements. These are primarily a consequence of changes in stock prices: falls in real stock prices in 1968 and 1970 augmented CCA profitability by introducing negative stock and monetary working capital adjustments, while the commodity price booms of 1973 and 1974, 1976 and 1979[3] significantly diminished CCA rates of return. The restatement of depreciation at replacement cost also affected the CCA figures, but not as appreciably as the stock price movements. Falling real plant and machinery prices over much of the period raised the CCA rate of return but the annual fluctuations are largely a consequence of volatile stock prices. The magnitude of these stock appreciation adjustments alerts us to the importance of including holding gains on stocks and choosing an appropriate price basis for monetary corrections. The RT figures, shown in column 4 of Table 6.4, do just that, and it can be seen that RT profitability in this example

Table 6.4. Constant nominal accounts, no inflation, actual movements in relative prices between 1966 and 1981

	HC (%)	CPP (%)	CCA (%)	RT (%)
1966	21.3	21.3	23.0	21.7
1967	21.3	21.3	22.2	21.8
1968	21.3	21.3	23.2	21.9
1969	21.3	21.3	22.8	21.8
1970	21.3	21.3	23.0	21.7
1971	21.3	21.3	23.7	21.7
1972	21.3	21.3	21.4	21.8
1973	21.3	21.3	15.0	21.8
1974	21.3	21.3	18.0	21.9
1975	21.3	21.3	23.7	21.8
1976	21.3	21.3	19.2	21.7
1977	21.3	21.3	24.4	21.7
1978	21.3	21.3	23.5	21.7
1979	21.3	21.3	21.6	22.1
1980	21.3	21.3	26.6	22.5
1981	21.3	21.3	24.2	22.6

is far more stable from year to year than CCA, while being consistently a little above the HC/CPP figures. The combined effect of revaluing depreciation and stocks used to current costs, together with inclusion of real holding gains and losses on assets and the exclusion of spurious monetary gains or losses resulting from specific price changes, is to produce a profitability figure which does take account of relative price movements but is not highly sensitive to them. In contrast CCA, which includes specific price effects in monetary gains and losses, exaggerates the effects of relative price movements on profitability. Table 6.4 therefore demonstrates that the choice of an index with which to deflate book values and cash flows is of much less significance than a systematic application of inflation corrections.

To summarize, these simple examples have illustrated the ways in which both CPP and CCA differ from RT, which we regard as the appropriate method of inflation accounting. CPP fails to revalue capital goods to current replacement cost and so, in general, produces an inappropriate depreciation figure and does not include real holding gains and losses. The monetary correction under CPP is, however, appropriate (although this conclusion depends on the assumption made in the above examples that liabilities have a value which is fixed in money terms). The two characteristic features of CCA, its financial correction and its use of specific prices in defining the capital to be maintained intact, have been seen to create severe distortions. The combination of the MWCA and the gearing adjustment produce a financial correction which is sensitive to the allocation of items between the two components and to the history of past inflation. Specific prices are inappropriate for measuring the loss on monetary assets and the gain on borrowing while their use in defining capital to be maintained intact eliminates real holding gains on stocks and capital goods which should be included in profit.

6.3 Illustrative inflation adjustments for a sample of UK firms

In this section we use the IFS Inflation Accounting model to calculate estimates of accounts on CPP, CCA, and RT bases over the period 1966–81 from published (HC) accounts for each of a group of 160 firms registered (and primarily operating) in the UK. The resulting profitability estimates should be regarded as no more than illustrative of the differences between the various systems of inflation accounting, not only for the reasons mentioned in Section 6.1, but for several others as well. In particular we had to link together two different sources of published accounting data. In order to produce inflation-adjusted accounts it is necessary to have a long run of annual accounts, because, as has already been discussed, the depreciation adjustment requires investment information for at least seventeen years prior to the year in question. There is only one database in the UK which provides a sufficiently long run of accounting information—the data bank assembled by the Department of Industry (DI) and standardized by the Department of Applied Economics (DAE) at Cambridge University. Unfortunately this database is currently only available to 1977 so that to produce results for more recent years it had to be linked with information provided by Datastream. There are considerable difficulties involved in linking together accounting series from different sources. Definitions, degrees of disaggregation, and methods of standardization vary, and while considerable efforts have been made to ensure as great a degree of consistency as possible, some series are impossible to match. This should be borne in mind when examining the results, which for 1966–75 are based on DI/DAE data and for 1976–81 on Datastream data. It was only possible to find data on 160 companies which had a complete record from 1948 to 1981 and were included on both the DI/DAE and Datastream original data sources. The resulting group of firms for which inflation-adjusted accounts have been estimated spans the main industrial classifications but cannot be regarded as a representative sample of UK industrial and commercial companies in terms of size or industry. Nevertheless, although the sample concentrates on relatively large firms, there is no reason to suppose that the conclusions about the effects of different inflation adjustments are systematically biased as a consequence.

Table 6.5 shows the average (across the 160 firms, weighted by opening shareholders' capital and reserves) estimate of HC, CPP, CCA, and RT annual

Table 6.5. Accounting rates of return 1966–81

Year	HC (%)	CPP (%)	CCA (%)	RT (%)
1966	7.3	4.1	5.0	4.5
1967	9.4	6.4	6.3	7.0
1968	11.5	7.2	8.0	8.0
1969	12.5	7.7	7.8	8.5
1970	12.5	7.1	7.3	7.7
1971	12.6	6.2	6.6	6.6
1972	15.6	8.4	6.1	8.7
1973	17.4	8.2	−2.9	8.2
1974	15.0	3.9	−2.1	4.0
1975	14.3	−0.3	−3.3	−0.1
1976	22.9	6.1	1.1	6.3
1977	20.6	4.4	6.8	4.7
1978	19.9	5.6	5.9	5.9
1979	18.5	3.3	0.2	3.9
1980	13.6	−1.0	0.3	0.1
1981	13.4	−0.3	−0.5	1.3
AVERAGE	14.8	4.8	3.3	5.3

accounting rates of return for the period 1966–81. The rate of return is defined as earnings (after tax, interest, and depreciation) on shareholders' capital and reserves. Earnings include both trading and investment income, and tax is based on stated amounts in company accounts.[4] Shareholders' reserves exclude goodwill. It is no surprise to observe the great difference between HC profitability in column 1 and the three inflation-adjusted profitability estimates in the other columns. One particularly interesting feature of the inflation-adjusted estimates in relation to their HC counterpart is the magnitude of the corrections in 1977 and 1978 when inflation was relatively low following the very high rates of 1974 and 1975. The reason for this is that the depreciation adjustment and revaluation of capital employed depend on the extent to which past investment expenditures have been revalued since acquisition, and so any change in prices will continue to create an adjustment to depreciation and capital employed as long as capital assets purchased before the price change are still being employed. These adjustments will reflect a weighted average of past rates of inflation and so may go on rising even if inflation is falling. Since fixed assets typically have a long service life (our estimate is that the average life of assets is seventeen years) a period of high inflation will involve significant adjustments to depreciation and capital employed for many years after it has passed. The rapid inflation of the late 1970s and early 1980s will continue to create significant inflation adjustments for several years to come, and the implications for the use of HC profitability figures in the latter half of the 1980s, even if the annual rate of inflation fades, are clear.

The other striking feature of Table 6.5 concerns the relations between the CPP, CCA, and RT profitability estimates. CPP and RT rates of return are very similar, with RT profitability being slightly above CPP in every year except 1973 (when the two are equal): this is what would be expected, given the results of Table 6.4, which show that the effect of excluding relative price changes in CPP profitability and including them in RT is, with the actual relative price movements over 1966–81, consistently to raise RT profitability above CPP. But the CCA rate of return diverges sharply from the other two inflation-adjusted ones in some years, particularly 1973, 1974, and 1979. The analysis in the previous section suggests why this might be so. On average CCA profitability lies below CPP and RT profitability, and this is precisely what we would have predicted on the basis of Tables 6.1 and 6.2 in a period in which inflation had substantially increased—the gearing adjustment includes monetary adjustments not covered by the MWCA only with reference to other inflation adjustments, and the relatively small depreciation correction which results when inflation is currently high relative to its historical level means that the gearing adjustment and inflation-adjusted profits are understated. Even if inflation had been constant, the allocation of financial adjustments between the MWCA and the gearing adjustment would have created a CCA average below that of CPP or RT as evidenced by the simulations in Table 6.2. During periods in which stock prices were displaying real rises (1973–6, 1979) CCA profitability falls dramatically below that of CPP and RT—CCA's entity concept of capital maintenance means that holding gains on stocks and fixed assets are not included in profit while the real capital which has to be maintained is based on specific price indices. At other times (1966–71) falling real stock and fixed asset prices result in lower depreciation charges under CCA and this, together with the exclusion of holding losses, raises CCA profitability above that of CPP or RT, outweighing the gearing adjustment understatement.

If we now simulate the effects of a constant 5 per cent inflation rate to 1972 followed by a constant 20 per cent inflation rate thereafter, and a zero inflation rate combined with actual relative price changes on the various profitability measures that would result from the actual accounts of our group of firms, we can confirm that the explanations for the differences between CCA, CPP, and RT suggested by the simple examples of the previous section hold good. Table 6.6 shows the profitability measures which would have resulted from the actual accounts of the 160 firms if inflation had been constant at 5 per cent p.a to 1972 and 20 per cent p.a. thereafter. With no changes in relative prices, CPP and RT profitability are identical. The first point to note is that even when inflation is constant, CCA rates of return are below their CPP/RT counterparts; this is a consequence of the inconsistent treatment of items in the MWCA and gearing adjustment mentioned above. More importantly, once

Table 6.6. Actual accounts, 5 per cent inflation to 1972, 20 per cent inflation from 1973

	HC (%)	CPP/RT (%)	CCA (%)
1966	7.3	2.7	2.4
1967	9.4	4.4	3.9
1968	11.5	5.8	5.6
1969	12.2	6.5	6.1
1970	12.5	6.6	6.2
1971	12.6	6.6	6.2
1972	15.6	8.7	7.9
1973	17.4	6.4	2.5
1974	15.0	2.4	−1.4
1975	14.3	−0.2	−3.2
1976	22.9	4.1	1.4
1977	20.6	1.8	−0.6
1978	19.9	0.8	−1.4
1979	18.5	−0.3	−2.3
1980	13.6	−4.1	−5.9
1981	13.4	−4.7	−6.6

inflation accelerates in 1973, the CPP/RT adjustment appropriately grows gradually, while CCA profitability drops suddenly from 7.9 per cent to 2.5 per cent between 1972 and 1973. The gearing adjustment thus makes CCA much too sensitive to changes in the rate of inflation and produces the tendency for CCA profitability to be below CPP and RT profitability that has been observed during the period of accelerating inflation.

Table 6.7 shows profitability measures for our group of firms on the assumption that there was no inflation over the period 1966–81 but the relative price movements of stocks and capital assets corresponded to the actual price changes over the period. As noted in the previous section CPP is unaffected by specific price changes so that CPP and HC rates of return are identical in this case. CCA and RT are both affected by relative price changes, but in different ways. Falling stock prices raised both CCA and RT profitability above CPP in the late 1960s and early 1970s, but by different amounts. The rapid increase in stock prices in 1973 led to a collapse in the CCA rate of return, but the RT rate of return increased above its 1972 value and was equal to the CPP figure. Rising stock prices also caused CCA profitability to fall below CPP profitability in 1976 and 1979, while RT profitability remained equal to CPP. Overall CCA can be seen to be highly sensitive to stock price movements, with the resulting rate of return being extremely volatile and often moving in the opposite direction to that of the appropriate measure, RT profitability. The failure of CPP to take account of

Table 6.7. Actual accounts, no inflation, actual relative price movements

	HC (%)	CPP (%)	CCA (%)	RT (%)
1966	7.3	7.3	8.5	7.7
1967	9.4	9.4	9.5	10.0
1968	11.5	11.5	13.1	12.2
1969	12.5	12.5	13.0	13.1
1970	12.5	12.5	14.3	13.1
1971	12.6	12.6	14.4	13.0
1972	15.6	15.6	14.2	15.9
1973	17.4	17.4	6.7	17.4
1974	15.0	15.0	12.6	14.7
1975	14.3	14.3	15.1	14.3
1976	22.9	22.9	19.3	22.9
1977	20.6	20.6	24.2	20.8
1978	19.9	19.9	21.1	20.2
1979	18.5	18.5	16.8	18.9
1980	13.6	13.6	16.0	14.6
1981	13.4	13.4	14.2	15.0

relative price changes results in there being some difference between the CPP and RT profitability measures, but these discrepancies are much less significant than those between CCA and RT.

6.4 Conclusion

The purpose of this chapter has been to provide a quantitative illustration of the nature and significance of the differences between HC, CPP, CCA, and RT profitability measures in order to supplement the theoretical arguments in favour of RT that were discussed in the previous chapter. We have seen that HC profitability figures are way in excess of the inflation-adjusted ones, emphasizing what is already well known, that HC accounts fail to record the real performance of companies. What is less well known, but emerges clearly from our analysis, is that despite the fact that inflation has abated substantially in recent years, the required inflation corrections to HC accounts remain important and will continue to do so for the rest of the 1980s, even if inflation falls to zero, as a consequence of the undervaluation of fixed assets and depreciation in HC statements.

The illustrations also show that, in quantitative terms, the most important difference between the three systems of inflation accounting is that between CPP and RT taken together and CCA. Although there are differences between CPP and RT as a result of CPP's use of historic costs rather than current values as its valuation base and its neglect of real holding gains and losses due to relative price changes these rarely produced a difference in average profitability across the 160 firms of more than one percentage point (although for some individual firms, of course, the differences were rather greater). The CCA profitability figures were, however, dramatically different from the CPP and RT ones in some years. One reason for this was the very curious properties of the CCA monetary corrections, with the gearing adjustment introducing a dependence of current corrections on the past history of the inflation rate, and the allocation of items between the MWCA and the gearing adjustment creating a discrepancy even once inflation had settled down to a constant level. Another was the use of a specific stock and fixed asset price index in CCA together with the exclusion of holding gains and losses on assets, which produced distorted profitability figures in certain years, particularly those when real commodity prices moved sharply. Evaluating CPP and CCA as methods of inflation accounting against the standard of RT, which we regard as the appropriate system, it is clear that CPP, although not ideal, is very much more useful than CCA in terms of the profit and profitability figures it produces. Although CCA balance sheet figures may have some value, the CCA profitability figures are at best crude approximations to an appropriate inflation-adjusted measure and at worst thoroughly misleading.

We have stressed throughout this chapter that the profitability measures which have been calculated are only to be regarded as illustrative. One reason for this is that they fail to deal adequately with the complications created by the appropriate treatment of deferred taxation in company accounts. It is to this issue that we turn in the next chapter.

Notes

1. An end-of-year error is introduced to the extent that nominal gains on stock holding from date of accumulation to accounting year end differ between opening and closing stocks. This will, in general, be small but can be avoided by including the net profit on stock holdings associated with revaluing to replacement cost at accounting year end.
2. Define DEP = Depreciation adjustment
   E = Equity capital
   K = Physical capital
   M = Net monetary assets = NTC − D
   NTC = Base of MWCA—essentially net trade credit extended
   D = Net monetary liabilities not included in NTC
   S = Stocks
   Π = Rate of inflation

   such that

$$S+\text{NTC}+K=D+E=E-(M-\text{NTC}) \qquad \text{(i)}$$

The total CCA adjustment is

$$\text{DEP} + \Pi(S + \text{NTC}) - ((\text{DEP} + \Pi(S + \text{NTC}))D)/(D + E)$$

where the last term is the gearing adjustment: from the identity (i) above this is equal to (for $D > 0$)

$$\text{DEP} + \Pi(S + M) - ((\text{DEP} - \Pi K)D)/(D + E).$$

The first three terms here are the depreciation, stock, and monetary adjustments respectively, while the last term is the inflation-rate-dependent distortion.

3. On an end-of-calendar-year basis (which is appropriate for most company accounts) the sharp rise in the cost of goods purchased by industry occurred in 1979.
4. This treatment of tax is another reason not to regard these profitability estimates as anything other than illustrative. The issues involved in recording tax appropriately in accounts are discussed in the next chapter.

7
Taxation and Accounting Profitability

7.1 Introduction

We noted in Chapter 2 that one of the reasons why accounting profits differ from net cash flows is that accountants adjust the net cash flows in an attempt to show profit as it is earned rather than when net cash flows are generated. One such adjustment concerns 'timing differences' between accounting and taxable profits: some items are included in the accounts in a period different from that in which they are dealt with for taxation. The need to provide for deferred taxation in arriving at accounting profits is regarded by many accountants as an integral part of the matching principle, by which all known costs are matched against income in deriving net profits for any period of time. According to this view the tax charge recorded in the accounts should be based on the profit figure stated in the accounts rather than the profit figure which is assessed for taxation, and when these figures differ, as is the case, for example, when the allowable depreciation charge for tax purposes exceeds the related charge in the financial statement, the tax effects of these timing differences must be accounted for as deferred taxation.

The appropriate way of accounting for deferred taxation has been an issue second only to inflation accounting in the degree of controversy which it has generated in the UK over the past decade or so. The purpose of the present chapter is to discuss this issue in the light of the general principles which, we have argued, make accounting profitability data directly relevant for economic analysis. We begin by outlining alternative methods of incorporating taxation into measures of post-tax accounting profits, and explaining the basic issues in accounting for deferred taxation. A brief description of the various proposals for standard accounting practice concerning deferred taxation which have been made in the UK since 1973 is also given. Then we provide a theoretical analysis of the appropriate treatment of deferred taxation in accounting profitability measures which parallels our earlier discussion in Chapters 2, 3, and 4 of the conditions under which such measures are relevant for economic analysis. As perhaps would have been expected, if we have complete accounting profitability data, including tax charges, over the entire lifetime of an activity, then it is possible to calculate the post-tax internal rate of return from the post-tax accounting profitability data so long as the accounting treatment of taxation is such that there is a fully articulated relationship between the tax charge in the profit and loss account and the tax liabilities in the balance sheet. There is thus no reason to prefer one fully articulated method of treating taxation in the accounts to another if one wishes to use accounting profitability data to calculate an activity's post-tax internal rate of return over its lifetime. But in many cases this is not what one is interested in when using accounting profitability data: rather one is trying to judge the performance of an activity over a relatively short segment of its life, and in this case it is no longer possible to be indifferent between various fully articulated methods of treating taxation in the accounts. We argue that the appropriate method of accounting for deferred tax is one which follows naturally when our analysis in Chapter 4 is adapted to take account of taxation. Finally we provide an illustrative calculation of a post-tax accounting profitability measure along these lines for a sample of UK companies which, although subject to certain qualifications, is in principle more satisfactory than other estimates of the profitability of UK industry which have used accounting data.

7.2 Accounting for deferred taxation: an introductory outline

Both the objective of accounting for deferred taxation, which is to match the tax charge in a period to that period's accounting profit, and the differences between alternative methods of doing so can be clearly seen in the following simple example. Suppose that there is an investment project involving the purchase for £100 at the end of period 0 of an asset which generates a positive cash flow of £50 at the end of each of the next four periods. The tax system is such that all positive cash flows are immediately subject to tax, while the asset can be depreciated for tax purposes in equal amounts of £50 in periods 1 and 2. The tax rate is 50 per cent in periods 1 and 2 but rises to 60 per cent in periods 3 and 4. Accounting depreciation is computed on a straight-line basis over the four periods, with £25 being written off in each period.

The top panel of Table 7.1 shows that if only the tax payable in a particular period is charged against the project's pre-tax accounting profits then there is considerable fluctuation in the post-tax accounting profit figure, which is equal to pre-tax accounting profit in periods 1 and 2 but becomes negative in periods 3 and 4. This method of treating taxation in accounts, by which only the tax payable in a period is charged in that period, is known as the 'nil provision' or 'flow through' method, and clearly does not involve the setting up of any deferred tax account.

The aim of accounting for deferred taxation is to reflect the amount by which the tax liability in respect of a particular accounting period's profit has been affected by timing differences. Timing differences between accounting and taxable profits arise because some items are included in financial statements in a period different from that in which they are dealt with for taxation purposes. When a tax saving arises from an 'originating timing difference' it represents a credit which does not correspond with the pre-tax accounting profit figure. For example, when the tax system gives accelerated

Table 7.1. Accounting for deferred tax on an investment project

	Period			
	1	2	3	4
Tax rate	0.5	0.5	0.6	0.6
Net cash flow	50	50	50	50
Accounting depreciation	25	25	25	25
Accounting profit before tax	25	25	25	25
Tax depreciation	50	50	0	0
Taxable profit	0	0	50	50
Tax payable	0	0	30	30
Accounting profit after tax payable	25	25	−5	−5
Originating (+)/reversing (−) timing difference	25	25	−25	−25
Deferral method				
Transfer to or from deferred tax account	12.5	12.5	−12.5	−12.5
Deferred tax balance at start of period	0	12.5	25	12.5
Accounting profit after tax payable and transfer to or from deferred tax account	12.5	12.5	7.5	7.5
Liability method				
Transfer to or from deferred tax account	12.5	12.5	−10	−15
Deferred tax balance at start of period	0	12.5	25	15
Accounting profit after tax payable and transfer to or from deferred tax account	12.5	12.5	5	10

depreciation allowances, the depreciation allowance is not properly matched with an associated expense, as the accounting depreciation charge is smaller than the tax depreciation charge. This is the situation illustrated in the first two columns of Table 7.1: in each of periods 1 and 2 tax depreciation exceeds accounting depreciation by 25, leading to two originating timing differences of this amount. The object of accounting for deferred taxation is to relate the tax charge in the accounts to the pre-tax profit figure stated in the accounts. In order to do this the amount of the tax saving resulting from an originating timing difference should not appear as a benefit of the period in which it was granted, but rather should be carried forward and credited to the profit and loss account (in the form of a reduction in the tax charge) in periods when there are 'reversing timing differences' (for instance, if the accounting depreciation charge exceeds that for tax purposes, as in periods 3 and 4 of the example in Table 7.1). Thus the tax charge against pre-tax accounting profit in a particular period should comprise both the tax actually payable as a result of that period's tax computations and transfers to (when there are originating timing differences) or from (when there are reversing timing differences) a deferred taxation account. These deferred taxation account balances should be shown separately in the balance sheet and not included as part of shareholders' funds.

There are two methods of calculating the deferred tax balances. The deferral method involves the calculation of the tax effect of each timing difference by recording the deferred taxation applicable to originating timing differences at the tax rate then current, and its reversal at the same rate, irrespective of the rate of tax in force in the period of reversal. Hence in the example of Table 7.1 under the deferral method there is a transfer to the deferred tax account of 12.5 (equal to the originating timing difference times the tax rate of 50 per cent) in each of periods 1 and 2, and a transfer from the deferred tax account of the same amount in periods 3 and 4 (when there are reversing timing differences) despite the rise in the tax rate to 60 per cent in these periods. The alternative to this approach is the liability method, which, instead of deferring the taxation effects of current timing differences to the profit and loss accounts of future periods when the timing differences reverse, regards the taxation effects as liabilities for taxes payable in the future subject to adjustment if taxes change in the future. Thus the liability method maintains deferred tax balances as the sum in any one period of a series of timing differences multiplied by the current tax rate, which is regarded as the best estimate of future tax rates. Under the liability method, therefore, there are revisions to the deferred tax balances when the tax rate changes which have to be reflected in the profit and loss account. In the example of Table 7.1, use of the liability method requires a change to the deferred tax balance at the end of period 3 as a result of the rise in the tax rate to 60 per cent. The deferred tax balance at the end of period 3 is 15 (equal to the sum of timing differences to that point (25) times 60 per cent) and as a result the transfer from the deferred tax account in period 3 is only 10.

The example in Table 7.1 relates to a single project in which two originating timing differences in periods 1 and 2 are subsequently offset by two reversing timing differences in periods 3 and 4, and hence does not illustrate an important issue in accounting for deferred taxation. Suppose that the tax system grants accelerated depreciation allowances, and consider a firm with stable or growing investment over time. Such a firm will have a hard core of timing differences as originating timing differences on the firm's more recently acquired assets offset reversing timing differences on its older assets, with the result that some tax is permanently deferred. Since there is little likelihood of a payment of deferred tax arising in such circumstances there are many advocates of the partial provision basis, which accounts for deferred tax only to the extent that it is probable that any tax liability will be temporarily deferred by timing differences which will reverse in the future without being replaced. Under partial provision, therefore, deferred tax is accounted for only in so far as it will actually become payable, and it is calculated on the liability method, as this is consistent with the aim of providing only for the deferred tax which is likely to be payable. In contrast the full provision basis involves establishing each year a balance of deferred tax which will be sufficient to meet the reversal of all originating timing differences irrespective of whether there will be a net reversal. Full provision therefore typically involves a larger deferred tax balance, a smaller value of shareholders' capital, and a higher tax charge in the profit and loss account than partial provision.

The discussion so far has focused on accelerated depreciation for tax purposes as the sole source of timing differences, but there are in fact several possible sources. As well as accelerated depreciation allowances, timing differences may result when the tax system grants stock relief, for which there is no equivalent accounting charge; when there are revaluation surpluses on fixed assets for which a tax charge does not arise until the gain is realized on disposal; when there are taxable losses in one period which can be offset against taxable profits earned in other periods; and when there are short-term timing differences due to the use of a receipts and payments basis for tax purposes and an accruals basis in accounts, which usually reverse in the next accounting period.

In the UK the appropriate treatment of deferred taxation has been a contentious matter in the accountancy profession since 1973 when ED11 'Accounting for Deferred Taxation' was issued. This proposed that there should be full provision for deferred taxation on all material timing differences using the deferral method. It was followed by SSAP11 in 1975 which differed only by giving companies the choice of computing deferred tax using either the deferral or the liability method. There was however, considerable opposition to SSAP11, because balance sheets were regarded as becoming increasingly unrealistic, with provisions being made for deferred tax liabilities which would in many cases never be paid because subsequent originating timing differences would offset the reversal of current ones. In October 1976 the 1 January 1976 starting date was removed from SSAP11 while the ASC undertook a review of it. This led to ED19 in 1977 and SSAP15 in 1978, which required deferred tax to be provided (using the liability method) on all short-term timing differences and all other material timing differences unless it could be demonstrated with reasonable probability that the tax effects of timing differences would continue in the future. This switch to a partial provision basis for deferred taxation in the UK became effective for accounting periods beginning on or after 1 January 1979.

In 1983 a new exposure draft on the subject, ED33, was issued, but its purpose was only to revise SSAP15 rather than to make drastic alterations. Controversy over the appropriate treatment of deferred tax resurfaced following the 1984 Budget in the UK, in which there were major changes to the corporation tax system, involving a phased reduction in both the statutory rate of tax and the capital allowances granted by the tax system (in the case of plant and machinery these allowances were to be reduced from 100 per cent first-year allowances to 25 per cent annual writing down allowances). For many companies this tax reform created the difficulty of calculating future tax liabilities for which deferred tax provisions had not been made under SSAP15. The problem was particularly severe for the clearing banks, for the leasing activities which they had been using to shelter their profits from tax were likely to be significantly curtailed by the reduction in capital allowances. The questions of how much unprovided deferred tax to bring into the accounts, and how this should be presented, led to some criticism of the partial provision basis: more generally it revealed the lack of a clear set of principles on which the appropriate treatment of deferred tax could be based. However the revised SSAP15 which became effective from 1 April 1985 did not involve any substantial changes from the original one.

It is clear from the above discussion that the accounting profession in the UK is by no means agreed as to how deferred tax should be accounted for, and a striking feature of the deferred taxation debate in the UK is that although it has been taking place contemporaneously with the inflation accounting debate the latter debate appears to have exerted no influence on the former. In particular there has been no discussion of whether or how deferred tax balances should be maintained on a current value basis. In the following section we consider deferred taxation in terms of our theoretical discussion in Chapters 2, 3, and 4 in order to see how post-tax accounting profitability measures which will be relevant for economic analysis can be computed, and in so doing we hope to be able to throw some light on the question of what basis there might be for choosing between various alternative methods of accounting for deferred tax. We will return to the controversy following the 1984 corporation tax reform in the UK as an illustration of the issues involved.

7.3 Economically relevant post-tax accounting profitability

We begin by considering the relationship between the post-tax internal rate of return (IRR) and the post-tax accounting rate of profit (ARP) in the case where the available accounting data cover the entire lifetime of the investment. This case is exactly parallel to that discussed in Section 2.4 of Chapter 2, and, as in that section, to simplify the discussion and avoid the need to distinguish between *ex ante* and *ex post* assessment of the investment we assume that there is perfect certainty. In Section 2.4 of Chapter 2 it was shown that, under certain conditions, a number of general results linking the pre-tax IRR and the pre-tax ARP could be derived: in particular an investment's pre-tax IRR could always be obtained from a complete series of the pre-tax ARP and book value of capital employed over the investment's lifetime. It seems reasonable to expect that a similar general result linking the post-tax IRR and ARP should hold under similar conditions, and we shall now show that it does.

The post-tax IRR is defined as that constant one-period discount rate which makes the net present value of the after-tax net cash flows associated with an investment project equal to zero. Throughout this chapter we will use a circumflex over a variable to indicate that it is measured after tax. The post-tax ARP in the period ending at t, $\hat{a}_t$, is defined by

$$\hat{a}_t = \hat{Y}_t/(G_{t-1} - \mathrm{DT}_{t-1}) \tag{7.1}$$

where $\hat{Y}_t$ is post-tax accounting profit in period t, G_{t-1} is the aggregate book value of capital employed, gross of deferred taxes, at the end of period $t-1$ (i.e. at the start of period t), and DT_{t-1} is the deferred tax balance at the end of period $t-1$. The book value of shareholders' capital, V_t, is thus given by

$$V_t = G_t - \mathrm{DT}_t. \tag{7.2}$$

In Chapter 2 we noted that the relationship between the accountant's definition of profit in a period and the change in the book value of capital employed over the period was crucial in establishing general results linking the pre-tax ARP and IRR, and a similar relationship is crucial in the post-tax case. We assume that the following relationship between accounting profit after tax, net cash flow, tax charge, depreciation, overall book value of capital employed, and deferred tax balances always holds:

$$\hat{Y}_t = F_t - K_t - X_t - (\mathrm{DT}_t - \mathrm{DT}_{t-1}) + (G_t - G_{t-1}). \tag{7.3}$$

Here F_t denotes net revenue generated in period t, K_t new capital required in period t, and X_t tax payable in t. Equation 7.3 implies that the depreciation charge in t, D_t, must be such that all changes in the overall book value of capital employed flow through the profit and loss account:

$$D_t = K_t - (G_t - G_{t-1}) \tag{7.4}$$

and the total tax charge in the profit and loss account in period t, TC_t, must be such that any charge different from the amount of tax actually payable in that period must be fully reflected in the change in deferred tax balances over the period:

$$\mathrm{TC}_t = X_t + (\mathrm{DT}_t - \mathrm{DT}_{t-1}). \tag{7.5}$$

To see the implications of equations 7.3–7.5 it is helpful to consider in more detail the relationship in any period between the transfer to or from the deferred tax account, the change in the deferred tax balance, and pre-tax and post-tax accounting profits. Define X_t, the amount of tax payable in period t, as

$$X_t = \tau(F_t - A_t) \tag{7.6}$$

where τ is the tax rate and A_t is depreciation allowances available for tax purposes claimed in period t. Note that A_t denotes allowances actually *claimed* in period t: this means that if the allowances to which a firm is notionally entitled in a particular period exceed its taxable profits—in which case the firm is unable to claim all its allowances and must carry the unclaimed allowances forward until such time as it has sufficient gross profits against which to offset them—then A_t must be interpreted as only the allowances actually claimed in t. The unclaimed allowances are carried forward and, if they are offset for tax purposes in period $t+n$, become part of A_{t+n}. The transfer to or from the deferred tax account in period t is equal to $\mathrm{DT}_t - \mathrm{DT}_{t-1}$, and can be written as

$$\mathrm{DT}_t - \mathrm{DT}_{t-1} = \tau(A_t - D_t) \quad (7.7)$$

where D_t is accounting depreciation in period t as defined in equation 7.4. Substituting equations 7.6 and 7.7 into 7.5 we find that

$$\mathrm{TC}_t = \tau(F_t - D_t) \quad (7.8)$$

so that the total tax charge in the profit and loss account is equal to the tax rate times pre-tax accounting profit, thus making clear the purpose of accounting for deferred tax as being to produce a tax charge which is directly related to pre-tax accounting profit. If equations 7.8 and 7.4 are substituted into 7.3 we see that

$$\hat{Y}_t = (1-\tau)(F_t - D_t) \quad (7.9)$$

so that the relationship which we are requiring to hold in equation 7.3 simply means that post-tax accounting profit is equal to one minus the tax rate times pre-tax accounting profit, where the latter is defined in such a way that all changes in the aggregate book value of capital employed flow through the profit and loss account.

If equation 7.3 holds then the post-tax IRR of an investment project is equal to a weighted average of the post-tax ARPs in the individual periods of the investment's life, with the weights being the book value of shareholders' capital employed discounted at the post-tax IRR. This result means that the post-tax IRR can be found iteratively from the post-tax ARPs and book values of shareholders' capital (net of deferred taxes) over the lifetime of the investment project. The result can be derived very easily along the lines of Franks and Hodges (1983). Suppose that all cash flows occur at the end of accounting periods. The post-tax IRR of a project, $\hat{r}_t$, is defined by the equation

$$-K_0 - X_0 + \frac{F_1 - K_1 - X_1}{(1+\hat{r})} + \frac{F_2 - K_2 - X_2}{(1+\hat{r})^2} + \ldots + \frac{F_n - K_n - X_n}{(1+\hat{r})^n} = 0 \quad (7.10)$$

where it has been assumed that $F_0 = 0$. Substituting equations 7.1 and 7.3 into 7.10, noting that $G_n = \mathrm{DT}_n = 0$ because the project is completed (i.e. generates its final cash flows) in period n, and rearranging gives

$$\sum_{t=1}^{n} \left[\frac{\hat{a}_t (G_{t-1} - \mathrm{DT}_{t-1})}{(1+\hat{r})^t} - \frac{\hat{r}(G_{t-1} - \mathrm{DT}_{t-1})}{(1+\hat{r})^t} \right] = 0$$

so that

$$\hat{r} = \frac{\sum_{t=1}^{n} \frac{\hat{a}_t(G_{t-1} - \mathrm{DT}_{t-1})}{(1+\hat{r})^t}}{\sum_{t=1}^{n} \frac{(G_{t-1} - \mathrm{DT}_{t-1})}{(1+\hat{r})^t}}. \tag{7.11}$$

Table 7.2 illustrates how the post-tax IRR can be calculated from suitably weighted ARPs and book values of shareholders' capital if the relationships in

Table 7.2. Example of calculation of an activity's post-tax IRR from post-tax accounting profitability data

	Period			
	0	1	2	3
New capital (K_t)	100	—	—	—
Net revenue (F_t)	—	48	63.2	69.12
Tax allowance claimed (A_t)	—	48	52	—
Tax paid ($\tau(F_t - A_t)$)	—	0	5.6	34.56
Post-tax net cash flow ($F_t - K_t - \tau(F_t - A_t)$)	−100	48	57.6	34.56
Accounting depreciation (D_t)	—	34	33	33
Originating (+)/reversing (−) timing difference ($A_t - D_t$)	—	14	19	−33
Transfer to deferred tax account ($\tau(A_t - D_t)$)	—	7	9.5	−16.5
Tax charge ($\tau(F_t - A_t) + \tau(A_t - D_t)$)	—	7	15.1	18.06
Pre-tax accounting profit ($F_t - D_t$)	—	14	30.2	36.12
Post-tax accounting profit ($F_t - D_t - \tau(F_t - A_t) - \tau(A_t - D_t)$)	—	7	15.1	18.06
Aggregate book value of capital employed at start of period (G_{t-1})	—	100	66	33
Deferred tax balance at start of period (DT_{t-1})	—	—	7	16.5
Book value of shareholders' capital employed at start of period (V_{t-1})	—	100	59	16.5
Post-tax accounting rate of profit ($\hat{a}_t$)	—	0.07	0.2559	1.0945
$\hat{a}_t(G_{t-1} - \mathrm{DT}_{t-1})/(1+\hat{r})^t$ ($\hat{r}=0.2$)	—	5.833	10.486	10.451
$(G_{t-1} - \mathrm{DT}_{t-1})/(1+\hat{r})^t$ ($\hat{r}=0.2$)	—	83.333	40.972	9.5486

$$\sum_{t=1}^{3} \hat{a}_t(G_{t-1} - \mathrm{DT}_{t-1})/(1+\hat{r})^t = 26.77; \quad \sum_{t=1}^{3} (G_{t-1} - \mathrm{DT}_{t-1})/(1+\hat{r})^t = 133.85$$

$$26.77/133.85 = 0.2$$

equations 7.3–7.5 hold. The activity in this example involves an initial investment of 100 in period 0 and generates net revenues in the following three periods, after which the activity ends. The tax system is assumed to be one in which net revenues are subject to a 50 per cent tax rate, but depreciation allowances for tax purposes are such that the book value of the activity can be written off in two equal amounts in periods 1 and 2, subject to the limitation that allowances claimed in any period cannot exceed net revenue in that period. Hence in period 1 only 48 of the 50 tax depreciation allowance notionally available can be claimed, because net revenue in period 1 is only 48. The remaining 2 is carried forward and claimed in period 2. The post-tax net cash flows of the activity are shown in line 5 of Table 7.2 and are such that the activity's post-tax IRR is 20 per cent.

The accounting profitability figures for this activity are shown in detail in Table 7.2. The activity is depreciated on an (approximately) straight-line basis, so that there are transfers to the deferred tax account in periods 1 and 2 (when tax depreciation exceeds accounting depreciation) and a transfer from it in period 3 (when tax depreciation is less than accounting depreciation). Pre-tax accounting profit in each period is given by net revenue less accounting depreciation, while post-tax accounting profit in each period is given by subtracting a tax charge equal to the sum of tax payable in the period plus (minus) the transfer to (from) the deferred tax account from pre-tax accounting profit. The aggregate book value of capital employed at the beginning of each period is equal to the sum of capital expenditure less accounting depreciation charges up to and including the previous period. The deferred tax balance at the start of each period is given by the sum of transfers to or from the deferred tax account up to and including the previous period. Subtracting the deferred tax balance at the beginning of each period gives the book value of shareholders' capital at the start of the period. The post-tax ARP in any period is given by dividing post-tax accounting profit in that period by the book value of shareholders' capital employed at the beginning of the period. The calculations at the bottom of Table 7.2 show that the post-tax IRR is equal to a weighted average of the post-tax ARPs, with the weights equal to the book value of shareholders' capital discounted at the post-tax IRR, and hence that it is possible to obtain the post-tax IRR iteratively if data for the post-tax ARP and book value of shareholders' capital are available for the entire lifetime for an activity.

The example in Table 7.2 simply illustrates the general point that any method of deferred tax accounting which satisfies equations 7.3–7.5 will produce post-tax accounting profitability data over the lifetime of an activity from which it is possible to obtain the post-tax IRR. In the example there was no change in the tax rate during the activity's lifetime, so the difference between the deferral and the liability methods of accounting for deferred tax does not arise. However if equation 7.5 holds, both methods will permit the post-tax IRR to be obtained: so long as any revision to the size of the deferred tax balances as a result of a change in the tax rate under the liability method passes through the profit and loss account as part of the tax charge, then equation 7.11 applies. It is also the case that the flow-through method of treating taxation in accounts, in which no deferred tax account is created, will produce post-tax accounting profitability data from which the post-tax IRR can be derived. Under this method DT is identically zero in equations 7.3 and 7.5 and the post-tax ARP is measured as $\hat{Y}_t/G_{t-1}$. It is straightforward to check that the argument used above to obtain equation 7.11 continues to apply even when there is no deferred tax account, and also that in the example of Table 7.2 if post-tax accounting profit is measured as pre-tax accounting profit less tax paid in any period the resulting ARP and aggregate book value of capital figures when suitably discounted yield a figure of 0.2.

Thus we can see that, just as in the no-tax case considered in Chapter 2 when interest was focused on depreciation, if we have accounting data for the complete lifetime of an activity the way in which deferred tax is accounted for is essentially irrelevant for the purpose of deducing the post-tax IRR from post-tax accounting profitability figures so long as the basic relationships of equations 7.3–7.5 are satisfied. There may, of course, be reasons other than whether the post-tax IRR can be inferred from the accounting profitability data for preferring one method of accounting for deferred tax to another, but as far as this particular criterion is concerned there is no reason to prefer any one of the deferral, liability or flow-through methods to the other two.

7.4 Valuing deferred taxes over limited periods

The result that the way in which deferred tax is accounted for is essentially irrelevant if one wishes to obtain the post-tax IRR and accounting data for the complete lifetime of an activity are available is not one of great practical value. In many cases the available accounting data will cover only a short segment of an activity's lifetime, and in any case, as we argued in Chapter 3, it is not clear that the post-tax IRR, which is defined as a single number irrespective of the length of life of an activity, can be meaningfully used to evaluate the performance of an activity over a relatively short part of its total life. Evaluation of performance of continuing operations over short segments of their lifetime is, of course, a central purpose of accounting data; in Chapter 3 we argued that the appropriate way to consider the relevance of accounting profitability measures was to ask what economic interpretation could be given to the accounting rate of return (ARR) over a segment of the life of an activity which is computed from the net cash flows during that segment and the accounting values of the capital stock at the beginning and end of it. We showed in Chapter 4 that if the value-to-the-owner conventions were used to value initial and terminal capital stocks the resulting ARR would be directly relevant for economic analysis. We now wish to consider how this general conclusion is affected by the presence of taxation, and in so doing we argue for a particular treatment of deferred taxation as being the appropriate one.

The post-tax accounting rate of return over a segment of an activity's lifetime is defined as that discount rate which makes the discounted value of the net cash flows over the segment plus the discounted book value of shareholders' capital employed at the end of the segment equal to the book value of shareholders' capital employed at the beginning of the segment. In formal terms the post-tax ARR over the segment from period 1 to period T is given by $\hat{\alpha}$ such that

$$G_0 - \mathrm{DT}_0 = \sum_{t=1}^{T} \frac{(F_t - K_t - X_t)}{(1+\hat{\alpha})^t} + \frac{G_T - \mathrm{DT}_T}{(1+\hat{\alpha})^T} \tag{7.12}$$

where G_t, DT_t, F_t, K_t and X_t are as defined above, and all cash flows are assumed to occur at the end of the period. The post-tax ARR over a segment is defined in terms of initial and terminal book values of shareholders' capital and net cash flows, but it can be deduced from accounting data over the segment so long as post-tax accounting profits are related to after-tax net cash flows and changes in both the overall book value of capital employed and the deferred tax balance in the manner of equation 7.3. This can be seen by substituting equations 7.1 and 7.3 into 7.12 and rearranging to give

$$\hat{\alpha} = \frac{\displaystyle\sum_{t=1}^{T} \frac{\hat{a}_t(G_{t-1} - \mathrm{DT}_{t-1})}{(1+\hat{\alpha})^t}}{\displaystyle\sum_{t=1}^{T} \frac{(G_{t-1} - \mathrm{DT}_{t-1})}{(1+\hat{\alpha})^t}} \tag{7.13}$$

so that the post-tax ARR over a segment of an activity's lifetime can be calculated iteratively from the post-tax ARPs and the book value of shareholders' capital employed over the segment.

The computation of the post-tax ARR is illustrated by the numerical example in Table 7.3, which shows a three-period segment in the life of an activity. The book value of shareholders' capital employed at the beginning of this segment is 1 000 and the terminal book value of shareholders' capital is 1 014.8. The tax system in this example differs from that assumed in the previous illustrations in this chapter: it now involves a 50 per cent tax rate on net revenues received with an immediate 100 per cent allowance for capital expenditure, subject to the restriction that if allowances in any period exceed net revenues the excess must be carried forward and claimed in some future period. The post-tax ARR over this segment is 10 per cent, as can be checked from the after-tax net cash flows and initial and terminal book values of shareholders' capital:

$$-1\,000 + \frac{300-80-110}{1.1} + \frac{392-150-121}{(1.1)^2} + \frac{200-100-50+1014.8}{(1.1)^3} = 0$$

Table 7.3. Example of calculation of an activity's post-tax ARR from post-tax accounting profitability data over a segment of its lifetime

	Period		
	1	2	3
Net revenue (F_t)	300	392	200
New capital (K_t)	80	150	100
Tax allowance claimed (A_t)	80	150	100
Tax paid ($\tau(F_t - A_t)$)	110	121	50
Accounting depreciation ($D_t = K_t - (G_t - G_{t-1})$)	100	120	80.4
Transfer to deferred tax account ($\tau(A_t - D_t)$)	−10	15	9.8
Total tax charge ($\tau(F_t - D_t)$)	100	136	59.8
Pre-tax accounting profit ($F_t - D_t$)	200	272	119.6
Post-tax accounting profit ($(1-\tau)(F_t - D_t)$)	100	136	59.8
Aggregate book value of capital employed at start of period (G_{t-1})	2000	1980	2010
Deferred tax balance at start of period (DT_{t-1})	1000	990	1005
Book value of shareholders' capital employed at start of period (V_{t-1})	1000	990	1005
Post-tax accounting rate of profit ($\hat{a}_t$)	0.1	0.1374	0.0595

$$\sum_{t=1}^{3} \hat{a}_t(G_{t-1} - \mathrm{DT}_{t-1})/(1+0.1)^t = 248.234$$

$$\sum_{t=1}^{3} (G_{t-1} - \mathrm{DT}_{t-1})/(1+0.1)^t = 2482.34$$

$$248.234/2482.34 = 0.1$$

and it can be deduced from the post-tax accounting data iteratively using equation 7.13, as is shown by the calculations at the bottom of Table 7.3, which confirm that a suitably weighted average of the individual post-tax ARPs will reveal the post-tax ARR to be 10 per cent.

What valuation conventions for the initial and terminal book value of shareholders' capital employed will enable the post-tax ARR to be given the significance attached to rates of return in economic theory? The discussion in Chapter 4 suggests that the appropriate conventions are the value-to-the-owner rules expressed on a post-tax basis, for it is clear that the analysis of Sections 4.2 and 4.4 of that chapter could be straightforwardly adapted to the case where taxes are involved by interpreting all variables on a post-tax basis. The value-to-the-owner rules on a post-tax basis can be expressed formally as:

$$V_t = \min\left\{\widehat{RC}_t, \widehat{EV}_t\right\} \text{ where } \widehat{EV}_t = \max\left\{\widehat{PV}_t, \widehat{NRV}_t\right\}. \tag{7.14}$$

Here V_t denotes the book value of shareholders' capital in t, $\widehat{RC}_t$ post-tax replacement cost in t, $\widehat{EV}_t$ post-tax economic value in t, $\widehat{PV}_t$ the present value in t (discounted at the after-tax cost of capital $\hat{\rho}$) of subsequent post-tax net cash flows, and $\widehat{NRV}_t$ post-tax net realizable value in t. Under the assumption that $\widehat{RC}_t \geqslant \widehat{NRV}_t$ for all t, the results of Chapter 4 all go through on a post-tax basis. Hence one can say, for instance, that if the *ex post* post-tax ARR calculated on the basis of the post-tax value-to-the-owner conventions is greater than the cost of capital (which in this case is the shareholders' after-tax discount rate) then either expectations were more than fulfilled during the segment over which the post-tax ARR was calculated, or post-tax present value at the start of the segment (based on expectations held at that time) exceeded post-tax replacement cost, providing prima-facie evidence of monopoly power.

The definitions of post-tax present value and post-tax net realizable value are straightforward. Post-tax present value is simply the discounted present value of all subsequent post-tax net cash flows associated with current assets, using the post-tax cost of capital as the discount rate. Post-tax net realizable value is simply the post-tax disposal value of current assets. Disposal of current assets may or may not involve a tax charge: in cases where assets have a tax written-down value of zero (because they have been fully depreciated for tax purposes) any receipt from their sale would attract a tax liability. The definition of post-tax replacement cost is a little more complicated. By replacement cost we mean the cost of acquiring assets which yield services equivalent to those used by the firm at their lowest current price. When the effects of taxation are considered it is necessary to take account of any allowances that the tax system grants on capital expenditures in defining post-tax replacement cost, such as annual writing-down allowances or initial allowances. These tax allowances mean that post-tax replacement cost is less than the cost of purchasing assets which yield equivalent services, but they will not be received until some time after the expenditure required to purchase the assets has been incurred, and hence these tax allowances must be discounted to reflect the cost involved in their receipt being delayed. Consistent with the definition of capitalization described in Chapter 3, the firm's tax liability is defined net of the present value of future allowances to which the acquisition of capital assets creates a legal claim. Post-tax replacement cost is therefore given by the current cost of acquiring assets which yield equivalent services to those currently used by the firm less the tax rate times the present value (discounted at the post-tax cost of capital) of the allowances granted by the tax system on the capital expenditure which would be required to purchase such assets. Note that post-tax replacement cost will depend on when in the future tax allowances can be claimed. This is particularly important when considering firms whose allowances exceed their taxable profits and so are subject to restrictions on the allowances that they can claim. The post-tax replacement cost of assets employed by such a tax-exhausted firm will be higher than that of identical assets employed by a firm which is not tax exhausted, because there will be a greater delay between incurring the expenditure required to purchase the assets and receiving the tax allowances for the former firm than for the latter.

This discussion of the conditions under which the post-tax ARR will be relevant for economic analysis has clear implications for the appropriate method of accounting for deferred taxation. If post-tax accounting profitability data are to provide appropriate signals about the performance of activities to investors and regulators then the deferred tax balance in any period must be such that when it is deducted from the overall book value of capital employed (determined on pre-tax value-to-the-owner conventions) the resulting book value of shareholders' capital employed is given by the value-to-the-owner rules on a post-tax basis. The total tax charge in the profit and loss account in any period is given by the sum of the tax payable and the transfer to or from the deferred tax account, where the latter is such that all changes in deferred tax balances from period to period are fully reflected in the transfer to or from the deferred tax account for that period. Thus we can add to our basic principles developed in Chapter 4 the following ones which relate to the treatment of taxation in the accounts: the deferred tax balance in any period must translate the book value of capital employed from value to the owner before tax to value to the owner after tax, and all changes in the deferred tax balance from period to period must flow through the profit and loss account via the transfer to or from the deferred tax account.

A consistent application of the value-to-the-owner rules on a post-tax basis involves the following procedure being followed. For assets valued at net realizable value any future tax liability incurred in the act of disposing of the assets, for example a balancing charge associated with a difference between net realizable and the tax depreciated value of the asset, should be recorded as a deferred tax liability in the balance sheet. For assets valued at replacement cost the expenditure incurred in replacing the firm's assets with ones that yield equivalent services will be diminished by the present value of the capital allowances that can be claimed on investing in these assets, as mentioned above. The deferred tax balance in this case should correspond to the present value of these allowances and hence show the reduction in the book value of the firm at replacement cost as a result of them. For assets valued at present value in their current operation the deferred tax balance is simply the present value of the expected future taxes associated with the net cash flows generated by the operation of these assets.

Broadly speaking the procedure employed when valuing assets at replacement cost can be described as a full tax provision, since the full discounted present value of allowances that can be claimed as a result of purchasing the assets is debited against replacement cost. Likewise the deferred tax recorded for assets valued at present value can be described as a full provision since no account is taken of returns accruing from future deferments of tax liabilities. Benefits accruing from the acquisition of assets at a future date will only be credited at the date that a legal claim is established. In any event the value-to-the-owner rules restrict the net valuation of an asset to be no greater than its post-tax replacement cost. It is the failure to ensure that this restriction is satisfied which has caused substantial errors and adjustments to have been made in the provision for deferred tax in the UK over the last decade.

It is helpful to illustrate how these conventions would apply in a simple example, which also demonstrates how substantial inaccuracies can result from other forms of deferred tax accounting. We take as our stylized example a bank which is engaging in the leasing of assets to other firms (i.e. is a lessor). We focus only on the leasing aspects of the bank's business, and consider the appropriate treatment of deferred tax around the time of the changes to the UK corporation tax system in 1984.

The example in Table 7.4 shows a case where the bank's leasing activities are in a steady state in the sense that new investment in leased assets is equal to depreciation on the existing stock. It is assumed that the value-to-the-owner rules result in leased assets being valued at replacement cost, which, given an assumption of no inflation, is equal to historic cost, and depreciation is assumed to take place on a straight line basis over four years. The leased assets are all assumed to be plant and machinery, and capital allowances have been computed on the basis of the provisions applying to this type of capital expenditure under the UK corporation tax system. Before 1984 100 per cent initial allowances were available on investment in plant and machinery. From 1984 the UK Government announced that initial allowances would be progressively phased out and investment allowances for plant and machinery would be restricted to annual writing down allowances computed on a declining balance basis. At the same time it was announced that the rate of corporation tax would be progressively reduced from 50 per cent to 35 per cent. The capital allowances and tax rates which have been assumed for the calculations in Table 7.4 are shown in the notes to the table.

The table shows that the effect of the tax changes is to reduce progressively the deferral provisions that the bank should make on a post-tax value-to-the-owner basis (assuming this involves replacement cost valuation). There are two reasons for this. The first is that the replacement of initial allowances by annual writing down allowances delays the date at which allowances can be claimed and hence reduces their present value. The second is that the rate at which allowances can be claimed is falling over the transition period thereby diminishing the value of the allowances. As a consequence of these two factors the balance sheet entry for deferred tax falls steadily, giving rise to a succession of negative entries under the overall tax charge in the profit and loss account.

Table 7.4. Illustration of a lessor's deferred tax provisions

	Investment in leased assets	Book value of leased assets	Deferred tax balance (a) Value-to-owner rules	Deferred tax balance (b) SSAP15 partial provision
1983	100	250	125	0
1984	100	250	104	52
1985	100	250	94	47
1986	100	250	62	31

Transfers to/from deferred tax account

	(a) Value-to-owner rules	(b) SSAP15 partial provision
1983	0	0
1984	−21	52
1985	−10	−5
1986	−32	−16

Notes

(i) Capital allowances have been computed on the basis of the following allowances and tax rates:

Year	Initial allowance (%)	Annual writing down allowance (%)	Corporation tax rate (%)
1983	100	n.a.	50
1984	75	25	45
1985	50	25	40
1986 and thereafter	0	25	35

(ii) The value-to-the-owner rules value the assets at replacement cost.

(iii) In determining the partial provision of the deferred tax it is assumed that the lessor expected to be able to defer liabilities associated with previous capital allowances indefinitely until 1983. From 1984 onwards it is assumed that the lessor anticipates being able to defer 50 per cent of the liabilities associated with past expenditure.

(iv) The present value of writing down allowances has been computed on the basis of an assumed 10 per cent cost of capital throughout.

Let us contrast the treatment of deferred tax under the post-tax value-to-the-owner rules with the following caricature of the procedures that many lessors followed in the UK. Before the tax changes in 1984 many lessors expected that they would be able to defer the subsequent tax liability associated with 100 per cent initial allowances 'for the foreseeable future'. Under SSAP15 they were therefore encouraged to make little or no provision for deferred taxation, and this is reflected in a zero deferred tax balance in the example of Table 7.4. In 1984 many lessors were alerted to the fact that with the reduced capital allowances they might no longer be able to defer tax liabilities indefinitely. As a result 'prudent accounting practice' required them to make at least a partial provision, and for the sake of argument we assume that they were minded to make provision for 50 per cent of the full liability. The balance sheet entry for deferred tax for our lessor in Table 7.4 thus shows a substantial *rise* in 1984 thereby creating an addition to the tax charge in the profit and loss account. In view of the fact that capital allowances were more valuable before 1984 than thereafter and, if anything, leasing activity can be expected to decline as a result of these changes, at least in the long run, an increase in the deferral provision can only be regarded as a rather curious product of a very unsatisfactory set of guidelines.

7.5 Post-tax accounting profitability figures for a sample of UK firms

In Section 6.3 of the previous chapter we gave illustrative inflation-adjusted accounting profitability figures for a sample of 160 UK firms over the period 1966–81. The figures presented there were designed simply to show the quantitative significance of the differences between the various systems of inflation accounting, and for that reason were based on the reported tax figures in company accounts. As will be clear from the discussion in this chapter we do not think that the actual treatment of taxation in UK company accounts has been, or is, appropriate in terms of producing economically meaningful post-tax profitability figures. In this section we therefore present estimates of post-tax accounting profitability for the sample of 160 UK companies which not only make inflation corrections in the Real Terms manner that we advocated in Chapters 5 and 6, but also treat taxation in the way that we have argued to be appropriate in this chapter.

The estimates of post-tax accounting profitability which are given in this section are intended to illustrate the quantitative significance of changing the treatment of taxation from that recorded in company accounts in the UK over the period 1966–81 to the system which we have advocated in this chapter. The procedure that we have used is as follows. For each company the IFS Inflation Accounting Model was used to obtain an estimate of the replacement cost of the firm's capital stock (gross of tax) in each year at constant prices, in the manner described in Section 6.1 of the previous chapter. Apart from taxation the other components of the Real Terms accounts for each firm were estimated in precisely the same way as in Chapter 6. However, recorded deferred tax was eliminated from the balance sheet of each firm, and in its place was substituted a new deferred tax entry obtained by calculating in each year the present value of the tax allowances that a firm would be entitled to if it incurred the capital expenditure required to replace its capital assets and stocks in that year, expressed in constant prices.[1] The book value of shareholders' capital was then obtained by subtracting the new deferred tax balance from the gross of tax replacement cost of the firm's capital stock. Post-tax profits were adjusted by the difference between the addition to deferred tax recorded in company accounts in each year and that computed on a Real Terms basis (in this case replacement cost). Thus the post-tax real accounting rate of return on shareholders' capital for each year was measured as:

$$\frac{\prod_t^{\mathrm{RT}} - (\mathrm{DT}_t - \mathrm{DT}_{t-1}) + (D_t^R - D_{t-1}^R)}{(G_{t-1} - \mathrm{DT}_{t-1})} \tag{7.15}$$

$$= \frac{F_t - D_t - X_t - (\mathrm{DT}_t - \mathrm{DT}_{t-1})}{(G_{t-1} - \mathrm{DT}_{t-1})} \tag{7.16}$$

where $\prod_t^{RT}$ is Real Terms profits in year t after recorded tax, as used in the column 'RT' in Table 6.5, D_t^R is the deferred tax balance in year t recorded in company accounts, DT_t is the deferred tax balance in year t obtained using value-to-the-owner rules and the other variables are as defined above. It is clear that the numerator of equation 7.16 corresponds to the definition of post-tax accounting profit in equation 7.3 (after substituting from equation 7.4) and the denominator corresponds to the post-tax measure of shareholders' capital at the end of the previous period. Equation 7.15 therefore represents the one-year post-tax ARP.

Table 7.5 records our estimates of Real Terms post-tax accounting profitability averaged across our sample of 160 firms (weighted by opening shareholders' capital and reserves). A number of considerations have to be borne in mind when interpreting these estimates. First, in valuing the deferred tax balance as the value of the capital allowances that can be claimed when incurring the expenditure required to replace a firm's assets, it is assumed that capital allowances can be realized in the year in which a claim arises. No account is therefore being taken of the effects of tax-exhaustion. As tax losses were widespread in the latter part of the 1970s and early 1980s (see the Green Paper on Corporation Tax, HMSO (1982)), measured profitability will tend to be understated in certain years.[2] Second, it is assumed throughout this section that an application of the value-to-the-owner rules leads to valuation on a replacement cost basis. In other words, Table 7.5 refers to the case of economic valuation being equal to or in excess of replacement cost for all firms in the sample. It is thus relevant to questions of investment, expansion, and entry, not those of disinvestment, exit, or retention of existing assets. A determination of how value-to-the-owner rules apply to a particular firm at a specific date requires more information than is available from company accounts.

Table 7.5 compares profitability estimates using the tax figures actually recorded in company accounts (as shown in Table 6.5 of the previous chapter) with those computed using post-tax value-to-the-owner principles. Rising interest rates at the end of the 1960s reduce the present value of writing down

Table 7.5. Post-tax accounting rates of return 1966–81

Year	RT with tax computed on value-to-owner principles	RT with tax computed on figures recorded in actual company accounts
1966	6.1	4.5
1967	5.4	7.0
1968	6.1	8.0
1969	12.6	8.5
1970	10.0	7.7
1971	2.3	6.6
1972	5.7	8.7
1973	−7.9	8.2
1974	3.4[a]	4.0
1975	2.1	−0.1
1976	9.4	6.3
1977	14.1	4.7
1978	9.0	5.9
1979	9.8	3.9
1980	3.0	0.1
1981	1.6[a]	1.3
AVERAGE	5.8	5.3

[a] The temporary implementation of a stock relief scheme in the UK between 1974 and 1980 creates a substantial timing effect in 1974 and 1981. This has been excluded from the above estimates.

allowances and raise the book value of shareholders' equity capital and profitability in relation to the figures obtained from unadjusted company accounts. At the beginning of the 1970s, investment incentives became steadily more generous, culminating in the introduction of 100 per cent first year allowances for investment in plant and machinery in 1972. The actual company accounts statements of shareholder capital are thus overstatements of tax-adjusted replacement cost measures, and this measurement error increases in size over the early years of the 1970s. Profitability computed on post-tax value-to-the-owner principles is therefore less than that obtained using stated tax liabilities. The lower profitability figures arising from the use of after-tax replacement cost measures of shareholders' capital are correctly indicating that the changes to investment incentives at the beginning of the 1970s encouraged deferment of capital expenditure to periods in which more generous allowances were available. Of course to the extent that the changes in investment allowances were unanticipated the *ex post* profitability estimates shown in Table 7.5 will differ from the *ex ante* ones and will not provide an accurate indication of the effect of changes in investment incentives on the timing of investment. The negative post-tax profitability estimate for 1973 using post-tax value-to-the-owner rules reflects the impact of the change in the statutory rate of corporation tax from 40 per cent to 52 per cent in this year: in combination with 100 per cent first year allowances this reduces the book value of shareholders' capital significantly and so leads to a large tax charge on profits via a transfer to the deferred tax account. Again this correctly indicates that if the tax change was anticipated then investment just before the change was very unprofitable by comparison with the alternative of deferring investment until after the tax change. After 1973 the value of tax allowances does not change appreciably but higher rates of return are recorded on lower valuations of shareholders' capital where full deferral provisions are made. In some years, tax adjustments result in quite small corrections to profitability but in others (for example 1977) the effects are appreciable. It is clear from the figures in Table 7.5 that evaluations of corporate performance can be sensitive to the rules that are used in accounting for deferred taxation.

7.6 Conclusion

The issue of how to provide for deferred tax in company accounts has been controversial over the past decade, and this chapter has attempted to show that the basic framework for the analysis of accounting profitability which was developed in earlier chapters of the book can provide clear guidance as to the appropriate treatment of deferred tax for the purposes of using post-tax accounting profitability figures in evaluating performance.

In Section 7.2 we explained the basic methods of accounting for deferred tax—the deferral and liability methods, and full and partial provision for such tax—and outlined the history of changes in official pronouncements on the approved form of accounting for deferred taxation in the UK over the 1970s. The major changes to the UK corporation tax system in 1984 highlighted the fact that the treatment of deferred tax in practice was not based on any clear set of principles. A particularly striking feature of the UK debate on deferred taxation was that although it was taking place at the same time as the debate on inflation accounting there was apparently no overlap between these two debates: in particular there was no discussion of whether deferred tax balances should be maintained on a current value basis.

In Section 7.3 of this chapter we applied the analysis of Chapter 2 to the case of an activity for which complete accounting profitability data were available over its entire lifetime, and showed that any method of accounting for deferred tax in which all changes in the deferred tax balance from period to period flow through the profit and loss account for that period will enable the activity's post-tax internal rate of return to be deduced from post-tax accounting profitability data. This might suggest that the question of the appropriate method of accounting for deferred tax is not one of any importance, but of course in most cases accounting data are being used to evaluate an activity's performance over a small part of its entire lifetime, and so the results from the complete lifetime analysis are of limited practical value. Section 7.4 of this chapter shows (following the lines of the analysis in Chapter 4) that if a post-tax accounting rate of return, defined in terms of initial and final book values of shareholders' capital (net of taxes) and intervening cash flows, is to be given the significance attached to rates of return in economic theory then initial and final book values of shareholders' capital must be measured in terms of the value-to-the-owner conventions on a post-tax basis. It follows from this that the deferred tax balance in any period is that amount which must be subtracted from the overall book value of capital (gross of taxes), which is found by applying the value-to-the-owner rules on a pre-tax basis, to give the book value of capital (net of taxes), which is obtained using the value-to-the-owner rules on a post-tax basis. This gives clear guidance as to how the deferred tax balance is to be computed on a current value basis: for assets with a book value of shareholders' capital given by post-tax replacement cost the deferred tax balance is given by the present value of the tax allowances that could be claimed if a company were to replace its assets by purchasing ones which yielded an equivalent service; for assets with a book value given by post-tax present value the deferred tax balance is the present value of expected future taxes associated with the net cash flows generated by the assets; and for assets with book value equal to post-tax net realizable value the deferred tax balance is given by the tax liability that would be involved in disposing of the assets.

If these principles are followed, and all changes in the deferred tax balances pass through the profit and loss account, post-tax accounting profitability figures can be given a meaningful economic interpretation. A simple example is given at the end of Section 7.4 to illustrate the difference between the treatment of deferred tax that was actually adopted by lessors in the UK following the 1984 corporation tax changes and the one which would be appropriate on the basis of post-tax value-to-the-owner conventions. In Section 7.5 we present estimates of post-tax Real Terms accounting profitability figures using post-tax value-to-the-owner rules for a sample of UK companies and contrast them with the corresponding figures obtained using the actual deferred tax entries in company accounts, which illustrate the qualitative significance of different treatments of deferred tax, and the importance of getting the treatment right if post-tax accounting profitability data are to be used for performance evaluation.

Notes

1. Statutory rates of initial and writing down allowances applicable in each year were used. The present value of writing down allowances was computed using the interest rate on 20 year government stock in the year of the investment as the discount rate.
2. For a description of how tax losses affect profitability measures see Mayer and Meadowcroft (1984).

8

Conclusion and Summary of Proposals

A LONG, complex, and at times acrimonious debate involving academics and practitioners in a range of disciplines has failed to resolve the question of the appropriate formulation of company accounts for measuring profitability, or indeed whether they should be formulated for this purpose at all. Such is the state of confusion that many have withdrawn from the debate claiming either that theoretical objections are irresolvable or that proposed solutions are impractical. The reluctance now of academics or regulators to employ accounting profitability data in economic analysis is a reflection of the former; the recent failure by the accounting profession in the UK to ratify widespread implementation of current cost accounting is an example of the latter. Instead, academics turn to other sources of information to evaluate performance, in particular market-based ones, and accountants return to former practices, hoping that previous problems will not re-emerge.

All of this is clearly very unsatisfactory and costly in terms of the quality of information provided and the purposes for which it is being applied. The object of this book has been to argue that the confusion and disillusionment are the result of a failure to specify sufficiently precisely the terms within which the debate is to be conducted. In particular a quite striking implication of this analysis is that much past discussion has failed to address the fundamental issue of the purpose for which accounts are being constructed.

To the extent that there has been any consideration of the objectives of accounting statements by economists it has usually been assumed that they are an attempt to approximate the Hicksian definition of profit. We argued in the introduction and elsewhere in the book that while the Hicksian concept is precisely appropriate for measurements of income, and possibly corporate distributions, it does not establish an appropriate basis for defining profit. Instead of wishing to be informed of what level of distributions can be maintained, the analyst of company performance is usually concerned about earnings in relation to what would have accrued in alternative activities.

Several examples of this have been provided throughout the text. The *ex ante* discussion considered questions of investment and disinvestment. The *ex post* sections referred to measurements of barriers to entry and exit and evidence of superior or inferior managerial performance. In each case performance is measured in relation to questions of the form what would have happened or will happen if the firm had done or does do something differently or if it did not have access to the resources which were actually at its disposal.

These counterfactuals or alternatives then define precisely the appropriate valuation bases for opening and closing stocks. As described at length they provide a persuasive justification for the application of replacement cost, present value, and net realizable value measurements of capital using the rules that are summarized below.

All of this is, of course, familiar and we are not arguing either that we have discovered a new measure of profit or that the accounting rules suggested are anything other than widely advocated. Instead, what the book has attempted to do is to marry the two and establish from basic principles the appropriate basis of accounting profitability measures. In the process, fortuitously or otherwise, we believe that a strong case has emerged for a particular set of accounting conventions. The conventions that have been suggested in the course of this book are summarized in the following section.

8.1 Summary of proposals

1. Value-to-the-owner rules should form the basis of the valuation of a company's assets and liabilities. These stipulate that if the replacement cost of the firm's assets exceeds their net realizable value on disposal then the assets of the firm should be valued at:

(i) net realizable value if the value of the firm's assets in their current use falls short of their net realizable value on disposal
(ii) replacement cost if their value in current use exceeds the cost of replacing the firm's assets with assets that generate an equivalent stream of services
(iii) present value of future earnings if the value of the firm's assets in their current use lies between net realizable value and replacement cost.

2. Value-to-the-owner rules can be applied to any economically meaningful set of assets—a firm, subsidiary, plant, industry, or economy, or to a single investment. When undertaking an *ex ante* investment appraisal, the rules should be applied to the group of assets as a whole, i.e. value the group at one of replacement cost, present value, or net realizable value. This reflects the fact that purchase or, in the case of disinvestment, disposal of the group is being evaluated. In an *ex post* assessment of performance, replication of the firm may involve the employment of existing assets. The value-to-the-owner rules should therefore be applied to the individual asset and then summed. In practice, accounts are constructed on an *ex post* basis and the latter conventions are the ones that are relevant to published statements.

3. All changes in book values including those resulting from holding gains and losses (whether realized or unrealized) should have corresponding entries in the profit and loss statement. The statement could perfectly justifiably distinguish between realized and unrealized gains or between exceptional and normal losses and gains and valuable information might thereby be conveyed.

But profit and loss statements are only economically meaningful if they correspond to changes in book values.

4. These valuation principles continue to apply during periods of inflation. Profit figures calculated on the basis of value-to-the-owner rules will always provide appropriate nominal measures. Inflation-adjusted profits can then be derived by merely subtracting the rate of inflation of a *general* price index (i.e. the retail price index, consumer price index, or ideally an index reflecting the basket of goods consumed by shareholders) multiplied by the net worth of the firm from nominal profit. This is described as Real Terms accounting. No further inflation adjustment is required.

5. Deferred taxation should be provided for on the same value-to-the-owner basis. Thus if the relevant asset is valued at replacement cost then deferred taxation is equal to the allowances (first year and the present value of subsequent depreciation allowances) that could be claimed on replacing the asset with one that yielded an equivalent stream of services. If the asset is valued on a disposal basis then deferred taxation should be recorded as the balancing charge that is due (if any) on the immediate disposal of the asset. If the asset is valued at its current operating value (gross of future taxes) then deferred taxation is equal to the present value of future taxes associated with the return on the assets.

6. Assets and liabilities should be capitalized in the balance sheet if activities to the date in question give rise to a future legal claim by or on the firm. Thus, for example, a contingent liability is a legal claim which, although of uncertain future amount, does have an associated present value, replacement cost and current termination value. It should therefore be capitalized at one of these valuations. Likewise, research and development should not be capitalized at less than the economic valuation of the activities undertaken to date but at no more than the current cost of replicating these activities.

7. Goodwill is valued according to the same principles. Where the cost of reproducing a firm's reputation is high in relation to economic value then goodwill will be valued at economic value. Where advertising, guarantees, or production techniques can be used to establish an equivalent reputation at lower cost than the associated economic value, then inclusion at replacement cost is appropriate.

These proposals are shown in tabular form in Table 8.1.

8.2 Implications of proposals

If these proposals are implemented then accounts will provide information that is of value to investors, managers, regulators, and economists.

Accounts that are constructed on an *ex ante* basis (i.e. are forward looking and based on expectations) will convey the following signals:

Table 8.1. Summary of proposals

A. VALUATION BASIS

	Asset	*Tax Liability*
(i) Present value net of taxes $>$ replacement cost less investment allowances	Replacement cost	First year allowances plus present value of future depreciation allowances
(ii) Present value net of taxes $<$ net realizable value net of balancing charge on disposal	Net realizable value	Balancing charge on disposal
(iii) Present value net of taxes between replacement cost and net realizable value	Present value of future earnings	Present value of future taxes

B. PROFIT AND LOSS STATEMENT

Nominal profit = Change in assets less change in liabilities
Real profit = Nominal profit less rate of inflation times net worth

C. ACCOUNTING RATE OF PROFIT

$$\text{The accounting rate of profit} = \frac{\text{Real profit}}{\text{Net worth}}$$

(i) an accounting rate of profit in excess of the cost of capital implies that new investment is profitable;
(ii) an accounting rate of profit equal to the cost of capital implies that the starting of a new activity is not profitable but existing activities should be continued;
(iii) if valuations are made on net realizable value basis then an accounting rate of profit less than the cost of capital implies that an existing activity should be curtailed.

Accounts that are constructed on an *ex post* basis (i.e. using actual out-turn data) convey the following signals, provided that expectations were fulfilled over the period in question:

(i) an accounting rate of profit in excess of the cost of capital is prima-facie evidence of a barrier to entry at the beginning of the period;
(ii) an accounting rate of profit less than the cost of capital is prima-facie evidence of a barrier to exit at the beginning of the period, provided that the closing assets are valued at economic value.

Persistence of abnormally high or low rates of return suggests barriers to entry or exit rather than unfulfilled expectations. Further indications of whether expectations were fulfilled may be available from valuations at market prices. Exceptional performance can be attributed to managerial skills if abnormal returns still persist when valuations are made on the basis of opportunities available to competitors. Furthermore, the principles of capitalization described above permit performance to be associated with activities undertaken in the relevant period. Thus legal claims created by past activities will already have been capitalized and included in a previous period's performance. On the other hand, in contrast to market valuations, anticipated but as yet unrealized claims will not be recorded until they are established.

We have noted that estimates of rates of profit are sensitive to the conventions that are employed. In particular we observed that the application of inappropriate price indices in inflation adjustments or valuations on bases other than the value-to-the-owner rules could result in seriously misleading rates of profit estimates. Neither of the two commonly advocated accounting systems, Current Cost accounting (CCA) and Constant Purchasing Power (CPP), accurately reflect rates of profit derived from value-to-the-owner and Real Terms accounting. CPP does not apply the value-to-the-owner rules consistently (at least not as it is commonly interpreted) and CCA uses inappropriate price indices and fails to ensure that all balance sheet changes are passed through the profit and loss statement. As implemented in the UK, CCA is also seriously distorted by the gearing adjustment which gives it a spurious dependence on past as well as current inflation rates. The importance of the correct application of Real Terms accounting is not merely restricted to periods of high inflation.

We saw that balance sheet valuations were sensitive to the manner in which deferred taxation was computed. For example, a lessor should not record the net value of a leased asset as being greater than the replacement cost of the asset less the capital allowances (first year and present value of depreciation allowances) associated with replacement. In other words the net value cannot be greater than that resulting from a full provision for deferred taxation on a replacement cost basis. If this convention had been followed in the late 1970s and early 1980s the major lessors would have recorded a very much lower net worth and would not have been required to make substantial deferred tax adjustments in 1984 when there was a fundamental revision to corporation tax in the UK.

References

Accounting Standards Committee (1977). *ED19 Accounting for Deferred Taxation.* London: ASC.

—— (1978). *Statement of Standard Accounting Practice No. 15, Accounting for Deferred Taxation (SSAP15).* London: ASC.

—— (1980). *Statement of Standard Accounting Practice No. 16, Current Cost Accounting (SSAP16).* London: ASC.

—— (1983). *ED33 Accounting for Deferred Tax.* London: ASC.

—— (1984). *ED35 Accounting for the Effects of Changing Prices.* London: ASC.

Accounting Standards Steering Committee (1973). *ED11 Accounting for Deferred Taxation.* London: ASSC.

—— (1975). *Statement of Standard Accounting Practice No. 11, Accounting for Deferred Taxation (SSAP11).* London: ASSC.

Baxter, W. T. (1967). 'Accounting values: sale price versus replacement cost', *Journal of Accounting Research* **5,** 208–14.

—— (1971). *Depreciation.* London: Sweet and Maxwell.

—— (1975). *Accounting Values and Inflation.* New York: McGraw-Hill.

Beaver, W. (1981). *Financial Reporting: An Accounting Revolution.* Englewood Cliffs: Prentice-Hall.

Bonbright, J. C. (1937). *Valuation of Property* (2 volumes). New York: McGraw-Hill.

Brealey, R. A., and Myers, S. C. (1981). *Principles of Corporate Finance.* New York: McGraw-Hill.

Bromwich, M. (1977). 'The use of present value valuation models in published accounting reports', *The Accounting Review* **52,** 587–96.

Canadian Institute of Chartered Accountants (1979). *Exposure Draft: Current Cost Accounting.*

—— (1982). *Reporting the Effects of Changing Prices.*

Canning, J. B. (1929). *The Economics of Accountancy: A Critical Analysis of Accounting Theory.* New York: Ronald Press.

CCAB (1975). *Initial Reactions to the Report of the Inflation Accounting Committee.* London: Accounting Standards Committee.

Chambers, R. J. (1966). *Accounting, Evaluation and Economic Behaviour.* Englewood Cliffs: Prentice-Hall.

Committee of Inquiry into Inflation and Taxation (1975). *Report: Inflation and Taxation* (The Mathews Report). Canberra: Australian Government Publishing Service.

ED11, see Accounting Standards Steering Committee (1973).

ED19, see Accounting Standards Committee (1977).

ED33, see Accounting Standards Committee (1983).

ED35, see Accounting Standards Committee (1984).

Edey, H. C. (1974). 'Deprival value and financial accounting' in H. C. Edey and B. S. Yamey (eds.), *Debits, Credits, Finance and Profits.* London: Sweet and Maxwell.

Edwards, E. O., and Bell, P. W. (1961). *The Theory and Measurement of Business Income*. University of California Press.

—— and Johnson, L. T. (1979). *Accounting for Economic Events*. Houston: Scholars Book Co.

Fairburn, J. (1985). 'Statutory monopolies and market power', unpublished paper, Institute for Fiscal Studies.

Fama, E. F. (1970). Efficient capital markets: a review of theory and empirical work', *Journal of Finance* **25,** 383–417.

—— (1972). 'Components of investment performance', *Journal of Finance* **27,** 557–68.

—— and Miller, M. H. (1972). *The Theory of Finance*. New York: Holt, Rinehart and Winston.

FASB (1978). *Proposed Statement of Financial Accounting Standards: Financial Reporting and Changing Prices*. Stamford: Financial Accounting Standards Board.

—— (1979). *Statement of Financial Accounting Standards No. 33 (FAS33): Financial Reporting and Changing Prices*. Stamford: Financial Accounting Standards Board.

Feldstein, M. S., and Summers, L. H. (1977). 'Is the rate of profit falling?', *Brookings Papers on Economic Activity*, No. 1, 211–28.

Fisher, F. M., and McGowan, J. J. (1983). 'On the misuse of accounting rates of return to infer monopoly profits', *American Economic Review* **73,** 82–97.

Flemming, J. S., and Wright, J. F. (1971). 'Uniqueness of the internal rate of return: a generalisation', *Economic Journal* **81,** 256–63.

Flemming, J. S., Price, L. D. D., and Ingram, D. H. A. (1976). 'Trends in company profitability', *Bank of England Quarterly Bulletin* **16,** 36–52.

Franks, J. R., and Hodges, S. D. (1983). 'The meaning of accounting numbers in target setting and performance measurement: implications for managers and regulators', unpublished paper, London Business School.

Gee, K. and Peasnell, K. V. (1976). 'A pragmatic defence of replacement cost', *Accounting and Business Research* **6,** 242–9.

Gibbs, M. (1976). 'A better answer to the problem of inflation accounting', *The Times*, 23 February 1976.

Gibbs, M., and Seward, W. (1979). *ED24—Morpeth's New Proposals*. London: Phillips and Drew.

Godley, W., and Cripps, T. F. (1975). 'Profits, stock appreciation and the Sandilands report', *The Times*, 1 October 1975.

Grossman, S. J., and Stiglitz, J. E. (1980). 'On the impossibility of informationally efficient markets', *American Economic Review* **70,** 393–408.

Harcourt, G. C. (1965). 'The accountant in a golden age', *Oxford Economic Papers* **17,** 66–80.

Hay, D. A., and Morris, D. J. (1979). *Industrial Economics: Theory and Evidence*. Oxford: Oxford University Press.

Hicks, J. R. (1946). *Value and Capital*. Oxford: Clarendon Press.

Hill, T. P. (1979). *Profits and Rates of Return*. Paris: Organisation for Economic Co-operation and Development.

Hirshleifer, J. (1958). 'On the theory of optimal investment decision', *Journal of Political Economy* **56,** 329–52.

HMSO (1982). *Corporation Tax*. Cmnd 8456. London: Her Majesty's Stationery Office.

Holland, D. M., and Myers, S. C. (1979). 'Trends in corporate profitability and capital costs' in R. Lindsay (ed), *The Nation's Capital Needs: Three Studies*. New York: Committee for Economic Development.

Hotelling, H. (1925). 'A general mathematical theory of depreciation', *Journal of the American Statistical Association* **20,** 340–53.

Institute of Chartered Accountants in Australia and Australian Society of Accountants (1976). *Provisional Accounting Standard: Current Cost Accounting*.

—— (1983). *Statement of Accounting Practice No. 1 (SAP1)*.

Kay, J. A. (1976). 'Accountants, too, could be happy in a golden age', *Oxford Economic Papers* **17,** 66–80.

—— (1977). 'Inflation accounting—a review article', *Economic Journal* **87,** 300–11.

—— and Mayer, C. P. (1986). 'On the application of accounting rates of return', *Economic Journal* **96,** 199–207.

Kennedy, C. (1978). 'Inflation accounting: retrospect and prospect', *Cambridge Economic Policy Review* **4,** 58–64.

Lindenberg, E., and Ross, S. (1981). 'Tobin's q ratio and industrial organisation', *Journal of Business* **54,** 1–32.

Livingstone, J. R., and Salamon, G. L. (1970). 'Relationship between the accounting and the internal rate of return measure: a synthesis and an analysis', *Journal of Accounting Research* **8,** 199–216.

Mayer, C. P. (1982). 'A program for inflation adjusting published accounts', *Institute for Fiscal Studies Working Paper No. 31*.

—— and Meadowcroft, S. (1984). 'Equity rates of return in the U.K.—evidence from panel data', *Recherches Economiques de Louvain* **50,** 363–98; and in D. Weiserbs (ed.), *Industrial Investment in Europe: Economic Theory and Measurement*, Martinus Nijhoff, 1985.

Meadowcroft, S. (1983). 'A program for inflation adjusting published company accounts: an interim report', unpublished paper, Institute for Fiscal Studies.

New Zealand Society of Accountants (1981). *Exposure Draft: Current Cost Accounting*.

—— (1982). *Current Cost Accounting Standard No. 1: Information Reflecting the Effects of Changing Prices*.

Parker, R. H., and Harcourt, G. C. (1969). *Readings in the Concept and Measurement of Income*. Cambridge: Cambridge University Press.

Peasnell, K. V. (1977). 'A note on the discounted present value concept', *The Accounting Review* **52,** 186–9.

—— (1982). 'Some formal connections between economic values and yields and accounting numbers', *Journal of Business Finance and Accounting* **9,** 361–81.

Richardson Committee Report (1976). *The Report of the Committee of Inquiry into Inflation Accounting*. Wellington: New Zealand Government Printer.

Salinger, M. A. (1984). 'Tobin's q, unionization, and the concentration-profits relationship', *The Rand Journal of Economics* **15,** 159–70.

Sandilands Committee (1975). *Inflation Accounting: Report of the Inflation Accounting Committee under the Chairmanship of F. E. P. Sandilands*. London: HMSO (Cmnd 6225).

Scott, M. F. G. (1976). *Some Economic Principles of Accounting: a Constructive Critique of the Sandilands Report*. London: Institute for Fiscal Studies (IFS Lecture Series No. 7).

SEC (1976). *Accounting Series Release No. 190 (ASR190), Amendments to Regulations S-X Requiring Certain Replacement Cost Data*. Washington: SEC.

Smirlock, M., Gilligan, T., and Marshall, W. (1984). 'Tobin's q and the structure-performance relationship', *American Economic Review* **74,** 1051–60.

Solomon, E. (1966). 'Return on investment: the relation of book yields to true value' in R. K. Jaedicke, Y. Ijiri, and O. Nielsen (eds.), *Research in Accounting Measurement*, American Accounting Association.

—— (1970). 'Alternative rate of return concepts and their implications for utility regulation', *Bell Journal of Economics and Management Science* **1,** 65–81.

Solomons, D. (1966). 'Economic and accounting concepts of cost and value' in M. Backer (ed.), *Modern Accounting Theory*. Englewood Cliffs, Prentice-Hall.

SSAP11, see Accounting Standards Steering Committee (1975).

SSAP15, see Accounting Standards Committee (1978).

SSAP16, see Accounting Standards Committee (1980).

Stamp, E. (1971). 'Income and value determination and changing price levels: an essay towards a theory', *The Accountant's Magazine*, 277–92.

Stauffer, T. R. (1971). 'The measurement of corporate rates of return: a generalised formulation', *Bell Journal of Economics and Management Science* **2,** 434–69.

Sweeney, H. W. (1936). *Stabilized Accounting*. New York: Harper.

Treynor, J. L. (1972). 'The trouble with earnings', *Financial Analysts' Journal* **28,** 41–3.

Turvey, R. (1971). *Economic Analysis and Public Enterprise*. London: George Allen and Unwin.

Tweedie, D., and Whittington, G. (1984). *The Debate on Inflation Accounting*. Cambridge: Cambridge University Press.

Whittington, G. (1983). *Inflation Accounting: An Introduction to the Debate*. Cambridge: Cambridge University Press.

Williams, N. P. (1981). 'Influences on the profitability of twenty-two industrial sectors', Bank of England Discussion Paper No. 5.

Wright, F. K. (1964). 'Towards a general theory of depreciation', *Journal of Accounting Research* **2,** 80–90.

—— (1970). 'A theory of financial accounting', *Journal of Business Finance* **2,** 57–69.

—— (1978). 'Accounting rate of profit and internal rate of return', *Oxford Economic Papers* **30,** 464–8.

Index

CREATE YOUR OWN STAGE FACES

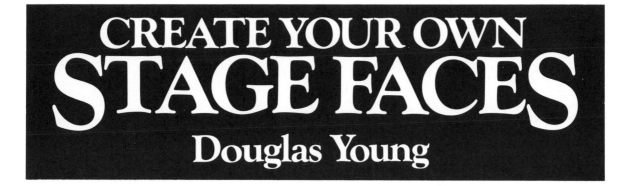

CREATE YOUR OWN STAGE FACES

Douglas Young

Bell & Hyman

First published 1985
Bell & Hyman Limited
Denmark House
37-39 Queen Elizabeth Street
London SE1 2QB

Published simultaneously in the USA
by Prentice-Hall, Inc.

British Library Cataloguing in Publication Data
Young, Douglas
Create your own stage faces
1. Make-up, Theatrical
I. Title
792'. 027 PN2068

ISBN 0-7135-2570-3

Create Your Own Stage Faces was conceived, edited, and designed by
Thames Head Limited,
Avening, Tetbury,
Gloucestershire,
Great Britain

Editorial and Marketing director
Martin Marix Evans

Design and Production director
David Playne

Art editor
Tony De Saulles

Editor
Gill Davies

Picture research
Jacquie Govier

Designers and illustrators
Heather Church
Jacquie Govier
Terry Thomas
Phil Evans
Nick Allen
Tracey Arnold
Nick Hand

Typesetting by
Optic, London

Reproduction by
Redsend Limited, Birmingham

Printed in Great Britain by
Purnell & Sons (Book Production) Limited, Paulton

Contents

Introducing a world of make-believe

The theater is a world of make-believe; a world in which everyone concerned — the author, director, set builder, costume designer, lighting engineer, property supervisor and so on — all do their best to make the audience believe that what they see is real.

The last link in this chain of experts is the actor, who has to make the audience believe in the character being portrayed. To do this, actors learn how to walk, talk and think like the character, dress like the character and finally, to look like the character. The actor will do this by creating a Stage Face with the aid of makeup.

Makeup has been used for the portrayal of characters in the theater from the earliest times, but in Roman and ancient Greek drama, much more reliance was placed on the use of masks. Each mask had its own shape and color to denote the character or emotion being depicted — the most well known of these are the masks of Comedy and Tragedy, which still symbolize the theater today.

Masks were also widely used through the Middle Ages, particularly for the performance of the miracle plays, and it was not until Elizabethan times that the actor was liberated from the mask and was able to use real facial expressions to convey feeling and character.

To emphasize these characters, powder and paint were used to create a mobile mask over the features. These paints were extremely crude, consisting of crushed earth colors and vegetable dyes mixed with animal fats or perfumed oils. Performers who had little money often smeared their faces with the fat from a piece of ham rind before applying brick dust or other colorants, which is how the expression "ham actor" came into being.

Since women were not permitted to act in the theater and performances in Shakespeare's "Wooden O" (the Globe Theater, London) were, more often than not, given in daylight or by candlelight, there was little need to improve this crude makeup, and it was not until the Restoration in 1660, when women were allowed to perform on the stage, that changes slowly began to take place.

Cosmetics were still crude and very limited, consisting of a whitening paste made of fat and white lead, white chalk for powdering, burnt cork for darkening the brows and lining the eyes, and carmine for the cheeks and lips. Samuel Pepys recorded in his diary that he watched Nell Gwyn and Mrs Knapp making up at the Kings Theater in Drury Lane and that,"It did much upset me, but what a show they made on stage by candlelight ".

The candlelight was eventually replaced by gaslight and during the nineteenth century electric light came into general use in the theater. Although makeup was now beginning to be produced commercially, it was still heavy and masklike in appearance. It was not until 1928, with the coming of the "talkies" to the cinema, that a big step forward was taken.

In the early days of the silent screen, actors and actresses used heavy stage makeup to counteract the harsh glare from the carbon arcs that were used to light the sets, but, once sound was introduced, the microphones picked up the sizzling noise of the arcs, so large and silent incandescent electric bulbs were created in their stead. This new light, and the

new panchromatic film which developed at the same time, revealed the heaviness and crudeness of the old stage makeup still being used, so Max Factor created a whole new range of finer cosmetics to meet these demands. Finding these new cosmetics more comfortable to wear, actors started to use them in the theater and, with the coming of color film and the great improvement in film techniques, makeup also became more refined — until it reached the high standard that we have today.

The main purpose of makeup in the theater is to make the actor "look the part", in relation to both the design of the production and the size and type of theater in which it is performed. The intensity and color of stage lighting, together with the distance of the audience from the stage, tend to wash out the natural color from an actor's face and to flatten the features.

So makeup can vary from the almost grotesquely heavy in a large opera or variety theater with brilliantly strong lighting, to almost no makeup at all in a very small theater or theater "in the round" with very low lighting.

Contrary to popular belief, it is not necessary to use a thicker coat of makeup in the theater than for other media, but it is necessary to use the right strength of color and correct intensity of light and shade so that the actor's face will look good to the audience, from the front row of the stalls to the back row of the circle.

Another common fallacy in the theater is that a crudely executed makeup will "look alright from the front" — this is just not true. Makeup in the theater should be as carefully applied and blended as for any other medium. Although the intensity of color will be greater and the demarcation of shadows and highlights more pronounced, the whole effect should be as acceptable at close range as at a distance, like a well-executed portrait in an art gallery.

Many actors these days start their careers in television or films where the majority of the makeup is done by skilled makeup artists. Often when they are called upon to perform on stage, these actors find that they are unable to do even the simplest of makeups. This is a

The impoverished "ham actor" used ham fat as a base

As cinema techniques improved, so new finer cosmetics were created

great pity because personal makeup is an essential part of an actor's craft. After all, who knows better than the actor how the character being portrayed ought to look and what effect the makeup will have on the face?

Naturally there are occasions when overall control of the makeup by a makeup artist is essential, such as in a stylized production where all the characters need to have a similar appearance. Generally speaking, it is very much better for individual performers to do their own makeup, taking time to slowly build up the character, paying attention to small details that no makeup artist, however skilled, could possibly have the time to do when making up a large number of artistes.

One other occasion when a makeup artist may be needed, is when the cast are students or amateurs who are not intending to take up acting professionally and do not wish to purchase a full set of makeup — which these days can prove quite expensive. This book has been written so that both individual performers and group makeup artists can use it to help them create their own Stage Faces.

The first half of the book describes all the materials and equipment needed for stage makeup and the techniques required to exploit these to the full. The second half of the book encompasses detailed projects on particular faces and also rather more specialized information on Stage Faces of many styles and ages.

Equipment and materials

The dressing room

In both the professional and amateur theater these are all too often inadequate, being small, uncomfortable and badly lit. A makeup table at the right height, a well-lit mirror and a comfortable chair are vital if you are to achieve a really good makeup, so do everything you can to make sure that you have all of these.

The makeup table, which can be a shelf attached to the wall, should be about 24 inches (60 cm) wide and approximately 30 inches (75cm) from the floor, with sufficient room underneath for the actor to draw a chair close up to the edge and rest his or her elbows on it.

The ideal mirror is of triptych design, as illustrated below. Note that light bulbs surround the central mirror and give an even, flat illumination of the face. The side mirrors are mounted on hinges so that the actor can not only see the face in profile, but also, by adjusting the angles, can see the overall effect at about 9 feet (275 cm) away and get an idea how the makeup will look from a distance. An added advantage would be to have the light bulbs recessed, in order that colored gelatins could be slipped in front of them to simulate actual stage lighting and show the effect of different colors on makeup.

If it is not possible to have such luxury as this, and it seldom is, at least make sure that your mirror is well illuminated. Ten 40-watt bulbs spaced along the top and sides of the mirror give a good light. This is virtually the same as the triptych arrangement without the side mirrors.

Failing all of this, two 100-watt bulbs in unshaded table lamps on either side of the mirror work quite well in an emergency.

Don't forget to have a waste basket for your used tissues and cotton balls.

Makeup kit

When choosing your first personal makeup kit, don't fall into the trap of buying a full range of colors and accessories to cover all the parts that you may be asked to play. This can be expensive and also wasteful because many of the things you buy will remain unused, become stale and have to be thrown away. Just choose the colors necessary for your immediate use and add colors as the need arises, with each new part that you play. The various types of cosmetics that can be used in the theater will be discussed later (see pages 14-17). It is up to you to decide which you prefer, either because of the ease with which you can use them or simply because they suit your skin best. Apart from the actual cosmetics, the following items will also be needed to complete your makeup kit.

Makeup robe

This is used to protect clothing. An old dressing gown or housecoat is ideal.

Hand towels

For hygienic reasons, only use these for washing purposes; never to remove makeup.

Brushes

A range of good quality brushes is indispensible when doing detailed eye makeup, character highlighting and shading, or applying lip color. Short-haired sable brushes are the best. A face-powder brush is also useful for removing excess powder or brushing away any specks of eyeshadow.

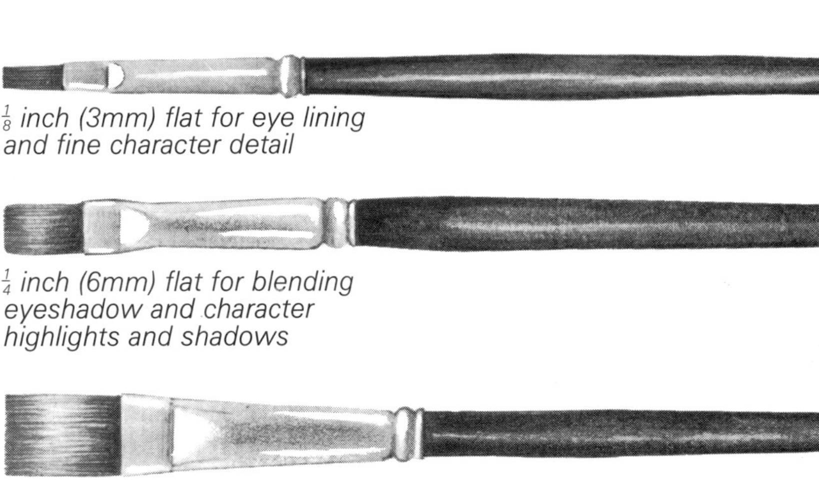

$\frac{1}{8}$ inch (3mm) flat for eye lining and fine character detail

$\frac{1}{4}$ inch (6mm) flat for blending eyeshadow and character highlights and shadows

$\frac{3}{8}$ inch (9mm) flat for blending large areas of light and shade

Number 2 filbert, for eye lining and fine character detail

Number 6 filbert for application of lip color, eyeshadow and character light and shade

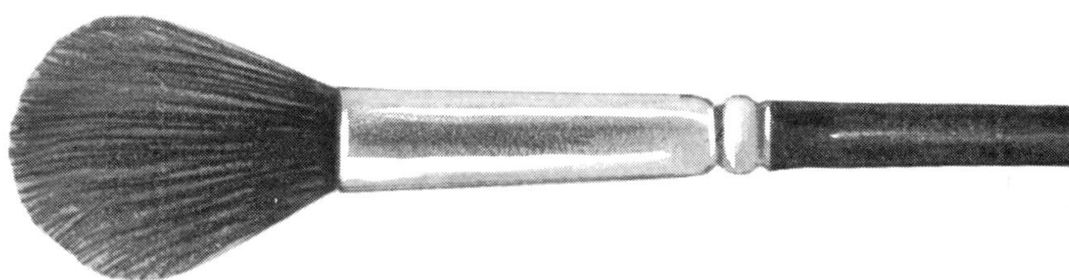

Rouge mop for application of dry rouge colors; this is usually made of pony or other less expensive hair, since sable would be too expensive and slightly too springy

Equipment and materials

Makeup remover

Both cream and liquid removers are equally efficient. Water-soluble cream removers leave the skin feeling refreshed but are usually a little more expensive. Baby oils or light mineral oils are favored by some actors, though a cosmetically balanced cleanser is better. People with skin problems should take great care with their cleansing routine and always use an antibacterial type of remover. The final choice is very much a matter of the actor's personal preference.

Skin tonic

This is used to remove final traces of makeup and remover after cleansing the face. It can be used, before makeup is applied on a naturally oily skin.

Cleansing tissues

Useful for the efficient removal of makeup.

Cotton balls

Helpful for applying skin tonic and so on.

Eye-makeup remover pads

These are useful for removing heavy eye makeup and also rectifying small mistakes.

Cotton buds

Extremely useful for removing smudged mascara and any other minor mistakes.

Powder puffs

The flat velour type is best. Have at least two so that they can be frequently washed.

Cosmetic sponges

These are used for the application of foundation and body makeup. Fine plastic foam sponges are best for the application of cake, cream and grease foundations. Natural silk sponges are excellent for the application of cake makeups if they are of a very fine texture with no large holes. Foam-rubber sponges can be used for cream and grease foundations but they sometimes disintegrate rather quickly.

Small bowl for water

This is essential when using cake makeup and is handy for moistening cotton buds and so on. The best type is a rigid, plastic cereal bowl which is unbreakable and easy to clean.

Small hand mirror

This is for applying mascara, eyelines, eyelashes, lips and so on. A round double-sided mirror with a flexible stand is the most useful. One side is usually magnifying — particularly helpful to those with poor sight.

When you have gathered together your accessories and cosmetics, you will need a box to keep them in. Cosmetic manufacturers sometimes sell special boxes designed to hold their own range of products and, although these are usually very good, they do limit your choice of materials. Plastic tool and fishing-tackle boxes, with cantilevered trays, are the most adaptable. They come in many different sizes, with a variable number of trays.

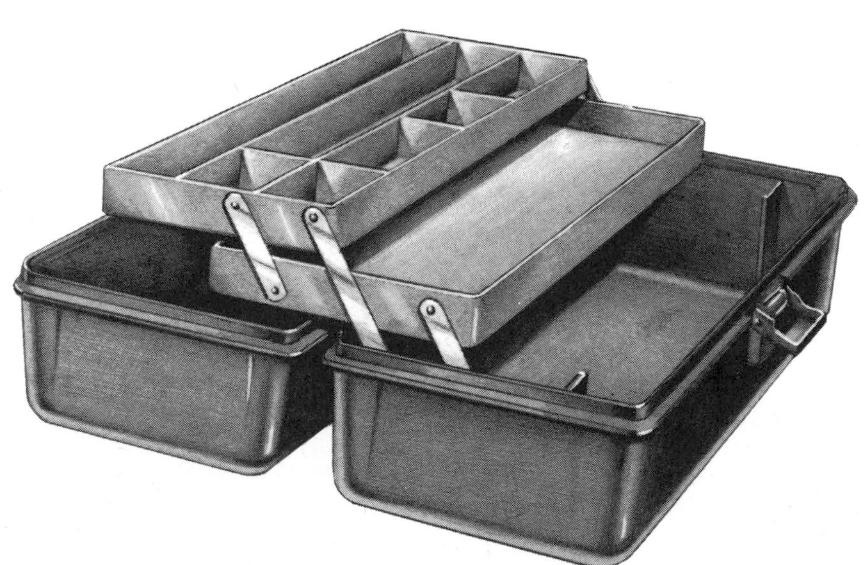

A small plastic fishing-tackle box is an ideal container for your makeup. Larger ones are suitable for group makeup

Choosing makeup

The choice of which cosmetics to use is a very personal thing and is governed by many factors such as: which type suits your skin best, which you find is easiest to use, the actual effect required, the cost, and above all, availability.

The recommendation of a specific shade and brand of makeup in any book is not very practical, since the availability of particular cosmetics is unpredictable. The following descriptions cover the types of cosmetics that are generally available and their use in the theater. The final choice of color must be left to the individual artist, but a simple system of color selection will be found in the section on color (see page 21).

Makeup bases (foundations)

Makeup bases are used to create the desired skin color, and are manufactured in many varied textures: hard greasepaint, soft greasepaint, creams, liquids and water-soluble cake makeup.

Hard greasepaint

One of the earliest forms of commercial stage makeup, this paint is packaged in stick form with a paper wrapping. It comes in a limited number of colors and it is necessary to blend two or more sticks together to achieve the desired skin tone. Since this is the least expensive type of cosmetic base on the market and many different skin colors can be achieved with a relatively small number of sticks, hard greasepaint is particularly attractive to someone with a small budget. However, it can give an old–fashioned masklike result unless it is used with great care.

Soft greasepaint

This soft, creamy-textured paint may be packaged in tubes, plastic pots or glass jars. It is much quicker and easier to apply than hard greasepaint but tends to be very shiny unless extremely well blended and generously powdered. Some manufacturers produce it in a limited range of colors that need blending in the same way as hard greases; others produce ranges of ready-blended colors which are more convenient to use.

Cream-stick makeups

These makeup bases, first created for film and television makeup, are now widely used in all mediums and are available in a large range of colors. Formulated on a non-greasy cream base, they are easy to apply, comfortable to wear and, when thoroughly powdered, they are long lasting. However, they are considerably more expensive than greasepaint.

Liquid makeups

The liquid-based makeups manufactured for stage purposes are mainly used for body

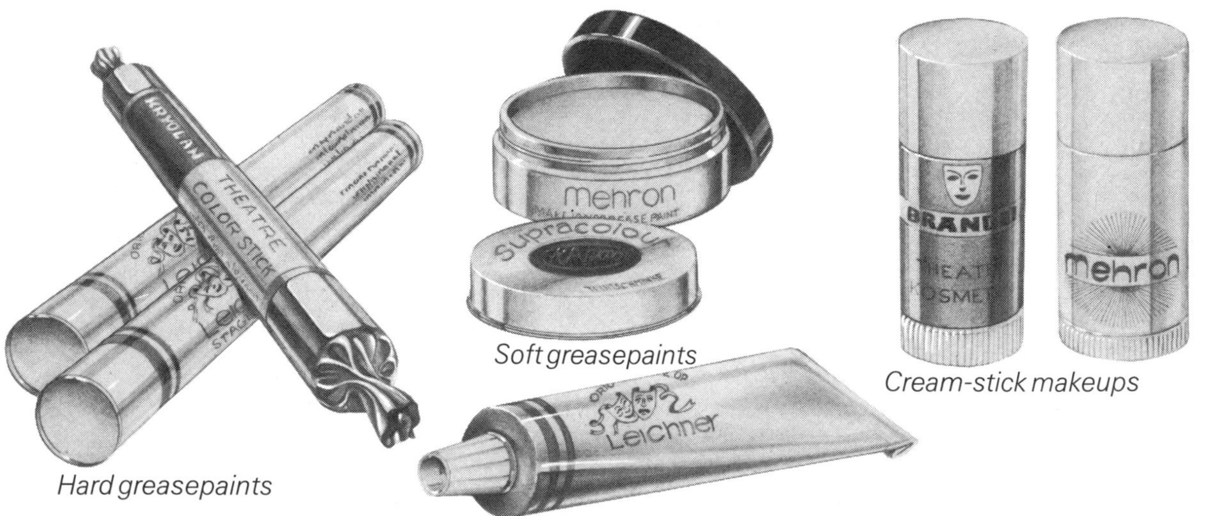

Hard greasepaints

Soft greasepaints

Cream-stick makeups

Equipment and materials

makeup and are produced in the same colors as greasepaint. There are a number of liquid bases in day makeup ranges that can be used effectively on stage, but, since the colors are made to be viewed in daylight or normal domestic lighting, they are not suitable for use on large stages with strong lighting.

Cake makeups

These are greaseless, water-soluble foundations that are applied with a wet sponge. Many actors prefer cake makeup to greasepaint because of its ease of application and removal. A non-greasy formulation, cake makeup does not encourage perspiration in the same way as greasepaint and so is extremely popular with dancers and performers who tend to perspire freely. Since cake makeups dry very quickly, it is difficult to mix the colors or to do detailed character work with them, so they tend to be used mostly for basic straight makeups. However, they are extremely useful for quick-change makeups and certain racial effects.

Although relatively expensive, cake makeups do not need to be powdered, and this balances the cost to some extent. They are also excellent for body makeup.

Lining colors

These colors are used to add detail to the makeup. They come in two basic forms — hard and soft greasepaint. Hard greasepaint liners are supplied in a very slim, stick form. Soft grease liners are supplied in small tins or pots. Both of these are available in a wide range of colors, including gray, brown, maroon, blue, green, black and white. There is also a range of reds available in both textures but these are usually referred to as lip colors.

Face powder

Face powder is used to set the foundation and lining colors and is available in a wide variety of shades and colors, in both professional and day makeup ranges. Generally speaking, these can all be ignored! One good translucent powder is all that is necessary in your makeup box. This can be used over all colors of foundation, from very pale to black, without seriously distorting the color. Many actors use inexpensive, white baby powder but this does tend to pale the makeup. A good translucent face powder is much better.

Eye makeup

Before the 1960s, eye makeup available for everyday use was quite limited and generally very subdued in color, so it was necessary to use the much stronger lining colors available for professional stage makeup.

Cake makeup

Liquid makeup

Face powder

Lining colors

Nowadays the selection of colors that can be bought at any cosmetic counter is so vast that there is no longer any need to buy special stage colors, no matter what effect is required.

Eyebrow pencils

These are used to reshape eyebrows and line the eyes. Although many different colors are available, black and dark brown are the only colors that are absolutely necessary. Any good, wooden eyebrow pencil is satisfactory, but professional pencils are usually longer and therefore more economical.

Mascara

All the various types of mascara available can be used in the theater, but with the water-soluble block form, smudges can be easily removed with a moistened cotton bud. Black and dark brown are the basic colors required.

Eyeshadow

Apart from the basic grease lining colors, there are many other different types of eyeshadow; powder, cream, creaseless liquids and eyeshadow pencils — all of which can be used to good effect in the theater, depending on the strength of color required.

Eyeliners

These, as their name suggests, are used only to line the eyes. Apart from pencils and greasepaint lining colors, there are water-soluble cake liners and liquid liners. Cake liners are the most versatile since they can be used to achieve sharp clear lines or blended away to a soft shadowy line. The liquid type of liner, which is usually packaged with an automatic wand applicator, is much more difficult to blend away but will achieve a very good clearly defined line.

False eyelashes

False eyelashes can be very effective on stage. These arc obtainable from any good cosmetic counter. Care must be taken to choose lashes that are heavy enough to register well from a distance but not so dense that they cast shadows over the eye. "Pointed" false lashes work very well. These have quite strong clumps of lashes spaced along the root so light can pass through them.

Cake rouge

Cake or dry powder rouge is used to touch up a completed makeup using a rouge mop or in conjunction with a cake makeup by using a moist sponge. There is a wide range of colors available from both professional and day-makeup manufacturers. Expensive types are often subtle in color so the less expensive and more basic colors are the most useful.

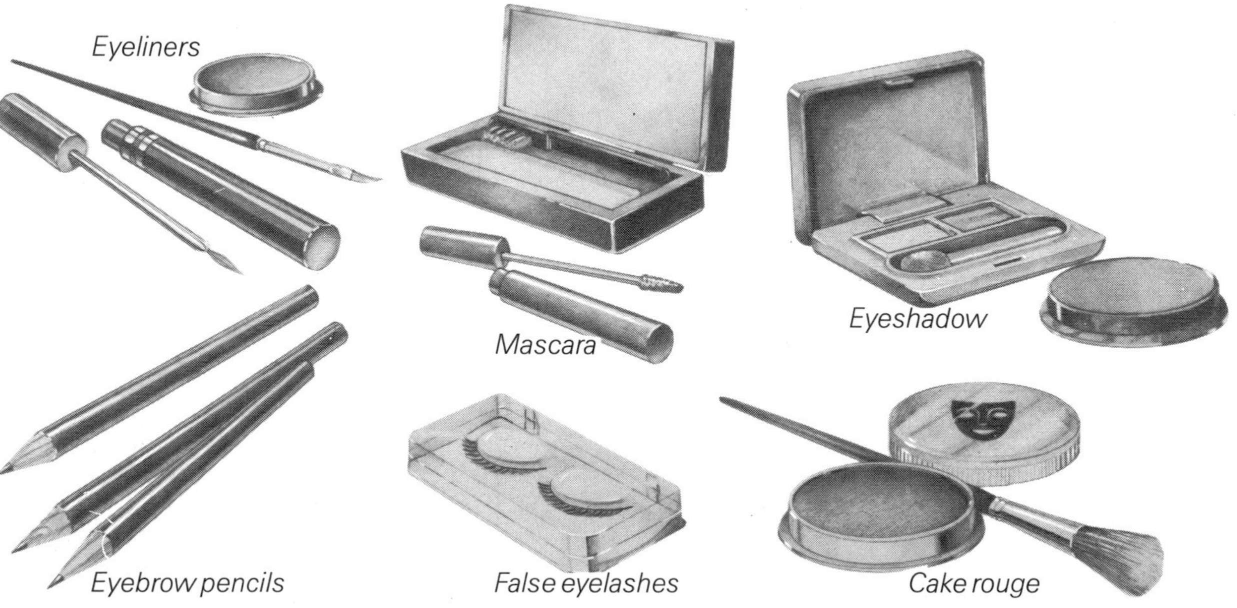
Eyeliners
Mascara
Eyeshadow
Eyebrow pencils
False eyelashes
Cake rouge

Color

Once you are aware of what makeup is available for use in the theater, the next task is to decide what colors you need for each particular job. Before you can do this, you should have at least an elementary knowledge of the principles of color in pigment and in light, and of the effects of light on pigment.

The three dimensions of color in pigment are hue, intensity and value. Each color or hue (that is simply the name by which we know it — red, yellow, green, blue or violet) and all the intermediate colors, such as reddish-orange or turquoise, can be very bright and intense, or very pale. Warm hues appear to come forward while cool hues recede. The simple color wheel below shows the primary colors (red, yellow and blue) and the secondary colors (those made by combining two primaries). The mixing of primary hues will also produce the intermediate colors.

Colors vary in intensity. Some are more brilliant than others and these move further from the center of the wheel as the color intensifies.

A very bright paint can be made paler by the addition of white. Blues, for example, can range from a very pale or desaturated blue to a very intense or saturated royal blue. Similarly, the darkness of a color is dependent upon the amount of black added to it.

The three dimensions of color are shown as two cones of color placed base-to-base with the color wheel in the middle. The top cone, which has white added, contains the tints; and the bottom cone, to which black is added, contains the shades.

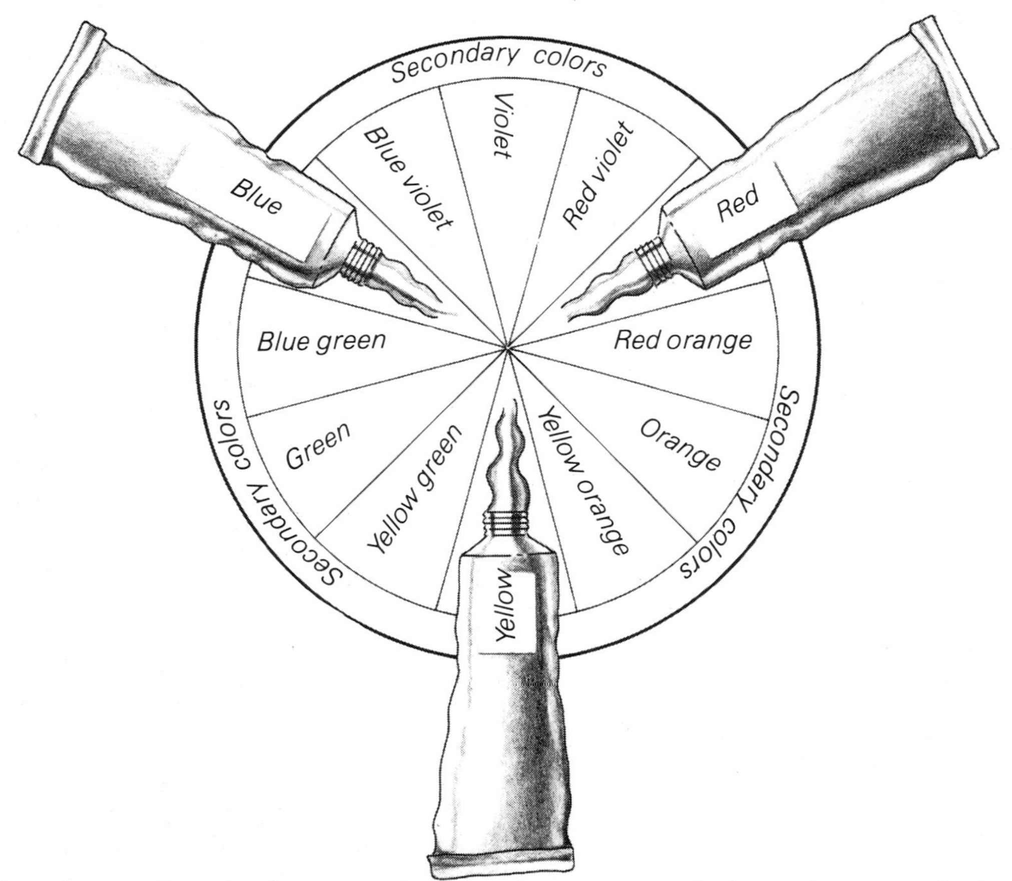

Opposite colors on the wheel contrast. As colors become more intense, they move further from the center of the wheel

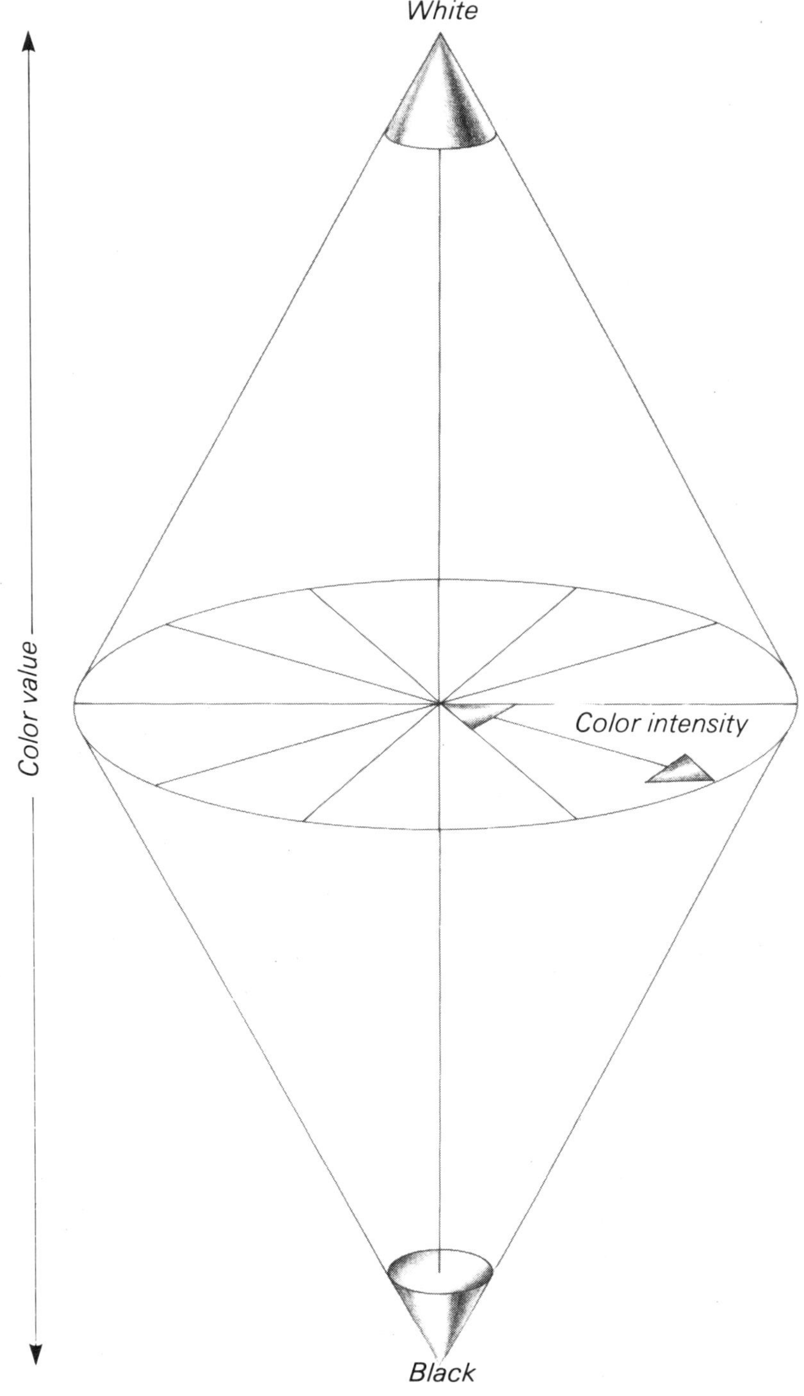

All hues and intensities appear within the color cone, which adds a third dimension to the color wheel

Color mixing

Given the three primary colors, you can mix any color you wish. Furthermore, given white and black, you can then mix any tint or shade of that color.

Fortunately it is not necessary when using cosmetics to mix your own colors since the manufacturers provide such a large range, but once you understand the principles of mixing, you can adjust a color by adding either black, white or a hue.

Color in light

As lighting plays an important part in stage makeup effects, it is very important to understand the difference between the primary colors in pigment and the primary colors in light — which are red, green and blue. Mix these together with equal intensity and they will produce white light.

In the theater, colored filters (or gelatines) are placed in front of incandescent lights to produce different color tints and shades. These color filters have the ability to absorb all the colors in the spectrum except their own. For example, a blue filter will allow only blue light to pass through on to the stage.

There are well over seventy different filters or "gels" to choose from. The most common and often-used colors when lighting are flesh (pale pink), surprise pink (cold neutral), daylight blue, steel blue, straw, gold and bastard amber (warm neutral).

Normal stage lighting generally contains a combination of cold and warm neutral lights — made up from ambers, straws, golds and surprise pink.

This neutral mixture, combined with the color of incandescent bulbs, tends to be yellow in tone, so that makeup should be slightly on the pink or warm side in order to appear as natural as possible under balanced stage lighting.

The following chart gives an indication of how colored lights will affect different colors of pigment.

Pigment colors in light

The chart below shows only the effect of strong colored light on brilliant hues. It does not take into account the subtleties of makeup colors and stage lighting.

However, by applying these basic principles, we can get close to appreciating just how certain colored filters will affect different makeups.

Flesh pink will have only a small effect on most makeups and is, generally speaking, one of the most flattering stage lights. Very strong red light will be disastrous to any makeup; skin tone will almost disappear, average rouging will totally fade away and dark reds become brown. However, since a strong red light is used only for very dramatic effects, the audience will expect the makeup to look strange.

Amber and orange filters will also ruin a good makeup. Skin tones will become yellowed and shading details look dirty. This

Pigment colors

Color of lights	Red	Orange	Yellow	Green	Blue	Violet
Red	Fades and disappears	Becomes lighter	Becomes white	Becomes much darker	Becomes dark-gray	Goes black
Yellow	Remains red	Fades slightly	Fades and disappears	Becomes dark-gray	Becomes dark-gray	Becomes nearly black
Green	Becomes much darker	Darkens	Darkens	Becomes very pale green	Turns dark-green	Becomes nearly black
Blue	Darkens	Becomes much darker	Turns light mauve	Lightens	Turns pale-blue	Turns light-mauve
Violet	Becomes pale-red	Lightens	Turns pink	Becomes pale-blue	Darkens	Becomes very pale
Neutral colors (black, brown and grays) remain almost the same under all lights, apart from a slight change in tone						

light should be used only to light the set. Bastard amber, on the other hand, is an extremely flattering light. It tends to intensify the pinks and flesh tones and adds life and sparkle to a makeup. Green light grays all skin tones and rouges and gives a macabre effect, but since this is usually why it is used, the audience will accept the effect quite willingly.

Blue light will give a sickly gray tone to the skin and will darken lip and cheek coloring, but since it is mostly used for moonlight effects, the audience will accept this. However, if a long love scene is to be played in moonlight, this color can be disturbing, so it will help if some supplementary warm light can be played on the actors' faces.

Straw and gold filters have very little effect on the makeup, except perhaps to warm it slightly. Violet light tends to intensify the reds, so play down the rouge and avoid pink skin tones which will become florid.

The biggest problem is that lighting can change very rapidly during the course of a play and obviously it is not possible to change the makeup as quickly. It is a good idea to make a careful check of your makeup during lighting rehearsals and try to modify it to suit all lighting changes. If, however, you find you are unable to do this and the lighting is really spoiling the makeup, then a word in the director's ear is necessary, so that some lighting changes can be made.

Choosing makeup colors

Manufacturers often discontinue colors without warning so no specific makeup shades can be recommended. Choosing colors is very personal as they look different on every skin and it is important that each makeup should be individual, not a stereotyped copy.

In recommending the colors to use for each different type of makeup described, the skin colors have been divided into the fifteen groups below.

However, it cannot be stressed strongly enough that when choosing and buying makeup colors, you must rely on your own judgment and the advice of your makeup supplier.

Lip and rouge colors are divided into the following four groups:

Light-red group
Clear light-reds with no blue undertones

Medium-red group
Strong, light blue-reds

Dark-red group
Dark-blue reds

Lake group
Dark-brown reds

All eye accent and special-effect colors are described by their actual color.

Pale group
Pale flesh colors that are neither strongly pink nor beige

Ivory group
Very pale ivory colors

Creamy group
Medium-beige colors

Pink group
Very strong, pink flesh tones

Peach group
Clear, warm-medium skin tones

Florid group
Strong, deep-red skin tones

Light-tan group
Light-tan skin tones

Deep-tan group
Strong tans

Warm-tan group
Very deep warm tans

Olive group
Mediterranean and Latin skin tones

Olive-brown group
Asiatic skin tones

Dark-brown group
Afro-Caribbean colors

Sallow group
Yellow-gray skin tones

Yellow group
Oriental skin tones

Drab group
Yellowy-gray browns

Character analysis

When actors start to rehearse a play together, they first read the script and then talk to the director and try to find out all they can about the characters; where they come from, how old and how fit they are, their temperament and anything else that will have an affect on the performances. Each actor should also work out how all of these things will affect pure physical appearance and how makeup will help to create the character.

The factors that determine our physical appearance can be divided into six main groups. These are heredity, ethnic groups, environment, health, temperament and age. Not all of these groups are necessarily of equal importance when analyzing a particular character, so just concentrate on those that you think will most influence your appearance.

Heredity

Heredity is a very complex field of study. For makeup purposes, all we need to know is that it gives us the mental and physical characteristics with which we are born. We have to decide which facial features will convey the most information to the audience about the character to be portrayed. (A fine aquiline nose, for instance, suggests noble breeding, while a coarse heavy nose indicates a coarse heavy character!) We should also take into consideration any resemblance necessary to relatives in the play.

Ethnic groups

Ethnic grouping is of course also part of heredity, but it raises many problems in its own right.We are apt to put ethnic groups into stereotyped compartments, with each group having a clearly-defined set of rules for skin color, type and color of hair, shape of features and other physical characteristics. However, this is totally inadequate, for within each group there is a wide variation from one individual to another.

For instance, in the north of India there is a strong Aryan influence from the invaders who swept across the north-west frontier; so the people tend to be tall with long narrow faces, large well-cut noses, straight hair and medium-brown skins.

The southern Indians, however, are generally shorter and much darker skinned, with small faces, broad snub noses and coarse, black wavy hair. These characteristics resulted from their being driven south by the invaders where they intermarried with migrating Africans and Indonesians.

Environment

Environment is also very important. A westernized black man from New York will look very different from an African tribesman; and a peasant working in the rice fields of China will not altogether resemble a wealthy Chinese merchant who lives in Singapore.

So many factors, apart from color and form, have to be taken into consideration. However, if it is important to the plot that the audience recognizes the particular race instantly, then the makeup must convey this information clearly and effectively.

Environment plays a vital part in determining the color and texture of the skin in all races. Fishermen, coal miners, office workers and athletes will all need to be portrayed by the use of different makeup. Moreover, an office worker on holiday in the south of France will look very different to one working in his London office. Therefore, the lifestyle of the character at that particular time must also be considered as part of the environmental influence on both makeup and hairstyling.

The first thing to decide is what sort of makeup the character would be wearing off-stage. Under normal circumstances, we assume that women wear cosmetics and men do not, but this is not always the case. During the Restoration period, men wore makeup, and in Victorian times well-bred ladies did not. In the 1980s, a man who is a "punk" or "new romantic" might wear makeup, and a feminist woman might well not!

Lengths and styles of hair, for both men and women, are affected by both period and social standing. Therefore, these points too must be studied very carefully as part of your character analysis.

Health

If there is no direct reference to the health of the character in the script, it can generally be assumed that he or she is in good health and no further research will be necessary. However, from time to time, the state of health of the person being portrayed is of vital importance to the plot so the makeup must reflect this.

In some instances, where specific diseases — such as tuberculosis, malaria or yellow fever — are quoted, it may be necessary to take advice from a medical expert as to what symptoms would be apparent. Then try to simulate these symptoms as closely as possible with makeup.

If a character is described as just being "ill" or suffering from some unspecified disease, simply make a change in the skin color and add a few shadows to give a "drawn" appearance, particularly around the eyes.

Of course it is not always ill health that needs to be shown; sometimes a character has to appear to be bursting with health and energy — and the makeup must exhibit this, as well as the performance.

Temperament

Our personalities, outlook on life and personal habits all play a big part in how we look. Rounded features with sparkling eyes, laughter lines and upturned corners to the mouth will show a happy personality, whereas drooping eyes and lips and drawn-in cheeks reveal a character sunk in melancholy.

Hairstyles, for both men and women, can be used to help reveal a character's personality and temperament. For instance, hair tightly pulled back into a bun can indicate severity of nature, but softly drawn back into a chignon can show a gentle reticent personality. On the other hand, allow the hair to fall loosely into voluptuous waves, and it instantly suggests an extrovert sexiness.

A man's hair which is slicked down with brilliantine and sharply parted indicates a very introverted and methodical character. The same man will look carefree and outgoing if his hair is blow-dried into a soft bouncy style.

Beards and mustaches can also be very useful character indicators. For example, a large bushy beard gives a wild bohemian appearance and a neat Vandyke a dapper and scholarly one.

Age

Although age is probably the most important single factor in analyzing a makeup, it must be remembered that the way in which we age is influenced by our heredity and environment, our temperament and even the race we belong to. So these factors must be considered first.

For example, try to imagine a bad-tempered ugly woman of fifty who suffers from asthma, lives in a tenement flat, works as a cleaner and couldn't care less how she looks. She will seem much older than a beautiful confident socialite of sixty who lives in luxury and takes care of her health and her appearance.

The descriptions of these two women have used all the analytical headings (apart from race) to summon up a mental picture of how they look.

Race may well be relevant, in some instances. The Chinese, for example, tend to look quite young well into middle age and often live to be very old indeed; the Asiatic Indian, on the other hand, is likely to age prematurely and will also have a comparatively short life expectancy.

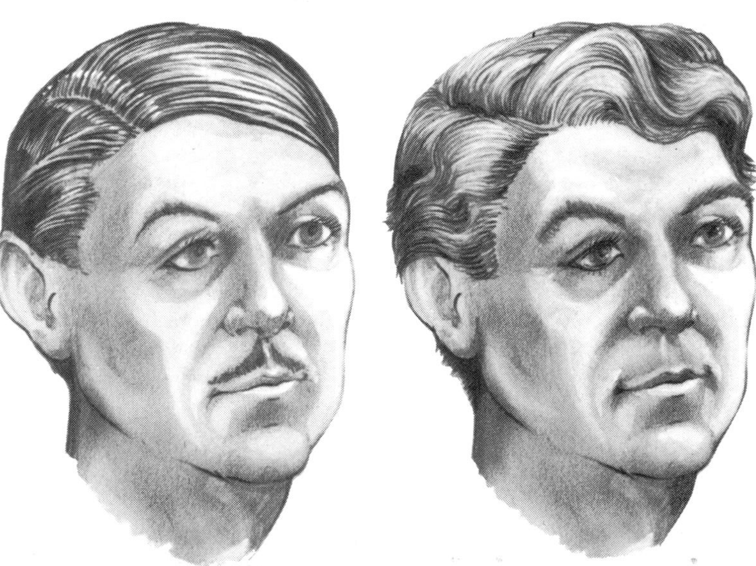

Sleek hair indicates a methodical character; a blow-dried style gives a carefree impression

Character analysis

Shakespeare wrote of the seven ages of man, but for our purposes we need consider only three classifications — youth, middle age and old age.

Youth

Youth covers a wide span from childhood to about thirty-five years of age. At one time in the theater all performers under the age of thirty-five were called juveniles and there was a further subdivision of straight and character juveniles. Being a straight juvenile meant you were of a reasonably pleasing appearance and expected only to play yourself, and so your makeup became known as a "straight makeup".

There is, however, no such thing as a straight makeup — every makeup sets out to do one of two things: either to create a character different from that of the performer, in which case it is a character makeup; or to make the performers look their best, in which case it is a corrective makeup — for none of us is perfect. It may be true that for the young and beautiful only a small amount of correction is necessary but as we grow older more and more correction is needed on this so-called straight makeup.

Middle age

Middle age is something the young never strive to achieve but, once achieved, it is something that we long to retain as long as possible. For theatrical purposes, middle age is usually a period of time between thirty-five and sixty-five years of age. The first major change during these years is that the bone structure begins to become more apparent and it is said that the face develops more character. Then, as time passes, the skin loses its youthful color and the hair turns gray. Wrinkles appear around the eye area and the corners of the mouth. Gradually the hair gets thinner and, in some cases, falls out. The muscles begin to sag and the flesh falls further away from the skull.

When analyzing your makeup, pick those features which will be most affected by the processes of aging and build up the degree of age you require.

Old age

Advanced old age in the theater is usually characterized by extreme thinness. As we advance in years, the subcutaneous fat under the skin becomes exhausted and then collapses while the skull structure becomes even more prominent, with the skin appearing to be draped over it. We lose teeth, the gums shrivel, the mouth and lips sink back into the face, and the neck becomes scrawny. The complexion is very pale or ivory in color, cheek color either disappears or becomes extremely livid. Lips may become colorless or turn blue if the heart is weak. Eyelids can turn pink and the end of the nose may droop and redden. Hair turns totally gray or white and falls out. Men's eyebrows become coarse and bushy and women's fall out.

There is also the type of extreme old age that comes with obesity, when the subcutaneous fat cells increase rather than decrease. The face then becomes swollen and flabby with the bone structure concealed beneath heavy folds of flesh. The eyes usually look small and are hidden by swollen lids. Men's noses tend to coarsen and swell while women's become button-like and buried between the puffy cheek muscles on either side. Necks shorten and the jawline disappears beneath numerous double chins.

Analyzing a character in the manner just described will obviously take time and patience, so working out a makeup should never be left until just before the dress rehearsal. Actors who are doing their own makeup will, of course, have to do a similar sort of analysis when they consider the performance, so it will be to their advantage to think about the makeup from the outset and to do a trial makeup as soon as possible.

For makeup artists, it is much more difficult, especially if they are not called in until the first dress rehearsal and are instantly expected to produce perfect makeups. This is of course quite impossible, especially if they have no previous knowledge of the play.

Ideally, the makeup artist should be present at the early run-throughs and have the opportunity of discussing the makeups with the director and each individual actor. Work can then begin on character analysis and charting out the makeup. With the more difficult character makeups, the makeup artist should aim to experiment with trial makeups on individual actors well in advance.

Making faces — a study of physiognomy

"Stop making that silly face, or you'll be stuck with it!" This threat is not as silly as it sounds, because the more we use certain expressions, the more the facial muscles become set in the direction in which we have pulled them. So an unhappy person who pulls down the corners of his mouth and raises the center of his eyebrows in an expression of melancholy will all too soon permanently display, just like Don Quixote, a "woeful countenance".

Because of these self-imposed masks of temperament that we make for our own faces, certain features and expressions have become associated with certain types of character — and we can make good use of this when creating a makeup. The following sketches and notes show which features and expressions you might use, but be wary of getting locked into makeup cliches or producing stereotyped faces. Use only those features that you think will fit the part. Collect all the references you find, in this book and elsewhere, and then build up your own Stage Face — not a stale "Greek mask".

Every feature on the face plays some part in reflecting the personality, but the areas around the eyes and mouth reveal the most about us. Since both areas are fairly easy to change with makeup, these are the features we should examine first of all.

Eyes

Normal eyes are not too deeply set in the orbital socket and are almond in shape. The upper and lower lid just cut off a small part of the iris. They are set apart by the width of an eye, gently framed by arching brows

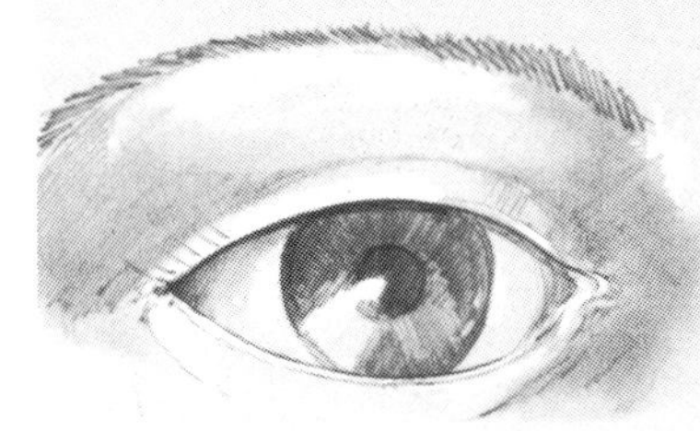
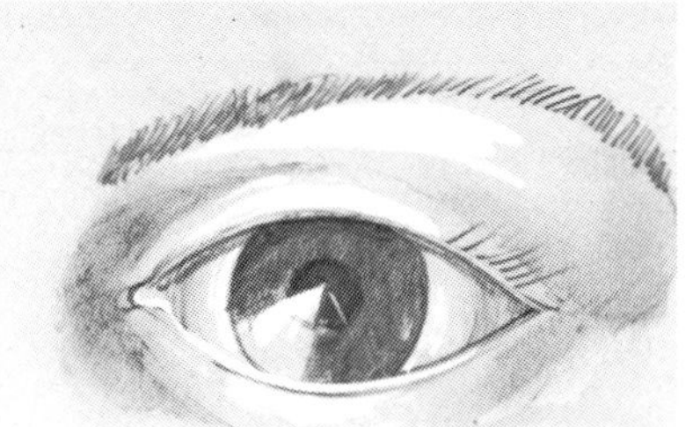

Deep-set eyes under straight lowered brows indicate the analytical and observant mind associated with writers and philosophers

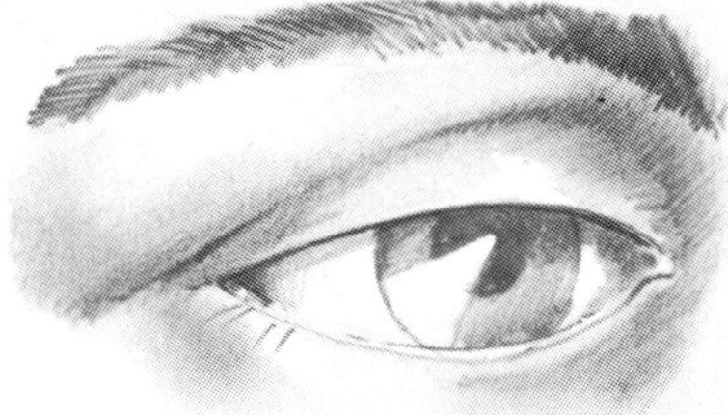

Eyes that are deep set and too close together can suggest a sullen and dishonest nature

Small, obliquely-narrowed eyes, with eyebrows winging up from the root of the nose, may be suggestive of a sinister and deceitful character

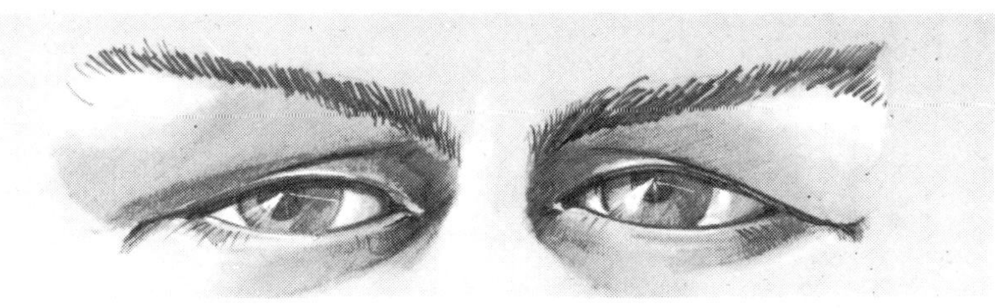

Slightly narrowed eyes, with wrinkles at the outer corner that tend to lift upward, are signs of a happy, pleasant, kind person — which is why we sometimes call them "laugh lines"

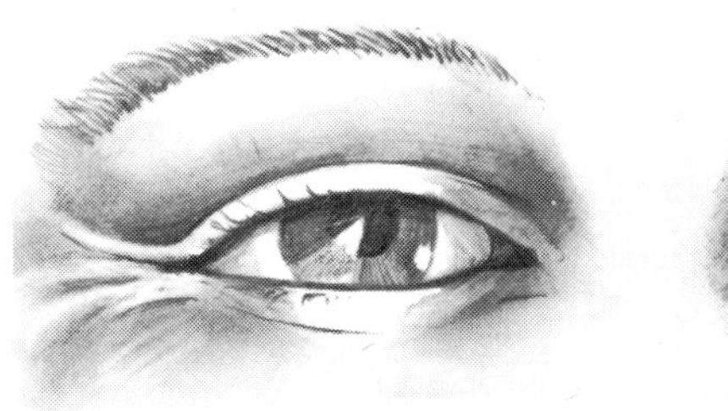
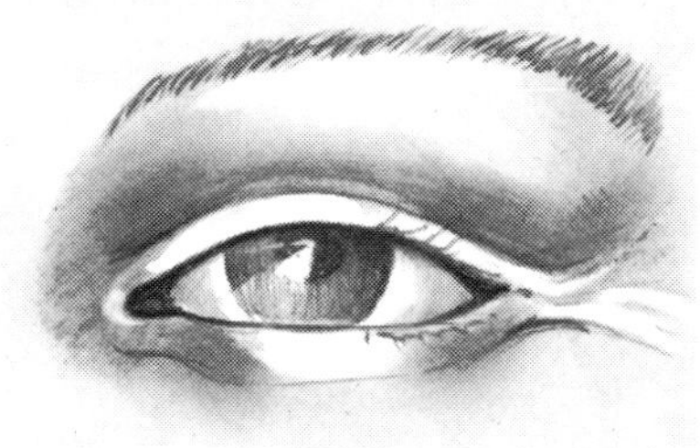

Prominent eyes with heavy lids are indicators of a languid aesthetic nature, associated with dreamers and poets

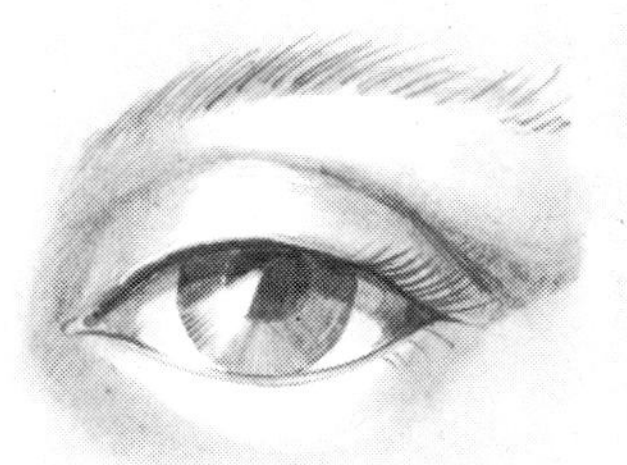

Prominent eyes, set too far apart with lifted brows, may convey an expression of stupidity or naivety

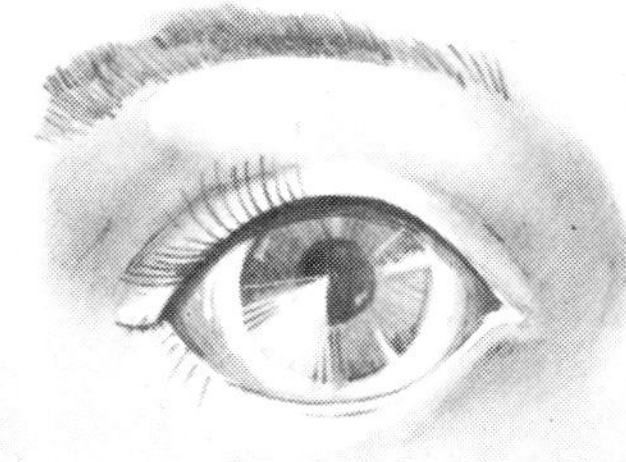

Downward-sloping eyes, with eyebrows that lift in the center, might denote anxiety, sadness or grief

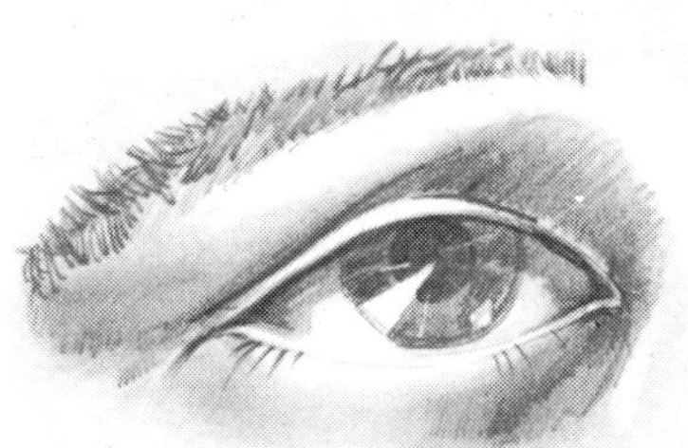
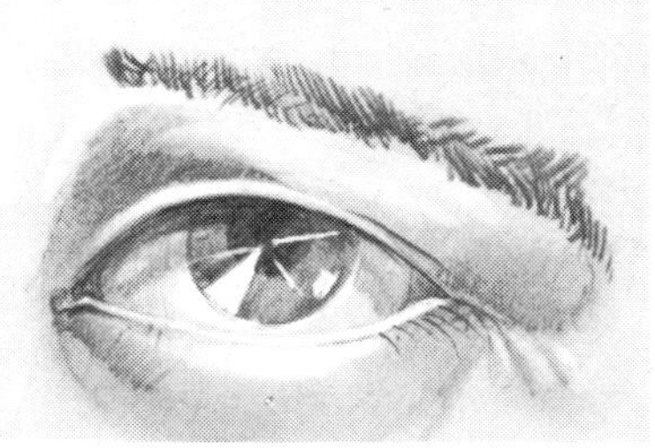

Making faces — a study of physiognomy

Eyebrows

After the eyes, the features which can change the face the most are the eyebrows. Because their shape is very easily altered, eyebrows are very useful to the actor and the makeup artist.

They vary in shape and may be arched, oblique or irregular; high or low on the face; close together, or far apart. Also the eyebrow hair itself can differ. There are bushy thick eyebrows and thin eyebrows; light and dark eyebrows of various shades — not always the same as the hair— and they grow in different directions.

The different shapes of eyebrows illustrated here are all shown over exactly the same eye shape, so you can see how dramatically they alter the appearance of the face.

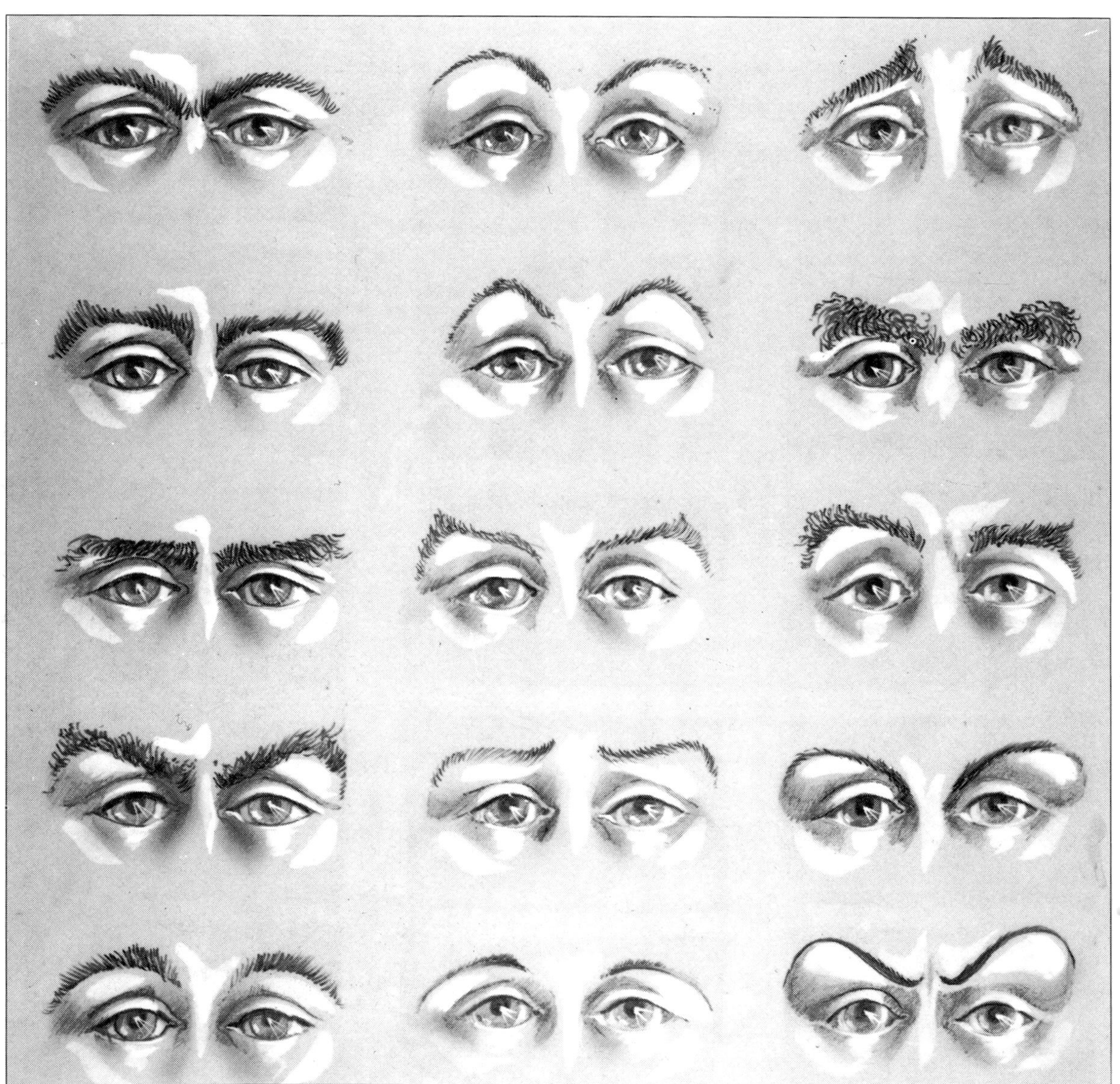

Mouth

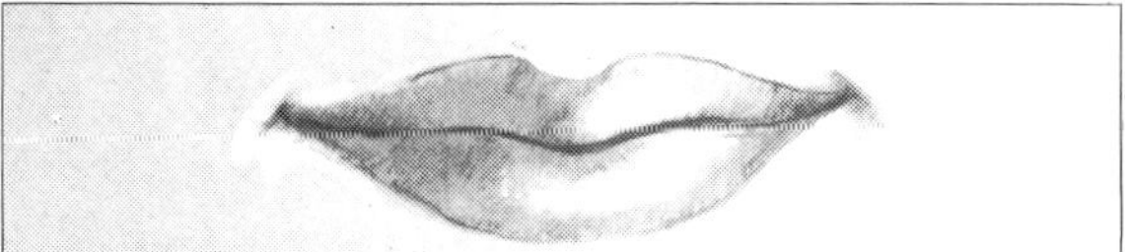

The classic female mouth has lips of moderate thickness with the top lip shaped like a cupid's bow and is considered very beautiful

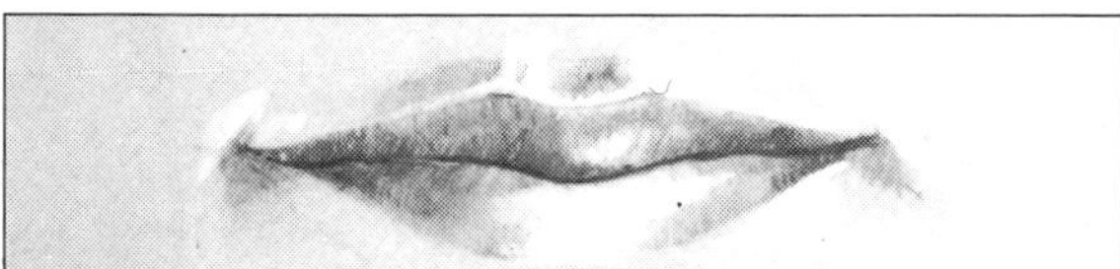

The classic male mouth is not so full and has a less bowed upper lip

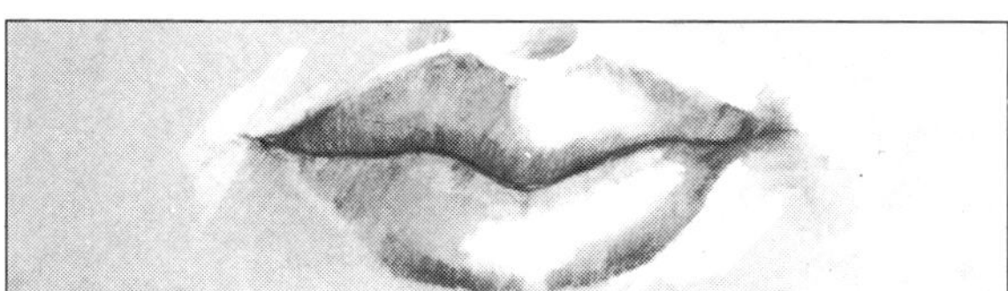

A large mouth with full lips suggests a sensual nature

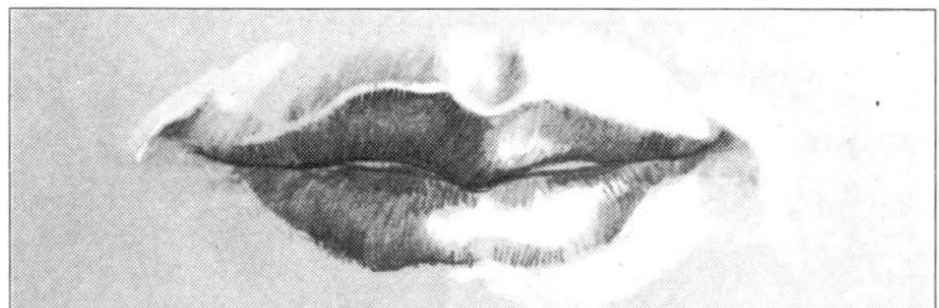

A wide mouth with curving lips can convey cunning, irony and malice

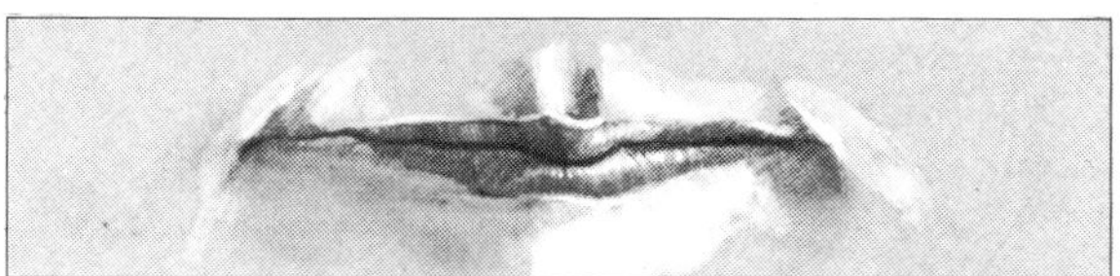

A very straight tightly-closed mouth shows firmness and willpower and is associated with meanness, cruelty and wickedness

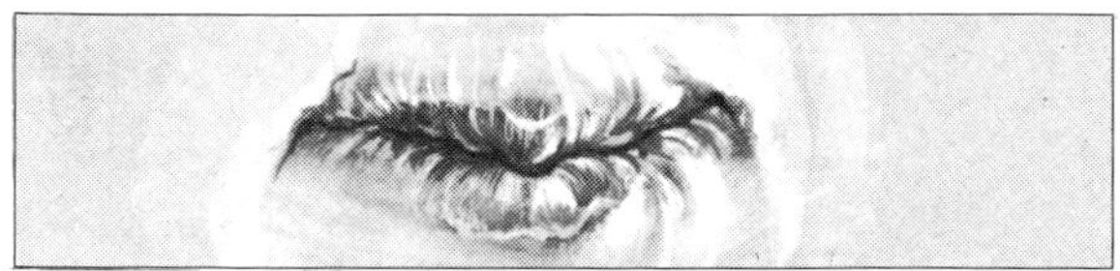

A receding wrinkled mouth denotes old age

A mouth with downward-drooping corners and a full lower lip gives the impression of petulance and selfishness

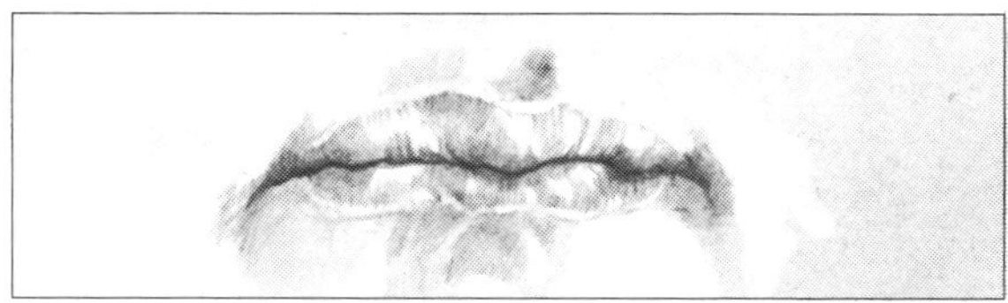

Downward-drooping corners with thin lower lips can show weariness, sorrow or old age

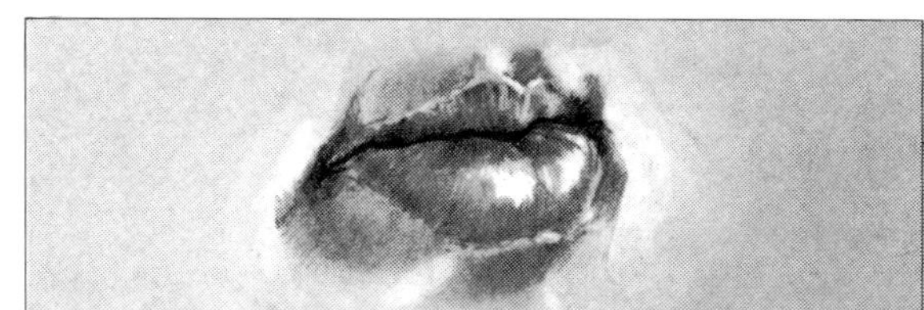

A mouth with a protruding lower lip raised up over the top lip will indicate determination and firmness of character

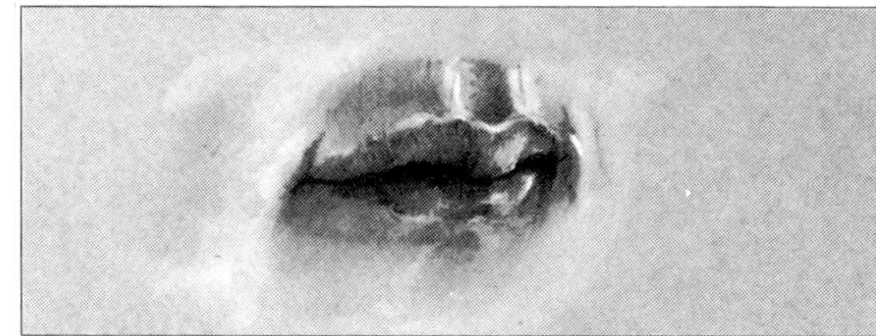

A mouth which has a protruding upper lip suggests disdain

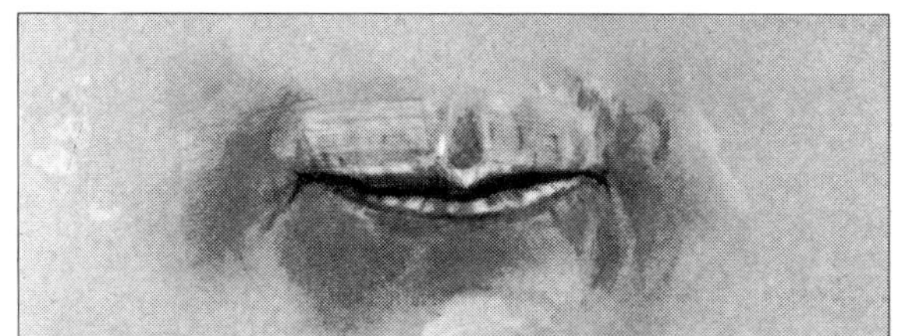

A small tight mouth could convey vindictiveness, obstinacy or selfishness

Making faces — a study of physiognomy

Nose

The nose, unlike the eyes and mouth, is relatively unaffected by the expressions we make, its shape being dictated primarily by our heredity. However, since it is a fairly rigid bony feature, it can be remodeled with a small amount of nose putty, making dramatic changes to the face.

Apart from obvious shapes dictated by heredity, such as the aquiline nose of an Arab or the broad flat nose of an Afro-Caribbean, certain shapes may suggest character traits to an audience.

The so-called Grecian nose is a conventional rather than an actual form found on statues sculpted in ancient Greece. It is hardly the thing of beauty that most people associate with the name. What they really have in mind is the straight or Augustian nose, of which there are four kinds: long, short, high tipped and low tipped — this last being considered to be the most beautiful shape of all.

Then there is the hooked or Roman nose, of which there are three variations; with the hook at the top, the middle or the end. Far from being just Roman, these can be Arabic, Semitic, Indian (both North American and Asiatic) or Melanesian.

The turned-up or snub nose also has three forms, with the depression in the upper, the middle or the lower part. Except in the last case (a *retroussé* nose), the effect is usually one of ugliness.

These shapes are of noses seen in profile and there are also innumerable variations on them when seen from the front. They can be symmetrical from root to tip, thick in the center, thick at the point, thin at the root: they may have narrow or wide nostrils, high or low nostrils, with flaring nasal openings very much in evidence or so tightly closed as to be almost invisible.

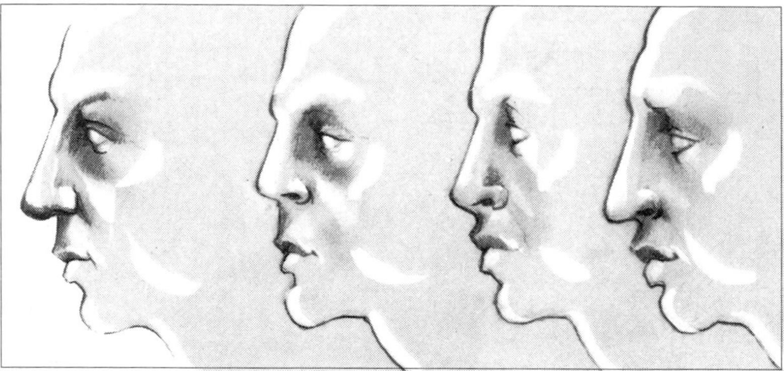

Augustian

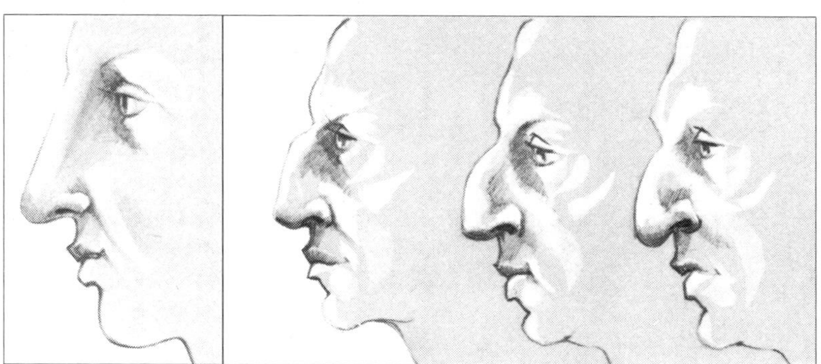

Grecian *Roman*

Snub

A The long straight Grecian or Augustine nose is considered to be an indication of noble birth, refinement, good taste and a sensitive nature.

B The short straight nose which is tipped up at the end suggests go-ahead enthusiasm and an eager curiosity.

C The long straight nose with a depressed tip can suggest a cold implacable nature and a grim determination to succeed. If it is associated with down-drooping eyes, it gives an air of melancholy.

D A short straight nose that is broad seems to indicate strength and vitality.

E The Roman nose with a hook in the center or at the top shows strength and determination and is very often associated with military leaders.

F The Roman nose with its hook at the tip conveys determination and strength but can also hint at shrewdness, cunning and treachery.

G The concave or snub nose with the depression at the tip may intimate a rather pert and mischievous nature.

H If the depression is in the center, it is more suggestive of immaturity and lack of ambition.

J When the depression is near the root of the nose, this tends to occur on broad flat faces with large ape-like nostrils. This rudimentary concave nose is associated with immaturity and underdevelopment, perhaps even lunacy. It is usually thought rather ugly.

Bone structure

"Alas! poor Yorick...I knew him well" — but alas, poor actor, you do not know him well enough! Without a good working knowledge of the structure of the skull, you cannot begin to remodel any of your features successfully. This knowledge is most important when you are aging the face, because, as we get older, the muscles covering the skull lose their firmness and begin to sag, the flesh sinks in and the shape of the skull gradually becomes more and more apparent.

Here is an illustration of a skull with each hollow and projection clearly named. Each of these features has a technical term, but for makeup purposes these everyday names will suffice!

Study this illustration as if you were looking into a mirror, and at the same time, with the fingertips, begin to trace the hollows and prominences of your head until you can identify and name each part.

Start at the top of the face where you should be able to identify the upper forehead **A** and below it the browbone **B.** Notice there is a slight depression between the two. This depression varies from person to person — in some it is very clearly marked and in others it is almost non-existent.

There is also a depression in the center of the brow, immediately above the nose. Place your two forefingers in this hollow and then, moving outwards, trace the line of the browbone until you reach the temple hollows **C,** just in front of which you will be able to feel the edge of the eye sockets **D** , which you can trace right around the eyes with your fingertips.

Between the eye sockets, you will find the bridge of the nose **E.** Grasp this between your finger and thumb and slowly move them down the nose and you will see that the lower section of the nose is not bone but a piece of flexible cartilage.

Front view

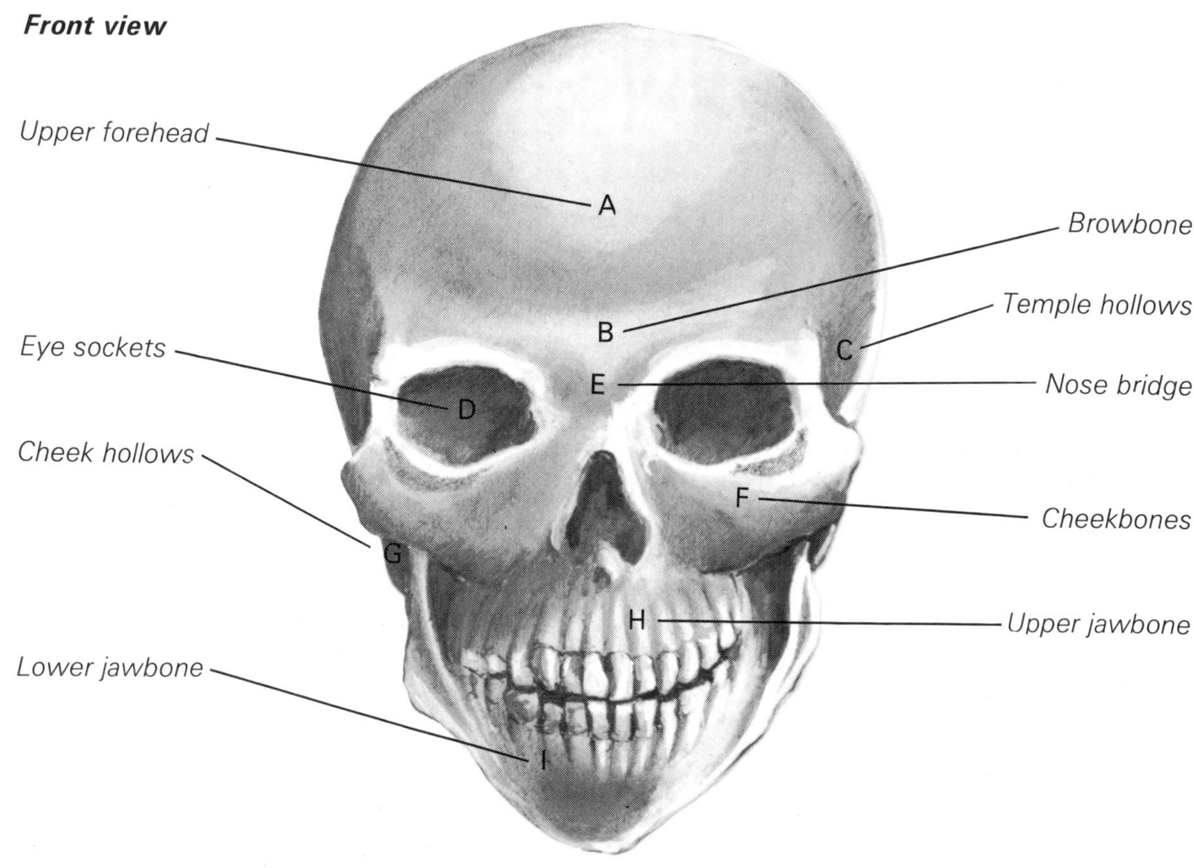

Immediately alongside the outer end of the eye sockets, you will be able to feel the high point of the cheekbones F which are the most important bones of the face as far as makeup is concerned. Spend as long as you can prodding along the whole length of the cheekbones, from the nose to the ear, until you can recognize their exact shape, noticing how they curve round underneath before disappearing into the cheek hollows G.

From these hollows, move the fingers forward underneath the nose until you can feel the upper jaw bone H, noticing how it falls back just beneath the crease between the nostrils and the corners of the mouth.

Finally, place your fingertips at the back of the lower jawbone I just below your ears, and trace the shape of the jaw right round to the point of the chin. Notice particularly the almost right-angled corner situated at the back of the jaw.

The area that most people find difficult to establish is the cheekbone and cheek hollow, so this section has been illustrated in profile.

Keep repeating this exercise until you really know the bones of your face. Remember, as you do so, that the hollows are the areas that need to be shadowed and the prominences the ones that need to be highlighted when remodeling the face.

When you feel you know your own bone structure, have a look around at other actors and notice how theirs may vary from yours and, if you can persuade them to allow you, repeat the tactile exercise on their heads. This is, of course, particularly important to makeup artists, as they will be working on many variations of face shapes and bone structures.

Profile

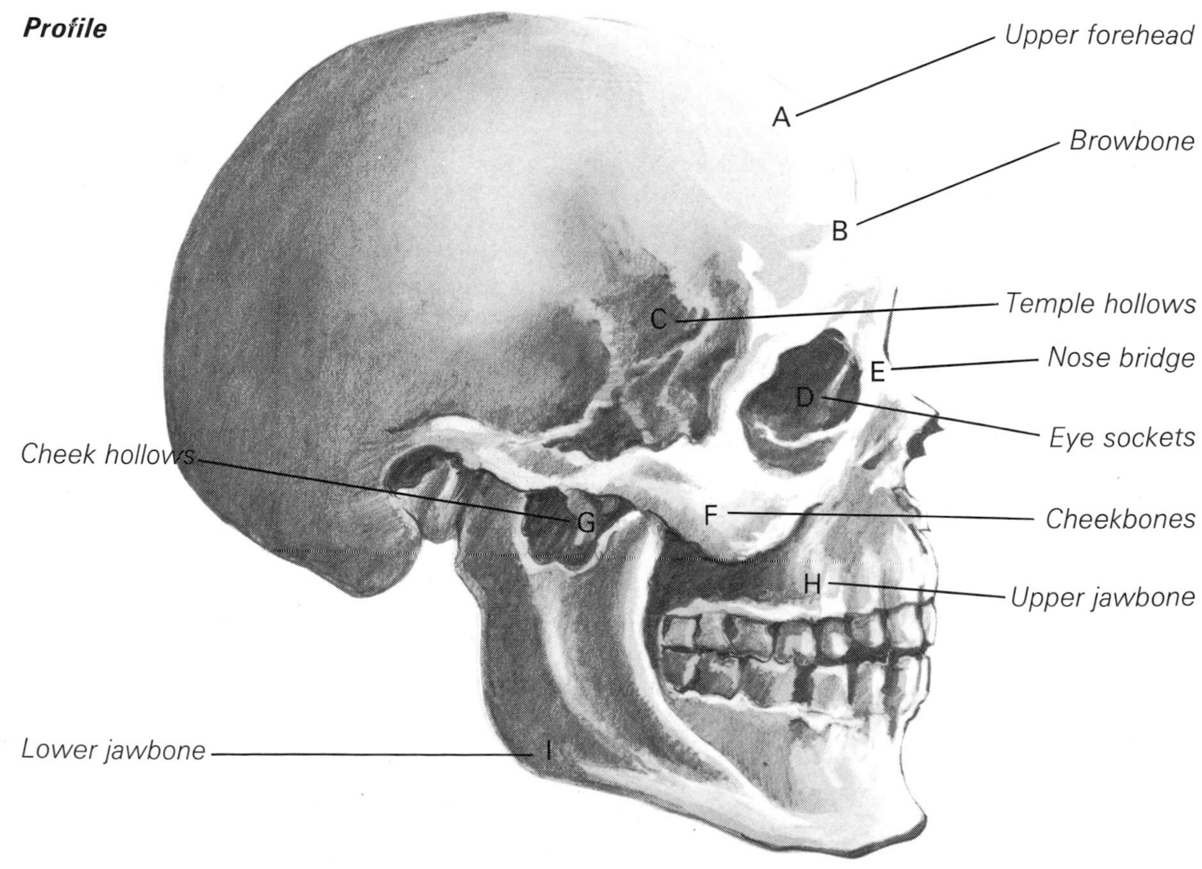

Putting on the "slap" — application techniques

Preparation

The term "slap" has, sadly, become synonymous with stage makeup, but the one thing you should never do is "slap it on". A hastily and badly applied makeup will always look messy and unprofessional and the longer you wear it, the worse it will look. So take time to apply your Stage Face properly.

Having taken off your street clothes, don a makeup robe or dressing gown and pull your hair away from your face with an elasticized head-band. You are ready to start.

Women should first thoroughly cleanse off all their day makeup, including mascara. Use a cleansing lotion or cream that does not leave the skin too greasy. The skin should then be toned with a gentle skin tonic. If the skin is normal to oily, there is no need for further preparation, but if it is very dry, apply a small amount of an under-makeup moisturizer, massaging it in gently until it is completely absorbed and leaves the skin feeling soft and velvety.

Men should ensure that they are clean shaven and that their skin is free from excess oil. It is not a good idea to apply makeup on to a freshly shaved face. If you have a strong beard and need to shave, try to do it at least an hour before the performance. If your skin is very oily, excess grease is best removed with skin tonic or after-shave lotion on a moist cotton ball.

Foundation

Once you are ready for your makeup, you will have to decide which foundation to use: hard or soft greasepaint, cream-stick, liquid or cake makeup.

(The order in which a makeup is applied when using a cake makeup is essentially quite different to that of grease, cream and liquid makeups so is dealt with separately at the end of this section, on pages 40-41.)

Hard greasepaint

Before applying hard greasepaint, you may first need to apply a thin film of cold cream to the skin to facilitate blending. (This is not necessary under warm conditions when the greasepaint becomes softer.) First remove the protective cellophane wrapper from the end of the stick and apply a few light strokes on to the forehead, cheeks, nose, chin and throat. Now, using the tips of the fingers, gently blend the color over the entire face and neck, fading it up into the hairline but taking great care not to get any on the hair itself.

When mixing two or more colors to obtain the desired skin tone, apply alternate strokes of color to the face and blend them together with your fingertips. Do not blend one color first and then add the second color over the top as this tends to give a heavy masklike result.

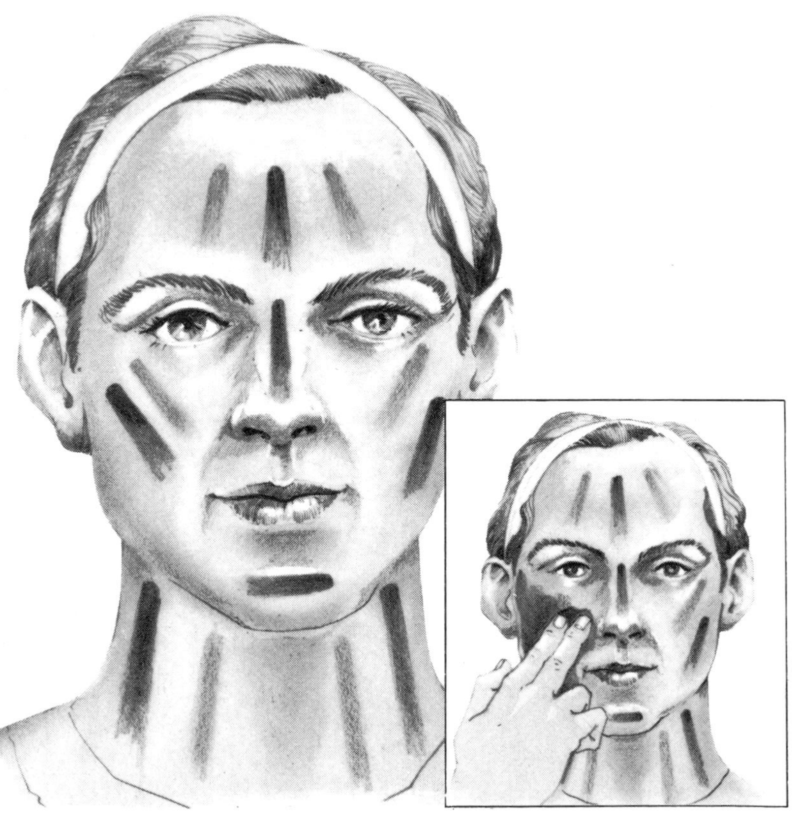

Apply a few strokes of color and blend in with the fingertips

Soft greasepaint

When applying soft greasepaint, always make sure the skin is completely dry and free from any grease.

If the paint is packaged in tubes, squeeze sufficient to complete the makeup on to the palm of the hand and then, with a fingertip, transfer it in small dots evenly all over the face and throat. If the paint is packaged in a jar, transfer sufficient color with a spatula into your hand and dot over the face in the same way. To mix colors, place the colors in the palm of your hand and stir them together with a fingertip before dotting on to the face.

Now blend the color gently and evenly all over the face and neck, using your fingertips or a damp cosmetic sponge. Make sure that you cover all exposed areas of skin. Gently fade the color up into the hairline, once more avoiding getting any color on the hair.

When you have finished blending the greasepaint (hard or soft), rub a clean fingertip over the surface of the makeup — if you leave a track in the makeup or there is a noticeable amount of color on your finger, you have used too much and it needs to be reduced.

To do this, blend once more, using all four fingers, until you have picked up a quantity of the greasepaint; remove this from your fingers with a tissue, and continue blending and wiping your fingers until you are no longer picking up any color from the face.

Do not be tempted to scrub color directly off the face with a tissue as this gives a patchy uneven result.

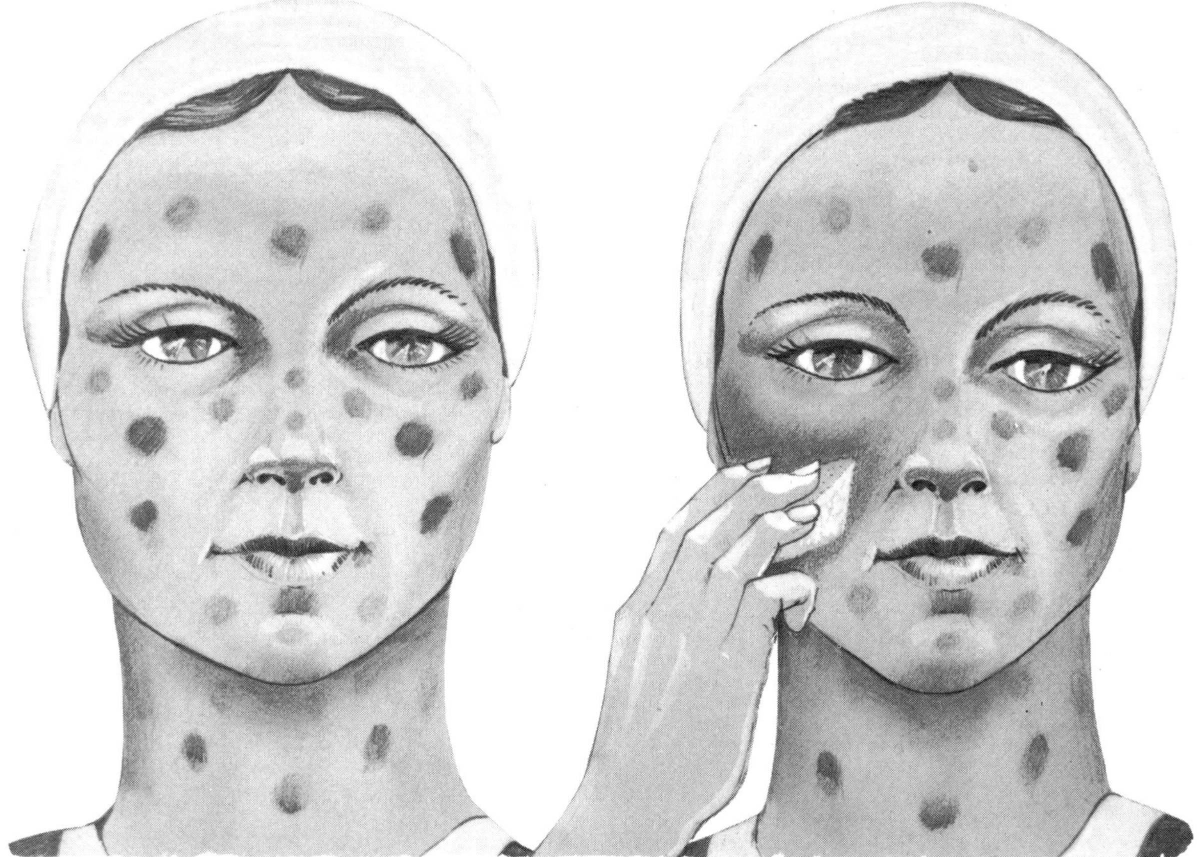

Dot the color over the face and neck, then blend in with a damp cosmetic sponge

Application techniques

Cream-stick foundation

This comes in a very wide range of skin tones and it is rarely necessary to mix them, so just choose the shade you need. Remove the plastic cover and wind the cream stick a short way out of the container; then apply it directly on to the face with broad strokes. Now blend the strokes into a fine even film over the entire face and throat, using a dampened cosmetic sponge. Use the product very sparingly to achieve the most natural result.

If you need to add more to conceal such blemishes as shadows under the eyes or broken veins, do so by picking up extra color from the end of the stick directly on to the sponge and then gently pat and stipple the cream over the required area.

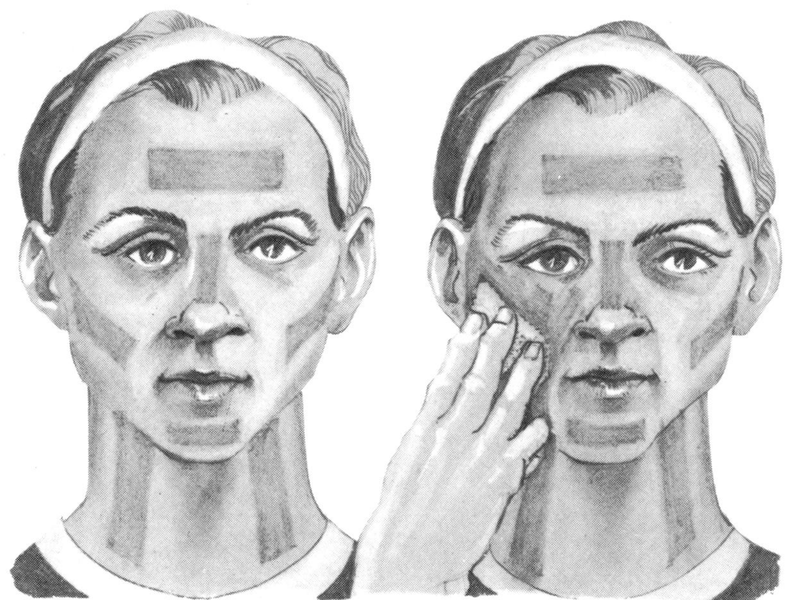

Apply the color in broad strokes directly from the stick and blend in with a damp sponge

Liquid makeups

These foundations, which are basically produced for day makeup, are too numerous to be individually named. They are generally water based so they should be applied with a dry cosmetic sponge. A damp sponge tends to dissolve the product and give a patchy uneven result.

Decant a small amount, about one inch (25mm) in diameter, into the palm of your hand, and dip a corner of your sponge into the product and apply to the face. Using a light stroking movement, blend it over the face and throat until a flawless finish is achieved. Extra cover can be obtained by patting and stippling in the liquid (as described above for the cream-stick foundation).

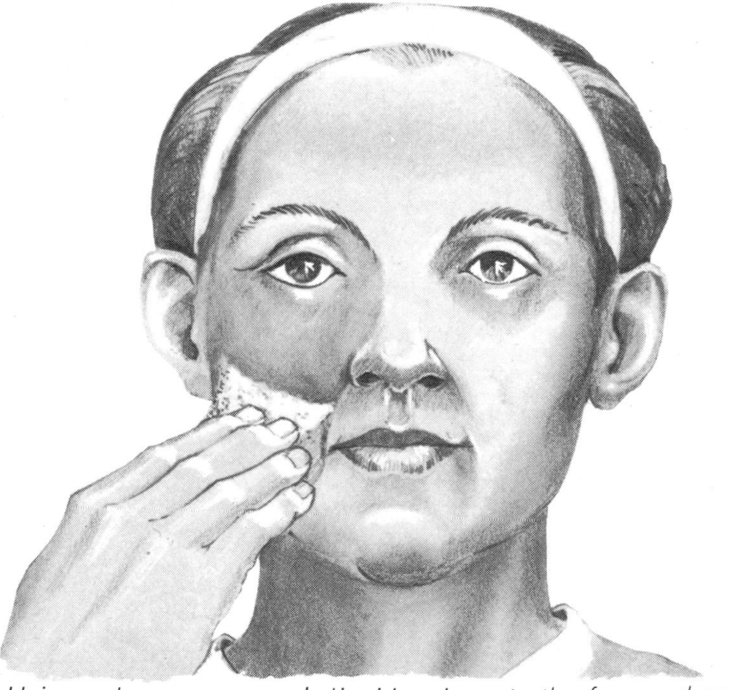

Using a dry sponge, apply liquid makeup to the face and neck

Rouge

After you have applied your foundation, using any of the four types of base described, the next step is to apply your moist or cream rouge. For a classic rouge application, pick up a small amount of the rouge on the tip of your forefinger and apply three dots of color along each cheekbone, as shown, starting on the high point of the cheekbone and working back along the bone towards the top of the ear. Now, with a clean finger, blend these three dots into a line of color along the cheekbone, using tiny little semicircular movements. Wipe the finger clean and blend this line of color away at the edges to produce a soft suffusion of color over the cheekbone, taking care not to take the color too close to the nose. If you need to add more color, do so by repeating the process in the same way, starting once again on the high point of the cheekbone.

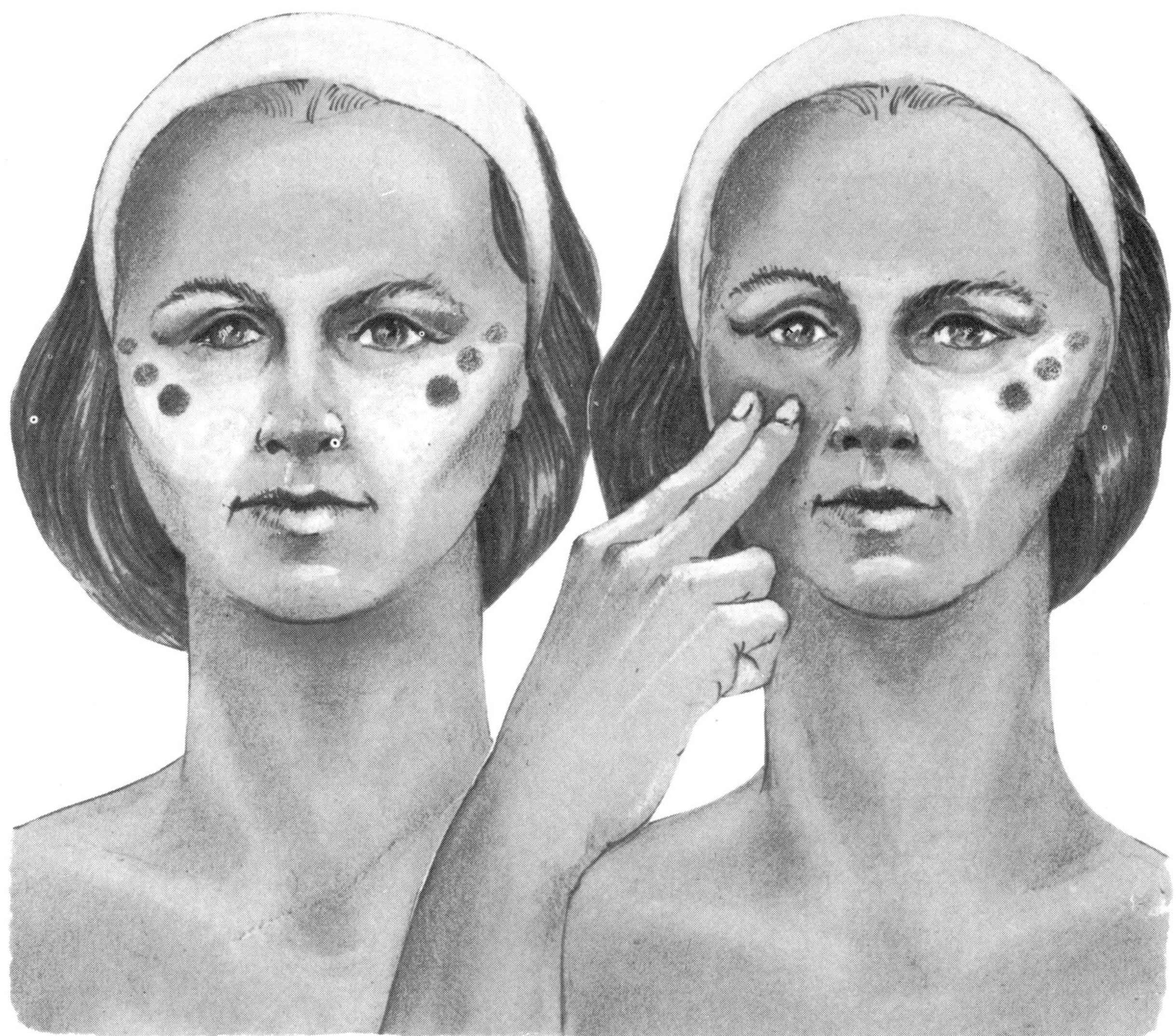

__1__ With a fingertip, apply three dots of color to the cheekbone

__2__ Blend dots into a line of color, wipe fingers and then fade out edges

Application techniques

Shadows and highlights

Once the rouge has been blended, the face can then be remodeled with highlights and shadows. First, apply the shadows. For this you can use your fingers or a brush; the choice depends upon the type and size of the shadow and on which you can use with the greatest skill. This you can find out only by experience and practice.

The best brush for large areas, such as the temples or cheek hollows, is the $\frac{3}{8}$ inch (9mm) square-ended sable. For lines and wrinkles use the $\frac{1}{4}$ inch (6mm) square-ended type.

Try using a combination of both brush and fingers when applying shadows and highlights. Apply color with the brush and use it for the early blending but finish off the final blending with your fingertips, using light stippling pats.

Now highlight these shadows, using first a brush and then your fingers in the same manner as before.

These highlights and shadows can be achieved in several ways. You can use either lining colors (see page 16) or colors chosen from the same range as your base — in which case the highlights would be about four shades lighter and the shadows about four shades darker. It is impossible to use this last method with liquid makeup as the range of colors available is too limited.

***1** Apply the shading color with a 3/8 inch (9mm)brush*

***2** Blend the shadow using a combination of both brush and fingertips*

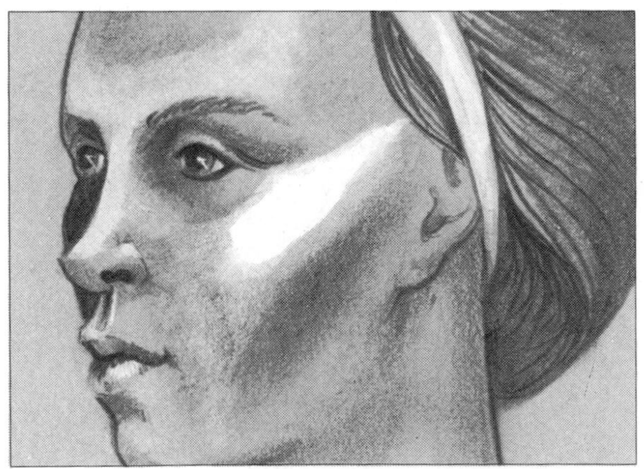

***3** Apply highlight with 3/8 inch (9mm) brush*

***4** Use brush and fingertips to blend highlight*

Powder

When you have completed the application of the base, the rouge, the highlights and shadows, it is necessary to "set" the makeup with a neutral translucent powder.

Pick up a generous amount of powder on your powder puff (which should be of the flat velour type), fold the puff in half and rub the powder back into the fibers of the puff, leaving no excess on the surface. Now pat and press the powder into the makeup with a firm rolling movement of the puff.

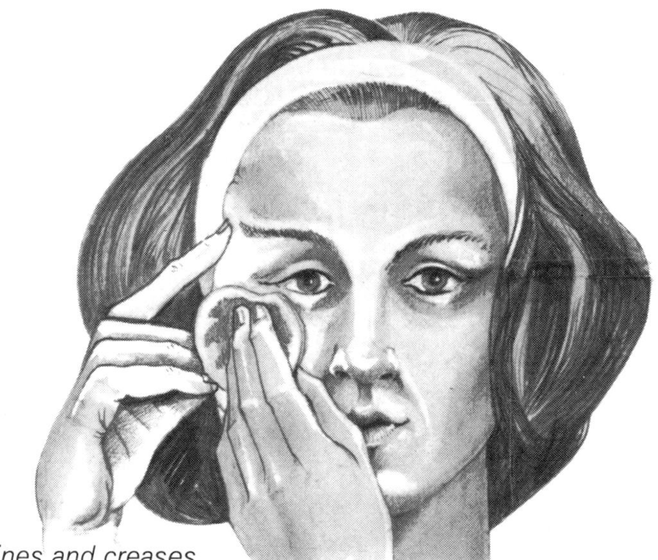

To avoid lines and creases, gently stretch skin, pat the makeup smooth and powder

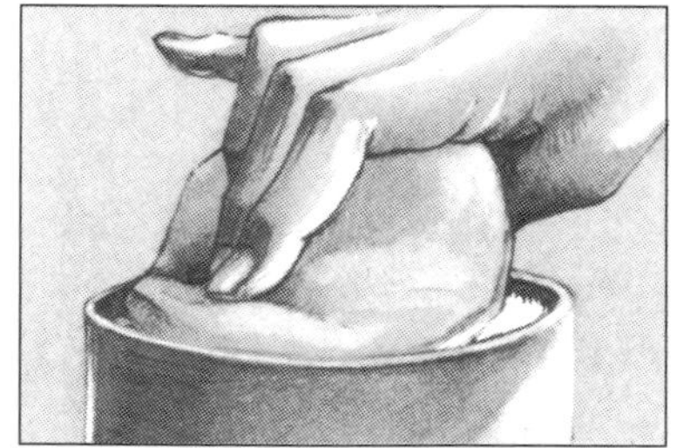

***1** Pick up powder on puff*

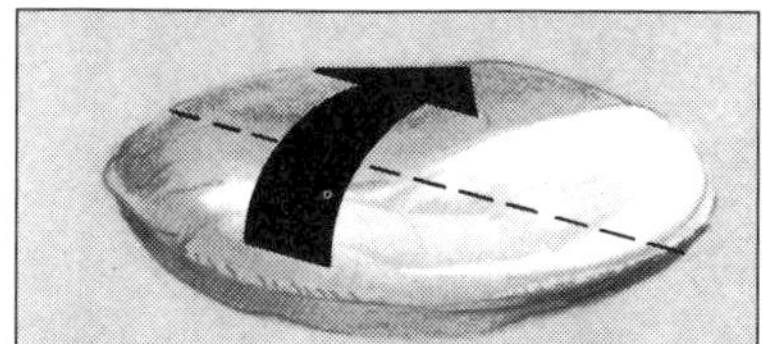

***2** Fold powder puff sides together to enclose powder*

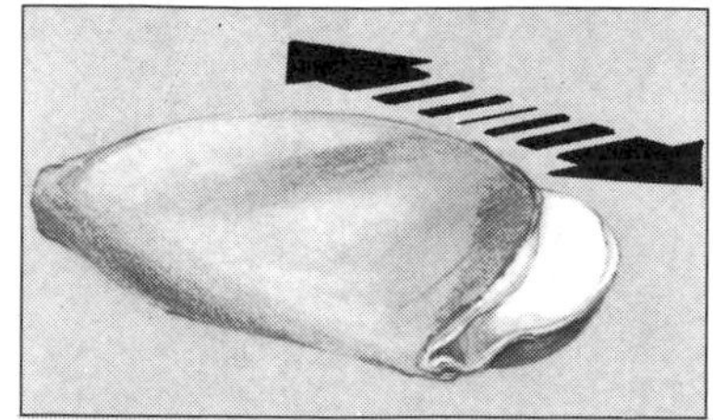

***3** Rub powder well into the fibers of powder puff*

Start on the throat at a point just below one ear and pat around the face in a decreasing circle, gradually working towards the nose which should be left until last. Never rub or smear the powder with your puff, as this will simply rub off the makeup.

Just before you powder the area around the eyes, make quite sure that the makeup is completely smooth and has not squeezed into any little lines and creases. If it has, then pat the makeup smooth with your finger and powder this area immediately, to prevent this lined appearance reoccurring.

This creasing of the makeup around the eyes will occur on even the youngest face, but on an older face there may also be lines on the forehead, in the fold between the nose and mouth and at the corners of the eyes, where the laugh lines are sometimes quite pronounced.

In these cases, gently stretch the lined area of skin between the first two fingers until the lines are flattened. Then pat the makeup smooth and thoroughly powder these areas while the skin is still taut. This will prevent the makeup "cracking" into these lines after it has been on a while. Otherwise the warmth of the skin could melt any unpowdered makeup.

When using hard or soft greasepaint, always remember to powder copiously, repeating this powdering process two or three times to ensure the makeup will remain set for as long as possible.

Cream-stick and liquid makeups require less powdering, but this does not mean that the powder should be skimped. Any excess powder which is not absorbed by the makeup can always be whisked away with a face-powder brush.

Application techniques

Cake makeup

Cake makeup is applied with a moistened cosmetic sponge. The best type is about three inches (75mm) in diameter and should be made of fine-textured foam plastic.

Dip the sponge into a bowl of water, squeeze it gently until it is just short of dripping and then work it over the surface of the cake in a circular movement until you obtain a soft creamy texture. Take up enough of the color from the cake to cover the entire face and throat. Then, working quickly, stroke it lightly and thinly over the broad areas of the face, forehead, cheek, chin and neck.

Fold the sponge in half around your forefinger and, using the small area of sponge under the fingertip, fill in the areas around the eyes, the nostrils and the corners of the mouth. Squeeze out all the surplus water from the sponge, turn it over and use the clean side to carefully blend the makeup into a really smooth flawless finish.

Still using the clean side, blend the color on the forehead up and into the hairline, taking care not to carry too much color on to the hair itself. Fade the color down the throat to avoid a masklike line where the makeup finishes.

Remember when choosing your color of cake makeup to pick a shade that looks several tones darker on the surface than the color you wish to achieve on the skin. This way you will find that the thinnest possible film of makeup will give you the correct color and the most natural finish.

Applying cake makeup

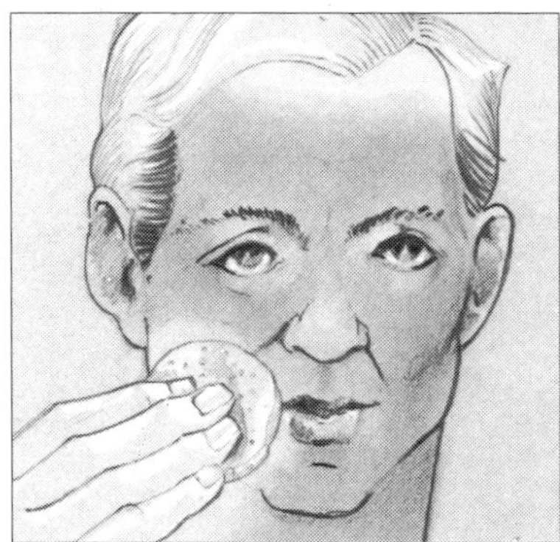

1 Sponge color over all the large areas

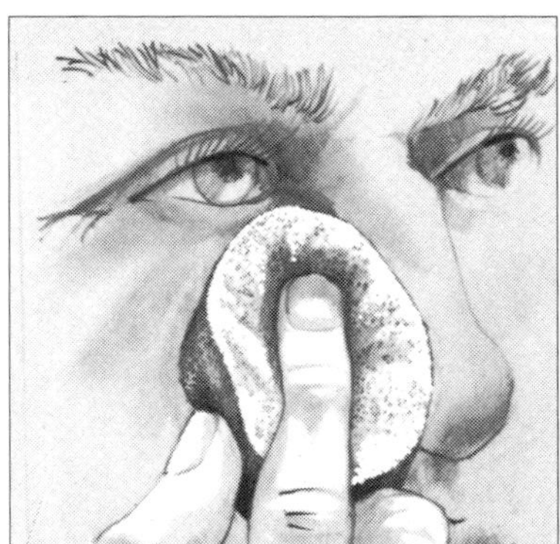

2 Fill in smaller details with a folded sponge

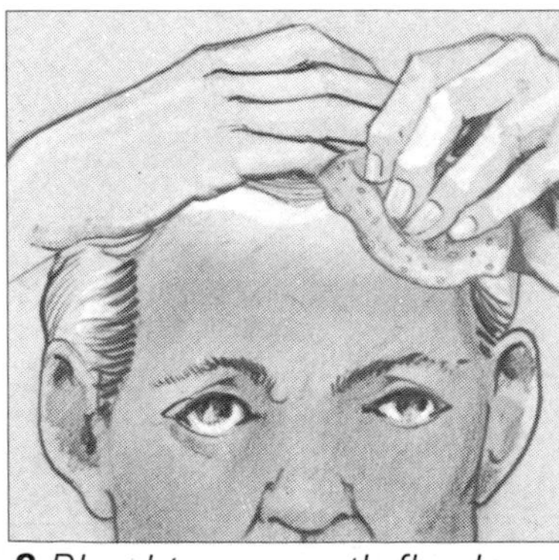

3 Blend to a smooth flawless finish with the clean side of the sponge

Powder

It is not normally necessary to use face powder over cake foundations since they dry with a matte finish anyway, but sometimes, when the skin tends to be over-greasy, a light powdering can be beneficial.

Retouching cake makeup

If necessary, cake makeup can be retouched using a small amount of the base color on your sponge, but great care must be taken not to obliterate any detail of the makeup when doing so.

Rouge with cake makeup

There are two methods of applying rouge with a cake makeup, using either moist rouge or dry cake rouge.

Moist rouge should be applied directly to the skin, using a stronger intensity of color than usual and then applying cake makeup over it. This method is useful because it gives the very natural effect of the blush appearing to come from beneath the skin.

Dry rouge can be applied over the top of the cake makeup, using either a rouge mop or the small puff sometimes provided with the product. Using your sponge and what is left of the cake color on it, blend the rouge softly into the foundation.

Most makeup artists prefer this second method as there is more control over the finished depth of color. However, do experiment with both of these methods until you decide which suits you best.

Highlighting and shading with cake makeup

There are two main methods of applying light and shade with cake makeup:

Method one

First apply your chosen base by the method already described and then apply your shadows, using a cake several shades darker than the base color. The highlights are then added, using a cake several shades lighter. These highlights and shadows are applied with either a $\frac{1}{4}$ inch (6mm) or $\frac{3}{8}$ inch (9mm), flat sable brush, depending on the size and type. Each shadow and highlight should be blended away, using either the brush or your fingertip, immediately the color has been applied. Should any of these details dry before you have finished blending, just wet the brush or finger with a little water and then continue the blending.

When using this method, do remember that color is much easier to add than to take away, so don't put on too much shadow or highlight to begin with. Apply a small amount, blend it and then add more until the desired depth of color is finally reached.

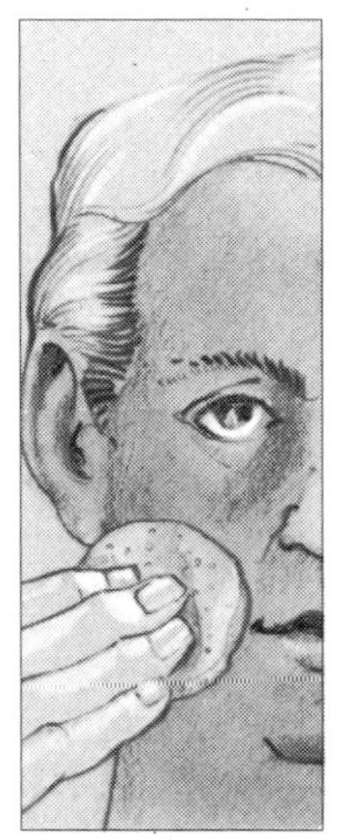

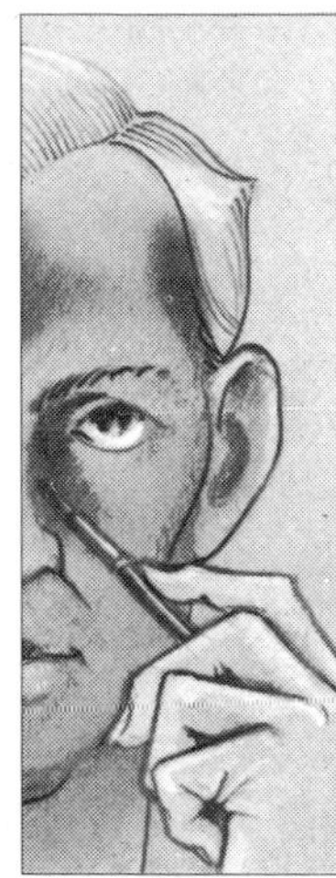

First apply cake base, then add shadows and highlights

Method two

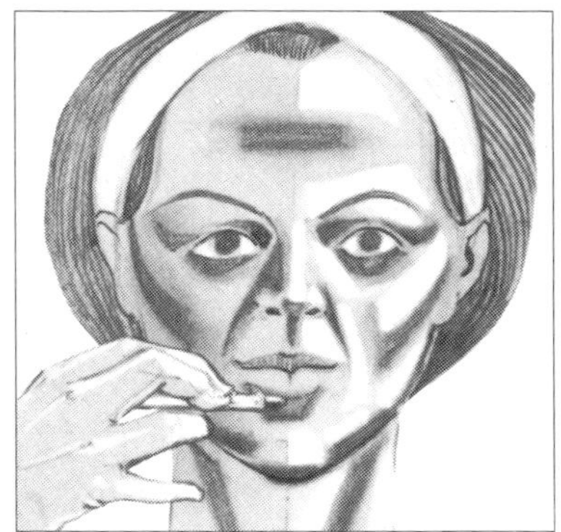

***1** Heavily apply shadows and highlights with grease liners*

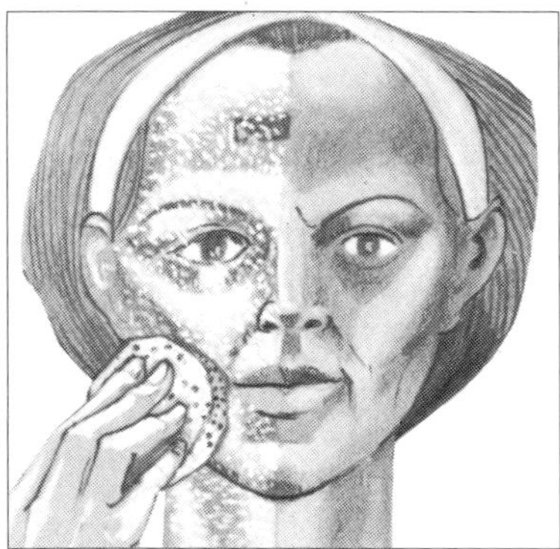

***2** Powder thoroughly before adding cake makeup*

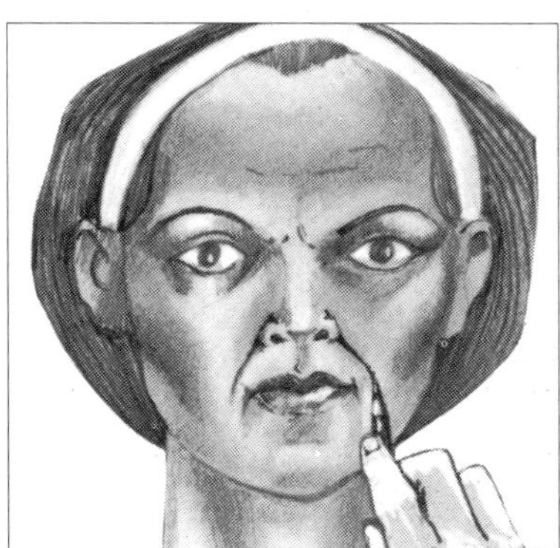

***3** Strengthen detail where needed with eyebrow pencil*

First apply your shadows and highlights directly on to the skin, using grease lining colors. The shadows should be a very dark shading color and the highlights a pure white.

Powder these highlights and shadows with translucent face powder or white talcum and then apply a thin film of your chosen color of cake makeup over the top. Do not be alarmed —you will not smudge the lining colors, providing that you remember to thoroughly powder them before applying the cake makeup.

Your character work should look slightly exaggerated before you apply the cake makeup, to enable it to show through the base color. The shadows and lines can be strengthened afterwards, using a dark-brown eyebrow pencil where greater clarity is desired.

This method is particularly effective in small theaters or theater in the round where a high degree of subtlety is needed, since the character work really seems to be "under the skin".

Application techniques

Eye makeup

The application of eye makeup and lip color involves exactly the same procedure for both grease and cake makeup, once these have been set.

Eyebrow pencil

Eyebrow pencils can be used for sketching in eyebrows and also for lining the eye. The first important thing to learn is how to sharpen them.

Although an ordinary pencil sharpener can be used, the resulting point will be most unsatisfactory. This is because the color content of these pencils is made from a soft wax formula which will become blunt after only a few strokes.

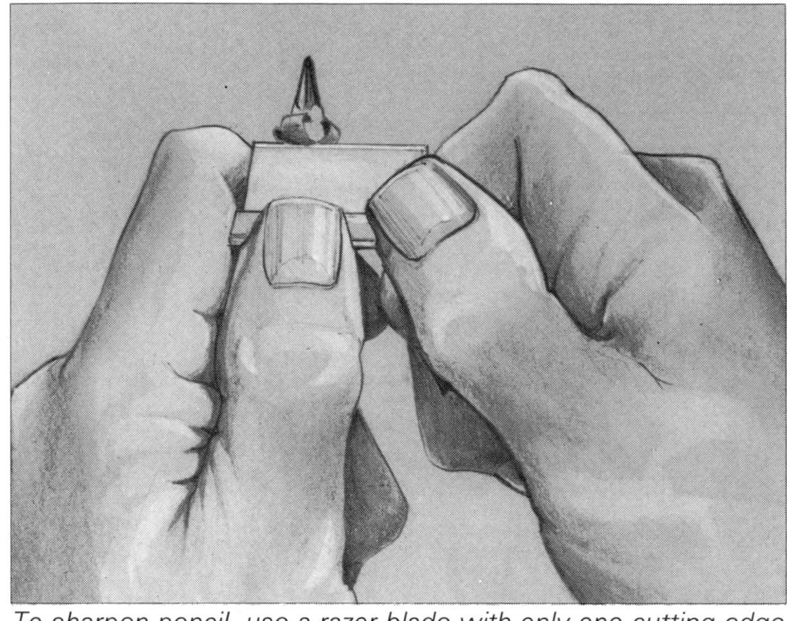

To sharpen pencil, use a razor blade with only one cutting edge

The best method of sharpening is to use a razor blade with only one cutting edge and a hard back, as illustrated. Holding the pencil in one hand and the blade in the other, press the blade into the wood of the pencil.

At the same time, pull back the pencil with the fingers, so the hand holding the blade only regulates its angle.

Using this pressing and pulling action, slowly pare away the wood but do not allow the blade to cut into the wax. When you have exposed about $\frac{3}{8}$ of an inch (9mm), gently scrape the wax down into the shape of a tiny, two-edged, flat-bladed sword. The point now has two sharp edges which can be used to sketch small hairlike strokes into the brows and also to draw soft broad lines, using the flat sides. These sharp edges can be easily resharpened by rubbing the wax over a fine emery board or gently scraping with the razor blade.

When using the pencil to reshape the brows, use only tiny hairlike strokes, remembering to lift the pencil away from the skin at the end of each stroke to simulate the natural growth of the brow. Never be tempted to use straight hard lines. This gives a "drawn on" look to the brows, which is very hard and artificial.

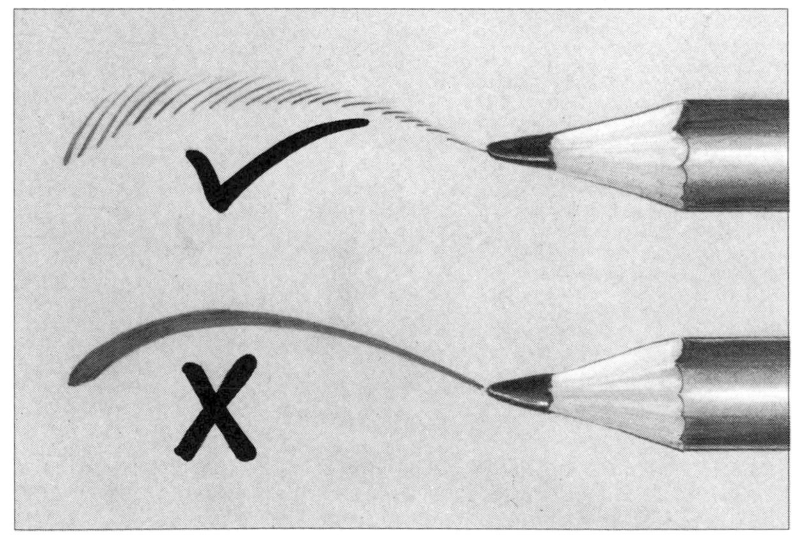

Eyeshadow

All the different types of eyeshadow available, apart from cosmetic eye pencils, are best applied with brushes. The number 6 filbert and the $\frac{1}{4}$ inch (6mm), square-ended sable are the most useful, but do remember that when you are using more than one shadow, you must use a separate brush for each color, otherwise the colors will mix together and look gray.

If grease liners, cream-type shadows, or soft, cosmetic eye pencils are used, they must be powdered to prevent creasing.

Powder shadows can be used on their own, but it is very difficult when using two or more colors together to prevent them smudging into each other and becoming gray.

A combination of cosmetic eye pencils and powder eyeshadows is the technique that I prefer to use. Note that these cosmetic pencils should be sharpened with a large pencil sharpener, obtainable from cosmetic manufacturers.

The eye pencil is first applied to the eyelid in the pattern required and then set with powder eyeshadow, applied with a $\frac{1}{4}$ inch (6mm) square-ended brush. This type of application is very long lasting and, by using a mixture of different colors, very subtle color combinations can be achieved. For example, by using a green pencil set with green powder shadow, a strong clear green is produced; use a brown pencil in combination with the green shadow and a more subtle hazel-green will result, and so on.

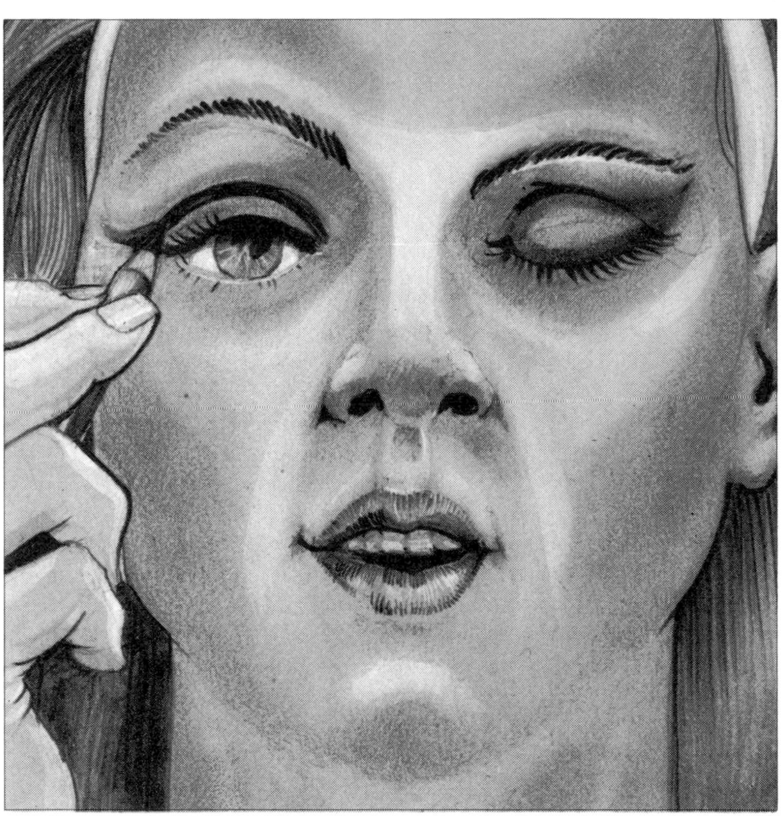

1 *Apply cosmetic pencil as shown*

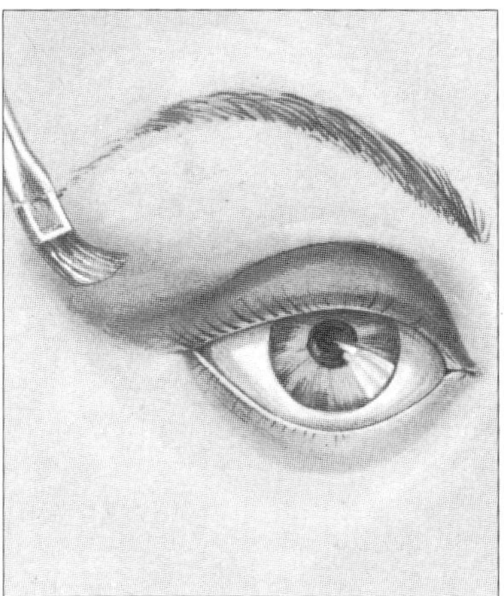

2 *Blend out pencil with a $\frac{1}{4}$ inch (6mm) brush, blending the color up and over the browline, softening edges*

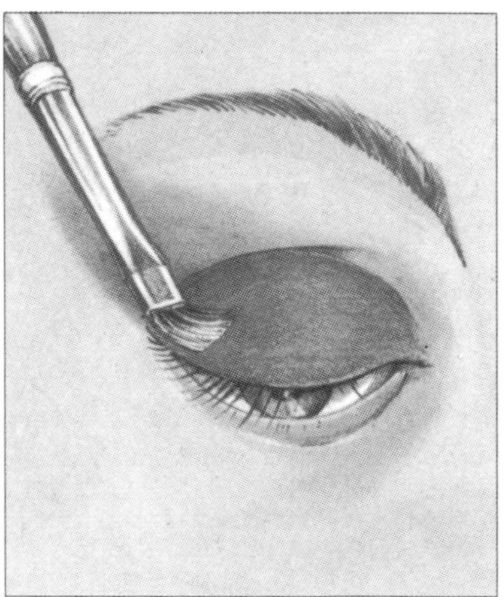

3 *Apply powder eyeshadow over pencil until the required depth of color is achieved and the pencil color set*

Application techniques

Eyelining

The eyes can be outlined using either a cosmetic pencil or a fine lining brush. The brush should be loaded with grease lining or water-soluble cake liner.

Eyebrow pencils are generally too hard to use around the eye area, but cosmetic eye pencils can be used quite effectively.

The finished eyeline must, however, be powdered and all too often the result can look smudged and dirty. Therefore cake or liquid liners are the best products to use.

A common mistake when applying eyeliner is to use too much color on the brush, which results in blobs along the edge of the eye. Fill the brush with color and then draw the hairs to a fine point, thereby removing excess color.

Tilt the head back and look down into the mirror so that the eyelids are stretched taut. Starting at the inner corner of the eye, draw a line close to the roots of the lashes. Follow the curve of the lid to a point just past the outer corner of the eye. Extend the line at the end of the eye up and out, as illustrated.

To line the lower lid, tilt your head downward and look up into the mirror so that you can get the brush under the lower lashes. Draw a line as shown.

In a large theater, eyelines should be drawn clearly and sharply, but in more intimate settings they look more natural if they are slightly softened with the tip of your little finger or a clean sable brush.

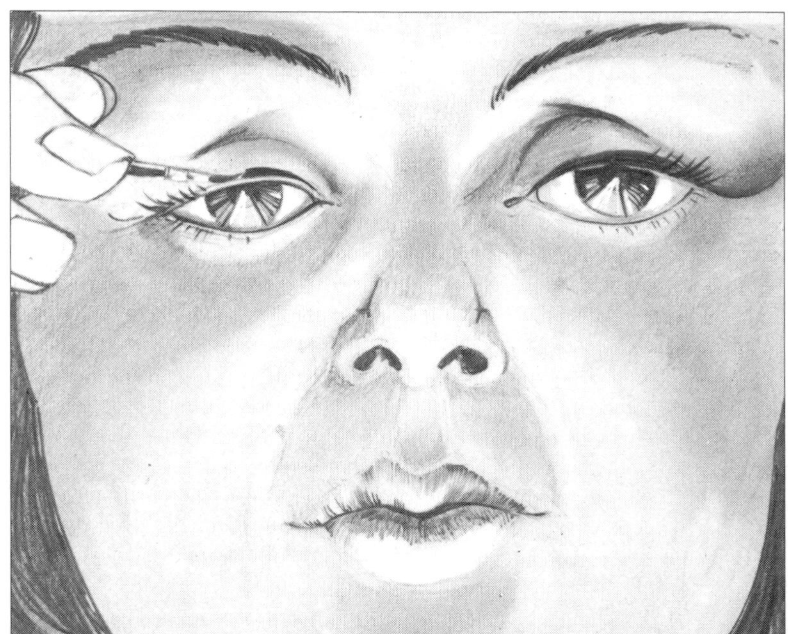

1 *Tilt the head back. Look down into the mirror and draw a line close to the lashes, following the curve of the eyelid*

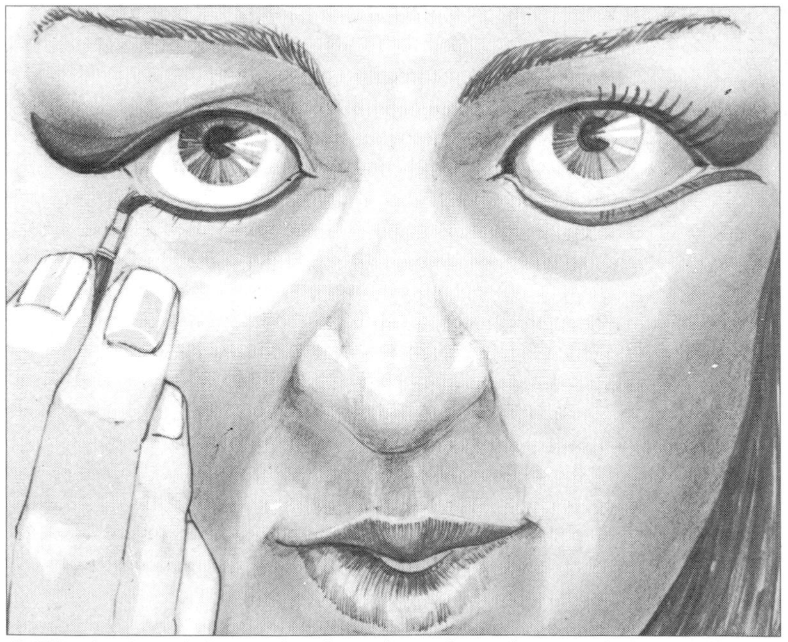

2 *Tilt the head down. Look up into the mirror and draw a line under the lower lashes*

Mascara

Whether you use a block mascara with a wet brush or an automatic wand type, the application is basically the same. (If using block mascara, first cream up the required amount with warm water on to the mascara brush.) Tilt back your head as for eyelining and apply the mascara generously on to the lashes, ensuring that the color goes right down to the roots of the lashes. Allow the first coat to dry and apply a second coat in the same way, repeating this until you have sufficient color on the lashes.

To make up the lower lashes, tuck your chin down as you did for the eyeliner and apply the mascara, using a sideways movement of the brush. Then brush downwards to separate the lashes. If your mascara is slow drying, it pays to make up the lower lashes before the top ones, so that when you look up into the mirror you don't smudge the color on to the browbones in little dots of black.

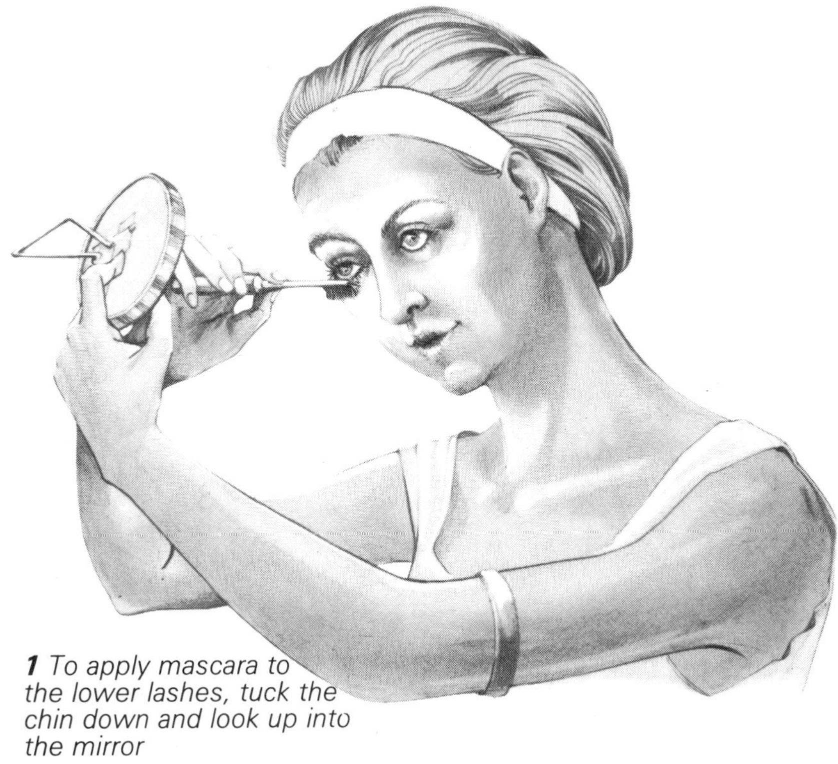

1 *To apply mascara to the lower lashes, tuck the chin down and look up into the mirror*

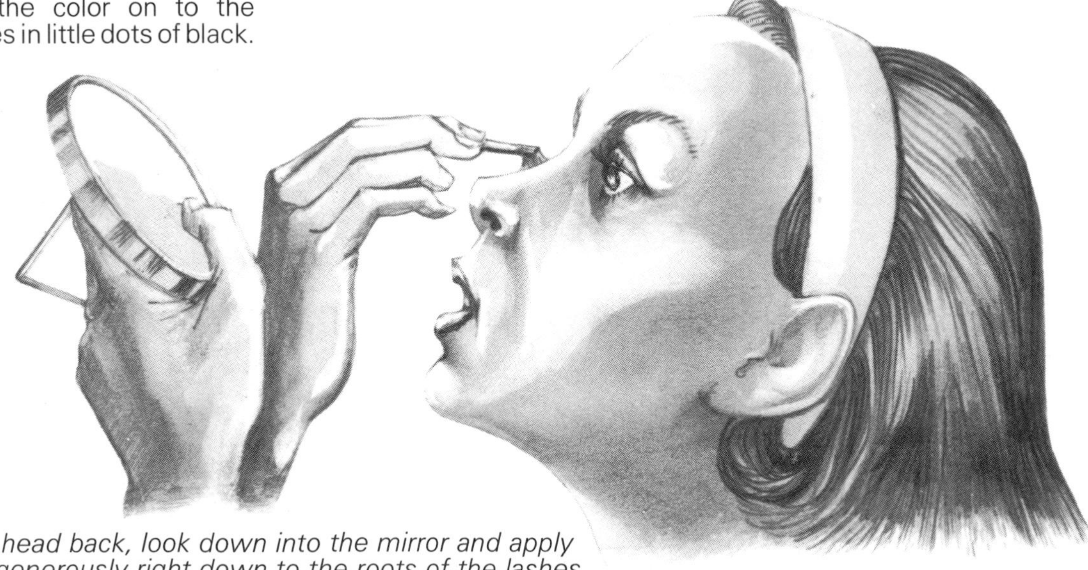

2 *Tilt the head back, look down into the mirror and apply mascara generously right down to the roots of the lashes*

Application techniques

Kohl

If you need to apply color to the inner edge of the eye, above the lower lashes, it should not be done until the mascara has completely dried. Look down into the mirror and gently pull the lower lid away from the eye with a fingertip. Apply the color with a cosmetic eye pencil or grease lining on an $\frac{1}{8}$ inch (3mm), square-ended brush. It is sometimes very effective to line the inside edge of the top lid, below the upper lashes. To do this, look down into the mirror and gently lift the lid away from the eye with a fingertip and apply the color in the same way as for the lower edge.

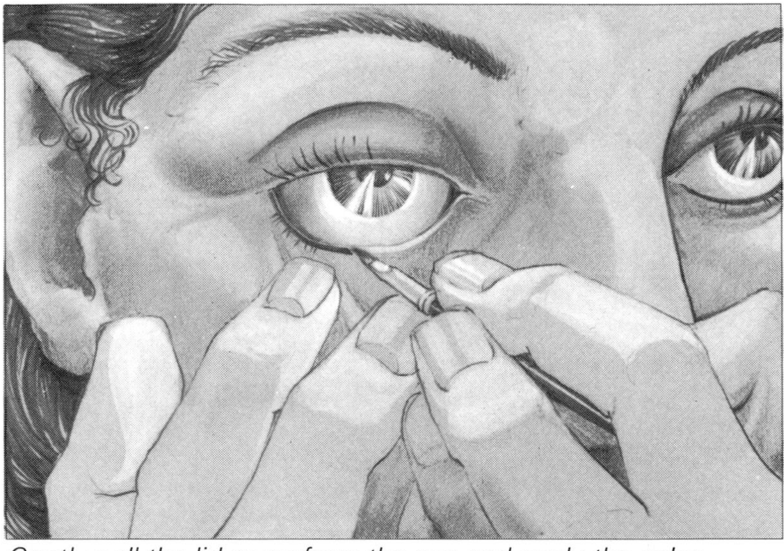

Gently pull the lid away from the eye and apply the color

Lip color

When reshaping a mouth, you need to use a lip brush to achieve a clear clean outline. Brushes sold as lip brushes are square ended and very slightly larger than $\frac{1}{8}$ inch (3mm), but these are generally too small. A number 6 filbert is better. Some people find it difficult to use a lip brush with ease, so here are a few tips to help you master the technique.

Always fully load the brush with color. Work your brush over the lipstick or lining color until the hairs are completely filled with the color, then stroke the brush into an even shape to enable you to draw a clear outline.

Practise drawing lip shapes on the back of your hand to give you the feel of the brush. Use the side of the brush rather than the tip and always remember to keep the head of the brush inside the lip shape.

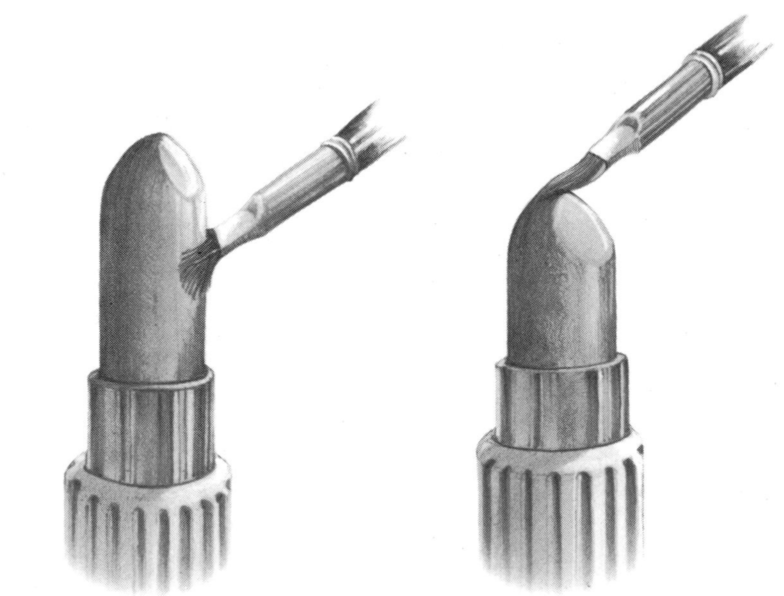

Load the brush with color and stroke into an even shape

To steady your hand, lean your elbow on a table and brace the tip of your little finger against your chin. Keep your mouth in a relaxed shape (not fully open, however, as this distorts the shape) and draw on the outline,working from the corners of the mouth inward toward the center. When your outline is

complete, fill in the center of the lips and gently blot the mouth with a tissue to remove any excess color.

When overpainting the lips to enlarge the mouth, the outline can be drawn with a darker lip-lining pencil than your chosen lip color. If you need a very hard look to the mouth, leave this as a sharp line.

For a softer effect, carefully blend the line with a brush in toward the center of the lips before filling in with the main lip color.

When a very soft unpainted look is required, especially for some male makeups, the color should be applied very sparingly, using the tip of your little finger.

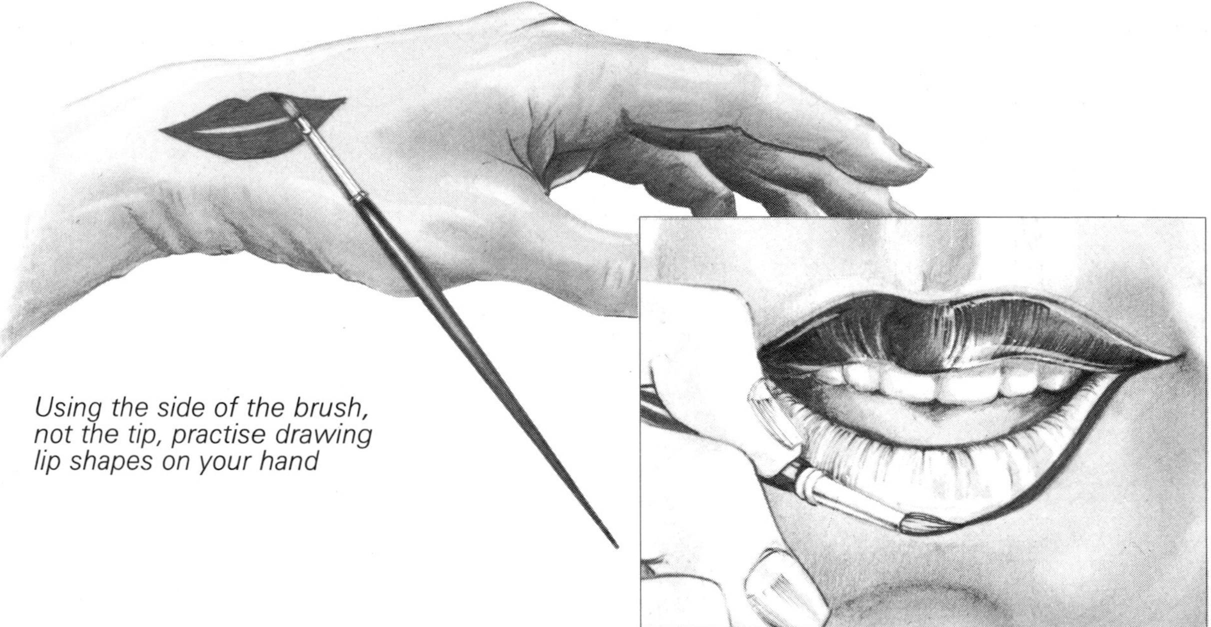

Using the side of the brush, not the tip, practise drawing lip shapes on your hand

Outline the mouth first and then fill in the center with color

Cake rouge

Once the makeup is completed and the lip color added, the original application of rouge may seem a little weak. This can be heightened by the addition of a touch of cake rouge at the last moment. This is applied with a rouge mop, using small semi-circular movements over the cheekbone, starting on the highest point and working back towards the top of the ear. Some corrective work can be done with cake rouge and this is described in fuller detail later.

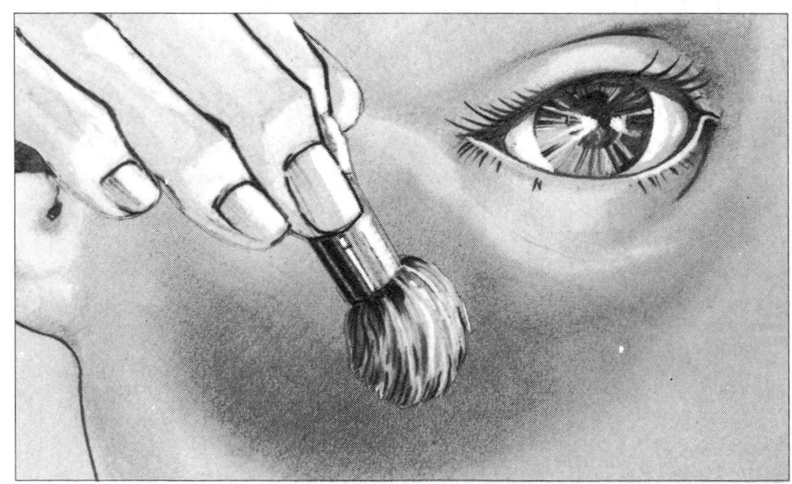

The art of application

When actors first have to create a new Stage Face, they initially use their acting ability and secondly a box of makeup. I say "secondly" because even the most well-conceived and beautifully executed makeup is not the be-all and end-all of a good characterization. The best makeup must have an actor underneath to breathe it into life. Makeup is only an aid to help reveal the characterization that has been built up through the weeks of rehearsal.

When you sit down in front of your mirror, before you apply the makeup, start to act the part. Use dialogue that gives you a clear indication of the character's personality, and observe what happens to your features as you say the lines; then you can gradually add the makeup, emphasizing and adding to what you see.

How do you use makeup to change your features; how do you slim down your face or make it look fatter, shorten your nose, widen your forehead or make your chin look more prominent? All of these problems become much easier if you apply what I consider to be the golden rule of makeup, "Anything you wish to look smaller, you make darker and anything you wish to look larger, you make lighter ".

This rule can be applied to every stage in a makeup. By using a light foundation color, you can make a face look larger and wider; a dark foundation will help you to make a large face look smaller. A touch of dark shading color on the tip of the nose will shorten it, while highlighting on the cheekbones will make them more prominent, and so on. The reason this happens is because we are making use of a simple optical illusion relating to the size of a given area.

Optical illusions

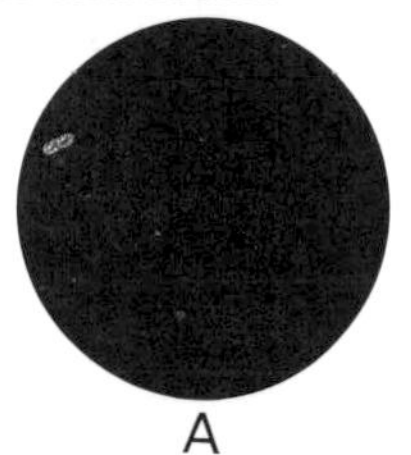

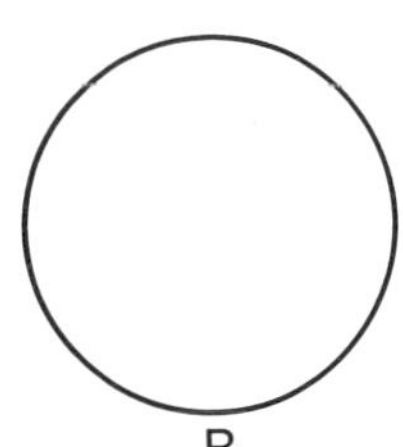

Both these circles are exactly the same size but A *appears to be smaller than* B *because black is a recessive color that reflects less light, thereby making the circle appear further away and smaller*

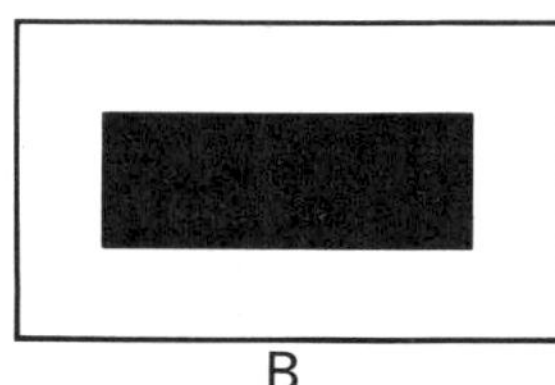

This effect becomes even more noticeable if a white area is placed against a black background and vice versa.
In this diagram the white rectangle in A *looks larger and nearer to your eye than the black rectangle in* B

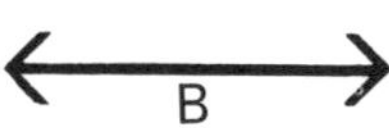

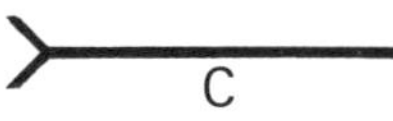

A second optical illusion that is used is one relating to the length of a given line. In this diagram the lines A, B *and* C *are all exactly the same length, but* B *looks smaller than both* A *and* C *because it is contained within closed acute angles.* C *looks longer than both* A *and* B *because it is between open acute angles*

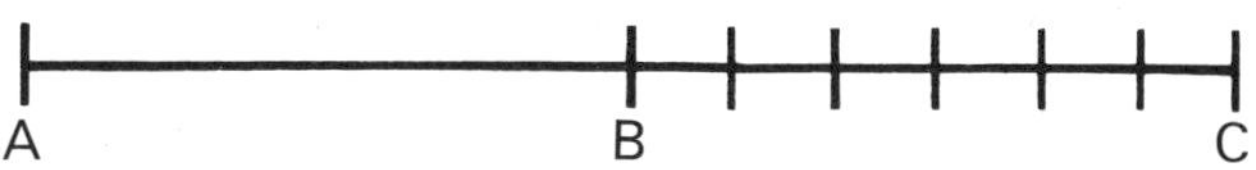

Yet another illusion is one of division. Here line A C *has been divided into two equal parts,* A B *and* B C. B C *has been further divided with several transversal lines, which makes* A B *seem shorter than* B C

These optical illusions are particularly useful when making up eyes. The effect can be seen in the drawing on the right. Both eyes are the same size but **A** looks smaller because it is contained in closed acute angles formed by the eyeliner and then surrounded by a light tone, which makes the eye look darker. Eye **B** looks larger because the dark eyeshadow makes the eye look lighter. The opened-out eyelines make the eye appear wider. Also, the illusion of division (illustrated on the previous page) is echoed by the emphasis of the made-up eyelashes.

One other optical illusion to be considered is the effect of horizontal and vertical details on the face. Shadows and lines used horizontally across the face tend to widen and flatten; vertical shadows and lines lengthen and narrow the face. This principle can be extended to include the use of hairstyles and beards and mustaches, as well as the actual light and shade on the face.

Furthermore, the shape of such things as hats, spectacles and jewelry can also influence the proportions of the face.

These two makeup designs for Sir Andrew Aguecheek and Sir Toby Belch in *Twelfth Night* show the use of horizontal and vertical details to create the illusion of thinness and fatness, respectively. Note particularly the use of hair and beards, the design of the hats and the necklines of the costumes.

Once you have mastered the fundamental principles of how to enlarge and diminish the features, you will be surprised just how much can be done with makeup, but bear in mind that there are limitations to what can be achieved. It is not always possible to create a makeup that exactly reproduces what the playwright or the designer had in mind. Naturally, the director, when casting the play, tries to choose an actor who has at least some physical resemblance to the character in question; after all, it would be sheer folly to cast a very short, fat actor to play the part of Sir Andrew Aguecheek and a very tall, thin actor to play Sir Toby Belch. On the other hand, an actor of medium build could, with suitably designed costumes and makeup, play either of these two parts quite successfully. However, bear in mind when creating a Stage Face, the more makeup you use, the more you will inhibit the natural facial expressions. Use just those features that can be changed most easily and with the most effect — and let the acting do the rest!

A

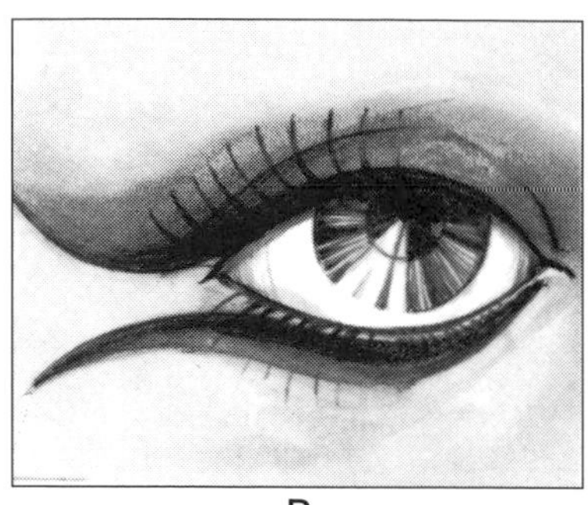

B

Sir Toby Belch *Sir Andrew Aguecheek*

Corrective makeup

The type of makeup that is most often required in the theater is one that enables both actors and actresses to project their own personalities and at the same time look as attractive as possible. In the professional theater this frequently means making them look younger!

Before we can correct a face, we need to discover its faults. To do this we should have a clear idea of just what is considered to be classically beautiful or good looking.

The classic face

There are two principal attributes to an ideal face — good health and harmonious proportions of the features.

Features of good health

A normal oval face — not too fat and not too thin — smooth elastic skin without blemishes, and a pink and even complexion are all signs of good health. The eyes should be open to a normal degree and be clear and bright; the lips should be red and the cheeks rosy.

Harmonious proportions

As shown on the right, the face can be divided horizontally into three equal parts:

1 From the hairline down to the eyebrows.

2 From the eyebrows to the tip of the nose.

3 From the tip of the nose to the base of the chin.

The face can also be divided vertically into five equal parts, with each part being the width of an eye, and with the eyes being the width of an eye apart.

The mouth should be slightly wider than the width of an eye so that imaginary lines drawn vertically from the corners of the mouth would just cross the inner edge of the pupils.

Ideally, the nose should be straight, in the exact center of the face and neither too broad nor too narrow.

The eyebrows should be slightly arched and just a little less than an eye's width apart. The eye sockets should not be too deeply sunken.

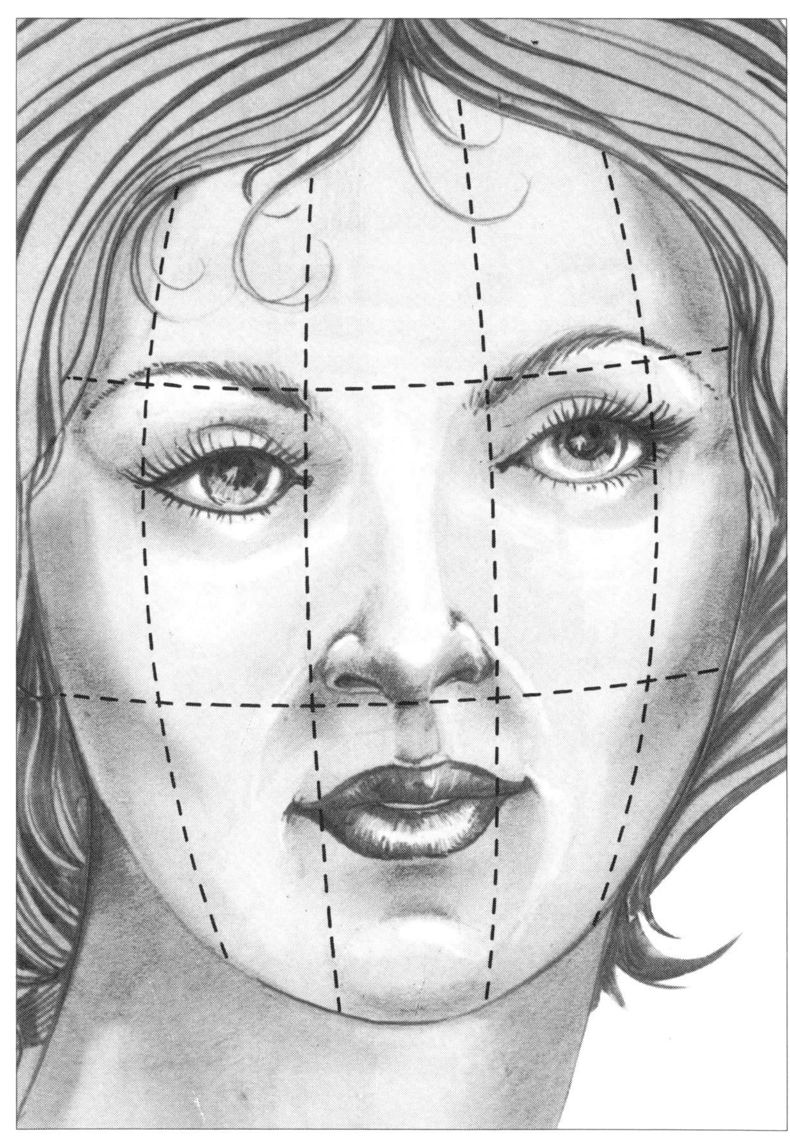

Complexion

The first thing to consider when applying a corrective makeup is the complexion. If the skin looks clean, healthy and perfectly unblemished, all that will be necessary is a light film of foundation, complimentary to the natural coloring of the performer and with sufficient strength of color to compensate for the effects of the lighting.

If, however, the complexion is uneven, sallow, ruddy or spotty, it must be corrected with a suitable foundation.

Uneven skin tones can be corrected with a slightly heavier application of a clean foundation color, carefully stippled over the skin with a moist sponge. Men, however, should take care not to make the complexion look too smooth and clear as this tends to destroy the masculinity of the face and gives too pretty an effect for a man.

Sallow skins need a fine film of foundation, complimentary to the natural coloring and then warmed by the addition of moist rouge stippled over the entire face. Start with a small amount of color, gradually adding more color until the required degree of healthiness is achieved, heightening the color on the cheeks, chin and forehead.

Ruddy complexions which have broken veins can be toned down by using an olive-based foundation, applied evenly all over the face. Stipple the color on with a moistened sponge and gradually add more foundation to the ruddiest areas of the skin.

Having toned down a ruddy complexion, place the rouge well back on the cheekbone, away from the cheek pad

Many people who have broken veins on their cheeks think it inadvisable to use rouge but, without it, the face looks flat and uninteresting. However, great care must be taken in applying the rouge.

It is best to use a tawny shade of dry cake rouge, gently dusted on with a rouge mop over well-powdered foundation (so as not to disturb the camouflage). Place the color well back along the cheekbone toward the ear to draw attention away from the cheek pad itself.

Under-eye shadows can be hidden, by using either a light colored cream-stick foundation or one of the specially designed cover creams available. Apply the color with a small sable brush directly on to the shadow itself and then softly blend away the edges with the tip of the little finger until the highlight merges imperceptibly into the foundation. Take care not to get the highlight on to the puffy areas on either side of the shadow as this would make the shadow look deeper.

Spots and blemishes can be disguised by using the same products, but in this case the color should not be lighter than your foundation as this would highlight the spot and make it look bigger.

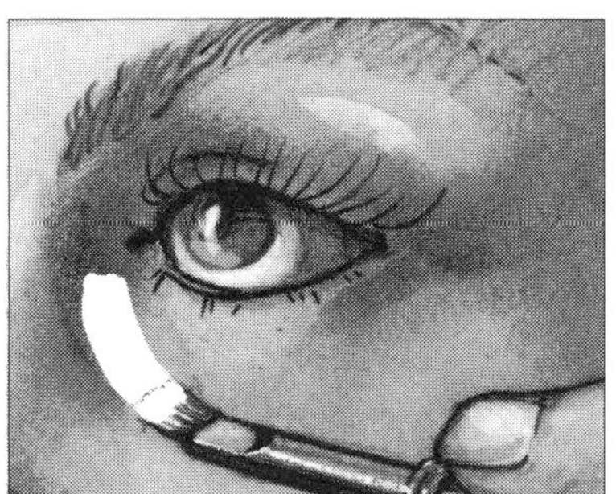

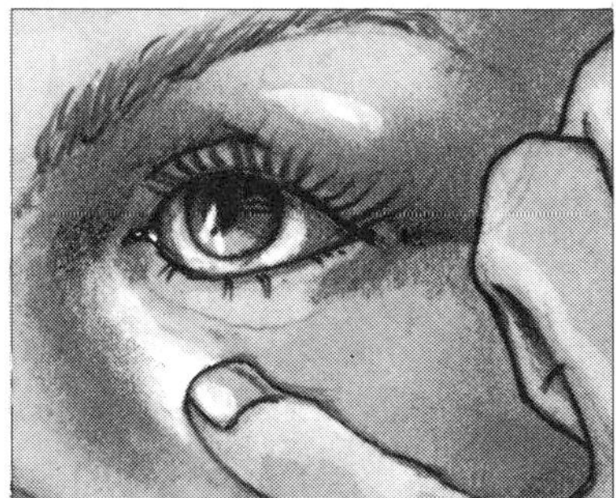

Apply a cover cream directly to under-eye shadows and blend away edges with the tip of the little finger.

Corrective makeup

Correcting facial proportions

If the horizontal and vertical divisions of the face are so unequal they upset the balance of the face, there are a number of ways these faults can be corrected.

Forehead

If the forehead is too high, it can be lowered by applying a fairly wide strip of shading color along the top edge of the forehead, close to the hairline. This band of shading can either be a foundation color two or three shades deeper than the base or a dark-brown rouge color. Blend the shading downwards on to the forehead until it merges into the foundation. The effect of this shadow can be heightened by dressing the front of the hair forward so that the lighting casts a shadow on to the top of the forehead.

If the forehead is too low, it can be heightened effectively by applying a highlight along the hairline. The hair should be dressed well back. This will allow the light to catch the highlight and make the forehead appear larger.

Too wide a forehead can be narrowed by simply shading the temple areas. Use a tawny shade of rouge, since brown shadows in the temples tend to add age to the face. Too narrow a forehead can be widened by highlighting the temple areas. This effect is also useful if you need to give a more youthful appearance to a face where the temples have become sunken with age.

If the forehead is too prominent, the whole area should be shaded with a darker base, fading the color away as it reaches the temples.

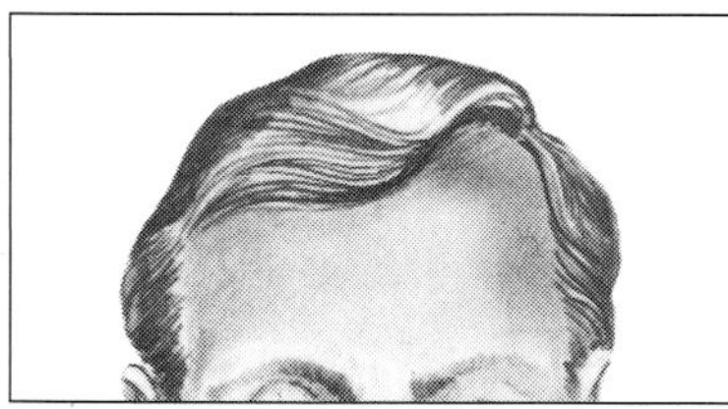

Shading along the hairline, with the hair dressed forward, will lower a high forehead

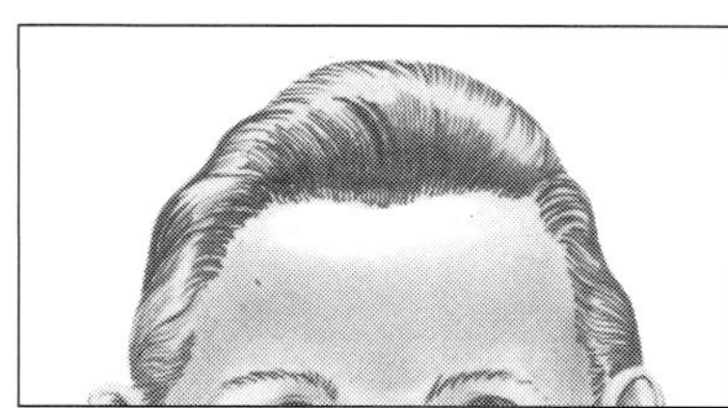

Hair dressed well back and a highlight along the hairline will heighten a low forehead

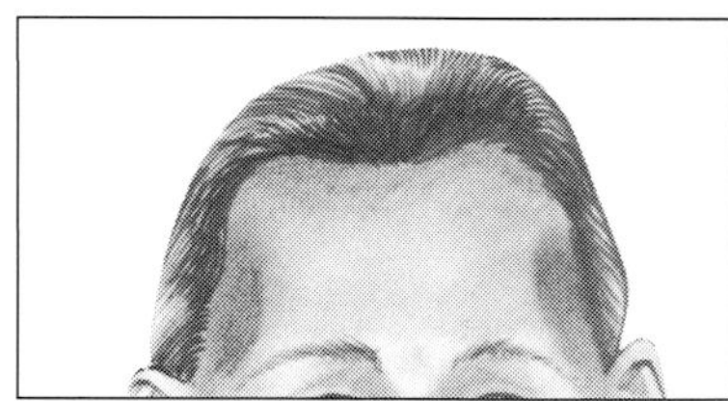

Shade the temple areas to narrow the forehead

Jawline

To strengthen a weak jawline, create a shadow immediately under the bone, fading it down on to the throat. Note the almost right-angled shape of the shadow applied just below the ear. A straight shadow here would be wrong as it gives a lantern-jawed effect

A sagging jawline can be corrected by highlighting the depressions and shading the jowls. If the jawline and throat have dropped badly, very little can be done with highlight and shadow. In this case temporary facial lifts should be used. The construction and use of these facial lifts is explained more fully in the chapter on special effects (see pages 96-97).

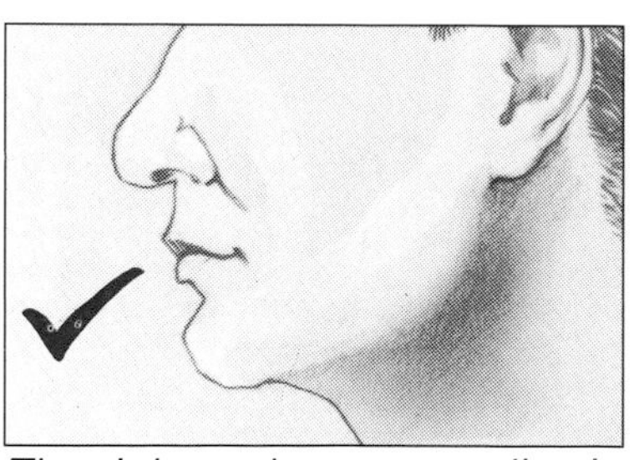

The right and wrong application of shadow to a weak jawline

Neck

If the neck shows signs of age, you can shade the prominent muscles and highlight the depressions, but this must be done with great care. One simple trick is to use a foundation two shades deeper than the color of the face over the whole neck area.

Nose

Too long a nose is shortened by applying a shadow under the tip and blending the edge up over the tip.

Too short a nose is lengthened by placing a highlight down the center of the nose and carrying it down and under the tip, making the highlight strongest right on the point.

Too broad a nose is narrowed by shading down the sides of the nose and over the nostrils and then running a narrow highlight down the center. A bulbous tip to the nose can be made to appear smaller by shading the tip on either side. Do take care not to carry the shadow up the sides of the nose.

A sharp thin nose is the most difficult to correct. First run a broad highlight down the center of the nose. Then very carefully pat a tiny amount of shadow just down the sharp bony ridge — to prevent the light catching it and so making it look sharper.

A broken or crooked nose can be corrected. Run a straight highlight down the nose, where it would be if the nose were straight and dead center. Then shade it on either side.

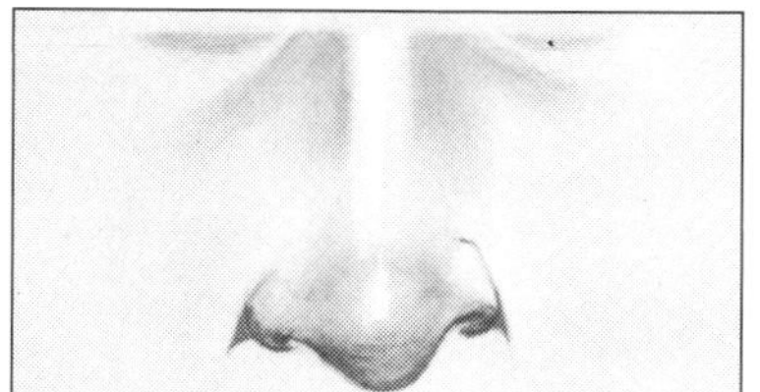
Long nose

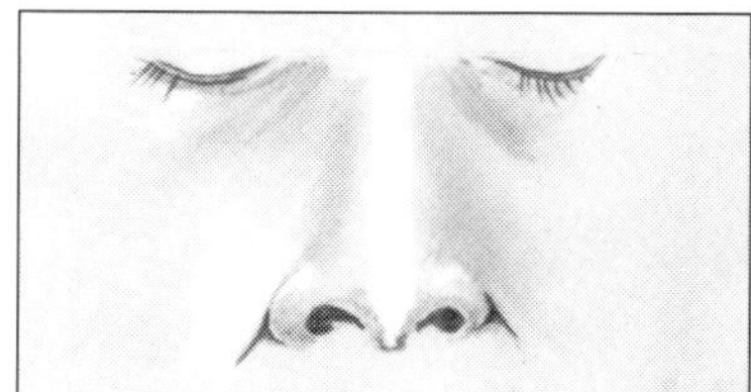
Short nose

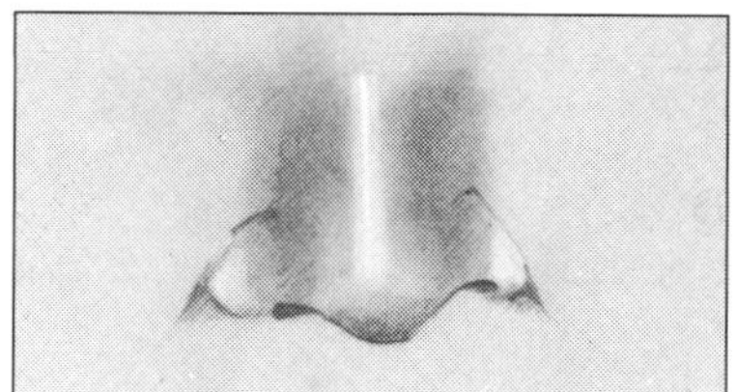
Broad nose

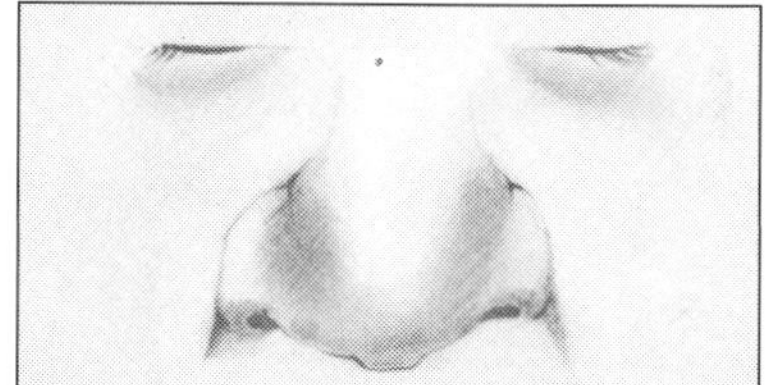
Bulbous-tipped nose

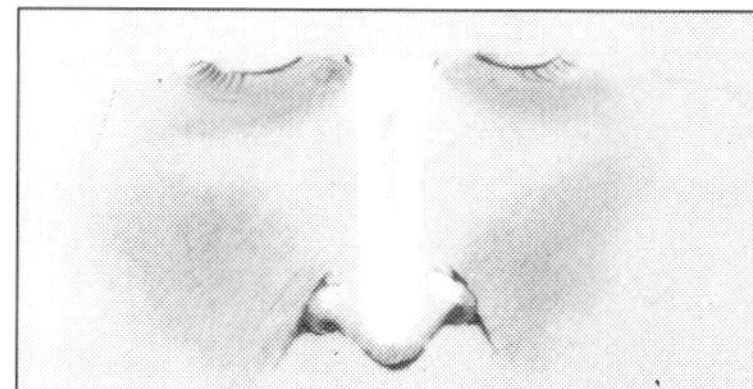
Sharp thin nose

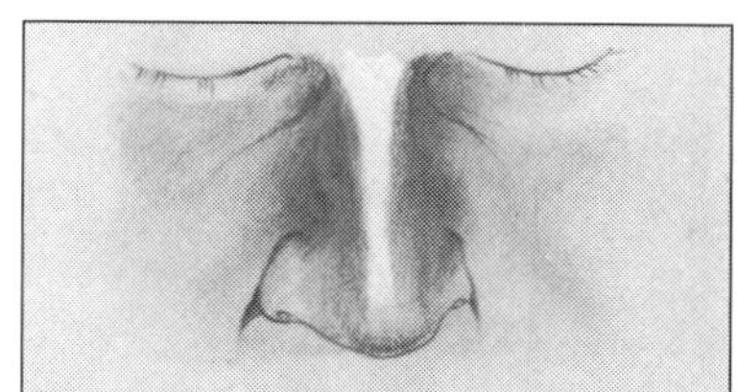
Crooked nose

Chin

Too prominent a chin can be reduced by shading it with a dark foundation. A receding chin can be brought forward by lightening it with a highlight.

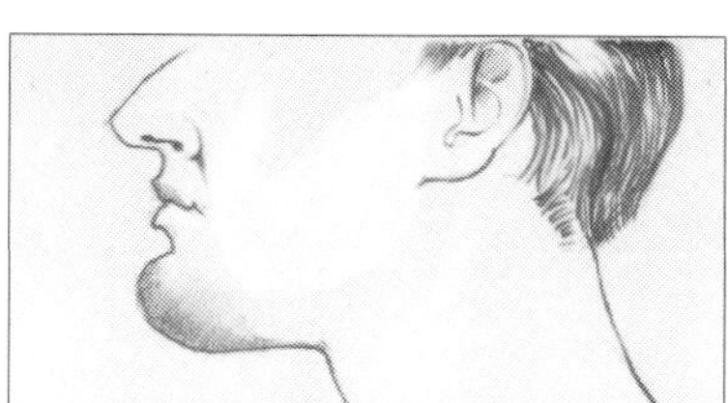
A prominent chin

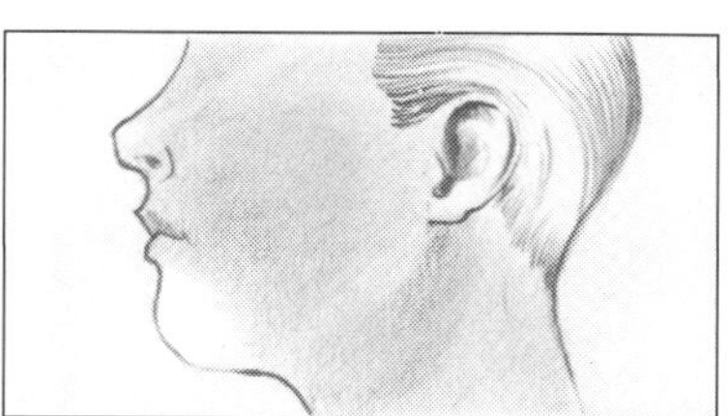
A receding chin

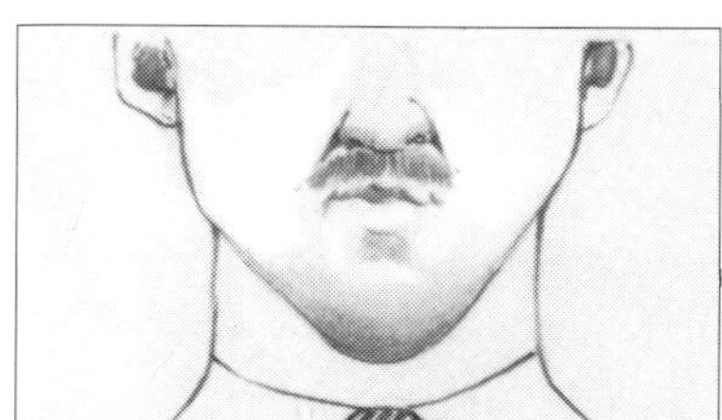
Too long or pointed a chin is shortened and squared off by shading the point

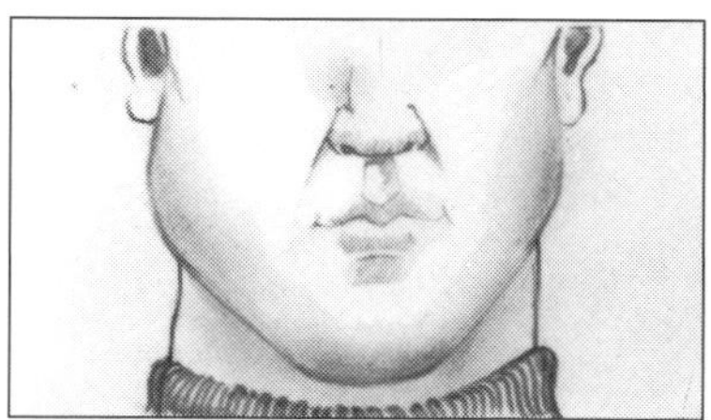
Too square a chin should be rounded off with a shadow on the corners

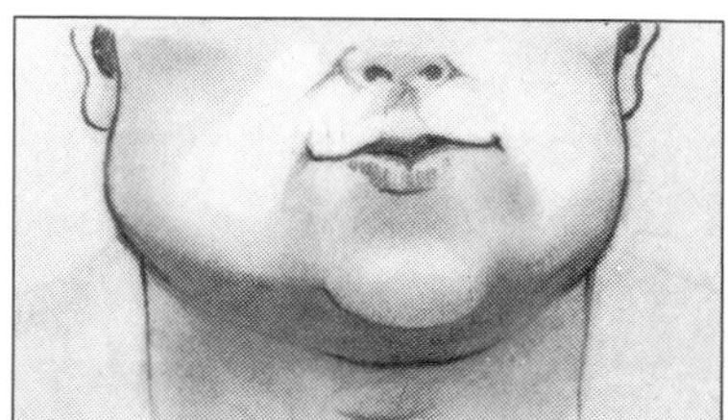
Disguise double chins with a strong shadow which is faded away down the throat

Corrective makeup

Eyes

The eyes are the most expressive and mobile features of the face and one of the most important assets that an actor possesses. It is vitally important to ensure that they look as good as possible and are able to be seen quite clearly from every seat in the house.

Since the male and the female orbital sockets are different and an actress can use makeup more obviously than an actor, we will deal with their problems separately. As a general rule, remember that dark colors are recessive so eye makeup for small eyes should be kept light in color. Also, if the eyes are too prominent, avoid highly iridescent shadows. These drawings show eyes before and after makeup is applied.

Male eyes

Before | After

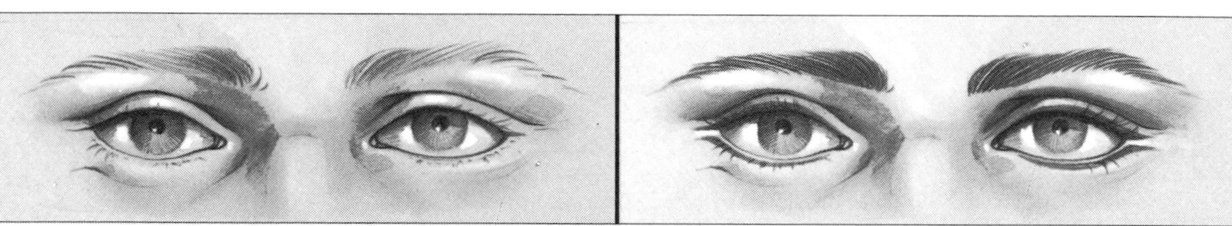

Average eyes

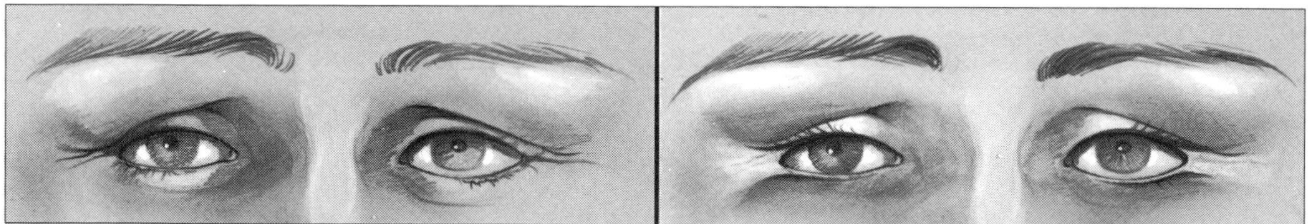

Small eyes

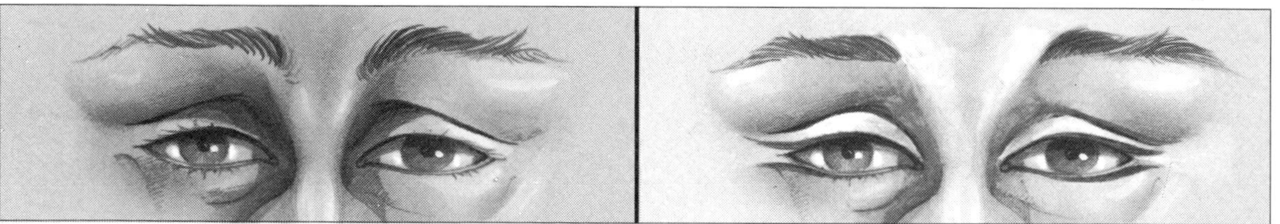

Deep and close-set eyes

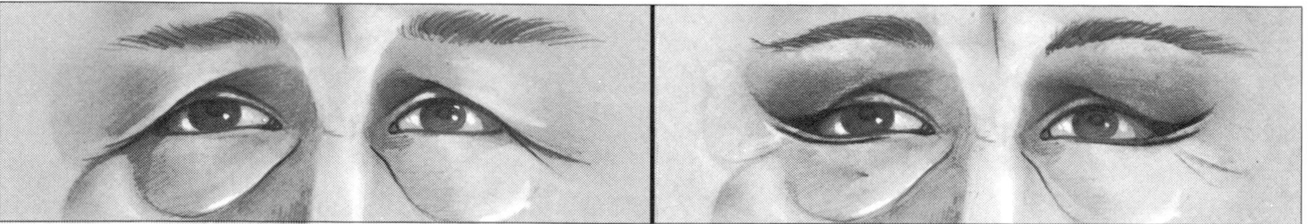

Drooping eyes

Female eyes

Before After

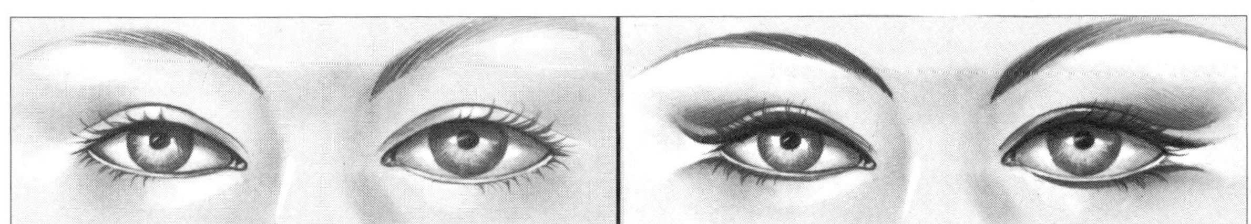

Classically lovely eyes

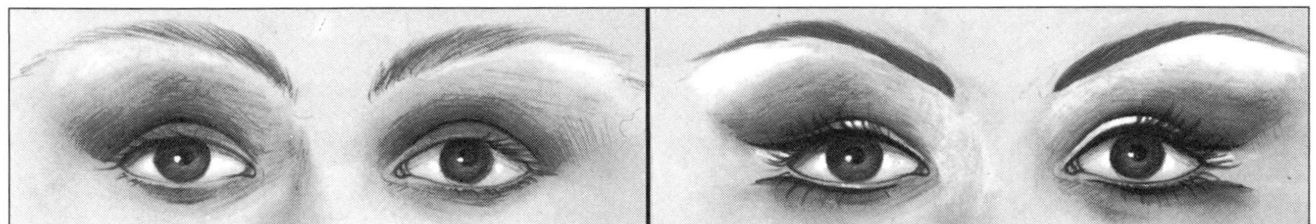

Small and deep-set eyes

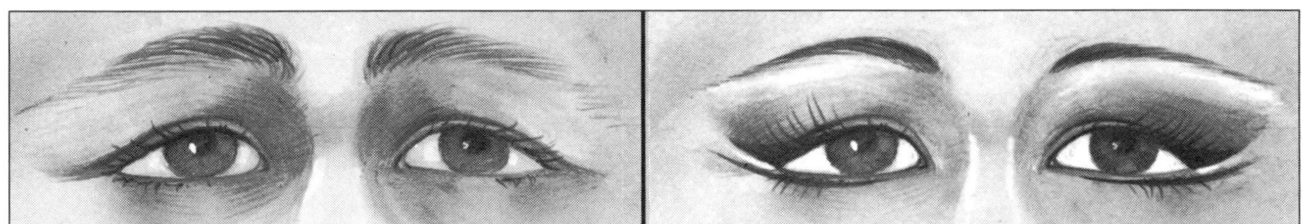

Close-set drooping eyes

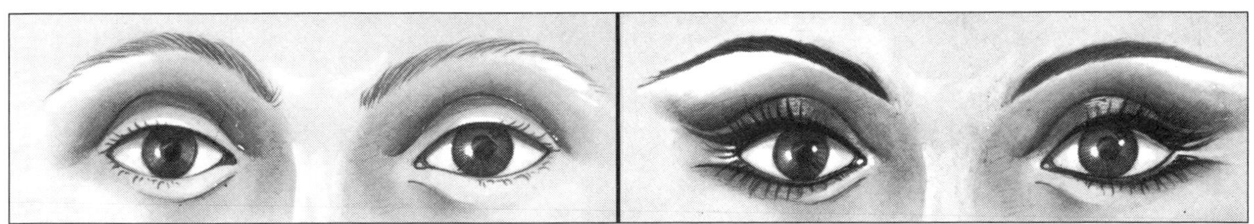

Round prominent eyes

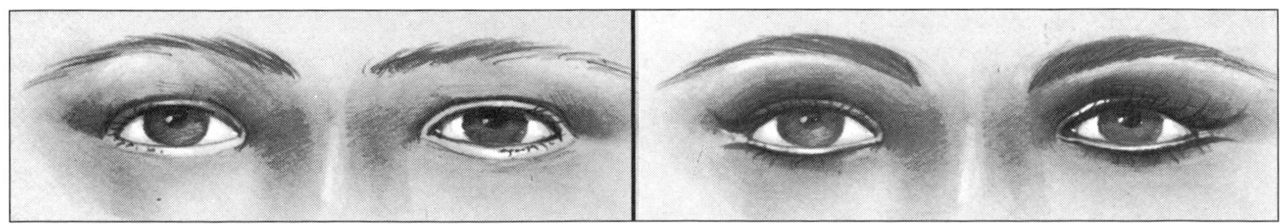

Wide-apart eyes

Corrective makeup

Eyebrows

The eyebrow creates a frame for the eye, clearly defining the area within which the eye makeup is applied. There are changing fashions in eyebrows for women; they can be thin and arched, heavy and straight, gently curving and so on (see page 28). One thing is constant, however, and that is that the brow must always harmonize with the eye makeup and the rest of the face.

Here we are concerned with creating natural-looking brows. There are a few rules that govern the shape of a well-balanced eyebrow. (These rules apply mainly to women's brows since men's usually need little corrective makeup.)

Generally, the eyebrow should start just above the inner corner of the eye. Brows that are too close together give a stern frowning look; those that are plucked too far apart give a vacuous empty look to the face and make the nose look thicker than it really is.

A perfectly-shaped brow points inward toward the other, never dipping downwards toward the nose. It then follows the natural arch of the browbone to a point about half an inch (12mm) beyond the outer end of the eye, winging slightly upwards at the outer end to prevent a downward droop — which would tend to age the face.

Hold the eyebrow pencil upright alongside the nose, with the point touching the browbone just above the inner corner of the eye. Ideally the eyebrow should start here, so mark this spot carefully.

Hold the pencil diagonally, from the side of the nostril alongside the outer corner of the eye. This is where the brow should end. Mark this spot.

To determine the high peak of the eyebrow, hold the pencil upright over the outer corner of the eye and mark the spot.

Using these three dots as a guide, lightly sketch in the shape of brow you require. Surplus hairs that detract from this shape can be plucked away from beneath the natural arch. (Plucking along the top of the brow gives a very hard unnatural look to the brow.)

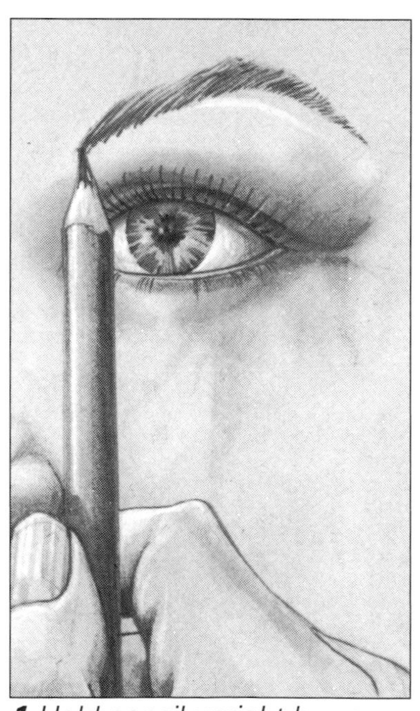

1 Hold pencil upright by nose

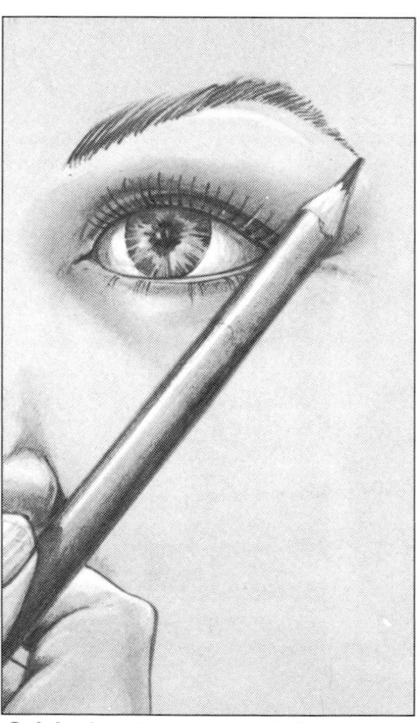

2 Mark where brow should end

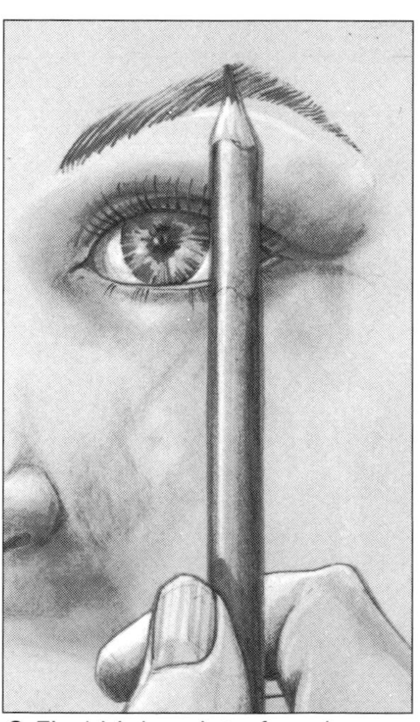

3 Find high point of eyebrow

Blocking out the eyebrows

Simple but very effective changes can be made to eyebrow shapes with pencil, paints and brushes, especially if the natural brows are fair and not strongly marked. Sometimes, the natural browline must be blocked out before a new shape can be drawn — very useful for character makeups.

There are several methods of doing this. The first is to rub a moistened bar of soap over the brows until they are flattened to the skin. Allow soap to dry and then cover brows with a thick coat of greasepaint and powder. This method is unsatisfactory for several reasons: first, the hairs can very quickly loosen and begin to show through during the performance; second, if the actor has very dark strongly-defined brows, these are almost impossible to hide; and last, if the stage is hot, perspiration can melt the soap, which may run into the actor's eyes and be extremely painful.

A safer method is to use a stick of Kryolan eyebrow plastic instead of soap, covering with greasepaint as before. However, this too can easily loosen and allow the hair to show.

The best method (shown on the right) is to use a combination of spirit gum and Derma Wax. If this method is used, the Derma Wax will require careful removal afterwards. First peel off the film of sealer and then gently work makeup remover into wax. Remove it with a cleansing tissue. Finally, dissolve the gum with spirit-gum remover, taking great care not to let it run down into the eyes.

Once the natural brow has been blocked out, a new browline can be drawn on, but whichever method of blocking out is used, great care must be taken not to disturb any of the camouflaged hairs. Eyebrow pencils are generally too hard for this purpose and will tend to cut into the wax and makeup. So the safest method is to paint on the brows with a number 2 sable brush, using grease or cake lining color. Build up the shape you require with tiny hairlike strokes of color to simulate natural growth.

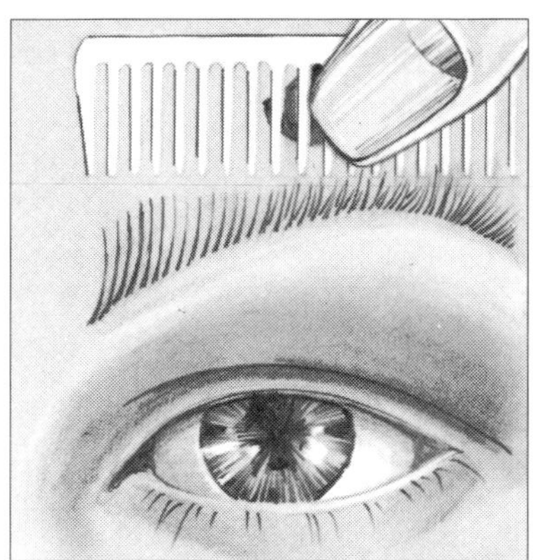

1 Brush spirit gum well into the brows and comb the hairs upwards until they are as flat to the skin of the forehead as possible. Use a metal comb so that the gum can easily be removed after use

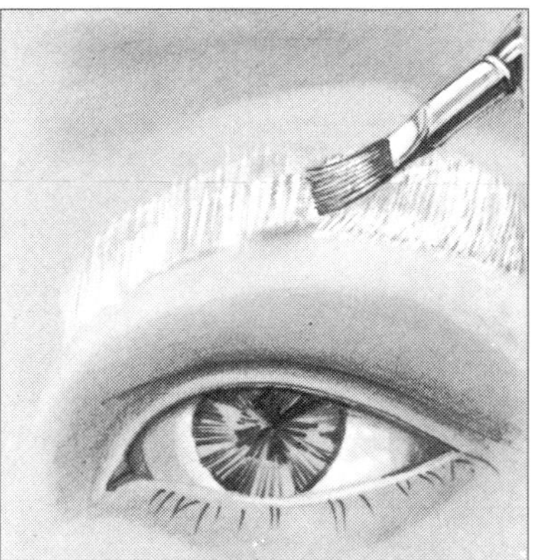

2 Allow gum to become tacky and press hairs firmly down on to skin with a damp lintless towel. Then apply a thin film of Derma Wax over the dry spirit gum. Cover with a fine film of sealer

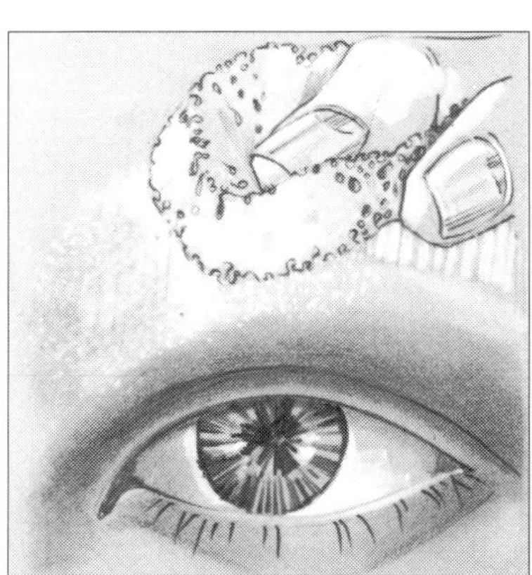

3 Once the sealer is really dry, gently stipple on a good covering of grease makeup. Use a small cosmetic sponge and then set with translucent face powder

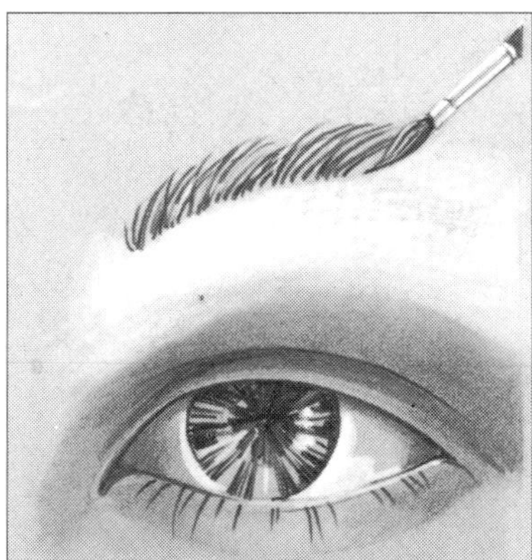

4 With the natural browline blocked out, the new eyebrows can be painted on with a brush, using tiny hairlike strokes and gradually building up the required shape

Corrective makeup

Cheeks

If the face is a normal oval, neither too fat nor too thin, and you wish to make the face look as young as possible, then a classic rouge application is all that is necessary (see page 37). However, if the face is either too fat or too thin, some corrective shading and highlighting must be used.

Slimming too full a face

Using your fingertips, trace the position of the cheekbone (see page 33). Then, with either your finger or a brush, lay a line of color along the underside of the bone from the ear to just under the high point of the cheekbone, slightly curving the line upward as you reach this point.

Soften the top edge of this shadow with a clean finger, brush or sponge, taking care not to carry the color up over the top of the bone. Then blend the bottom of the shadow downward into the cheek hollow until it merges into the foundation.

Using a clean finger or brush, highlight the cheekbone, blending the upper edge so that it merges with the foundation and softening the lower edge into the upper edge of the shadow. There should be no hard line between the two.

To give a softer and more glamorous effect on a female makeup, apply cake rouge after the highlights and shadows have been powdered. Keep the color light over the highlighted area; intensify the color in the shadow area. For a stronger effect, a dark shading rouge can be used in the shadow.

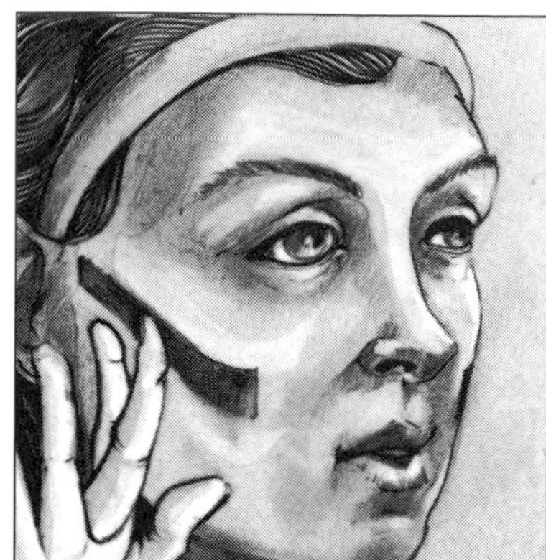

***1** Lay a line of color along underside of cheekbone*

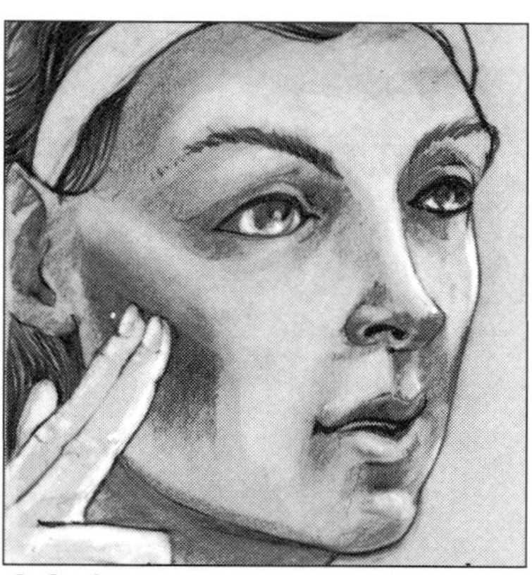

***2** Soften top edge and blend shadow into cheek hollow*

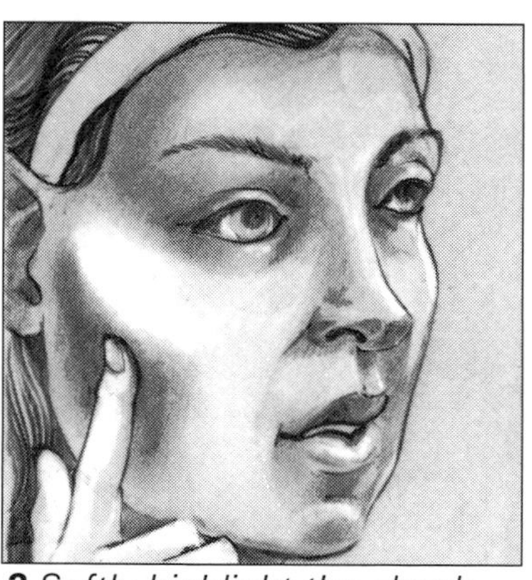

***3** Softly highlight the cheekbone above the shading*

Filling out too thin a face

If the cheek hollows are too sunken, a highlight two or three shades lighter than the base color should be applied to the shadowed area below the cheekbone. Women should then apply a light dusting of rouge over the cheekbone.

Highlight below cheekbone

Teeth

Unattractive dark or discolored teeth or gold caps can be disguised with a light tooth enamel. However, great care should be taken to use a creamy shade that matches the good teeth — pure white tooth enamel looks grotesque.

If the teeth are uneven in length, the line can be straightened by using black tooth enamel on the tips of the long teeth. However, these effects can be used only in very large theaters. Since good teeth are essential to an artiste playing anything but character roles, a visit to the dentist might be in order!

Mouths

Correcting the shape of the mouth is obviously much easier for women than for men since the lips can be boldly over or under-painted with a strong lipstick color to achieve the desired shape. As a general rule the male mouth should be underplayed so correction may not be necessary. If it is needed, then care should be taken to make the lip makeup as natural as possible, using a brownish-red tone of lip color or even a brown eye pencil.

The following illustrations are shown for the female mouth but also apply to the male mouth, providing the corrections are done as subtly as possible.

Thin lips

If the lips are too thin, draw outside the natural line of the lips but don't change the shape. This overpaint should be drawn on with a darker shade of lipstick or lip liner and the center filled in with a lighter shade to give fullness.

Thick lips

If the mouth needs to be slimmed, apply your base cover over the outside edge of the lips and draw on a new outline just inside the natural rim, using a muted tone of lipstick.

Small mouth

If the mouth is too small and narrow, then carry the color right to the extreme corners, and just beyond on the top lip. Very slightly overpaint the whole bottom lip, following its natural shape.

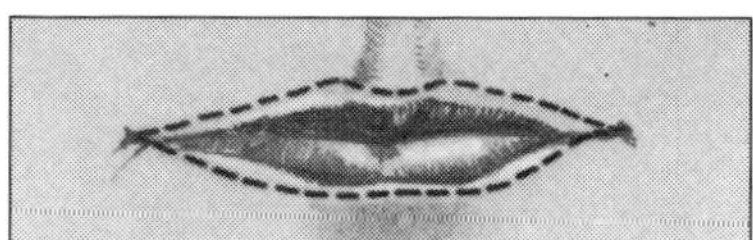

Thin lips

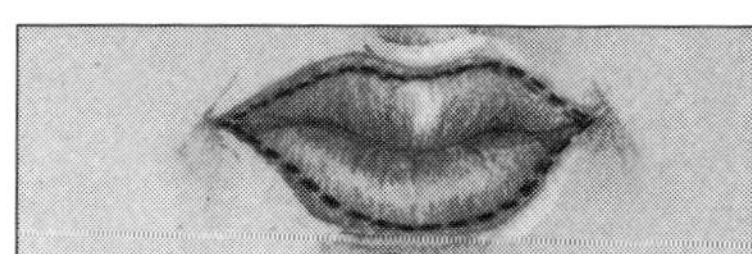

Thick lips

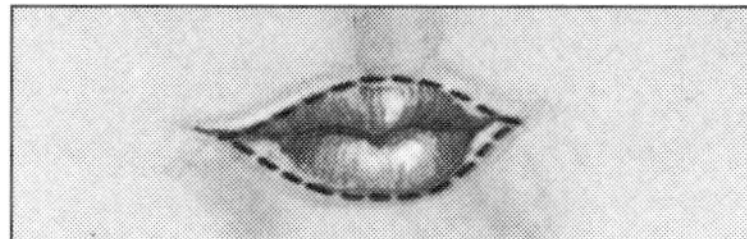

Small mouth

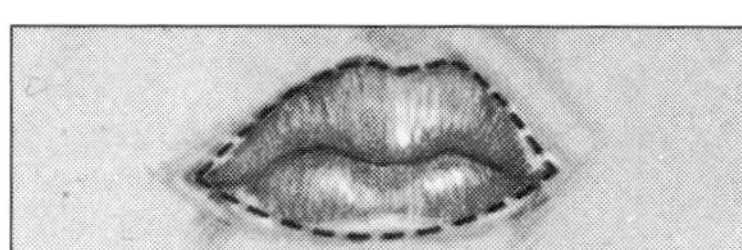

Droopy mouth

Too wide a mouth

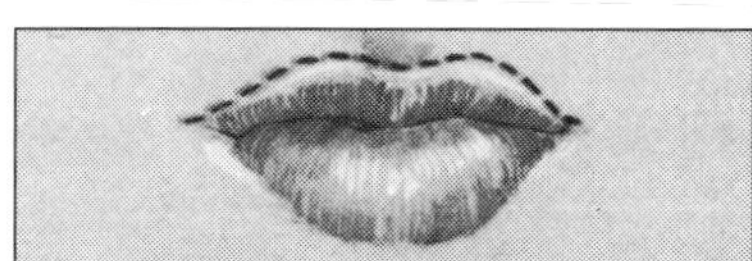

Thin top lip

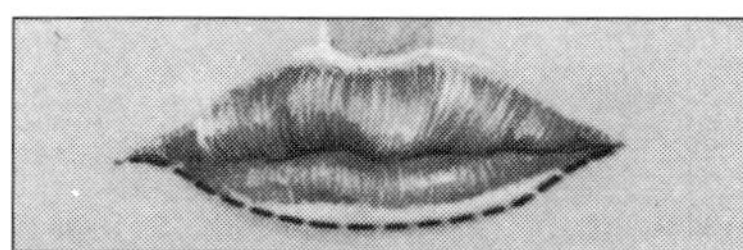

Thin lower lip

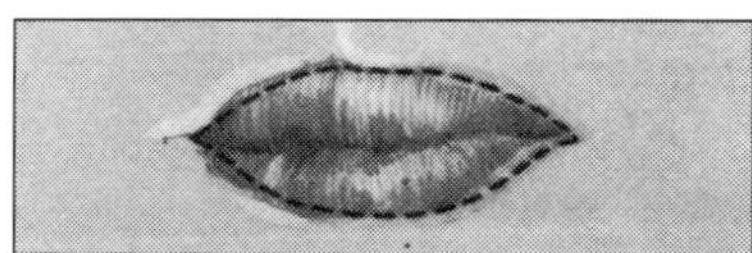

Crooked lip

Droopy mouth

If the mouth has a heavy upper lip, a thin lower lip, and the corners turn down, overpaint the lower lip to meet the upper one and turn up the corners of the top lip with your color.

Too wide a mouth

If lips are too wide, cover outer corners with foundation: do not carry lip color into corners.

Thin top lip

If the upper lip is too thin or straight, add fullness until it balances the lower lip.

Thin lower lip

If the lower lip is too thin, draw outside the lower lip to balance the top and highlight the center of the lower lip with a pale iridescent lipstick.

Crooked lips

If the mouth is crooked, slightly underpaint the high side and slightly overpaint the low side — never do the correction on just one side.

Hair

Many facial faults can be disguised with cosmetics but hairstyles can help too. This is particularly true for women, but men can also benefit from rethinking their hairstyles.

Some hints on corrective hairstyles are included in the chapter on hair (pages 78-83).

Reshaping the face with light and shade

So far only straight makeups have been described, and how the proportions of the face can be changed by optical illusion to look more attractive. Perhaps the most important aspect of makeup, however, is using cosmetics to create character and age a face. All too often, age is represented by a maze of dark-brown lines drawn on the face with an orange-stick and then highlighted with lines of white greasepaint. This can look grotesque and heavy when viewed from the front stalls, while from the back of the theater it all but disappears and merely makes the face look dirty. However, highlights and shadows skillfully applied and blended will look effective from every part of the house.

To do this well you must understand the effects of light and shade and know how to use them to create shape. First of all, study the drawing of a square column and a round column lit by the same electric light bulb. Notice how the lamp creates highlights and shadows on both columns. In A the division between light and dark is sharp and immediate. In B it is soft and gradual. These are known as hard and soft-edged shadows. Now look at the drawing of draped curtains lit by the same light. Here the artist has created the effect of folds and swags by using both soft and hard-edged shadows and highlights. It is by using a combination of these two types of shadow that a makeup artist can create wrinkles, pouches and sagging flesh. When creating a simple depression or hollow, a shadow with only soft edges is used — to suggest, for example, hollow cheeks.

A *A hard-edged shadow* B *A soft-edged shadow*

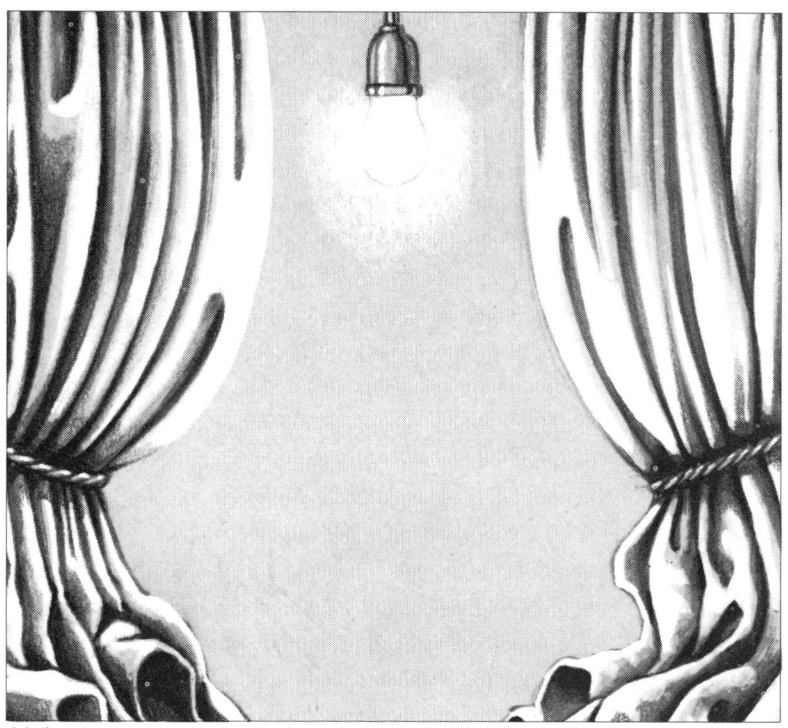

Using a combination of hard and soft-edged shadows to create the effect of folds

Creating hollow cheeks with shadow

Suck in the cheeks to discover the hollow and apply a dark shading color with a $\frac{1}{4}$ inch or $\frac{3}{8}$ inch (6-9mm) brush in the Y pattern shown. Blend the outside edges of this Y shape until it resembles a realistic hollow. Note that the top edge is only slightly blended, without the shadow being allowed to rise on to the cheekbone. The lower edges, however, are allowed to fade out almost completely into the foundation, creating a soft-edged shadow.

Apply a strong band of highlight along the cheekbone. Blend the top edge of this highlight until it merges into the foundation and then gently blend the lower edge with small tapping movements of your fingertips, until it merges with the top edge of your shadow.

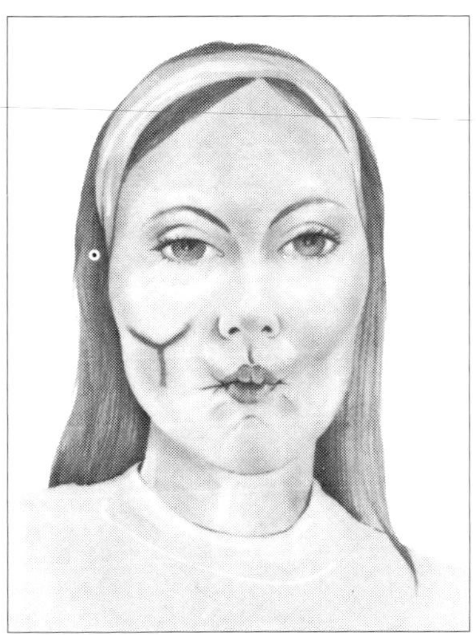

__1__ Suck in cheeks and apply shadow, as shown

__2__ Blend away the shadow, as illustrated

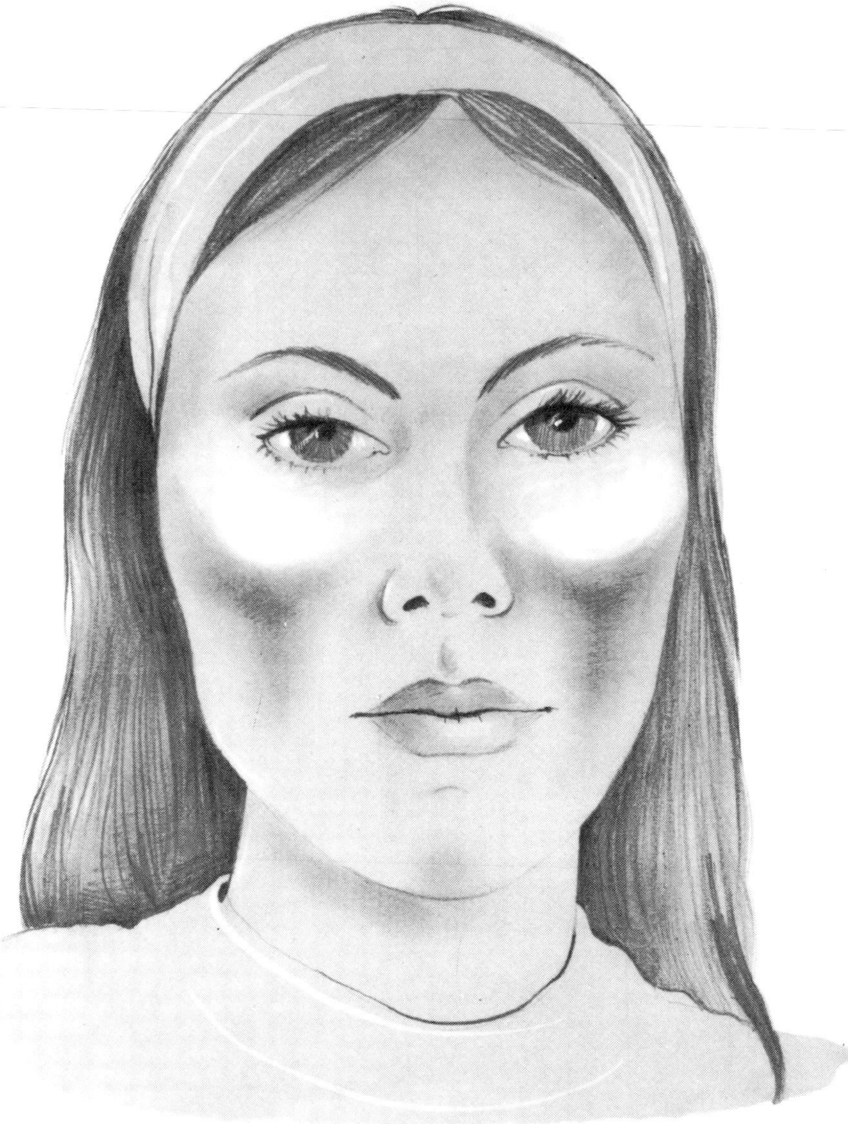

__3__ Apply highlight to cheekbones and blend away, as shown

Reshaping the face with light and shade

Lines, wrinkles and pouches are created by using a combination of both hard and soft-edged shadows and highlights. This is well illustrated when makeup is used to create the creases that run from the nostril down to the corners of the mouth — known as the "nasolabial fold".

The nasolabial fold

Using a square-ended brush, draw a line of dark shading color along the crease of the nasolabial fold, so that the lower edge of this line is directly through the center of the crease. Using a clean brush, carefully blend the top edge of this line upwards, away from the crease, on to the cheek.

Now apply a highlight. This should be directly adjacent to the lower sharp edge of the shadow. Blend this highlight away along the top lip.

The next step is to apply a line of highlight along the top of the nasolabial fold.

Blend both edges of this highlight, as shown, and you will see how this combination of soft and hard edges can reproduce a very realistic deep crease.

The principles of shading and highlighting can be applied to all the features of the face in order to age them.

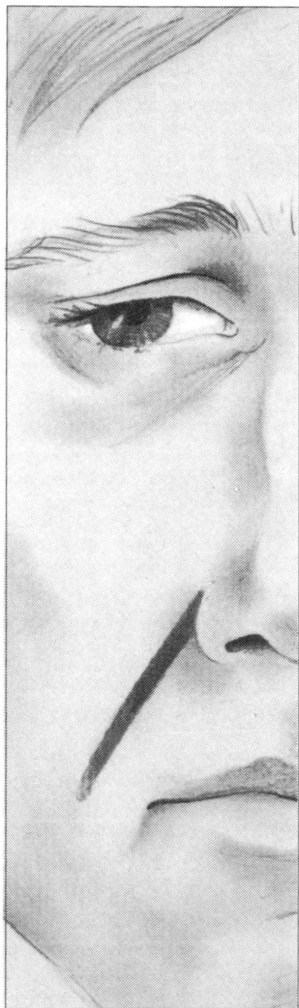

1 Draw a line of shadow along center of the crease

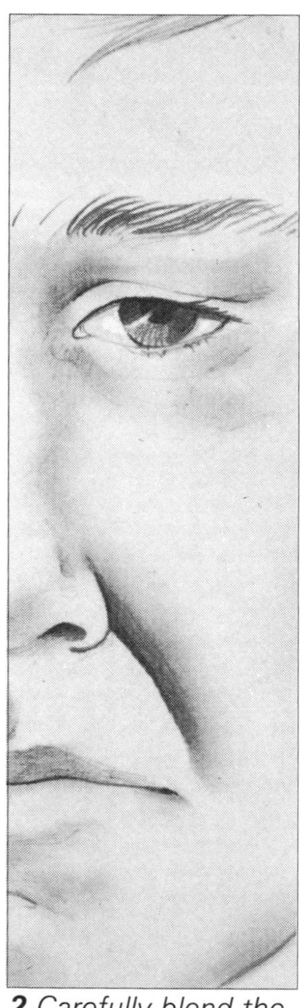

2 Carefully blend the top edge upwards, on to the cheek

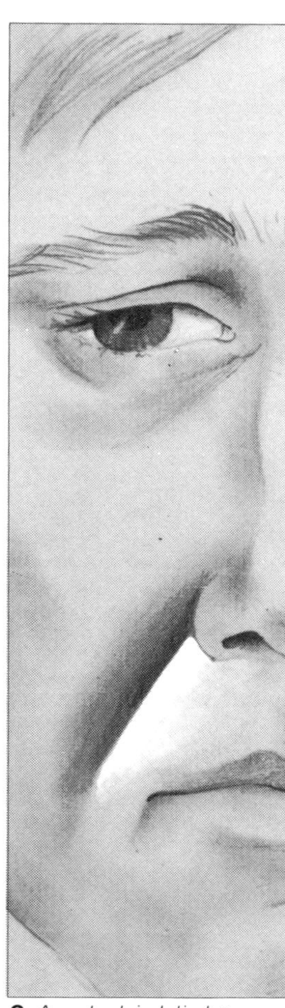

3 Apply highlight below shadow and blend along lip

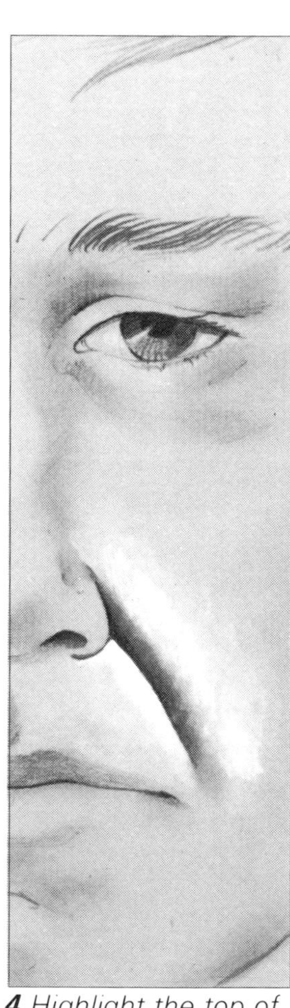

4 Highlight the top of the fold and then blend, as shown

The forehead

One of the most effective methods of aging the forehead is simply to highlight and shadow the prominences and depressions of the skull, as shown on the right.

The effect of a wrinkled forehead is created by using a combination of hard and soft shadows, as shown. Always remember to follow the line of the natural wrinkles so that when the eyebrows are raised, the lines will appear to deepen. The method is illustrated below.

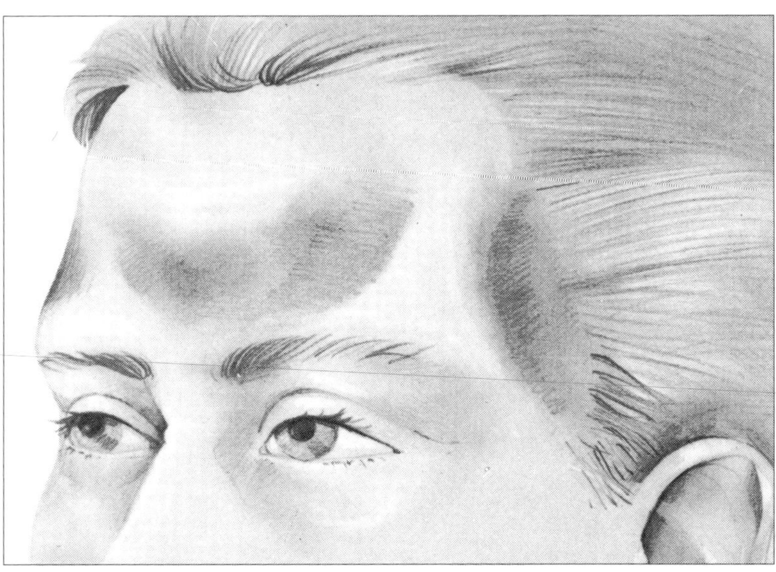

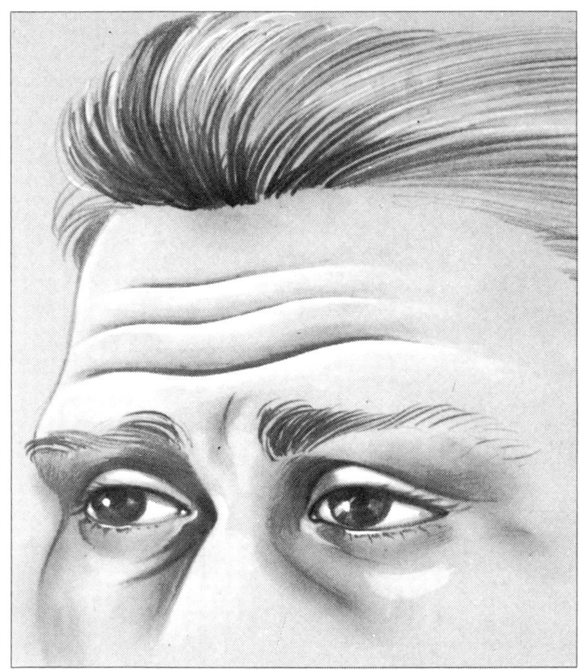

1 With a $\frac{1}{4}$ inch (6mm) square-ended brush, draw a highlight immediately below each wrinkle, fading the colour out at each end. Using a clean brush, blend the lower edge into your foundation

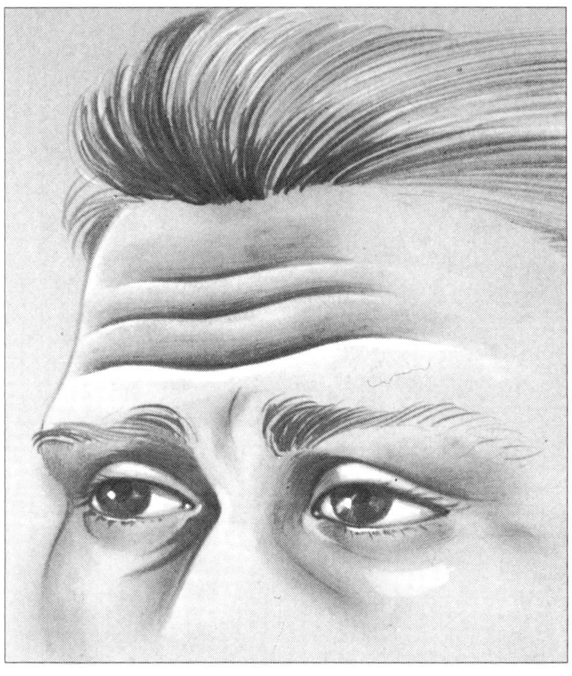

2 Using a number 2 filbert brush, draw a line of shadow into the heart of each wrinkle, fading the colour out at each end. With a clean $\frac{1}{4}$ inch (6mm) brush, blend these lines upward so that they merge into the adjacent highlight

Reshaping the face with light and shade

Eyes

The eyes can be aged in many ways (pages 114-121) but first let us look at a step-by-step application of a makeup, showing the early stages of aging around the eye, using both soft, and hard-edged shadows.

The best type of brushes to use for this are number 6 filberts since they can be either drawn to a point or splayed out to create fine or wide shadows, both of which will be required to create the effect of pouches and wrinkles around the eyes.

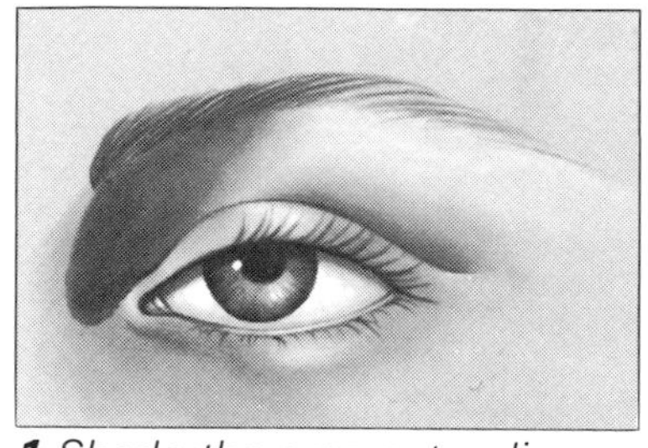

1 *Shade the area extending from the inner corner of the eye towards the bridge of the nose. This sinks the eye back into the socket. The deeper the shading, the greater the effect of aging*

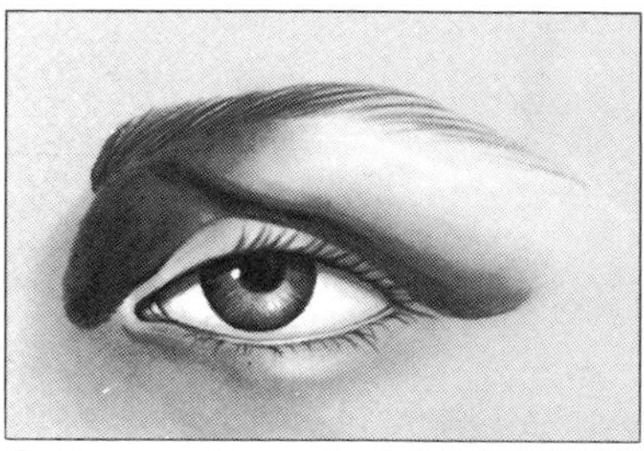

2 *Draw a line of shadow along the eyelid crease as shown; carry it downwards over the eyelid as close to the corner of the eye as possible before winging it gently upwards*

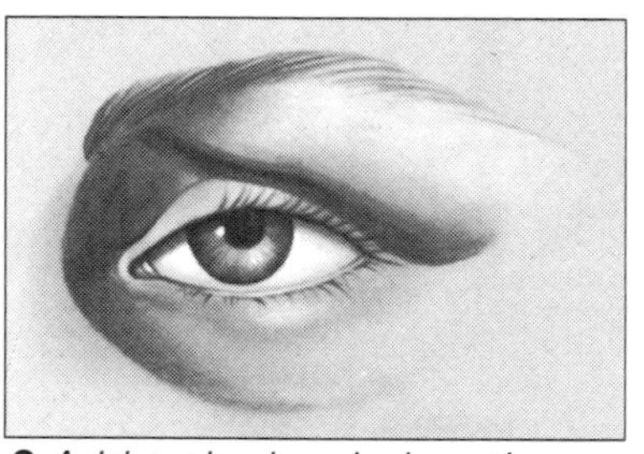

3 *Add a shadow below the eye, starting at the inner corner and following the edge of the eye socket. Fade the shadow out before reaching the outer corner*

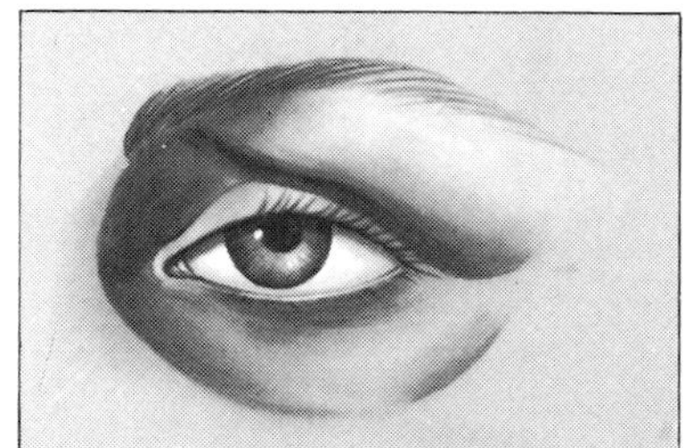

4 *Add a small touch of shadow in between the end of this last shadow and the outer corner of the eye, along the edge of the eye socket. Also shade along the edge of the lower lid*

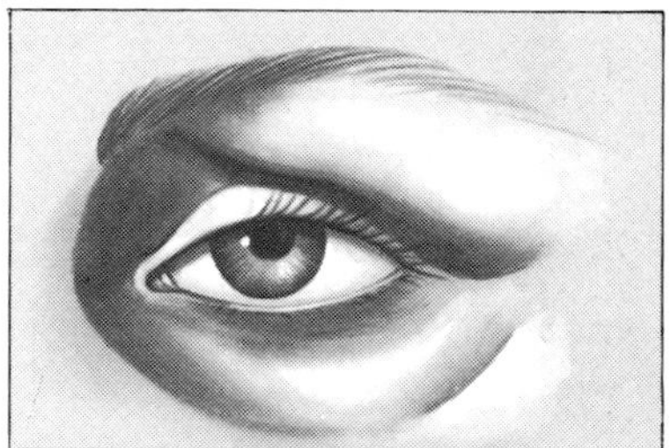

5 *Now apply highlights, noting the different degrees of intensity of each highlight. Powder these highlights and shadows immediately to prevent them being displaced by the movement of the eye*

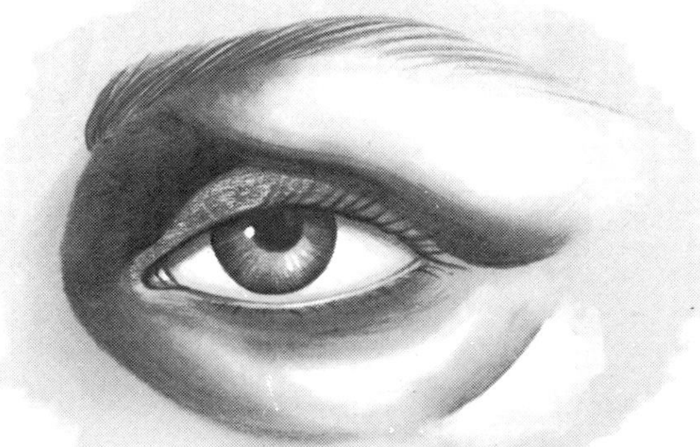

6 *This type of eye can be made to look more deep-set by replacing the highlight on the actual eyelid with shadow, as shown here. Remember to use separate brushes for each color*

Modeling an under-eye pouch

To create bags under the eyes, you need to use very sharp-edged shadows and these are best applied after the highlights. Note: it is very important when modeling the eye area with cream or grease makeup to set the finished details with powder as soon as possible, to prevent your work being displaced by the movement of the eye.

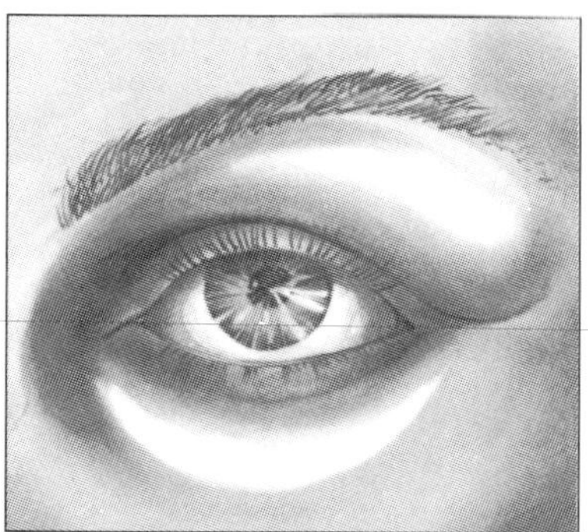

***1** First outline the bag or pouch with a line of highlight. If a pouch is already present, the highlight should follow the natural outline. If, however, no pouch is apparent, the best outline to suit the eye can only be discovered by trial and error*

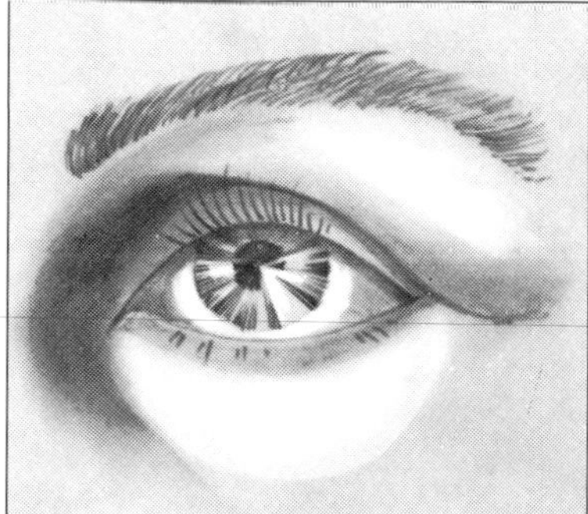

***2** Blend lower edge of highlight away with a clean square-ended brush until it fades into the surrounding foundation. Then apply a highlight to the center of the pouch area to create a puffy appearance. Intensify the highlight in the center to gain the maximum effect*

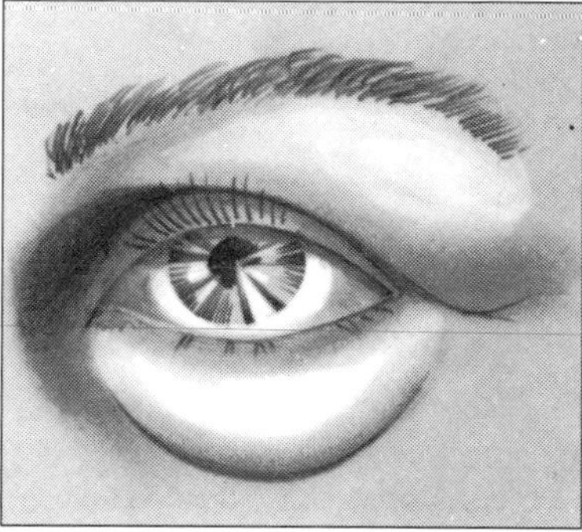

***3** With a fine pointed brush, draw a sharp-edged shadow along the bottom edge of the pouch, making the shadow deepest in the center and fading it away as it reaches the outer corners. Blend the upper edge of this shadow up over the pouch area to create roundness, fading it into the central highlight*

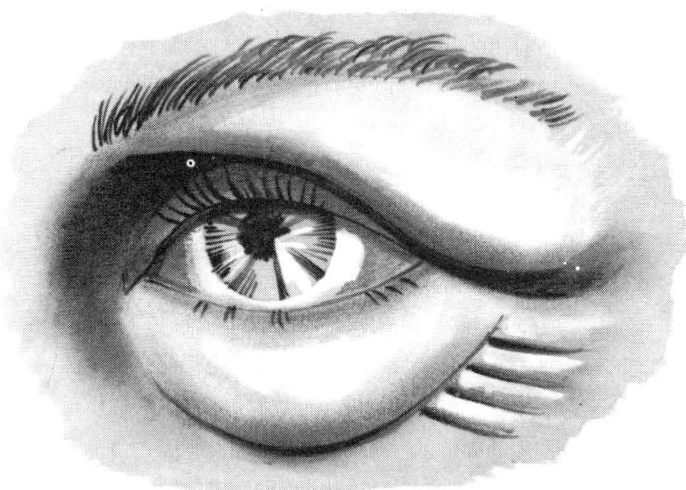

The effect of age can be further dramatized by creating laugh lines at the outer corner of the eye, and intensifying the fold above the eye by deepening the shadow and strengthening the highlight

Reshaping the face with light and shade

Nose

When modeling the nose with light and shade, the first area to consider is the small depression between the brows at the top of the nose. The simplest treatment for this area is to use shade so the top of the nose appears to be sunken. Then add one or more vertical creases, depending on the natural formation when frowning.

Using the number 2 filbert brush, draw shadows into the lines which are created at the top of the nose by frowning, and then blend these away. Highlight all the prominences in between and at either side of these lines, blending as shown in the drawing on the right.

The nose can be further aged by using makeup to sharpen and narrow the center.

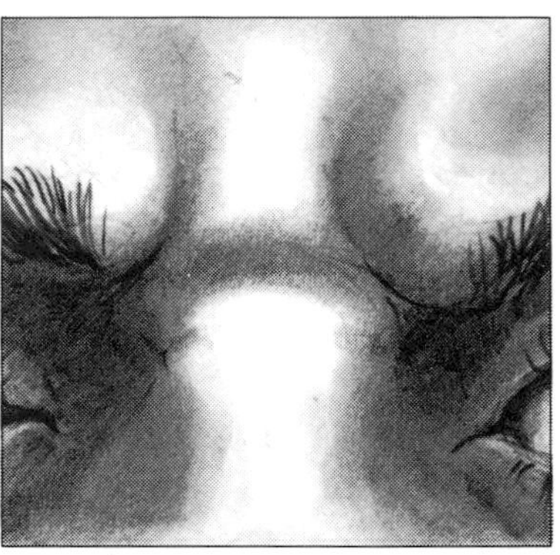

Aging a nose

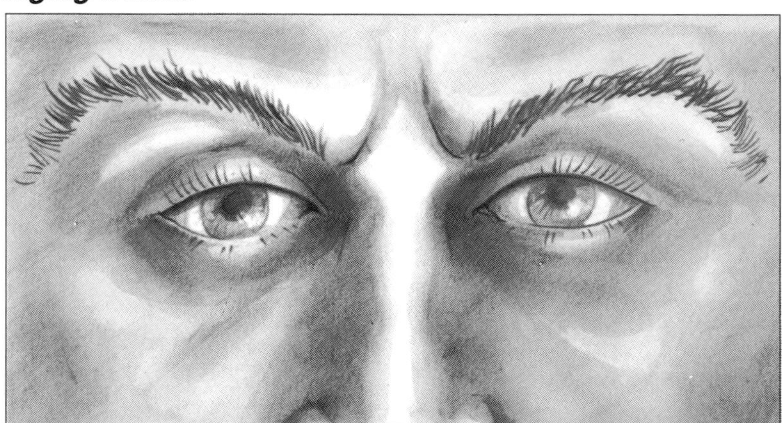

__1__ Apply shadows on each side of nose, narrowing the shape above and below the bridge, and highlight the center bone

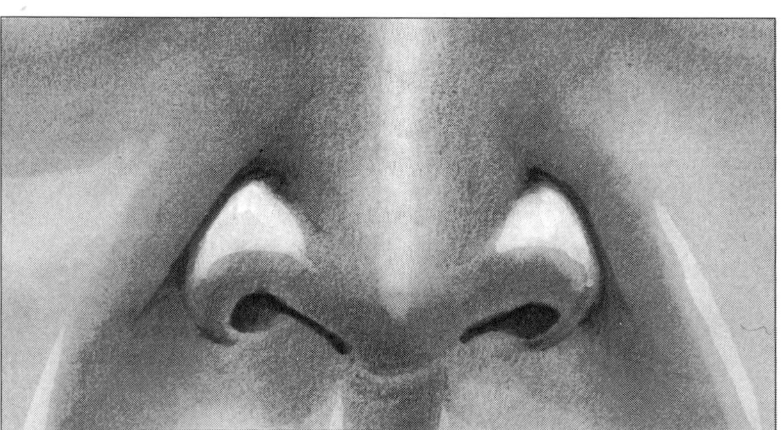

__2__ Deepen the creases around the nostrils, making the shadow deepest at the back. Apply a highlight to the top of nostril

Creating a broken-nose effect

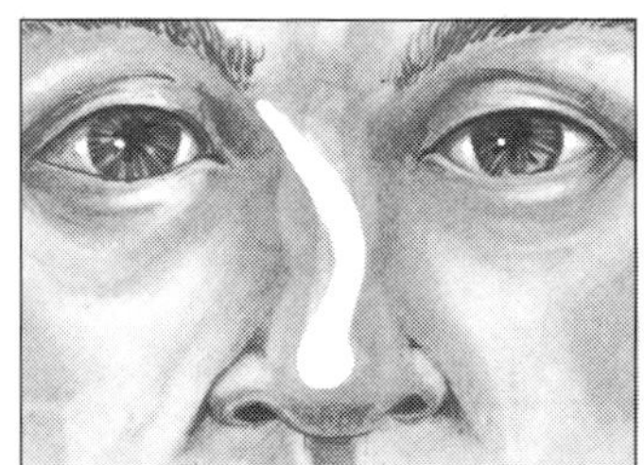

__1__ Using a $\frac{1}{4}$ inch (6mm) square-ended brush, draw a strong highlight down the center of the nose, creating the shape that you require

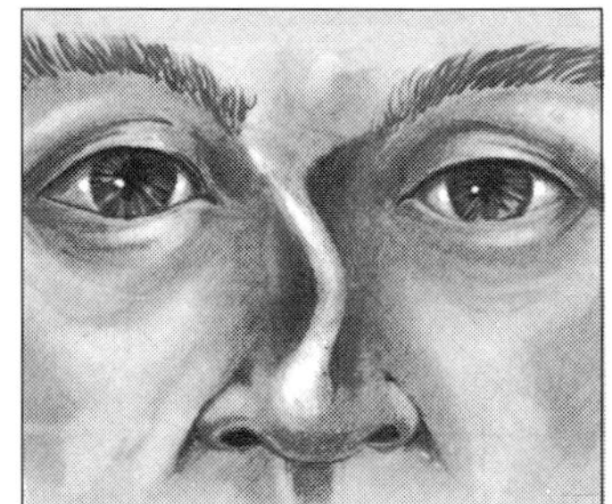

__2__ Shade the areas on either side of highlight, where a natural highlight would be if the nose was supposed to be straight

Cheeks

We have already examined how to create the impression of hollow cheeks at the beginning of this chapter (see page 61), but some simple aging effects can be achieved, especially for women, with the strategic placement of rouge.

Apply a dark-brown shading rouge well back under the cheekbone to create a gaunt hollow look. Apply a slightly blue tone of rouge immediately below the cheek, fading it downwards to give a drawn look to the face.

Apply a hot crimson tone of rouge below the smile pad, in the pattern shown, to give a plump, middle-aged fullness.

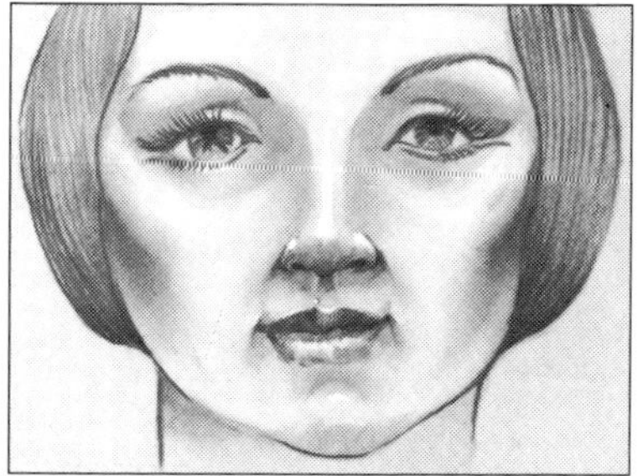

Create a hollow look by using dark rouge below cheekbone

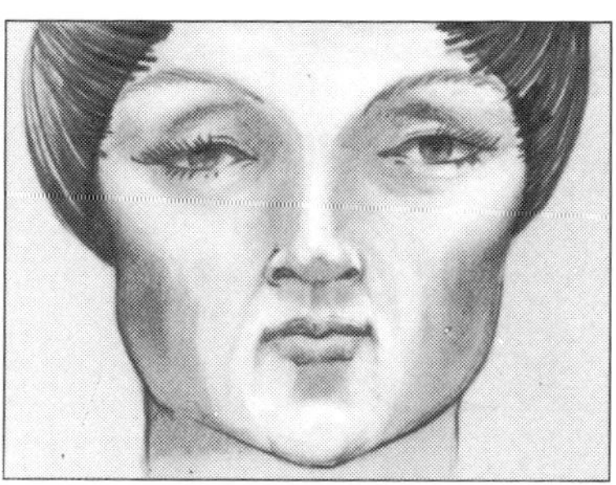

Bluish rouge faded down the cheek creates a drawn look

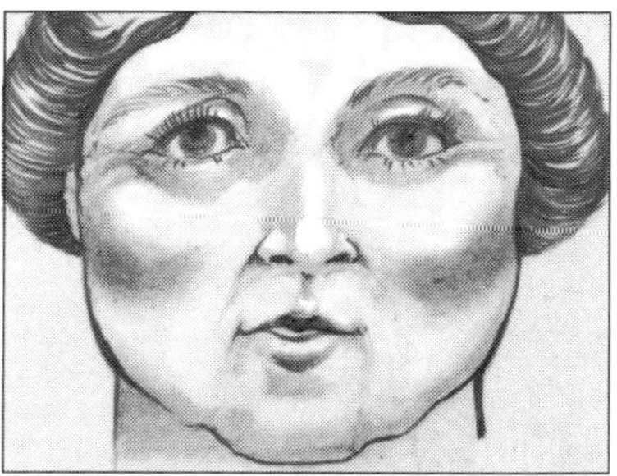

Strong brilliant rouge below smile pad creates plumpness

Aging the jawline

To age the jawline, you need to create the illusion of sagging jowls. Once again it is important to place the shadows where the natural ones will eventually fall. To discover these, pull the chin back into the throat until creases and folds are created and then accentuate these with your highlights and shadows.

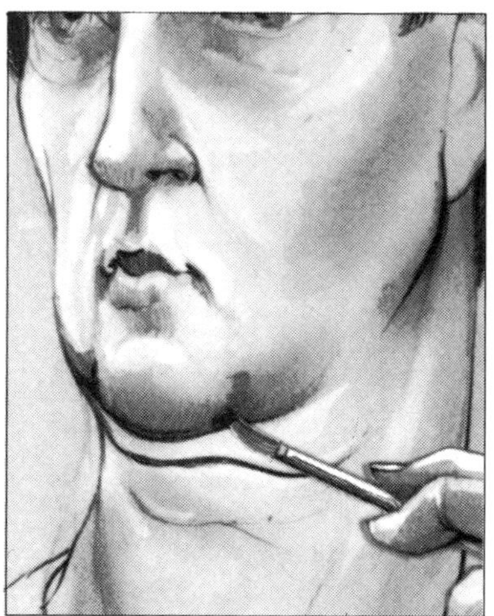

***1** Using a $\frac{1}{4}$ inch (6mm) or $\frac{3}{8}$ inch (9mm) brush, apply a hard-edged shadow under the folds created when tucking in the chin. Blend the top edge away up over the bulges*

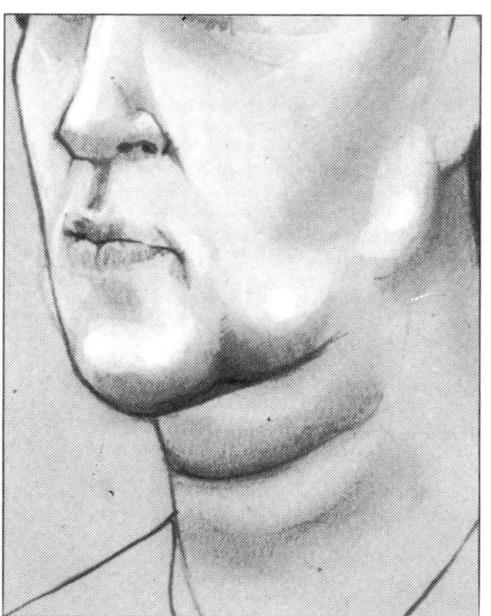

***2** Highlight the center of the bulges and blend the top edge of this up towards the cheek area. Then soften the lower edge of the highlight until it merges with the shadow*

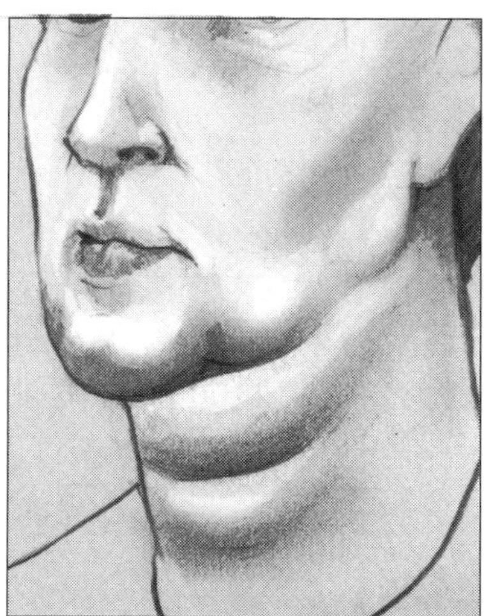

***3** Finally, add highlights under the jowl shadows, with a reasonably hard edge meeting the lower hard edge of the shadows and then blend the lower edge down the neck*

Reshaping the face with light and shade

Aging the chin

Just how jowls are formed will naturally vary from face to face. In some instances, deep vertical creases will rise up from them over the sides of the chin or into the center of the cheek. When signs of these natural creases begin to appear as the chin is pulled back, they can be used to create a greater aging effect on the jawline.

The chin itself can be aged in various ways, and once again it is important to contract the muscles to see where the natural creases occur before accentuating them.

If chins are painted on to a very firm throat, the actor must remember to continue to pull the chin down during the performance to gain the maximum effect from the makeup.

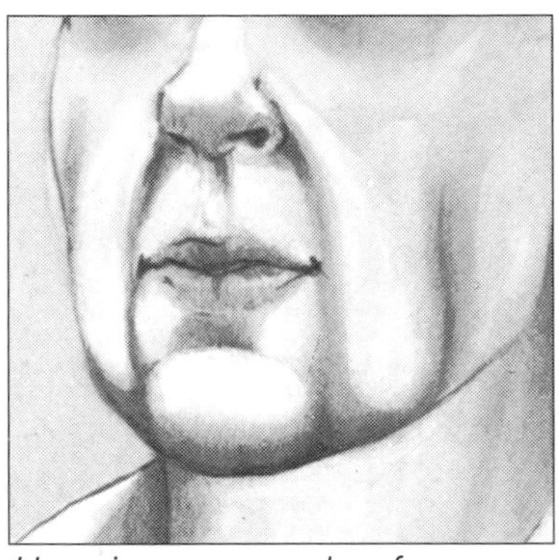

Here is an example of a crease forming alongside the chin and rising up to meet the crease of the nasolabial fold at the corner of the mouth and another crease rising at the back of the jowl up into the cheek area

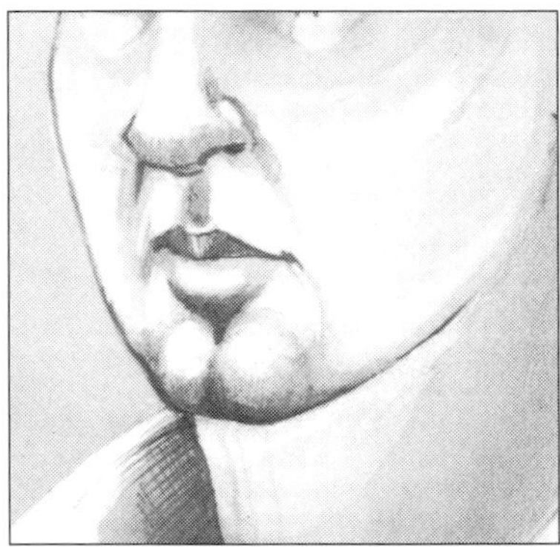

Here is another chin to consider. In this instance you will notice that the chin has been deeply creased just below the lower lip. Note also the small triangular shadow which has been placed on the point of the chin

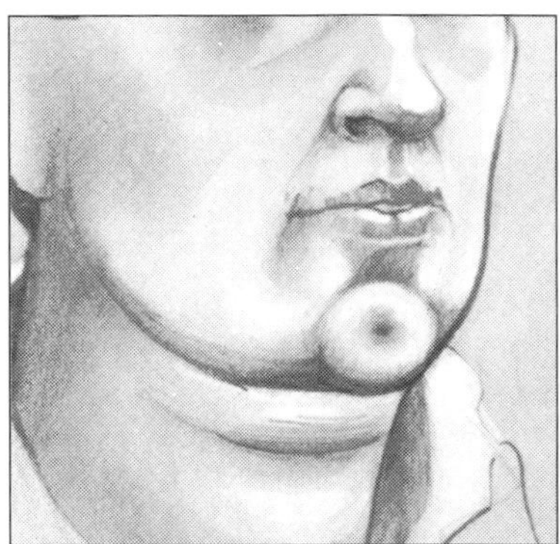

Here light and shade have been used to create a small round pad with a deep dimple. The pad is then stippled with dots of strong blue-red rouge. To add a double chin, pull chin back and shade and highlight the natural folds

Aging the mouth

One of the simplest methods of adding age to the mouth is to conceal the natural color with your foundation and so give the impression of the mouth sinking back into the face. This can be further exaggerated by painting a very thin dark lip-shape inside the natural outline.

With age, the muscles at the corners of the mouth sag, causing deep creases to form. These creases can be simulated with shadows and highlights , similar to those used to create the nasolabial fold.

Draw a hard-edged shadow down from the corners of the mouth, softening the top edge . Then place a hard-edged highlight alongside this line, blending it away at the bottom edge. Highlight the fold above crease, using two soft edges.

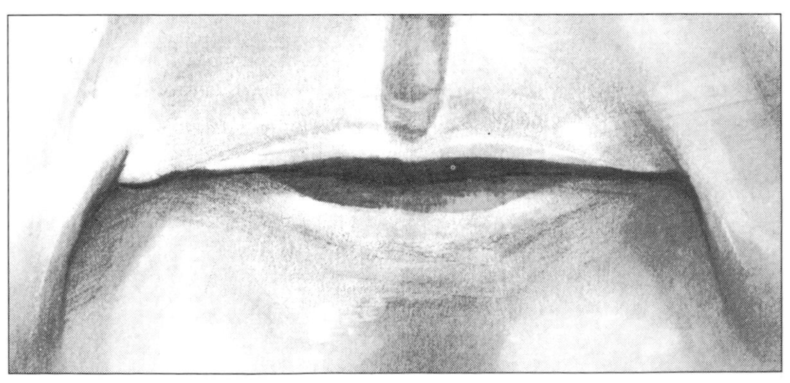

The mouth can be aged by painting on wrinkles which cut vertically into the lips, but this must be very carefully done, or the wrinkles will look like teeth in a skull!

To find out exactly where the creases should be, tightly pucker up the lips. Lightly brush a white highlight over the resulting wrinkles with a $\frac{3}{8}$ inch (9mm) brush or your fingertips.

Relax the mouth and add vertical shadows between the highlights. A sharp dark-brown eyebrow pencil will be less easily displaced by the lips moving than a grease liner.

Using clean $\frac{1}{8}$ inch (3mm) brushes, blend out your highlights and shadows to create the desired wrinkles. Then powder immediately.

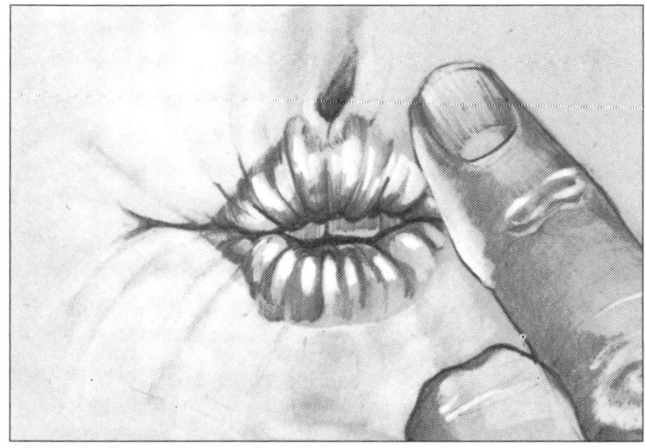

1 Tightly pucker the lips and paint white highlight over resulting wrinkles, using a $\frac{3}{8}$ inch (9mm) brush or the fingertips

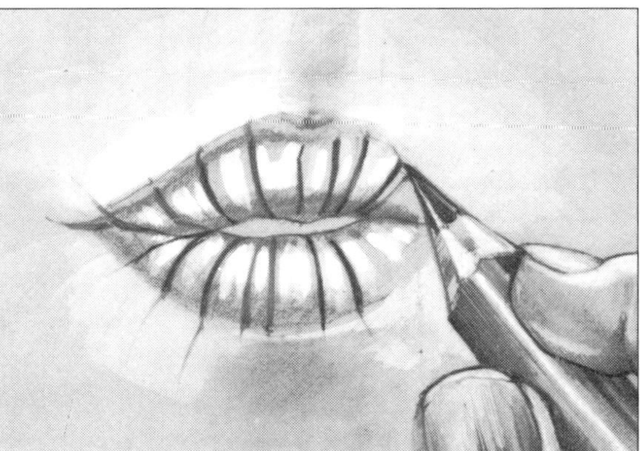

2 Relax the mouth and add vertical shadows between the highlights, using a dark-brown eyebrow pencil

Teeth

Very white even teeth can look out of place in a character makeup. This can be corrected by applying a film of dark-brown wax pencil over the teeth to give them a dingy appearance. For extreme old age and ugliness, teeth can be blocked out with black tooth enamel.

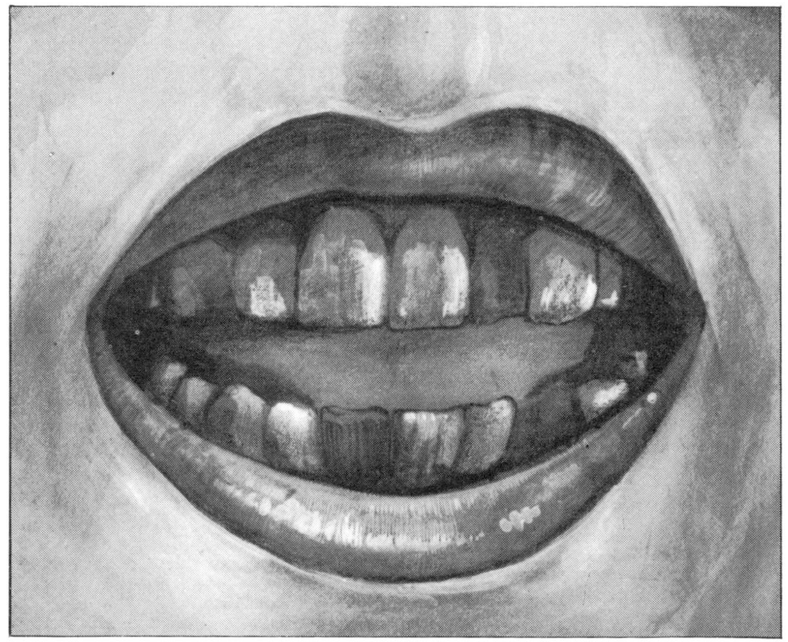

Reshaping the face with light and shade

Aging the neck

The neck often tends to show age before the face and it is therefore most important not to neglect this area. All too often one sees an actor with an incredibly aged face supported on a slim young neck.

First accentuate the transverse wrinkles across the throat, fading them back toward the ears, using a combination of soft and hard edges.

If the larynx is fairly prominent, it should be highlighted and shadowed as much as possible to accentuate its sharpness.

Now turn head sideways to reveal the muscle running from below the ear to the hollow in the center of the breastbone. Highlight and shade this muscle to create a cylindrical effect.

If the costume has a very low neckline, then the breastbone hollow and the "salt cellars" (the small hollows above the collarbone) should be shadowed, and the breastbone highlighted.

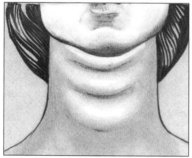

__1__ Accentuate all the transverse wrinkles, using both hard and soft edges

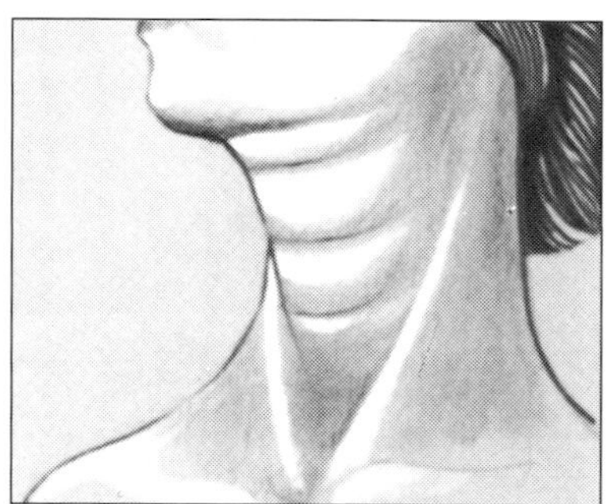

__2__ Turn the head to reveal neck muscle and then shade and highlight this

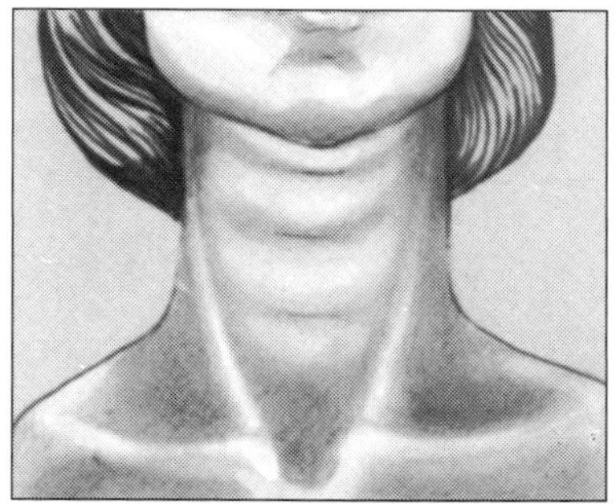

__3__ Highlight and shade the "salt cellars" immediately above the breastbone

Aging the hands

Hands are also sometimes neglected when applying makeup. Whatever age is being portrayed, the hands should always be made up with a color which tones with the face.

Just how much the hands will need to be modeled will depend both on the age and the lifestyle of the character being portrayed. Except where the character is very obese, hands tend to become thinner and bonier with age and the veins become more prominent. The lifestyle and environment of the character will govern just how cared-for the hands should look, and attention must therefore be paid to this aspect.

Since the modeling needed to age hands can be very complex, it is best to approach the problem in three stages.

The first stage is to highlight and shade the bone structure to give a skeletal appearance.

The second stage is to age the knuckles by applying a combination of hard and soft-edged shadows and highlights.

Finally, the veins are added. Use lining colors, or colored pencils (my personal preference). Try a bluey-mauve pencil for delicate fair-skinned hands, a greenish-blue for sallow or oriental hands and a bluish-black or maroon for tanned hands. The veins are given a three-dimensional look by highlighting one side and shading the other. In reality, the position of these highlights and shadows on the veins would depend on the direction of the source of light — which is impossible to predict as it constantly changes. These changes cannot, of course, be represented by makeup. Therefore you should decide on a fixed source of light and paint the shadows and highlights accordingly.

As the hands are frequently held horizontally across the body, thumbs uppermost, and as the main source of light comes from above, always highlight the veins on the sides nearest the thumbs and shadow the sides nearest the little fingers.

Accentuating the bone structure

Highlight and shade the hands, accentuating the natural bone structure. Note how the bones of the fingers are highlighted along the top and shadowed either side to give a skeletal appearance

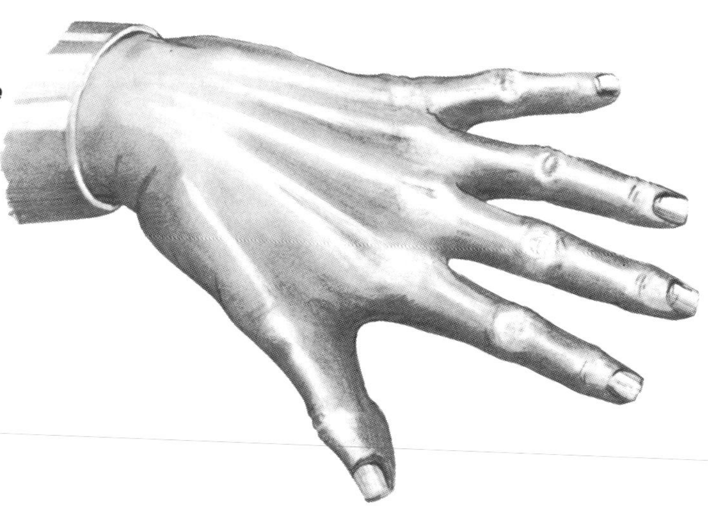

Aging the knuckles

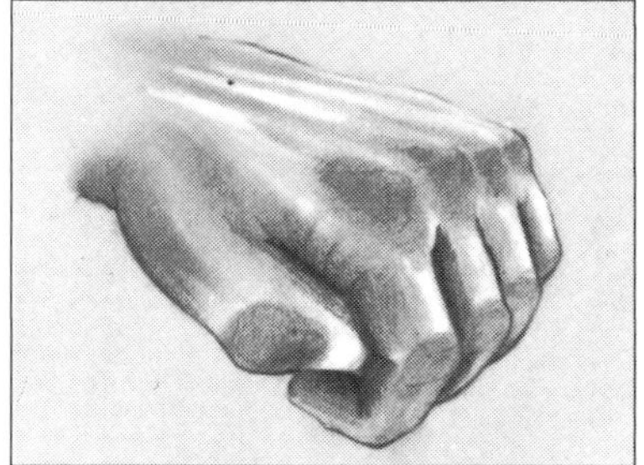

__1__ Here is a quick method of wrinkling the knuckles. First of all,make a fist so that the skin is stretched tightly over the knuckles and then apply a circular patch of shadow over each knuckle

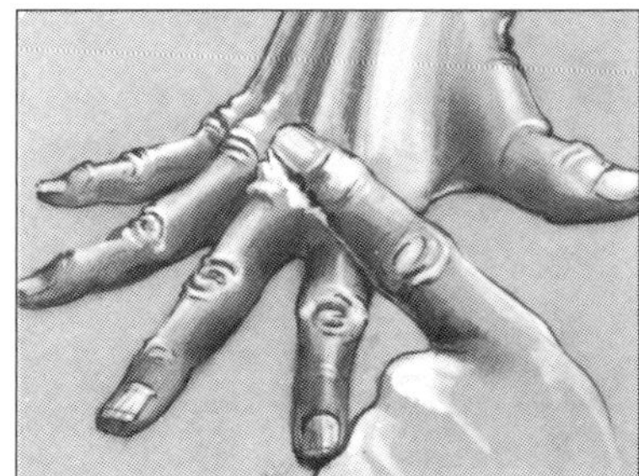

__2__ Relax the fingers and press them down on to the makeup table, so that the knuckle creases are exaggerated, and then apply a thin film of highlight over the creases with your fingertips

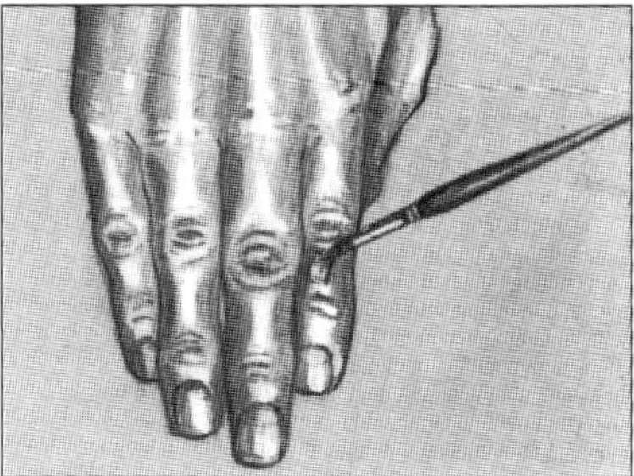

__3__ Blend the edges of all these highlights and shadows with an $\frac{1}{8}$ inch (3mm) brush. When the knuckles need to be reddened, use a touch of cake rouge, dusted on with a $\frac{3}{8}$ inch (9mm) brush

Painting the veins

Create the veins with highlight and shadow, as illustrated, using lining colors or colored pencils. It helps age the hands if the actor holds the tips of the thumbs against the tips of the little fingers underneath the palms. This gives a narrow clawlike look to the hand

Three-dimensional makeup

A great many changes can be made to an actor's face simply by modeling it with light and shade, but these changes are merely optical illusions and do not actually change the physical outlines of the face. Sometimes this is not completely convincing, particularly with features such as the nose or chin — especially in profile. So it may be necessary to make physical changes with false pieces, premade from rubber latex or from plastic, or by applying nose putty or Derma Wax.

False pieces

The most satisfactory method of building up the features is with false pieces, providing that they are well made and fit the actor's face.

There are many advantages of such premade pieces. They are quick and easy to apply and remove, and they always give a constant shape. Most actors find them light and comfortable to wear. Also they usually stay firmly in place and are not very susceptible to damage, so the actor wears them with confidence. Most important of all, they can be used for such things as eye pouches, double chins, sagging throats, false eyelids, and so on, which cannot be made from putty and wax.

They have two main disadvantages. Firstly, they are expensive to buy. Secondly, they are difficult to obtain, since, ideally, they ought to be made-to-measure and this means a visit to a specialist in this field. Of course it is possible to make them for yourself but this can be very time-consuming and complicated. For those who wish to try, there are a number of excellent books on the subject. (See Bibliography.)

False latex pieces should be stuck into place before any makeup has been applied to the skin. Spirit gum or latex adhesive can be used for this, but since latex adhesive can be more easily loosened by perspiration and muscular movement under the piece, spirit gum is the better choice.

As noses are the most usual false pieces to be used, the following illustrations show a nose being applied, but the method remains the same for other pieces — such as eye pouches, chins, and so on.

Applying false pieces

First place the piece in position on the nose to check the fit, noting how much excess latex is around the edge of the piece. Next trim away this excess edging with very sharp scissors, keeping the outline as irregular as possible because straight edges are hard to camouflage. Apply a thin film of spirit gum about ½ inch (12mm) wide along the inside edge of the piece and allow the gum to become tacky before placing the false piece on the skin.

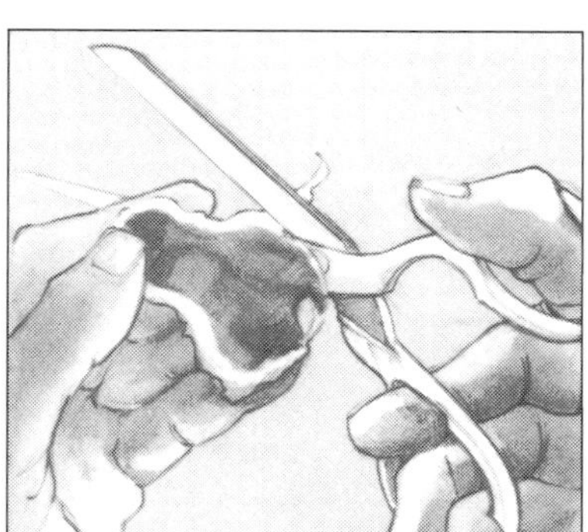

***1** Trim edges from false nose, making them slightly ragged*

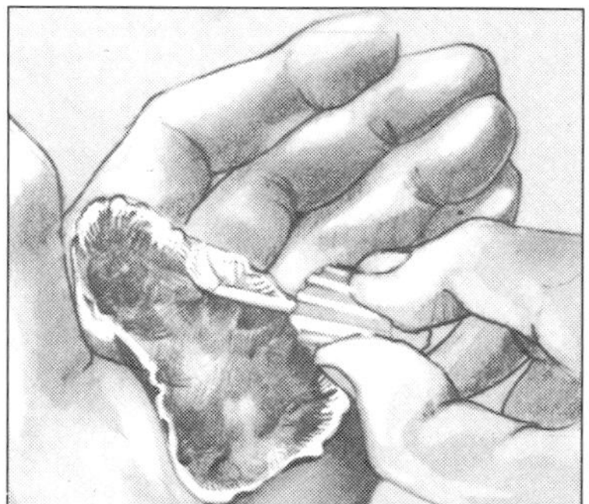

***2** Apply spirit gum to inside edge. Allow to become tacky*

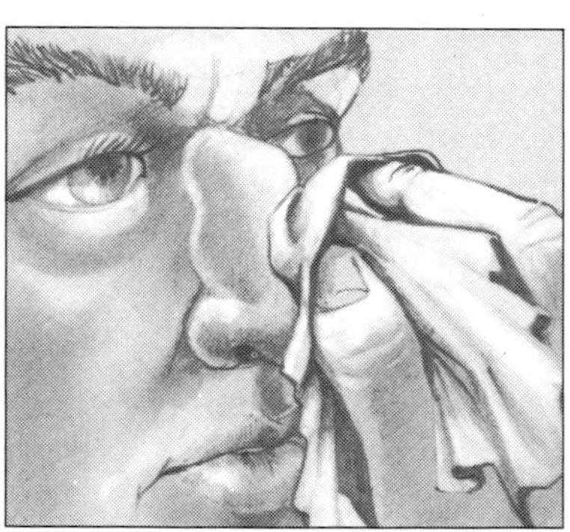

***3** Press the nose into the exact position required with a damp lintless towel*

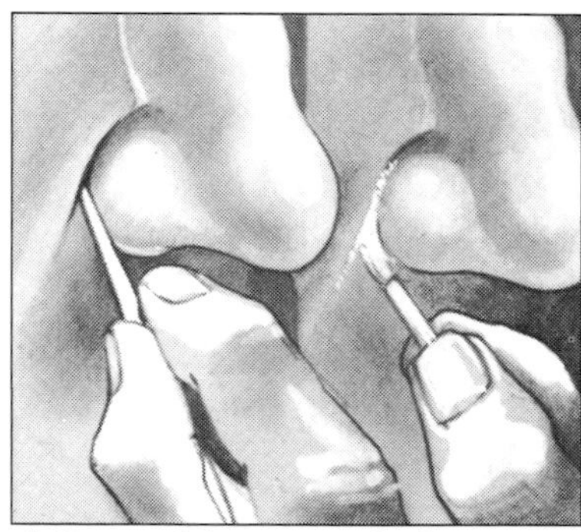

***4** Press false nostrils into place with an orange stick and cover join with latex adhesive*

Now place the false nose very carefully in the exact position required. Do not adjust the position once it is is in place, as this wrinkles the edges, making them more difficult to conceal.

Using a dampened lintless towel wrapped around your fingertip, press the edges into place.Areas such as the crease at the back of the nostrils can be pressed in place using the blunt end of an orange-stick or hoof-stick. If the edges of the piece are thick, they can be concealed with a small amount of liquid latex adhesive stippled along the join. This must be allowed to dry completely before applying makeup to the piece.

Applying makeup to false pieces

As greasepaint tends to make rubber latex deteriorate, it is best to make up false pieces with a special rubber-mask greasepaint which is based on castor oil. This can prove to be quite expensive as it is often necessary to use two or three different shades of paint to camouflage a false piece. If this proves too much for your budget, a good substitute is cream-based stick makeup, applied with a little castor oil.

First apply your chosen base to the rest of the face, stopping just short of the edge of your applied piece.

With your fingertip, work a small amount of castor oil over the top of the stick makeup until it is well mixed. Then stipple the mixture over the false piece, carefully blending the color into the foundation already applied. Powder well.

Now observe the color difference between the makeup on the piece and on the skin. Adjust by stippling on darker and lighter shades of your original base color with a stippling sponge. Then powder again.

It is sometimes necessary to add a little rouge to features such as the nose or ears. This can be done by stippling on cream rouge when you adjust the color to the skin, or by applying cake rouge with a rouge mop, after powdering. (This should be done very carefully, gradually building up the depth of color required, as it is very difficult to remove.)

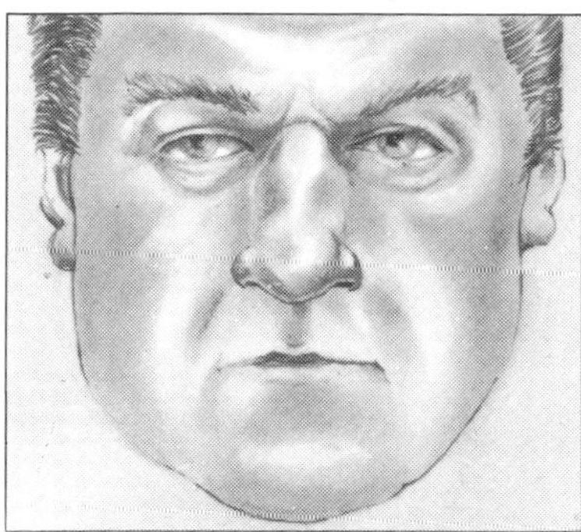

Make up the false piece with rubber-mask greasepaint until the color blends with the foundation. Use a stippling sponge to give a slightly uneven texture. Set makeup with translucent powder

Removing a false piece

A false piece that has been attached with spirit gum should never be pulled off the face or the edges will inevitably tear.

Dip a flat bristle brush (an artist's oil brush will do) in spirit-gum remover and gently work it between the edge of the piece and the skin. Gradually work the bristles along the edge, lifting the piece very gently away as you go.

Remove any spirit gum left on the skin with a pad of cotton that has been moistened with spirit-gum remover.

Lay the piece on a lintless towel and gently remove the spirit gum with a cotton pad moistened with surgical spirit, before replacing the false piece in its storage box.

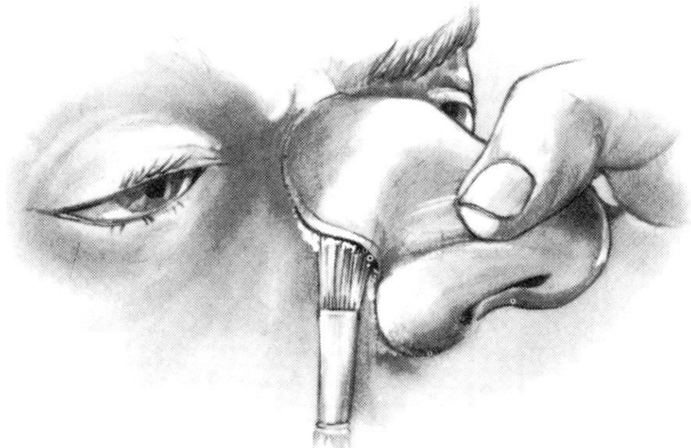

Use solvent on a bristle brush to remove false pieces

Three-dimensional makeup

Nose putty

Sometimes false pieces are too expensive for your budget or difficult to obtain. If you do not have the time or skill to manufacture your own false pieces, then nose putty or Derma Wax can be used to good effect. However, both these "builds" require a certain amount of expertise and skill. If using them for the first time, don't leave it too late to practise before the opening night.

Nose putty, as its name implies, is generally used to build up and change the shape of the nose, but it can be used for other features as well, providing that they have a firm bony base and are not subject to a lot of muscular movement which would dislodge the putty.

You will be surprised how little putty is needed to make quite startling changes to the shape of the nose, and it is a good idea to practise with small quantities of putty before embarking on really big builds.

Before starting to build up the nose, you must first decide on the shape you need. (See pages 30-31.) If no available picture suits the part, then make a profile sketch of the shape required. Tape your sketch or reference picture to the makeup mirror for easy referal and have a small hand mirror nearby — so that you can study your profile as you are working.

Make sure that the area to which you are applying the putty is clean and free from grease by cleansing the skin beforehand with a little toning lotion on a cotton ball.

Applying the putty

Take a small piece of putty from the stick and gently knead it with the fingertips until it is pliable. If it tends to stick to the fingers, this can be prevented with a fine film of nongreasy hairdressing gel rubbed over the fingertips.

Press the resulting ball of putty on the part of the nose to be built up and gently start to press it down at the sides, using the first finger and thumb. Continue to blend and shape the nose in this way, thinning the edges of the putty into the skin.

Once the edges of the putty are blended into the skin, adjust the shape by squeezing and pressing the putty until it resembles your sketched outline.

Now take some of the chosen makeup base on to a fingertip and gently stipple the color on to the putty nose, carefully massaging the surface to smooth out any unwanted bumps or cracks, and then gently powder it. Now apply the makeup to the rest of the face.

The putty is usually much lighter than the natural skin color and it is often necessary to adjust the coloring on the build by stippling on a deeper shade of your chosen base color.

If you accidentally knock or rub the surface of the nose during the performance, the makeup can be disturbed and the underlying pale putty shows through. Avoid this by adding a small amount of a very dark cream-stick makeup to the putty when you first knead it, changing its color to something nearer the natural skin tone.

Removing a putty nose

Hold the build between your finger and thumb and gently rock the putty until it works loose. Lift the nose away and squeeze it into a ball — which you can then use to lift away any remaining pieces of putty left around the edges of the build. Any small fragments that then remain can be massaged with removing cream and wiped off with a facial tissue.

The putty ball can be kept and re-used a number of times, although eventually the successive addition of makeup base will make it too sticky and pliable to use.

***1** Press the ball of putty on the part to be built up*

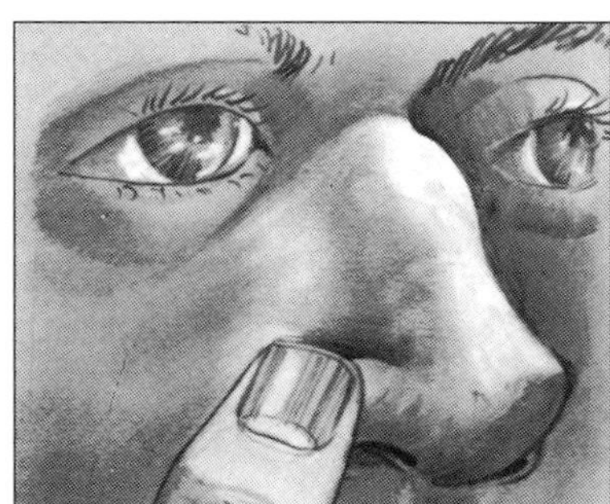

***2** Shape the nose and blend the edges into the skin*

Derma Wax

Derma Wax has a much softer texture than nose putty and it can be molded and shaped more easily. At the same time, it is much more easily damaged if accidentally knocked, so it needs to have a protective film of sealer painted over it before the makeup is applied. Since perspiration, and even a very small amount of muscular movement at the sides of the build, can easily dislodge this protective film, it is better not to use this type of build for stage work. However, because of its slightly translucent appearance, it can be almost indetectable in close-up and is therefore invaluable for film or photographic makeup or drama in the round — so here is the method of application.

To prevent wax being easily dislodged with perspiration, it is necessary to create a "key" (a base which aids adhesion) to the skin before starting the build. This is done as follows:

Paint the area of the build with spirit gum and apply a thin layer of cotton (cotton wool) over gummed area. Press gently into place and allow to dry.

Pull off excess cotton, to leave a slightly fluffy surface over the build area. This will provide a key to which the wax will more safely adhere.

Knead a small amount of a very dark cream-stick foundation into a lump of Derma Wax. (Use a palette knife on a plastic palette, rather than fingers, which can make the wax too warm and soft.) Carry on until the wax is approximately the same color as the natural skin tone, then roll the wax into a ball and press on to the fluffy key.

Blend and shape the wax into the shape required, in the same manner as with nose putty but using a lighter touch. When working with wax, do not apply cream or gel to the fingers but dip them in cold water to prevent the wax adhering to them. Even then there is a tendency for the wax to pull away, and a good tip is to use the handle of a teaspoon, dipped in cold water, as a spatula to mold the wax.

Paint a fine film of sealer over the entire build, using a flat-ended, soft bristle brush. (It is worth keeping a cheap brush for this purpose as the sealer and solvent used for cleaning will soon ruin a good sable brush.) Once the sealer is completely dry, the build can be made up as described before.

Removal of Derma Wax

If you do not wish to re-use the wax, the build can simply be removed by pulling it away with a tissue.

If you wish to retain the wax for further use, the sealer must first be carefully lifted and peeled away from the wax, before it is removed. Final traces of wax and sealer should be massaged with makeup cleanser and wiped away with a tissue.

Building a nose with Derma Wax

1 *Using spirit gum,paint the area to be built*

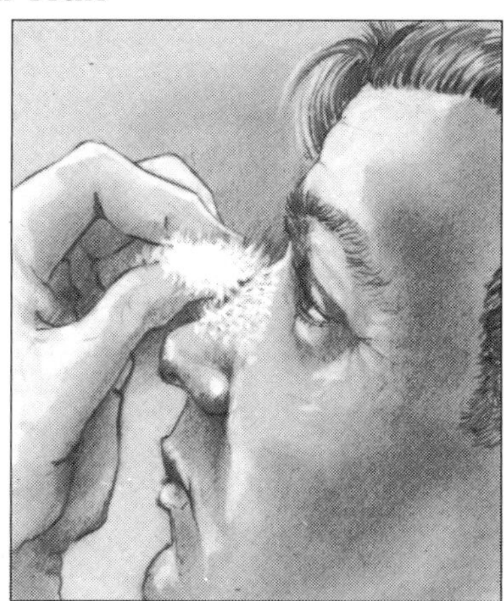

2 *Apply a layer of cotton (cotton wool) over the gum*

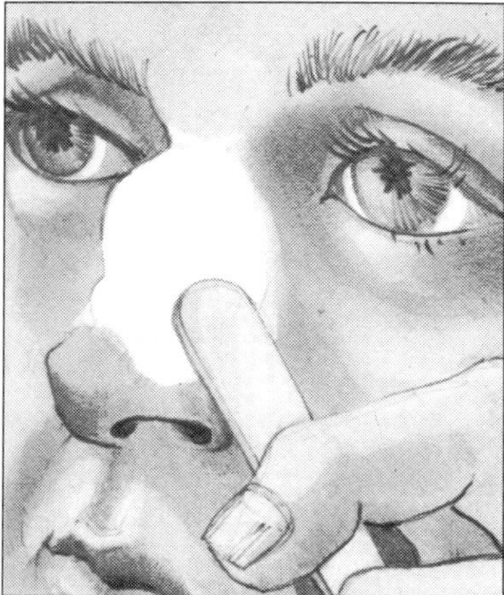

3 *Press ball of wax on to nose; then shape and blend*

Three-dimensional makeup

Creating a wrinkled skin

Many actors think that their skins are too smooth to be effectively aged by using just light and shade and feel that physically wrinkling the skin will achieve a really old look. But, however effective a finely wrinkled surface on the skin may look in your mirror or when seen on film or television, under stage lighting and viewed from a distance, it will become almost invisible.

There are techniques that can be used to wrinkle the skin coarsely enough for it to show in the theater, but it needs a good deal of patience and skill to make the wrinkling look natural, and often the result looks more like a horror mask than graceful old age. However, for those who wish to try it, here is the simplest method of wrinkling — applying cleansing tissue over liquid latex or spirit gum.

First tear a single thickness of facial cleansing tissue into sections to cover the right shape and area of skin.

(Do not be tempted to use very large sections as they quickly become unmanageable. Using peach or brown colored tissue will give the best results.)

Stretch a small area of skin taut between the first finger and the thumb and paint it with a fine film of liquid latex or spirit gum.

When the gummed area has become slightly tacky, apply a section of the torn tissue to the area. Then apply a second coat of latex or gum over the surface of the tissue and, with the skin still stretched taut, dry the area with a hairdrier.

Release the skin and note how the skin will wrinkle. Then repeat the process on adjacent areas of skin.

Once the whole face has been covered with the gummed tissue and has completely dried, it can be made up, with grease or cream-stick makeup stippled over the surface.

Using a shade lighter than the color of the gummed tissue, it is possible to highlight just the tops of the wrinkles. In this way the wrinkled effect can be emphasized.

If latex and tissue has been used, the wrinkled skin can very simply be peeled away from the face, but if spirit gum is used then a spirit-gum solvent is necessary to soften the application before removal.

Note: It is not advisable to use this wrinkling technique over a sensitive skin or a skin covered with fine facial hair.

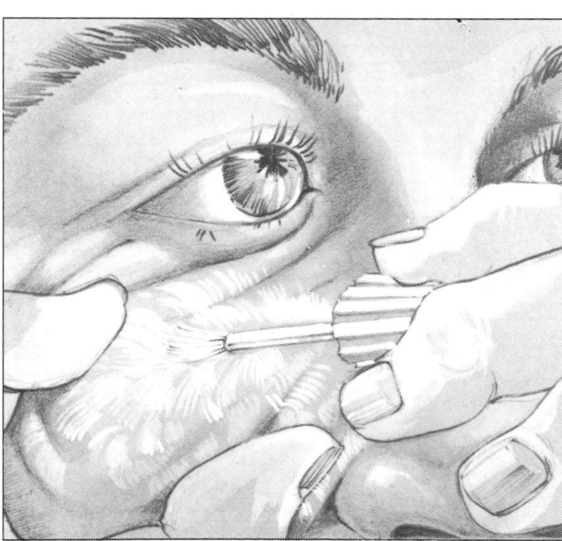

__1__ Stretch a small area of skin and paint with liquid latex or spirit gum

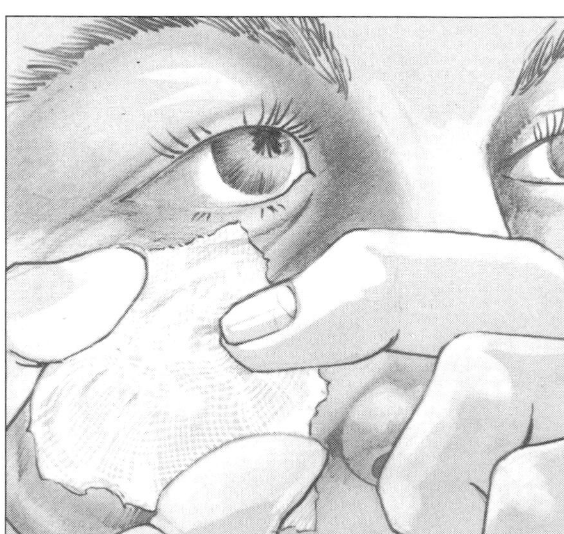

__2__ Apply a piece of tissue, paint on more gum and dry with a hairdrier

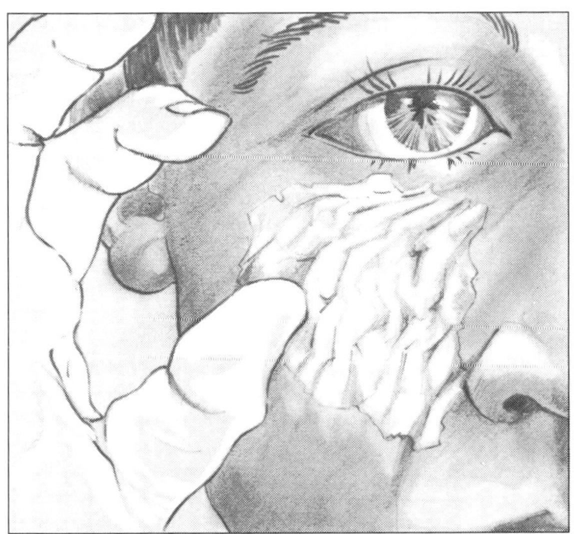

__3__ Release the skin and repeat process until all the face is wrinkled and dry

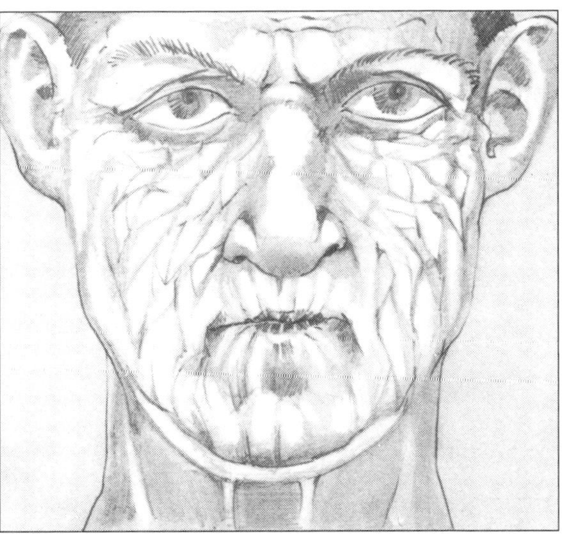

__4__ Stipple skin with a pale grease makeup to highlight the wrinkles

Nose plugs

Nostrils can be enlarged and coarsened by the insertion of nose plugs. These plugs can be made from a number of different items, such as a small plastic thimble with a hole drilled through the top or a small plastic curtain ring. The most effective to use, and the most comfortable to wear, are made from the tip of a baby's pacifier or a section of rubber teat from a baby's feeding bottle.

Cut a section from the middle of the teat, as shown. (The actual size of this section should be varied according to the size of the performer's nostril and how much you wish to enlarge it.) Insert the plug by placing it on the tip of your little finger and gently inserting it into the nostril. The inside of the plug and the visible edge should then be darkened with makeup to conceal the rubber.

When using a baby's pacifier, make a hole in the tip, cut off the top of the bulb and proceed as before. Remember to make the hole in the tip or the actor will have difficulty breathing!

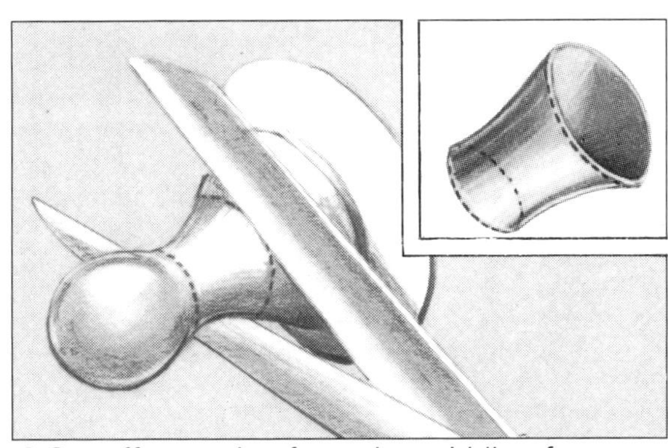

__1__ Cut off a section from the middle of a baby's bottle teat

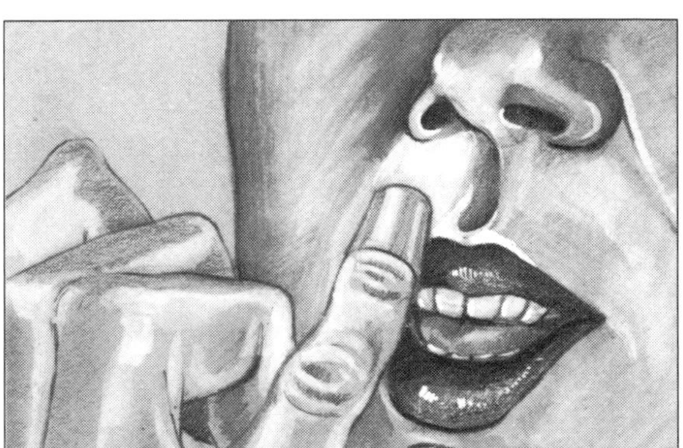

__2__ Gently insert the plug into the nostril with the fingertip

Hair and wigs

Using your own hair

The right hairstyle and hair color are very important considerations when working out a makeup. They can help to suggest age, personality and period. A simple change of hairstyle may transform an actor into a brand new personality.

Wigs can be used to good effect but the cheapest and simplest method is to use your own hair and restyle it. This is much better than using a bad wig. Simple changes can easily be made with a brush and comb, hairspray and water. Modern home-hairdressing appliances (such as heated rollers, electric curling tongs, setting gels, foams and temporary hair-colorants mean that quite big changes in style can be achieved at home without enormous expense. It is not necessary to go into detail on the techniques of home hairdressing as there are already many books on this subject, but one fact should be remembered — in any good style it is the cut that is most important and it pays to have this done by a really first-class hairstylist. Do not attempt to cut hair yourself unless you have had training.

Many facial faults can be helped by the right hairstyle and both men and women can benefit from rethinking the shape of their hair.

If the actor is lucky enough to have an oval face, almost any hairstyle will look good. All that needs to be considered is the suitability of the style for the particular character.

Hairstyles to suit face shapes

before *after*

A round face

A round face needs height on top. An asymmetrical side-sweep is also very slimming to the face. Long hair can be cut shorter at the sides to fall over the cheeks like a curtain. Short hair should be built up on top and should hug the ears closely

A square face

A lift on top and an asymmetrical side-sweep, with extra width at the temples, detracts from the square look. Medium-length hair cut to taper along the jawline will soften a square jaw

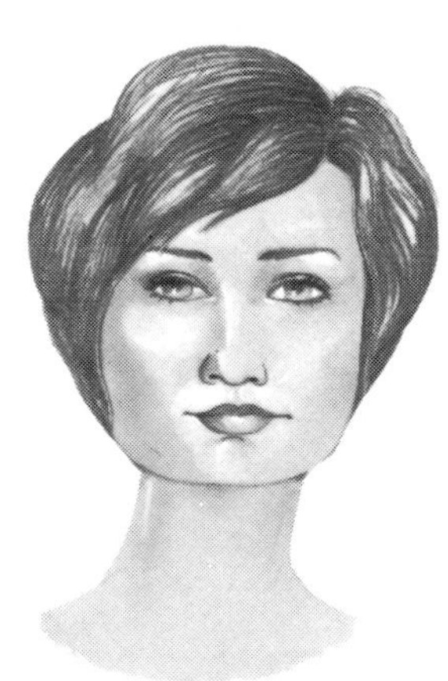

A pear-shaped face

Hair at chin level, sweeping forward, hides the fullness of the jaw. Build the top slightly and add width at the temples to balance the face

before

after

An oblong face

Keep the top flat and add width and volume at eye level. Flick up the ends at jaw level

A heart-shaped face

Curve the hair forward over the temples to cut forehead width and balance the chin with softness behind the ears

Hair and wigs

Hairstyles to disguise specific features

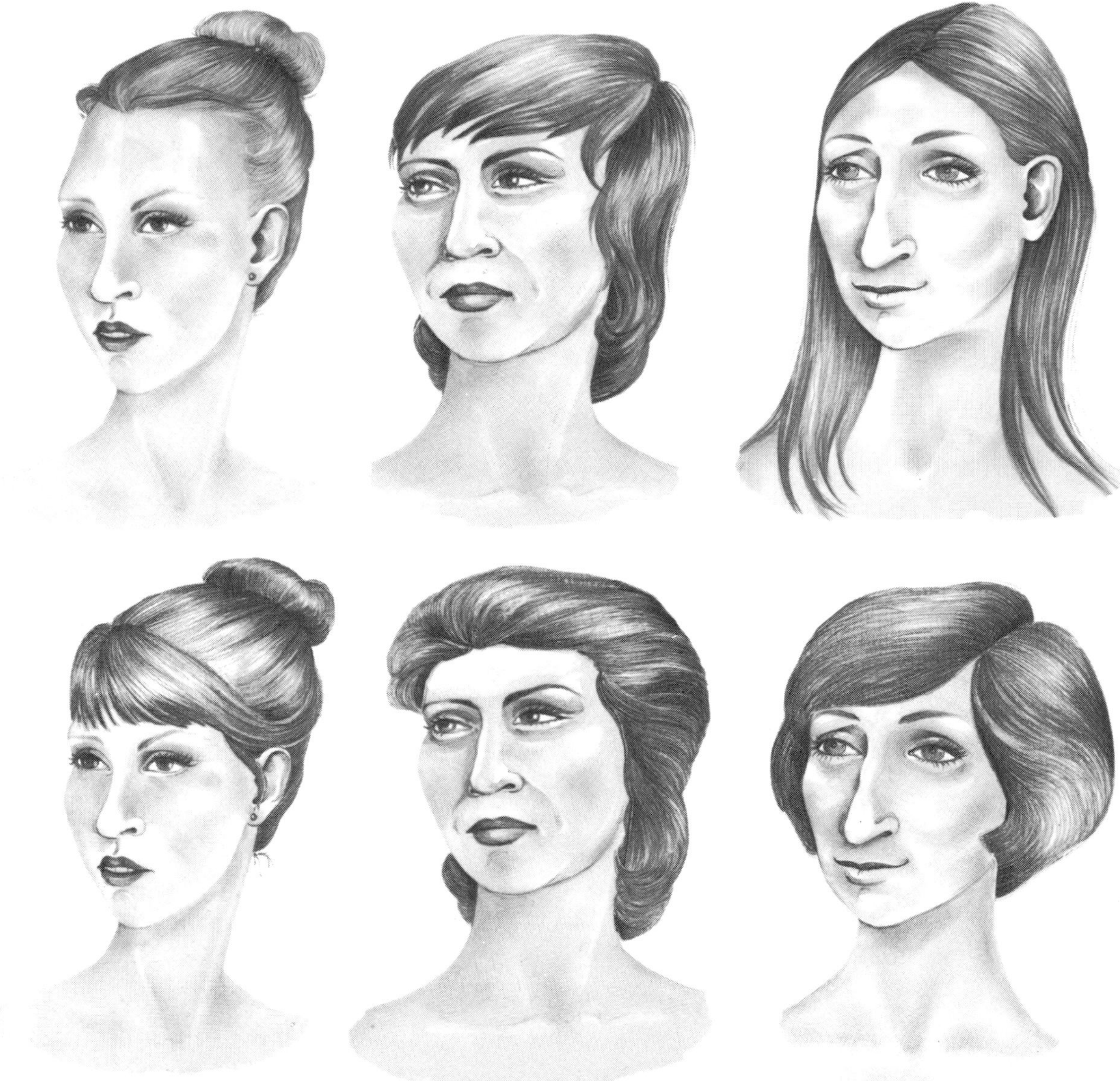

A high or domed forehead can be cut down with a casual half-fringe or a full fringe

A low forehead can be heightened by sweeping the hair up and off the face and adding extra height to the top

If you have a long pointed nose, avoid long straight styles and center partings. Medium-length hair with an asymmetrical parting and a side-swept fringe will make the nose look smaller

A very prominent chin is accentuated by short hair. Medium-length hair swept forward to hug the jawline will help

A long thin neck can be disguised with hair taken just below chin level and curved under the jawbone to shorten the length of the neck

A short thick neck can be elongated by short hair cut into a V at the back. Medium-length hair should be swirled up and out over the ears. Long hair swept up into a topknot will also lengthen the neck

Hair and wigs

Corrective hairstyles for men

Although men do not have the same scope as women to influence the shape of the face by dramatic changes of hairstyle, there are still a number of things that can be done.

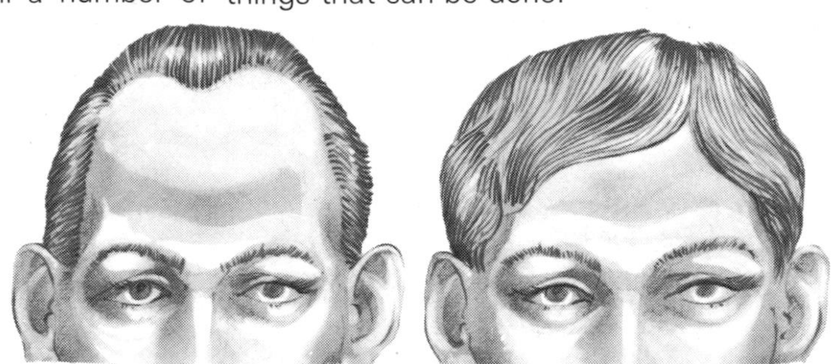

If the forehead is too high, keep the hair flat on top and full at the sides and dressed forward over the forehead

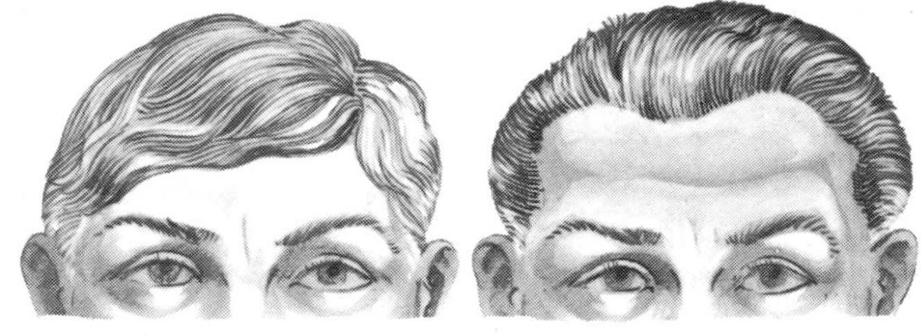

A low forehead can be heightened by dressing the hair well back

A round face can be slimmed by keeping the hair full on top and short at the sides

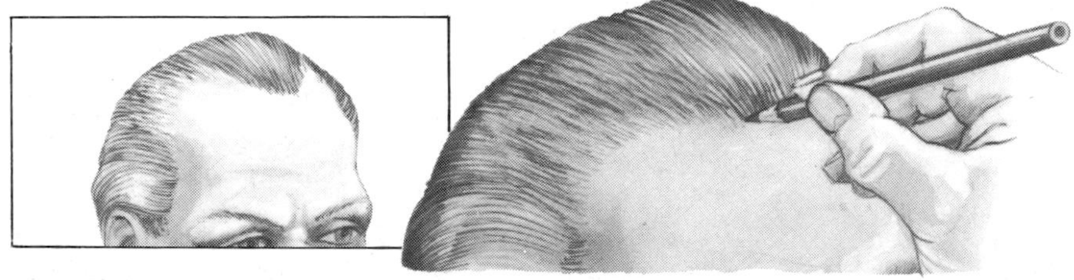

If the hairline is receding, it can be corrected by penciling in a new line with an eyebrow pencil that matches the natural color. Using the edge of a well-sharpened eyebrow pencil, sketch in tiny hairlike strokes in the same direction as the natural growth. Bald spots on the crown of the head can be disguised by darkening the scalp with a color which will blend in with natural hair. You can use either a colored hairspray, cake makeup or masque. (Masque is a product similar to mascara, which can also be used to darken graying hair.)

Graying and coloring the hair

The simplest method of graying the hair is with white talcum powder but this is usually most unsatisfactory as it gives the hair a lifeless dull appearance and it is very easily displaced.

Whitener applied with a tinting brush is much better because the application can very easily be localized to a particular section of hair and does not easily come off.

However, this method can be long and tedious when graying a full head of hair and the hair is subsequently quite difficult to style. It is sometimes easier to use one of the temporary sprays of haircolor. They come in a wide variety of colors, including silver, white and gray.

When using these sprays, it is most important to avoid getting the color on to the face. The best solution is to cut a template of cardboard to match the hairline and use this to mask the face as you spray the front sections of hair.

To create a streak in the hair, take a sheet of foolscap paper and cut a slit about two inches (50mm) long in the middle. Pull a lock of hair through this hole and press the paper as close to the scalp as possible.

Spread the lock of hair over the paper and spray with the chosen color. Allow it to dry, remove the paper and comb the lock back into the hair.

One other method of graying the hair is by using greasepaint or cream-stick makeup. This is particularly effective for small localized applications such as at the temples or for streaks, but it must be remembered that it will rub off on hats, or on the hands if it is touched.

Whichever of these methods you use, take care that you do not make the graying look too white or it will appear blue and slightly artificial when seen under stage lighting.

Apart from graying the hair, sprays can be used to change the hair to almost any color. However, it is sometimes difficult to make very dark hair look effectively lighter.

In such cases, it may be preferable to have the hair professionally lightened and then given a temporary color rinse.

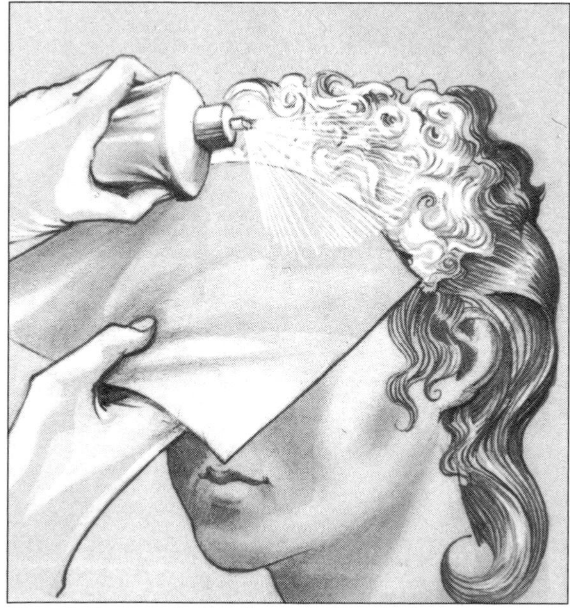

Carefully mask the face with a template when spraying hair

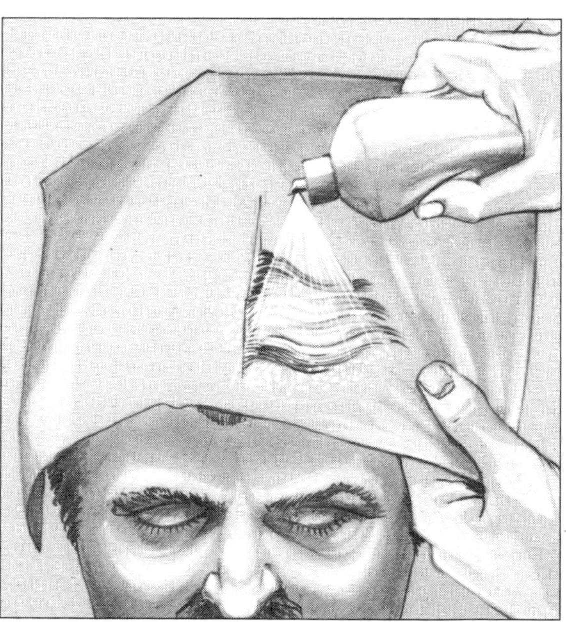

To create streaks, isolate locks of hair and color with a spray

Hair and wigs

Hairpieces

It may not always be possible to change your own hair to the required style so a wig or hairpiece may be needed. Wigs cover natural hair completely, while hairpieces just supplement the natural growth.

There are several types of hairpieces: toupees, falls and backpieces for men; and switches, chignons, falls and curls for women. Hairpieces must blend into the natural hair, so when ordering from a wigmaker, enclose a snippet of your own hair to ensure a true match.

Switches and chignons

These are the easiest hairpieces to use. They are simply pinned into position without having to be blended into the natural hair.

Falls

These can be used by both men and women. They are useful for period styles when loose flowing hair is needed at the back of the head. Part the hair across the top of the head from ear to ear and securely pin the fall along the parting and into the back hair. The hair in front of the parting is then combed back over the edge of the fall and into the false hair, and pinned in place with fine hairpins. This is often more effective than using a full wig, since the front hairline is natural and there is no wig-join to conceal.

Curls

Curls are very simple to use. They can be fixed in a number of ways, either pinned under the natural curls or loops of hair, tied into place with ribbons or simply fastened underneath bonnets or headdresses.

Toupees

These are used to disguise a receding hairline. Good toupees have a fine hair-lace front, are expensive and need to be treated carefully. Less expensive toupees do not have lace fronts, are much stronger and easier to apply. Unfortunately these cheaper toupees can look very false, unless the front hair can be dressed forward in a fringe to hide the hairline.

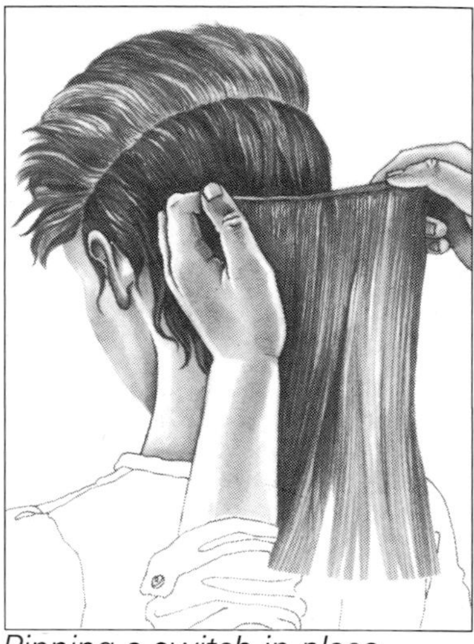

Pinning a switch in place

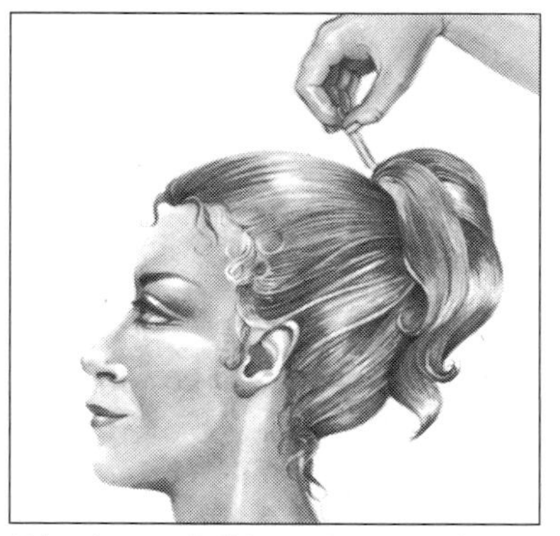

Pinning a fall into back hair

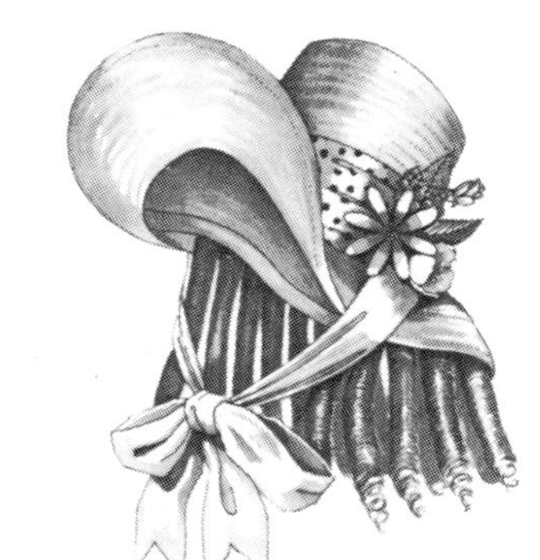

False curls fixed to a bonnet

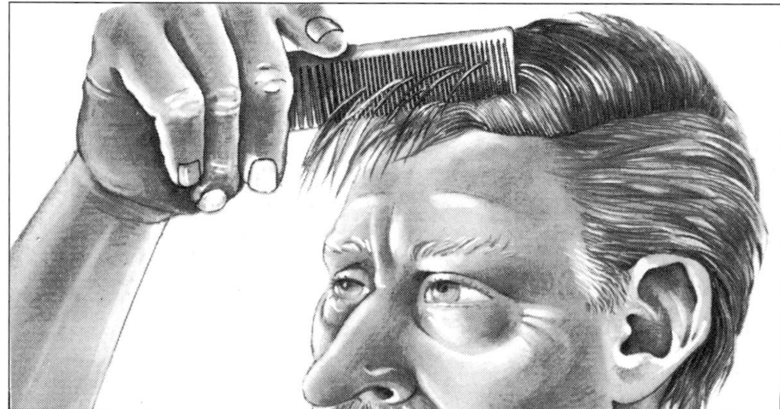

Disguising a hard-edged toupee

Wigs

Should it not be practical to augment your own hair with a false piece, a full wig must be used. Generally these are hired from a theatrical wigmaker but nowadays there are many very good women's wigs, made from artificial hair, on sale in beauty parlors and in some departmental stores. Providing that they suit the part, these wigs are perfectly satisfactory.

Full wigs are available with three different fronts or "joins".

Hard edge

The first type has a so-called "hard edge" where the hair is knotted directly to the front of the wig foundation and does not have a natural-looking hairline. This edge can be concealed in two different ways.

The first method is simply to dress the wig hair forward into a fringe or a set of curls so the hard edge is concealed.

The second method is to comb forward a narrow section of your own hair over the face, along the natural hairline. Put on the wig with the hard edge along this parting, fastening it in place with hairpins or grips.

Now brush the natural hair back over the wig until it blends into it, pinning it into place with fine pins, if necessary. If the natural hair is not the same color as the wig, this can be corrected by using a colored hairspray.

Providing the wig is a good fit, this method usually works better than any other type of join on a woman's wig.

Wigs with this type of hard edge are not usually practical for men. The only exception to this is when the wig is actually supposed to be obvious.

For example, a hard-edged wig could be used when the role demands a legal wig or the sort which would have been worn by an aristocrat in the seventeenth or eighteenth century

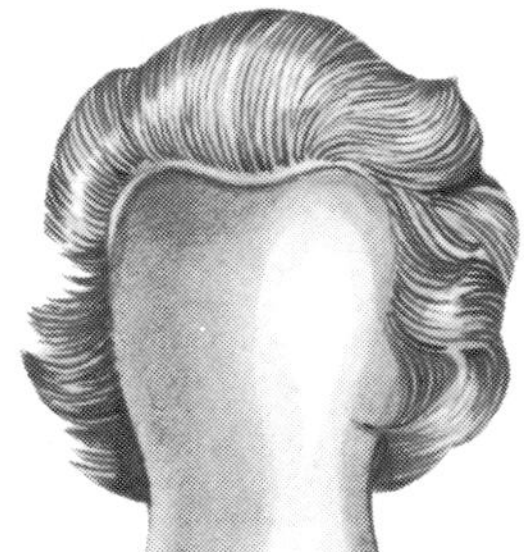

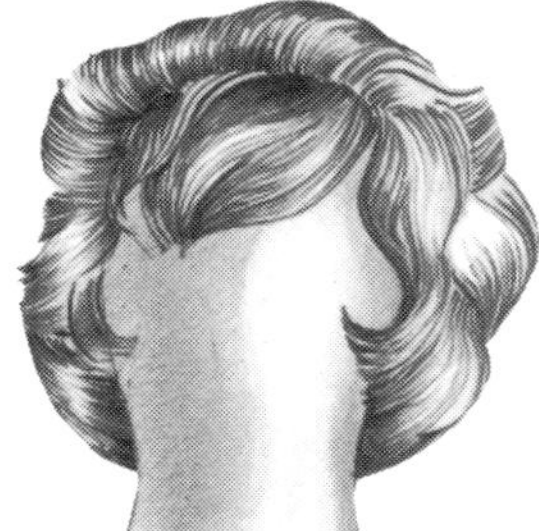

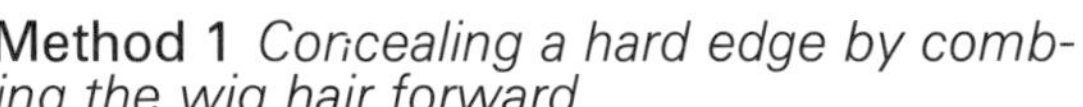

Method 1 *Concealing a hard edge by combing the wig hair forward*

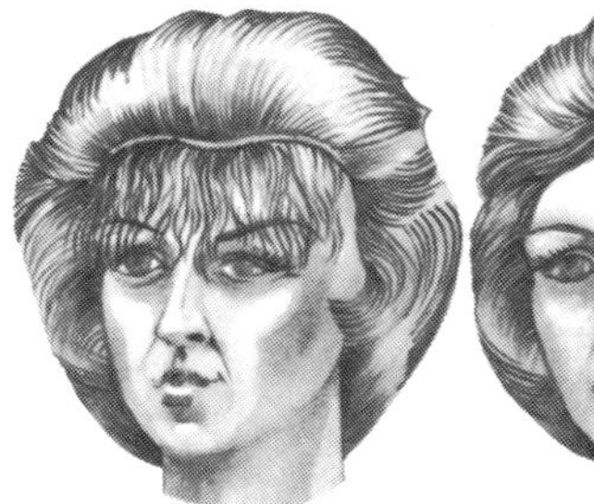

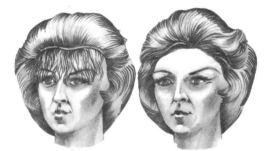

Method 2 *Concealing a hard edge with the natural hair combed back into the wig*

Lace front

This type has a fine hair- lace or nylon-net join, similar to the join on a toupee, which is stuck to the forehead with spirit gum.

Blender

This type has a blender, which is made of tightly woven gauze stretched across the forehead. This blender must be covered with makeup so that it matches the rest of the face.

The blender front is usually found in character wigs where the hairline is receding and the gauze masks the performer's natural hair.

These wigs are particularly useful if the character being portrayed requires a bald head or a very high forehead.

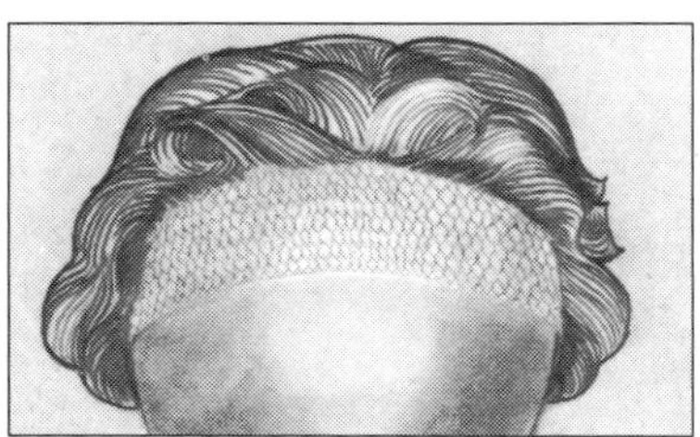

Lace front

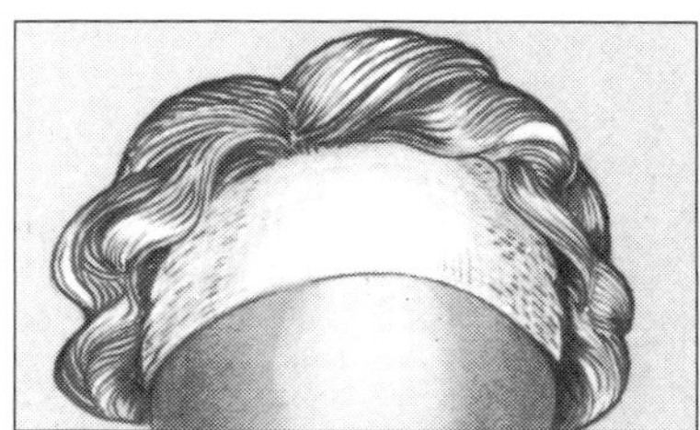

Blender front

Hair and wigs

Putting on a lace-front wig

Before putting on a wig, the natural hair must be flattened to the head as much as possible. Men with short hair do not usually need to do this, but if a very heavy periwig is being worn, a strip of bandage wound twice around the head provides a base to which the wig can be firmly pinned in position.

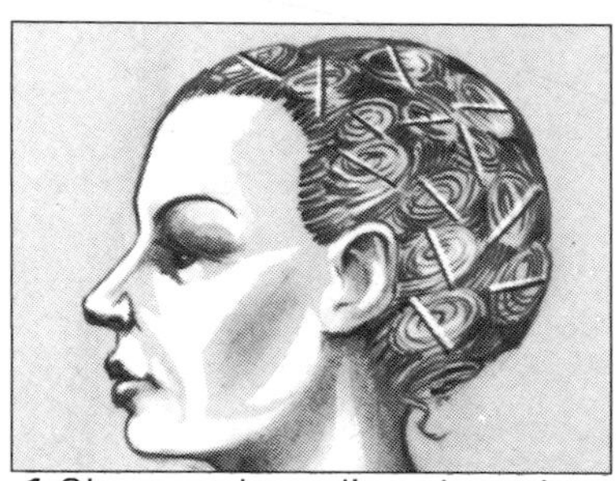

1 Short and medium-length hair should be pinned in small circular curls, flat to the scalp, evenly all over. This keeps the hair tidy and provides the best shape for the wig

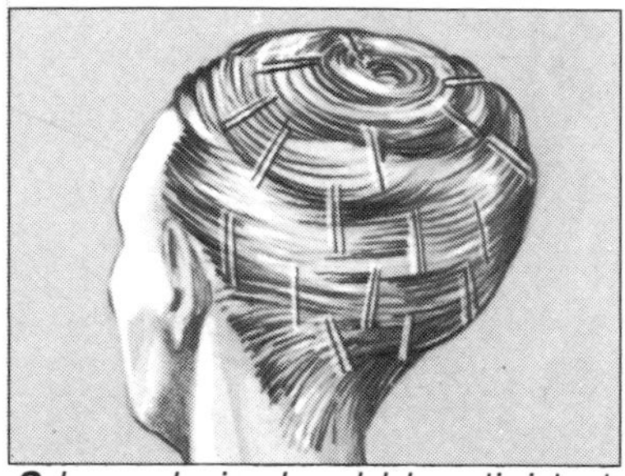

2 Long hair should be divided right down the center and wound round the head, folding the two sections over each other at the back and firmly pinning them in place

3 Cover the flattened hair with a cotton gauze or crepe bandage wound firmly round the head, or with the top of an old stocking made into a cap — to act as a base for the wig

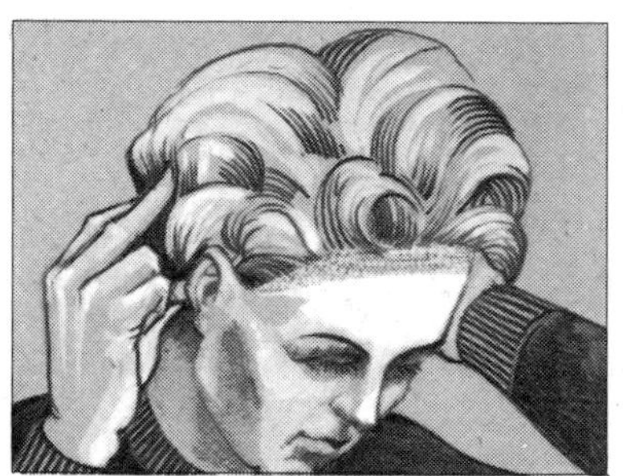

4 Grasp the wig by the two springs at the back edge and carefully position front join so it is touching the center of the forehead. Pull wig firmly but gently backwards with both hands, as if putting on a bathing cap, until the springs are nestling comfortably into the nape of the neck. The lace front should now be in roughly the right position

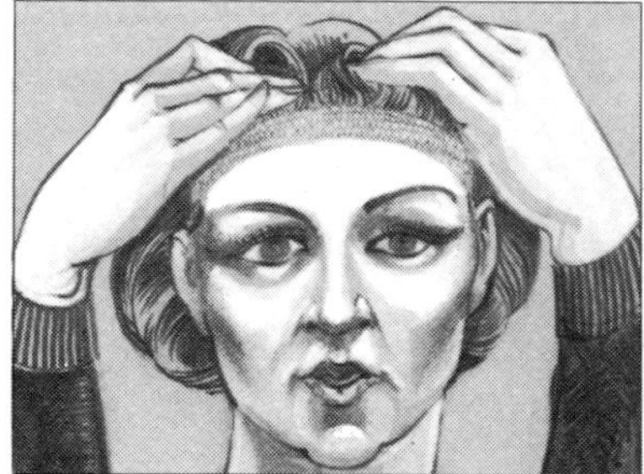

5 Now place both hands on top of the wig and adjust its position by very gently easing it back until the join is exactly where it is required. If the wig is pulled too far back and the natural hairline shows, it will be necessary to take off the wig and start again. Never try to pull the wig forward, as it will not sit properly and you may damage the lace front

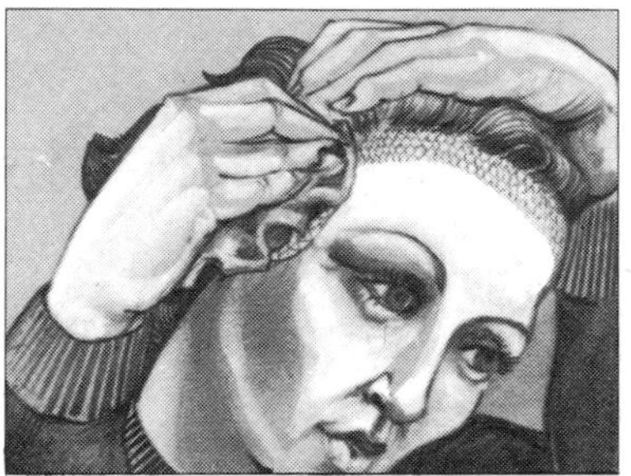

6 Take hold of the springs at each side of the face and pull them gently into position (just in front of the ears). Pin them securely to the bandage. Now the wig can be pinned into place, taking care the pins do not damage the foundation. Fasten the two net side-flaps to the skin with spirit gum, pressing them firmly into place with a damp towel

If the wig is a good fit, the net front will be stretched firmly across the forehead. Gum the center of the join to the forehead to prevent the wig riding up.

If the join is not tight, fasten it with spirit gum around the hairline. Do this carefully or it may pucker the lace front, stain the net or reveal the join. Never use latex.

How to conceal a blender front with makeup

When using a blender front, it is first necessary to cover the gauze with makeup to match the color on your face.

Apply foundation color to the face, carrying the color on to the forehead, well above the line where the join of the wig will be. Thoroughly powder forehead.

Put on the wig, using a piece of thin tissue or greaseproof wrapping-paper between the blender and your own hair to prevent the makeup sinking through the gauze into the hair.

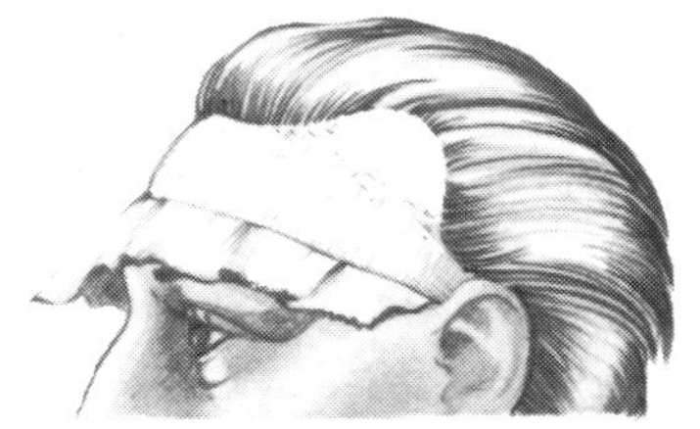

Make up the gauze front or bald top with a greasepaint foundation, adjusting the color so that it matches the makeup on the forehead, and do any character work that is needed (see page 63). Now thoroughly powder the front until the greasepaint is set. Carefully remove the wig, lift away protective paper, and powder the inside of the blender which will still be greasy.

It is not necessary or advisable to make up the front for every performance. This would cause too big a build-up of foundation on the gauze — and the join would begin to show. It should only be repainted about once a week or when it becomes discolored. It is a good idea to remove some of the first application of greasepaint with surgical spirit or acetone before renewing the makeup so the build-up is kept to a minimum.

Putting on a blender wig

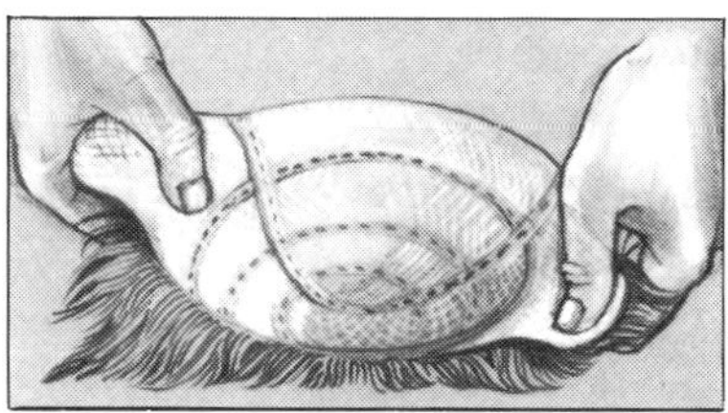

1 Make sure your own hair is flat to the head. Hold the wig with a thumb and forefinger positioned on either side of the blender front

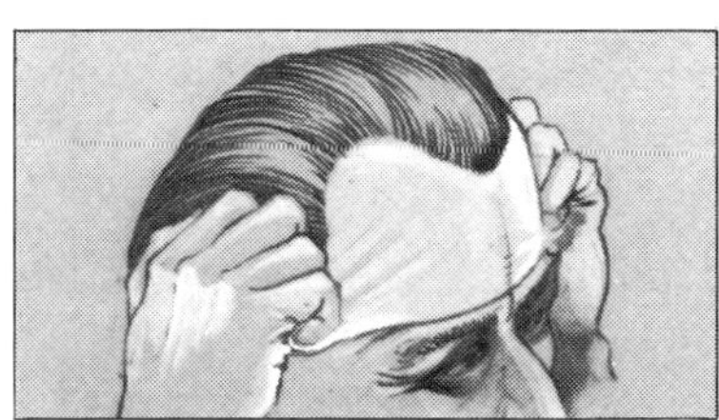

2 Keeping the wig as open as possible, position the edge of the blender just above eyebrows, making sure wig is centered properly on the head

3 Hold the blender edge firmly on the forehead, using the thumb and forefinger, and gently pull down the wig on to the head with the other hand

4 Gently ease wig back until firmly positioned, with the edge of blender in the right place. Check back fits snugly into the nape of the neck

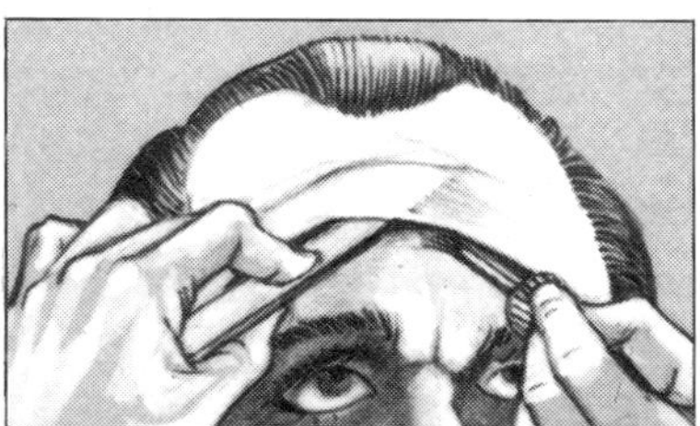

5 With an orange-stick or thin wooden spatula, lift the gauze and apply a thin film of spirit gum underneath the edge, right along the blender

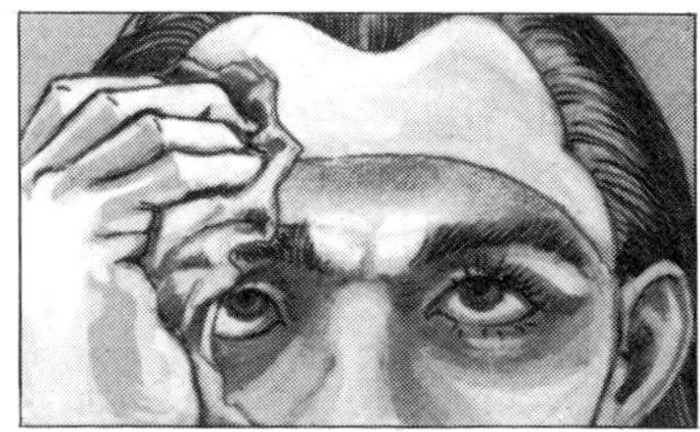

6 Press into place with a dampened towel until the gum is dry and the wig solidly fastened in place. Then retouch makeup to hide join

Hair and wigs

Putting on a toupee

Take care that the toupee sits where the natural hairline would be, or even slightly higher. A toupee worn too far forward changes the shape of the face and looks unnatural.

If the toupee has a lace front, place it in position and brush a thin coat of spirit gum on to the dry skin, devoid of any makeup, immediately below the lace. Do not apply the gum over the lace and never use latex-based adhesives. Allow the spirit gum to dry slightly and then press the lace front into position, using a dampened lintless towel. Continue to press the lace down with the towel, using small rolling movements of the fingers, until the spirit gum has lost its shine.

The back of the toupee must now be fastened in place, using either double-sided toupee tape directly on to the scalp or pinning the toupee to the back hair with a grip sewn on to the back edge of the foundation.

Hard-fronted toupees should be attached with toupee tape both at the front and back.

Dressing and caring for wigs

When a wig arrives from the wigmaker, it is usually in a cardboard box, carefully packed in tissue paper and with a ball of tissue inside the wig so that it will keep its shape. Once unpacked, it should be kept on a wig block so that it does not lose its shape and can be easily redressed. If you do not have a wig block, the wig should be returned to its box and packed as it arrived so that it remains in good order.

A rented wig often arrives unsuitably dressed but, providing that it is a reasonably good wig made of human hair, it can be redressed to the style required. After a few wearings, even a correctly dressed wig begins to lose its set and needs to be redressed to look its best. It is therefore important to have a little knowledge of how to dress a wig.

Pin the wig to wig block with wig pins. Brush and comb it out thoroughly, taking care not to let the comb dig into the foundation by holding the comb with the teeth pointing away from you.

For a softly-waved style, simply curl with an electric curling iron. If a stronger wave is required, put the hair up into pin curls or on rollers, first moistening each section of hair by spraying it with water or hair-setting lotion. The curls or rollers should be placed in the direction in which the hair is to be combed out when dry.

When all the rollers and pin curls are in place, cover the wig with a net and dry thoroughly with a hairdrier. Then remove all rollers and pins, brush out the hair and style as required. Spray with light hairspray to preserve set.

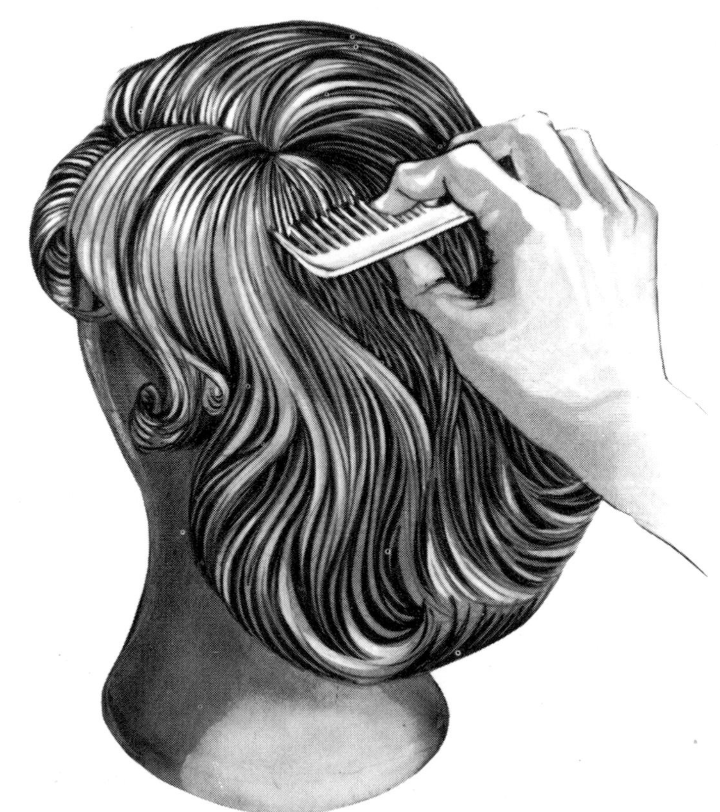

Dress wig carefully, with the comb's teeth pointing away from you so they do not dig into the wig foundation

Removing wigs and toupees

To remove wigs and toupees with lace fronts, apply spirit-gum solvent with a brush to the gummed areas until the lace begins to lift, and then, with both hands, grasp the foundation at the back of the wig or toupee and pull it gently forward and off. Never be tempted to push the wig backwards as this may tear the lace — and never pull it off by the hair.

When removing a wig with a blender front, work some spirit-gum solvent underneath one end of the blender edge with a flat brush and gradually ease the brush along under the edge as the solvent dissolves the gum. Then remove the wig in the same manner as for a lace-fronted wig.

Cleaning wigs and toupees

Immediately after removing a wig or toupee, clean the spirit gum off the join with acetone or carbon tetrachloride. Lay the lace front on a piece of blotting paper or a lintless towel and dab the cleaner on to the gum with a brush or a piece of lintless material until the lace is clean.

Do not use cotton balls because the fibers stick to the lace and are very difficult to remove.

Once the lace is cleaned, the wig should be put on a wig block or stuffed with tissue paper and returned to its box.

A wig needs to be kept clean but under no circumstances ever shampooed. Rubbing the hair in water will cause matting and tangling, and the hair tends to creep through the foundation inside the wig so the whole wig can easily be ruined.

The best method of cleaning a wig is to dip it in and out of a bath of carbon tetrachloride.

Shake it dry and put it on a wig block to be restyled. Remember to use this solvent only in a well-ventilated room. Avoid getting it on the skin and do not expose it to an open flame.

Ordering wigs and hairpieces

When ordering wigs, hairpieces, beards and so on from a wigmaker, it is essential to supply accurate measurements as well as the style, color and period required. Allow as much time as possible when ordering so the wigmaker has time to clean and dress the wig and to mail it. All the measurements needed are shown below.

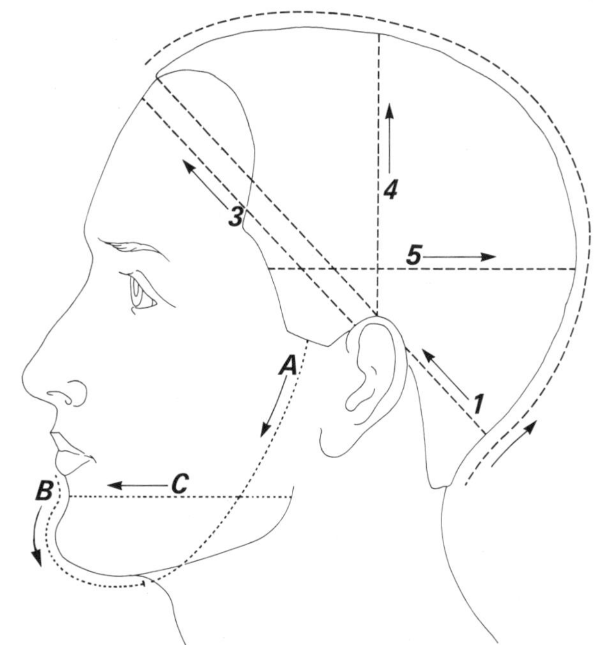

Wig measurements

1 *Circumference of the head (average 22 inches: 560mm)*

2 *Front hairline to nape of neck (average 14 inches: 355mm)*

3 *Ear to ear across forehead*

4 *From ear to ear over the top of the head (average 12 inches: 305mm)*

5 *Temple to temple round back of head (average 16 inches: 405mm)*

Beard measurements

A *Sideburn to sideburn under the chin*

B *Lip to end of beardline under the chin*

C *Round the front to back of the jawbone*

Beards and mustaches

The most realistic false beards, mustaches and sidewhiskers are those knotted on to fine hair or nylon lace and are obtainable from wigmakers. They should always be stuck on with spirit gum (not latex which would ruin the hair lace).

Many people recommend that you clean off the foundation where you are going to apply a beard or mustache but it is better to leave a fine film of well-powdered foundation on the skin as this acts as a barrier to the spirit gum, making it more comfortable to apply.

Usually when you receive a beard, a mustache or side-whiskers from a wigmaker, you will find a very wide margin of hair lace around the actual shape of the piece. This must be carefully trimmed. Do this in a good light so you can see the very fine knots of fairer hair at the hairline. You need to trim the lace about two or three holes away from the actual hairline.

Once the piece has been trimmed, the technique of application is as follows:

How to attach a nylon-lace beard

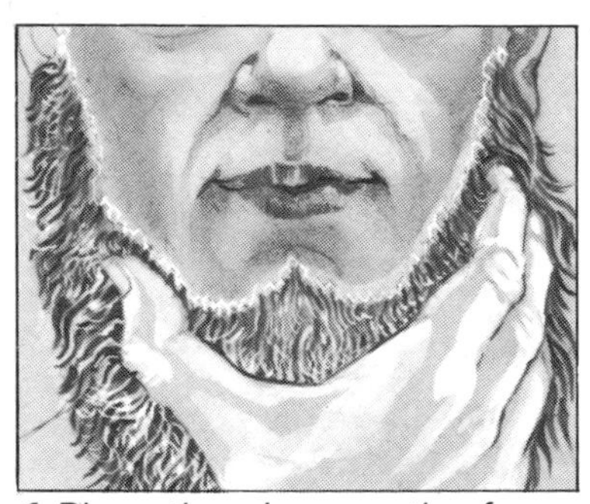

1 *Place the piece on the face, exactly where it needs to be stuck, and note the area covered by the lace so that you can determine where to apply the spirit gum*

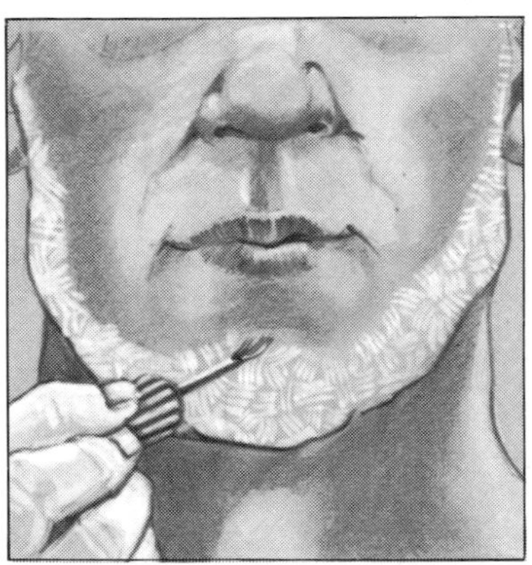

2 *Brush a thin film of spirit gum exactly where the lace will go. Allow it to dry completely. Lightly load brush with spirit gum and remoisten the gummed area*

3 *Make sure your hands are clean. Place the hairpiece carefully in position , pressing the edges firmly on to the face with the dampened corner of a linen towel*

4 *Where a beard or side-whiskers meet the natural sideburns, lift the bottom edge of the sideburns with a comb and stick the lace under the growth of hair. Then comb the natural hair into the false hair until they blend together. If there still is a gap between the false beard and the natural growth, fill this in with a small amount of crepe hair or by adding a few strokes of matching eyebrow pencil*

Removing and cleaning a hairpiece

To remove a hairpiece woven on to a lace foundation, moisten the lace with spirit-gum solvent until the gum is dissolved and the piece can be gently peeled away. The edge of the lace should then be thoroughly cleaned with acetone so it is ready to be used again.

Between performances, these pieces should be stored in the wigmaker's boxes so they do not become flattened or the lace damaged.

Using crepe hair for beards and mustaches

Well-made hair-lace pieces are quite expensive to buy and, because of their fragile nature, are not hired out by wigmakers. If your budget does not allow you to purchase them, you must learn to use wool-crepe hair, which is relatively inexpensive but must be applied with skill if it is to look natural.

When using crepe hair to make beards and mustaches, as well as spirit gum and solvent, you will need a small pair of very sharp hairdressing or mustache scissors, a small lintless towel and a selection of crepe hair in different colors. (Solid colors do not look natural so always buy crepe hair with mixed colors in the braid. The only exceptions are black hair for an Afro-Caribbean makeup or primary colors for stylized makeups.)

Preparation of wool crepe

1 *Crepe hair is supplied in tight braids bound with string and needs straightening before use. First undo the string and cut off a piece about six inches (150mm) long when stretched out*

Holding both ends of the piece, immerse it in a bowl of warm water and move it gently around until it begins to lose its strong curl. Now tease it out into the shape shown, still floating it on the surface of the water

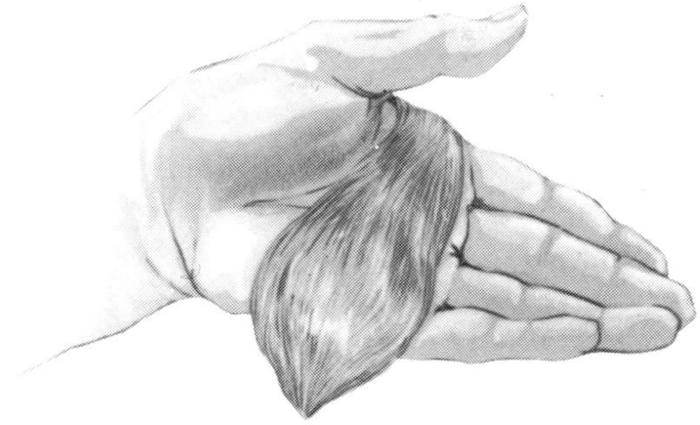

2 *Lift the "mat" of hair out of the water and lay it on a piece of towel or blotting paper. Repeat this process until you have sufficient "mats" for your use*

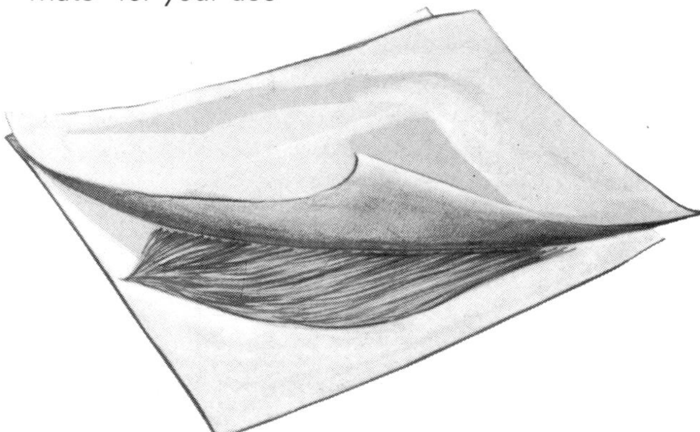

3 *Allow the "mats" to dry completely and store them between the pages of an old book, secured with a rubber band*

Beards and mustaches

Making a chin beard

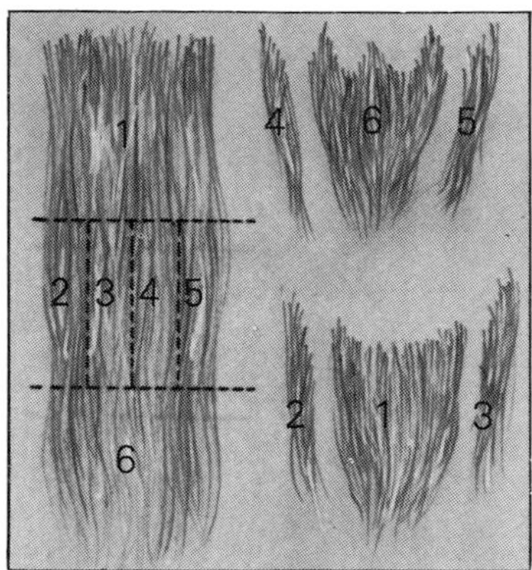

1 *Divide the mat of crepe hair, as shown, cutting off the two ends l and 6 and then breaking the middle section into four equal pieces with your fingers. Separate each section into the shapes shown*

2 *Paint the entire area of the chin to be bearded with the spirit gum lightly loaded on a brush. Always allow the chin to dry completely*

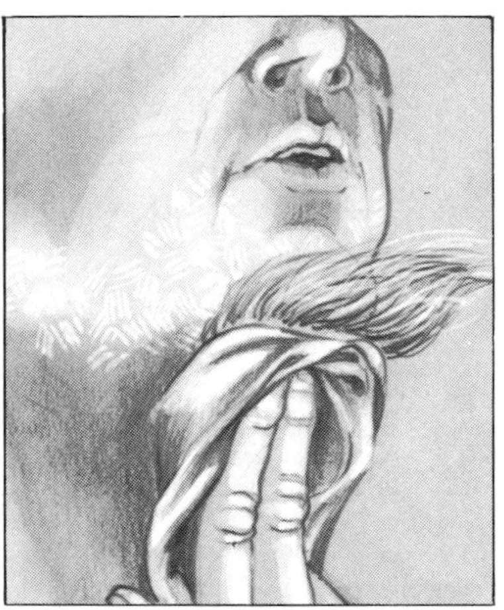

3 *Remoisten the underpart of the chin with a lightly loaded brush and lay section 1 in place, with the hair coming forward from the top of the throat to the point of the chin. Press firmly in place with a moistened towel*

4 *Remoisten the sides of the jaw just above section l and lay sections 2 and 3 in place, parallel to and touching section l. Press into place with the moistened towel*

5 *Remoisten the areas just above section 2 and 3, along the top of the jawbone and rising towards the corners of the mouth. Lay sections 4 and 5 in place, touching 2 and 3. Press into position*

6 *Remoisten front of chin and lay section 6 in place, with the center point just below the center of lower lip and the two outside points joining sections 4 and 5 at the corners of the mouth. Once more, press into place with a moistened towel*

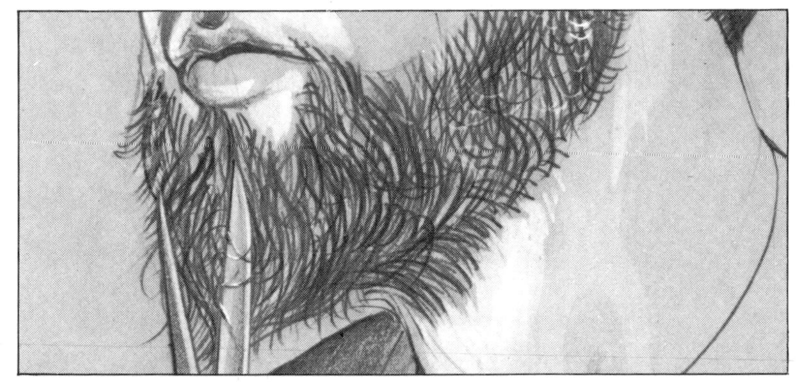

__7__ Allow all the sections to dry completely. Then gently stroke the beard with your fingers, blending all the sections together and removing any loose hairs. Trim and shape the beard with sharp hairdressing scissors to the required style. For a full facial beard, simply continue this process up the side of the face as far as the sideburn, with short sections of hair overlapping like roof tiles

Stubble beards

A four-day-old stubble beard can be simulated by using crepe hair.

Pull a length of crepe hair out of the braid and snip it into pieces approximately $\frac{1}{4}$ inch (6mm) in length. Store these clippings in a small box.

Apply a thin film of spirit gum over the beard and mustache area and allow to become tacky.

Pick up a ball of the hair clippings with your fingertips and pull it in half.

Dab the clippings on to the gummed face. Start by the sideburns on each side of the face and use both hands. Avoid getting gum on the fingertips. After about six dabs, pick up a new ball of clippings and continue the process, working down the sides of the face.

Continue on to the top lip, the chin and down the throat until the required density of stubble has been applied. If the gum becomes too dry for the hair to adhere after a while, stop at once and remoisten it.

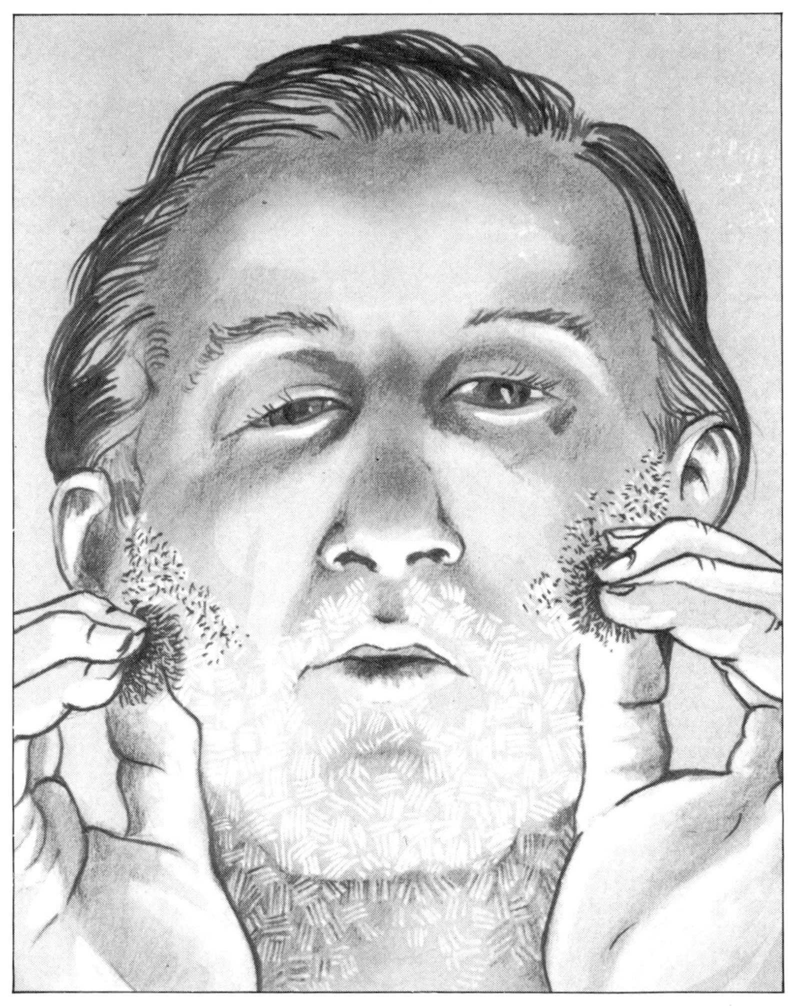

Beards and mustaches

Laying a simple wool-crepe mustache

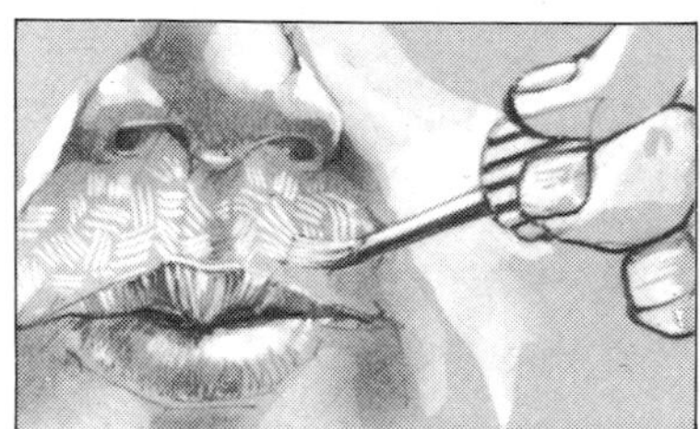

***1** Apply a thin coat of spirit gum to the entire top lip and allow it to dry*

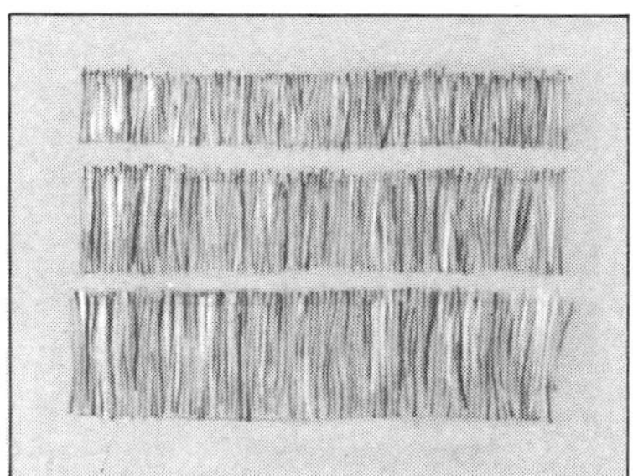

***2** Cut three straight sections from a mat of crepe hair, approximately $\frac{1}{2}$ inch (12mm), $\frac{3}{4}$ inch (18mm) and 1 inch (25mm)*

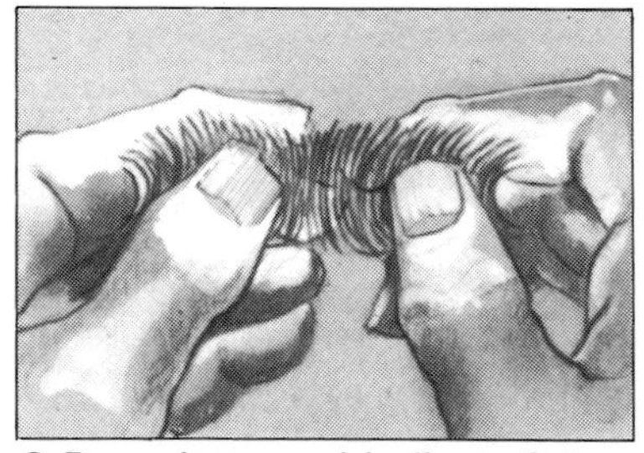

***3** Remoisten a thin line of the gum just above the mouth. Hold the $\frac{1}{2}$ inch (12mm) section of hair between your first fingers and thumbs. Gently pull down with your thumbs and push up with your fingers so that the straight cut becomes beveled and all the hair-ends are visible*

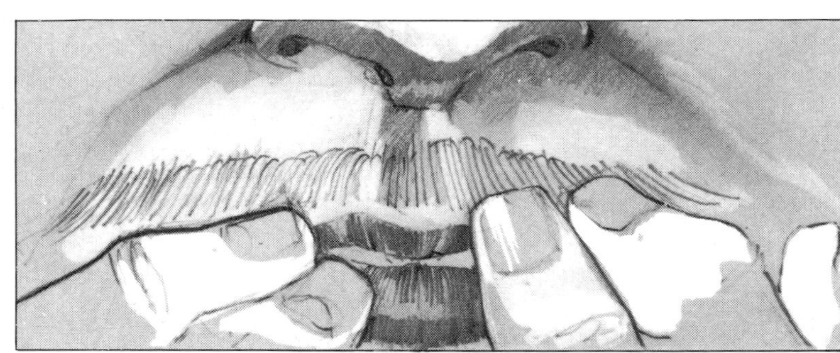

***4** Lay this strip of hair along the moistened edge of the lip, slightly twisting the hair outwards in the direction shown. Then press it in place with the moistened corner of your towel*

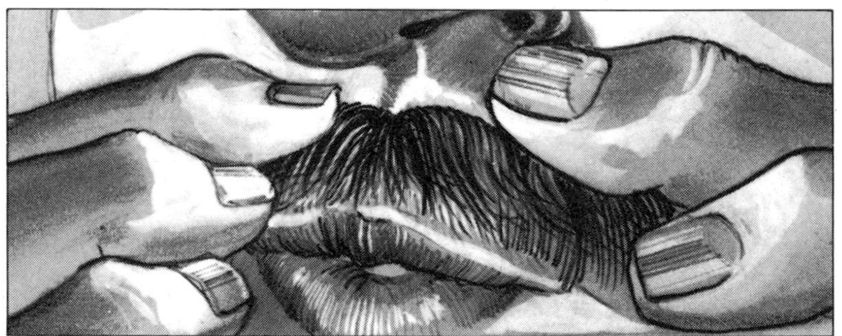

***5** Remoisten the gum just above the first section, allowing the gum to go over the ends of the first layer of hair. Lay the $\frac{1}{2}$ inch (12mm) section of hair in place, beveling the edge as before and twisting the hair outwards again. Press into place with a damp towel. Remoisten remaining gummed area, once more allowing gum to cover the ends of the previous section. This area will be divided in two by the center wing of the nostrils*

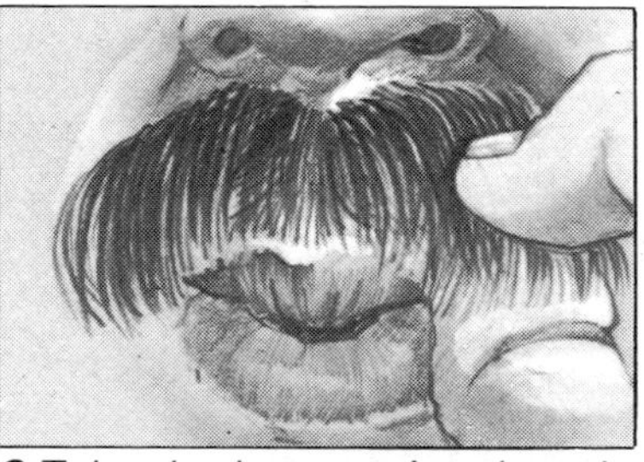

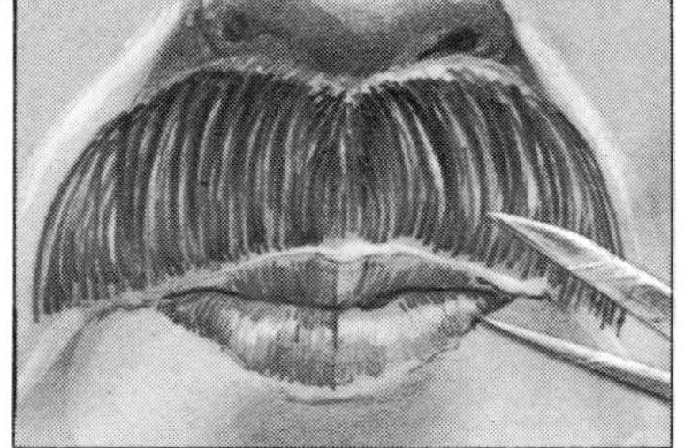

***6** Take the last section, bevel as before, and then separate it into two halves. Apply each half to either side of the lip, turning the hair well outwards to simulate natural growth. Press into place with a dampened towel. Allow to dry completely and tease out any loose hairs with thumb and forefinger. Trim along the base of the mustache with hairdressing scissors and remove any long hairs that might irritate the nose*

Laying a longer wool-crepe mustache

1 First cut off the end of the mat of hair, at $1\frac{1}{2}$-2 inches (35-50 mm), depending on how long the mustache is to be.

Divide this section lengthwise into four. Take two pieces and pull them between your finger and thumb until the wide end of the section is beveled. Twist the thin end into a point

2 Following the same gumming and pressing technique, apply these two shaped sections as shown. (The remaining two pieces can be used for your next mustache)

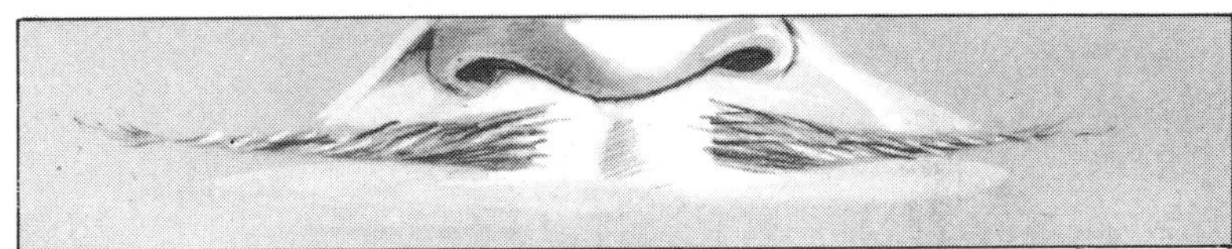

3 Now overlay short sections of hair over the center area, angling them so that they flow in the direction of growth of the two side-pieces. Gum and press as before

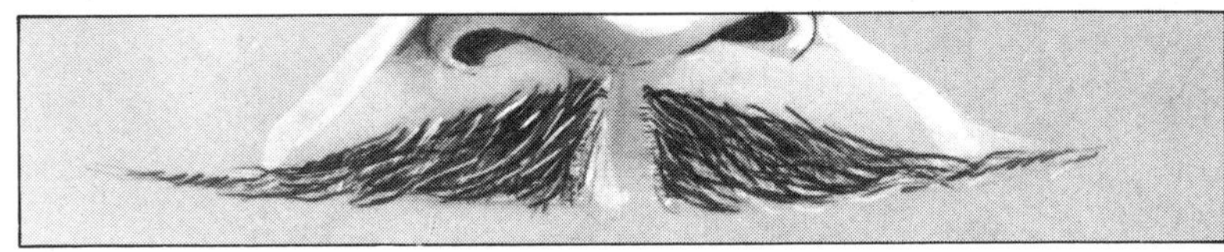

Mutton-chop whiskers

1 These can be simulated with unstraightened crepe, pulled directly from the braid and molded with fingers

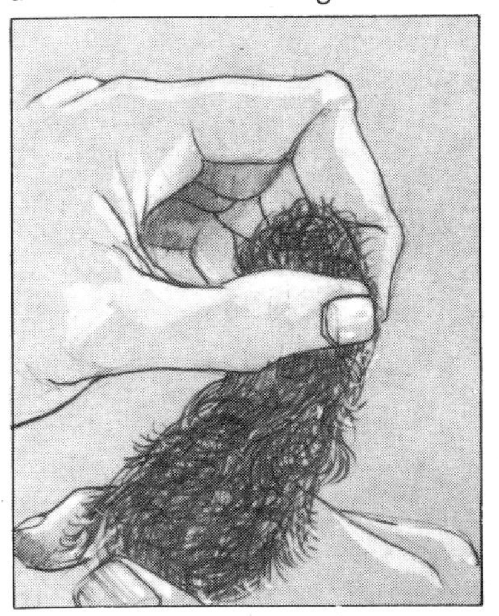

2 Attach the fluffy sections along the jawline, double gumming but not pressing the hair too firmly with your towel

3 Now add small sections of hair up to the natural side-burns, overlapping like tiles as in a full facial beard

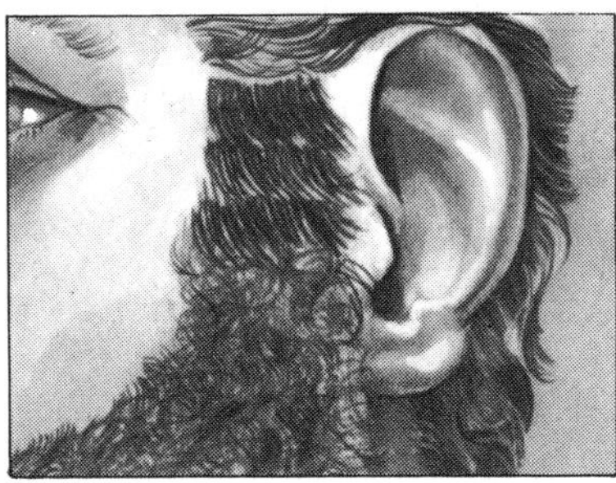

Important Remember when working with crepe hair to keep your fingers and scissors absolutely clean and free from spirit gum by wiping them with solvent as you proceed.

Special effects

This is a very interesting aspect of makeup, which gives great scope for the makeup artist to use his ingenuity. Here are a few examples of the many things that can be done.

Temporary face lifts

If shading and highlighting cannot conceal a sagging jawline or throat, temporary face lifts can be used. You will first need to obtain some fish skin. This is a strong animal tissue, obtainable from musical-instrument repair shops or makeup stockists. (Silk muslin can be used as a substitute.) You will also need some fine invisible hairpins, a one inch (25mm) roll of adhesive tape, some small elastic bands and a reel of button thread.

__1__ Cut pieces of fish skin with scissors and pinking shears into the shape shown.
Using electrician's wire cutters, cut fine invisible hairpins into 1 inch (25mm) lengths.
Cut adhesive tape into $\frac{1}{4}$ inch (6mm) sections

__2__ Roll top $\frac{1}{4}$ inch (6mm) of fish skin around a section of hairpin. Lay the hairpin section across the center of adhesive tape and fold the tape over it

__3__ Sew a short length of button thread (in a similar color to the actor's hair) to one end of the adhesive tape and tie off around hairpin. Drop a $\frac{3}{8}$ inch (9mm) elastic band over the needle and thread. Sew into the other end of the adhesive tape and tie off. Attach about 10 inches (25cms) of button thread to the elastic band.
Two of these tabs are required for each "lifting operation"

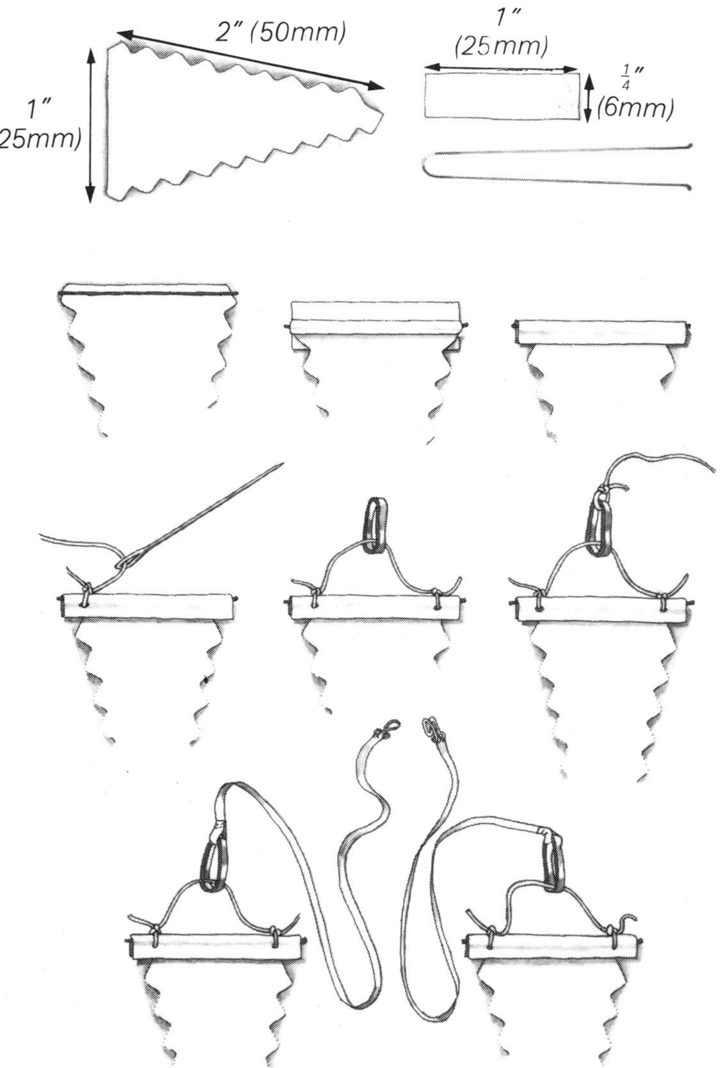

__4__ Fish skin is very fine so it is easy to conceal with makeup once it has been stuck to the face. However, each pair of fish-skin tabs are only usable once, while silk-muslin tabs can be cleaned with acetone and reused. The elastic band and button-thread fastening can then be replaced with lengths of cotton elastic, and a dressmaker's hook-and-eye used to fasten off. The exact position of the hook-and-eye can, of course, only be determined when the tabs have actually been fastened to the face, on the first occasion they are used

Using the face lifts

To lift a sagging jawline and heavy nasolabial folds, the tabs should be attached to the face with spirit gum just below the hair, in front of the ears. The top of the tab with the elastic band should be high enough to be covered when the hair or sides of a wig are dressed over it. To ensure strong adhesion, paint the skin with the spirit gum, allow to dry completely and then remoisten with your spirit-gum brush before pressing tab in place with a moistened lintless towel. Leave gum to dry for as long as possible before pulling up tabs and fastening off.

Part the hair in a line across the top of the head from ear to ear and plait a small braid on the crown of the head. Then gently pull the two lengths of thread up together at the crown until the right degree of tension has been reached, and tie off in a bow.

Pull the braid of hair over the bow and fasten in place with a grip. The tabs can then be covered with foundation to conceal them and the makeup completed. The hair should then be dressed or a wig used to conceal the fastenings.

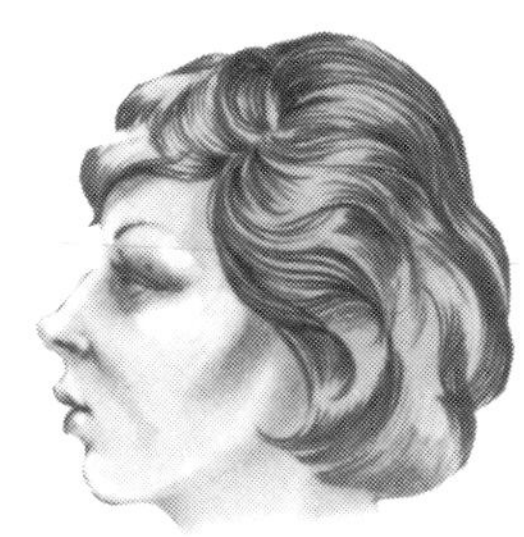

Blindness

Although it is possible for an actor to simulate blindness by keeping the eyes nearly closed, this imposes a very big physical and mental strain if the performance lasts very long. Here is a simple way of overcoming this :

Cut a piece of fabric-backed adhesive tape into a D shape to fit the actual eyelid.

Apply the tape to the eyelid so that it holds the lid almost closed. This enables the actor to see, while at the same time appearing to be blind. Since the adhesive tape is usually flesh-colored, to conceal the join you need only shade the edges away with a dark-brown liner.

When removing the tape afterwards, always lift the top edge and pull it gently downwards, so as not to damage the eyelid.

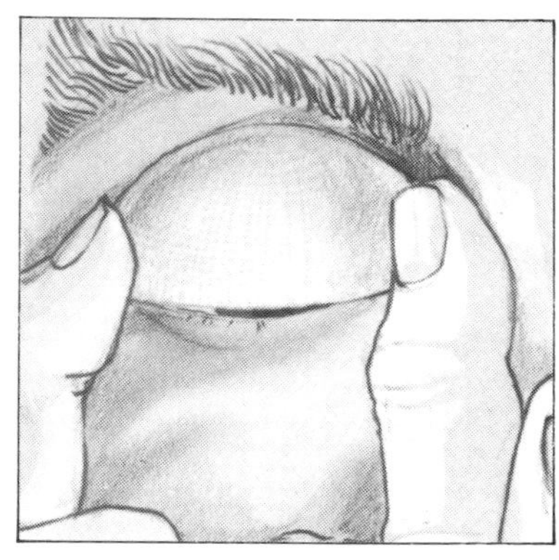

Creating a disfigured eye

1 *Cut an oval piece of gauze bandage, about the same size as the eye socket. Paint the gauze to represent whatever is required — a closed eye, a staring eye or a disfigured eye*

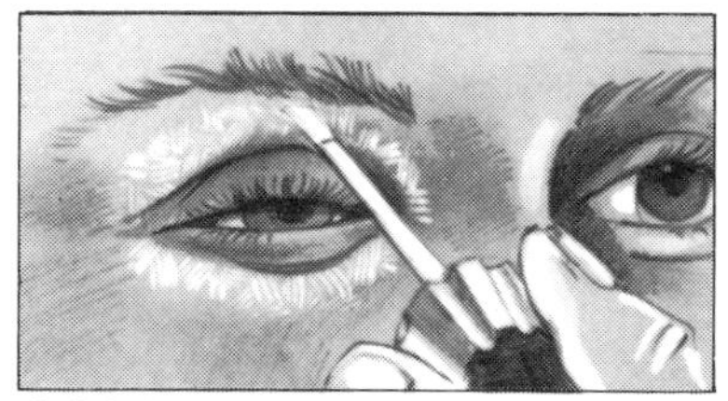

2 *Make sure the painted, disfigured eye is dry. Check it fits and gives the desired effect. Now paint spirit gum in a circle around the eye area, avoiding the lid and lashes*

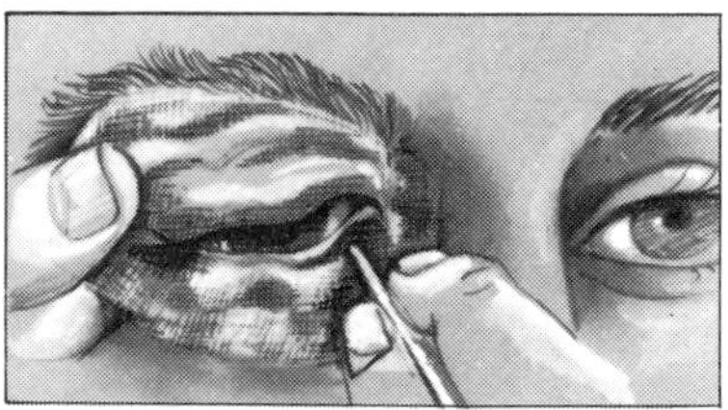

3 *Position the gauze in place with the end of a spatula. Allow the gum to dry and apply makeup to blend the edges of the patch into the skin color*

Special effects

Scars

Scars can be suggested with the use of greasepaint but to be fully effective they need to be three-dimensional.

The simplest method is to use nonflexible collodion. Paint the area to be scarred with collodion and allow it to dry. As it dries, it contracts and puckers the skin. If the effect is not deep enough, apply a number of successive coats, allowing each application to dry completely before applying the next.

This indented scar can be further accentuated with makeup by shadowing the depression and highlighting the edges.

The problem with this method is that, after continuous use, it may damage the skin and leave a permanent mark, so it is recommended only for very occasional use.

Very good scars can be made by squeezing liquid latex adhesive on to a glass plate and, with a spatula or orange-stick, molding the shape required. Allow this to dry, peel it off the plate and apply to skin with spirit gum, accentuating the scar with makeup, as for collodion scars.

With practice, very effective eye pouches or bags can also be made using this method.

One slight disadvantage of latex scars made in this way is that they are almost transparent, but this can be corrected by adding a small amount of colored pigment to the latex during the molding stage. If you do not have a ready source of powder pigments, a good substitute is to scrape a small amount of color off the surface of a suitable cake makeup with a scalpel. If the scar needs to be very livid, a scraping from the surface of a cake of dry rouge will produce the required effect.

Open cuts and wounds

Good latex wounds can usually be obtained from makeup suppliers but very often they are not exactly the type of wound that is required, so creating them yourself is usually more satisfactory. It is a comparatively straightforward procedure.

First paint with spirit gum the area where the wound is to be placed and allow to dry.

Then spread a thin layer of Derma Wax over the gummed area, and, using a spatula, carefully thin out the edge, making it as fine as possible.

Make a cut in the wax, using the blunt edge of a modeling scalpel, and very carefully open out the wound.

Color the inside of the cut, using a dark-maroon lining color on a brush. If the lining color you are using is of a very firm texture, soften it with a little cold cream so that the color can be gently brushed into the cut without disturbing the wax.

Paint a thin film of sealer over the wound and allow to dry completely.

Makeup can now be applied to blend the wound into the surrounding skin color and the actual cut can be accentuated with highlights applied along the edges.

Stage blood may now be introduced into the cut, using an eyedropper. Plastic blood, which dries very quickly, should be squeezed directly from its tube into the cut or wound.

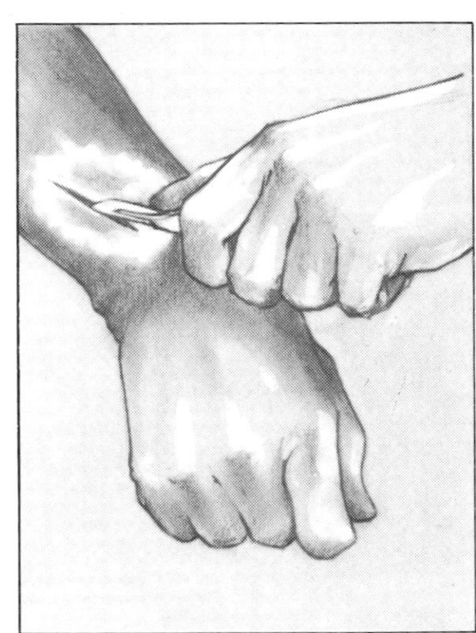

1 Apply Derma Wax and make a cut in it with the blunt end of a modeling scalpel

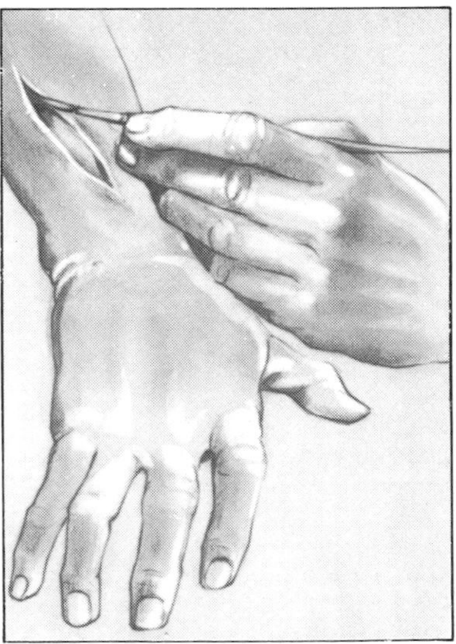

2 Having carefully opened out the wound, paint the inside to resemble bleeding tissue

Bullet wounds

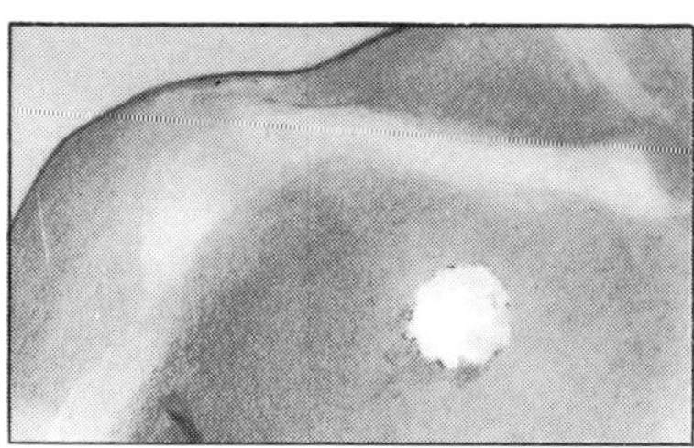

1 Paint a circle of spirit gum on to the skin and allow it to dry. Spread a thin layer of Derma Wax over the gummed circle, thinning out the edges until they merge into the surrounding skin

2 Press the blunt end of a pencil into the wax to make the required hole

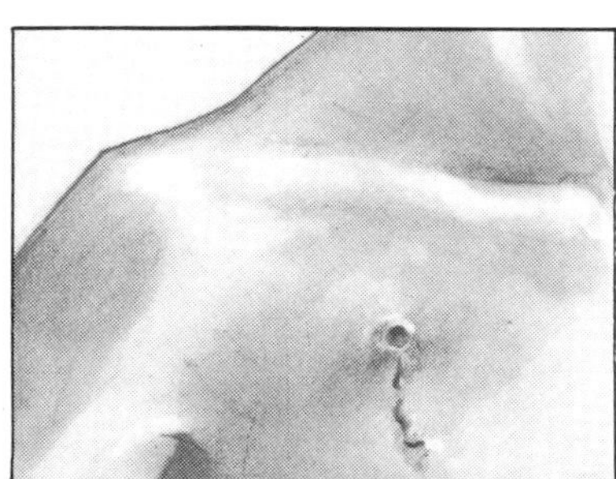

3 Paint inside the hole with a mixture of red and black lining color to simulate blood and the charring of the flesh. Cover the bullet wound with a thin film of sealer and add a thin trickle of blood, using a dark plastic blood

Instant "on stage" effects

Bullet wounds and open cuts must obviously be prepared in advance but there are occasions when instant effects are required on stage. Here are a few hints on how to achieve some of these effects.

Blood flowing from the mouth is best achieved by using empty gelatine capsules purchased from your local pharmacy. Fill these with stage blood suitable for internal use (checking this with your makeup supplier). These capsules can be retained in the mouth and then simply crushed between the teeth to release a flow of blood.

External bleeding, such as a bloody nose or a sword cut, can be simulated by using a small sponge, saturated in blood, which can be squeezed on to the area required. When it is not convenient for the actor to carry a blood sponge for a long period it can sometimes be concealed in the scenery or stage furniture until it is needed.

When blood is needed to seep out of, say, a shirt front, a blood sponge should be inserted into a small plastic bag with one or more small holes punched in one side. This package is then taped to the actor's body, holes uppermost, underneath the shirt. All the actor then needs to do is to press on the area to release a slow ooze of blood through the holes. Remember to use blood that will not permanently stain the clothing!

The effect of flesh being cut and blood flowing from the cut can be simulated as follows:

First make sure that the blade being used will not actually cut the skin by protecting the cutting edge with a strip of cellophane tape.

Tape an eye-dropper filled with stage blood on to the underside of the blade, with the tip lying just alongside the cutting edge and the bulb conveniently placed by the hilt — so that it can easily be depressed by the actor's thumb or first finger.

When the effect is required, the actor simply draws the blade along the flesh, with the eye dropper concealed on the under side, and at the same time depresses the bulb, so a stream of blood is drawn along the flesh from the tip of the dropper.

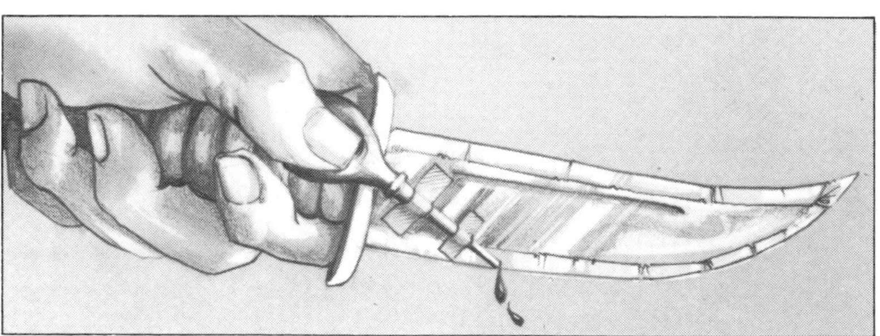

An eye dropper containing stage blood concealed behind a knife blade is used to simulate cutting flesh. Note the protective cellophane tape

Special effects

Burns

Burns can be simulated by first stippling the area with maroon lining color and then covering this with a layer of liquid latex or sealer and allowing it to dry completely.

Break holes in the dry latex or sealer, lifting patches away from the skin to form broken blisters and peeling skin. Black cake makeup, carefully stippled on, will help give the appearance of charring.

Black eyes and bruises

Fresh black eyes and bruises can be simulated with dark-red, purple, and blue-gray lining colors applied in that order, one on top of the other, slightly decreasing the area covered with each application. This should be left unpowdered so the area looks very moist and inflamed.

Older bruises and black eyes change color as time passes; the inflammation fades and the surrounding areas of flesh become a rather yellowish-green. Start your application with a mixture of chrome-yellow and green, followed by blue-gray and purple, and finally add patches of dark red to the area closest to the eye or the center of the bruise.

Warts and moles

Warts and moles can be created from many different materials, such as preformed latex pieces, Derma Wax, cotton balls and spirit gum (or even Rice Krispies or Puffed Wheat) stuck to the skin with spirit gum and then suitably colored. When the offending appendage needs to be hairy, you can attach the hairs to the material being used, before sticking it to the skin, but as such detail is scarcely visible to the audience, it's really not worth the trouble!

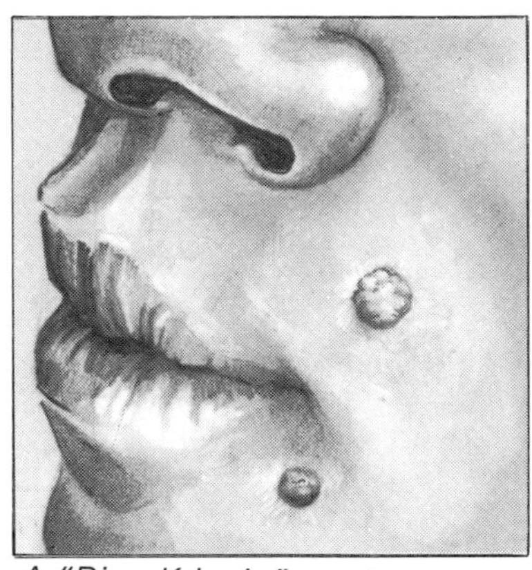

A "Rice Krispie" wart

Gold teeth

A gold tooth, which looks very effective on a pirate or Mexican bandit makeup, can easily be simulated by sticking a small piece of gold foil from a chocolate bar over the tooth, using spirit gum.

Perspiration

This is easily represented by spraying the face or body with glycerine, taking care to shield the eyes. A greasy sweaty appearance is achieved by rubbing the body with mineral oil, and a dirty greasy look by adding dark grease makeup to the oil as it is applied.

Bronzed sun-tan effects

Although liquid body makeups or body tints give a good color to the skin, they tend to look dull and matte. The best tanned effect is achieved with those body-powder makeups containing special ingredients which, if applied wet, allowed to dry, and then polished with the hands or a chiffon scarf, give off a gleaming shine.

Long fingernails

Extra long fingernails, used for witches and Chinese mandarins, are difficult, if not impossible, to buy. You will need to cut them out of acetate or old photographic film. They can then be glued to the natural nails with false-fingernail glue or spirit gum, and colored with nail varnish or the quick-drying acetate paint used by modelmakers.

Tattoos

Tattoos can be drawn on to the skin with colored eye-makeup pencils but remember that most tattoos are small works of art, so they need to be drawn very carefully. One method of getting a good shape for every performance is to trace the outline on to tracing paper and prick out the pattern with a thickish needle Then lay the pattern over the skin (which should first be lightly covered with a film of cold cream) and pat black face powder on to the paper. The face powder will go through the holes and give a dotted outline of the pattern, which you can then fill in with colored pencils.

The tattoos illustrated on the opposite page make useful reference for tattoo design. You might like to experiment by tracing these and practising on a suitable "victim"!

A few examples of tattoo design

Makeup gallery

Once you are familiar with all the basic techniques of makeup described in the preceding pages, you will be ready to put this knowledge into practice, so the second section of this book concentrates on detailed step-by-step descriptions of how to apply makeup to create particular Stage Faces. The range covers many age groups and nationalities, from glamorous young makeups to aged character roles, from the pampered Restoration fop to Frankenstein's monster.

To help you organize each makeup routine, the next two pages contain blank makeup charts. These can be photocopied and used to record all the relevant information and color details for each new Stage Face. (Water-color pencils are useful for this.) Some completed charts appear on page 174. (Pages 104–105 have been released from the copyright regulations applying to the rest of the book.)

Remember that all the makeup ideas which follow are for guidance only. Develop your own style, using as much imagination as possible. Do not merely reproduce standard characters with stereotyped masks. Experiment; explore the effects of makeup. Use these step-by-step routines as a starting point, a foundation on which to build individual new Stage Faces so that you create a fresh interpretation for each role.

Makeup chart for men

Production
Character
Actor

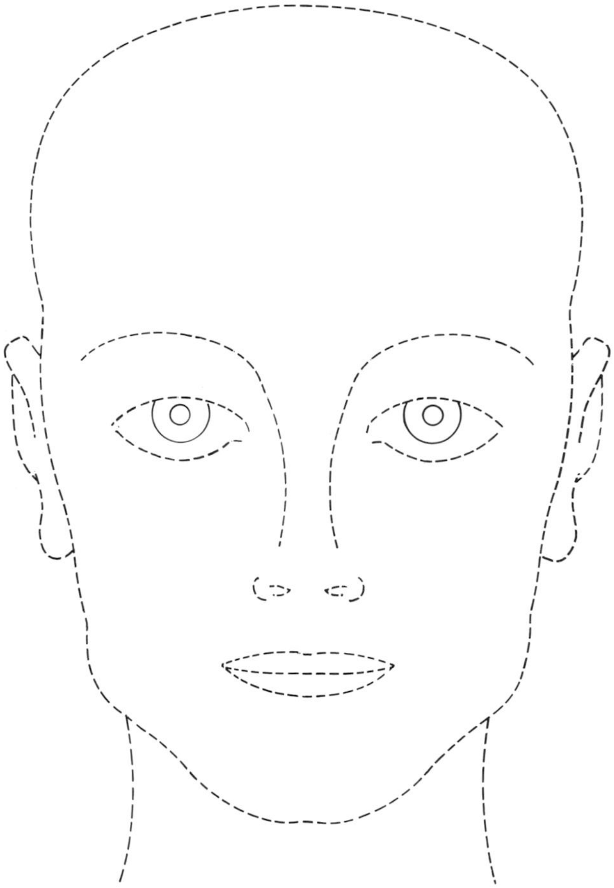

Base

Highlight

Shading

Powder

Moist rouge

Dry rouge

Lip color

Eye makeup

Body makeup

Hair

Notes

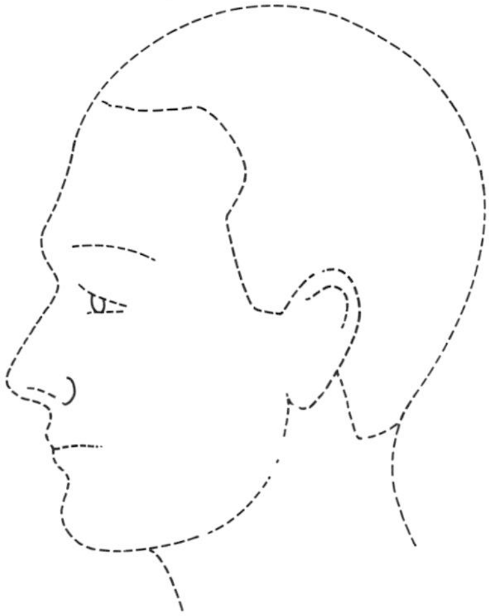

Makeup chart for women

Production
Character
Actress

Base

Highlight

Shading

Powder

Moist rouge

Dry rouge

Lip color

Eye makeup

Body makeup

Hair

Notes

Straight makeup for women

There is no such thing as a straight makeup in the theater — or for that matter, in any of the acting media — since every makeup should be designed to portray a character.

Of course if you have been cast "to type", not only for your acting ability but also for your physical appearance, then it will not be necessary for you to put on a character makeup. But you will still have to use a makeup that is strong enough to offset the draining effect of the stage lighting and to define your features enough for them to be seen quite clearly from every seat in the theater.

In addition to these practicalities, the actress will wish to look as attractive as possible to the audience, and as none of us can claim to have physical perfection, every so-called straight makeup becomes a corrective makeup.

Straight roles for women can vary from the woman who wears no makeup at all, or those who use just a dab of lipstick and a touch of eyeshadow, on to those who don a complete maquillage but still look natural by today's standards. Hopefully, you will have discovered during your character analysis which makeup type the part demands.

The following step-by-step routine is designed to be adaptable to whichever degree of artifice is required to put your best face forward.

Color guide

Foundation Peach, creamy or light-tan groups

Rouge and lip color Light or medium-red groups

Highlights Pale groups

Shading Warm, brown shading color

Eyeshadow Neutral gray or brown for natural look, or a color to harmonize with the costume

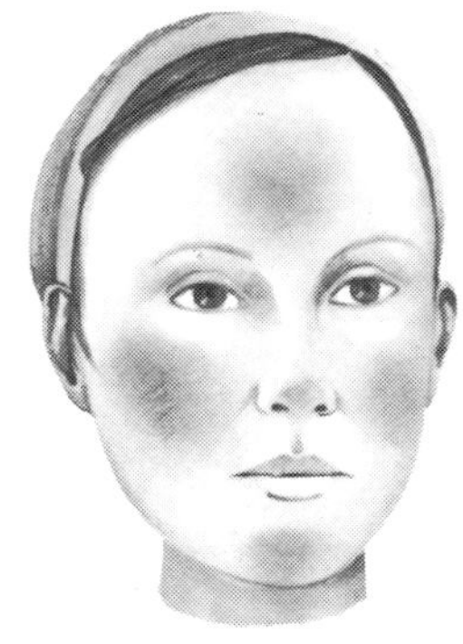

__1__ Prepare the skin and apply a smooth, light film of foundation. Add moist rouge to cheeks and a touch of color to browbone, forehead and chin. Highlight and shade, then powder face well

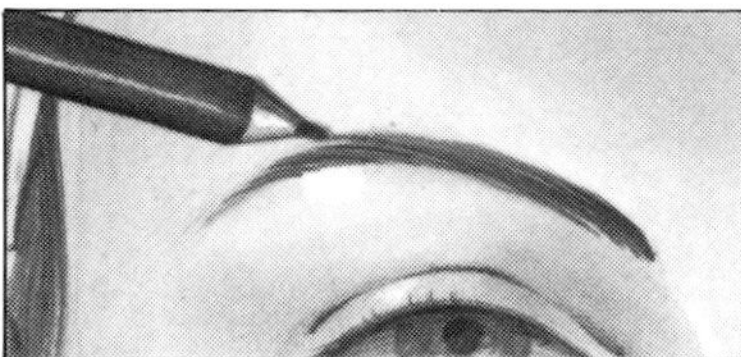

__2__ Reshape the brows with eyebrow pencil, using tiny hairlike strokes. Follow natural growth of brow

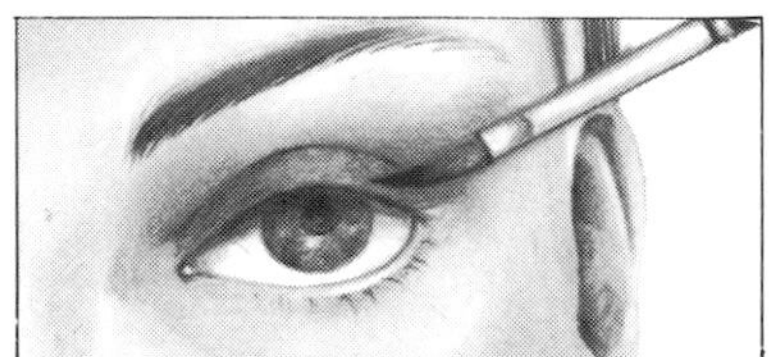

__3__ Apply eyeshadow to top lid, using a number 6 filbert brush. Use a separate brush for each individual color

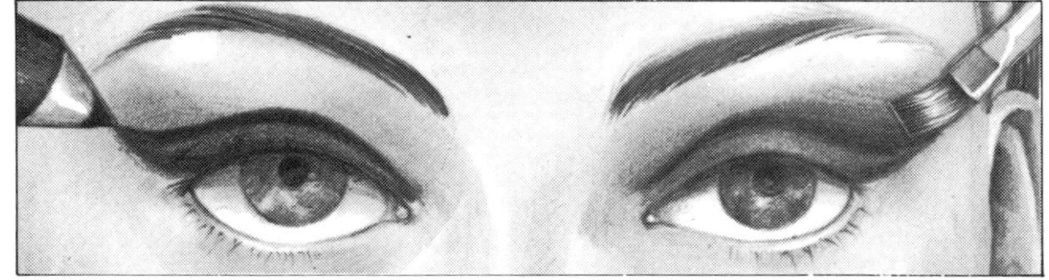

__4__ Draw in contour line with pencil or lining color and blend away on to browbone with a $\frac{1}{4}$ inch (6mm) flat-ended brush

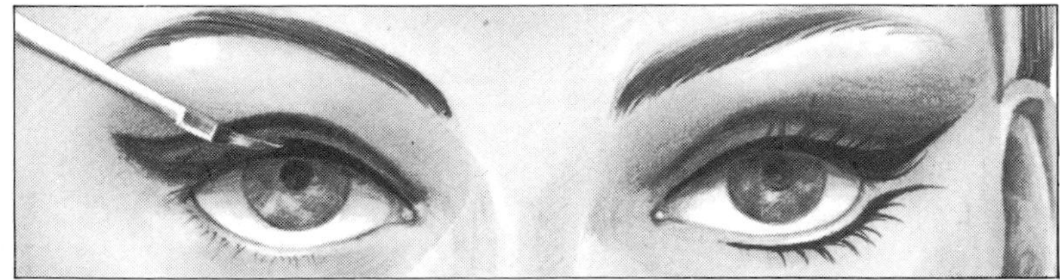

__5__ Outline the eye with eyeliner, keeping the outer ends open as shown. Then mascara top and bottom lashes

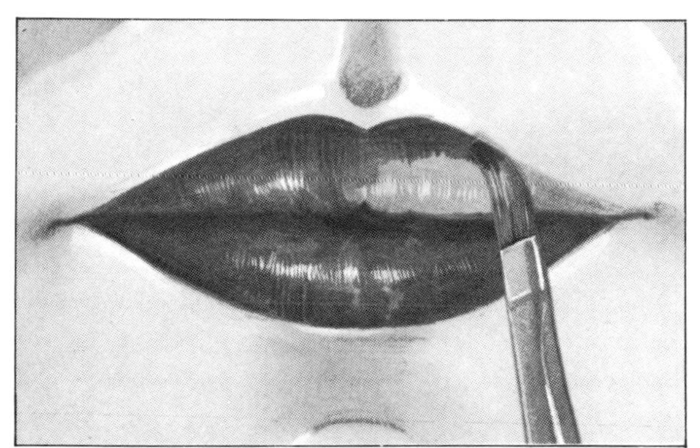

***6** Apply lip color with a number 6 filbert brush, doing any correction needed*

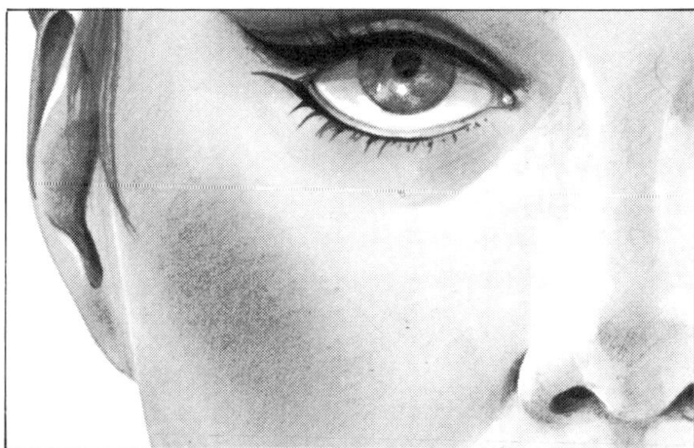

***7** Strengthen cheek color with dry cake rouge if needed. Don't forget to make up hands*

Straight makeup for men

Everything that has been said about straight makeup for women applies equally to men, but a man's makeup must look completely natural and in no way over-madeup. So it is important to use as little makeup as possible but to gain the maximum effect from it.

Choose a foundation color that looks much darker in the stick or cake than you think you need, and then apply the thinnest possible film of color so that it gives a very natural and unmadeup look to the skin. At the same time, ensure that the color flatters the natural skin tone.

Keep eye makeup to an absolute minimum. Only neutral browns and grays should be used for shadow, and eyelining should give the appearance of shadows rather than a hard line, except when the makeup is for a very large theater.

Lips should be treated with great care since even the tiniest amount of lip color can give a lipsticked appearance to the mouth. When lips are naturally well formed and strongly colored, they are best left without any makeup at all, but if they do need color just the smallest amount of a dark brown-red, applied with the finger rather than a brush, will give a good natural result.

Rouge should be used to give the face shape rather than color, placing it under the cheekbones, in the temple hollows and along the browbone.

If the face has a good bone structure, modeling is usually unnecessary since modern stage lighting is very flattering, so use modeling only when there is a need for correction.

In this step-by-step routine a certain amount of corrective modeling has been added — just how much of this is needed must be left to each individual actor's discretion.

Colour guide

Foundation
Choose from light, deep and warm-tan groups or olive groups for Latin characters

Modeling color
Use lake groups or choose from warm-tan or deep-brown groups

Highlights
Use pale or ivory groups

Eyeshadow
Dark-browns or grays

Lip color
Dark-red or lake groups

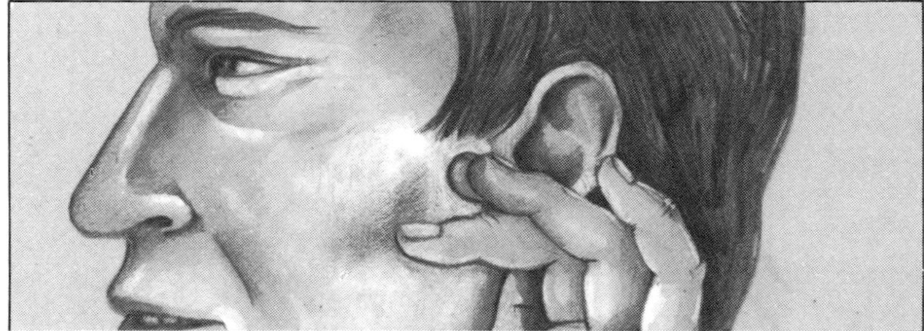

***1** Apply your chosen foundation to a cleanshaven and grease-free face. Remember to keep the foundation as light and natural-looking as possible. Add modeling color, using either a moist rouge or a warmer deeper tone of your foundation. Add corrective highlighting and shading where considered necessary. If grease or cream-stick foundation is being used, then the makeup must be thoroughly powdered at this stage. Cake makeup applications do not need powdering*

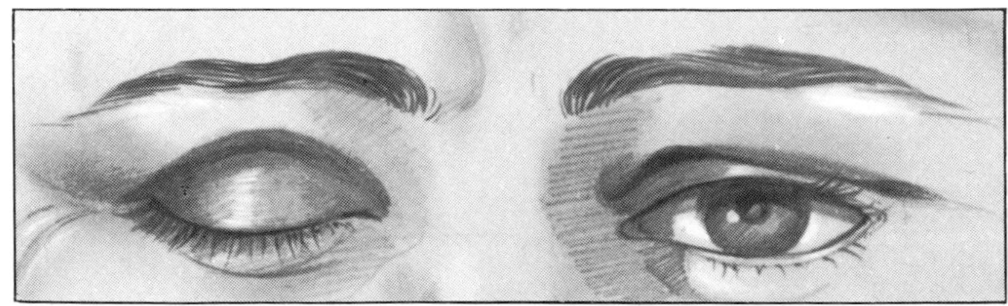

***2** Where eyebrows need to be strengthened, sketch in with short hairlike strokes to simulate natural growth. Take care not to make brows too dark. Apply neutral eyeshadow to the eyelid, intensifying the color in the contour crease*

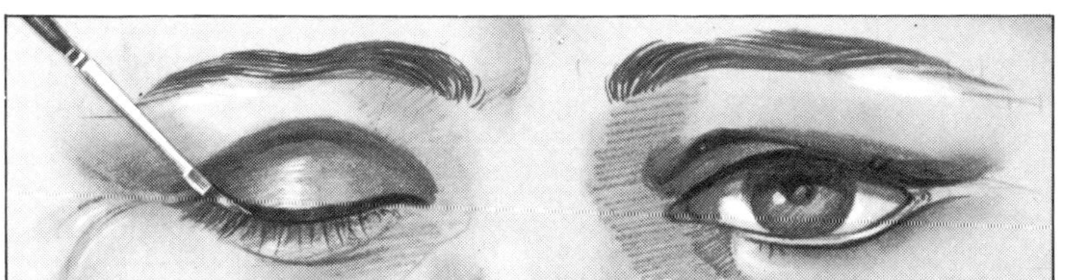

3 Draw in eyelines, blending away the edges with a sable brush or fingertip. The larger the theater, the stronger the lines — while for small intimate stages they should be kept to the barest minimum. If the lashes are fair or poorly defined, a light coating of mascara can be applied, but take care not to make the lashes look over-madeup

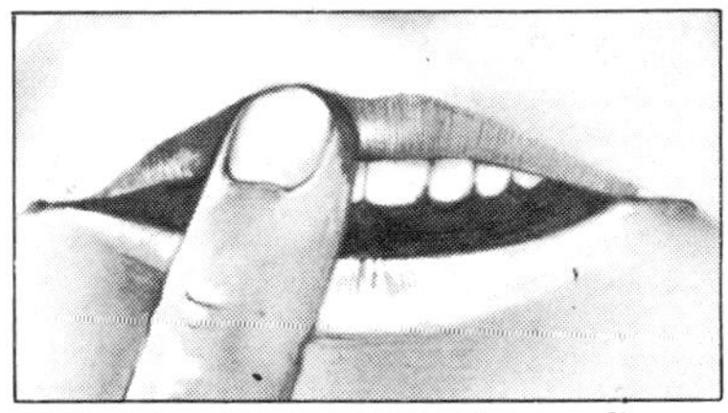

4 Apply lip color, using a fingertip or brush. Make the top lip slightly darker than the lower. If the lips are naturally well formed, remove excess foundation from the lips

5 Dress the hair. Add cake rouge if the cheek coloring needs to be intensified. Make up hands and all exposed skin, including the back of the neck which is so often neglected in a man's makeup

Middle-age makeup

Women

Middle age is an undefined period of time between thirty-five and sixty-five years, and just how old a woman will look at any given age depends on her lifestyle, her health and how she cares for her appearance. So, before embarking on this type of makeup, character analysis is absolutely vital. A mature actress playing a middle-aged character needs only to put on a makeup suitable to the character's way of life.

The following routine however, is designed to show a younger actress how to age her face when called upon to play a more mature character.

Once there is a clear picture in your mind of how the character should look, the first consideration should be what to do with the hair. A good wig, of gray or graying hair in a mature style, is usually the best solution but you may feel that you can easily restyle and gray your own hair.

Once you have decided which to do, have a look at yourself in a suitable wig or hairstyle, with no makeup on your face.

If the skin is naturally pale and colorless, you may not need to use a foundation; just the addition of shadows and highlights will give the effect you need.

If, however, the skin still looks very youthful, then you will need to apply a suitable foundation to drain the bloom of youth. With the skin color suitably adjusted, return the wig to its block and start to shade the face, applying shadows where needed with a ¼ inch (6mm) sable brush.

Color guide

Foundation For warm, healthy middle age use peach or pink groups muted with a small amount of sallow or ivory groups

For pale sallow tones use sallow or ivory groups mixed with a small amount of peach or pink groups

Shading Use olive and lake groups

Highlights Use ivory or pale groups

Rouge and lips Dark or medium-red groups

Eyeshadow Dark-mauves, blue-grays, browns, dark-green or blue

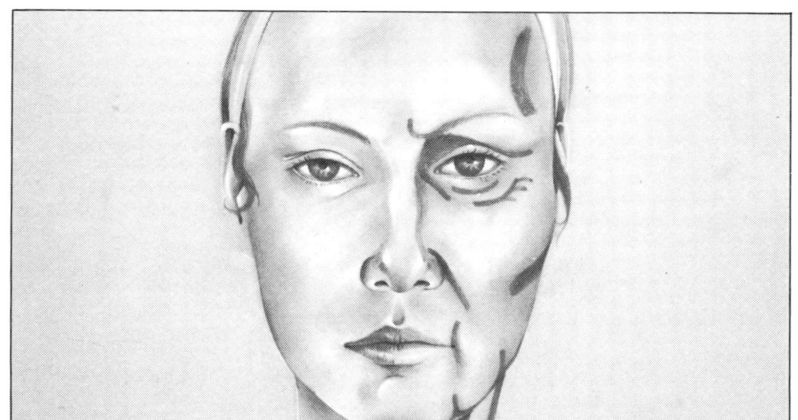

1 Here you can see suitable aging shadows, before blending, applied to one side of the face only

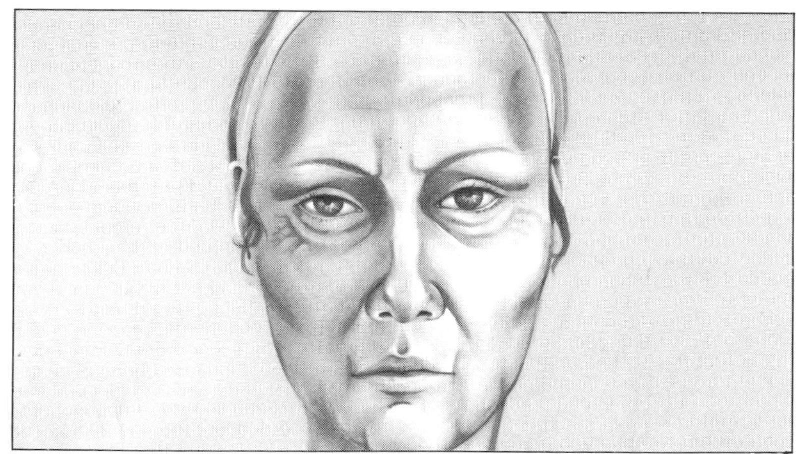

2 Blend out the shadows and apply highlights to give them depth and roundness. Thoroughly powder makeup

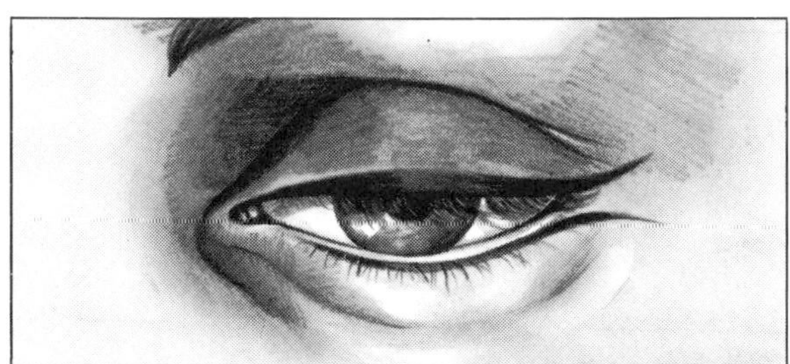

3 *If required, use powder eye-shadows in aging colors such as mauve or gray-blues, and keep eyelining and mascara to a minimum*

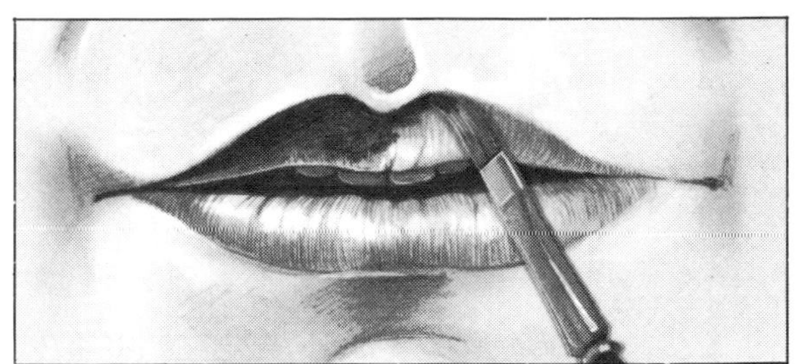

4 *Apply a small amount of a dark, aging lip color, using a number 6 sable brush*

5 *Restyle hair or replace wig, fastening in place with pins and clips and securing lace with spirit gum. Remember to make up hands and all exposed skin areas to tone in with the face*

Middle-age makeup

Men

A man's appearance in middle age will vary according to his lifestyle, health, and his pride in his appearance. So it is very important to study the character and analyze just how he is meant to look.

First of all, take a careful look at the hair and see what can be achieved with just a small amount of restyling.

Color guide

Foundation For sallow skin tones use creamy or sallow groups

For healthy skin tones use light-tan groups mixed with florid groups

Shading For sallow skins use olive-brown groups

For healthy skins use lake groups

Highlights Use ivory or pale groups

Eyeshadow Brown plus lake groups

Lip color Use lake or florid groups

Dressing the hair back from the forehead will often reveal the early signs of receding hair. Add a touch of gray at the temples and maybe a mustache, and you will often give sufficient maturity without resorting to a full character makeup. If the hair looks too youthful to be successfully restyled, then a very good wig will be needed

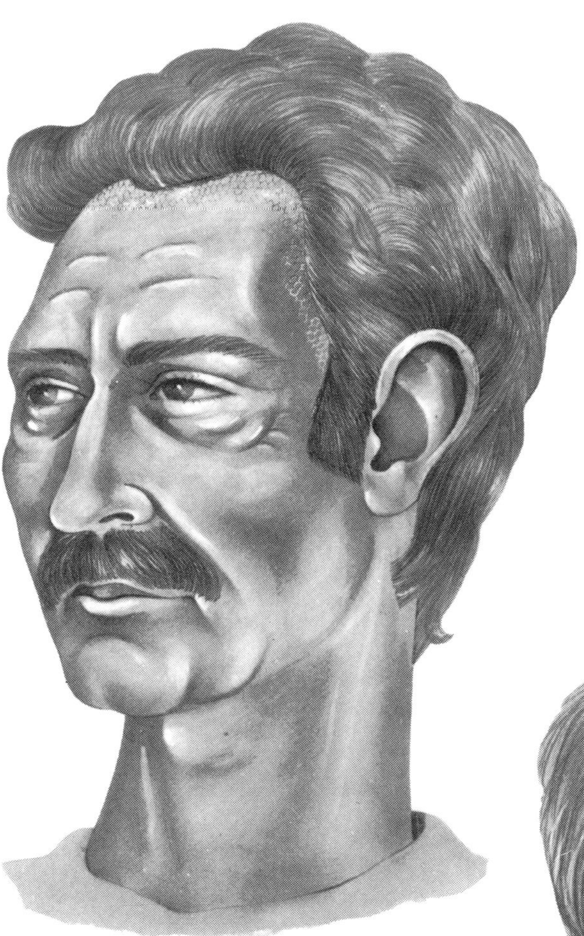

For this more mature look, a wig has been used. Shadows and highlights have been added, together with a rather fuller mustache. Note particularly the shadows and highlights around the eyes and the way that the jawline and neck have been aged

Middle-aged makeup for the fuller face does not rely so heavily on shadows and lines. More use is made of broad planes of ruddy color, with the eye makeup giving a puffy look to the eyes. The full beard round the sides of the face gives a widening effect

Thin old age

Advanced old age is usually characterized in the theater by extreme thinness, since a very thin bony appearance gives a greater illusion of age than one of fatness and obesity.

To achieve this effect, the skin must be made pale and parchmentlike and appear to be draped over the bone structure, giving the face a skull-like appearance. Men and women age in a similar manner so we can look at a step-by-step routine for a woman and then examine finished thin old-age makeup for both sexes.

Try on the wig and study the general effect on the face. Then remove the wig and keep it on its block until all the makeup is completed.

Apply a pale sallow foundation over the entire face, draining all natural color from the skin.

Then, using a $\frac{1}{4}$ inch (6mm), flat-ended sable brush, start to apply shadows to the eye area, sinking the eye back into the socket as far as possible.

Continue to shadow the face, sinking in the temples and cheek hollows and thinning down the nose. Now you are ready to add lines to the forehead, under the eyes and around the mouth.

The next stage is to break up the jawline with jowls and add shading to the neck and throat.

Using a clean $\frac{1}{4}$ inch (6mm), flat-ended sable brush, add highlights to each of the shadows already applied, giving extra emphasis to all bony edges and heavy folds of flesh. When all the highlighting is finished, thoroughly powder the makeup with translucent powder.

If you need broken veins, they should be stippled on now with dark-red liner or lake, using a coarse stippling sponge. Next, add wrinkles to the lips (see page 69) and then replace the wig. Fasten it into position with pins, grips and spirit gum.

Whiten the brows and lashes with white lining color, using a small mascara brush.

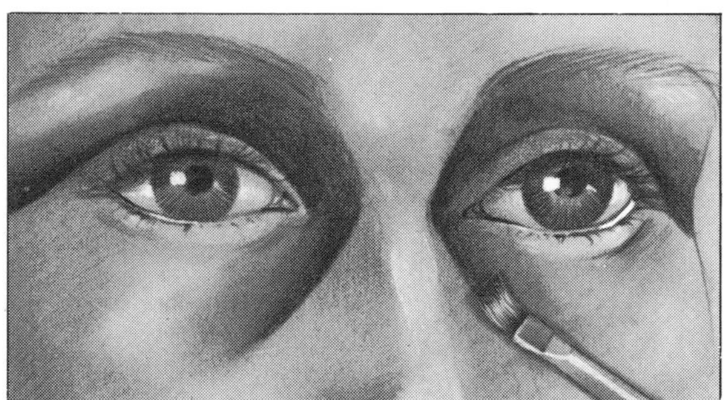

1 *Shade eye area, sinking eye back into socket*

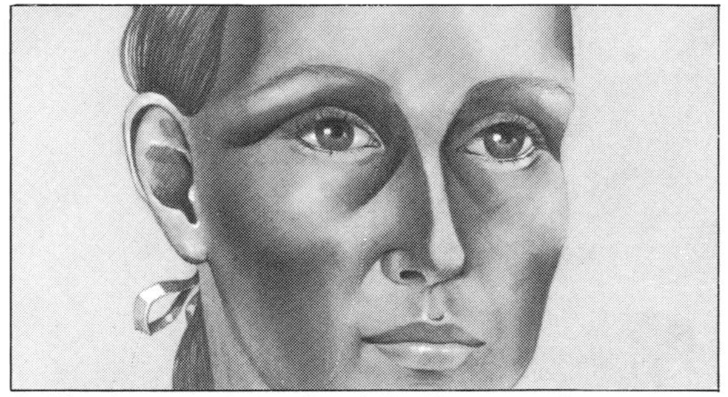

2 *Shade temples, cheek hollows and nose*

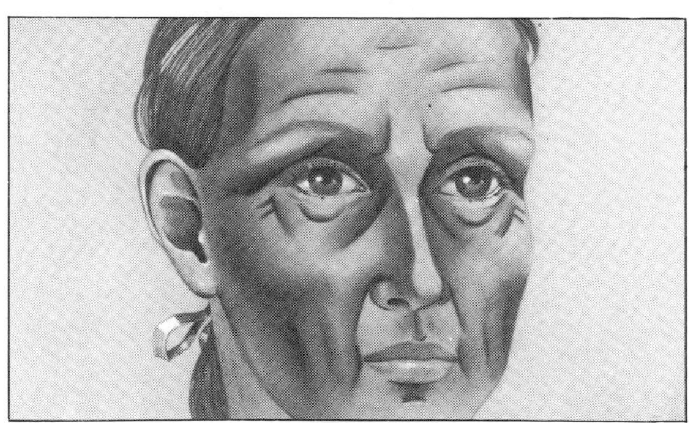

3 *Line forehead, eye area and around mouth*

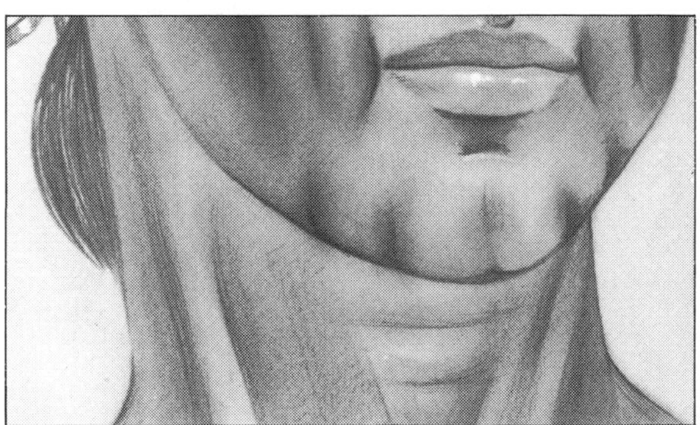

4 *Add jowls. Shade neck and throat*

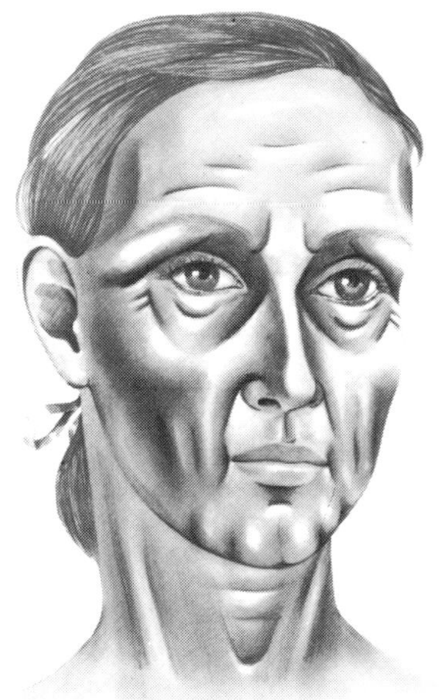

5 *Highlight shadows to emphasize bone structure*

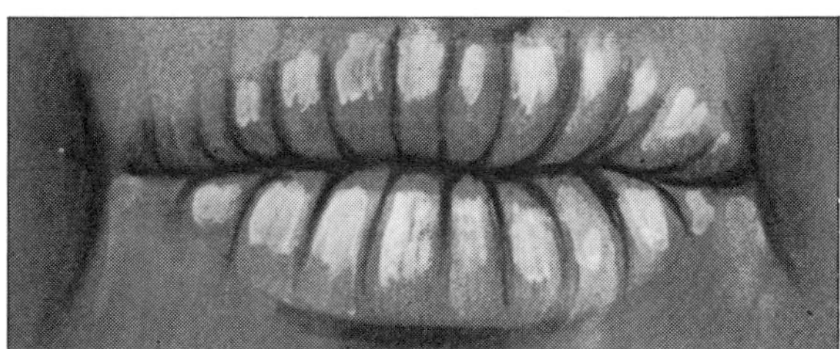

6 *Stipple on broken veins*

7 *Add wrinkles to the lips*

Additional effects

When a rheumy-eyed effect is required, a thin line of a medium-red liner can be added to the inside edge of the lower lid; gently pull the lid away from the eye with the tip of the little finger and add the color with a $\frac{1}{8}$ inch (3mm), flat-ended sable brush.

A tiny touch of the same red can be applied to the top lid to give a weak sore look to the entire eye.

Where shading is insufficient to slim the nose effectively (this can occur on a very juvenile snub nose) a thin aquiline effect can be obtained with the application of nose putty, before starting to apply your foundation (see page 74). These additional effects can be used for both men and women.

Paint a thin red line on inside edge of eyelid

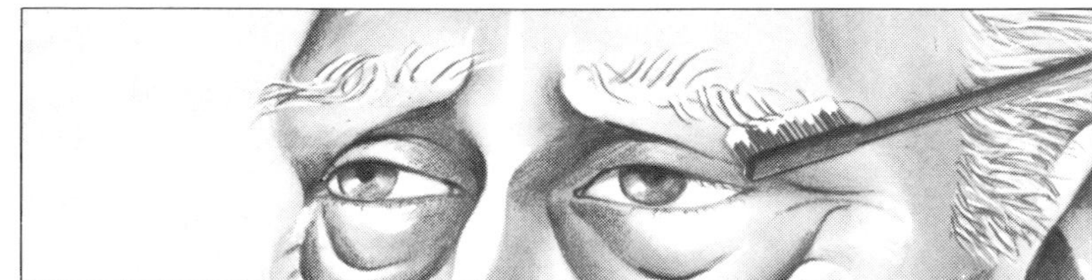

Whiten the brows and lashes

Nose putty slims a snub nose

Thin old age

Thin old women

Note how the vertical treatment of the majority of the shadows and highlights, and the style of the wig with its center parting, contribute to the overall thinness of the face. Also note how the hand has been aged (see page 71).

Color guide

Foundation For a pink and white complexion use pink groups mixed with white or pale groups

For sallow, ivory skin tones use ivory or sallow groups

Shading Olive-brown and lake groups

Highlights White

Cheeks and lips Dark-red or lake groups

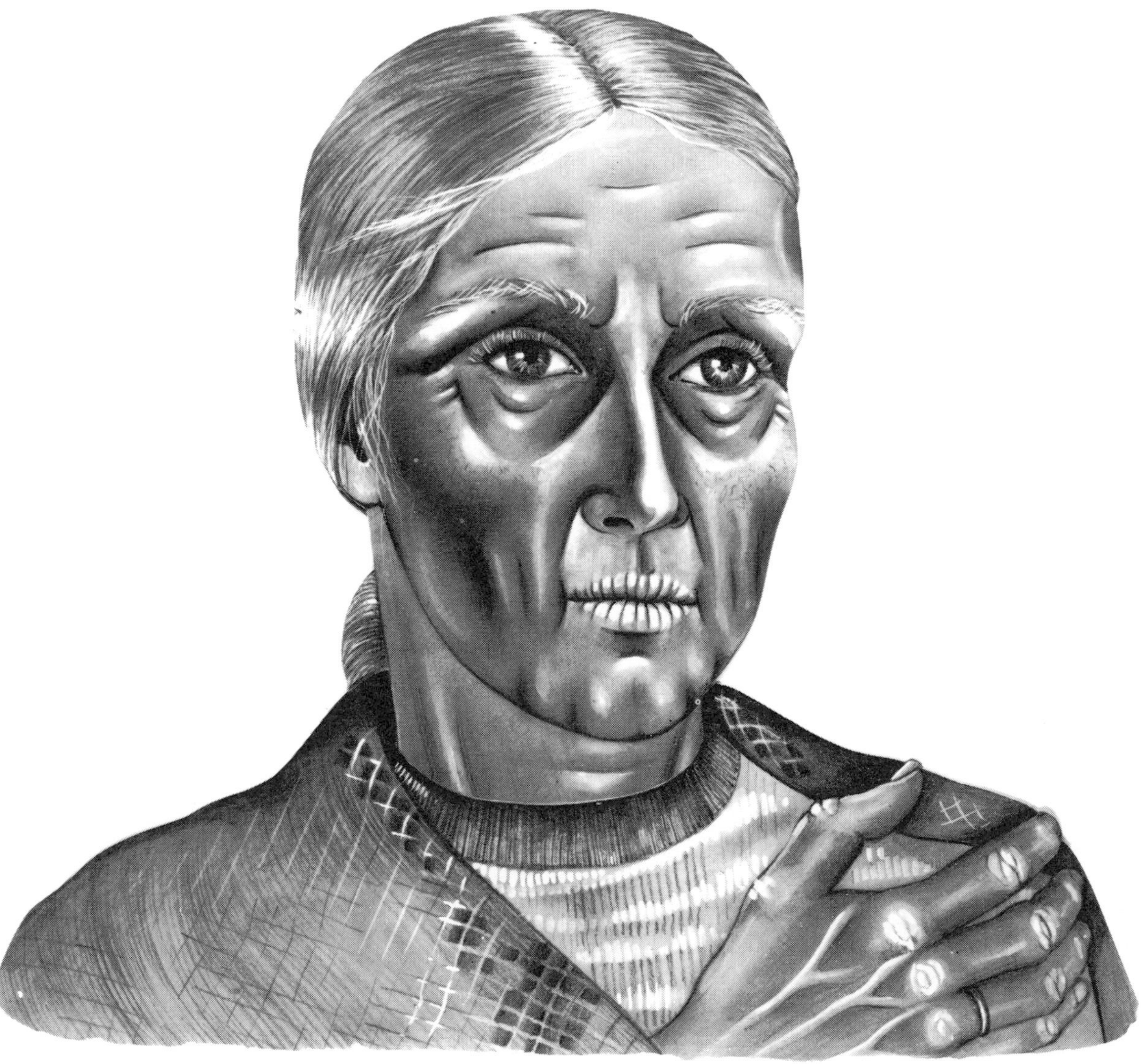

Thin old men

The highlights and shadows are almost identical to those on the female chart, the only major difference being the balding wig, the thickening and coarsening of the eyebrows and, of course, the mustache.

Color guide

Foundation For pinkish complexions use ivory or pale groups together with florid groups

For sallow tones use sallow or ivory groups

Shading Olive-brown and lake groups

Highlights Use white or ivory groups

Cheeks and lips Dark-red or lake groups

Fat old age

Obesity and old age together present a number of makeup problems. First of all, fat people, both men and women, tend to look much younger than thin people of the same age, so it is very difficult for a young thin actor or actress to be made to look both fat and old at the same time. It is best, when casting this type of role, to choose an actor who is already slightly overweight, or, at the very least, has a full round face.

Also very young performers tend, unless they are extremely overweight, not to have the necessary maturity to carry off the illusion of heaviness needed for this type of part; so it is generally best to cast more mature artistes for these roles.

There are two main optical illusions used to create the illusion of extreme stoutness in the theater. The first is the use of horizontal detail to give maximum width to the features (see page 49). Apply all your lines, wrinkles and folds of flesh in as horizontal a direction as possible. Hairstyles and beards and mustaches can also be used to increase the width of the face, using this same principle.

The second optical illusion to use is comparison of size. By making the eyes and mouth as small as possible, the rest of the face will appear bigger by way of contrast.

Fat old women

Choose a wig that is full at the sides and fairly flat on the top, with the hairline as far back as possible from the sides of the face. Try it on and check the general effect that it has on the shape of the face, then return it to the wig block before commencing the actual makeup.

First apply the foundation, which should be as light and bright as possible. Grease-based makeups are the best sort to use since they can be left slightly underpowdered to give the skin a suitably shiny and hot look.

Apply moist rouge in a circle of color on to the fullness of the cheek pads, keeping the strongest accent of color around the outside of your circular pattern.

Using a warm, brown shading color, shade the nose at the side and around the nostrils to give a small buttonlike appearance. Then apply shadows and lines to the eye area, keeping them as horizontal and wide as possible. Now you can add lines to the forehead, if necessary, keeping these lines as long and horizontal as possible to add to the broadening effect.

Pull the chin back into the throat and paint on jowls and double chins with your shading color. Highlight all your shadows, paying particular attention to the fullness of the cheeks and the puffy areas around the eyes.

Paint on a small rounded mouth, highlighting the center to give it as pouting an appearance as possible. Now add shadows and highlights to the corners of the mouth and to the flesh surrounding the lips to give as puffy an effect as possible.

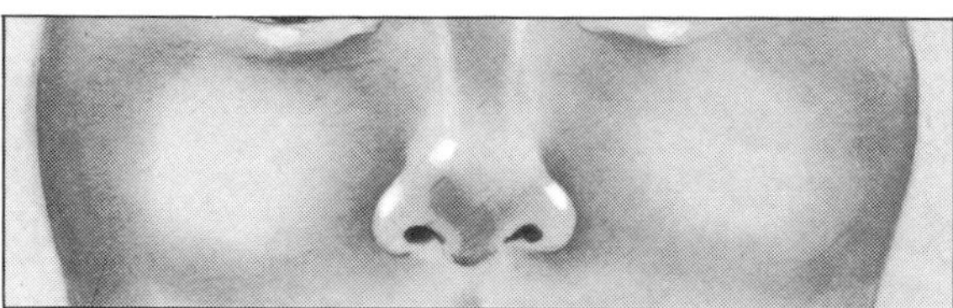

1 *Apply moist rouge in a circle on cheek pads*

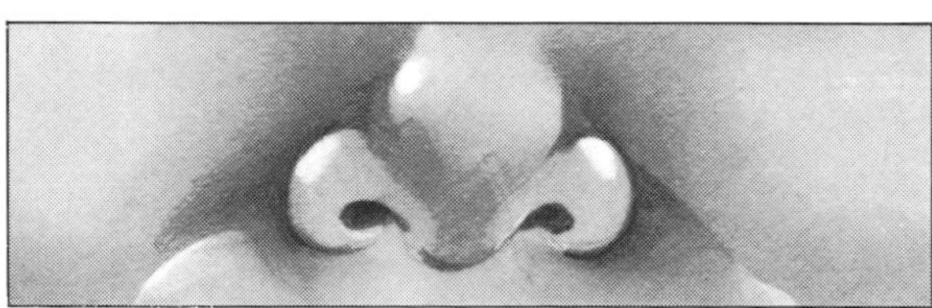

2 *Shade nose at the side and around nostrils*

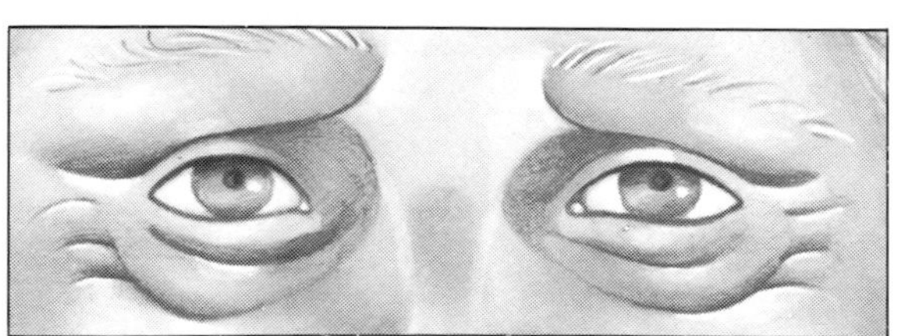

3 *Add lines and shadows to eye area*

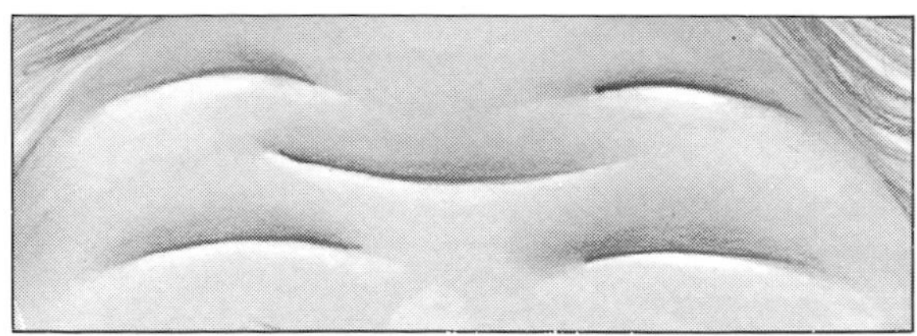

4 *Apply long, horizontal lines to forehead*

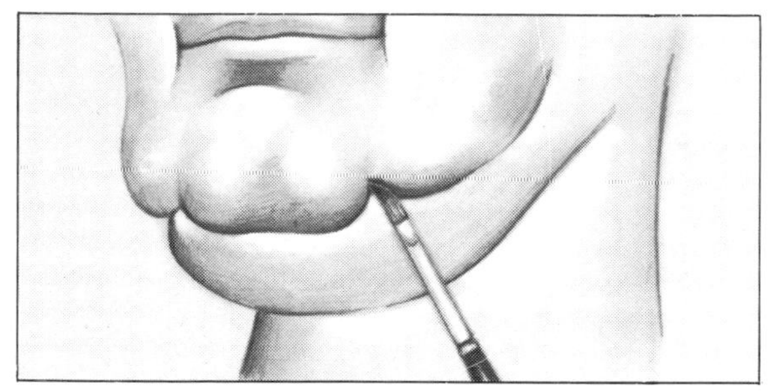

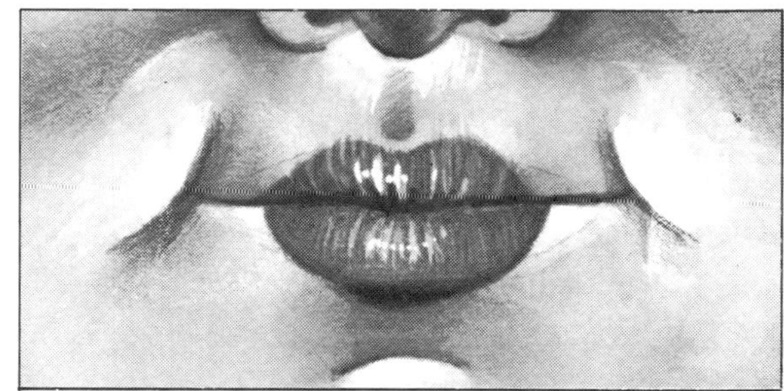

Color guide

Foundation For pink and white complexions use pale or pink groups mixed with florid groups. For ruddy florid complexions use sallow groups with florid and lake groups

Shading Use olive-brown groups mixed with lake groups

Highlights Use pale or ivory groups

Lips and cheeks Dark-red or lake groups

Eyeshadow Mauve tone

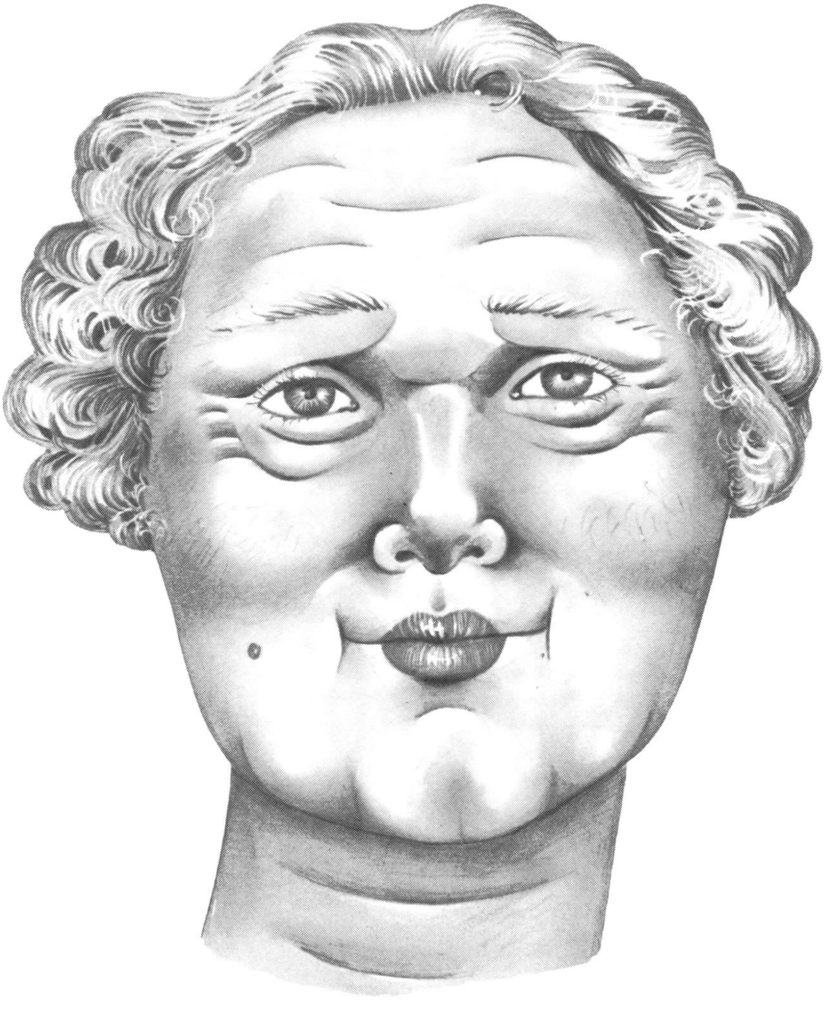

Fat old age

Fat old men

Try on the chosen wig and study the general effect on the shape of the face. A bald wig that has a hard dome, a wide forehead, and the hair puffed out at the sides and back will help the illusion of fatness. The best type has the dome built right down to the browbone with bushy eyebrows fastened along the edge. Remove the wig to a wig block until the makeup is completed.

If you are using a false nose or nose putty, it should be applied now (see pages 72-75). An enlarged and coarsened nose helps this type of makeup enormously. If it is possible to make or obtain false double chins, they will contribute to the overall effect and should be applied at this stage.

Apply your foundation, mixing the colors with a stippling technique to give the complexion a really broken appearance, and adding your rouge with the same technique until the foundation is built up. Note the shape of the rouge pattern around the lower fullness of the cheek pad.

Using a $\frac{1}{4}$ inch (6mm) sable brush, apply the shadows, which should be very red in tone. Keep all the shadows as horizontal as possible to give maximum width to the face.

Apply highlights with a clean $\frac{1}{4}$ inch (6mm) sable brush. Give maximum emphasis to the cheek pads, folds of the double chin and puffiness around the eyes. Lightly powder makeup with translucent face powder.

Stipple on broken veins, using lake lining color on a coarse stippling sponge. Then paint on a small well-rounded mouth. Intensify the shadow below the lower lip, using a very dark-brown pencil or lining color, and highlight center of mouth to give maximum fullness.

If the natural eyebrows are being used, whiten these with white lining color or greasepaint on a mascara brush. Brush the color on to the brows in the opposite direction of the natural growth, to make them as fluffy and full as possible.

Replace the wig and fasten it securely in place with spirit gum and grips.

Make up hands with pink-toned body makeup. Then redden the knuckles to give a rounded puffy effect.

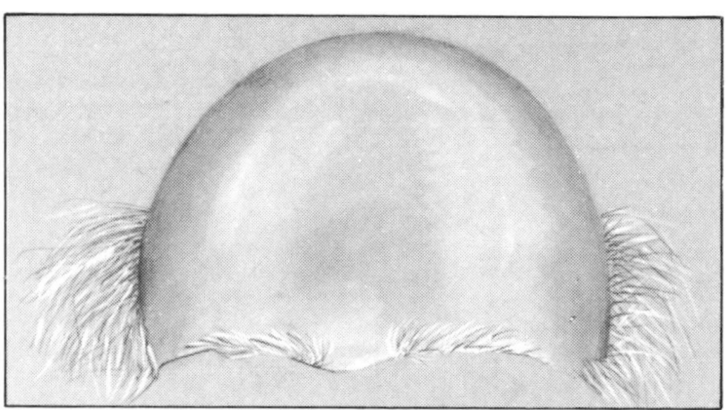

***1** Hard-domed wig with eyebrows attached*

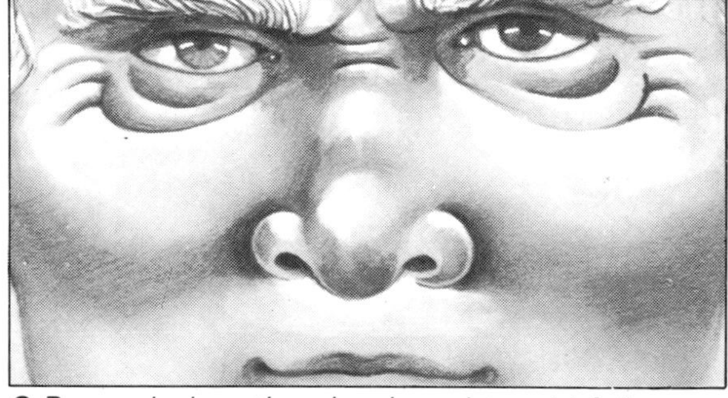

***2** Rouge below the cheek pad to add fullness*

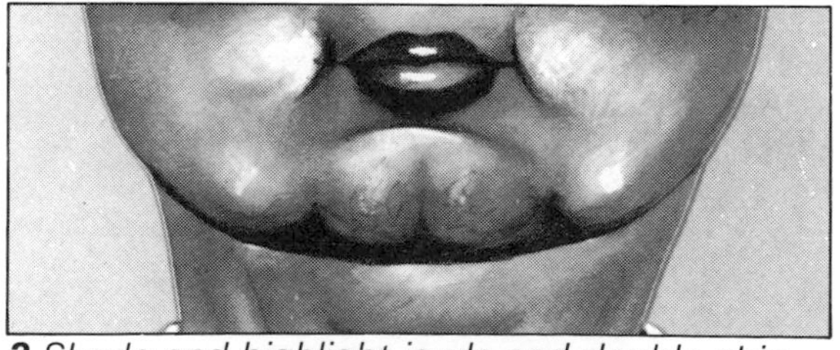

***3** Shade and highlight jowls and double chin*

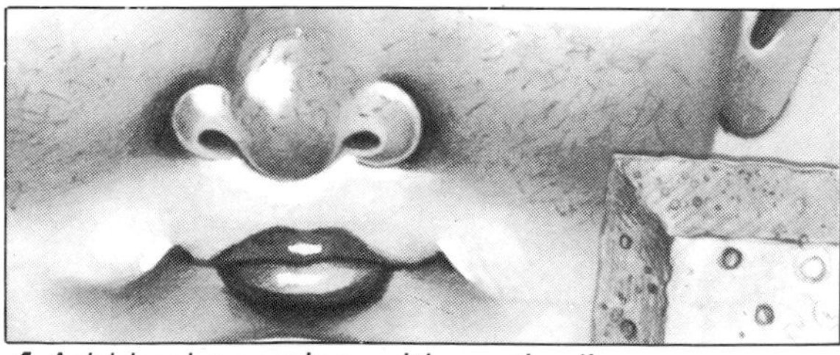

***4** Add broken veins with a stippling sponge*

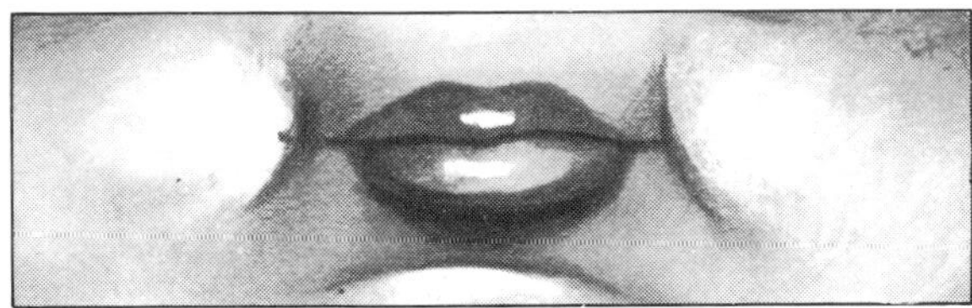

5 *Shade below the lower lip to add fullness to the mouth*

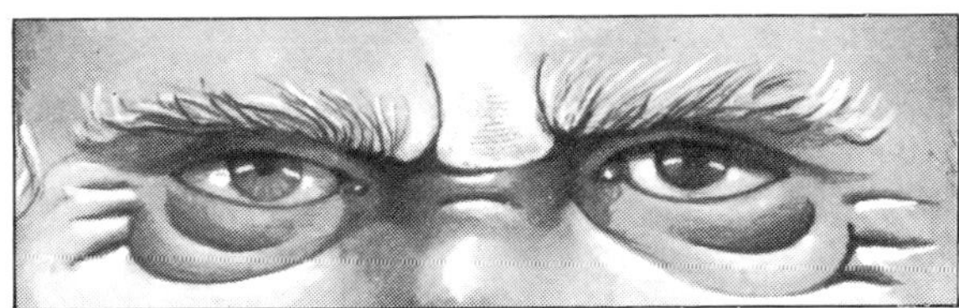

6 *Apply white lining color or greasepaint to dark brows*

Additional effects

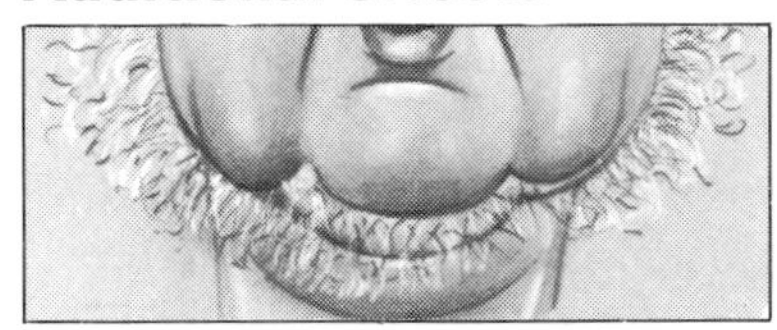

Some fat characters will benefit from a "moonraker" beard. Apply to the outermost edge of the jawline to emphasize the fullness of the cheeks and the heaviness of the jowls

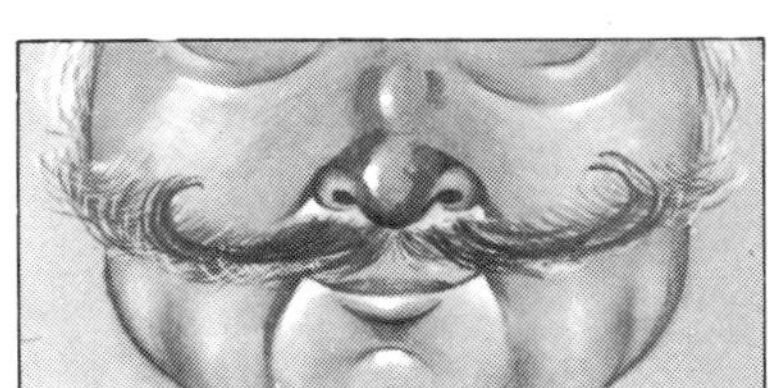

Very full mustaches sweeping outwards and upwards under the cheek pads will give them added fullness and add to the overall wideness of the face *(see pages 94-95)*

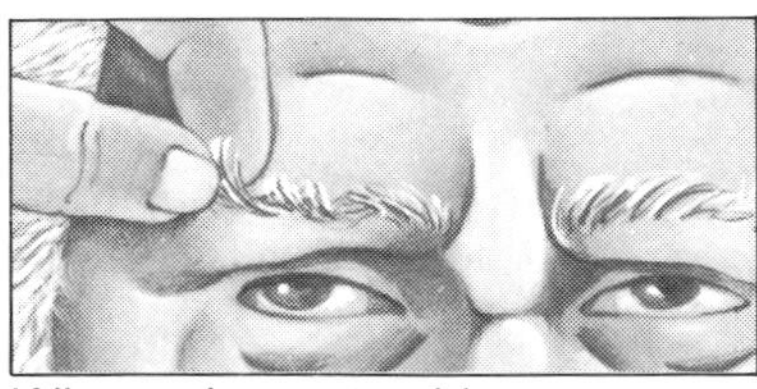

Where the natural brows are not strong enough, teased-out white or gray crepe hair can be used to give a bushy effect. Extra width is added to the face by exaggerating the fullness at the outer ends of the brows

Color guide

Foundation For highly florid complexions use pink stippled with florid and lake groups. For sallow skins with florid overtones use ivory or sallow stippled with dark-red or lake groups

Shading Lake mixed with olive-brown groups

Highlights Use ivory or pale groups

Lips Use lake or dark-red groups

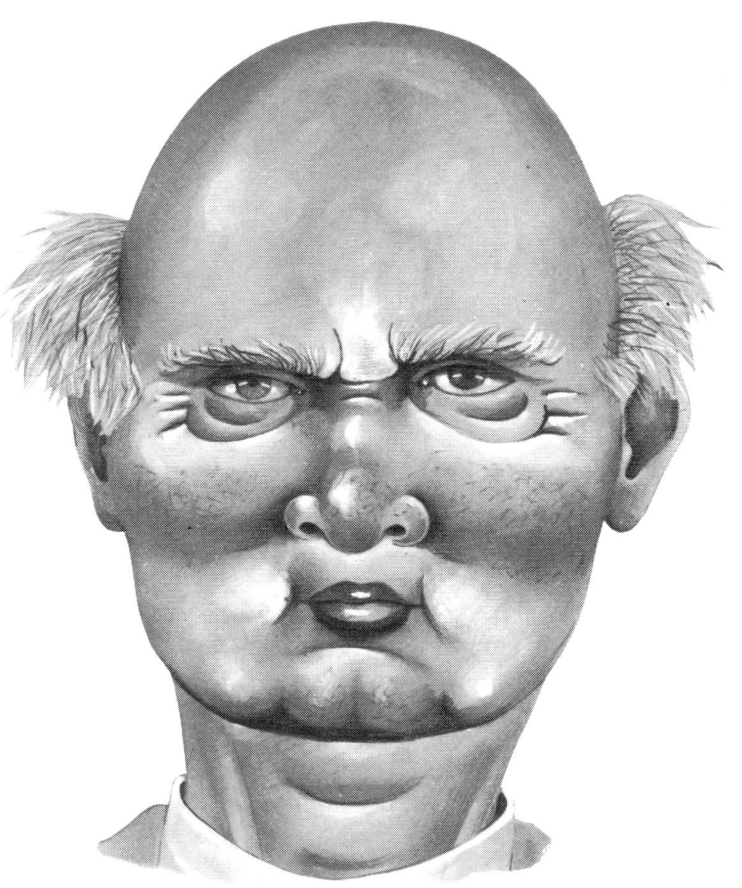

Glamor on stage

The makeup techniques shown in this section are unashamedly artificial and intended to make the actress look as glamorous and beautiful as possible. They are basically intended for use on very large stages for musicals and opera so they must be bold in design and strongly colored to be in keeping with the costumes and scenery.

Remember that the lighting for this type of production is usually very bright and colorful, so make sure that the foundation color is very clear and strong and considerably warmer than the one you would use on a smaller stage.

Eye makeup should be strong and bright and very clearly defined. False lashes give a glamorous look to the eyes but be careful with your choice of style. Very heavy dense lashes tend to cast dark shadows over the eyes and make them all but disappear. Pointed lashes with well-spaced clumps are best.

Corrective highlighting and shading plays an important part in this type of makeup and can be used boldly and strongly.

Lip color should compliment both costume and complexion but at the same time it must be strong, clear and bright. Soft subtle colors may look attractive at close quarters but will inevitably disappear under strong lights on a large stage. Lip gloss is also very useful for this type of makeup. The general rule throughout is to use strong clear colors and warm tones. Be bold in design.

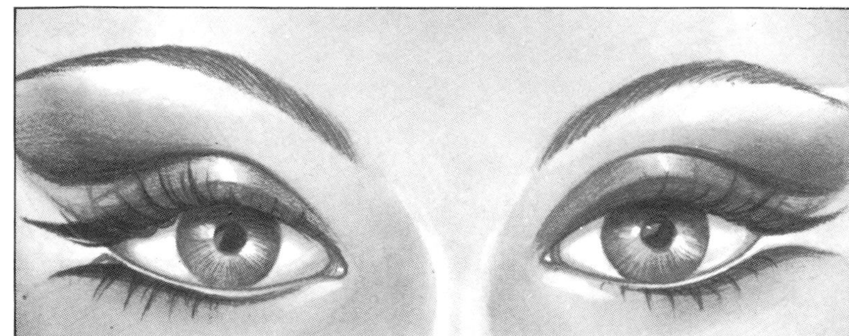

An example of glamorous eye makeup

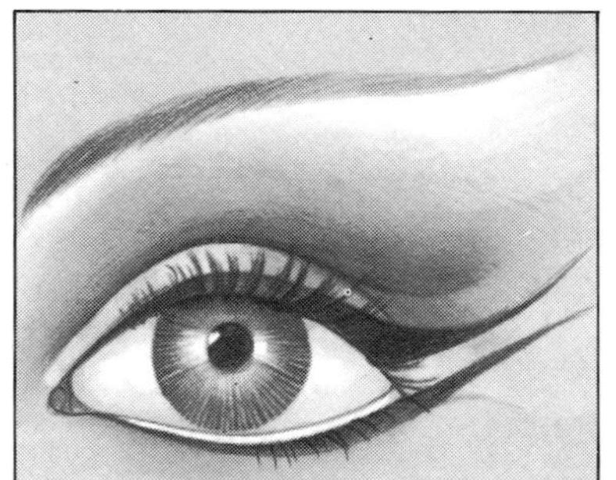

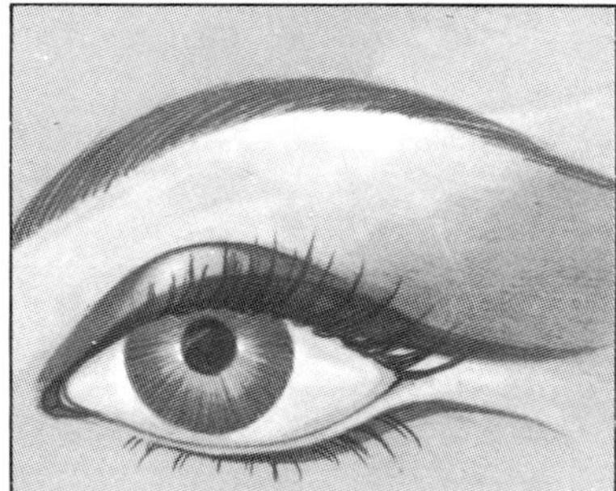

Suggested variations on eye makeup

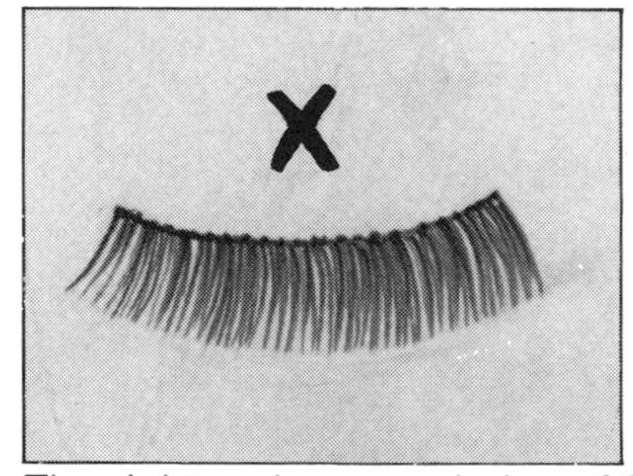

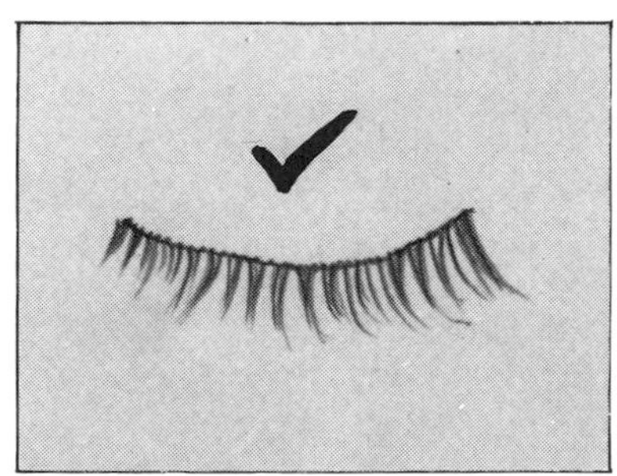

The right and wrong choice of false lashes

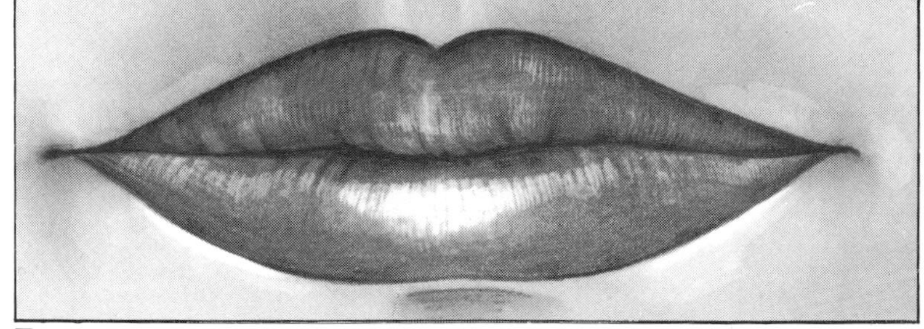

Treatment of mouth for glamor makeup

Color guide to makeup

Foundation Choose from the peach, creamy and light-tan groups

Rouge Light and medium-red groups

Lip color Light or medium-red groups, or lipstick to harmonize with costume

Eyeshadow To harmonize with natural eye coloring or costume. Iridescent colors are particularly good

Black artistes

Black actors and actresses have for many years found it very difficult to get help and advice on makeup for the theater, and in consequence many choose not to use any at all. This imposes severe limitations on the roles they can play — which is a great pity, because, apart from the actual skin coloring, all the principles that we have already discussed apply to the black-skinned player as well as to the white-skinned caucasian.

The black actor has one big advantage over his white counterpart in that very often the natural skin color looks fine under stage lighting, without the use of any foundation. All that is needed is a small amount of highlighting and shading to accentuate the features. However, there are many more variations in the coloring of black skins than white. These range from the pale coffee-colored complexion, through yellowy and reddish browns, to the very dark black skin; it is when these colors need adjusting that difficulties may arise.

Since dark colors are recessive, very dark skins tend to make the features disappear on stage. It is necessary to lighten the skin tone so that the artiste can be seen at his or her best — but often, when a dark skin is lightened, it looks dull and chalky and has a very dead appearance. This is because light-brown makeup has a great deal of white pigment added to make it light and this white pigment gives the black skin its chalky appearance. So, when choosing a makeup for this purpose, make sure it contains strong yellows or reds, according to the natural coloring of the skin. These colors (which in the stick tend to look overbright and unnatural) are most effective in lightening a black skin, but the exact shade and color required can be determined only by trial and error.

Conversely, a black actor with a light-brown complexion may sometimes need to darken the skin tone to suit the role. Very often the resulting makeup makes the skin look dull and muddy. Avoid this by using a color which, although darker, is also brighter, with more depth of color than the natural skin.

When the skin tone is the right color but the complexion is slightly uneven, a normal makeup base may make the face look masklike. Use instead a "face glosser" or "gleamer". These products contain a low level of dark pigment mixed with iridescent material which imparts an attractive gleam to the skin and, at the same time, evens out any patchiness in the complexion.

The general rule for black performers is to add brightness to the skin and this also applies when using cheek color, eyeshadow and lipstick. Muted subtle colors tend to become muddy and disappear, so keep the choice of colors clear, clean and bright.

Straight makeup for the black actress

***1** Study the skin coloring closely to determine whether it contains yellow or red undertones and apply a foundation that is complimentary: on a yellow-toned complexion use a bright golden-yellow tan; on a reddy-brown complexion use a bright orange-red tan. Keep the application as fine as possible to prevent a masklike appearance or use one of the face-glosser products mentioned above*

Powder the makeup with a translucent face powder containing a small amount of iridescent material, which will help to retain the attractive gleam of a black skin

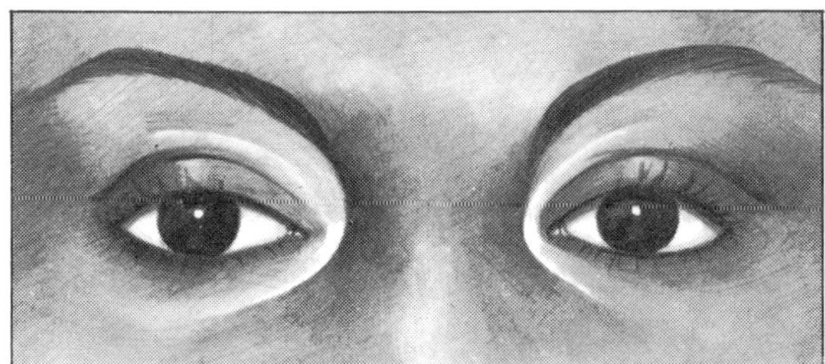

2 *If the brows are poorly defined, sketch them in with black eyebrow pencil, using short hairlike strokes, to simulate the natural growth (see page 42)*

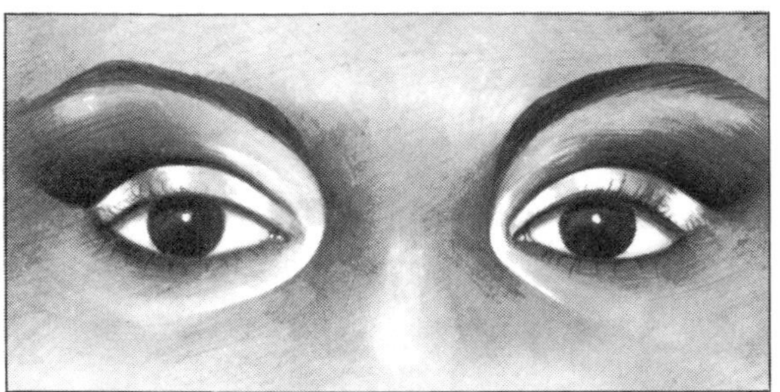

3 *Apply a clear, bright eyeshadow color to the upper lid. All iridescent colors, including metallic golds and silver, are especially attractive on black skin. Using very dark lining colors or eye pencils, draw in the contour crease, blending the shadow up and over the browbone at the outer end of the eye. (If the skin color is particularly dark, black kohl pencil can be used for this contour shadow)*

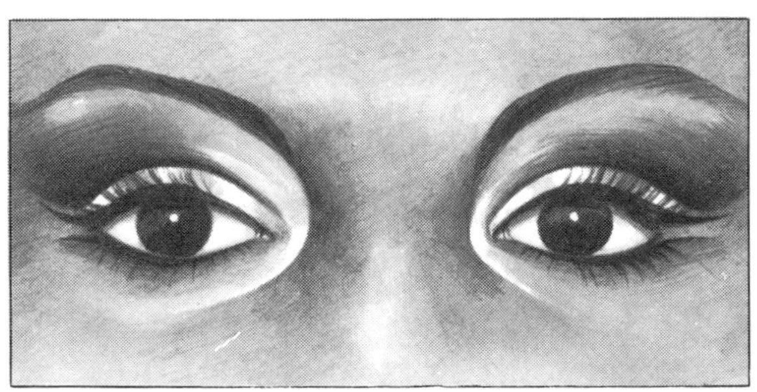

4 *Clearly outline the eyes, using black lining color (see page 44). Paint the top and bottom lashes with black mascara. If the eyelashes are very short and sparse, false lashes can be used to good advantage, particularly when a very glamorous makeup is required*

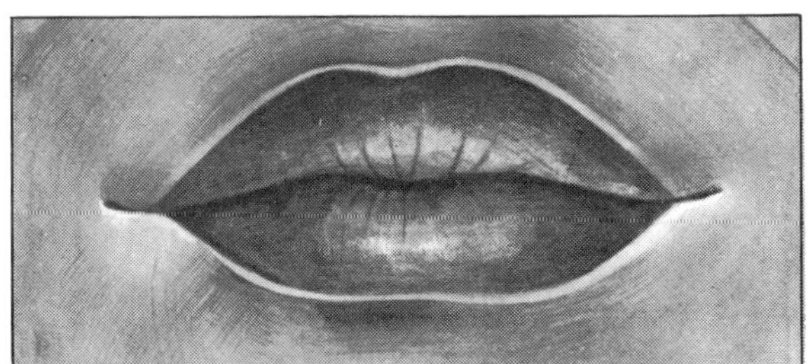

5 *Apply a strong shade of lip color with a number 6 sable brush. If, however, the lips are overlarge, keep the outline just inside the natural shape and avoid overbright or very pale colors, as these tend to enlarge a mouth*

6 *Brush a bright, strong powder rouge over the cheekbone, adding a touch to the forehead and chin. Where corrective contouring is needed, a dark-brown shading rouge should be strongly applied under the cheekbone (before applying the normal cheek color over the cheek area) and over the top of the shading rouge already applied. Generally, there is no need for hand and body makeup, although occasionally the pigmentation on the hands can be broken and uneven, in which case body makeup should be used to correct this*

Black artistes

Straight makeup for the black actor

Corrective makeup for the black actor should be kept to the absolute minimum. Bear in mind that the foundation should be as fine as possible to avoid any suggestion of an over-madeup appearance.

1 *Apply a fine film of foundation when needed, using light liquid foundations or face glosser. If the skin tones are particularly uneven, a very thin film of a strong, bright cake foundation can be used but choose colors carefully. Eyebrows on the black male may be rather undefined and, although this looks completely natural at close quarters, it can look strange on stage. A slightly stronger amount of definition may be applied with a black eyebrow pencil, taking care not to overdraw the brows as this can give a comical look to the eyes*

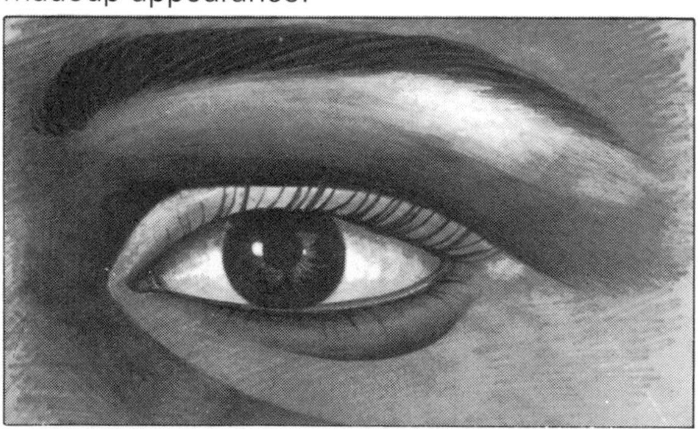

2 *Apply a highlight to the actual lid area and the browbone. This highlight should be some four shades lighter than the skin color and contain golden-yellow tones. Metallic gold eyeshadow, used discreetly, can often work very well*

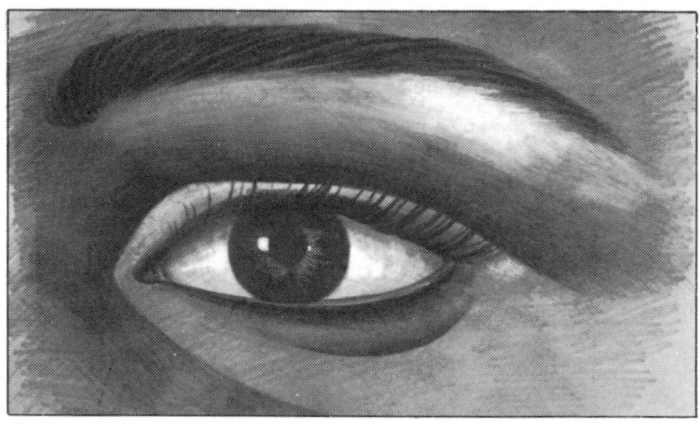

3 *Darken the contour crease if needed, using very dark-brown or black pencil or lining color. Fade the edges away, using a $\frac{1}{4}$ inch (6mm) sable brush. Then outline the eyes with black pencil and soften away the edges, again using a $\frac{1}{4}$ inch (6 mm) sable brush*

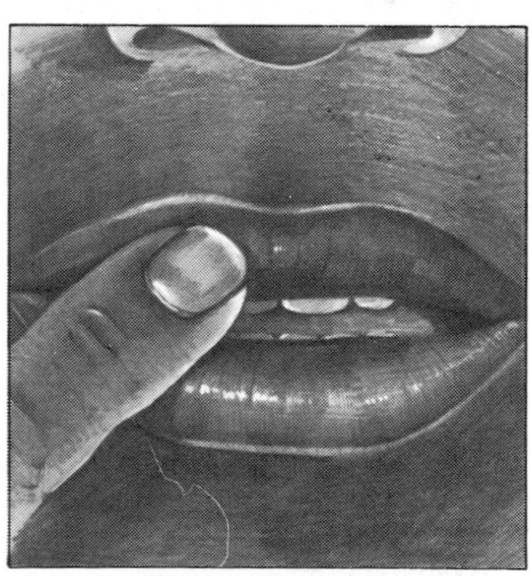

4 *If the lips lack definition and color, a small amount of very dark brown-red rouge can be added with the fingertips. Be careful not to over-redden the mouth. (If the mouth looks too red, add a touch of black pencil to tone it down)*

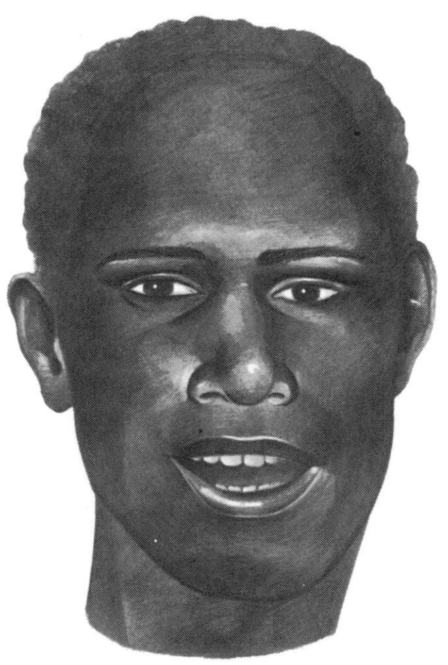

Aging makeup for black performers

The principles of aging apply equally to the black actor and actress but the makeup will vary according to the darkness of the skin tones.

If the actor has relatively light skin coloring with yellow undertones, it is possible to highlight and shade directly on to the skin. If the skin has warm red undertones, use a base color to drain the color from the skin before applying the shadows and highlights.

Medium-dark skin tones can be effectively aged by using a dark shading color into which a small amount of black lining has been mixed (this will give extra depth to the shadows). Then highlight with a pale-yellowish highlight.

Very dark skin tones can be treated in two ways. First use an overall base color (several shades lighter than the natural skin color) to give a dull gray appearance to the skin. Then add aging shadows and highlights. Or you can add highlights directly to the skin, allowing the natural dark coloring to act as shading, with just a touch of black to give extra depth to eye pouches, jowls and lines.

The easiest way to gray the black actor's hair is to use a spray. Too white a color will look unnaturally blue on black hair, so a silvery spray is best. It may be better to dress the hair flat in braids and use a good gray wig.

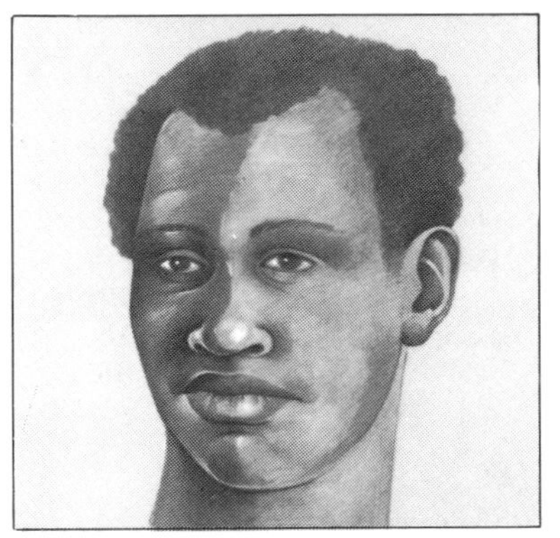

1 Gray the skin tone with a suitable color of foundation. Note change of skin tone on right of face

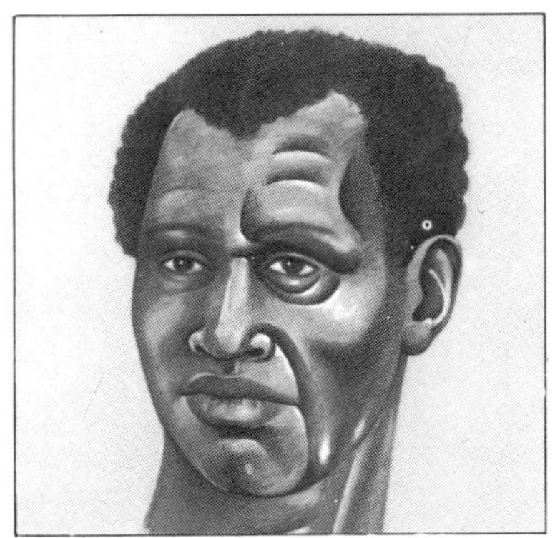

2 Apply shadows and highlights, following the normal aging principles (see pages 61-71)

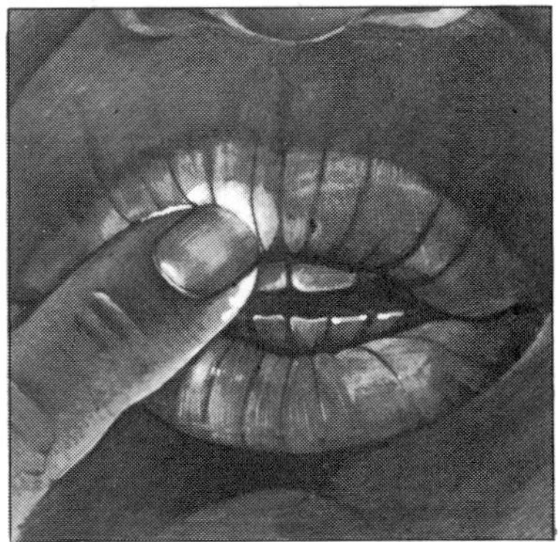

3 Apply highlight over puckered lips with a fingertip and powder immediately with translucent face powder

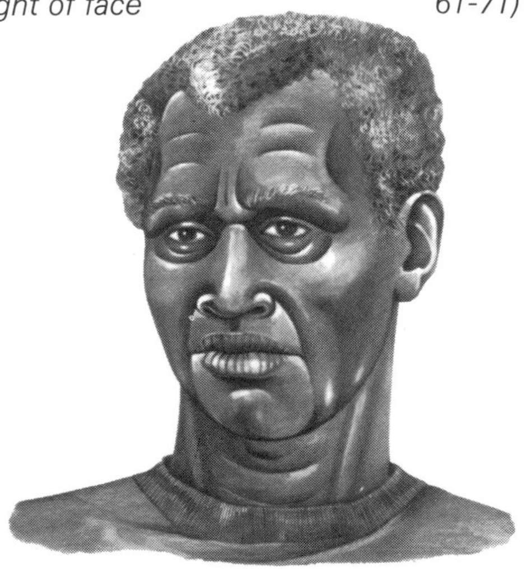

Mediterranean makeup

The Mediterranean or Latin races include the Spaniards, Portuguese, Italians and the Greeks. All these nationalities have many characteristics in common, so the following makeups can be easily adapted to suit the country of origin.

They can also be applied to South American characters of European descent.

All the races we are looking at have good, strong bone structures with dark golden-olive complexions. The hair is generally very dark and glossy and Mediterranean people usually have dark expressive eyes and strong sensuous lips.

Mediterranean women

Many of the Spanish, Italian and South-American roles for women are strong, fiery, and temperamental, and this should be reflected in the makeup.

Apply a dark golden-tan foundation, adding corrective highlighting and shading to emphasize the bone structure as much as possible. Powder with an iridescent translucent face powder.

Sketch on the eyebrows, lifting them as high as possible, making them dark and well defined.

Apply a strong eyeshadow to the top eyelid and along the edge of the lower lid, beneath the lashes, to enlarge the eye as much as possible. Highlight the center of the top lid to give it prominence.

Outline the eyes with black eyeliner, keeping the outer ends wide apart in the fishtail shape shown. Then use white eyeliner along the inside edge of the lower lid, continuing it out between the open ends of the eyeliner at the outer corner of the eye. Now apply mascara to top and bottom lashes and apply false lashes if required.

Outline the mouth with a dark-red lip pencil or lip color. Fill in the center of the lips with clear bright red and apply lip gloss.

Accentuate the cheek shading with dark shading rouge and then add plenty of accent rouge to the cheekbone to give a good strong color to the makeup.

Finally, dress the hair in the required style or, if the natural hair is unsuitable, use a wig. The hairstyle in illustration A, with its elaborate curls around the face, is very appropriate for a South-American or Spanish character. The next illustration, B, shows how, by dressing the hair flatter to the head and taking it back into a chignon, the character becomes less flamboyant; if, at the same time, a neutral brown eyeshadow is used and the lips and rouge are more subdued, the makeup is changed to one more suited to an austere Greek woman or an Italian peasant.

***1** Apply a dark golden base and accentuate bone structure with highlight and shading*

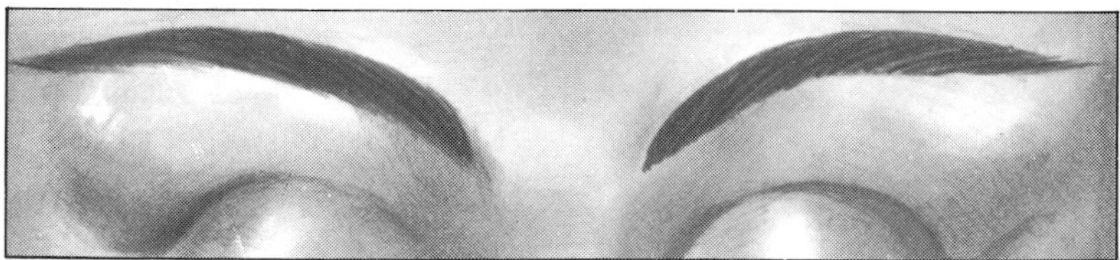

***2** Sketch on high, dark well-defined eyebrows*

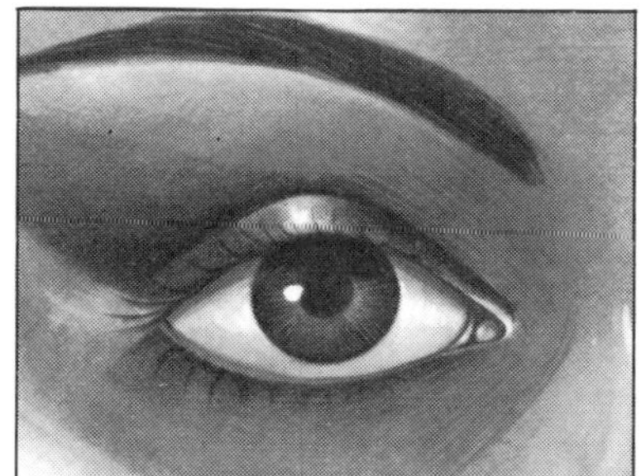
3 *Use eyeshadow to enlarge eye as much as possible*

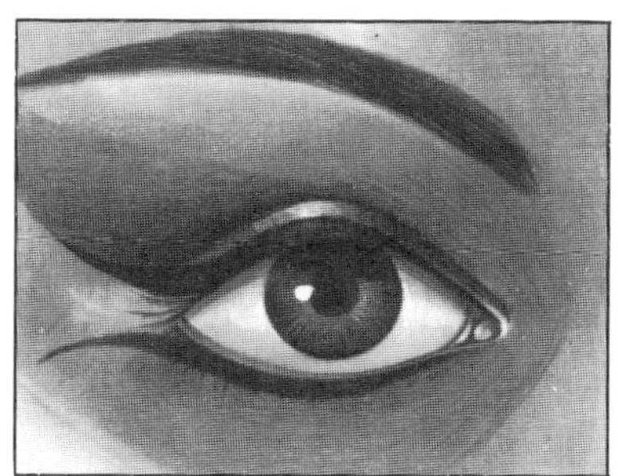
4 *Apply black eyeliner in a fishtail shape*

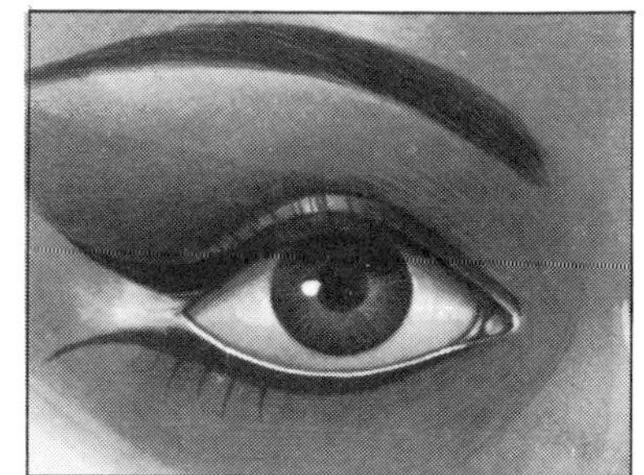
5 *Add white liner to inside of lower lid, and beyond outer corner*

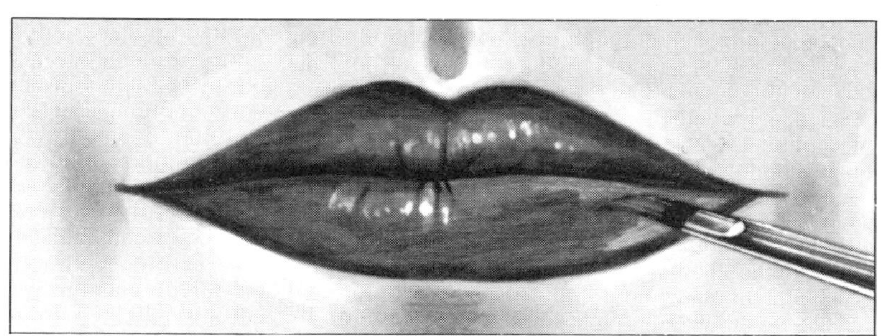
6 *Outline mouth with dark red. Fill in with clear red and gloss*

7 *Apply cheek shading and rouge*

An elaborate hairstyle, with very strongly accented features, is highly suitable for a South-American or Spanish role, while a severe chignon, with subdued eyes and lips, transforms the makeup to one more suitable for a Greek or Italian peasant

A

B

Mediterranean makeup

Mediterranean men

Latin men, like the women, tend to be portrayed as having strong fiery temperaments, and this must be made apparent with the makeup. The bone structure must be emphasized as much as possible.

Nose putty or false noses can be used to strengthen the profile, particularly for the more aristocratic type of character.

The eyes need to be very dark, deep and as fascinating as possible. Therefore rather more eye makeup can be used than usual.

Sketch in very dark wide brows, keeping the pattern of growth low under the browbone and maintaining the same width along the whole of the brow, just slightly decreasing the density of growth at the outer end. A few strokes of pencil added between the brows will give a heavy menacing look.

Give the top lid a strong highlight and then sink in the contour crease with a strong line of black pencil or lining color, fading it up toward the browbone.

Line both top and bottom lids very strongly with black, opening the outer corner in a fishtail shape. Blend away the edges of these lines to give a dark smoldering look to the eyes. Men with fair lashes should darken them with black mascara.

For large stages and operatic roles, white lining can be added along the inside edge of the lower lid and between the open ends of the eyeliner.

Lips need to be made very strong and quite full. Where the outline is weak, the mouth should be lined with dark-brown pencil, fading the color inward toward the middle of the mouth before filling in the center with a very dark brown-red.

Hair is a very important part of the whole look, so careful attention should be paid to it. Wigs for this type of makeup, unless they are of absolutely top quality, often look very artificial, so darkening the natural hair with a water rinse and then redressing it is usually best. Use plenty of brilliantine dressing to give it a high gloss. Long sideburns running down the sides of the face and curving forward under the cheekbones, accompanied by a thin dark mustache, are immediately recognizable as being typically South American or Spanish.

Although real hairpieces are the best, especially for small stages and theater in the round, in larger theaters, mustaches and sideburns can be quite convincingly drawn in with black eyebrow pencil. Sketch them in with small hairlike strokes applied one on top of another, gradually building up the shape and density required.

Most Latin men have very strong well-marked beardlines. This gives them a dark swarthy appearance but, when using makeup to simulate this, care should be taken not to make the character look too villainous.

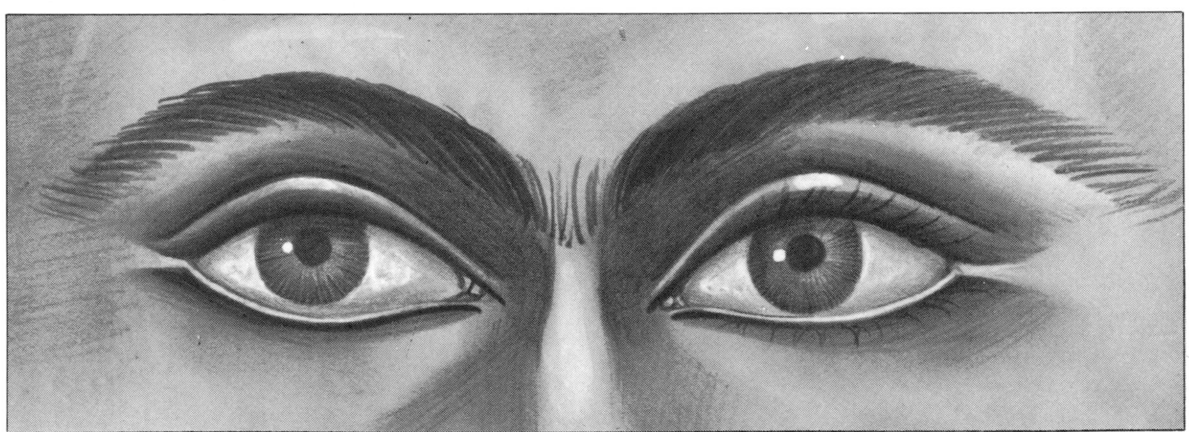

__1__ Create a dark, fascinating eye makeup with very heavy brows and a strong highlight on the lids. Use well-defined contour creases and eyeliner, smudged away to give a dark smoldering look. Apply plenty of black mascara to complete the dramatic effect

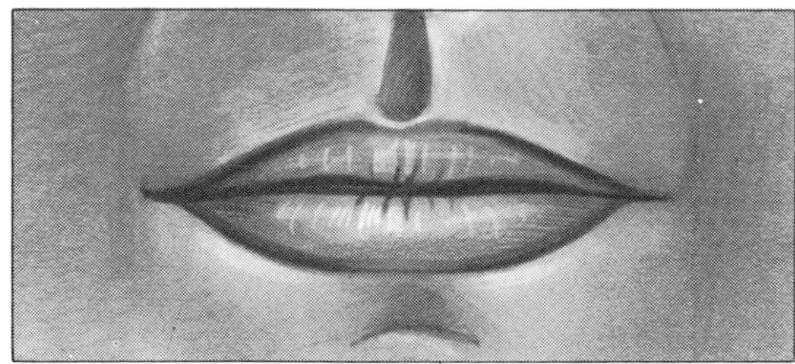

2 Outline the lips with dark-brown pencil, filling in the center with a dark brown-red

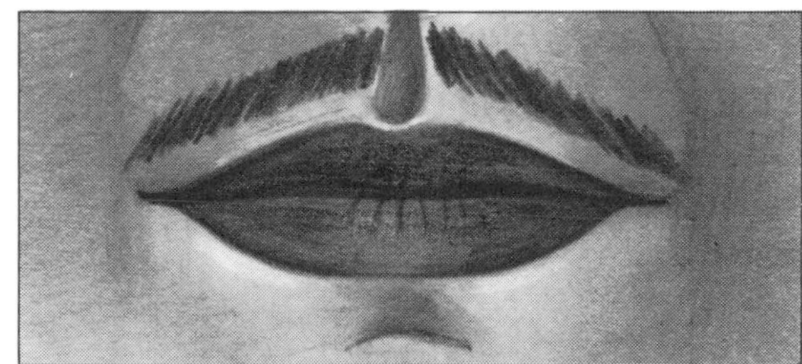

3 Sketch in mustaches with small hairlike strokes, using a black eyebrow pencil

A Greek man

Greek men, although they have very similar coloring to the other Latin races, look different on account of their hair, which is often curly and rather unruly, and their mustaches, which are usually large and luxuriously flamboyant

Oriental makeup

The oriental races include the Chinese, the Japanese and the numerous different peoples of south-east Asia. The most important of these, so far as the theater is concerned, are the Chinese and Japanese. The other Asian races are so numerous and varied that it would be almost impossible to show the subtle differences in makeup on an occidental face.

Although orientals are often thought to have yellow skin, this is not strictly true, as their complexions actually vary from very pale olive to dark yellowish-brown. Pure yellow foundations should not be used, except for very stylized makeups, such as those used in *The Mikado.*

The other mistaken idea is that oriental eyes slope obliquely upwards. They are in fact almond-shaped, horizontal and narrow, with a tendency, if anything, to slope downwards. The fact that they appear to slope upwards is an optical illusion caused by three factors:

Firstly, the Mongolian fold curves downward over the inner corner of the eye. Secondly, there is an upward-sloping curve to the shadow cast by the prominent, bulging upper lid at the outer corner. Thirdly, there is the shape of the eyebrow; although this does not slope up any more than an occidental brow, having risen, it is cut short and does not go down again.

Since the bone structure of the occidental face is very much stronger than that of the oriental, it is very difficult to be completely convincing with makeup when trying to show the difference between the Chinese and Japanese races. Often the best we can do is to rely on hairstyles and costume.

However, there are a number of differences that can be borne in mind. The Chinese face is inclined to be plumper and rounder than that of the Japanese. The Japanese nose is much more aquiline than the Chinese smaller, flatter nose.

Generally speaking, the Japanese skin is darker and much more olive than the Chinese skin, which is inclined to be pale and sallow olive. The Japanese eye is widest at the inner corner, giving it a very decided downward slope.

Finally, the Chinese jawline is rather weak and often recedes, while the Japanese jawline is usually strong with a long upper lip and a strong simian thrust to the lower jaw.

The one factor that both races have in common is that their features are very smooth and bland. The easiest way to achieve this is with a very even and slightly heavy application of cake makeup, which will give an overall flatness to the face.

The most noticeable and striking thing about the oriental eye is the shallowness and flatness of the orbital socket. This flatness can be simulated on the occidental face by applying a strong highlight to the entire orbital area or by using artificial oriental eyelids, as shown on the right.

The one problem with artificial eyelids is that they tend to close the eye so much that all expression is lost, particularly in a very large theater. (Of course this can sometimes be very useful if the role portrays an inscrutable oriental personality.)

Young orientals' hair is very straight, very black and shiny, and much coarser than European hair, so wigs are essential to a good makeup.

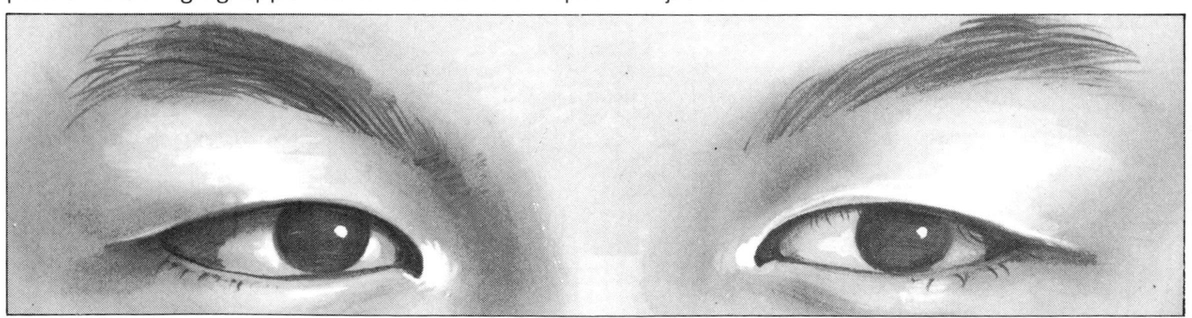

This drawing shows the actual shape of oriental eyes. Note the Mongolian fold and the tendency to slope down rather than up

Oriental eyelids

It is difficult to create the appearance of an oriental eye with just highlight and shadow if an actor's eye socket is particularly deep.

Made-to-measure rubber eyelids are very effective but are difficult to obtain and expensive. A good substitute can be made from adhesive tape or fine chamois leather.

Using a piece of surgical adhesive tape or chamois leather about $2\frac{1}{2}$ inches x $1\frac{1}{8}$ inches (50x28mm), cut out the shape shown by heavy line A.

(When using adhesive tape, first cover shaded area B with a small piece of tissue paper or press powder over it, so that this area is non-adhesive.)

To apply chamois-leather lids, paint the area C with spirit gum and press the lid in place so that it covers the end of the eyebrow. (If using adhesive tape, the false lid is just pressed into place with its own adhesive.) Lift a few eyebrow hairs from under the false lid where they are trapped, at point D, and allow them to fall over the edge of the piece.

The false lid should now be made up with base color. Then shade along the edge of the eye opening and highlight the center of the lid to create the slightly swollen, puffy look of an oriental eyelid, as can be seen in the completed eye makeup.

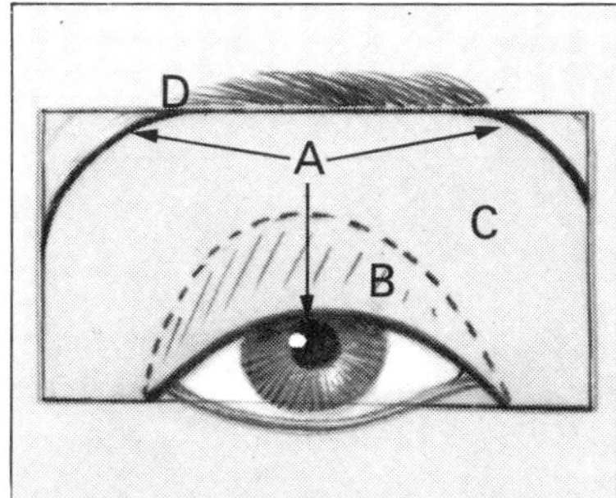

1 *Cut out the shape shown by heavy line A*

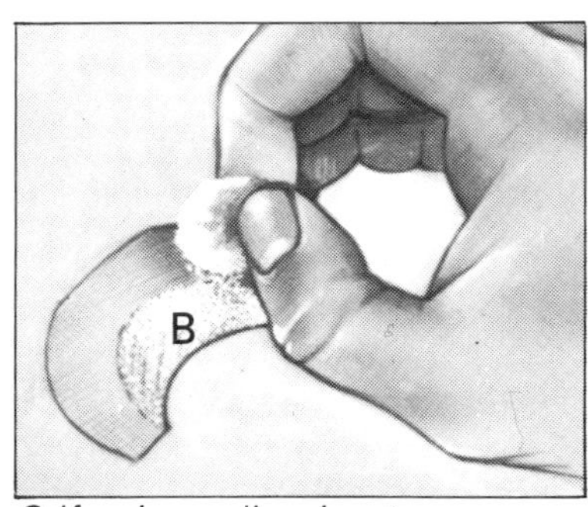

2 *If using adhesive tape, powder shaded area B*

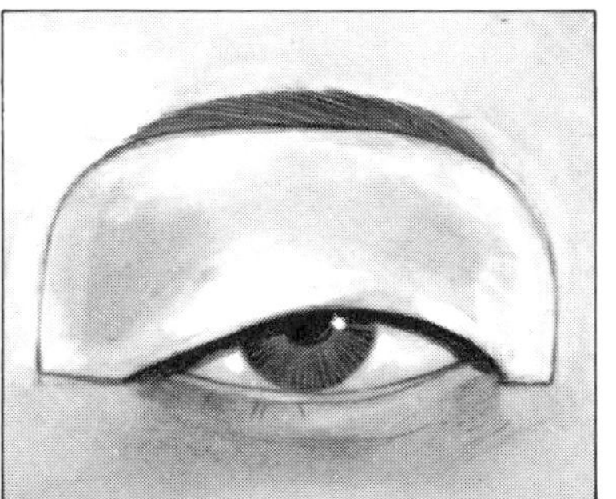

3 *Press or stick the lid into place, covering the end of each eyebrow*

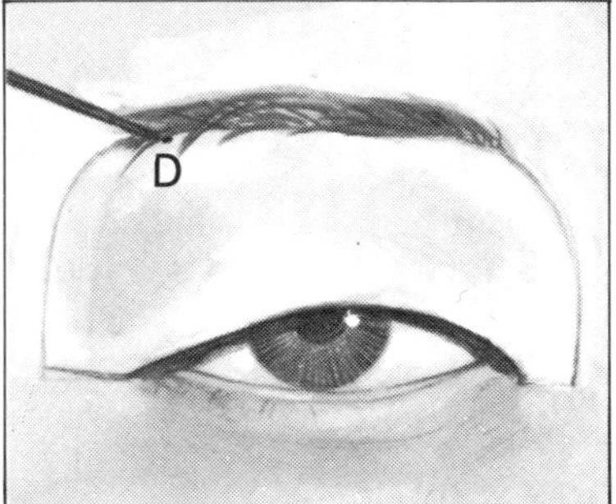

4 *Using the end of a tail comb, release eyebrow hairs at D*

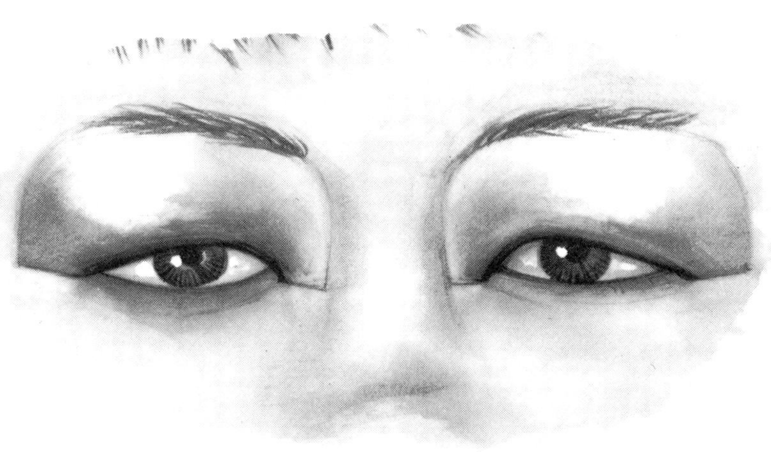

5 *Emphasize the puffy look of oriental eyelids with highlights*

Oriental makeup

Young oriental women

This step-by-step routine shows an oriental makeup using just light and shade. If artificial lids are used, apply these first (see page 133).

Block out the end of the eyebrows (see page 57), and apply a smooth even layer of cake makeup over the entire face and throat with a cosmetic sponge.

Highlight the entire orbital area with white cake makeup, using a $\frac{1}{4}$ inch (6mm), flat-ended sable brush. Carry the highlight up over the blocked-out eyebrow and down over the edge of the eye socket below the outer end of the eye.

Highlight and shade the nose to flatten and shorten it. Then sketch in eyebrows with black pencil, starting at a point low down near the nose, below the natural growth of hair. Curve the line up in a crescent shape, stopping well short of the end of the browbone.

Draw a fine black line along the edge of the top lid, as close to the roots of the lashes as possible, using a number 2 sable brush. At the outer corner of the eye, extend the line in a slightly downward direction before winging it up under the strong highlight on the browbone. Fade the top edge of the line to give the bulging effect shown.

At the inner corner of the eye, drop the line of black under the edge of the top lid, continuing it down over the corner of the eye to simulate the mongolian fold. Then darken the inside edge of the lower lid with kohl pencil to narrow the eye shape. Add a small triangle of black lining at the outer corner of the eye to blend with the upper line.

Accentuate the highlight immediately above the mongolian fold with an extra touch of white cake makeup. Paint in the mouth with an exaggerated rosebud shape, highlighting the center of the lower lip for extra fullness. Deepen shadow under the lower lip, using a brown eyebrow pencil. Now brush on cake rouge at an oblique angle over the cheekbone to accentuate the flatness of the bone structure. Finally, put on the wig and fasten it in place with pins and spirit gum.

With the face makeup complete, make up the hands and all exposed skin with a toning body makeup. The oriental hand is slim and graceful so you might add false fingernails to lengthen and slim the hand.

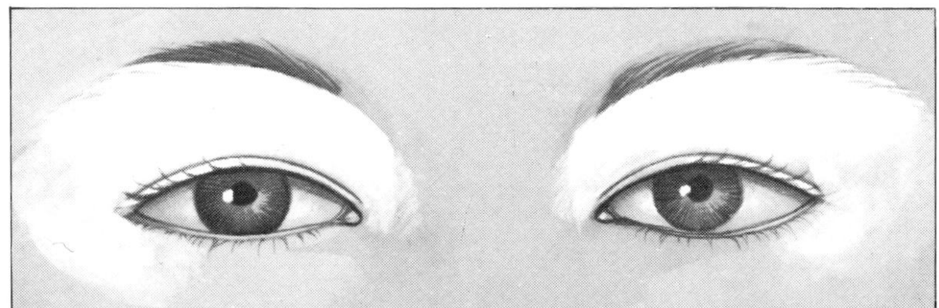

1 *Block out end of eyebrows and apply cake makeup. Apply highlight to orbital area and over blocked-out brows*

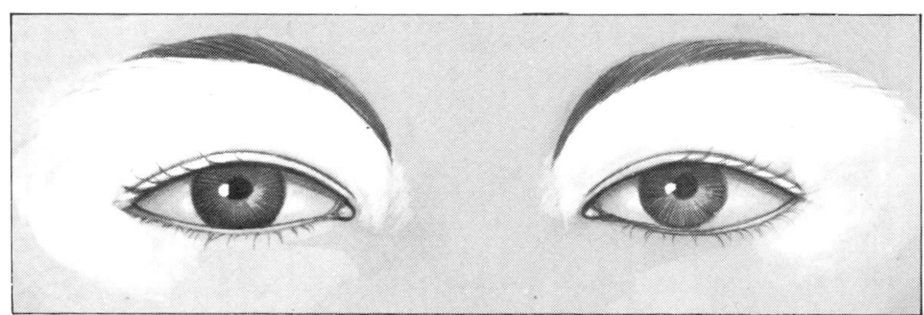

2 *Sketch in crescent-shaped eyebrows as shown here*

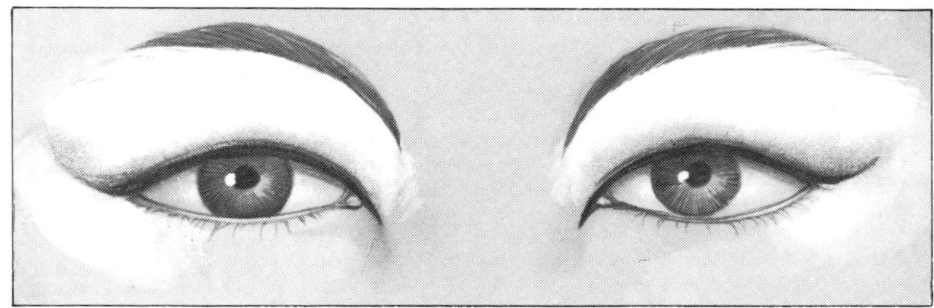

3 *Draw fine eyelines on top lid, blending them away to create the bulging shape illustrated*

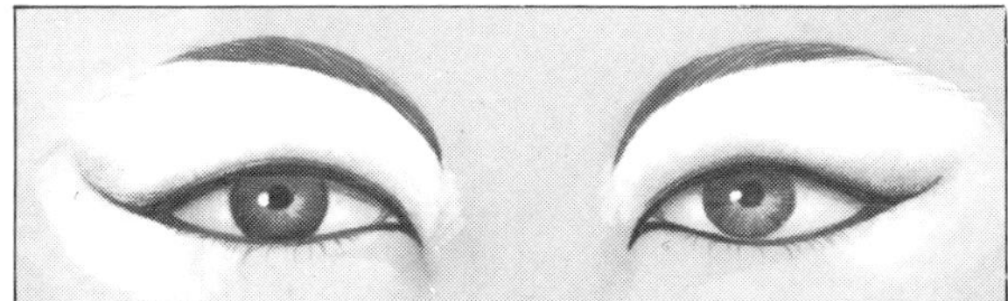

4 *Apply kohl to lower lid, as shown, to narrow the eye shape*

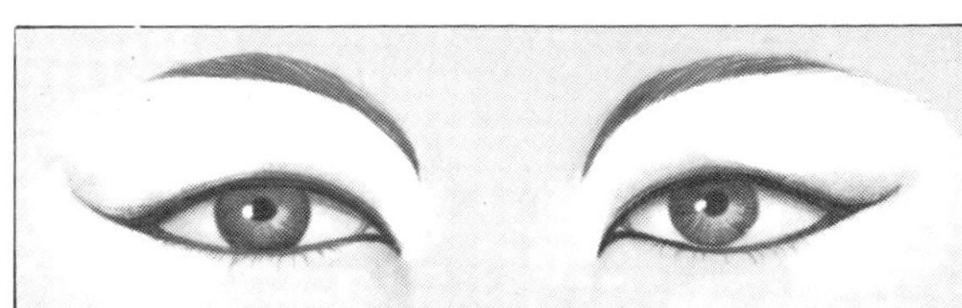

5 *Accentuate highlight above mongolian fold with white cake makeup*

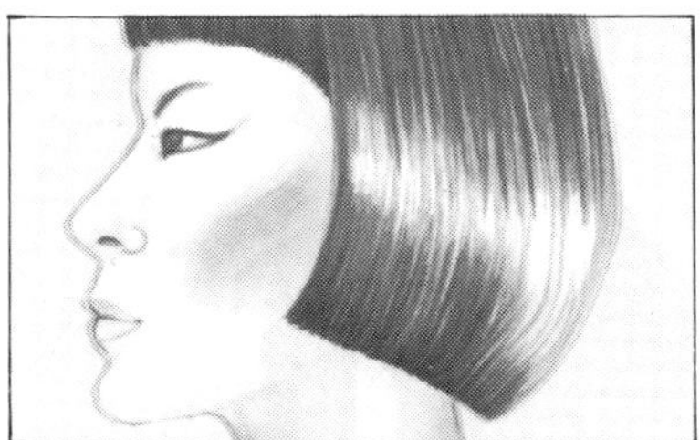

6 *Apply cake rouge at an oblique angle to flatten the bone structure*

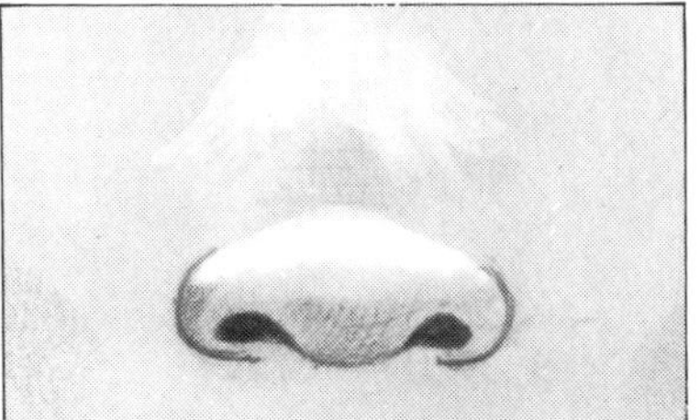

7 *Broaden and shorten the nose with highlights and shadows*

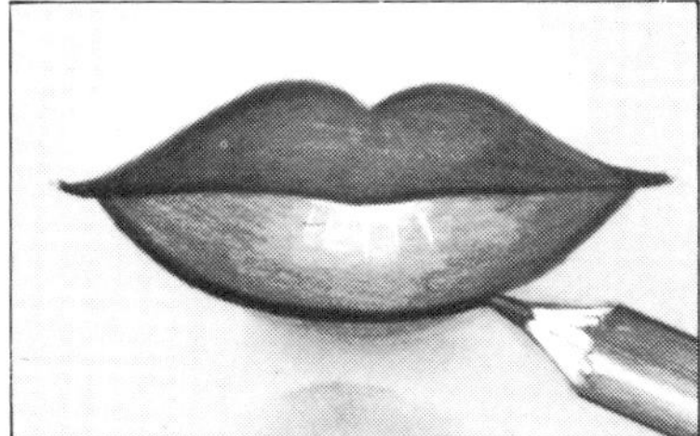

8 *Apply lip color in a full rounded shape and add shadow under lower lip*

Color guide

Foundation Mix ivory with peach or yellow groups for Chinese,and ivory with peach, olive or yellow for Japanese

Highlights White or ivory group

Shading Olive-brown or lake groups

Lips and cheeks Light or medium-red groups

Fit the wig to complete the makeup

Oriental makeup

Young oriental men

In this step-by-step routine artificial lids are used. If you do not wish to use them, follow the instructions given in the preceding makeup.

Apply the artificial oriental eyelids (see page 133), using the false lid to block out the ends of the eyebrows.

Smooth an even layer of foundation over the entire face and throat. Cake makeup can be used for a stylized look but cream-stick or grease will look more natural and also blend more easily over the false lids.

Highlight the false lids, giving emphasis to the center and the puffy overhang. Now apply a shadow along the edge of the artificial lid, extending the shadow downward at the outer end of the piece to exaggerate the puffiness of the lid. Apply a narrow highlight along the edge of the lower lid, immediately below lashes, and add a shadow below this highlight to give the illusion of puffiness to the lower lid.

Highlight and shade the nose to flatten and shorten it as much as possible, keeping the shadows at the sides of the nostrils as horizontal as possible.

Highlight the top lip to make it as long as possible. A thin strip of moistened cosmetic sponge can be inserted under the upper lip at the top of the gum to accentuate this illusion. (This will also help to give a lisping oriental intonation to the voice.)

Paint on a shorter, fuller lip shape, keeping the upper lip narrow and dark and the lower lip full and rounded. Deepen the shadow below the lower lip with brown eyebrow pencil.

Brush on dark shading rouge at an oblique angle over the back of the cheekbone to flatten the bone structure. Now you are ready to put on the wig and fasten it in place with pins and spirit gum.

Make up the hands and all exposed skin areas with body makeup to tone with the face.

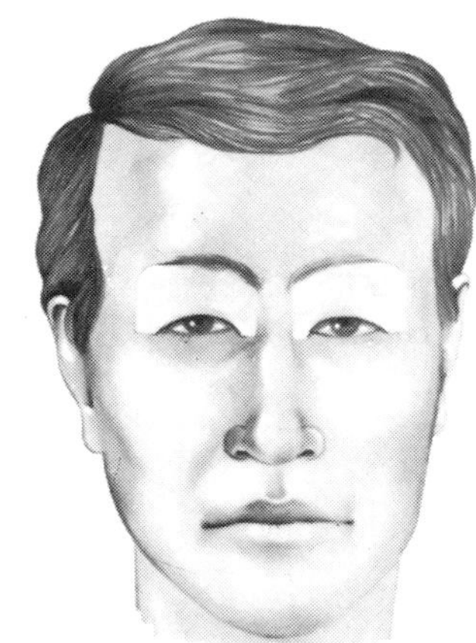

***1** Apply false eyelids and foundation*

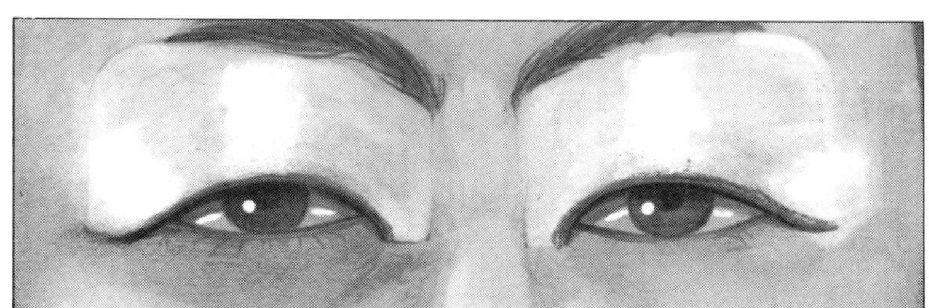

***2** Make up artificial lids in the pattern shown here*

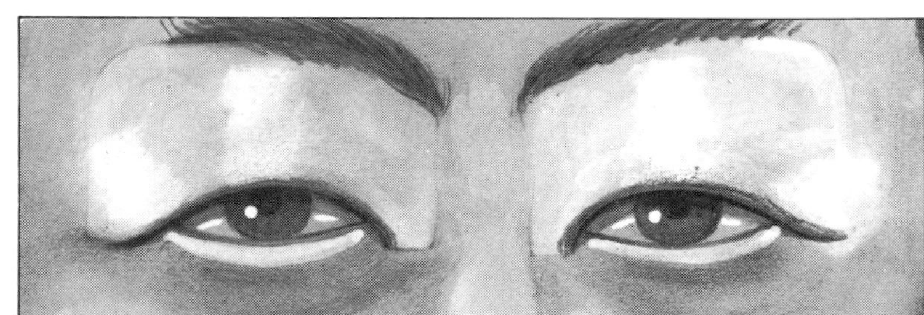

***3** Create a puffy under-eye with light and shade as shown*

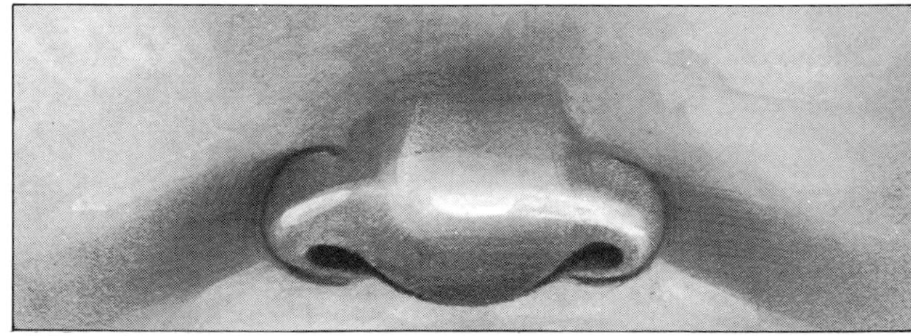

***4** Broaden and shorten the nose with highlights and shadows*

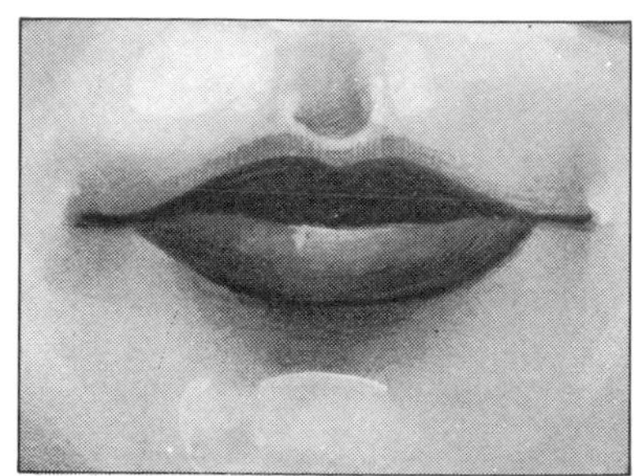

__5__ Apply lip color in the shape illustrated here and add shadow under the lower lip

Color guide

Foundation Mix ivory or olive groups with warm tan or yellow groups

Highlights White or ivory groups

Shading Olive-brown mixed with lake groups

Lips and cheeks Lake groups

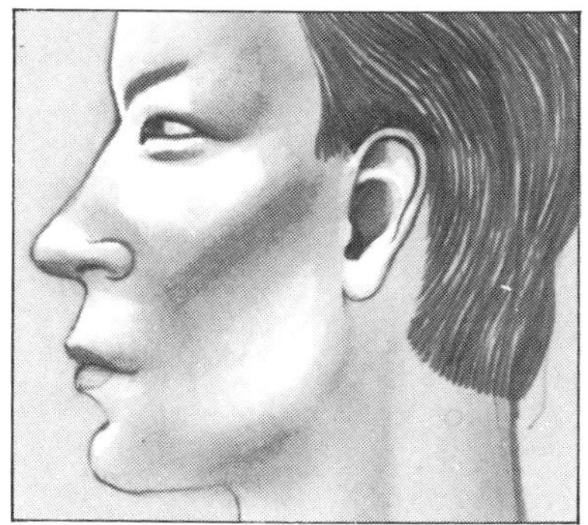

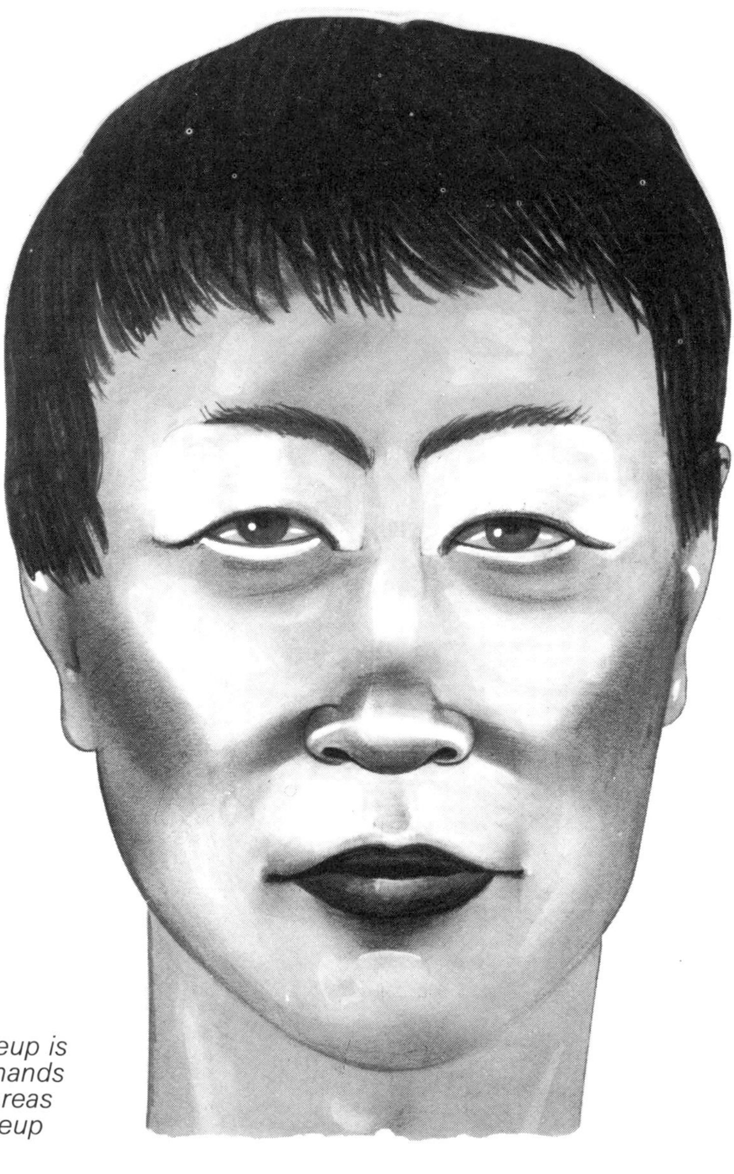

__6__ Apply shading rouge to flatten the bone structure

__7__ When the face makeup is completed, make up hands and all exposed skin areas with toning body makeup

Oriental makeup

The aging oriental

The aging oriental has an almost colorless face with very pale yellowy-white skin and thin, wispy gray hair practically blending into the skin color. Oriental women tend towards obesity while oriental men can become very thin and skeletal.

Elderly oriental men

1 *Apply false oriental eyelids (see page 133) made from latex rubber with exaggerated overhanging folds. Once these are firmly in place, the face must be made to look very pale. Drain all natural color from the skin with a very pale ivory foundation*

2 *Apply shadows and highlights to give an exaggerated skull-like appearance to the face. Set with translucent face powder. Now add a very small colorless mouth with deep wrinkles, using highlights and vertical shadows (see pages 68-69)*

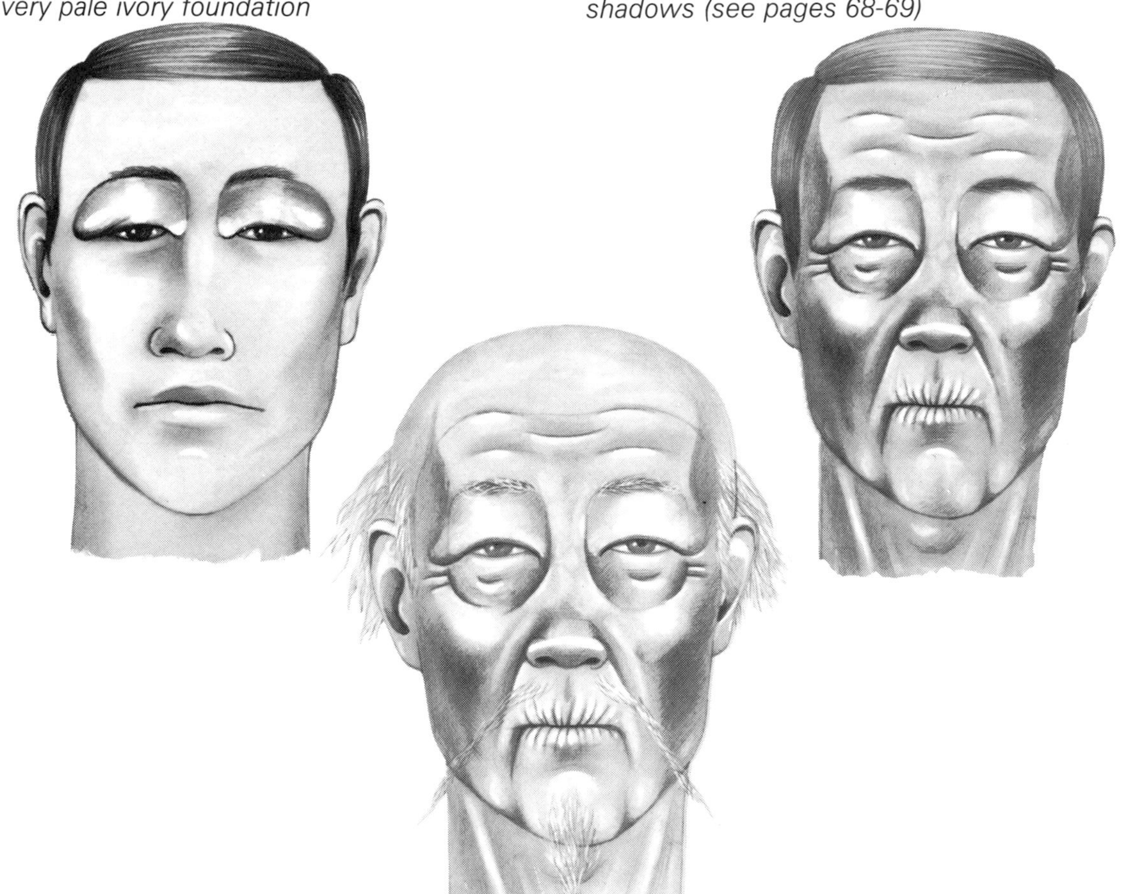

3 *Put on a bald wig with long, wispy side hair. Hide blender edge with shading at temples and exaggerated forehead lines. Apply thin wispy beard and mustache, using thin sections of straightened real crepe hair rather than wool crepe. Make up the hands to give a skeletal look to the fingers and add long fingernails (see page 100)*

Elderly oriental women

1 *Apply false oriental eyelids, made full enough to almost cover the natural eyebrow and very puffy over the eye itself (see page 133). Apply a pale ivory foundation over the entire face and throat, draining the whole area of color*

2 *Add highlights and shadows to give heavy folds and puffiness to the face. Note the fullness of the cheek pads and the heavy neck folds. Apply a very small dark mouth with exaggerated puffiness at the mouth corners*

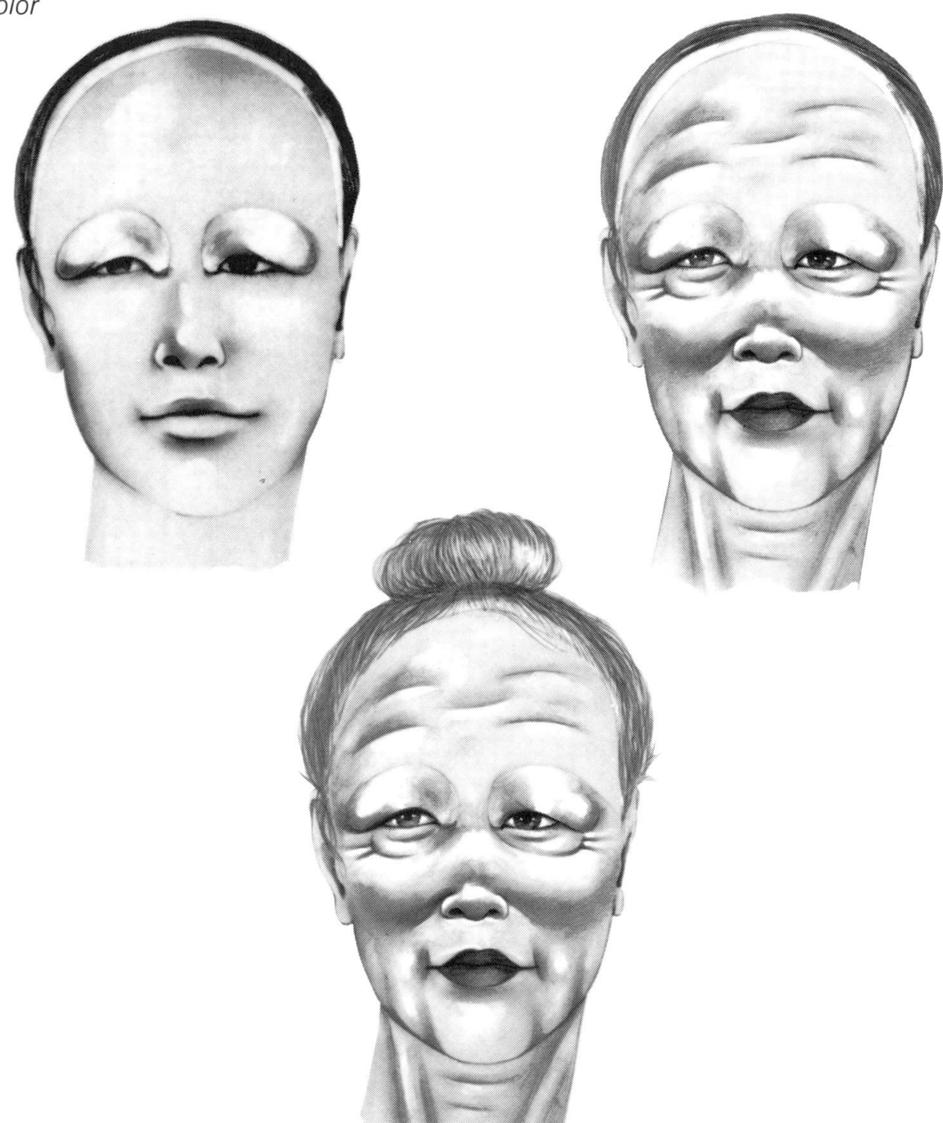

3 *Stipple broken veins under cheek pads. Then use a wig with very fine hair over a balding pate. If this type of wig is difficult to obtain, use one dressed back into a tight bun with a blender front to give height to the forehead. Make up the hands with very pale, ivory body makeup*

Asian makeup

The bone structure of the Indian and the European is similar so we need consider only skin and hair color and the shape of eyebrows and eyes,which are the most easily recognized of the Asian features.

The eyebrows are very well defined, heavy, and straight. With the aquiline nose, this gives a T-shaped frame to the deep-set, almond-shaped eyes.

The skin around the eye is much darker than the rest of the face. This gives an intense, mystical look to the eyes, heightened by the use of kajal in the eye itself. Kajal is made by mixing lamp carbon with aromatic oils and protects the eye from disease and the sun's glare.

The lips, although well shaped, are thin and dark, with a purple undertone. The skin near the mouth is dark, and Indian men have a very strong beardline. Caste marks are worn by all Hindu women except widows. Often they are just small red dots but they can be ornate and bejeweled. Men may also use caste marks. Married Bengali women redden the center parting of their hair.

Asiatic Indian hair is very dark, but is not like the intense blue-black of the oriental. The native Hindu male shaves his hair close to the scalp, leaving a single lock at the crown, while the Sikh male never cuts his hair, concealing it beneath his turban. The beard too is left uncut and the more sophisticated Sikh curls it around elastic in a tight roll close to the jaw. The skin at the edge of the hairline has the same darkening as the eye and mouth areas.

Asian men

If a turban is being worn, a wig may not be necessary but any hair showing must be darkened with spray or masque. So try on the turban or wig, then remove it to the block until the makeup is completed.

Apply a very dark olive-brown foundation in a fine film over the entire face. Then, with the same color, darken the areas around the eyes, nose, mouth and also the hairline.

Using a pale yellow-toned highlighter, emphasize the bone structure. Note the long highlight down the nose and the highlight along the top lid, which is slightly extended at the outer end. Now thoroughly powder all over, especially if using grease makeup.

Sketch in the eyebrows with black pencil, starting high above the nose with the inner ends fairly close together. Keep the shape as straight and as horizontal as possible, emphasizing the growth of hair under the browbone.

Starting right at the inner corner of the eye, strongly outline both top and bottom lids. Carry the color around the eye to meet at the outer corner, where it should be extended straight out to give as horizontal a look to the eye as possible. Then apply black mascara to the lashes.

Clearly define the mouth, adding black or dark-blue to intensify the color and outlining the lips with pencil, if needed.

Next, using a coarse stippling sponge, stipple beard and mustache area with black to emphasize the beardline.

Replace wig or turban and secure firmly in place. In some cases it may be possible to color and restyle the natural hair, in which case it should be sprayed with brilliantine dressing to impart a gloss.

Finally, make up hands and any exposed body areas.

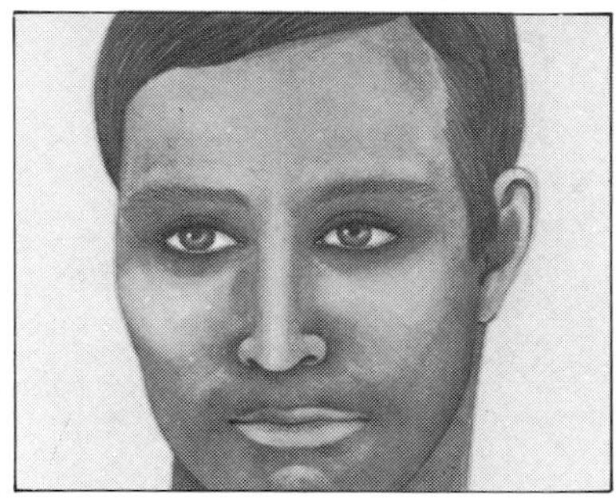

***1** Apply foundation over entire face, darkening the areas around the eyes, nose, mouth and hairline*

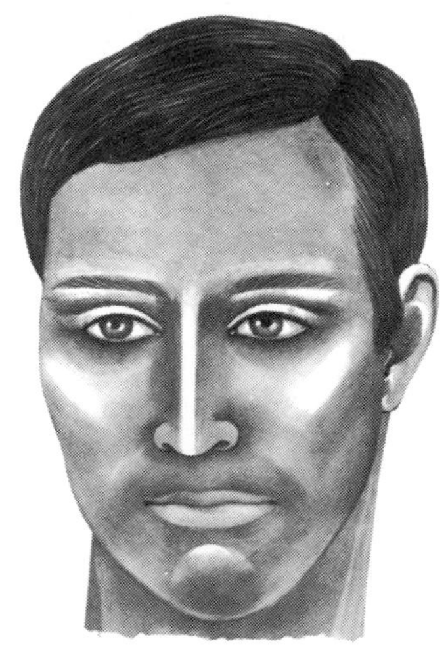

***2** Emphasize the bone structure with a yellow-toned highlighter. Note the long highlight down nose and along top lid*

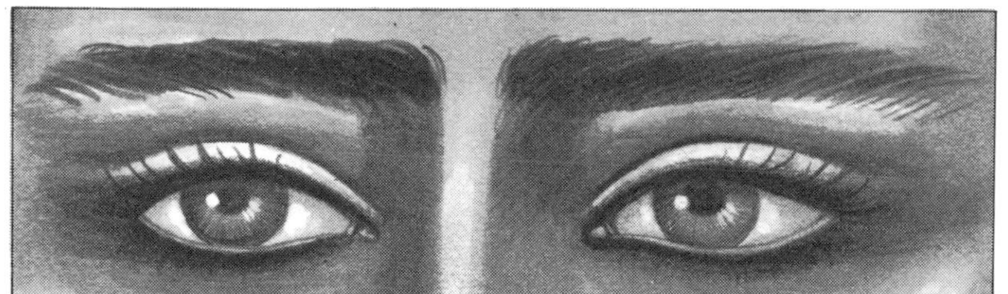

3 *Sketch in the eyebrows, keeping the shape straight and horizontal*

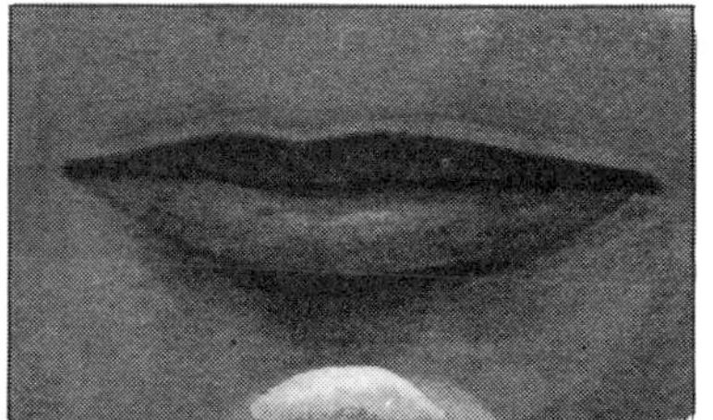

4 *Clearly define the mouth, deepening the color with black or dark blue*

Sikh men

The Asian makeup can be adapted for a Sikh man with the addition of a strong aquiline putty nose and a luxuriant beard and mustache

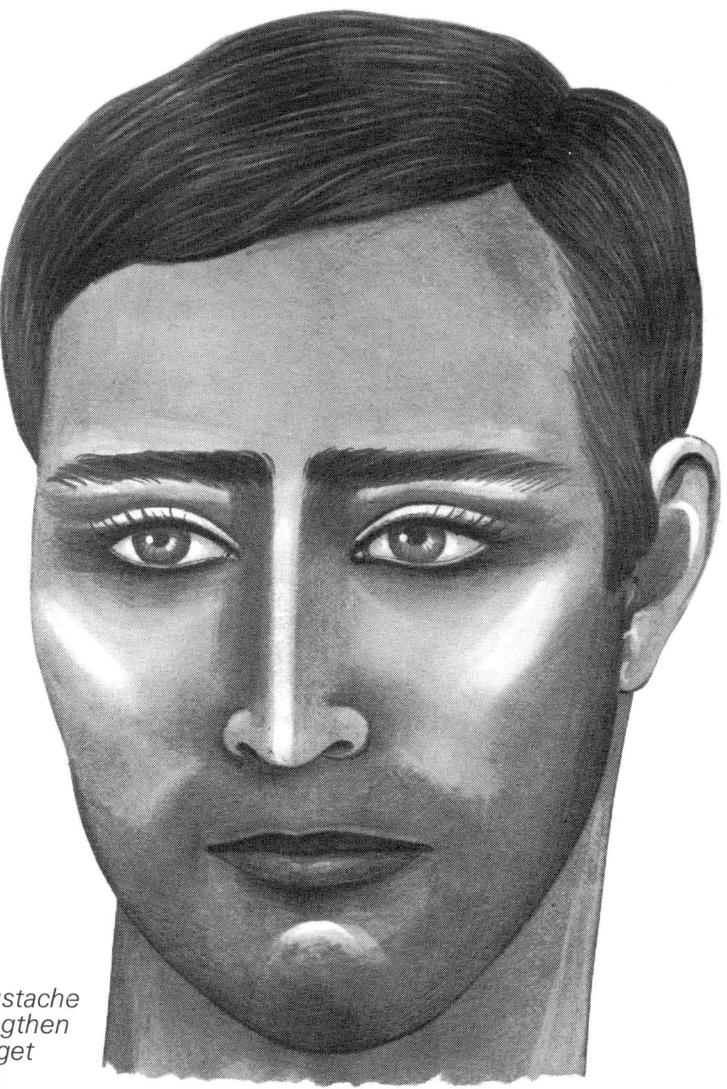

5 *Stipple beard and mustache area with black to strengthen the beardline. Don't forget hand and body makeup*

Asian makeup

Asian women

If using conventional makeup, the underlying duskiness of the asian skin is difficult to achieve without the face appearing to be "dirtied". This step-by-step routine explains how to overcome this problem and is particularly effective when the makeup is for a fair-skinned Asiatic Indian woman.

Check the wig and return it to the block until the completion of the makeup. Then apply a thin film of dark olive-brown grease or cream-stick makeup over the entire face, darkening the areas around the eye sockets, the nostrils, the sides of the mouth and along the hairline with the addition of extra foundation.

Thoroughly powder this grease foundation with translucent face powder, and apply a film of a clear golden-tan cake makeup over the face with a sponge.

Then, with a $\frac{1}{4}$ inch(6mm) brush, apply highlights to the nose, chin and cheekbones, using a lighter tone of cake makeup. Apply the same highlight color to the top eyelid, extending it out horizontally beyond the outer corner of the eye.

Outline the eye with black eyeliner, opening the lines at the outer end in the parallel shape shown. Then, starting at the inner corner of the eye, draw a contour crease line around the back of the top eyelid, extending it at the outer end, parallel with the top eyeline. Blend away the top edge upwards over the browbone.

Sketch the eyebrows in a clear outline. Follow the same horizontal pattern created by the eyelining and contour creases.

Apply a highlight along the browbone between the eyebrow and the contour crease, once more extending it horizontally out at the outer end. Also, add a touch of highlight along the top of the eyebrow.

Make up top and bottom lashes with several coats of black mascara and add kohl pencil to the inside edge of the lower lid. Extra intensity can be added to the eye makeup by applying kohl pencil to the inner edge of the top lid, underneath the lashes. This is done by rolling the top eyelid up and back with the fingertips, before applying the kohl pencil.

Outline the lips with dark-brown eyebrow pencil, keeping the top lip long and thin. Slightly darken over both lips with the pencil and fill in your chosen lip color with a number 6 filbert brush.

Shade under the cheekbone with a dark-brown shader blusher. Replace the wig and secure it with pins, grips and spirit gum.

Apply a caste mark to the center of the forehead, between the ends of the brows. The blunt end of a grease liner gives the ideal shape. Failing that, the blunt end of a pencil or the head of a large nail rubbed with color both make excellent substitutes. Finally, make up hands and all exposed areas of skin.

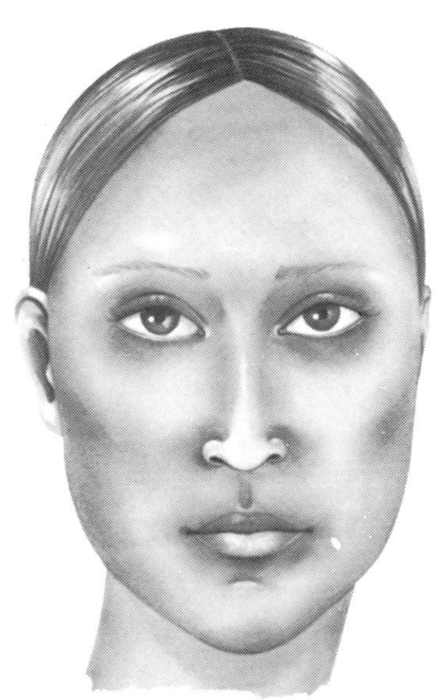

__1__ Apply dark olive-brown grease or cream-stick makeup over entire face, darkening the areas around the eyes, nostrils, mouth and hairline. Set with powder

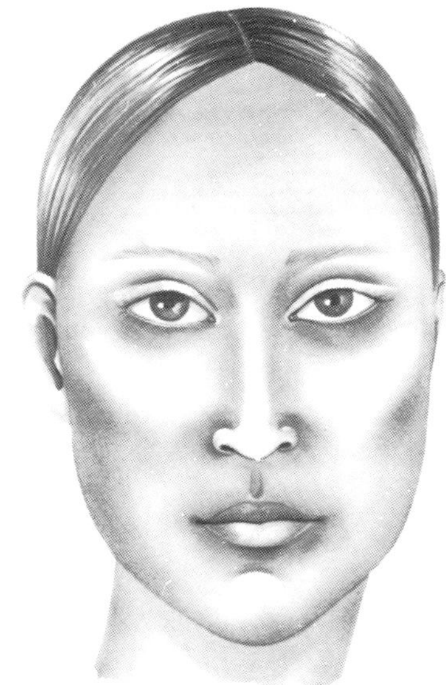

__2__ Sponge a thin film of a clear, golden cake makeup over the entire face. Apply highlights to the nose, chin, cheekbones and to the top eyelids, using a lighter tone of cake makeup

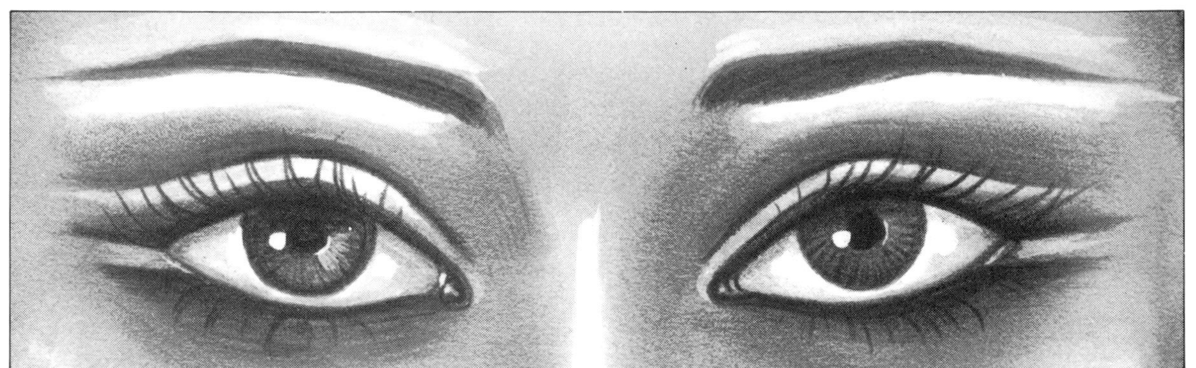

3 *Make up the eyes with highlights, contour creases, eyelines and eyebrows all following the horizontal pattern shown here. Apply kohl to the inside of the eyelids and generously mascara the lashes*

4 *After finishing the lip makeup and cheek shading, a red caste mark completes the makeup for an Asiatic woman*

Afro-Caribbean makeup

There are many types of Afro-Caribbean men and women with varying bone structure, coloring and hair formation. But it is generally accepted that most have thick prominent lips, flat broad noses, low foreheads and tight, black curly hair.

When a caucasian performer is called upon to play a black role, it is not necessary to adapt every one of these characteristics — this would probably be impracticable, anyway. Therefore the actor's face should be very carefully studied to discover which features can most easily be changed.

The first thing to avoid is making the skin too black since this will prevent you from effectively broadening and flattening the features with shading. Afro-Caribbean makeup can be applied by any of the methods described earlier but there is one very serious drawback; if a very dark base color is highlighted, the highlight tends to look chalky and dead and to sit on the surface — just as light colors do when applied to a naturally dark skin.

Secondly, do not be tempted to use unnecessary false pieces (such as noses and lips) as these tend to inhibit the movement of the features and the character may easily be lost behind the makeup.

If you study an Afro-Caribbean complexion, you will see that the natural highlights have a pale, and almost translucent appearance. This effect can be simulated with makeup, and the particular technique described below was created for Sir Laurence Olivier in the role of Othello at the National Theatre in London.

First apply the cake makeup with a cosmetic sponge that has been moistened with a transparent, liquid body makeup instead of water. These transparent liquid makeups can be removed from the skin only with soap and water, so the dark makeup cannot be accidentally rubbed off to reveal the white actor beneath the surface!

However, it is possible to rub away the cake makeup with a cotton pad moistened with the body tint only. This process removes the cake makeup but leaves behind the lighter, transparent body tint.

If a stronger lighter highlight is required, simply use a pad of cotton moistened with water, which will also remove some of the tint.

Shadows can be applied to this type of makeup by painting them on with black cake makeup. Use a sable brush that has been moistened with the transparent body makeup.

The body can also be made up with this combination of cake and transparent body makeup. When it is dry, the surface can be polished to a high sheen, using the palms of the hands or, better still, a piece of silk chiffon.

If you can wear rubber gloves when applying this makeup, you will avoid staining the fingertips and nails.

One popular misconception about Afro-Caribbeans is that they have very large shining whites to their eyes. In fact, generally speaking, Afro-Caribbeans have quite small eyes and the whites are often discolored. The eyes just look large and white in contrast to the dark skin. Do not, therefore, make the mistake of applying a white line along the lower edge of the eyelid unless the makeup is for a Black and White Minstrel Show. A much more natural effect can be achieved by lining the inside edge of the lid with brown kohl pencil.

Afro-Caribbean hair is usually short and close to the head so make sure that wigs do not have too much hair. The actor's hair must be dressed as flat as possible or the top of the head will look too bulky. (This may be difficult for a woman with very long hair so, in these instances, try an Afro-style wig instead.)

Sir Laurence Olivier as Othello

Afro-Caribbean makeup

Young Afro-Caribbean men

Try on the wig, keeping the hairline as low on the forehead as possible and paying particular attention to fit so that all natural hair is concealed. If any does inadvertently show, it must be darkened with spray or black masque. Remove wig to block until makeup is completed.

Apply your chosen cake makeup with transparent body makeup, using the technique on page 144. Then highlight the base color by rubbing away the cake makeup with body tint or water on a small cotton ball. Check width of highlight on nose and chin and the strong highlights on the browbone, cheekbones and jawline.

Apply black pancake on a $\frac{1}{4}$ inch (6mm) sable brush, moistened with body tint, to shade the face very strongly. Now draw on strong eyebrows with black pencil, rubbing through the drawn-on shape with your fingertip to give a blurred outline.

Heavily outline the eyes with black pencil or lining color, blending away the edges as shown. Apply kohl pencil on to the inside edge of the lower lid. Then make up top lashes with black mascara or masque.

Outline the lips with black eyebrow pencil, enlarging the shape as shown. Darken both lips with the pencil, making the top lip quite dark. Then cover the mouth with your cake makeup. Now, using an $\frac{1}{8}$ inch (3mm) sable brush, draw a line of white lining color around the enlarged lip shape as shown, and intensify the shadow under the lower lip with a black pencil.

Replace the wig and fasten with spirit gum. Your makeup is nearly ready; all that remains is to broaden the nostrils. Nose plugs are best added after the rest of the makeup has been completed.

To make these, first cut the tips from two pacifiers or baby's bottle teats (see page 77) and blacken the inside with eyebrow pencil. Now insert these into the nostrils with the little fingertip.

Conceal the edge with black eyebrow pencil, at the same time carrying the color out over the nostril edge to give maximum emphasis to the nostril opening.

Make up the hands and all exposed body areas with the cake and body-tint combination, removing cake color from the palms of the hands and soles of the feet (if seen) with a cotton ball moistened with the appropriate tint or water.

If a beard or mustache is required, it should be remembered that facial hair on an Afro-Caribbean is usually very sparse and lies close to the skin. The best method of application is as follows:

First cut up a quantity of black crepe hair, straight from the untreated braid so that it is as curly as possible and about $\frac{1}{8}$ inch (3mm) in length.

Paint the exact shape you require for both beard and mustache on to the skin with spirit gum and allow it to become slightly tacky.

Pick up small clumps of the crepe hair with your fingertips and press it into the gummed pattern with little stippling pats. Note how the shape of the mustache makes the top lip recede and so increases the apparent fullness of the mouth.

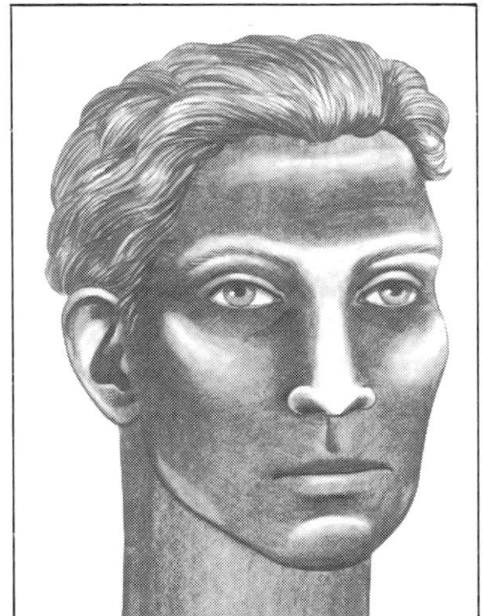

***1** Apply base makeup. Then highlight by rubbing away the color*

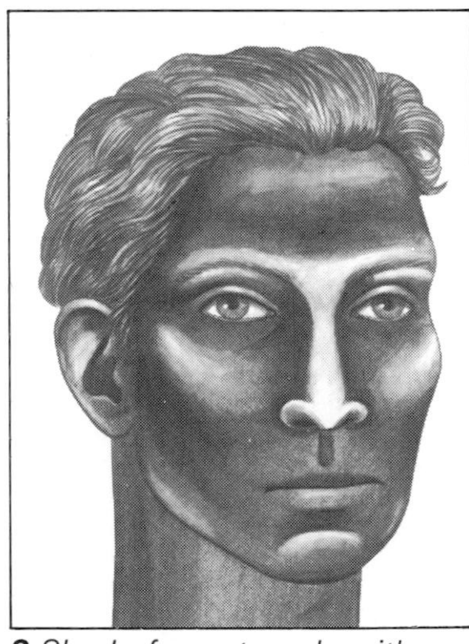

***2** Shade face strongly with black pancake applied with body tint*

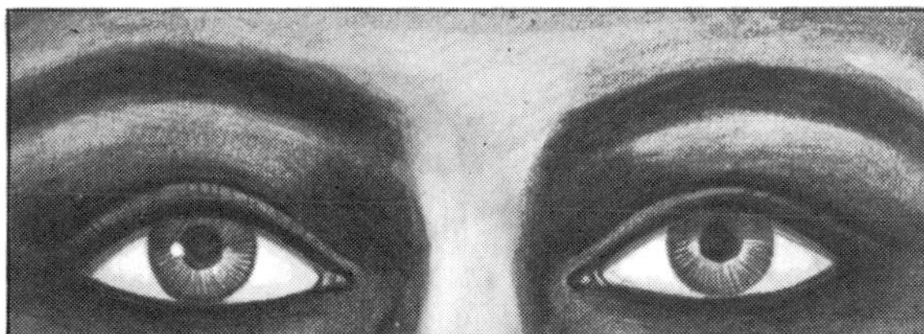

3 *Darken eyebrows and apply eye makeup as described in text*

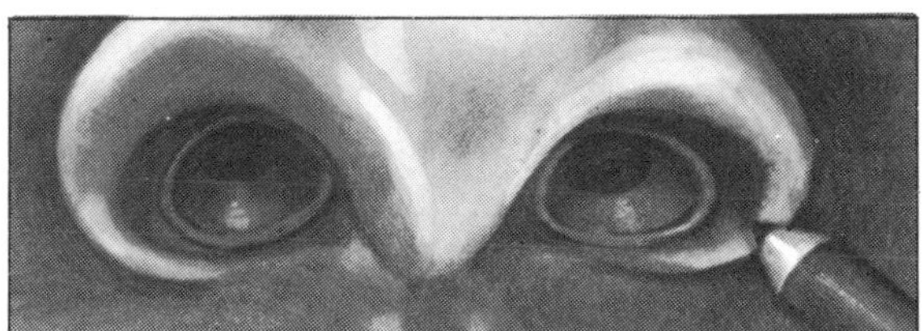

4 *Widen nostrils with nose plugs and with black makeup*

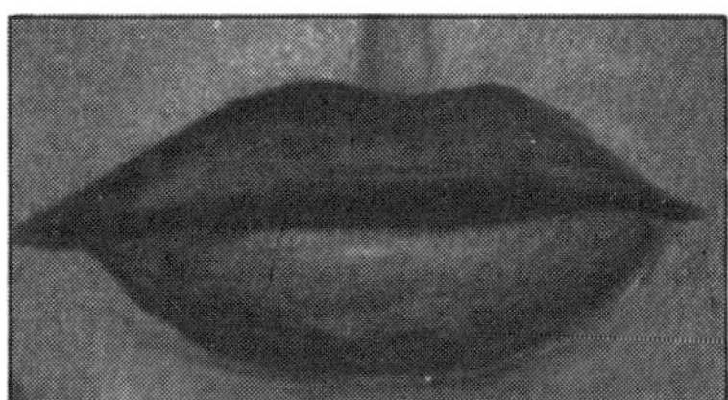

5 *Apply lip makeup to enlarge the mouth, using the method described in the text*

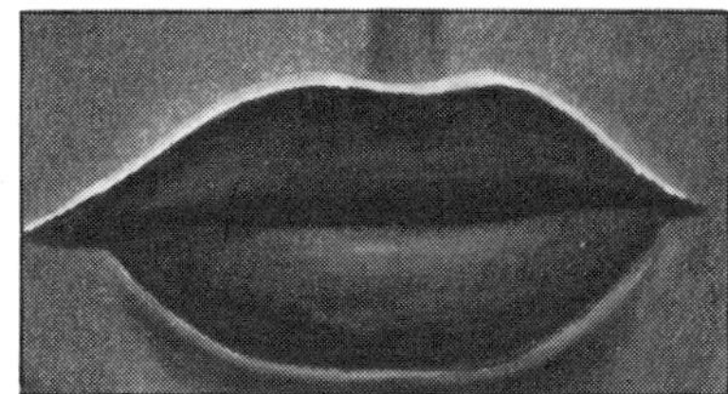

6 *Sponge cake makeup over new mouth shape, and highlight and shade as shown*

Color guide

Foundation Dark-brown groups applied with dark body tint

Lips Lake groups if warmer color is needed

Afro-Caribbean makeup

Young Afro-Caribbean women

First try on the wig, making sure the hair is fairly low (to shorten the forehead). Remove to the wig block. Then apply cake makeup with transparent body tint, taking care to take the color around the back of the neck, behind the ears and well beyond the wig line. The inside of the ears can be colored, using a sable brush. Cover the lips with foundation. Now, using a cotton ball moistened with transparent body tint, rub away cake makeup from the areas to be highlighted.

Apply shading with black cake and tint. Widen the nose by drawing in the nostril line about $\frac{1}{8}$ inch (3mm) away from the natural crease. Keep the shadows on the sides of the nose well apart. Shade the chin to give it maximum width and darken the skin around the eye. Keep the shadows in the cheek hollows high and well to the back of the face to add width and heighten the cheekbones.

Sketch in the brows quite strongly, and then shade in contour creases at the back of the top lids, fading the color up over the browbone. Outline the eyes strongly with black pencil or eyeliner, blending away the edges to give a softer look. Apply black mascara to top and bottom lashes and add false lashes, if required. Then apply kohl pencil to the inside edge of the lower lid.

Using black pencil, blacken inside nostrils. Carry the color out over the edge of the openings so they seem larger.

With black pencil, draw an outline around the lips to enlarge their shape, working a little pencil over the top lip. Now apply your lip color over this new shape. Add a touch of highlight to the center of the lower lip to increase its fullness. With an $\frac{1}{8}$ inch (3mm) sable brush draw a line of white liner above the outline of the top lip. Then carefully blend it upwards away from the lips. Now intensify the shadow under the bottom lip, using black eyebrow pencil.

Replace the wig and fasten it in place with pins and spirit gum. Lastly, make up the hands and any other exposed areas of flesh, using the same combination of cake and body tint as used on the face. Then, using a piece of cotton moistened with tint, rub away the cake from the palms of the hands so that they are a pinky brown.

Color guide

Foundation For light coloring use warm-tan groups or olive-brown groups, applied with medium-dark body tint. For very dark coloring use dark-brown groups applied with dark body tint

Cheeks Dark-red or lake groups

Lips Dark-red or lake groups or lipstick of choice

Portraying age

Since the application techniques just described are designed to give maximum depth and gloss to the skin tones, they are not suitable when a makeup is required to simulate aging skin. The best bases for this type of makeup are either cream-stick or greasepaint. Many different skin tones have to be considered when a black performer has to be aged, but when a caucasian actor is portraying an aging Afro-Caribbean character, these subtleties do not need to be taken into consideration. However, care needs to be taken with the choice of base color, because a warm dark base is very difficult to age. The best colors are very dark olive-browns, with yellow undertones rather than red.

Once the correct base color has been chosen, the makeup is very similar to aging a white character — except that each shadow and highlight must broaden and flatten the face, as well as suggesting age. Fortunately this sort of character is not often encountered, and hopefully, a more mature actor or actress will be cast in the role. You are then left only with the problem of applying an Afro-Caribbean makeup, using good graying wigs, with gray crepe for facial hair. Nose plugs (for both male and female performers) will probably be needed because, as the Afro-Caribbean ages, so the features often coarsen and broaden.

An aged Afro-Caribbean man

An aged Afro-Caribbean woman

Arabian Men

The predominant race in the Middle East is the Arab. Arabian characters are frequently found in the theater, particularly in musicals, so the makeup shown here is deliberately flamboyant.

The conventional stage image of the Arab sheik is hawk-nosed, lean-faced and usually bearded and mustached, but there are, of course, many other types of Arab. The makeup described can easily be adapted by changing the shape of the beard, the nose, or the eyebrow — to suit the particular part being played.

Most of the Arabian characters in musicals wear national costume and their hair is usually covered by a turban or head-dress — so wigs are not always necessary.

In straight plays, the Arab is very often portrayed as a westernized character. In these cases the hair should be dark and wavy, and heavily brilliantined to give it a suitably slicked-down oily appearance.

For an Arabian sheik makeup, you will need to apply a false nose, using either nose putty or a latex piece (see pages 72-75).

Next, using a $\frac{1}{4}$ inch (6mm) brush, apply shading to slim the face and strongly accentuate the bone structure. Highlight the shadows very strongly and sharply. Clearly emphasize the cheekbones and browbones, and use a strong highlight on the top lid.

Sketch on the eyebrows with a black pencil. (The shape shown here will add to the hawklike appearance of the face.)

Now outline the eyes with black liner or eye pencil. Use a downward extension of the lines in the inner corners and a strong, upward winging shape at the outer corner, again emphasizing the hawklike look.

Draw in a contour crease with liner or pencil, blending away the top edge in an outward winging pattern. Fair lashes should now have mascara applied to them.

Strongly define the mouth with dark-lake liner. Deepen the lips with black or dark blue.

Last but not least, apply the beard and mustache. The shape illustrated is yet another hawkish detail but there are many variations.

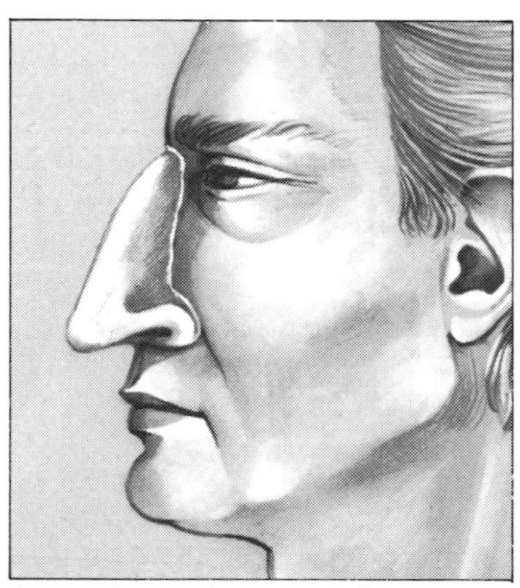

1 *Apply a false nose for a hawklike appearance*

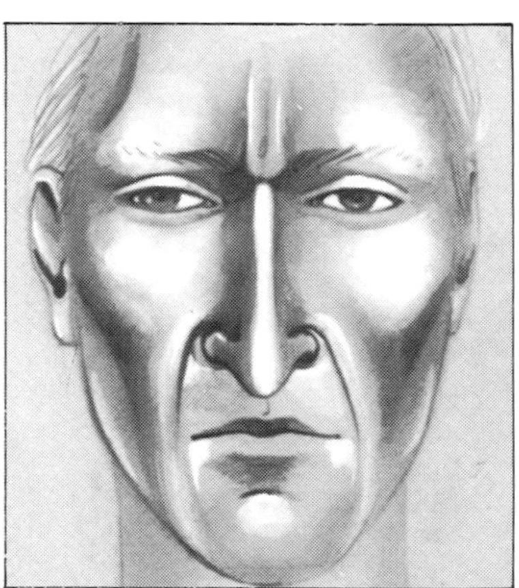

2 *Accentuate bone structure with shadows and highlights*

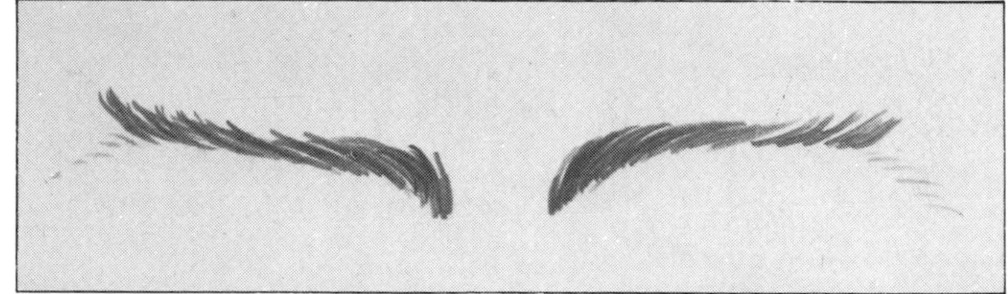

3 *Boldly sketch on eyebrows with a black pencil*

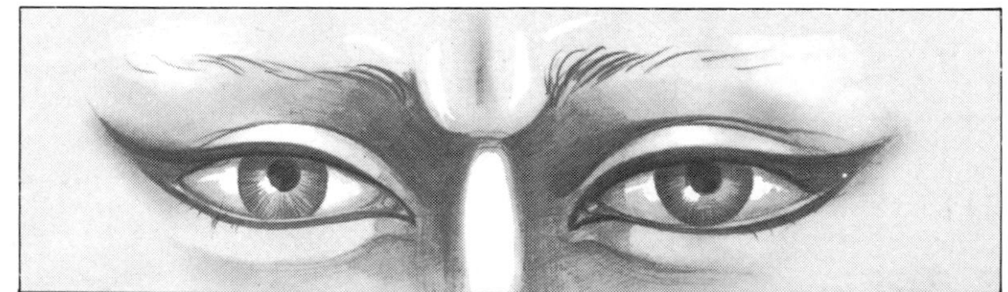

4 *Outline the eyes into a strong upward-winging shape*

5 *Draw in contour crease and darken lashes with mascara*

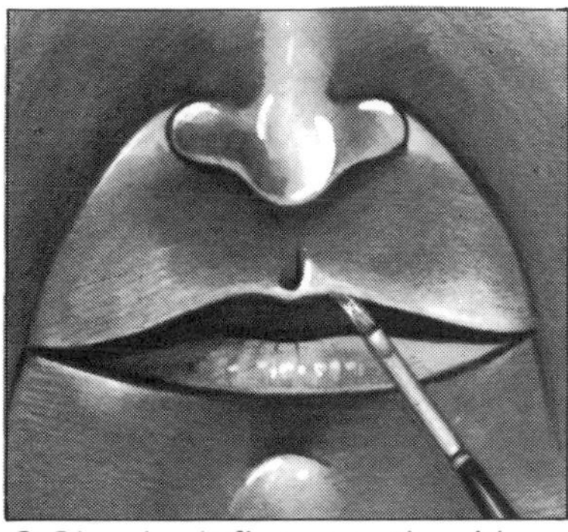

6 *Clearly define mouth with liner and darken lips*

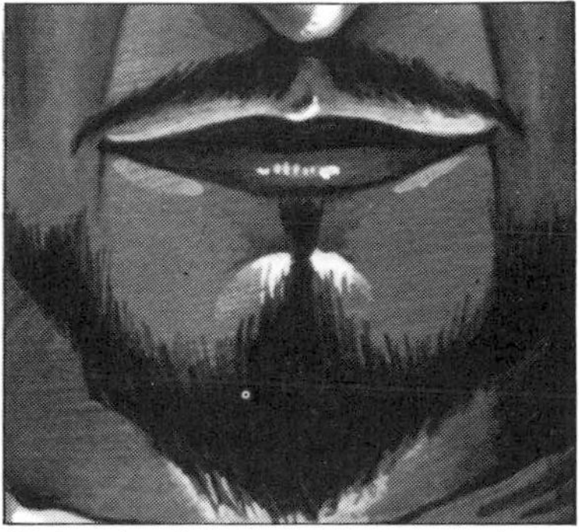

7 *Apply the mustache and beard (see pages 90-95)*

An Egyptian Pharaoh

This makeup can be adapted for an Egyptian Pharaoh by applying the eye makeup shown here, leaving the chin clean-shaven and adding an obviously false beard.

Harem girl

True Middle-Eastern women are seldom found in the theater, and if they are, their faces are hidden by the all-concealing yashmak. To accompany the very theatrical sheik, however, there is that glorious theatrical invention of the glamorous slave or harem girl. This character, like the alluring leading lady, has a totally artificial face, and the actress or makeup artist need have no inhibitions about what may be used to achieve the end result. Glitter, jewels, outrageously false lashes, gold and silver makeup can all be added — so long as the result is beautiful, glamorous, and very seductive.

Since slaves were captured from every part of the world known to their captors, they can be of any color or race, and the more exotic and mysterious they look, the better. Skin color is of no matter, so long as it is flattering. The slaves can be fair like the Persian women who bleached their skins and stayed out of the sun; they can be beautifully tanned, or dark and bronzed like the Amazons, or oriental, or black.

If the women who play this type of part are dancers, the makeup can be very balletic, giving scope for elaborate and exotic eye makeup.

The winged-up fly-away shape shown on this chart looks very exotic and attractive but it must be done clearly and cleanly.

Before starting the makeup, the end of the natural brows must either be plucked or blocked out to allow the eye makeup to be swept up and out towards the temples. You can use any colors you choose for the eyes, so long as they are strong and clean. Iridescent and metallic shadows are particularly good, especially if the costume is very glittery or shiny.

Note the very strong angle of shading and highlighting on the cheekbones, with the eyelines, eyebrows and eyeshadow all following the same angle upward and outward toward the temples.

The lips should be very full and sensuously curved, using strong light colors with plenty of lip gloss.

Slave-girl costumes are usually very brief, flimsy and revealing, so good body makeup is essential. If the show is to have a long run, it is often worth while using a sun-bed to achieve a good strong tan and so obviate the need for nightly body makeup. But if makeup has to be used, cake or pigmented, liquid body-makeup is better than the transparent type of tints. These give a smoother and more glamorous finish to the skin. Gleaming body powder can also look very effective, as can the addition of body gels containing glitter.

Jewels and glitter dust can be applied to the face, using either spirit gum or liquid latex adhesive. The best type of jewels are those that have a flat back so that they will adhere easily to the skin. Apply spirit gum to both the jewel and the skin and allow it to become tacky before pressing the jewel into place.

To apply glitter to the skin, paint spirit gum or latex adhesive over the required area, allow it to become slightly tacky, and then pick up the glitter on an old brush. Lightly press the glitter into place.

If you use latex it can easily be removed by lifting an edge of the gum away from the skin and peeling it off. Spirit gum, however, must be dissolved with solvent and then gently massaged away with a facial tissue. Take great care not to let the glitter scratch the skin. Also be very careful not to get the solvent into the eye — the best way to do this is for the actress to lean well forward, putting the head down so that the brow-bone is below the eye, then carefully use the solvent.

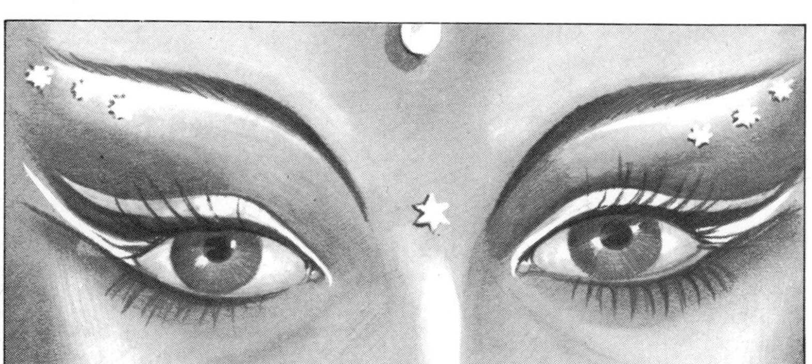

This shows the use of jewels on an exotic eye makeup. Glitter dust can be used instead of individual stones if preferred

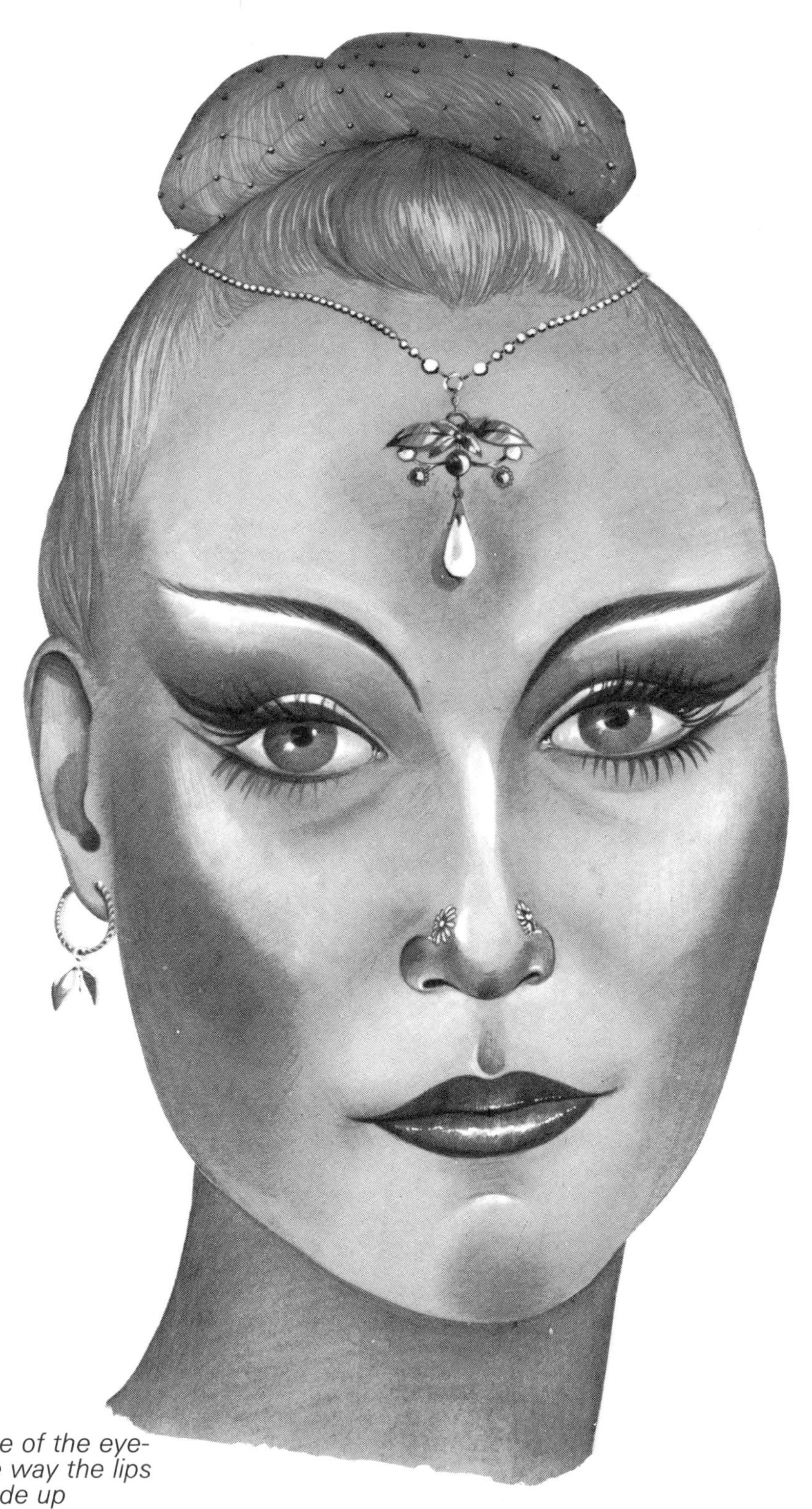

Note the shape of the eyebrows and the way the lips have been made up

Makeup for Restoration comedy

As a general rule, historical periods in the theater do not call for a change in makeup style as such, merely for a change of hairstyle and costume. There is, however, one very important exception to the rule — and this is the Restoration period.

During this time, makeup was worn by both men and women from many different walks of life, and the amount and style of makeup clearly denoted social standing. Since there are a very large number of plays and operas which were written during or about this period, and these are constantly being performed, it is very important to have a good understanding of the makeups needed.

Young country girls and boys did not use makeup so these characters need no more than to look healthy and natural.

Women in towns, from both the upper and lower classes, wore makeup and made no attempt to conceal the fact. Dark complexions were considered common so skins were whitened with rice powder, chalk or sinister washes made from white lead or zinc oxide.

Cheeks were heavily rouged. Ladies of delicacy and breeding used rosy pinks. Lower-class women tended to use strong ugly reds, as did older women struggling to retain their youth.

Eyebrows were often darkened with carbon sticks and colored eyeshadow was used by the upper classes.

Many people during this period suffered from smallpox (which was then raging through Europe) or the disfiguring effects of venereal disease, so men also wore heavy concoctions of lead and white zinc oxide to cover the scars, and the more dandified they were, the heavier the makeup became. But, in any case, elegant men of fashion all wore flesh-colored powder and a touch of rouge on cheeks and lips.

Patches were worn by both sexes, some for pure ornamentation, some to hide spots and pimples. Where they were placed on the face often had some significance, either sexual or political, for the Whigs patched to the right and the Tories patched to the left. The patches were made variously from velvet, silk or even black paper and were gummed to the face with mastic.

Wigs were used extensively, particularly by men who wore them over closely shaved heads. Styles varied from the very simple type worn by the working classes to the exaggerated extravagances of the Restoration fop.

Restoration fop

Makeup for the Restoration fop in the theater can be approached in many ways; from the rather genteel, slightly effeminate look to the clown-like, pantomime-dame type of face. Which of these you use must be determined by the style of the production, the play and the actual character.

However, they should all look as though they are using cosmetics and have spent a long time in front of a mirror caring for their appearance.

The over-madeup look can be achieved in several ways. A most effective method is to use a heavy application of a pale-pink cake foundation and stop the application short at the jawline — to give the face a mask-like look.

Arched eyebrows and an exaggeratedly tip-tilted nose can all add to the required effect. To arch the brows, block out the natural browline (see page 57) and boldly draw in the new browline with black pencil or liner. Latex or putty noses should be applied before putting on the foundation.

The eyelids can be shaded with colored shadow, the eyes boldly outlined with black liner and the lashes heavily mascared.

The lips should always be obviously made up, with the shape suiting the character. For a soft effeminate look, use clear bright-red colors painted into a cupid's bow. For a more sardonic cruel character, the lips can be painted into a large sneering shape, using strong dark-red colors.

The cheeks should be obviously rouged with bright colors; soft and pretty for the effeminate types, strongly scarlet for the more evil characters.

Patches can be cut from black flocked paper and stuck on with spirit gum or simply drawn on with black eyebrow pencil.

Hands and other exposed body areas can be made up, if needed, but sometimes it is effective to leave the hands unmadeup in order to accentuate the over-madeup face.

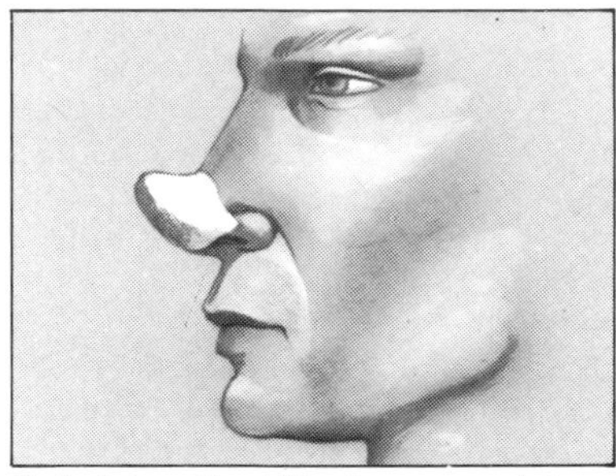

1 *A false tip-tilted nose adds to the comic effect*

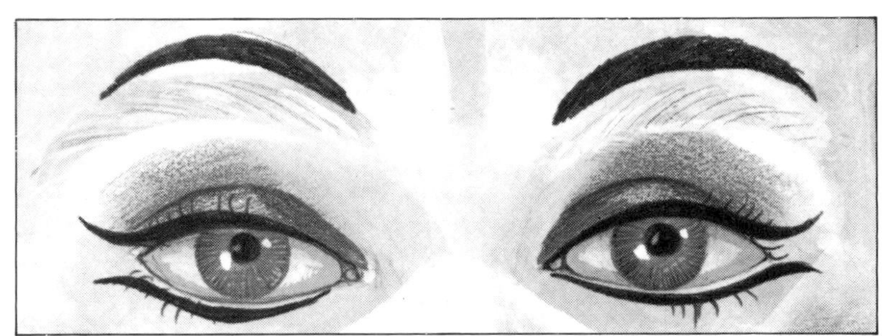

2 *Bold black eyeliner and arched brows, with mascara and clear shadow, give an obvious madeup appearance*

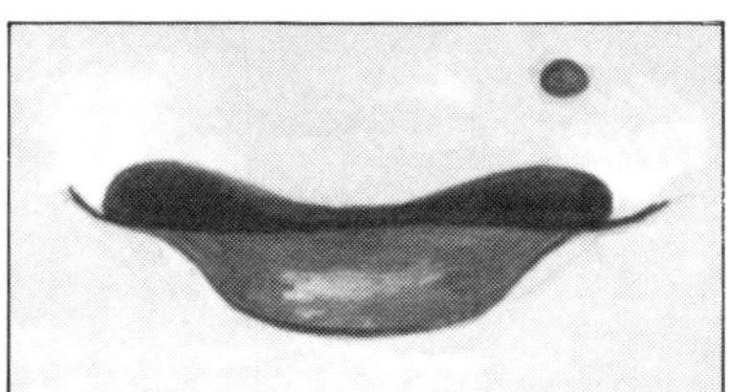

3 *This sneeringly shaped mouth can be used for a sardonic cruel character*

4 *A wig and patch complete the foppish makeup, with the masklike foundation stopping at the jawline to emphasize the over-madeup appearance*

Makeup for Restoration comedy

Elegant and sophisticated women

In Restoration times, sophisticated women wore heavy and obvious makeup, which by today's standards would be thought rather crude. When making up these characters in a modern production, there is a tendency to make them rather more subdued and attractive, but it is still very important to retain the appearance of an obvious makeup.

Apply a very pale pink-toned foundation, using either cream-stick or cake until an absolutely flawless finish has been achieved. If using cream-stick foundation, powder thoroughly. Use a very pale or white pigmented powder, rather than a translucent one, to give a porcelain finish to the makeup.

Delicately sketch in the brows, using very dark-brown or black eyebrow pencil. Keep the arch high and gracefully curved.

Highlight the top lid with white liner or cake makeup. If white liner is used, powder with white face powder. Depending on the finished look required, this highlight can be left white or very lightly colored with a pale-blue or lilac powder shadow.

Draw in the contour crease, keeping the shape high and well rounded to give a prominent hooded look to the lid.

Very finely outline the eyes. The line on the top lid should be kept very thin and as close to the roots of the lashes as possible. The lower line should be widest in the middle to give the eye a wide and round appearance. Mascara both the top and the bottom lashes.

Paint on a generous and well-curved mouth, using bright clear reds or strong clear pinks, depending on the costume color. Then brush on powder rouge to tone with lip color, adding color to achieve a good, strong rouged appearance. Put on the wig and fasten it in place. Depending on the character, this can look like natural hair dressed in the period style or, alternatively, it can be an elaborately dressed artificial wig in silver, gray or white.

Make up hands and all exposed skin areas with cake or pigmented, liquid body-makeup,

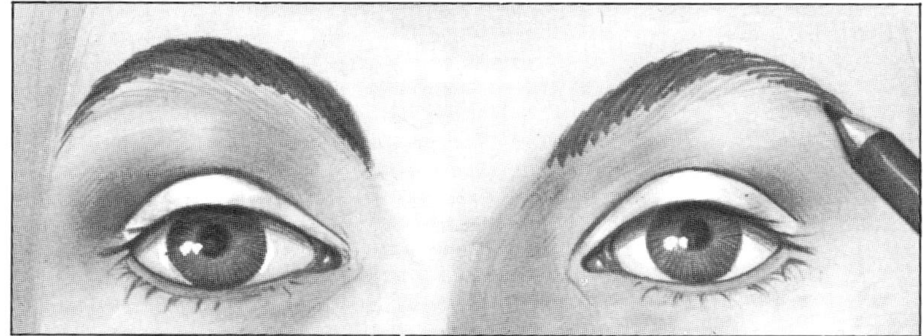

***1** Sketch brows into a graceful high arch. Highlight top lids with white and add pale-blue or lilac eyeshadow, if required*

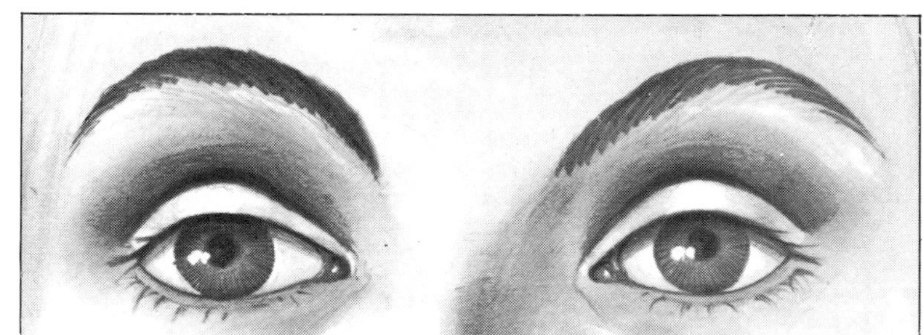

***2** Draw a high, well-rounded contour crease to give a prominent, hooded look to the lid*

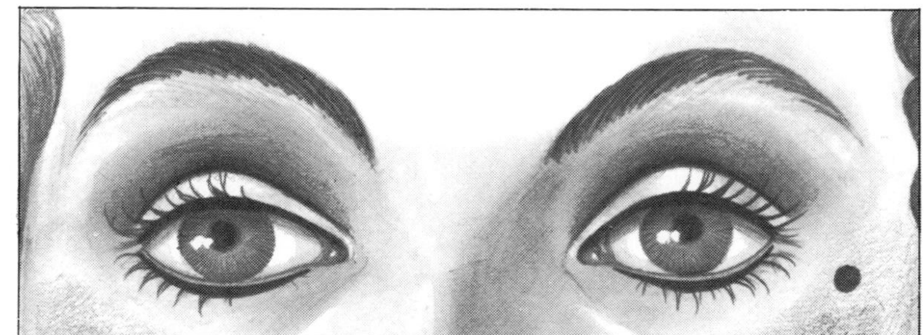

***3** Outline eyes to give a wide, round look. Keep top line thin and close to lashes and thicken center of lower line*

using a very pale color so that the skin is almost white, with the merest hint of pink.

A small black patch (made of flock or drawn on with eyebrow pencil) may be used to complete the overall sophisticated appearance.

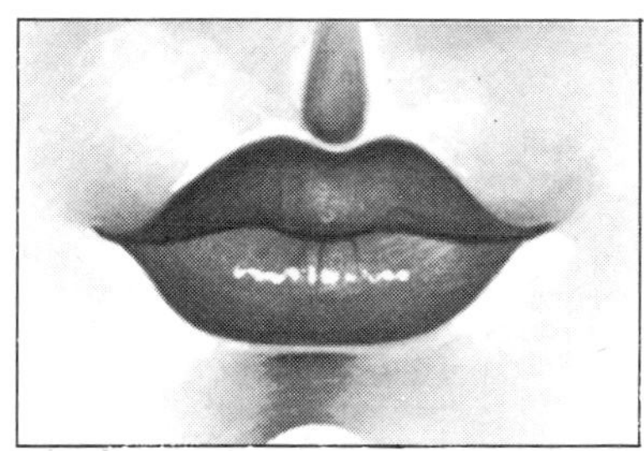

***4** Keep lips full and generous*

***5** Strongly rouge cheekbones*

***6** An elaborately dressed wig completes the artificial appearance of the makeup*

Makeup for Restoration comedy

Over-madeup elderly women

One other very important character that is frequently met in Restoration drama is that of the aging old harridan who uses every artifice to recapture her lost youth and looks.

The technique required to achieve this makeup varies according to the age of the actress playing the part. If she is young, it is first necessary to age the face very strongly and to make it as unattractive as possible. Then apply the over-madeup look over the top, using cake foundation.

If, however, the actress is already mature, it is necessary only to exaggerate the highlights and shadows already present on the face and at the same time make it as ugly as possible. Then, once more, apply the over-madeup look over the top.

The addition of a grotesquely ugly false nose is often useful to achieve the required look and this should be applied before aging the face.

The aging makeup should be executed with grease liners, using very dark brown for the shadows and pure white for the highlights, which should then be thoroughly powdered with translucent face powder.

With a fairly wet cosmetic sponge, apply a wash of a very pale, almost white, cake makeup over the aging makeup.

Stop the application short at the jawline so that the aging on the neck has maximum emphasis.

Draw on eyebrows with black pencil in one continuous hard line, arching them well up above the natural line of growth. If the natural brow is particularly heavy, block it out before starting the makeup (see page 57).

Apply a vivid splotch of very bright eyeshadow to the top lid and strongly outline the eye with black liner on a number 6 filbert brush. Extend the line on the top lid beyond the outer corner of the eye in a downward direction. Make up both top and bottom lashes with a heavy application of black mascara.

Outline the mouth with black eyebrow pencil. Lift the center of the exaggerated cupid's bow almost up to the nostrils and allow the ends to droop down at the corners of the mouth. The bottom lip should be well rounded but small. Fill in the lips with strong dark-red color, using a number 6 filbert brush.

With a rouge mop or a pad of cotton, very crudely apply the rouge to the center of the cheeks, keeping the color slightly low on the face.

Put on the wig, which can be very elaborately styled and made of obviously dyed hair. Patches can then be added, using black pencil or gummed flock paper. Finally, the hands should be aged (see page 71).

This type of makeup needs a certain amount of practice in order to get the right effect but, whatever you do, don't be afraid to overdo it. What may look overpainted and harsh in the mirror can often look quite pretty to the audience.

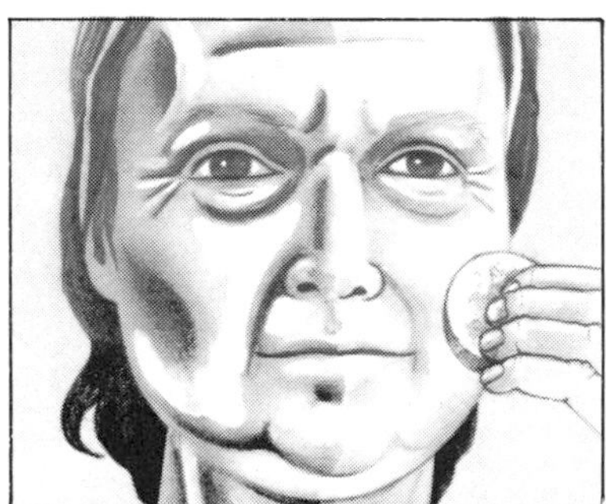

***1** Apply a pale cake makeup over a strong aging makeup*

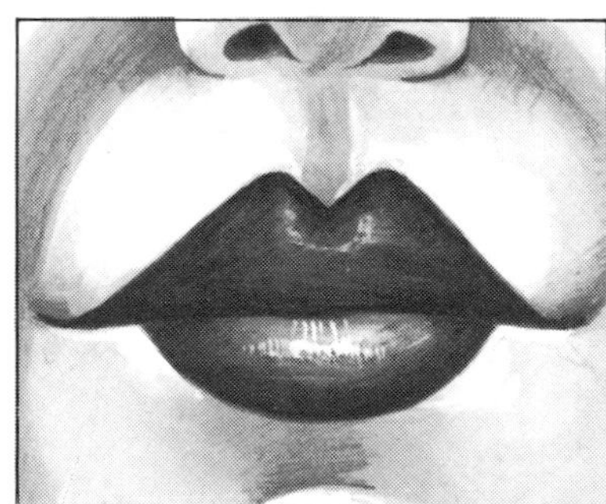

***2** Overpaint the mouth in an exaggerated shape*

***3** Draw on a new browline above blocked-out natural brows and apply a patch of vivid eyeshadow*

4 A grotesque wig and large patches complete the makeup

Dressing-room scenes

Some Restoration plays require the actress to make up on stage. This may be tricky, but with a little practice and a few short cuts, a very good effect can be achieved.

The aging makeup, complete with blocked-out brows and false nose, will need to be applied before curtain up. (If the wig is put on or taken off during the performance, a bald cap with wispy graying hair looks very bizarre.) Just how much makeup can be done on stage depends on the time available.

Foundation could be already applied and the actress need only mime a few pats of a powder puff to indicate whitening the skin. If there is time to apply the foundation, load it on to a natural sponge, placed in a porcelain bowl. (Modern cosmetics and packaging did not exist in Restoration times!) Eyeliner and mascara usually take too long to apply and need to be on at the beginning. Then the actress has only to add a splotch of eyeshadow and crudely draw on the brows, using a black wax crayon, which will look like a charcoal stick from the front.

Lip shaping can be very difficult at speed, so a good idea is to have the outline already sketched on lightly with brown pencil and just add the color with a brush. Rouge can be added quickly and crudely but remember to use a rabbit's foot rather than a rouge mop.

Wigs should be an easy fit and preferably be on an elasticized base to prevent the need for a great deal of immediate fixing.

Makeup for rough characters

The makeup in this section covers a wide range of characters, such as tramps and winos, drug addicts, pirates, bandits, thieves, and so on. Every character will vary according to environment, temperament, health and age; so careful character analysis is vitally important in order to determine the right degree of coarseness and ill health. Race is also important; a black tramp and Mexican bandit, for instance, apart from both being dirty and unkempt, must at the same time look Mexican or black. It is obviously impossible to detail every variation. Having learned how to coarsen the average caucasian face, the actor must superimpose these effects over the social and racial characteristics needed for the character being portrayed.

Most rough characters need to look unshaven. Although stubble can be applied (see page 93), a natural growth of beard, two or three days old, looks better and is much less trouble.

Tramps and winos usually have dirty, unkempt and matted hair. This can be simulated by rubbing solidified brilliantine into the hair and then dusting it with fuller's earth (available in most drugstores).

The look of unwashed skin with deeply ingrained dirt can be created by using fuller's earth, with dark-brown or black face powder added to it, and then mixing it into a moist paste with a little water. This can then be rubbed into the skin and allowed to dry. If the face is pulled into exaggerated expressions while this paste is being applied, the expression lines will be left lighter when the face is relaxed, giving a really good broken effect.

Broken or flattened noses help to coarsen the features and can be applied either with light and shade or by using a false nose (see pages 72-75). An effective distorted look can be given to the nose by inserting a single nose plug into one nostril (see page 77) and then exaggerating the distortion with highlights and shadows.

A menacing and ugly look can be given to the mouth by drawing crooked lips with an eyebrow pencil, twisting one corner down and lifting up the other.

Distorted eyes can be very effective on makeups for pirates, brigands and other villains. These can be simply done with lines and moist rouges painted on to transparent gauze (see page 97).

One other method is to take a small narrow strip of fish skin or silk muslin, approximately $\frac{1}{4}$ by 2 inches (6mm x 50mm), and stick one end of it just below the lashes at the outer corner of the eye with spirit gum. Pull the strip down until the eye is sufficiently distorted and stick the other end to the cheek, holding it in place with a dampened towel until the gum is completely dry. The strip can then be hidden with makeup and the distorted edge of the eye can be accentuated with eyeliner and moist rouge.

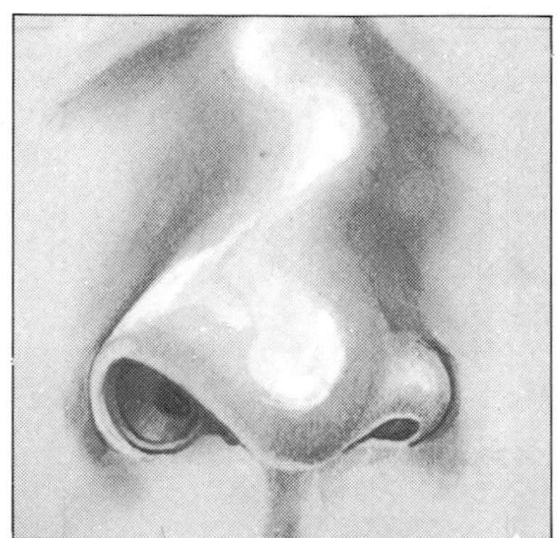

1 *A broken-nose effect, created with a single nose plug and suitable highlights and shadows*

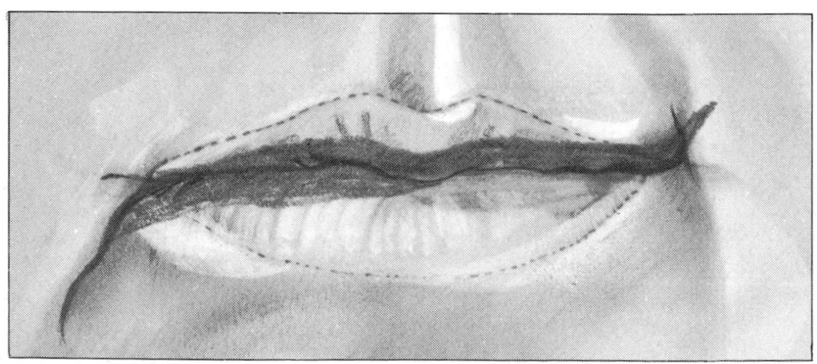

2 *A twisted mouth drawn with eyebrow pencil and highlights*

Other deforming scars and special effects can be added if the character needs to look particularly villainous and tough (see page 98).

A gleaming white smile will look totally out of place on rough makeups, so the teeth must be blackened or dirtied. Dark-brown wax pencil rubbed on will stay in place for quite a while and looks very effective; it can be more permanently fixed with a thin coat of spirit gum. Broken uneven teeth can be created with black tooth enamel painted along the edge of the teeth in a jagged line, or whole teeth can be completely blocked out.

All exposed areas of the body must be "dirtied" in keeping with the face makeup. Give particular attention to the hands and nails, working dark grease liner around the cuticles and under the nail.

Body tattoos can be used for many of the characters in this area. Character analysis will provide clues as to the style of tattoo. (For how to apply them see pages 100-101.) Seafaring types will have anchors, mermaids and sailing ships; pirates may well sport the skull and crossbones; while regimental crests, daggers, serpents and crossed swords all indicate a military background.

Drug addicts and alcoholics often have crude, rudimentary tattoos, obviously self-inflicted.

If the body is to be dirty as well as tattooed, then the tattoos must be covered with a film of sealer (before the dirtying makeup is applied) to prevent smudging them away.

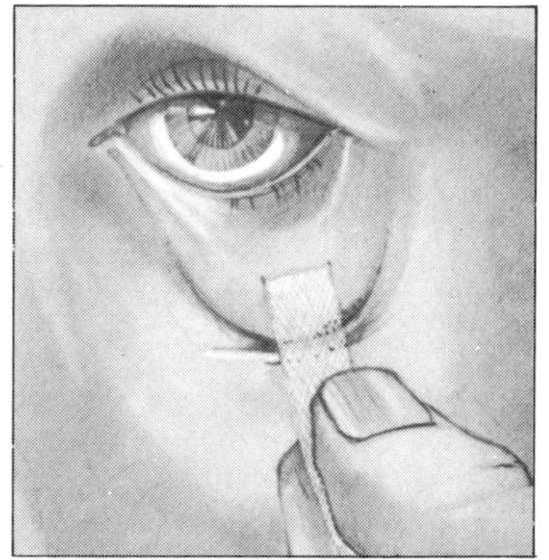

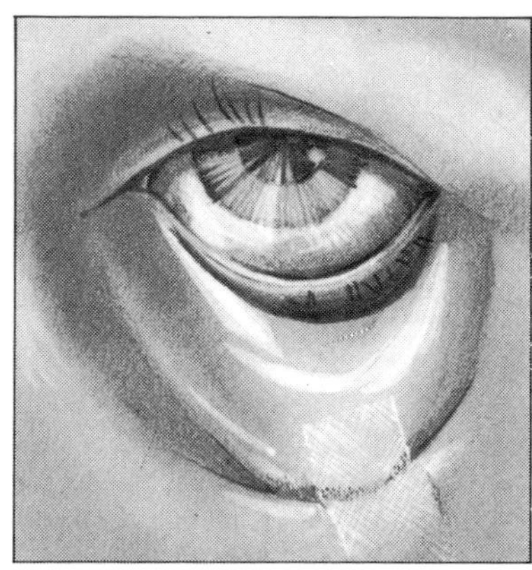

***3** Distort the shape of the eye with a strip of fish skin stuck to the cheek and then concealed with makeup. The distortion can then be exaggerated with makeup*

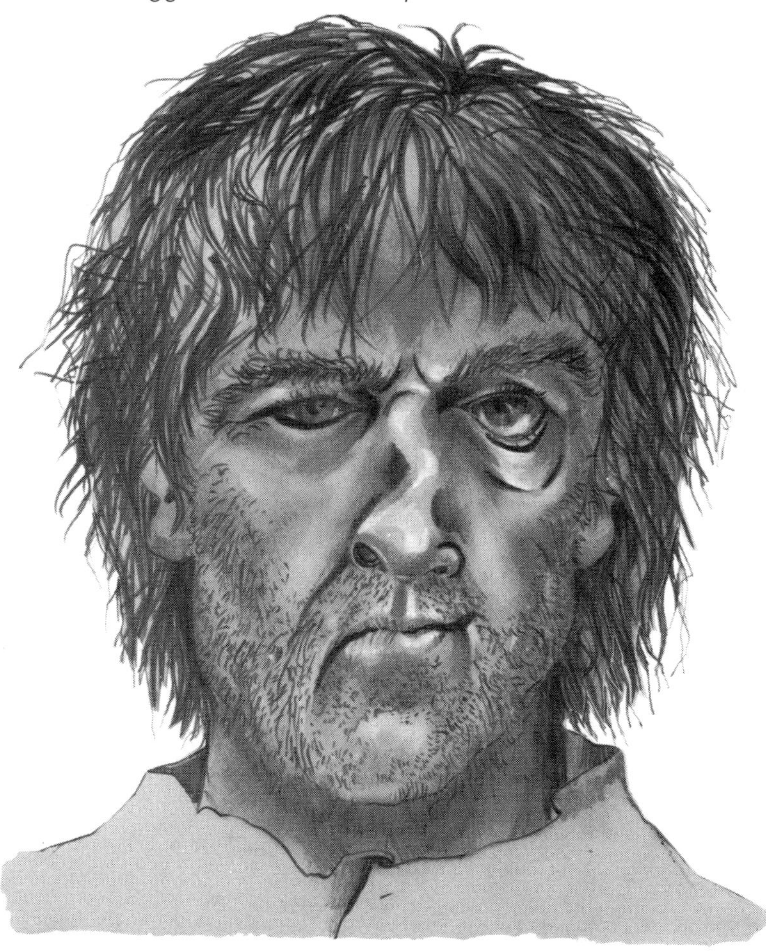

Fantasy and non-realistic makeup

The makeups in this section give the actor and the makeup artist great opportunities to be imaginative and to create something new and original.

Fantasy and non-realistic makeups can vary from very theatrical exaggeration of normal human features to stylized representation of non-human forms. Animals, abstract paintings, mosaic floors, stained-glass windows and so on all come into this category.

The first thing to remember when creating this sort of makeup is that it must fit in with the production as a whole, so an overall guiding influence, such as the director or a makeup artist, is most important.

Another vital point to watch is whether the characters have become so familiar to the audience that any change in their appearance would be totally unacceptable. For instance, the monster in Frankenstein will be for ever the character as portrayed by Boris Karloff; and the Mad Hatter and all his friends in Wonderland will always be the characters illustrated so well by Tenniel. However, the three witches in *Macbeth* have no definitive portrait and so their appearance is always open to a new interpretation.

It would be impossible to cover every character that an actor may be called on to create, so here are just a few of the more obvious ones to give some guidelines on how to approach this especially fascinating area of stage makeup.

Witches

Witches can be both good and bad, beautiful or ugly, but this makeup is for the evil and ugly witch so often seen in the theater. Traditional witches have large hooked noses, sharp pointed chins, sunken cheek hollows, and tiny, deep-set evil eyes. Their heavily wrinkled skin is covered in hairy warts, and tight thin lips conceal almost toothless gums. They have long straggly hair, clawlike hands with long, curved dirty fingernails and dark dingy complexions with sallow-yellow or green undertones.

Before you begin the makeup, apply false noses and chins, using nose putty or prosthetic pieces(see pages 72-75). (Since long noses and pointed chins are easily knocked, using the prosthetic type is definitely preferable.) Now put on foundation color, using grease or cream sticks, with a stippling technique to give a broken appearance. Shade and highlight the face very strongly, using black or very dark olive-brown for shadows, and white or yellow for highlights.

Next sketch on very heavy eyebrows with a black pencil, or use false brows. Intensify the eyes with black liner and add red liner to the inside edge of the lower lid. Attach warts (see page 100) with spirit gum or latex adhesive, and apply strands of dark-gray crepe hair to the chin with spirit gum. Then draw in a thin mouth with black eyebrow pencil and blacken the teeth with tooth enamel (see page 69).

Now you can fasten the wig in place. Alternatively, use raffia, gray wool or teased-out sisal string — dyed a suitable color and sewn around the edge of the witch's hat or hood.

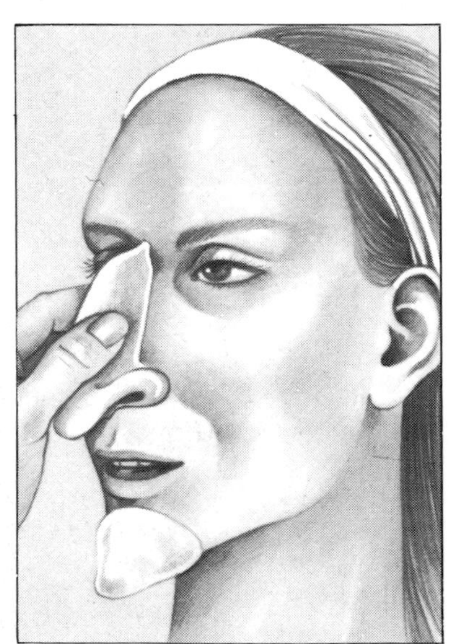

1 Apply a false nose and chin. Prosthetics are best

2 Stipple on foundation. Shade and highlight strongly

3 *Last but not least, the hands need attention. Use an exaggerated version of aging makeup (see pages 114-116). Bony knuckles look effective. To make these, first paint the knuckles with spirit gum, allow it to dry slightly and add a small ball of cotton (cotton wool) to each knuckle. Cover the cotton ball with a coat of sealer and allow it to dry. Then make up the hands, highlighting and shading the false knuckles to make them as bony as possible. Long witches' fingernails can be added, using old photographic film (see page 100). Paint the nails with black, gray or green nail enamel, or try using model-airplane paint*

If time is short, a simpler way of dealing with the hands is to wear ragged dirty mittens, leaving just the fingertips and nails to be made up

4 *Redden the inside edge of the lower eyelid with lining color. Blacken the teeth with pencil or tooth enamel and add warts. Then apply crepe hair to the chin*

Fantasy and non-realistic makeup

Demons and devils

Mephistopheles is the archetypal devil with a long thin face, sharp pointed features, a long nose and narrow well-defined lips. His black eyebrows are close together, curving dramatically upwards over dark deep-set eyes that wing in the same direction as the eyebrows. He usually has a thin mustache and a small, pointed goatee beard and he may have horns.

To achieve this makeup, first block out the ends of the eyebrows to allow the browline to be winged up. Then apply a very pale foundation with green undertones. Paint in highlights and shadows very strongly to give maximum strength to the bone structure (note the angle of the cheekbone shading), using dark olive-brown or black for shading and white or ivory for highlights.

Sketch on the eyebrows with black pencil, starting very low down by the top of the nose and winging the end dramatically upward over the browbone.

Outline the eyes with black liner, starting well in at the inner corner, close to the nose, and winging the outer corner up towards the browbone, parallel with the brows. Now mascara the lashes and add red liner to the inside edge of the lower lid.

Outline the mouth with black pencil, keeping the top lip long and thin. Fill in the lip shape with very dark lake liner and darken the top lip with the pencil.

Apply a beard and mustache (see pages 90-95), and then put on the wig and fasten it in place.

If using the natural hair, draw in the widow's peak with an eyebrow pencil.

Make up the hands to tone in with the face, accentuating the bone structure with shading to make the hands look as thin and long as possible.

This makeup can be adapted to create many different characters such as Dracula, Richard III, Iago from *Othello* or the Demon King in pantomime.

For Dracula, leave off the beard and mustache and add the vampire's teeth. For Iago, make the foundation dark and swarthy. For the Demon King, the foundation can be red and a red sequin stuck to the center of each eyelid will give a fiery flash as it catches the light.

Death

The character of Death normally wears an all-enveloping black cloak and hood, with just the skull and hands visible.

First of all, block out the eyebrows completely. Then apply a heavy, pale ivory foundation over the entire face, stopping short at the jawline.

Shade the temple and cheek hollows deeply, with dark-gray liner. Draw in the eye sockets in a sloping-down pattern. Lightly shade the depressions in the center of the forehead and just below the lower lip on either side of the chin.

Using black liner, intensify the temple and cheek hollows and completely blacken in the top of the eye socket as shown. Then draw in the nostril openings, starting just below the bridge of the nose, in a triangular shape over the sides of the nose. Blacken the inside of the nostrils but leave a hairline of pale foundation down the center of the nostril flange.

Using black eyebrow pencil, draw in the teeth along the top and bottom lips, extending them out at the corners of the mouth to a point immediately below the end of the eye. Blacken the center of the mouth with a line of black pencil, extending this out at the corners of the mouth, between the two sets of teeth.

Apply black foundation over the neck, meeting the ivory face color in a sharp line along the jawbone. Finally, make up the hands as illustrated.

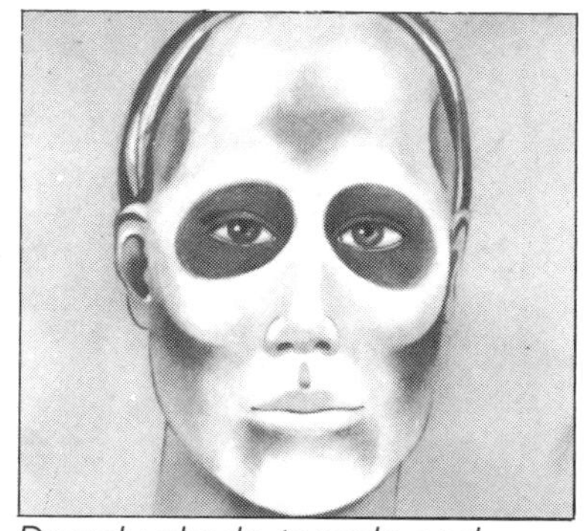

Deeply shade temple and cheek hollows and blacken eye sockets

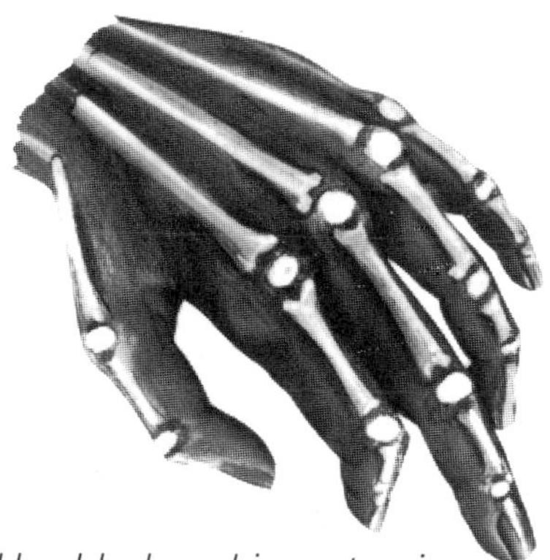

Use black and ivory to give hands a skeletal appearance

Fantasy and non-realistic makeup

Monsters

Just how far to go with monster makeup depends on the style of the production. If it is an adult horror play, then you can make the monster as frightening as possible but a more sympathetic approach should be used for children's entertainment. Many special effects can be used — such as nose plugs to flatten and coarsen the nose, open wounds with streaming blood, distorted eyes, and so on.

Werewolves

Werewolf wigs can be made to resemble animal hair growing low on the forehead or with hair which appears to grow from the browbone and then covers the entire face with an abundance of facial hair. These, with fang-like teeth and coarse flattened noses, can be very effective.

Teeth for monster makeups are best made by a dental technician so that they fit comfortably in the actor's mouth, but they can be very expensive. If the actor does not have to speak a great deal, quite effective teeth can be made by embedding animal teeth (which can usually be purchased from taxidermists) into a thin strip of foam rubber, using a strong glue. This strip is then pushed up under the top lip, in front of the gums.

Frankenstein's monster

This well-known monster needs a good wig with a built-up forehead. This should be made to fit right over the eyebrows to give the classic hairless browbone effect. Heavy false eyelids can be made from adhesive plaster in a similar manner to the lids for a blind person (see page 97).

Since the flesh should appear to be "stitched together", long cuts can be applied with Derma Wax (see page 98). The stitching can be simulated by using staples or small pieces of a fine hairpin bent into shape and pressed into the wax.

The neck bolts can be made by taking the caps off old electric-light bulbs and sticking them to rubber washers. The washer provides a suitable surface to stick to the neck with spirit gum.

Werewolf

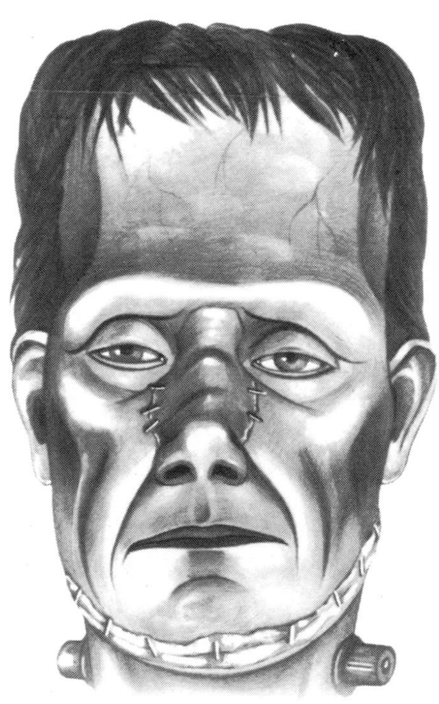

Frankenstein's monster

Animals

Makeup for animal characters can be approached in two ways: realistically or non-realistically. For the realistic approach, a fur-covered latex mask or headpiece needs to be made by a modelmaker and possibly the eyes and mouth made up to blend in. This approach is best for such roles as the lion in *Androcles and the Lion* or for the cat in *Dick Whittington,* which are non-speaking characters. However, animals like Toad and Badger in *Toad of Toad Hall* need a stylized face makeup that blends in with a suitable head-dress or hat; perhaps even the actor's own hair might be dressed in a suitable style.

Toad

Block out brows with Derma Wax to create prominent brow-bones, and then apply a yellow foundation.

Draw on heavy lids with black pencil and white highlight and add pouches under the eyes. Now add eyebrows with a black pencil and darken the inside of the nostrils.

Draw on a toad's mouth in the shape shown, using lake liner and black pencil and then highlight the top lip with white liner.

Dress the hair down well with solidified brilliantine and make a center parting or side parting, whichever flattens the top of the head most. A wig can be used and dressed this way if the natural hair is unsuitable.

Badger

Apply a very pale or white foundation. Then shade the face with dark gray or brownish black to create the striped pattern as shown below.

Outline the eyes with black liner and apply a beard and mustache. False eyebrows can now be added.

Finally, dress the hair with hair whitener in the striped effect shown, brushing the hair up as much as possible before spraying with lacquer. A wig would be the simplest solution but they are very difficult to find in the style and colors needed, so a very dark-brown wig that has been sprayed with silver may well be the answer.

Do not make up the mouth.

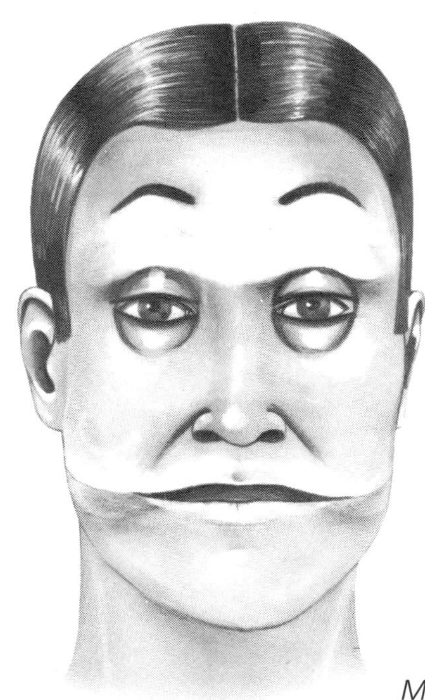

Makeup for Toad and Badger in "Toad of Toad Hall"

Fantasy and non-realistic makeup

Clowns

Clown makeup is basically divided into two groups: white-faced clowns and tramps. Both these groups can be further sub-divided into sad and happy clowns. Sad clowns have mouths and eye makeups that slant downwards, and happy clowns have wide-awake eyes and mouths which have upturned corners.

White-faced clowns are usually painted with "clown white", a special, very opaque grease makeup, but other white foundations can be used. If clown white is not available, a good method of whitening the face is as follows:

Apply a thin film of white grease or cream-stick makeup evenly over the face and thoroughly powder with white face powder. Then apply a wash of white cake makeup over the top. This method overcomes the problem of the base color "splitting" and allowing the natural skin tone to show through.

No shading is used and any cheek color is usually drawn on in clear geometrical shapes, which are often outlined with black pencil.

The natural browline is either heavily overpainted or blocked out and a completely new shape drawn in.

The new brows can be almost any shape — large half circles, inverted V's, sinuous curves and flashes of lightning. The brows may even be completely asymmetrical.

The eyes themselves are usually very simple, with vertical "blips" or dots on top and bottom lids, or just basically outlined in black with an upward or downward slant — according to the character. A single wash in a very bright color can be used for eyeshadow.

Mouths are generally small, neat and well defined and are executed in clear red with an outline of black pencil.

Tramp clowns usually have a strongly colored foundation and the makeup is, more often than not, very comic, with huge overpainted mouths in red or white, their corners turned up or down and surrounded by an obviously painted-on beard line. The eyebrows are generally very high and in the shape of an inverted U, which is often infilled with white or a very bright clear color. The eyes themselves can be shaped like stars, triangles, or complete circles — in fact, any shape that takes your fancy.

Most tramp clowns have big red bulbous noses, which may be bought ready-made from joke shops. Alternatively, the end of the nose can simply be painted bright red.

Wigs are worn by both white-faced and tramp clowns and can be as exaggerated as you wish.

Examples of a white-faced clown and a tramp clown

Dolls

A doll-like makeup can be achieved by using very pale pink or creamy-white foundation, applied quite heavily to give a porcelain finish to the skin. Pink rouge should then be applied in a round spot to the center of each cheek and very softly blended around the edges.

Eyes should look as round as possible. Draw on rounded eyebrows, blocking out the natural brows if necessary (see page 57). With a black eyebrow pencil, draw a line in the crease at the back of the top lid, in as round a shape as possible. Draw a circular line under the lower lashes and fill inside this circular pattern, using a white cake makeup.

Now draw on false lashes, as shown in the sketch, and paint the mouth in a small, exaggerated cupid-bow shape. An inexpensive wig made of nylon, with braids or a mass of curls, will complete the effect.

Fairies and elves

Fairies, elves and other kindred spirits can, like witches, be good or evil. If they are evil, a modified form of witch's makeup will suffice, with pointed noses and slanting evil eyes. Good fairies, however, are more difficult since they really should look diminutive and ethereal. Good casting is the first essential and then the makeup should be delicate and precise.

Foundations need to be very pale and pretty and can vary from the palest pink to pale blue, green or mauve. Sometimes, designers suggest metallic gold or silver but a complete metallic face makeup can look very heavy; so it is better to use a very pale base with gold or silver highlighting. A tiny tip-tilted nose looks very elfish or fairylike and can be made with a small amount of nose putty.

Pointed elf ears can be made from latex but it is also possible to make them from adhesive plaster and hairpins. Cut a strip of 2 inch (50mm) wide adhesive tape about 4 $\frac{1}{4}$ inches (105mm) long. Place it sticky-side up and lay a two-inch fine hairpin on it, bent into the shape shown here, with the open ends $\frac{1}{8}$ inch (3mm) from the end of the tape. Now cut a circle of paper 1 $\frac{1}{2}$ inches (37mm) in diameter, fold it in half, and lay it along the bottom edge of your strip.

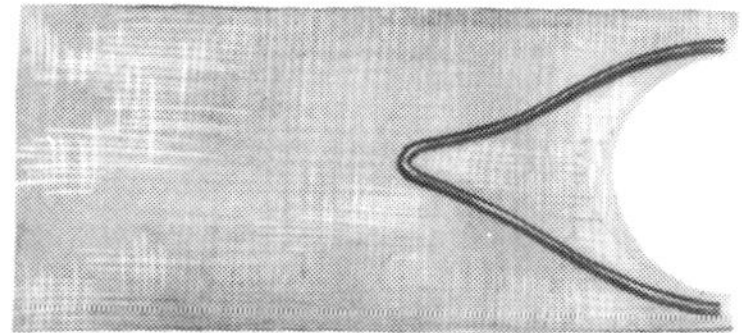

Fold the top half of the strip over the hairpin and the paper and press the two sticky surfaces together, trapping the hairpin and the paper between them. Then cut around the shape of the bent hairpin and along the bottom edge, to cut through the folded edge of the paper.

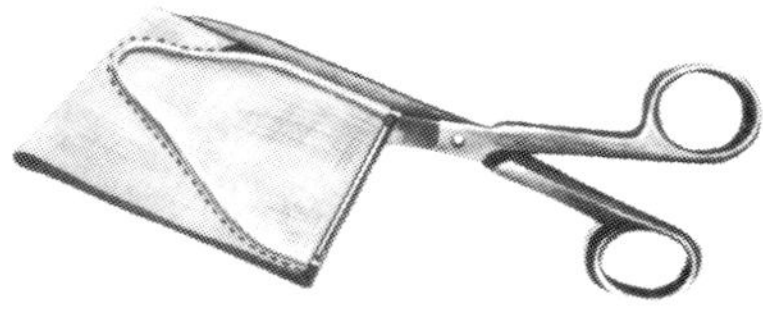

Open out the end of the resulting ear shape and cut away some of the tape and paper on one side to make the shape fit the front of the natural ear.

Color the tape with greasepaint to match the skin color and stick it on to the natural ear with spirit-gum. These ears can be removed with spirit-gum solvent and reused several times if handled with care.

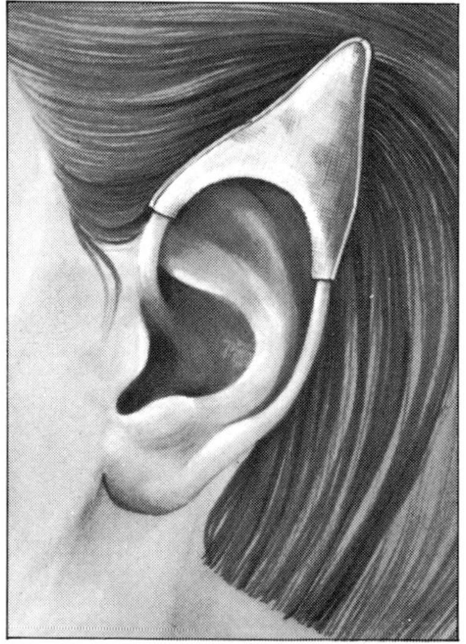

What a drag — male and female impersonation

Men and women reverse roles in the theatre for a number of different reasons, giving rise to many varying styles of makeup. These may be used for glamorous female impersonation, slapstick pantomime dames, straight sex reversal in a Shakespearean production and breeches parts in opera. They may simply be used, of course, for the purpose of disguise.

Female impersonation

Hopefully, the performer playing a glamorous female impersonation role will have a suitable bone structure — one that is not too aggressively masculine. Then all that is necessary is to apply a glamor type of makeup (see pages 122 and 152) and at the same time to follow the principles laid down in the section on corrective makeups (see pages 50-59). Pay particular attention to the eyes (page 54), eyebrows (page 56) and lips (page 59).

The first step is to conceal the beardline. The actor should shave about half an hour before applying the makeup, and, if the beardline is not too strong, it is necessary to add only just a touch more foundation to the beard area. If the beardline is very dark, first stipple a covering film of cream-stick or grease foundation (approximately the same tone as the natural complexion color) on to the beard area and thoroughly powder.

Then apply cake makeup over the entire face and throat, powder once more, and proceed with the rest of the makeup.

A good wig is usually essential to complete this type of makeup, but if the actor's hair is sufficiently long, it can be dressed into a feminine style.

Pantomime dames

The traditional dame of British pantomime needs a different approach since no attempt is made to conceal the fact that the part is played by a man. Every actor playing a dame tends to develop his own individual style of makeup, which can vary from simply putting on a wig and perhaps a lipsticked mouth, through to a complete makeup — similar to that used for over-madeup old women in Restoration comedy (see pages 158-159).

Kenneth Connor as one of the ugly sisters in Cinderella

Danny La Rue in his glamorous cabaret makeup

Male impersonation

Makeup for male impersonation varies enormously. There is the simple masquerade used in Shakespearean productions, when a masculine costume is donned, the hair concealed beneath a hat or a man's wig, and makeup kept to a minimum. A glamorous principal boy in pantomime may wear a man's costume but the makeup is essentially feminine. However, for full male impersonation, very detailed makeup should be used, as shown .

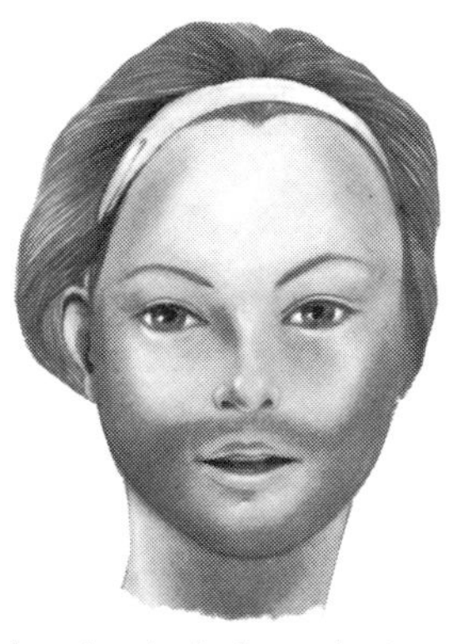

__1__ Apply dark foundation (see page 108) and stipple in beardline with medium-gray lining color. Cover natural lip line with the foundation

__2__ Highlight and shade the bone structure, paying special attention to the jawline, brow-bone and nose. Nose putty or a false nose can be used

__3__ Lightly sketch in the eye-brows to give a fuller, more masculine shape and then draw in the eyelines (see page 109), blending away edges

__4__ Add a false beard and mustache, if required, and put on a masculine-styled wig

Quick-change makeup

When a makeup has to be changed during the course of the performance, this often has to be done at speed. Careful planning and, in some cases, a complete change from normal techniques may be required. Because the reasons for makeup changes are so varied, there are no hard and fast rules that must be followed. However, here are a few points that should be remembered:

The changing room should not be too far from the stage, and the change should be kept as simple as possible, using the minimum of equipment.

Only those items required for the change should be on the makeup table and they should be placed in the order in which they are to be used. Finally, the change should be rehearsed and timed to ensure that it is possible. If there are any doubts, then either the change should be simplified or the script should be adjusted to allow more time.

There are also a number of short cuts that can be used with the equipment. Try to choose those materials that can be applied directly to the skin — rather than those which are applied with brushes and sponges. (If brushes and sponges do have to be used, they should be already loaded with the required colors so that no time is wasted.)

Brushes used for highlighting and shading should be color-coded on their handles for easy identification. All the brushes should be kept upright in containers, rather than left lying flat on the table, so that they are less likely to roll off.

If there are a number of changes during the play, the actor should have a helper (usually a dresser) who can lay out the equipment in the right sequence and load the brushes and sponges so everything is ready and waiting for the next change.

Quick-change methods

Depending on the type of change needed, there are a number of different techniques that can be used. Complete removal of the first makeup is very time-consuming and should be avoided wherever possible. Cake makeup is invaluable for this because the colors can so easily be sponged one over another.

Changing complexion color

Method one
Using cake foundations

Simply sponge a new color over the first makeup, using a slightly wetter sponge than usual. Remember, when using this method, that the foundation color already on the skin is still water-soluble. Therefore a certain amount of the color will be picked up and mixed with the second application, affecting the final color. So, if you need to lighten the skin tone, the second cake makeup should be lighter than the actual color required, and vice versa if you need to darken the skin. You will need to determine the color to use by trial and error.

Method two
Using grease and cake foundation together

For the first makeup, use grease or cream-stick makeup, which is thoroughly powdered. The skin tone can then be changed by sponging a film of cake makeup over the top in whatever color is required.

Method three
Using only grease foundation

When changing the skin tone, using only grease or cream-stick foundation, the first makeup should be left unpowdered to facilitate blending the second color into the base.

Changing the details

When details such as eye makeup, lipstick or rouge need to be removed, this removal should be effected before any other change is done. Makeup-remover pads are ideal for this purpose, and a clean pad should be used for each detail so that none of the removed makeup is wiped back on to the face. Any excess removal oil should then be wiped off with a pad of cotton moistened with skin tonic. If cake makeup is being used, the areas from which the detail has been removed should then be powdered to ensure a really smooth application.

Wigs, beards and mustaches

Wigs used for quick changes should be easy to put on and remove and need as little fixing as possible. They should also be dressed in a style that will not easily become displaced.

Prepared beards and mustaches should be used. If they need to be quickly removed, make sure they are on as strong a foundation as possible to prevent damage. For very quick application or removal, double-sided adhesive tape can be very useful, but it should be remembered that such applications will stay safely in place only for short periods. Also, great care should be taken to place the hairpiece in exactly the right spot the first time; if it is pulled off and the position adjusted, the adhesive quality of the tape is badly impaired.

Costume changes

One very important point to remember when a makeup change is needed is that there will, almost always, be a change of costume as well. So it is imperative, when planning the makeups, to work in close co-operation with the wardrobe department to ensure that there is sufficient time for both types of change. Remember that the style of costume may help to give a strong indication of the age and temperament of the character. In this way a very complicated makeup change can be avoided.

Plotting quick changes

In order to demonstrate how to plot a series of quick changes, I have chosen the character of Stella in Peter Ustinov's *Photo Finish*, a part requiring six makeup and costume changes.

At the beginning of Act One, Stella is eighty years of age. After a stage wait of approximately twenty-five minutes, she appears at the age of twenty. She is next seen after an interval (and a stage wait of ten minutes) at forty, but uncaring about her appearance.

She then has fourteen minutes before re-appearing as a twenty year-old. After the second interval (and a stage wait of twenty minutes), Stella is once more forty, but now attractive and well groomed. Then, with a wait of ten minutes, she is eighty again. After which, she has just three minutes to become the attractive forty year-old for her final appearance!

As there is a reasonable amount of time for the first four changes, they can be conveniently effected in her normal dressing room and quite carefully executed. The last two changes, however, need to be done in a quick-change room beside the stage. As only a limited number of features can be changed in the time available, attention should be paid to the stage lighting so that the face of the actress is not too well illuminated. This allows the wig and costume to convey the message of age to the audience.

Before going into the makeup details, let us look at the costume changes. For her first appearance at the age of eighty, Stella can wear a loose-fitting dress, suitably styled for an older woman, with a high neck and a knitted shawl over the shoulders. (Underneath this dress, the actress can wear the necessary foundation garments to give her figure a youthful appearance for her second change. These can remain on throughout the entire play.) For the two appearances at the age of twenty, use a figure-hugging Edwardian suit in light pastel tones, with a high-necked blouse (which can be a false front attached to the suit lapels). As Stella is "visiting", this outfit needs a pretty boater-style hat, a parasol and a handbag.

For her first appearance at the age of forty, Stella should look slightly slovenly and as if she has just tumbled out of bed. This can be achieved with a loose-fitting nightdress and a slightly crumpled peignoir.

For her second appearance at the age of forty, she appears more attractive and well groomed. A smart, sophisticated Edwardian suit in russet or green over a neat pleated blouse will give the right effect.

The time available for the next change — to eighty years of age — is very short (ten minutes) and the subsequent change back to forty is even shorter (three minutes). Therefore, the Edwardian suit should be left on and overdressed with a heavy dressing gown and the knitted shawl from Act One clasped at the throat, to conceal the blouse. These are simply discarded for the last change, leaving most of the available time for the makeup.

Quick-change makeups, that are necessary in a play such as this,demand good organization or panic will reign! To achieve a smooth-running routine, plan exactly what is required at each stage, as in the plots and makeup charts for *Photofinish* shown on the next page.

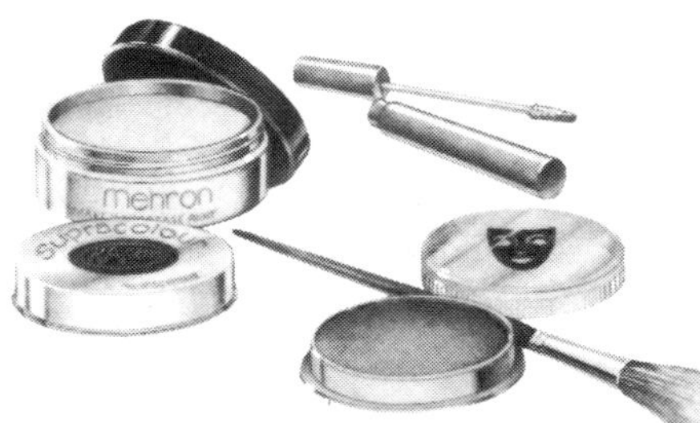

Quick-change makeup

Character	Stella at 80
Base	None
Highlight	Ivory
Shading	Olive brown and lake
Powder	Translucent
Rouge	None
Lip color	Highlights and shading
Eye makeup	None
Body makeup	None
Hair	Gray wig with fringe and bun at the back
Notes	Half-frame reading glasses

Character	Stella at 40
Base	As for 20 Plus pale peach cake makeup (Kryolan)
Highlight	Pale pink
Shading	Warm brown
Powder	Translucent
Rouge	Medium red
Lip color	Medium red
Eye makeup	Pink highlight Warm brown shadow Brown/black pencil. Black mascara
Body makeup	None
Hair	2 chestnut wigs with a touch of gray. One loosely dressed, falling to shoulders. The other dressed in fashionable Edwardian style
Notes	

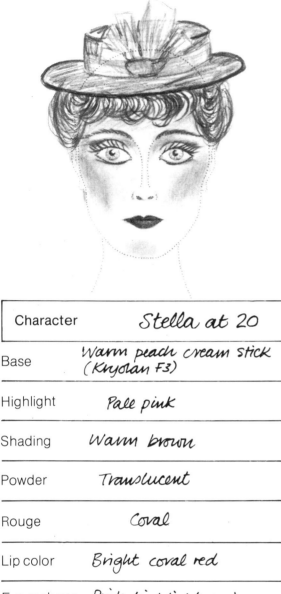

Character	Stella at 20
Base	Warm peach cream stick (Kryolan F3)
Highlight	Pale pink
Shading	Warm brown
Powder	Translucent
Rouge	Coral
Lip color	Bright coral red
Eye makeup	Pink highlight and warm brown shading. Black mascara. Brown/black pencil fine false lashes
Body makeup	None
Hair	Chestnut wig in young upswept Edwardian style
Notes	

Makeup plot

Eighty year-old makeup applied before curtain up

Change One Twenty year-old
(25 minutes)
Remove gray wig, spectacles and all character work
Apply straight corrective makeup, as charted, and young wig

Change Two Slovenly forty year-old
(20 minutes)
Remove young wig, lip color, and ends of brow. Smudge eye makeup. Remove false eyelashes if there is time
Apply pale cake makeup over rouge and add shadows. Apply loose-style middle-aged wig

Change Three Twenty year-old
(14 minutes)
Remove middle-aged wig and shadows. Redraw eyebrows and sharpen eye makeup, coral lipstick and rouge
Apply young wig and false lashes (if removed)

Change Four Smart forty year-old
(30 minutes)
Remove young wig, lip color and end of brows. Smudge eye makeup slightly
Apply new eyebrow shape, medium-red lip color and rouge. Apply fashionable middle-aged wig

Change Five Eighty year-old
(10 minutes)
Remove middle-aged wig and lip color
Apply pale cake makeup over lips and cheeks. Apply gray wig and spectacles

Change Six Forty year-old
(3 minutes)
Remove gray wig and spectacles
Apply middle-aged fashionable wig, lip color and rouge

Makeup through the ages

When the play being produced is set in any other than contemporary times, it is vitally important to ensure that costumes, hairstyles and makeup are all historically correct. So here is a brief guide to the fashions in hair and makeup from Ancient Egypt to the 1980s.

Egyptians

As can be clearly seen by studying the wall paintings found in Egyptian tombs, the civilized Egyptian, both the men and women, made extensive use of cosmetics. The eyes were heavily outlined with black galena and the lids colored with green malachite. The cheeks were rouged with powdered red earth or henna leaves crushed in cream, and the lips were colored with carmine. Although skin was sometimes whitened with a ceruse of white lead for ceremonial purposes, most Egyptians preferred their own suntanned complexions.

Hairstyles play a very big part in Egyptian makeup since most men and women shaved their heads and wore elaborately styled wigs, or cut their hair in careful geometric tiers. Eyebrows were also shaved and new ones drawn on. Most men were cleanshaven but patently false beards were worn for ceremonial purposes — even by Egyptian queens.

Romans

Both men and women in Roman society whitened their skins, and rouged their lips and cheeks. They also dyed their hair and darkened their brows. Theatrically speaking, however, makeups do not need to be grossly exaggerated — except perhaps for the more decadent characters. Women's hairstyles became more elaborate and complicated as the Roman Empire developed, with extensive use of false braids and curls piled on top of the head.

Men's hairstyles tended to be short, dressed close to the head, and combed forward over the forehead. Longer hair was bound with a fillet. Most mature men were cleanshaven, but the younger men sometimes allowed their beards to grow until they attained their majority when they were ritualistically shaved and their beards were dedicated to the gods.

Assyrians and Persians

These Middle-Eastern people used cosmetics as extensively as the Egyptians. Both men and women lined the eyes with antimony, but less extravagantly than in Egypt. Brows, however, were very heavily darkened, often meeting in the middle, which gave them a stern and forbidding appearance.

Hairstyles were elaborately crimped and tonged for both sexes. Wigs were extensively worn and natural hair was dyed — the Assyrians favoring black, and the Persians, red. Beards gave an indication of rank, with slaves and soldiers being cleanshaven while court officials and kings wore extravagantly long and curly beards, both natural and false.

Ancient Greeks

Compared to the other ancient civilizations, the Greeks used cosmetics sparingly, so in the theater the makeup is usually very natural, particularly for men. As far as the women are concerned, the makeup is not unlike that used in the 1960s, with unrouged cheeks and muted lip makeup. The eyes have the contour crease well defined, thus giving the lid a sculpted look.

Hairstyles were comparatively simple. Women piled their hair high on the top or back of the head and allowed spirals and ringlets to fall down their backs or loosely over the shoulders. Low foreheads were more fashionable than high ones, so the hair was often dressed forward with curls.

Men generally kept the hair short, tightly curled, close to the head and, like the women, dressed forward over the forehead. Most men were bearded and mustached, the styles being long and softly curled.

Egyptians

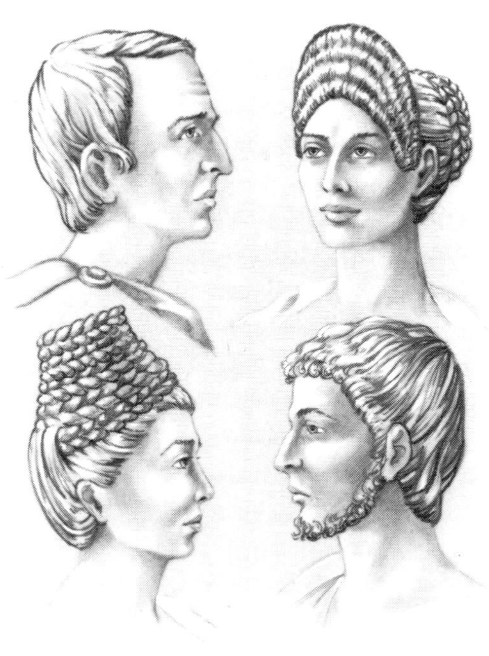

Romans

Assyrians and Persians

Ancient Greeks

Makeup through the ages

The Middle Ages

Our knowledge about the use of cosmetics and hairstyles worn in early medieval times is very limited as we have few pictorial records of that period. We know that with the passing of the Roman Empire, there was a return to barbarism and much less care and attention was paid to personal appearance during the Dark Ages. Men allowed their hair and beards to grow unchecked and bathing became a thing of the past.

With the arrival of the Middle Ages, women still wanted to look pale but, more likely than not, they were bled rather than painted. They seldom added any color to their cheeks or eyes; they lightened their hair or (after marriage) hid it away beneath a veil or "mentonniere", a kind of chin strap. This exaggerated pallor was further accentuated by plucking out the eyebrows and the hairline, so that the face was smooth, white and without definition — like a large white egg with eyes which resembled stuck-on beads.

Unmarried women wore their hair long and flowing or woven into heavy long braids bound with ribbons. Sometimes they added false pieces so that the hair fell well below the waist or even the knees. Later in this period, these braids were often wound round the head, or coiled into elaborate chignons or pads over the ears.

In the fourteenth century, the miracle play required actors to make up with incredible realism and ingenuity as devils and saints, animals and angels.

The sixteenth century

The Renaissance brought a renewed interest in cosmetics and, with the opening up of new trade routes, makeup materials became more readily available to those who could afford to buy them. So, while women still plucked their brows and hairlines, the pale wan look was banished in the courts and replaced by Indian red or Spanish rouge over a skin whitened with Venetian ceruse. Regrettably, these materials were far from safe, so to hide the resultant damaged skin, the makeup became even heavier.

By the middle of the sixteenth century, hair had begun to be brushed high up over wire frames and pads. The whole effect was framed in crescent-shaped headdresses, heavily bejeweled with pearls and precious stones, or else with tiny hats pinned to the summit. By the end of Elizabeth I's reign, wigs were in fashion, some tightly curled like the monarch's, or smooth and winged like those of Mary, Queen of Scots.

Men's fashion was centered around the beard, so hair was cut short and the beard allowed to grow so that it could be elaborately styled.

During Henry VIII's reign, beards were generally very full and generously curled, but in the Elizabethan court they were trimmed into countless different shapes — the Spanish spade beard, the English square-cut, the forked beard, the stiletto beard and so on; sometimes they were even dyed red as a tribute to Queen Elizabeth.

The seventeenth century

The seventeenth century saw many changes in fashion, with the pendulum swinging back and forth from Jacobean melancholy to Restoration baroque. Early in the century, hair and makeup still bore a look of the Elizabethan age — with high hairstyles and heavily painted faces for the women. For men, the beard was still all-important but the hair was now worn longer and fell to the shoulders.

By the middle of the century, the beard had almost disappeared and the hair became the dominant feature, with wigs becoming more and more fashionable. For women, hairstyles became lower and wider — often with wire supports to allow the cascades of curls to stand well away from the face. The faces themselves became fuller and more voluptuous. Gone was the whitened complexion; instead the milkmaid's "peaches and cream" became the fashion, with ruby-red lips and dark flashing eyes.

Then came the Puritans, the men with cropped hair and square-cut beards, the women looking pure and scrubbed, hiding their hair beneath their bonnets. With the Restoration, and onwards to the end of the century, the excesses of fashion that we have already discussed became the order of the day. Hairstyles rose higher and higher and wigs became ever longer and more voluminous.

The sixteenth century

The Middle Ages

The seventeenth century

Makeup through the ages

The eighteenth century

The excesses begun in the previous century continued to grow until they reached a peak of almost total absurdity in the late eighteenth century. Women's hair was at first disarmingly simple but then, like a vehicle out of control, the styles became more and more extravagant, adorned with galleons in full sail, baskets of fruit, bouquets of flowers — anything, in fact, that took the fancy of the court milliners.

For men the eighteenth century was, as in the seventeenth century, the age of the wig. Although not so voluminous and bulky as the wigs of the seventeenth century, the styles were endless in their variety — with bag wigs, bob wigs, club wigs, pigtail wigs, brigadier wigs, scratch wigs and others too numerous to mention. The scratch wig was an inexpensive wig favored by the working classes and the name has passed into theatrical parlance, to mean a cheap wig used by the low comics in old-fashioned melodrama.

Makeup was used extensively and extravagantly by men and women. Both sexes whitened their skins with dangerous layers of white lead, and deaths were recorded as a result of the use of these white paints.

Cheeks were over-rouged in a completely unnatural manner, with no attempt to blend away the edges of patterns that were sometimes circular, sometimes triangular or sometimes just wild slashes of color.

Brows were heavily blackened and eyelids brightly colored. Makeup for men reached its zenith with the coming of the so-called "Macaronis" around the seventies, with their elaborate powdered wigs, grotesque makeups and foppish dress.

However, by the late eighteenth century, all these excesses had passed and makeup once again became more natural. Wigs disappeared, and since they had often covered shaven heads, hairstyles became very short for both men and women.

The nineteenth century

In the early part of the nineteenth century, the pendulum of fashion had swung away from the artificial-looking makeups and extravagant hairstyles of the eighteenth century. Makeup was just subtly deceptive and hair, though short, was very carefully dressed.

The women, however, regretted having their hair short, and soon false pieces were being added to supplement the natural hair. Topknots became fashionable, braids and chignons were pinned in place, and bejeweled bandeaus encircled the head. Feathers, jewels and flowers were used in profusion. With the coming of the Victorian era, cosmetics were frowned upon and obvious makeup was rarely seen. Hair grew naturally longer and was braided and knotted close to the head.

Later, however, during the 1870s, more and more false hair was worn, with enormous chignons and falls of false curls being pinned on to the natural hair. Gradually this practise decreased until towards the end of the century, with the introduction of Marcel waving, the false piece all but disappeared. The hair, now softly waved, was swept up over the ears to the crown of the head in soft voluminous topknots, often being dressed well forward to give a very high full look to the front of the hair.

During the first part of the century, men remained clean-shaven with short natural hair but, as the century advanced, facial hair became increasingly fashionable again and, by the middle of the century, beards and mustaches were almost universally worn.

It was the side whiskers that dominated the fashion scene, with their innumerable variations. Men sported "mutton chops", looking remarkably like their name sakes; or they wore "Piccadilly weepers" or "Dundrearies" (named after an actor playing the character of Lord Dundreary), which were long and flowing. "Burnsides", which crossed the cheek to join the mustache, were named after General Burnside in the American Civil War.

By the end of the century, the beard had almost disappeared, leaving just the mustache.

The eighteenth century *The nineteenth century*

Makeup through the ages

The Edwardians

With the passing of Queen Victoria, artifice started to creep back but since cosmetics were now of a much higher standard, the general effect was still very natural for younger women, while older women, although looking madeup, did not seem garish in appearance.

Hair became fuller and wider, rather than higher, at the beginning of the period but by the time of the First World War, the full, heavy look had gone. Although still worn wide rather than high, the hair followed the natural shape of the head, lapping over the ears in soft coils.

Men in the Edwardian era were, in the main, cleanshaven, with the occasional beard and mustache still to be seen on the older man. The hair itself was of moderate length and, on the whole, unremarkable.

The twenties

Makeup in the twenties once more became obvious. Eyebrows were plucked, mascara generously applied to lashes, eyeshadow was openly worn, lips were strongly colored and rosebud shaped, and cheek rouge was no longer regarded as sinful.

Hair was bobbed or shingled. Fringes, bangs and curls were brilliantined on to the face and a tight bejeweled bandeau encircled the head. The men sported pencil mustaches and the hair was cut short and brilliantined close to the head or sometimes artificially waved.

The thirties

By the thirties, the mannish bob was outmoded and longer, softly-waved hair was all the rage. Makeup was strongly influenced by Hollywood. Gone were the bee-stung lips and the very exaggerated cupid bows; instead the lips were larger and more sensuous, like those of Joan Crawford. The brows were still plucked but, instead of being highly arched, they were now longer and curved softly downward, giving a sad and langorous look to the face.

The hair was parted on the side or in the center and was gently finger-waved at the sides, ending in soft fluffy curls.

For men the glossy patent-leather look was out and the hair, though still short, was allowed to wave softly. Mustaches became fuller in England, while in America they had all but disappeared.

The forties

Despite the many restrictions imposed on the cosmetic industry during the Second World War, women still managed to imitate the stars of the silver screen. Makeup became more colorful and slightly theatrical in appearance. Hairstyles varied from the Veronica Lake "bang" to the topknot of Alice Faye. The snood which was used to protect long hair in the munition factories became a fashionable accessory.

The war influenced men's hairstyles too, introducing the short back and sides. The top of the hair was still allowed to wave, often being carefully dressed into place with finger and water waves.

The Edwardians

The twenties

The thirties

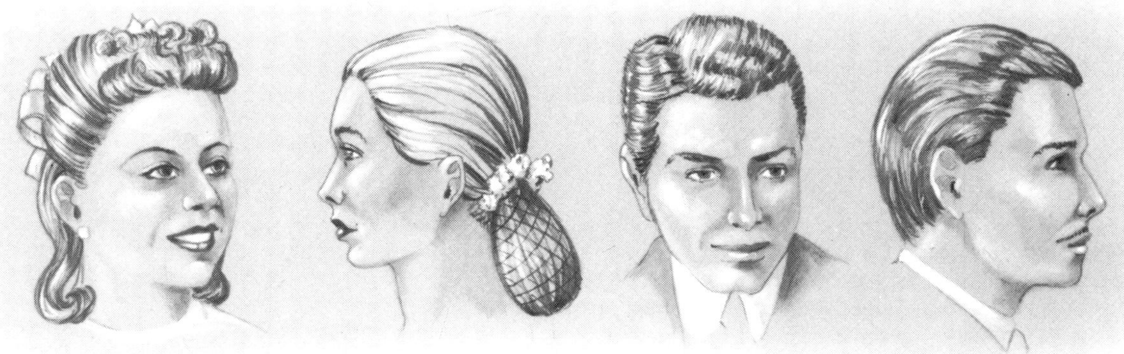

The forties

Makeup through the ages

The fifties

The fifties heralded dramatic changes in both makeup and hair. With the introduction of the doe-eyed look, eye makeup became all important. More and more eye cosmetics appeared on the market — the painted look was back! Lip colors became more exciting. Rouge went right out of fashion and was used less and less.

Hair was also most important in the fifties, with constantly changing styles, lengths and colors. First came the urchin cut and the butch cut, to be rapidly followed by longer styles, such as the beehive and the chignon. Hair cannot grow overnight, so these longer styles brought back the wig and false piece.

Men in the fifties had a wide variety of hairstyles to choose from — the Elvis Presley quiff, the crew-cut, the flat top and all the various styles now possible with the new blow-dry techniques. Makeup for men also made a comeback at this time, with the introduction of artificial tanning agents.

The sixties

In the early sixties, the trends already felt in the fifties were developed and eventually distorted into the styles of the Swinging Sixties. Complexions became deathly white and unrouged. Lips were pale, even to the point of being whiter than the complexion. The eyes, on the other hand, were so heavily made up with black liner and fringed with so many pairs of false lashes, they became almost invisible. The eyebrows were plucked or bleached to the point of extinction. The hair was tinted and teased into monstrous beehives or mounds of false pieces.

For men, the sixties brought the Beatle haircut and the long hair associated with the beatnik and the flower children.

Towards the end of the decade, the extravagant hairstyles and over-madeup faces were once more outmoded and there was a return to a more natural look, with long straight hair framing a softly madeup face. The eyes, however, were still heavily belashed — the leggy, round-eyed "dolly-bird" had arrived.

The seventies and eighties

Throughout these years, the changes in makeup and hair have been so numerous and so frequent that no real image of the period is possible. Suffice to say, there has been a great wave of nostalgia, with each of the decades of the twentieth century having their turn for revival. Therefore, if presenting a modern production, the choice of hairstyle and makeup must depend on the decisions taken by the directors and designers, and the personal preferences of the individual performers.

Two strong influences that have made themselves felt in recent years are punk fashion and ethnic fashion.

Punk fashion in makeup and hair can range from the humorous, through the bizarre, to the downright ugly — but all must be executed with great panache and skill to be effective.

Ethnic fashion can be represented by hair with cornrow styles, hanging braids, teased-out Afro styles or "Rastafarian dreadlocks".

The fifties

The sixties

Punk and ethnic fashion in the seventies and eighties

Organizing group makeups

So far we have concentrated on makeups for individual performers, but problems in amateur theater frequently stem from not knowing how to organize makeup for large casts. All too often, not enough care and attention is paid to planning how makeup is to be done when a large number of actors are involved. The result is that chaos reigns and many of those taking part go on stage wearing a makeup that they feel is quite dreadful and, in consequence, give an embarrassed and inhibited performance.

Naturally, the exact procedure that should be adopted varies according to the size of the cast, the number of competent makeup artists and what facilities are available for doing the work. Basically, there are two ways of tackling the problem:

The first, and without doubt the most artistically satisfying method, is for each makeup artist to completely make up a number of specific characters — which should then be checked and approved by the chief makeup artist. However, when very large groups are involved, this method requires a large number of good makeup artists and a great deal of makeup and equipment — since each artist will need his or her own kit.

It is then probably far more practical to use the "conveyor belt" system, where each makeup artist is alloted a specific step in the makeup sequence. The performers move down the line of artists, having one step at a time added, until they reach the chief makeup artist at the end of the line — who checks the makeup and makes any final adjustments or corrections. This method, which is excellent for straight makeups, still needs to be carefully organized. Every performer should have a chart, explaining exactly what makeup is required, which can be shown to each makeup artist as the actor passes down the line.

Ideally, there should be one or two assistant stage managers, who make sure that there is always someone ready and waiting to be made up and then keep those not required clear of the makeup area.

The more difficult character makeups should still be done individually, since to create a character you need to see the work through from start to finish. These detailed makeups should be allocated to the more experienced members of the makeup team, leaving the "conveyor belt" to willing (but often untrained) helpers, who can easily apply a straightforward base or blusher.

Having decided just how the makeups are to be done, the next important thing to take into consideration is the makeup area. This should, ideally, be a large airy room with sufficient space to accommodate the makeup team and the actors in comfort — preferably situated fairly close to the stage itself, so that if any retouching or makeup changes are required during the performance, the actors do not have to go a long way.

There should be sufficient well-lit mirrors, makeup tables and chairs for each of the makeup artists to have a separate working area and, if possible, a supply of running water. Finally, ensure that each makeup artist has a waste basket ready for the disposal of used tissues and cotton balls.

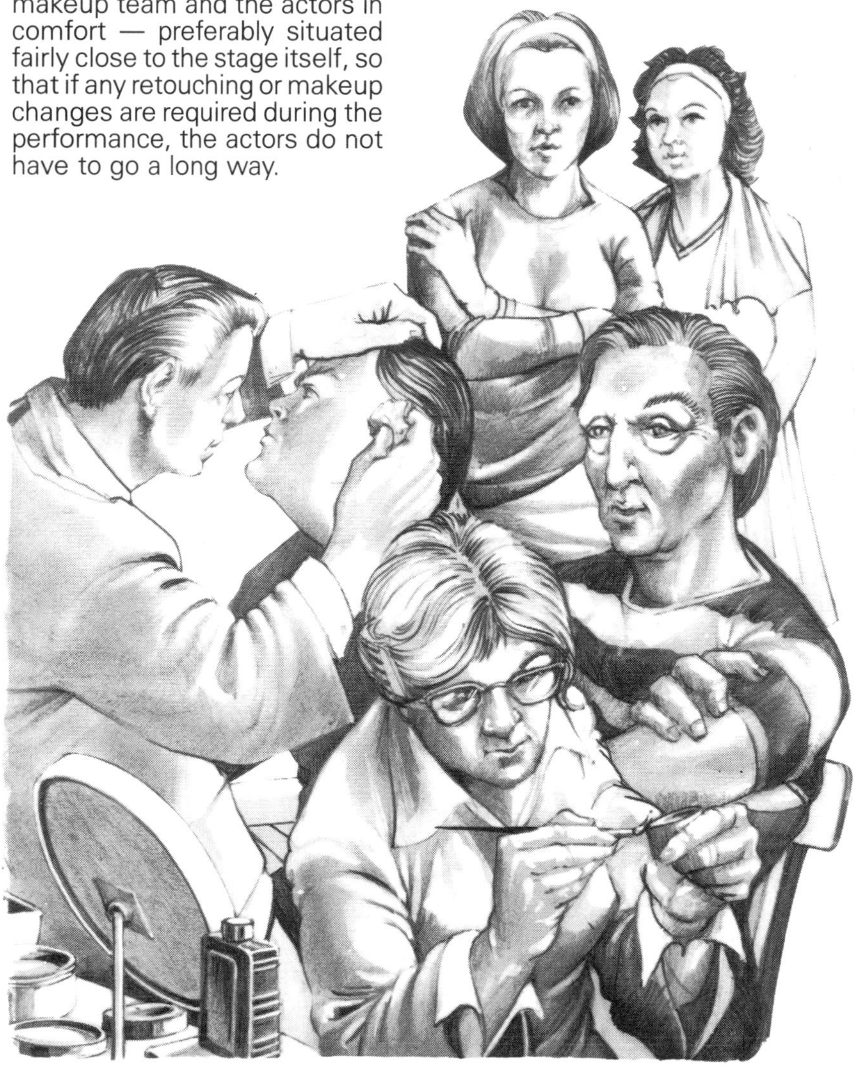

General information

Glossary

Accent rouge rouge used to highlight the high point of the cheekbone

Antimony a brittle, bluish-white, metallic substance

Brilliantine a hair cosmetic which imparts a gloss

Carmine a crimson color, originally made from cochineal

Ceruse a white paint derived from lead

Cotton wool British term for cotton balls or cotton

Eye pouches bags which form under the eyes

Filbert brushes brushes which are broad at the base but taper to a fine point

Fishskin a very strong, fine animal tissue

Fuller's earth a white-to-brown natural substance which resembles potters' clay when mixed with water

Galena common lead ore

Gelatines the colored filters which can be placed in front of a light

Key a base which will aid adhesion

Malachite a green mineral derived from copper

Masque black coloring, similar to mascara, used to darken the hair and scalp

Neutral lights those which may affect the makeup but of which the audience is unaware

Orbital the overall area of the eye socket

Pacifier a baby's dummy

Pantomine dame a comic matronly character, usually played by a male comedian

Pate top or crown of the head

Physiognomy the art of judging character from the features of the face

Pigment coloring matter

Shading rouge rouge which is used to hollow the cheeks

Smile pad the raised cheek area which is formed on the face by a smile

Snood a hairband or net which confines the hair at the back of the head

Subcutaneous beneath the surface of the skin

Triptych mirror a hinged, triple mirror

Reference files

Every makeup artist, and any actor required to create character makeup, needs to be very observant and to have a good memory for faces; but it is not always possible to carry everything in the mind's eye. It is a good idea to build up a collection of reference pictures to help create the characters that you need.

It is very helpful to have a number of indexed correspondence files in which to store any photographs, drawings and illustrations of interesting faces and characters.

Keep your filing as simple as possible, without too many subdivisions. Use a small indexed notebook with cross-references for each illustration under different headings. For example, some pictures of Abraham Lincoln could be found under Historical, or under Beards, Noses, Foreheads, Mouths or Eyebrows — all of which were very distinctive features of Lincoln. These could be used not only to create Lincoln's look-alike, but also as individual features for some other characters.

This organization, together with a sound knowledge of makeup and its application, will all help in the creation of your own Stage Face.

Bibliography

Baygan, Lee
Techniques of Three-Dimensional Makeup
Watson-Guptill 1982
An excellent reference book for those who may wish to manufacture their own prosthetic false pieces

Corson, Richard
Fashions in Hair
Peter Owen Ltd 1965
Excellent reference book of period hairstyles

Corson, Richard
Stage Makeup (Sixth Edition)
Prentice-Hall, Inc. 1981
Excellent text-book for makeup artists, especially those wishing to make their own hairpieces, wigs and prosthetic appliances

Diakonoff, Serge
The Diakonoff
Published 1978
British suppliers: Kryolan
Very good examples of fantasy makeups

Jans, Martin
Faces, Fantasy Makeup
Published 1983
British suppliers: Kryolan
Excellent examples of fantasy makeups

Young, Douglas
ABC of Stage Makeup for Men
ABC of Stage Makeup for Women
Samuel French 1976
Handy reference cards of individual makeups, for use in the makeup room

Suppliers

Charles Fox Ltd
22, Tavistock St, London WC2
Stockists of most leading brands of professional makeup. Efficient and fast mail-order service. Catalogue available

Theatre Zoo
28, New Row, London WC2
Suppliers of masks, prosthetic pieces, inexpensive wigs and makeup

Wig Creations Ltd and Wig Studios Ltd
12, Old Burlington Street, London W1
Wigmakers, supplying a full range of top-quality hairpieces and wigs for purchase or hire

Wig Specialities Ltd
173, Seymour Place, London W1
Wigmakers, supplying a full range of top-quality wigs and hairpieces for purchase or hire

L. Leichner (London) Ltd
202, Terminus Road, Eastbourne, East Sussex, BN21 3DF
Manufacturers of a full range of theatrical makeup. List of stockists available

Dauphine Stage Hire Ltd
8-24, West Street, Old Market, Bristol

S.B. Watts Ltd
Princess House, 144, Princess Street, Manchester M1 7EN

California Theatrical Supply
256, Sutter Street, San Francisco, California 94102
Distributors of Kryolan makeup range

Bob Kelly Cosmetics Inc.
151, West 46th Street, New York City, New York 10036
Manufacturers of a complete range of stage makeup. Also wigs and hairpieces. Available from professional makeup sales outlets

Makeup Center Ltd
150, West 55th Street, New York City 10019
Handy source of makeup supplies in New York

Ben Nye Inc.
11571, Santa Monica Blvd., Los Angeles, California 90025
Manufacturer of a complete range of professional makeup. Available from professional makeup sales outlets

Paramount Theatrical Supplies (Alcone Company)
575, Eighth Ave, New York 10018
Mail-order service for most brands of professional makeup. Catalogue available

M. Stein Cosmetic Company
430, Broome Street, New York City 10013
Complete range of theatrical makeup. Available by mail-order only

Kryolan GMBH
D. 1000 Berlin 51
10, Paperstrasse
Federal Republic of Germany
Manufacturers of a complete range of professional makeup, including materials for prosthetic use. Available in UK and USA

Index

G

H

I

J

K

L

M

N